MAKING
THE BEST
OF THINGS

Making the Best of Things

The Autobiography of a Camberwell Lad

Len Williams
1907–1986

FrameCharge Press

Copyright © 2013 FrameCharge Press

Apart from fair dealing for the purposes of research or private study for non-commercial purposes, or criticism or review, as permitted under the Copyright, Designs and Patents Act 1988 and the Copyright and Related Rights Regulations 2003, this publication may only be reproduced, stored or transmitted, in any form or by any means, with the prior permission in writing of the Publisher or in the case of reprographic reproduction in accordance with the terms of licences issued by the Copyright Licensing Agency in the UK.

ISBN: 978-0-9555777-2-7

British Library Cataloguing in Publication Data. A catalogue record for this book is available from the British Library.

Published by:	FrameCharge Press
	Ely, UK
	editor@framecharge.com
	http://www.framecharge.com

Technical Editor:	Peter White
Editor/Designer:	Jeff White

Produced using Open Source Software

Printed and bound by Lightning Source

The tea tin had pride of place on the overmantle, a sort of shelf over the fireplace with a frilly dado hanging from it. On this was displayed our few treasures—a box with seashells embedded in it, a decorated biscuit tin (full of hairpins and junk), a nine-inch statue of Psyche (chipped) and our money boxes (usually empty). Below was the kitchen range which in winter time was kept alight continuously, usually with our iron kettle singing away on it. Mum liked her cup of tea and she often said that she hoped there would be tea in heaven.

Editor's Foreword

About the Author

Leonard Ernest Williams was born on 14 October 1907, at No. 3 Wren Road, Camberwell, and was the second of two sons in a family which eventually numbered nine in all. His mother, Ellen Williams (*née* Bierton), came from the village of Aston Abbotts, Buckinghamshire, and his father, Frederick Williams (also known as Frederick William Lacey), born in Berkhamsted, lived and worked in London. At the age of three, Len, with his family, moved a short distance to Stobart Mansions in Kimpton Road, Camberwell, which was to remain his home for the next twenty-five years until his marriage in 1935. It was during this period that he gained the intimate knowledge of Camberwell and its environs that he would draw upon when he began writing the following memoirs, almost seventy years later. The whole family received their fairly basic education at Denmark Hill School, Grove Lane, apart from a gap of four years during the 1914–1918 war, when the school was requisitioned by the Government. During this time the pupils were transferred to another school, Lyndhurst Grove School, receiving only part-time education as a result. The family's social life revolved around Kimpton Mission (a branch of the Shaftesbury Society), just a few doors away, and it became an important part of their lives. At the age of fourteen, Len left school and eventually obtained his first permanent job as a shop assistant with the local Co-operative Society. On the outbreak of war in 1939, he served in the Auxiliary Fire Service and then joined the Royal Air Force in November 1940, where he became a Leading Aircraftsman. He spent the war years in England, and for much of this time he was billeted with the Misses Illingworth and Dunnington at their bungalow, 'Mardale', in the village of Tollerton, near York. After the war, Len joined the GPO and later the Ministry of Health, where he became an Executive Officer.

He met Elsie Ruth Squires at Kimpton Mission in 1930 and they married at Wren Road Congregational Church on 7 September 1935. They celebrated their Golden Wedding in 1985 with their three daughters, Doreen, Brenda, and Janet, and their husbands, eight grandchildren, friends and relatives.

Len started writing his memoirs during his retirement and would have been delighted to see them published as a book for his family. For our part, we couldn't have wished for a better legacy.

About this Book

The manuscript I inherited from Dad was typed by him in the 1970s and 1980s. They were the carbon copies and I have never seen the original top copies. The script I received had very few alterations and transferring it to the computer was a lengthy, but not difficult process. I had to rearrange some sentences to make them flow more easily, and in some cases he repeated details and events. I made the decision as to which place in his story they were best suited. With my son Peter's help we made a few grammatical changes, but in all cases our aim was not to compromise the integrity of Dad's work.

Brenda White
June 2011

Author's Foreword

What I am recording here is, to the best of my knowledge, completely true, and it has taken a lot of courage and soul-searching to even think of writing it down; but in the hope that some day, by some quirk of fate, the rights of the family may be acknowledged, I have overcome my reluctance to open up unpleasant memories, and the anger that goes hand in hand with them, and trust that my sisters and I will be forgiven for the reluctance we have shown to discuss our past.

As children, we had a fairly happy life in an area that had some mean streets and its share of squalor and hardship. The mansions where we lived were only a few yards away from busy Church Street, Camberwell, the main shopping area and the main road to and from the centre of London. Trams clattered along the centre of the street and buses moved along nearer the kerbs. It was a lively area, separating South Camberwell from the poverty and slums of the northern area. People glibly talk these days of the poverty and deprivation of the so-called third world, but sixty years ago there were people near us who were on the verge of starvation; children walked the streets barefooted and went to school in rags and without any breakfast, and folk died because they could not afford to call the doctor...and the money-lenders were worse than leeches.

It is not easy to get things in true perspective and memory tries to forget the unpleasant and unhappy things, and recall only the pleasant and heart-warming times that stand out like great peaks from the mass of the surrounding foothills. As children, and by children I refer to the four oldest children of my family, we lived a reasonable and comfortable life until the outbreak of the First World War, when our way of life suddenly shattered and we learned the meaning of hardship and poverty. It left scars that nothing has been able to erase, and it changed our mother from a vivacious young woman to a drudge working all hours doing menial tasks, like cleaning other people's houses and taking in washing and mangling.

We were told that Dad, by trade or profession, was a commercial traveller whose business took him on long journeys and necessitated him being away from home for quite long periods. We had no reason to question this and accepted it. In any case children in those days never questioned their parents on such matters.

Dad was a thick-set man, but short in stature. In height he only reached my shoulder. He was more or less bald, having lost his hair, so he said, when he was about twenty-one years of age. He wore a goatee beard and was a chain-smoker, and liked a drop of whiskey. He possessed a fine head and piercing eyes, and was very, very intelligent; could speak French fluently, had knowledge of German and Spanish, and often paid visits to the Continent. In looks he reminded me a little of Captain Mainwaring of *Dad's Army*. He was a

Freemason, an organist, and a member of the Royal College of Music; he was also, in his day, a well known astrologer, having founded a magazine on the subject with Alan Leo. Of course, I knew nothing of this until after his death.

I believe he considered my brother Reg and I to be mental lightweights, and was often impatient with us. He was not averse to giving us a beating if we stepped out of line, which we frequently did. He mellowed as we grew older and I like to think that I was nearest to him. Even so, he left us in complete ignorance of his life outside the walls of the family home and never brought friends to meet us, discussed business matters with us, or helped us to find employment when we left school. Never once were we taken to meet any of his business colleagues. Some Friday nights, Mum would go to meet him in town and they would go to Henekeys in the Strand. But I never knew any member of the family join them. We understood that Dad's office was somewhere nearby, but we never went there.

How was it, folk may ask, that the members of the family never suspected that Dad was leading a double life? I reply, 'Why should we have done so?' We believed what we were told and left it at that. Sister Con, with womanly intuition, must have realised that Dad was not playing the game by us, but she never confided in me, although Brother Reg probably was told. I understood, long afterwards, the reasons for the bitter rows that took place between Con and Dad and because I, in my ignorance, tried to defend Dad, I brought about my sister's wrath on my head, and caused an estrangement that lasted for many years.

It was probably also the reason for the hostility between Reg and Dad, and why eventually Reg left home and joined the Army. When I stumbled on the cause of the trouble and spoke to him about it, he said he thought I knew. Unfortunately Reg and I seldom met because we were living some way away from each other and so had little opportunity to talk things over. When Elsie and I held our Ruby Wedding celebration at Kingsway, Reg said he had delved into the family histories and would let me have a copy of his researches. Unfortunately he died shortly afterwards, and although my sisters and I have often asked his wife Betty for the papers, they have never been handed over.

Reg told me that he had traced the Bierton side of the family back for hundreds of years, and that on Dad's side, we were related to 'some of the highest in the land'. He said that Dad's mother's family was originally De Lacey, and could trace its line back to the Norman Conquest. Around the turn of the eighteenth century the family had extensive interests in the brewing industry centred around Rickmansworth in Hertfordshire. There were strong French connections. As a young woman, Dad's mother, Frances Lacey, kept company with a young Lord Carrington, who lived in nearby Bledlow. As a result of this liaison, Frances had a son and was disowned by her family; she took a cottage in Prospect Street, Berkhamsted, where she and Dad lived in near poverty.

By all accounts their times were very hard. Dad said that one Christmas all they had for their dinner was a kipper. Dad was furious with his mother's family and said that no matter what happened, he wanted nothing to do with them. On one occasion, Dad nearly drowned in the Rickmansworth watercress beds. He always said that his mother had strange psychic powers, some of which Dad inherited.

How long this situation lasted I do not know, or even when his mother died, but it seems that Dad's family finally acknowledged their responsibility and gave him an expensive education. Sister Con says that she has seen his name in the records of Balliol College, Oxford.[1] One thing is certain, Dad moved in some high circles. We believe he was in the shipping business, and Brother Reg always said that he was a silk merchant in Paris.

By the time of his marriage to Florence Marshall he was a well-to-do man. His wife was the daughter of a landowner with extensive properties in the East End of London. They lived first in West Ham, spent some time in Godstone, before settling in Tulse Hill, at this time a very select area.

There were nine children to the marriage. Three died in infancy, all the others were expensively educated. Charles, the eldest, became the African representative of Lever Brothers. It was he who brought Polly, our grey parrot, home (of course, it was many years before the bird came our way). He married and had a daughter, Muriel. As a boy, I once met Muriel and her mother; Muriel was about my age, but I cannot remember anything about her mother.

The second eldest, Harold Ernest, whom Mum always said I closely resembled, and whose second name I was given, died in South America. By all accounts he was the family favourite. Two other sons were killed in the war. The two youngest daughters we knew well, for they often came to the Mansions to visit my mother. They were around my sister Con's age. They spoke beautifully; Dora was a trained singer and on one occasion sang at the women's meeting at Kimpton Mission. Mary was, I believe, a demonstrator and buyer. I never for one moment thought that they were my step-sisters. On one occasion, Dora remarked to Mum: 'In all the many times we have been to see you, we have never once met your husband, Ellen.'

That is a very brief summary of the Lacey side of the family. Where did the Biertons come into the picture? The Bierton family tree is reasonably easy to trace because of the unusual name (which is the name of a village just outside the town of Aylesbury). I have written elsewhere about the Bierton family history; suffice it here to say that my mother, her sister and brother were illegitimate. Their father's name was Higgs. Who he was I do not know; probably Higgs was already married. If that was so, this probably explains

---

1 Frederick William Lacey is not, however, listed in *Alumni Oxonienses: the members of the University of Oxford 1715–1886: their parentage, birthplace and year of birth, with a record of their degrees* (Oxford: 1887).

why my mother and her brother and sister were all christened Bierton. Mary Bierton was born in 1843, and died on 29 August 1927 aged eighty-four.

It would seem that Higgs's wife died around 1898, and Grandfather Higgs moved in with Mary Bierton. My Mother was the only one of the children still living at home, for Aunt Rebecca had married Joseph Hornsby and was living in Rushden in Northamptonshire, and Uncle George was also married and living in Aston Abbotts. Whether the village gossip was too much for my grandparents I do not know, but they left the village, taking my mother with them. They settled in Brixton in Treherne Road, and Higgs became an employee of Lambeth Council. Mum said he was made a foreman in the cleansing department responsible for sending the water carts around the borough to lay the dust and wash down the roads. Mum chummed up with two sisters living nearby – we knew them as Aunt Ethel and Aunt […].[2]

My mother was then about eighteen years of age, and, by all accounts, a most attractive young woman. She applied for the position of children's nurse to a well-to-do family living in Tulse Hill. This was the Lacey family. Mrs Lacey was a strict employer but treated my mother kindly. Mum's real work was to care for the two younger daughters, Dora and Mary, and it says much for her devotion to them that they frequently visited her up until the time the family left Stobart Mansions to live in Herne Hill in the 1930s.

I believe Mum's years with the Laceys were fairly happy. The sons of the family thought the world of her and teased her a lot. Her chief favourite was the second son, Harold Ernest. She found favour also in the eyes of the master of the house. Mrs Lacey's health became poor and she developed TB, and Mum took over the running of the household.

We have reason to believe that Grandfather Higgs died around 1900, as Mary Bierton returned to her native Aston Abbots and took the tenancy of a cottage in Church Row at a rent of 1s 6d per week. Her son George lived two or three doors away. She now called herself Mary Higgs, or perhaps she had indeed married her man before he died. I believe Mum sent her a few shillings a week to make her life a little easier.

Now comes a puzzling part. On 24 February 1901, 'Ethel' comes into the picture. Who she was, or what her connection to us was, is not clear. Dad was of course her father. Sister Con is of the opinion that Mum was Ethel's mother, but this I do not believe. Mum really disliked her for the way she treated my grandmother. In appearances, she was completely different to members of my family and whereas at birth we were all fair-complexioned, she was dark and sallow. She was tall and thin and had black hair. She was fond of the expression 'why bless yer gal'.

I am proud to say that my brother and sisters were all generous to a fault, but Ethel was hard and grasping. I possess an excellent memory and can recall forgotten glimpses of the past. I remember one of my mother's few

---

2 Len's memory evidently failed him here, as the typescript is blank at this point.

outbursts against Ethel and her bad-tempered ways. It happened when she had a letter from her mother Mary Higgs, who was complaining of Ethel's treatment of her. I did not read the letter, but Mum, in a sudden outburst, said 'Your father has been married twice, and Ethel is the daughter of his first wife'. She was certainly christened Ethel Williams. In later years she married Frank Halsey – but she always referred to me as her brother.

I have mentioned that in appearance, the actor Arthur Lowe bears a startling resemblance to my father: the same stocky figure, nearly bald head, full face and a moustache, blue-grey eyes and a goatee beard. Not really my idea of an Apollo or Zeus, but no doubt in his youth, Dad was handsome enough. Be that as it may, women used to find my father fascinating, which rather surprised me, but I used to note how many of my mother's friends regarded him with awe and hung on to his every word.

At the time of Dad's death, Charles and Dora and Mary were the only surviving members of his first family. There was only one grandchild, Muriel.

The news of Dad's death was brought to Mum by, I believe, Charles Lacey. I heard afterwards that a gentleman called at the flat, so he must have known the set-up, or at least suspected something. Whether Dad asked him to assist our family after his death I do not know, for we were completely ignored.

Dad was buried in the Lacey family grave in Norwood Cemetery. Brother Reg and I went to the Memorial Service. Reg, who must have known what was going on, was home on leave at the time. It was a Thursday morning and I was busy at the provisions counter of the shop when he came in and saw Clarke the manager. I was called to the office and Reg told me that Dad had died. I was shocked and couldn't think clearly. Reg went on and told me that Dad was being buried 'by the Masons' at Littlehampton. He continued by saying that Mr Lacey had also died and was being buried this afternoon at Norwood and Mum wanted the two of us to go.

The memorial service was well attended and as far as I can recall, was an all-male affair. Why Dora and Mary were absent I do not know; I expect Charles Lacey was there but I did not know him and he did not introduce himself to us. The proceedings were of very little interest to me and my mind was full of other thoughts. Had I known that Mr Lacey was my father, the future pattern of my life would have been very different. As it was I was in complete ignorance. Con and Reg must have known, but for some obscure reason they did not confide in me.

We went with the other mourners to the graveside and whilst I did not take much interest in the last rites, I did notice how wealthy and influential the other mourners seemed to be. Most of them were probably Masons as well as business colleagues. In the days when motor cars were the prerogative of the wealthy there were quite a number at the gates, many chauffeur-driven. Nobody spoke to my brother or myself and so we left and boarded a tram opposite the cemetery gates and made our way back to Camberwell Green and home.

Naturally questions were asked for which I had no answers, and I felt sick at heart. I hoped that Mum when she recovered from the shock would enlighten me and answer the many questions that perplexed me. That evening, in the kitchen, I tried to talk with the others. Con was very caustic, but did not enlighten me and the other younger members of the family. It took us a very long time to believe that Dad was dead. In the days that followed, Mum kept silent. About a week later she came into my room, and, without saying anything, gave me Dad's cash box and a sealed letter. The cash box was empty. I broke the seal of the letter; inside was a sealed envelope addressed to Mum. The letter to me was no answer to my hopes. It was an instruction for me to see that my two youngest sisters were educated according to his wishes and saying 'ample funds would be forthcoming for this purpose'; that when Mum died I was to dispose of the home as I saw fit. In the event I never received one penny to carry out his wishes. I gave Mum the letter and said I would do my best to look after her and the girls. This I tried to do.

L. E. Williams
July 1978

CONTENTS

The Early Years 1907–1914..1
    First Memories..1
    High Days and Holidays...2
    Fun and Games..10
    At Home..12
    The Local Neighbourhood...16
    Shopping..19
    Demon Drink and Sweet Treats..22
    Outings with Reg...25
    Music and Song...26

Camberwell Remembered...29
    More about Stobart Mansions..29
    Kimpton Road and Beyond...32
    Camberwell Green...36
    Further Afield...40
    Denmark Hill..42
    Popular Entertainments...44
    Wren Road...45
    Contrasts and Changes..46

The War Years 1914–1918...49
    1914..49
    1915..53
    1916..72
    1917..84
    1918..92

The Post-War Years 1919–1921..99
    1919..99
    1920–1921..114

The Years of Change 1921–1930...117

Sunshine and Shadow 1930–1935...159
    1930..159
    1931..177
    1932..182
    1933..191
    1934..197
    1935 (up to 7 September)...202

The War Years 1939–1945 209
  1939 210
    Saturday 26 August to Saturday 2 September 210
    Sunday 3rd September 217
    Monday 4 September 221
    Tuesday 5 September 222
    Wednesday 6 September 223
    Thursday 7 September 224
    Sunday 10 September 224
    Monday 11 September to 31 December 225
  1940 230
  1941 249
    RAF Hednesford 249
    Home on Leave 258
    On Active Service 260
    Calshot Camp 268
    Garforth 271
    Shipton 273
    Handley Page Factory 279
  1942 281
    Shipton 283
    Linton-on-Ouse 284
  1943 301
    Sutton-on-Hull 302
    Hutton Cranswick 307
    Dishforth 308
    Snaith 310
    Rufforth 311
    On Leave 314
    St Eval 316
    Lindholme 321
    Upper Heyford 322
  1944 326
    RAF Tarrant Rushton, Dorset 326
    RAF Shipton 331
    RAF Stansted 332
    RAF Hunsdon 336
    RAF West Malling 339
    RAF Breighton 343
    RAF Woodbridge 345
    RAF Westcott 347
    RAF Clifton 349

    1945..350
        Junior Leaders' Course, Woolsington, Newcastle..............................352
        Earls Colne...353
        RAF Lindholme..355
        RAF Lissett...356
        The End of Hostilities in Europe...357
        RAF Odiham..359
        RAF St Athan, South Wales...360
        Weeton Hospital...364
        Goodbye to the RAF...366
        Christmas at Home...367
    Civvy Street..368

Appendix I: The Family Research of Janet Eaton......................371
    Frederick William Lacey..371

Appendix II: The Recollections of Mary Lacey...........................373
    Ellen...373
    Grandma Lacey 376

Appendix III: The Recollections of Sandra Pearse......................379
    Pamela's Story..379

Index...381

THE EARLY YEARS
1907–1914

First Memories

It is impossible to say with certainty when I first became conscious of my surroundings, of my parents, my sister or my brother or of what was happening around me. Hazy elusive pictures float almost within reach, only to fade and vanish when I try to steady and retain them. Most people can remember something of their early childhood, when the mists of time part to reveal a scene or happening that, at the time, was strong enough emotionally to imprint itself on the awakening memory.

I have three such memories, and can be fairly certain about when they happened because in later life I discussed them with my mother. The first was on Christmas morning of the year 1909 when I was just over two years old. I recall sitting on the floor playing with a toy tradesman's van and pushing it to and fro on its tin wheels whilst my parents, towering over me, showed me how to right it when it tumbled on to its side. Then I must have knocked it over in some way for suddenly the roof of the van slid off, cascading a lot of lovely coloured sugar-coated biscuits decorated with fairy-tale animals. I can still recall the laughter of my parents, sister and brother as they witnessed my delight at the unexpected discovery of so many good things to eat.

The next recollection was in the spring of 1911. My brother Reg had been told to take me to play in Brunswick Park, a little green oasis not far from home. Reg was two years older than me and he probably resented the responsibility of having to mind his younger brother when he would have preferred playing with his friends. In the park he told me to sit on a bench while he went off to join in the fun on the nearby field. It was eventide and as the light gradually faded from the sky I began to get cold and fidgety. After a while I got down from the bench and trotted off to find my mother. Unfortunately for me I went in the wrong direction and left the park by the Glebe Road gate. I retain a glimpse of the hospital wall with its railings as I wandered on in the darkness. Somebody must have found me for my next memory is in the police station at Peckham eating sweets. How Brother Reg fared when he returned home without me I know not, but when in the course of time my parents arrived to collect their wandering boy, they found me fast asleep in the interview room clutching a bag of sweets in a very grubby hand.

Later that same year, probably during the school holidays in August, Mother took her four children on a visit to see her mother, who lived in a cottage in Church Row, Aston Abbotts, a small village about six miles from Aylesbury in Buckinghamshire. I liked my grandmother because she knew small boys were always hungry and she did her best to give me the odd cake and piece of pie, despite my mother's protests.

One afternoon after playing alone in the garden, I went indoors but could not find my mother. On asking Granny where she was I was told she had gone to Nordock Farm to get some milk. I had been that way a couple of times with my sister and on impulse decided to go and meet her. The farm was about a mile away, across several fields. Many years later I retraced my early steps. I must have walked down the garden path and along the little footway that led to the road. Then past the pump that supplied water to the cottages, across the sandy road and round the churchyard wall and the schoolmistress's house. A kissing gate led into a field where the local lads played cricket on a Saturday afternoon, but where cattle grazed during the week.

At this point my memory returns. The footpath wound its way to another stile which I climbed over and dropped down onto the grass. Then I saw that between me and the next stile a herd of cows and some horses were grazing. The huge beasts frightened me and I hesitated by the stile. It seemed I stood there for an eternity wondering whether to go on or retrace my steps to Granny's cottage. Everything went suddenly quiet and I felt as if the whole world was watching me. The birds in the hedgerow hushed their singing, the butterflies their flickering, and out of the corner of my eye I saw a rabbit motionless, ears erect, by a clump of nettles in the corner of the field. The only sound was a soft breeze sighing through the uppermost branches of the trees.

I stood in the shadow of the stile, still hesitating and undecided what to do. The cattle and horses ceased to graze and stood watching me with lowered heads and unblinking eyes. Fear of these huge animals with their big horns urged me to go back, but the desire to find my mother was equally strong. This uncertainty seemed to last forever but was probably only a minute or two. Then with beating heart and unsteady legs I left the shadow and came out into the sunshine.

As I did so the world sprang back into life. The birds renewed their song, the butterflies continued dancing over the blackberry flowers, the rabbit disappeared into the nettles and the cows and horses moved away from the path as I approached. With pounding heart I passed safely through them and reached the further stile. As I climbed the rails I saw Mother and Ethel coming towards me with the milk in an enamelled can. I was overjoyed and ran the few yards to meet them. Hand in hand we walked back to the cottage and I was praised for being 'a brave little boy'.

High Days and Holidays

From what I remember of those far-off days, my early childhood was happy and carefree. My mother told me we used to spend our summer holidays at

Deal in Kent, but of this I have no recollection whatever. I do recall wearing a little sailor suit, being taken to the zoo, watching the squirrels in Regent's Park and having a ride on a camel.

The family gradually increased in number and holidays and outings became fewer, but we were always treated to a visit to a pantomime in the new year. We always went to the Kennington Theatre for this. We would join the queue outside the entrance and fidget impatiently until it was time to enter and see the show. Like children of all ages, my sisters, brother and I joined in the singing of the songs and thoroughly enjoyed ourselves. Between us we managed to remember most of the words of the comic songs and the melody. Long after this land of make-believe had become a distant memory, we would still be singing the songs we had learned around the flat. One such, from a production of *Cinderella* and sung by Buttons (who stuttered a lot), went something like this:

> *Brown bread, brown bread, brown bread, brown bread,*
> *I used to stutter, just the same as you,*
> *But by persevering, out of it I grew,*
> *I said 'Brown bread', every time I stuttered,*
> *So all you have to say is 'Brown bread, brown bread,*
> *Brown bread, well buttered'*

Our mother always tried to spend a few days each year with her mother in Aston Abbotts. Grandma Higgs (née Mary Bierton) was our only grandparent, the others having died before we were born. She was a dear soul. She dressed in black, had lots of wrinkles on her face and looked ever so old. One or two of us children always accompanied Mother and there was keen competition among us as to who should go. Mother tried to be fair but it wasn't easy. Sister Con was expected to look after the youngest sisters. I usually managed to get Mother to take me with her and I think this led to some friction with the others who believed, not unnaturally, that the younger son received preferential treatment.

There was one visit to Granny's, when Sister Grace was a toddler, when the five of us went with Mum because Dad was going to Paris on business. We were terribly excited at the prospect and Sister Con obtained a railway timetable and recited to the rest of us the names of the stations between Baker Street and Aylesbury railway station. She went through it so often that we came to know the stations by heart—St John's Wood, Finchley Road, Harrow on the Hill and so on. We were told that the Metropolitan Line was electrified only as far as Rickmansworth and that a steam locomotive hauled the train from that point on the line. There were other stations with romantic, strange-sounding names like Moor Park, Amersham, Great Missenden and Stoke Mandeville, and in our imagination we pictured them as places where witches brewed spells and elves and fairies danced in the morning dew. The reality proved to be somewhat different and there were no witches in black hats flying their broomsticks across the face of the moon.

When the long-awaited day came we went by tramcar to the Elephant and Castle and then by Underground to Baker Street. Dad saw us on to the train then left to return to his office somewhere in the City. Thinking back I cannot recall his ever accompanying us to the village. Evidently the rural life had no appeal for him.

Mother certainly had her hands full. Eileen was a baby in arms. Grace, I suppose, was aged about four years. Con, who was nearly ten, was a great help with our little sister. Reg, who was eight years old and full of energy, reckoned he was in charge. We were full of high spirits and were constantly being told to sit down and not to lean out of the window.

I had inherited from Mother a love of the countryside and was soon absorbed in the fields and woods sliding past the carriage window. We watched intently when the time came to attach the locomotive to the front of the train. When all was secure, it gave a great snort and we started the final part of our journey.

The rail journey to Aylesbury took about an hour and a half. When the train reached the county town we jumped down on to the platform and Reg and I passed our luggage to each other. I observed (for the first time) that in addition to our address, the labels bore the words 'Passenger to Aylesbury', a precaution I suppose against losing it.

We left the station and with our cases and bags struggled up the road known as Station Approach to the market square with its cobblestones. Mum shepherded us into the Temperance Hotel for some refreshments. To sit down and have a cup of tea in such a posh place was a real thrill and we felt most important. When we came out into the square we found that sister Grace (perhaps showing the first signs of her collector instincts) was clutching one of the hotel's teaspoons in her chubby hand. After a call into the nearby Home and Colonial Stores for some provisions we were ready for the final stage of our journey.

The motor omnibus which was to end the isolation of many villages and hamlets was still some years away and the link between the rural communities and the town was by a carrier and his horse-drawn cart. There was also a 'packman' who travelled from farm to farm and village to village with his wares in a pack on his back. He carried small items like bootlaces, cottons, tape, bottles of lotion, pencils and pegs. He was useful too, acting as a sort of postman carrying letters and messages to the outlying cottages and farms. Folk were a bit wary of the one who included Aston Abbotts in his round for he was a gossip and had prying eyes. His was already a vanishing race and as communications improved the end of the packman was inevitable.

The carrier, on the other hand, was a useful member of the village community. He belonged to a hardy race of men who faced all weathers to make a living by serving his small community. These carriers transported anything from passengers to sacks of cereals and livestock. They took corn to the miller and brought back the flour, took produce to town from the market gardens, and on market day would go shopping on behalf of the villagers. The one who served Aston Abbotts was Ned Kent. His family had the licence of the Royal Oak Inn at the entrance to the village. On the evenings before market days (Wednesdays or Saturdays) he would go around the houses and the lady of the house would give him a list of the items she wanted that could not be obtained from the village store.

About 9 a.m. on the morning of market day the carrier would take on passengers from outside the Bull and Butcher pub in the middle of the village opposite the blacksmith. He had a wooden form fixed on either side of his cart and the passengers, usually about twelve in number, would sit facing each other chatting and exchanging the latest gossip as the horse jogged them into town. There was space beneath the forms for luggage, parcels, boxes, anything in fact that could be described as portable. The cart was usually well down on its springs and hills were a bit tricky, causing the passengers to get out and walk up the steeper slopes. On arrival in Aylesbury the people would go their own ways while the carrier would go to the various shops with his clients' lists, leave them with the shopkeepers, and call back later in the day for the completed orders. What the financial arrangements were I know not. No doubt the carrier received a small commission from the shopkeeper as well as the charge he made to the customer for his services.

Opposite the north end of market square, across Bourbon Street, was the parking area for all sorts of horse-drawn conveyances. Here also were the premises of corn chandlers and hay and seed merchants. It was a lively, bustling place smelling strongly of horses and manure. Mother knew her way around these parts and soon found the place where the village carrier was stationed. It seemed we were expected. No doubt she had written to Ned Kent informing him that we were coming. She and he were old friends having been taught in the same village school. We squeezed on board and somehow space was found for our luggage. As Mum chatted with folk she knew and proudly presented her children to them her cares seemed to slip away and she looked years younger.

When the time for departure came the carrier released the brake and the horse slowly pulled the heavily laden cart. We turned left into Cambridge Street toward the Bierton Road. Just outside Aylesbury is a steep hill and most able-bodied folk, including Reg and I, alighted from the cart and walked to the summit as the horse was not equal to the load. Mum told us that one winter's day when the road was slippery with ice, there was a fire nearby. The Aylesbury fire appliance was called to the blaze but halfway up the hill the horses slipped and the engine overturned causing casualties among the crew.

On the left-hand side of the road we passed the entrance to the Women's Prison, a grim-looking building surrounded by a high wall with large iron gates across the entrance. However, we soon left it behind and entered the village of Bierton. It appeared to be a sleepy place with many old cottages and a very ancient public house. I remembered that Mother's name before she married was Bierton, and I wondered what the connection was, but I didn't have the opportunity to ask her as she was deep in conversation with another lady. The horse plodded on and soon Bierton disappeared around a bend in the road.

This part of Buckinghamshire was very rural. There were thick hedges bordering the road and in the meadows behind, cattle and sheep were grazing. Once we passed a flock of sheep moving over the road like a slow grey wave with a collie dog fussing around his charges. The shepherd exchanged a word or two with the driver and some of the passengers. On the right a weather-beaten sign pointed an arm to a village called Hulcott. It struck a chord for I remember Mum telling me that Granny Higgs had been born there. Although I looked for houses none were visible from the road we were on. Next we came to the hamlet of Rowsham where we stopped for a few minutes for the horse to have a breather.

On we went in very leisurely fashion. No one was in a hurry. It was undulating countryside and the road wound about to avoid the steeper inclines. Then we came to the Wingrave crossroads. The road to the right led to the village of Wingrave, the one to the left to Aston Abbotts whilst the road we had been travelling on continued to Wing and Leighton Buzzard. As we turned into the home stretch some of the passengers alighted once again, for the sandy road to Aston went up a steep hill. Once the hill was behind us our journey was almost over. We passed some old cottages on our left, strangely called New Zealand Cottages, I never found out why. Almost opposite was an area of land known as No-Mans which the Parish Council let out in plots to the men of the village for growing vegetables and fruit. Around a left-hand bend in the road was the Royal Oak Inn at the entrance to the village. The Inn looked very ancient with its thatched roof, and had a lot of land around it. Opposite the Inn was a grand house with a row of stables, called The Firs. Much of it was hidden behind high hedges. Soon after, we disembarked near the village green, on which grew some huge oak trees. I learned later that these were called the Town Trees and on them were pinned, or nailed, notices relating to village matters. Granny's cottage was only a few yards away and soon we were sitting down with a very welcome drink, whilst Mother and Granny hugged each other in joyful reunion.

Perhaps I could digress here with a few lines about Aston Abbotts as I knew it in those days. The Church of St James was built of stone with a square tower, and to me it looked a very dull building. It was surrounded by a churchyard and wall that bordered the road to Cublington. I presumed that many of my ancestors were laid to rest here but could find no trace of 'Bierton' or 'Higgs'. I suppose many of them were interred in the numerous humble mounds in the churchyard, as poor families could seldom afford a headstone. One monument stood apart from the others. It marked the burial place of the Arctic explorer Sir John Ross, who discovered the magnetic pole.[3]

On one side of the churchyard was the village school, only a small building, with two gabled roofs. I think there was only ever one teacher, but the standard of teaching was unusually high. On the other side was the vicarage. The incumbent at that time, named Paxton, was a generous man and keen horticulturist, who was held in high esteem by the village folk. His garden was a riot of colour. In front of the vicarage was the small church hall built in 1902. In all my visits to the village over many years I can only remember being inside once and that was years later when I had the honour of entertaining Aston's Senior Citizens.

Next to the village hall was the house of the schoolmistress in whose garden was one of the largest walnut trees I have seen. Away from the road leading up to Lines Hill (the highest point of the Chilterns), behind high hedges, across a lake, and hidden from view, was the Abbey, the great house around which the village was built. I have never been inside the Abbey, or even its gardens, for the owners did not encourage visits from the peasantry, although they relied on them to keep the place functioning. When I was about seventeen years old and spending a holiday in the village, I met the owner of the Abbey, a Major Morton, when strolling around the wooded area known as 'Fox Cover'. He very impolitely told me to 'clear off'.

The history of the Abbey, as I understand it, was that centuries ago the land belonged to a Saxon nobleman who, under spiritual pressure from the monks of St Albans, handed the land and buildings to them in return for the promise of an honourable place in Heaven. It was a common form of blackmail practised by the monastic leaders who thereby increased their possessions, and power. Presumably it remained in their clutches until the dissolution of the monasteries by Henry VIII, when the Abbey came into private ownership. During the Second World War it became the headquarters of the Czechoslovakian Government in exile and its leader, Dr Beneš,[4] was frequently seen around the village. My youngest sister, Pamela, married one of his bodyguards, a Charles Spalenka. When the war ended Dr Beneš erected a bus shelter for the villagers at the Wingrave crossroads.

At one time the villagers lived at the bottom of Lines Hill on the way to Weedon, but after a disastrous fire which destroyed most of the cottages they moved uphill to where the village now stands. From the summit of Lines Hill one could look across the vale of Aylesbury to the cross on the hill above Amersham. Most of the land, which was mainly pastoral, was owned by the Rothschilds, the merchant bankers. Their great house was at Mentmore, the

---

3 Sir John Ross (1777–1856) was buried at Kensal Green cemetery according to the Oxford Dictionary of National Biography. The magnetic pole was actually discovered by Sir James Clark Ross (1800–1862) on a voyage with Sir John Ross. It is James C. Ross who is buried at Aston Abbotts.
4 Dr Edvard Beneš (1884–1948).

other side of Wingrave. It followed that most of the men who worked the land were tenant farmers and the majority of the village males, farm labourers and shepherds. Many of the village houses had been erected about 1850 and were in terraces of four. Above the porches were the initials 'H.E.' (for Hilda Rothschild, the lady who had them built). Each house had four rooms, two up, two down, plus a large barn, a pigsty and a huge garden. To every block there was a pump and a bakehouse. These were 'tied cottages' (the house went with the job), and if a man left his employment he had also to leave his home. The rent in those days was 2*s.* 6*d.* a week. The wages of a man working on the land was 30*s.* 4*d.* a week plus 2*s.* 6*d.* for Sunday working.

There were, of course, other houses, some a lot older. A few were thatched. The Firs, the fine residence opposite the Royal Oak, was a much newer building. It was once owned by a Belgian millionaire named Lowenfeldt who, in mysterious circumstances, fell to his death from an aeroplane over the Channel in the First World War.[5] After that it came into the possession of the Steele family. There were two public houses, the Royal Oak (already mentioned) and the Bull and Butcher. The publican of the latter was also the village baker and he supplied bread to most of the nearby villages and hamlets.

A tiny Primitive Methodist chapel was near the village green and catered for the needs of the dissenters, who were few in number. I once went to a service there and preferred it to the one held in St James's. I think it was the smallest chapel I have ever been in. Nearby was the Post-Office-cum-village-store and opposite, the blacksmith's forge. He was a key figure in village life for he kept most of the agricultural machines and implements in working order. The population of Aston Abbotts, men, women and children, was about 200. I would not call it a pretty village, but it was clean and quiet and of generous proportions.

But to return to this particular visit. Granny made us very welcome and had laid on a nice tea which, after our long journey, was very welcome. The house itself was very small and like most cottages, had four rooms, a tiny kitchen and a little room with a bucket toilet. But this was home to Mother for she had been born here with her sister Rebecca and brother George, and she loved everything about it. There was a long front garden but the back garden was no longer part of the house because some time before, these back gardens had been taken in lieu of payment for a debt owed by the landlord. At the end of the terrace of cottages was a row of roomy barns, one for each cottage. In these, the family mangle and tin bath, plus the bits and pieces which could not be accommodated indoors, were kept. It was also the fuel store. Most people burned wood as coal was too expensive.

Mum's brother, George Bierton, with his wife Sarah and their family, lived

---

5 Probably Alfred Lowenstein or Loewenstein (1877–1928), Belgian soldier, aviator, sportsman and industrialist, who disappeared during a flight across the English Channel in his private aeroplane ('Captain Loewenstein', Obituary, *The Times*, 6 July 1928, 18b).

in the cottage next to the last one in the row. I believe they had four children, two sons and two daughters. They had little to do with us and, after some initial overtures to the boys, which evoked little response, we ignored each other. The girls were more friendly. Uncle George was a Parish Councillor but as the Council was run by the Lord of the Manor, it only rubber-stamped what the great man decided.

Most tenants of the cottages had large families. How they were reared in such small dwellings is beyond my comprehension. There was no piped water. A pump, which often froze in icy weather, was situated at the entrance to the common path, and from this the families drew their water in buckets. There was no gas or electricity. All cooking was done on a kitchen range and the rooms were illuminated by candles or paraffin oil lamps. Despite these primitive conditions the villagers seemed healthy enough.

I used to listen a lot to the adults' conversations and the general moan was the lowness of the farm workers' wage, which as I have said previously, was about thirty shillings a week. Even so, their standard of living seemed higher than that of the town dweller. Most men grew their own fruit and vegetables, many kept a few hens. Four men usually combined to keep a pig. The fields were alive with rabbits and whilst the farmers took a poor view of poaching, the odd bunny and occasional hedgehog often supplemented the family diet. There were times, like harvest, when extra money could be earned. Blackberries added flavour and colour to an apple pie, whilst mushrooms abounded in the fields. The townsman had little opportunity to vary his diet compared with the countryman.

During these halcyon days Mum would take us 'wooding' for Granny. Most folk relied on wood for heating and cooking. There were lots of trees around and after a gale, they would go and collect the dead branches that had blown down. We could only carry back the small stuff, but this was useful for kindling; the branches brought back by the adults were broken up and stored in the barns. Men would form a team and cut up any larger boughs where they had fallen. Some would be given to the elderly folk. As most villagers were related, either by blood or marriage, it was natural they should work toward the common good.

Brother Reg and I spent as much time as we could chasing rabbits. On hot days the rabbits would lie up in thick clumps of grass, and we would try to creep up silently, and then whack their hides with sticks. Many a sleeping rabbit must have had its dreams rudely shattered by us and, as it bounded away to the safety of the hedge, wondered who these horrible humans were. Once we disturbed a fox and watched his bushy tail bobbing away from us through the tall grass. Despite our enthusiasm and energy we never brought anything home for Granny's pot. Her cat was much more successful and often brought home a young rabbit.

One day, in a field on the Cublington side of the village called Coldharbour, we found some huge mushrooms. They were as big as dinner plates.

People called them horse mushrooms. They were quite distinct from the small button variety that grew in abundance in late spring and early autumn. That evening we feasted on fried mushrooms but unfortunately, during the night, I was terribly sick. Many years were to pass before I could bring myself to taste another and, even today, I prefer to leave mushrooms alone.

They were happy carefree days which passed all too quickly. As we boarded the carrier's cart for the first leg of our return journey it seemed only a few hours had passed since our arrival. There were tears in the eyes of Mother and Granny at the parting, but after we had said our farewells and murmured our thanks, we were soon chatting excitedly about our adventures, each clutching a bag of apples to take home with us.

Fun and Games

Whilst this holiday left many lasting memories my mind goes blank after it. Of the journey home my memory has no picture, so presumably our return was uneventful, and life continued much as before.

School seemed to fill my life from that time. I used to go along with Con and Reg, but was inclined to dawdle and this would often infuriate my sister, who did not suffer fools gladly. Getting up in the morning was a problem for I was usually too warm and cosy. Breakfast was normally a bowl of porridge with a sprinkling of sugar, although I much preferred golden syrup. In winter time I was always cold and suffered from chilblains a lot. I wore short trousers and a grey jersey but it did not keep the cold out. Cold was my Enemy Number One. It was demoralising and deadening. No one showed any sympathy, I was told to keep moving, slap my hands across my chest and jump up and down. People who were warm could not imagine anyone else feeling cold.

At my first school Christmas in 1912, we were each given an orange when we broke up for the holiday. This was a gift from the teacher and was a sort of tradition among primary teachers. It was only for children in their first year, and so the following year I was not so privileged.

At home sister Eileen (born 10 December 1912) was the baby. She was small, had auburn hair and seemed to cry a lot. I recall that one day she cried so hard and for so long that Mum, who had more than her share of patience, was in tears herself as she tried to pacify her. What caused this outburst I have no idea, nor, I think, did anyone else. However, after this she gradually calmed down and became quite a favourite. I did not get along too well with sisters Grace and Con, but Eileen and I were to have an excellent relationship.

During the summer of 1913 the flat across the landing, No. 23, Stobart Mansions became vacant and Mum and Dad took the opportunity to take the tenancy of it. Flat No. 21 had become rather cramped as there were now seven of us in the family, and although the number of rooms were the same, two bedrooms, a living room and kitchen, those in No. 23 were larger. On moving day we were sent out to play but, being curious, I came upstairs during the morning to see what was going on and saw Dad and Mum pushing furniture across the landing. When Dad looked up and saw me I was curtly told to keep out of the way and go and play in the yard. Dad was not blessed with much patience. Perhaps he found moving flats a big bore.

The yard was a concreted area between the two blocks of flats and this is where the children played their games. These were usually hide-and-seek (although there were few places to hide) and skipping, which was always popular amongst the girls. They would skip alone or together, and in the latter play, a girl at either end swung a rope whilst the rest, jumping together, tried to avoid getting their feet entangled in the rope as it came round. The unlucky ones would then change places with the ones turning the rope.

Hopscotch was popular although I never understood the finer points of the game. An oblong was drawn on the ground in chalk and subdivided into squares numbered 1 to 8, with a semicircular box at the top. A competitor would throw a stone into one of the squares then hop from box to box trying to retrieve it without getting the hopping foot on a chalk line. Another game was five-stones. These stones were five china or earthenware cubes with scalloped sides. They were placed in the flat of your hand, tossed in the air and then, with fingers outstretched, caught on the back of your hand. Those that landed on the ground could be retrieved in the time it took to toss a stone in the air and catch it again.

Marbles, when they could be obtained, were popular with the boys. Some were of earthenware but the best were made of glass, called 'alleys',[6] and were treasured. Some had thin coloured threads running through the glass making pretty patterns. If marbles were unobtainable the lads collected cherry stones and bowled them at metal screws; if you knocked the screw down you kept it. Playing with tops was equally popular. There were two kinds, spinning and whipping. The spinning tops were usually made of boxwood and were pear shaped, with a continuous groove running down from the domed top to a metal stem about a half inch long. To spin it, a length of string was wound through the groove then, holding it upside down, it would be flung away whilst pulling back sharply on the string. Once the art was acquired it gave hours of pleasure. The whipping top was much cruder; a small cylinder of wood with a metal stud at one end and a rounded piece of wood at the other end for a cap. The cap was usually coloured with chalk. One whipped it along by using a piece of string tied to a stick.

Hoops, made of wood or iron, came in many sizes and were played with by both sexes. One ran along the street with it using a hook or hitting it with a piece of wood to propel it. Provided one kept away from the main roads there wasn't much danger from traffic. In any case, what traffic there was was

---

6 *Ally* or *alley*, 'a choice playing-marble of marble, alabaster, or glass' (*Concise Oxford Dictionary*).

horse-drawn, plus a few bicycles. Only on the major roads were there tramcars and omnibuses.

Sometimes a child would obtain an old tennis ball and this would provide a lot of fun in the yard, although most tenants frowned upon ball games because of the danger of broken windows, which had to be repaired by the householder. The old-type tennis balls were of poor quality and soon lost their bounce. The 'Sorbo', or sponge rubber ball, did not come along until around 1919. There were community games like 'Mothers and Fathers', 'Poor Jenny is a Weeping', 'The Farmer wants a Wife' and 'I'm on Tom Tiddler's Ground Picking up Gold and Silver'. These, together with counting games, kept children amused during their leisure. The resulting noise was terrific but we were seldom asked to keep quiet. Most people in the flats had children so, I suppose, they shut their ears to babble and din.

The collecting of cigarette cards was a national hobby and any male walking along the street smoking was a target for small boys with the universal request of 'Got any cigarette cards, guv'nor?'. Sometimes one was lucky but most times not. Collecting a set was a must and a lot of swapping went on with this aim in mind. I remember one boy selling a set of Army Badge cards for 2½d. In those days that was a lot of money.

At Home

The family soon settled in to No. 23 and we were to stay there for the next fifteen years. By present-day standards our furnishings were meagre. There was a plain wood-top table in the kitchen with half a dozen chairs. To the side stood a built-in wooden dresser reaching to the ceiling; its upper section had open shelves for keeping plates and saucers, and hooks screwed into the front held cups and jugs. Below were two drawers for keeping cutlery and cloths and, underneath, two cupboards for storing dishes and containers. A little wooden food safe on four legs with a metal gauze in the door kept perishable food, although everything cooked by Mum was usually consumed at one sitting. In hot weather keeping food fresh was a major problem and flies were an awful nuisance. People who could made daily visits to the shops.

Each room had a fireplace of sorts although those in the bedrooms were rarely used. The kitchen range had a strip of green tiles on either side, and above it was a board known as the mantelshelf. This had a frilly coloured dado hanging from it, whilst on the board were displayed the few family mementoes—a vase or two, some decorated tins, including the tea caddy, a jar containing pins and old buttons which Mum had cut from worn-out clothes, and some gas bill receipts and the like. On another wall hung the 'Eagle' bracket. This was a very handsome piece with an eagle carved from wood supporting a small shelf, and an upright mirror with a smaller version of the eagle crowning the surrounding carving. I have often wondered what became of this family treasure.

The colour of the paint on doors and woodwork was either dark brown or dark green. Today we would find it most depressing but then we accepted it without question for it was the norm. The wallpaper was of poor quality, very thin, and had vertical lines of coloured flowers, mostly roses, running from ceiling to skirting board. Most of the walls were covered by large pictures, mostly by an artist of the Victorian period called Arthur J. Elsey. Mum liked the works of this man but they tended to follow a standard pattern—a young woman with long flowing tresses, wearing an ethereal expression as she gazed heavenward whilst clasping a book (presumably the Bible) in a slender hand. There was always an animal in these pictures, a horse or dog, and I think it was this feature that appealed to Mum, for she loved the natural world.

On a side table was our aspidistra plant, which had its leaves regularly sponged. I cannot recall it ever having any flowers, but these plants were very popular and a specimen could be seen in most houses. The Kimpton Mission used to give us every year a large illustrated paper calendar containing a text for each day of the year, and this was proudly displayed until it was torn or defaced with pencil, or crayon, or became dirty from smoke or flies.

In the kitchen was the cooking range with an oven at its side. It was very efficient, burning almost anything, from bits of old wood to vegetable waste. The fire had an iron plate in front that could be hinged down to support an iron, kettle or saucepan. The top of the range was a steel plate with a couple of removable rings in it, over which stood the big iron kettle and saucepan. A 'damper', like a small swivelled plate, could be used to direct the heat from the fire over the top of the oven. Some kitchen ranges also had a water container on the other side of the fire. This had to be filled manually, but there was a tap for drawing off the hot water.

To my way of thinking, the kitchen range was a godsend, for its small fire provided not only warmth but the means of cooking and baking at a low cost. Even the flatirons could be heated either in front of the fire or on top, although one had to be sure no bits of dirt attached themselves to the iron during the process of heating.

Most housewives took a personal pride in their ranges, which were kept polished with blacklead; the edges were rubbed with emery cloth to make them gleam. The iron fender that kept ashes and cinders confined to the hearth received similar treatment. There was a big ash box beneath the fire and when this was full Brother Reg or I took it down to the yard and emptied it into one of the dustbins. When the ashes had been disposed of, the hearth would be washed, then rubbed with a piece of rough hearthstone and smoothed with a damp cloth to give it a white surface when dry. It was work that never ended. Periodically, the chimney had to be swept, although a flue brush helped to keep the chimney sweep's visits to a minimum. Some folk seldom called on the services of the sweep and chimney fires often resulted, filling the air with burning soot and obnoxious fumes which smelt horrible and made eyes burn and smart.

Next to the range, in the corner by the window, was a primitive kind of boiler known as the 'copper'. It was like a deep bowl made of zinc and enclosed in a casing of brick and mortar. Below was a small firebox for heating the water, the smoke exit of which was linked to the kitchen range. The fire took a lot of lighting and often a down draught would send a tongue of flame spurting out into the room. Singed hair and eyebrows were not unknown. The copper had a wooden lid and a piece of broom handle served as a 'copper stick' to push the washing down into the water when it ballooned up. Mother always used 'Hudson's Soap Powder' when boiling the clothes. It cost 1½d. a packet and weighed about three-quarters of a pound.

On the opposite wall were pipes leading to a black monster—the gas stove. It had three burners and an oven. Like the range, parts of it were blackleaded and the showy bits kept shiny by repeated rubbings with Oakey's emery paper. This gas stove burnt a lot of gas when in use for it had large burners when lit; these spurted out great jets of flame, which gave off a horrible sulphurous smell. Most folk disliked using the oven, which became spattered with burnt fat and (unlike the enamelled ones today, with removable linings) had to be cleaned by scraping – a most unpleasant job. As a result, people either used the range oven or took the Sunday joint, or meat pie, to Kranz the baker for cooking. His shop was on the right hand corner of Kimpton Road and D'Eynsford Road. We used to buy our bread there. The bread was always weighed, and if it was below the standard weight of two pounds, a small roll or piece of bread was put on the scales as 'make-weight'.

I think gas may have been installed in the flats after they were built for the ugly iron pipes were not buried out of sight but were fixed in the angle of walls and ceiling. In time these pipes became covered with a coating of whitewash and dirt which flaked off, fell on the floor and made a mess. Periodically, these pipes had to be 'blown' to get rid of the rust and foreign matter that accumulated inside them, causing a lowering of pressure. Just inside the entrance door was the gas meter which had an insatiable appetite for pennies. The charge to householders for gas was 1s. 8d. a therm, or 1,000 feet of gas (a therm was once described as a germ which got into gas meters and caused rapid consumption).

The householder did not get a full pennyworth when a coin was put in the meter because the Company charged for fixtures and fittings, which were included in the price, and it made sure that they were always on the right side by making the consumer pay for more gas than he received. About once a month, the gasman called to empty the meter. He would unlock the securing padlock, take out the coin box and tip the pennies out on to the kitchen table. The coins would be counted and stacked into piles of fifteen, and then four of these piles would be neatly stowed into a 5s. paper bank bag. After calculating how much had been overpaid he would issue a receipt and return the surplus pennies. If any foreign coins had found their way into the coin box they were returned as part of the surplus. Often the pennies returned by the collector made the difference between having a meal or going hungry. I know it happened on more than one occasion to us.

Illumination of the flat when daylight faded and night closed in was by gas or candle-light. Before the coming of the incandescent gas mantle, the gas came from brackets on the walls. One turned a little tap and applied a lighted match or taper, and the gas ignited in a naked semicircular flame. Although an enamelled plate, blue on top and white underneath, was hung from the ceiling to catch the soot from the jet, the ceilings always looked grubby. These gas flames were dangerous and the cause of many fires. The gas supplier for our area was the South Metropolitan Gas Company which had its headquarters, gasholders and retorts in the Old Kent Road at Peckham. The incandescent mantle, when it arrived, was quite a big advance in lighting. There were two types, upright and inverted. Before use, they had to be 'burnt off'. Their main drawback was their fragility, for they would fall to pieces at the slightest knock.

Mother never liked her children walking about with lighted candles but, on the odd occasion when any of us did, it always had to be carried in a candlestick, which was a saucer-shaped enamelled dish with a holder for the candle in its centre and a finger ring on the outside for carrying.

Electricity for the domestic consumer came to the Mansions in 1928. Despite promises that it would be no dearer than gas, we found it expensive – it worked out at sixpence a unit. The landlord, or the Electricity company, or (as I suspect) both in collusion, pulled a fast one on all the tenants, who had been led to believe that installation would be free, whereas in practice, the cost was hidden in the charge per unit. In the end, we paid for the installation and fittings, paid a quarterly charge and for the amount of light we used.

The floor of the kitchen was solid concrete but those of the living room and bedrooms were of wood. In the beginning, when, presumably, finances were better, all were covered with linoleum, but as this wore out, it was replaced with oilcloth. This oilcloth came in attractive colours and pleasing patterns, and was cheap. It was the standard covering for the floors in most homes. Alas, it was not made to last and once the decorative surface wore off the black, tarry under-surface became exposed and it looked horrible. Where the floorboards were uneven their lines showed through in a series of ridges. We had a few rugs scattered around, the largest of which graced the area in front of the living room fire.

A door in the kitchen opposite the copper led to the toilet. In front of the toilet door was a space about six feet by four feet. Here we stored the mangle, brooms and pails and, from a nail in the wall, the galvanised bath. This space had an outside wall about four feet high, and overlooked the yard. It was open to all the winds that blew and although some neighbours enclosed their space, we never got round to doing ours. It would have made the flat much warmer had we done so.

The sink was sited in front of the kitchen window, was made of a yellow stone and was very shallow, with the only tap over it. Water splashed over the sides very easily and we often had to mop the floor if anyone was clumsy. Hot water came from the big black kettle that stood permanently on the range, or from the copper when it was lit. A few shelves were fixed to the walls. Hanging by the side of the range was a large ladle used when Mother made one of her stews. It had the initials 'M.B.' engraved on it but what they stood for I never did find out.

None of the flats possessed a bathroom but in each of the bedrooms was a washstand with a marble top on which stood a large decorated china basin and jug with a soap dish to match. The girls used this, but Reg and I washed at the kitchen sink. At weekends, the copper would be lit and the hot water scooped out into the bath. It was not unknown for two or three of us to use the same water.

I suppose by modern day standards, our accommodation would be termed as inadequate, but we never gave it any thought. We were better off than most. While we were small, brother Reg and I shared the same room as our sisters, but as we grew older we put up our bed in the living room. In the end the living room became the third bedroom and we lived in the kitchen, although Reg and I sometimes slept on the floor in front of the fire. This sufficed us until mid-1928 when we moved downstairs to No. 14, where I had my own room.

The Local Neighbourhood

In those early days we children would often sit at one of the windows overlooking Kimpton Road and watch the animated scene below. We took a keen interest in all the exciting happenings. Now and again a small herd of cattle went by and we laughed to see people scatter as the animals charged into gardens or came up on the pavements. One morning there was great excitement as a flock of sheep, fussed over by two collie dogs with a shepherd at the rear, came up Kimpton Road and disappeared round the corner into Church Street. Where these animals went to I know not, but the countryside was not so far away. There were still farms in Dulwich and open spaces where animals were rested. I recall seeing some cattle grazing in a small meadow at the top of Fowler Street, and for some years cattle were kept for milking purposes in Lugard Street, Peckham. Sheep were often brought to Hyde Park to graze in summer.

All types of itinerant traders, struggling to earn a living, pushed their wares around streets on costers' barrows. The air was full of noise as each man called or shouted out, to acquaint the public with the goods or services they had to offer. Many sold fruit or vegetables, others firewood or cats' meat on skewers. There were coalmen, knife grinders, sellers of pots and pans, and out-of-date comics or magazines at reduced prices. Once some young women in Victorian or Georgian costume came selling sprays of lavender, singing one of London's old street songs:

> *Won't you buy my sweet lavender,*
> *Sixteen branches for a penny...*

It was lovely to hear and it made a great impression on me. I never forgot the scene. Another time a group of Welsh miners sang in harmony, but their songs I cannot recall.

As soon as they were old enough every member of the family was expected to share in the household chores. One of my jobs was to clean the knives on a Saturday morning. These knives were made of steel and stained easily. In days to come the addition of nickel into knife-making was to make them stainless, but when I was a child that process was some years away. I would sprinkle some Oakey's knife polish on to a strip of leather fixed to a piece of board and rub the knives forward and backward until the stains were removed. Sometimes emery paper was needed if the knives were heavily impregnated, and this made them very sharp.

Occasionally a cleaner of knives would come round the streets. He had a hand-propelled cart on top of which was a circular box with slots in it for inserting the knives up to their handles. Inside the box were two drums covered with leather and impregnated with powder. The drums revolved either by a foot pedal or a handle. How I used to wish he would clean our knives and leave me more time to play.

Another regular workman was the chair repairer. He would sing out:

> *Old chairs to mend,*
> *Old chairs to mend,*
> *Rush or cane bottomed,*
> *Old chairs to mend.*

He would sit on the pavement or on a doorstep and quietly re-weave any chair passed to him. Some of our chairs started life with rush bottoms but as these frayed, Mum replaced the rush with thin shaped wooden seats which were nailed to the frame and stained with Jackson's Varnish Stain.

Milkmen were the first roundsmen of the day. Their first delivery started about 6 a.m., the second, after breakfast. As clocks were not plentiful, some were unofficial 'knockers-up'. They brought the milk in a large churn which bore the name of the supplier. It was carried on a 'pram', something like a tricycle. Around the pram were racks for carrying the milk cans, each of which was engraved with the name of the dairy. As I recall it, the first milk bottle came into use around 1920 and were much thicker round the neck than present-day counterparts. Inside the neck of the bottle was a rim, and a cardboard disc was pressed on to it for a seal.

Some milkmen had lovely yodelling voices, and their call 'Milko' was a joy to hear. They sang out, not for the benefit of their regular customers, but in the hope of attracting 'chance trade'. I gathered their wages were small, but they boosted their earnings with commission on sales.

Many people had a poor opinion of the milk roundsmen for it was believed that they not only watered the milk, but gave short measure as well. One day at the pantomime, where we had been taken to see *Ali Baba*, one of the company came to the front of the stage and shouted, 'I'm one of the forty thieves, the other thirty-nine are milkmen'. He received great applause from the audience.

We bought our milk from the Farmers and Cleveland Dairy whose manager was a Kimpton Mission stalwart. His son once gave me a brown and white rabbit whom we nicknamed 'Buckshee Bunce', after a character in a comic. The dairy was in Camberwell Road, just past Wyndham Road, but the entrance to the milk yard was round the back in Crown Street. In this area of Sultan Street, Wyndham Road, Toulon Street and Crown Street were Camberwell's worst slums.

Often we purchased the odd pint from Jackson's Dairies, whose man came around in a milkcart called a 'Chariot'. The name aptly described the vehicle. It was two-wheeled, had a sloping floor and long shafts for the horse, and was driven at an angle. It carried two churns. Riding in it gave one quite a thrill.

Barrel-organs playing the latest tunes came down the road regularly and there were always men, down on their luck, croaking out a sentimental ballad in the hope of getting a penny or two from a sympathetic listener or someone who wished them further. One day, brother Reg, who was always enterprising, heated a halfpenny in the fire then threw it down to a street singer who acknowledged the gift with a wave of his hand. When he stooped and picked up the coin, he quickly dropped it. How we laughed when he looked up and shook his fist. The next time we tried it he kicked the coin first into the nearest puddle.

Besides the itinerant street traders, there were always men or women knocking on the door with something to sell, or with a hard luck story to tell. One day, when Reg was indoors on his own (the rest of us being out with Mum), a knock came on the door and on opening it a woman selling 'Hair tidies' confronted Reg. I presume these hair tidies were grips or combs which ladies used for keeping their long hair under control. Finding Mum out she got Reg into conversation and extracted from him where Mum kept the rent money. When we returned home, the rent money had been taken and a few hair tidies left in its place. Mum was very bitter to think a woman could have so taken advantage of a boy's trust.

These door-to-door salespeople had a reputation for dishonesty. One day, Harry Moon. who lived on the ground floor of the opposite block, bought for 1*s.* 6*d.* a quart beer bottle of French polish from a man at the door. When he went to use it he found only the top inch or so was polish, the rest was water. These sharp practices were all too common.

Shopping

It was the heyday of the small shopkeeper and their little businesses were to be found on the corners of most of the back streets. They opened their shops early and shut them late as the competition for trade was very keen. They found it hard going for there was little money about. They used all sorts of minor attractions, mainly for children, to lure the customers. Among the gifts they offered were balloons, paper windmills, packets of paper flowers (which opened when immersed in water) and little butterflies that had a tiny metal ball in the hollow cylinder that formed the body, and which, by letting it descend down a piece of cardboard at an acute angle, would flutter over and over.

Mum liked to take one or two of us with her when she went shopping, mainly to help carry home her purchases. She used to visit Waterloo Street, which was a busy little market just on the north-east side of Camberwell Green. On one side, the row of shops backed on to the Greencoat School and the Marmite factory (which smelled horrible). A large greengrocer's, Priest's, had their premises at the 'Green' end. They also specialised in removals, and owned a large pantechnicon drawn by two horses. There was keen rivalry between Priest's and another greengrocer's at the further end whose prices were a little cheaper and where Mum usually bought her potatoes and greens. In between was a row of small shops and a yard that sold jumble items of furniture and the like. A proportion of the yard's profits were said to help King's College Hospital.

Outside these shops, in the gutter, were about twenty stalls selling a wide range of foodstuffs. I was always fascinated by the woman who kept the rabbit stall. She could skin and chop a rabbit in about half a minute. We ate lots of her rabbit, which sold at 6d. a pound and was very tasty. The fish stall sold herrings, kippers and haddock (Dad's favourite). He preferred a cut from a large fish to a small whole one. One of the shops sold fish and chips which was as popular then as it is today. The usual charge was 1d. for chips and 2d., 3d. or 4d. for fish, according to size.

Because there were no refrigerators in those days, many folk would hang around the butchers, fishmongers and fruit stalls on a Saturday evening waiting for the shopkeepers to sell off their remaining stock cheaply. It was part of the way of life. There was so little money in the average purse that every penny had to buy as much as it possibly could.

As a special treat we were occasionally taken to Brixton on a tramcar. At that time many theatrical folk lived in the Brixton area because it gave easy access to the London theatres. From Camberwell Green to the stop by the police station at the end of Gresham Road, the fare was 1d. for adults and ½d. for children. There were two big stores in the Brixton Road, Quin and Axtens, and the Bon Marche. We did not go into them very often but usually made our way to the market stalls in Atlantic Road. Under one of the railway arches Marks and Spencer had their 'Bazaar', and we often walked round it whilst the trains rattled by overhead. A little further along, under another arch, was Woolworth's. Everything they sold was sixpence or less. We loved going round although we had no money to buy anything. Across the road was a turning called Electric Avenue. Mum often told us that at one time its illuminations fair dazzled the eyes, but I never saw it thus.

Unfortunately, Brixton had its share of pickpockets and bag-snatchers even in those days, and a tight grip had to be maintained on one's purse, whilst an open shopping basket was an invitation to the light-fingered who hovered around ready to steal at the slightest opportunity that presented itself. Trams leaving Brixton were always crowded, and with no orderly queues, in the rush and struggle to get aboard, many a packet of tea or bag of sugar was 'lifted' by a human predator. Mum herself suffered this on more than one occasion and sometimes she pinned a cover over the top of the basket.

Now and again we made a shopping expedition to Westmoreland Road, a turning out of Walworth Road, near Camberwell Gate, where the turnpike once stood. Here were more stalls, mainly of vegetables and fruit. Nearby was Arments, the eel and pie shop. It was a real treat to be taken there for a pie and mash for the shop specialised in steak and kidney pies which cost $2d.$ each. Mash was $1d.$ Their stewed or jellied eels were almost as popular. Pieces of eel about an inch long were encased in a green jelly, and my tummy turned over when I looked at them. But how I loved those pies. All their food was said to be made on the premises. An order for pie and mash would result in a pie being tipped out of its tin dish on to a plate, a spoonful of mash would be flopped at its side and the whole lot covered with 'liquor', a sort of white sauce with bits of parsley floating in it. One took the plate to a high-backed bench where tin cans of salt and pepper stood on the table. The cutlery, as one can imagine, was not exactly silver-plated, but it sufficed.

Although I was no lover of the liquor the pies were excellent, with a good meat filling and thick dark gravy. In after years, memory often reminded me of them, especially during the last war when food was monotonous and scarce. Many years later when I was working at the Elephant and Castle I decided to visit Arments and sample their wares. I went in, ordered a pie but declined the mash and liquor. Alas, the pie bore no resemblance to its ancestor of fifty-five years ago and although its price had increased twenty-fold, it tasted nothing like the pies of my memory. Arments still flourishes although it has moved from the Walworth Road into Westmorland Road.[7]

In those days men employed on manual work had to put in very long hours, often from early morning until late at night. Mechanical aids to assist the masses with their daily toil were, with few exceptions, still locked away in the future and consequently labour for man and beast was arduous and endless. Many jobs like road making and repair, ditching and excavating

---

[7] Arments trades at 7–9 Westmorland Road (see http://www.armentspieandmash.com).

were carried out by gangs of 'Navvies' (a name handed down from the Navigators who built Britain's canals and railways). Some of these men were huge and could wield a pickaxe, sledgehammer or shovel for hours without seeming to weary. Some of them sang, rather unmusically, as they worked. One of their songs, probably learned from some of the old time navvies, went something like this:

I'm a navvy, I'm a navvy working on the line,
Four and twenty bob a week including overtime,
Pease pudding, mutton chops, every dinner time,
That is what a navvy gets for working on the line.

The biggest men I ever saw were the draymen employed by the breweries. These men, who drove the great shire horses that pulled the heavily-laden drays over the cobbles, could lift the heavy beer casks from the dray and slide them down wooden chutes into public house cellars without any seeming effort. Sometimes if the cellar was deep they wove a thick rope around the barrel and lowered it to the cellarman in the gloom below. These men wore leather aprons, caps and heavy boots. Most had ruddy complexions and large red bulbous noses. The horses usually had a feed from a nosebag whilst the deliveries were made.

Household coal came by train from the collieries and was dumped on railway sidings. It was brought around the streets by horse and cart although here and there were little coal yards where small quantities of fuel could be purchased, and most poor folk bought fourteen pounds of coal at a time. The coalman carried different kinds of coal and these were marked in chalk at the side of the driver's seat. The most common, and cheapest, were 'Kitchen Nuts'. Others were 'Silkstone', 'Derby Brights' and 'Tyne Main Cobbles'. The coalman also carried a pair of heavy scales which came into use when a Local Authority Inspector checked the weight of the coal in the sacks. People distrusted coalmen who always seemed to leave a few lumps behind on the cart when making a delivery.

Most greengrocers obtained their supplies of vegetables and fruit from the Borough Market in Southwark. The market began business early and was usually finished by 8 a.m. The potatoes came in two-hundredweight sacks and because they were never very clean, the greengrocer would tip some on to a large sieve and give them a good riddle to get rid of the surplus dirt, before putting them on sale. Apples came in large barrels, or bushel baskets, and it was a common sight to see a man carrying several baskets on his head. Spanish oranges came in boxes which had a partition in the middle. The greengrocer would throw out these orange boxes and they were often used to house a child's pet rabbit or guinea pig.

Sugar came to the shops from the refinery in two-hundredweight sacks which bore the name of the well-known firm of Tate and Lyle in big black letters on the hessian. The grocer always said he made no profit on sugar. The sack was the only thing on which he made a few pence. Women often bought these sacks and made them into coarse aprons to wear when doing dirty work such as cleaning the grate or scrubbing the scullery floor. They were especially useful to women who worked on the market stalls. Tea came from India and Ceylon in chests made of plywood and bound with metal strips to protect the edges. Inside was a tinfoil lining to keep the 100 lb of tea away from the wood. Removal men were always keen to purchase these chests for transporting breakable items like china and glass, but most chests went back to the tea blenders and importers.

Demon Drink and Sweet Treats

What to do with their small amount of spare time posed problems for many overworked men and women who were not content to relax in their own homes. Their choice of recreation and entertainment was limited. There was the music hall or the bioscope,[8] but many of them gravitated to the local taverns. The best public houses had much to offer beside drink, for in them local trade union branches conducted their business. Fraternities like the Buffaloes and Oddfellows held their lodge meetings on the premises.[9] Landlords organised 'slate clubs', a form of saving that was shared out at Christmas. Here too were the darts and billiard teams who competed with other hostelries in the league. There was always a piano, and music and entertainment were part and parcel of the old time pub. No doubt many political and social views were aired over a pint of old and mild.

Although the reputation of such establishments was high there were many less well appointed public houses where men and women were encouraged to drink to excess. The resulting drunkenness was a terrible social evil, for the money that some working-class parents should have spent on food, clothing and rent was squandered on the altar of the great god alcohol. Many desperate women knew from bitter experience, that once the man of the house went boozing with his pals on the evening of a pay day, there would be little money left for her to provide for the family when he reeled home drunk and aggressive after the pub closed. These tragic women would wait outside their man's place of employment to get some of his wages before he had the opportunity to drink it away. If both husband and wife were heavy drinkers their children suffered greatly and home conditions were pitiful.

I have some vivid memories of drunken brawls in the streets and the screams of women and children who were punished for being in the way

---

8 An early form of cinema popular from the late 1890s through to the First World War. Bioscope shows formed part of the entertainment on offer at music halls, such as the 2,000-seater Camberwell Empire on Denmark Hill.

9 The Royal Antidiluvian Order of Buffaloes (RAOB), a quasi-Masonic fraternity founded during the 1820s, philanthropic in aim; The Oddfellows, one of the oldest of the friendly societies.

when the drunk reeled home. Many had to run to neighbours for safety until the man's drunkenness wore off. Stories of such brutal treatment of loved ones were commonplace and they frightened me. I would hurriedly cross the road to avoid contact if I saw a reeling figure heading my way. Once I saw a little girl trying to lead her drunken father home and her cries were heart-rending as he kept falling into the gutter. For once I tried to comfort the little lass and helped the man home.

One man who lived in the opposite block of the Mansions, and who always drank to excess at weekends, smashed up his piano one lunchtime and threw the pieces out of the window of his third floor flat into the yard, much to the amusement of some residents but to the astonishment and consternation of others.

Much of the poverty in our neighbourhood was due to drink. Men stole for it, others pawned clothes and treasured possessions to buy it. Children in rags and barefooted went hungry because of it and many men and women became social outcasts because their will to resist it had gone. There was no Alcoholics Anonymous to help in those days. As children we were not allowed to be out after dark unless we were at the Mission, but on occasion, when we had been out with Mum and we came home through the ill-lit streets, we would see little children in threadbare clothes, looking tired and hungry, standing or sitting on the pavement outside the Hermit's Cave or the Artichoke,[10] waiting for their parents to come out and take them home. It was a sight that made my Mother, normally a quiet and placid woman, extremely volatile and angry.

But the public conscience on this problem was slowly awakening and, led by the Salvation Army, the Mission Halls and the Temperance League, a vigorous campaign was under way to educate young people on the effects and evils of excess drinking. The Band of Hope was in the forefront of the attack and branches were formed at most of the Shaftesbury Missions. Resources were limited and at first seemed to have little impact on the problem, but progress was made. As children we joined the Mission's Band of Hope, not for any convictions about drink, but because it was another evening out. To become a member one had to make a promise, something like this; 'I promise to refrain from drinking intoxicating liquors as beverages'. It didn't mean much to us. We went for the social side and the annual tea and entertainment that went with it. Mr Scurr was the leader, with Miss Mulley as his secretary and deputy.

Dad enjoyed a glass of Scotch or Irish whisky, whilst Mum, for medicinal reasons, enjoyed a glass of Hammerton's Stout, which was reckoned to be beneficial for nursing mothers. There was a small off-licence on the corner of Harvey Road and Sansom Street and that was where we used to go for Mum's beverage. However, our parents were moderate in all things and they put the

---

10 Both on Church Street, Camberwell, at nos. 28 and 25 respectively.

needs of their children first. At a very early age I took an intense dislike to the smell of beer, porter and all kinds of liquor, and instantly resented any person who had been drinking breathing alcoholic fumes over me.

As I grew older the resentment against strong drink did not diminish, rather it increased, and has stayed with me to this day. Often as I ran errands for Mum or for neighbours, I would see a man who had spent his money so unwisely as to become inebriated, pitched into the street by the bouncer. Such unpleasant incidents strengthened my determination that the demon drink would not have me as a disciple.

The favourite children's drink was lemonade and was similar to its modern counterpart. Another soft drink was cherry cider, bright red in colour. There were two mineral water firms in the neighbourhood, R. White of Albany Road and Batey of East Dulwich Road. The latter firm specialised in Koala, possibly an ancestor of today's Coca Cola or Pepsi Cola. As a child it was a real treat to have a drink of lemonade from a bottle. These bottles were called 'Codds' after their inventor Hiram Codd, and the drink nicknamed 'Cods Wallop'.[11] The fizzy drink was sealed inside the bottle by a glass marble held tightly against a rubber collar in the neck by the gas pressure from the pop. To get to the contents, the marble was forced down by a plunger and two little lugs prevented it from reblocking the neck of the bottle when the liquid was poured out. It was said that thousands of these bottles were smashed by boys in order to get at the glass marble. Codd bottles are now quite rare and are very collectable.

By present day standards sweets were cheap. Toffees, favours, American gums and the like sold at 6*d*. a pound and the confectioner would always sell a child a 'ha'porth'. I loved coconut ice, a mixture of sugar and desiccated coconut, which was made into oblong slabs, pink on top with a white base. It also sold at 6*d*. a pound. Then there was coconut candy, strips of coconut in a mould of brown sugar, but it was inclined to be gritty. A finer type of this confection was Indian Cream made of coconut flour and sugar and sold in pink and white lumps about the size of a tennis ball, at 8*d*. a pound.

Then, as today, the main ingredient of confectionery was sugar, which sold in the shops at 2*d*. a pound. Some people made their own sweets like bullseyes or acid drops. Beside the sugar-based sweets there were liquorice sticks and Pontefract cakes (little circles of liquorice about the size of a penny). Then there were aniseed balls, linseed, liquorice and chlorodyne lozenges (popular in winter). Also heavily-scented cachous for sweetening the breath, sherbet sucks and sweethearts, little flat round sweets which bore slogans in red lettering, such as 'I love you' or 'meet me tonight'.

Chocolate was very expensive and the best varieties like Cadbury's and Rowntree's were out of reach for the less well off. The cheaper brands, as I remember them, were coarse in texture, tasted of cocoa and had a slightly

---

11 Hiram Codd (1838–1887) perfected the 'Codd' bottle in 1872.

bitter taste. Peppermint rock was popular but American gums stuck to the teeth like glue. Then there were toffee apples, tiger nuts and monkey nuts (peanuts that came in their shells and were unroasted). Many sweets sold at two ounces for a penny but as pocket money (when you got it) was only a half-penny a week one had to be very selective before spending it. Often I would gaze in a shop window for a long time trying to decide which of the attractive wares on display should receive my patronage.

Jam and marmalade jars were returnable to the shops. Jam was almost a staple food. It sold in one-, two-, three- and seven-pound jars. Two pounds of Laurie's Marmalade cost 6½d. but Hartley's, Chivers' and Robertson's Golden Shred (a real luxury) was 8½d. Mixed fruit jam, said by the people who knew to be only flavoured turnips, was 3 lb for a shilling. One was not allowed margarine and jam on the same slice of bread, it was one or the other. Sometimes if we ran errands for neighbours they would give us an empty jar which we would take back to the shop. A halfpenny was refunded on a 1 lb jar and a penny on a 3 lb jar but we did not get many of the latter size. When the cash was in our hands we would deliberate on what to buy. It was seldom sweets, more likely it was stale cake, broken biscuits or broken saveloys. We would share the spoils with our friends and often had our feast in the yard or Brunswick Park.

Ice-cream was in its infancy and was watery, icy stuff which had little taste and was like flavoured water. I suppose the confection called 'hokey pokey', which was coloured and sold in little blocks by the Italians, was the forerunner of today's ice-cream. We once had an ice-cream freezer at home. It was a wooden tub with a revolving canister in the middle. Mum would make a thin custard and pour it into the canister. The lid was fixed on and freezing salt and ice packed in the space between the canister and the side of the tub. We took turns with the handle which, when turned, revolved the drum. It was hard work and it took about two hours before the custard solidified. Mum was always generous with it and she would send us with a saucerful to friendly neighbours.

Outings with Reg

One day Brother Reg, who was an enterprising and energetic lad, decided to go to One Tree Hill, the highest point of the Borough, and he took me along. I think I was about five years old at the time and Mum would have had a fit if she had known his intended destination. I had no idea where we were going and do not recall much of the walk except some shops in Grove Vale. Here we met Mr Scurr, the superintendent of Kimpton Missions' Band of Hope. After a little chat he gave us a penny each and we felt on top of the world. It was a long, long walk and I was tired out when we got there. We gathered some blackberries in fields which are now covered by houses. All the time I was afraid that Reg would run off and leave me for I had no idea where we were. Fortunately my fears were unfounded and an exhausted Leonard staggered home to tea and bed.

On another occasion I recall Reg being sent with a parcel to Durlstone Manor, a large and imposing house on the Champion Hill estate, and I went with him. When we arrived we were shown into the servants quarters where we were given a piece of cake, which was always acceptable. It was an enormous room with a large table in the middle and dressers all round the walls, but what took my attention was an oblong box on one of the walls. The box had a glass front behind which was an indicator panel with lots of numbers.

Whilst we were there a bell sited above the box rang, causing a miniature shutter to fall across one of the numbers. The maid who had been sitting at the table immediately sprang to her feet and, pausing only to reset the indicator board, left the room to answer the summons from above.

In time I was to see more such boxes and came to realise the vast difference between the 'Haves' and 'Have Nots'. I saw it as the hallmark of a society which insisted that everyone below stairs should know their place and answer a summons without question. I hated the thought that one day my sisters might have to answer the call of the indicator panel, and in later years I would express my contempt of the system in no uncertain manner. However, my fears were largely unfounded, for a new society was to rise which would all but eliminate the servitude to the indicator board.

Music and Song

This period of my life cannot be left without fond recollection of the music and songs of ordinary people. However distressing their living standards, however poor they were or meagre their amount of food, they went about their daily duties with a melody in their hearts and a song on their lips. Few folk expected much from life. They had been born to adversity and to a life of toil, with the spectre of the workhouse at the end of their days, but from infancy they had been told of the glories of the life to come and rejoiced in the promise of the hereafter, raising their hearts and voices in song.

It was a time when every child was encouraged to express themselves and make the most of the talents God had given them. Housewives with dust caps on their heads sang as they beat the carpet or cleaned the grate. Carmen sang softly to their horses, errand and delivery boys went their several ways whistling the latest tunes. Children danced in the streets to the music of a barrel-organ while destitute men went around playing jews harps, mouth organs or tin whistles in the hope of collecting a few coins. Walk down any street after school hours and you could hear a child scraping a bow across a violin string or practising a piano scale in the hope of becoming a great name in the musical world of the future.

In the evenings, music and song would echo from the Mission Hall as the choir practised or the Sunday School rehearsed. From every public house as the night wore on would come the babble of distorted music-hall songs, tunes on a honky-tonk piano and ribald laughter.

Sunday morning was a time for the bands to display their prowess. Boy Scouts, Boys' Brigades, Salvation Army, Free Salvationists, and others marched through the streets with a large following of children. In summer, bands would play in the bandstand in Ruskin Park, and prior to evening service, the Salvationists would come and play in Artichoke Place before marching off to their Citadel in George Street (Lomond Grove).

What songs do I remember people singing? Strangely they were, in the main, hymns or sacred songs from the Sankey hymn book.[12] Today it is almost impossible for anyone to imagine what a hold they had on ordinary folk. We sang them at the opening and closing of day school. They were included in the repertoire of barrel-organs. People walked along the streets singing them or humming the tunes without any embarrassment. Street singers sang the more heart-rending ones but the big bands loved to let rip with the more exuberant ones, like 'Bringing in the sheaves' or 'Work, for the night is coming'.

Mother had a soft melodious voice and like most housewives she sang as she performed her household duties. She also had a liking for Sankey tunes, but her special favourite was 'Pretty little girl from nowhere'. Others were the 'Tin Soldier' and 'Grace Darling'. This latter song recorded the heroism of a young woman who, with her father, a lighthouse keeper, rescued the crew of the *Forfarshire* which came to grief on rocks near Longstone one terrible stormy night. I had believed that this song recorded a recent event and was amazed to read one day that the rescue took place in the 1830s, and that Grace died in 1842 when she was only twenty-nine years old. Songs lasted a long time in those far-off days.

As there was no radio or television, and only a small minority of households possessed a phonograph, most songs were learned from other people, often at parties. Sheet music was expensive and most ballads sold at two shillings a copy, which was out of the reach of poor people. An artist could take a successful song round the music halls and variety theatres in the cities and country towns for years, and it would always be fresh to someone. Provided their voice didn't give out, a hit song would provide a living for a long time.

If one was invited to a party, one always took along a 'party piece' to sing or recite during the evening. Most young women numbered piano playing among their accomplishments and there were always young men on hand to turn the pages of music for them. The sopranos, contraltos, tenors and baritones all helped the evening along. One difficulty was that in an effort to put one over the others and sing the latest hit, many came to the party with

---

12 *Sacred Songs and Solos* (1873), by Ira David Sankey (1840–1908).

the same song, which was embarrassing. Dad told me once that at a party he went to as a young man no less than eighteen of the male guests came armed with the song 'Nancy Lee'.[13] Who had the dubious honour of extolling the virtues of this popular lady, and what happened to the unlucky seventeen, I never did get to hear.

---

13 *Nancy Lee* ('Of all the wives as e'er you know'), words by Frederick E. Weatherly (1848–1929), music by Stephen Adams (1844–1913), published 1876.

Camberwell Remembered

More about Stobart Mansions

Stobart Mansions, where our family resided from 1910 to 1937, were comprised of two blocks of flats and were built, I believe, in the final years of the nineteenth century. They were well designed and each flat had good-sized rooms. At the time of their erection they were no doubt considered modern, in contrast to many other tenements in the area. They were probably named after someone, but who 'Stobart' was I have no idea. It could be that the architect named them after the person who financed the building.

Why my parents came to live there I never thought to ask but most likely it was because Camberwell Green, with its buses and trams radiating to all points of the compass, was an ideal centre, and the Mansions were only five minutes' walk away. Although I have been curious about it since, at the time I was living there it didn't seem important. The logical answer (to me) is that when my sister Grace was born on 2 June 1910, the Wren Road flat became too small for a family of six. In their search for roomier accommodation they must have come across the Mansions, which were only a minute or two's walk away, and No. 21 being vacant, rented it. I wonder if they thought, when making their decision, that Stobart Mansions would house their growing family for the next quarter of a century.

The entrance to our block of flats was in Kimpton Road and just a few yards from busy Church Street, Camberwell's shopping area and the main artery for public transport. The other block of flats had its entrance in Artichoke place and the block was sandwiched between the Artichoke public house and the entrance to Camberwell Baths. Opposite this entrance was a cobbled area, known locally as the 'Stables'. On one side carts and wagons were parked whilst on the other side were the stables where the horses were kept at night. Above the stables, with its mangers and hay stores, were flats where many large families dwelt. It must have been awfully smelly for these people but I never heard anyone complain.

The name 'Stobart Mansions' was proudly displayed in huge letters across the face of both buildings and at first, the property was well maintained and never short of tenants; but over the years, and partly due to the lack of maintenance in the 1914–18 war, the fabric began to deteriorate. In between the two blocks was a large concreted area known to the residents as 'The Yard'. At the northern end of the yard a number of large refuse bins were kept and in these the families put their fire ash and household waste. The Council dustmen came on a Monday to collect all the garbage, and as the entrances to the yard were narrow and the height of the entrance doors only about average height, a lot of rubbish, much to people's annoyance, was spilt along the passageway.

The yard was the children's playground and as most flats had several youngsters, the noise they made could, at times, be deafening. A small amount of privacy was given to the occupiers of the ground-floor flats by the immediate area of yard outside their windows being walled off with bricks and iron railings. Time and weather had corroded these railings and they presented a very sorry spectacle.

In these reserved areas of the ground-floor flats were the rainwater drains, and there were small openings in the low walls to allow water from the yard to flow into the drains. Children were warned by their parents not to play around these openings for they believed they were a source of infection and illness. One of the tenants, Harry Moon, who lived at No. 3 with his wife, son and daughter, kept about a dozen hens in his reserved area and these birds used to squeeze through the drain opening into the main yard and peck around the dustbins in search of anything edible. This doesn't sound very hygienic, but in those days many people kept animals and birds as a source of supplementary food.

The backyard walls of the Church Street shops formed the southern perimeter of the yard, whilst the high brick wall behind the dustbins gave seclusion to an olde-worlde cottage that must have been built in the days when Camberwell was a rural village. The brick wall was not continuous for at the Kimpton Road side were a pair of high wooden gates used in times past for access to the yard from Kimpton Road. However, I cannot recall ever having seen them open. The brickwork hereabouts was very broken, caused by people hammering in nails to support their washing lines. Frequently the weight of the wet clothes would drag the nail from the wall, and as the surface of the yard was seldom clean, there would be angry words and occasional tears. It was not unknown for naughty boys to throw pellets of mud and bits of refuse at the washing flapping in the breeze, but their misdemeanours seldom went unpunished as most flats had two windows overlooking the yard and there was always someone surveying the scene below.

The Mansions comprised twenty-three flats of which 12 (Nos. 1 to 12) were in the Artichoke Place block, whilst the other eleven (Nos. 13 to 23) faced Kimpton Road. Except for the ground floor of the Kimpton Road block, where there were only two flats, each floor contained three flats of three or four rooms. The largest flat was No. 14 which our family occupied from mid 1928 at a rent of £1 a week, which was expensive.

To reach the upper flats from the ground floor one had to ascend a wide stone staircase of six flights comprising forty-eight stairs. As usual with Victorian buildings the number of stairs to each flight varied in number. The first flight of ten stairs led to a landing where two tall windows looked out on to the yard. In between the windows was a gas jet which, when lit, illuminated the stairs after dark. Then a flight of six steps led up to the first floor flats. The doorway of the centre flat overlooked the stairs, with the doors to the other two flats on either side of it.

This pattern was repeated for the next two floors although the number of stairs in the four flights was nine and seven, then seven and nine. The walls of the staircases were painted in a dark green up to halfway and cream from thence to the ceiling which, very occasionally, was given a coat of whitewash by the landlord. The occupants of the flats took turns in keeping their section of the stairways and windows clean.

As a youngster I never gave a second thought to climbing the forty-eight stairs to No. 21 where we lived, but it must have been exhausting for my parents, tradesmen and occasional visitors. The milkman trudged up and down every morning and the coalman, carrying a hundredweight of kitchen nuts on his back, must have mused that there ought to be easier ways of earning a living. It was small wonder that my mother relied on her children to do odd bits of shopping and to take the ashes and household waste down to the dustbins in the yard.

The interior of the flats was fairly uniform. The landing door opened into the kitchen-cum-scullery (how I hated the word *scullery*). Behind the door was a brick coal bunker of one hundredweight capacity. On a shelf above the bunker rested the gas meter, the property of the South Metropolitan Gas Company. We only used gas for quickness for the meter had an insatiable appetite for pennies.

Round the corner was the gas stove and beside it stood the mangle, an iron giant with a big iron wheel and wooden rollers. Next was a door to a small store room and toilet. The store room had a wall about waist height then a gaping square above open to all weathers. Here we kept our firewood, brooms and brushes.

In front of the window overlooking the yard was the kitchen sink. The water supply was a single lead pipe direct from the main, which fractured easily in cold weather, and next to it, in the corner of the room, stood the copper, in which mother boiled the clothes on washdays (usually Mondays). The firebox that heated the copper was so dangerous that in the end Mother bought a zinc clothes boiler that she could heat on the gas stove.

Occupying most of the other wall was the kitchen range. It was like a maid of all work and rendered us yeoman service. Its top consisted of a large steel plate with circular openings. These had removable covers for feeding the fire and cleaning, and on this we kept a large iron saucepan and a black iron kettle. The large teapot usually resided in the hearth when not in use. Above the kitchen range was a mantle shelf covered with a wooden board with rounded edges and decorated with a frilly dado.

Away from the kitchen were the two bedrooms and the parlour. In the bedroom were marble washstands on which rested large floral water jugs and basins to match, with a soap dish and glass. The beds were iron with brass knobs and took up most of the floor space. A rug or two protected the feet from the cold oilcloth. As the family grew in number the parlour was turned into a third bedroom and the scullery became our living room.

The flats were lit by gas and, as mentioned previously, I believe it may have been installed after the Mansions were built. In my early years illumination was by gas jets burning in a half circle of blue flame from brackets on the walls, but in the course of time the gas jets were succeeded by mantles. The first ones were known as 'uprights'. They had to be burnt off before use and were very fragile, crumbling to white dust at the slightest touch. They were superseded by inverted mantles fixed in coloured brackets and they became an accepted part of household equipment. Electricity was not introduced to the flats until 1928.

Falls of soot and brick dust from the chimneys was a constant source of irritation to Mother who seemed to be on her knees continually brushing and sweeping. The fire always died in the night and had to be relit next morning. One of the last jobs before bed was to put some kindling wood in the oven to make fire lighting easier with tinder dry wood. In every room there was a fireplace and this accounted for a feature of the city skyline—row upon row of chimney stacks and chimney pots.

A wide variety of soft coal was a available for burning in domestic grates. Coalmen would come around with a horse-drawn cart laden with sacks of fuel. The cart would bear the name of the supplier and a board on which was chalked the name of the colliery or fuel, and the cost per hundredweight. Our coalman usually earned an extra 2*d*. gratuity for lugging a hundredweight up the forty-eight stairs to our flat.

Windows were of the up-and-down type with counter-balance weights in the framework. This type of casement let in draughts and sash cords had a very short life. They often broke without warning and caused many a bruise to an unwary cleaner sitting on the sill. The Mansions had a sort of odd-job man but he was seldom to be found when wanted. Few people could afford a window cleaner and we always cleaned our own. Sitting out on a sill fifty feet above the ground was nerve-wrecking and I used to hang on to the frame tightly with one hand whilst trying to wash the glass with the other. It was alright as long as one didn't look down. All the same, I was never happy doing it.

I have mentioned before that the entrance to our flats was in Kimpton Road. Where the name Kimpton originated I do not know. There is a village of that name in Hertfordshire so perhaps the developer came from there. The top end led into Church Street, the other end to D'Eynsford Road. Its length was about 150 yards.

Most likely it was a rural lane in times past.

Kimpton Road and Beyond

There was a street lamp outside the entrance to the Mansions. These lamps were spaced at forty-yard intervals along most roads in the neighbourhood, and consisted of a tall standard with a four-faced lantern on top. One of the sides was hinged to allow for cleaning. Maintenance was carried out during the daylight hours. The cleaner would arrive with his ladder, cloth and pail of water. A metal arm protruded from the top of the post at the base of the lantern and overhung the pavement, and the cleaner leaned his ladder against this, mounted the rungs, hooked his pail onto the top rung and proceeded to wash the four panes of glass, clean the jet or renew the mantle or do what ever was required. At dusk a lamplighter, carrying a long pole, would go around the streets with a leisurely stride and, with his pole would trip the switch to ignite the gas from a pilot light. Sometimes the pilot light would have gone out so he would affix a taper to the end of the pole, light it with a match, open the lantern door and light the gas jet. Some lamplighters came round on bicycles. They were very expert and, without getting off their bikes, could use their pole like a lance, switching on with a single thrust. In the darkness the little pools of yellow light gave one a feeling of warmth and security. I worked in the West End of London during the 1950s and was surprised to see the lamplighter still at work in Regent Street and the surrounding streets. The lamps outside Buckingham Palace were also gas-lit. In Camberwell the street lighting was converted to electricity in 1938. To watch the lamplighters' persuing their calling in the 1950s took me back in my imagination to those far-off days when I was very young.

Opposite the Mansions were four large nondescript houses which did not boast any architectural merit, but the majority of houses in the road and surrounding streets were small terraced types erected in about 1840. Like many houses of this period their design too left much to be desired. It would seem the builder erected one, liked it, then followed the same pattern without much variation. Usually the street door was next to the bay-windowed parlour, with two windows above. The interior was uniform. A passage from the front door led to the kitchen and scullery. Off this passage was the door to the parlour and one to a small back room. This back room was dark, for the kitchen and scullery extended beyond it to the garden, where the toilet was sited. The gardens were about fifty feet in length and mostly kept in good order. Many families kept a few hens, some rabbits and pigeons, the majority of which ended their lives on the dinner table. Upstairs were two bedrooms and a box room. Often two families, usually related to each other, shared the house.

Next to the Mansions was a derelict area giving access to the 'Yard'. Alongside were three olde-worlde houses, then a smithy, or forge. As children we often stood around and watched the blacksmith at work. He must have been a kindly man for he never sent us away but kept an old wooden form for us to sit on. It was lovely and warm by his fire and when he blew it up with bellows a shower of sparks would soar up the chimney.

In my early days the horse was still the beast of burden and our blacksmith was always busy. He wore a leather apron and would hold the animal's hoof between his legs, using a large pair of pincers to rip away the worn shoe and a sharp knife to trim the hoof. He would search through his stock of horseshoes for one of approximate size, heat it in the fire until red hot, hammer it into shape and apply it to the horse's hoof with a pair of tongs. The resulting acrid smell of burning hoof I found most offensive and always held my nose. I wondered why the animal did not rear or shy in pain. Once the smith was satisfied with the fitting he would toss the hot shoe into the water and when it was cool would nail it on and file off any rough edges. The re-shod horse would then clip-clop away and another be led in for attention.

Next to the smithy was Kimpton Mission, a beacon of light in a dark area. Its four halls were in constant use as a social centre every day of the week; on Sunday, services were held morning, afternoon and evening. Its influence among the poor folk of the neighbourhood was profound. For over a hundred years it carried high the torch of Faith and practical Christianity.

The small shopkeepers and their businesses flourished at this time and Kimpton Road alone boasted two grocers, a baker, a greengrocer and a dairy, plus the inevitable pub, the Camberwell Arms. These little shops drew their custom from the people who lived nearby. They kept their heads above water by giving credit, and 'on the slate' was an everyday expression among the working poor. Nobody had a very high standard of living and as there was no such thing as social security one worked hard to keep the wolf, or landlord, from the door.

To the north of our immediate area was a small street market called Waterloo Street, and stalls lined one side of it. Nearby was a very depressed area with high, dark tenement blocks. At one time the main thoroughfare was named after King George but it was later re-titled Lomond Grove. It was here that the Salvation Army had its citadel.

Unemployment was rife and living standards depressed. There was little money to earn and many mouths to feed. Many families existed on a monotonous diet of potatoes and stale bread, with consequent malnutrition. Hungry children in rags and often barefoot were a common sight around these streets. Charitable workers did what they could and all praise to them, but they had neither the money nor the resources to be really effective. It was not until the outbreak of the First World War that the authorities began to take note and deal with the appalling conditions. Most people feared eviction more than hunger and the first call on a family's resources was the rent. In these conditions the moneylender, tallyman and pawnbroker flourished.

At the nearer end of the street market was the premises of George Priest, a large greengrocers and fruiterers. He was also the local removals man and owned a large wooden pantechnicon drawn by two heavy horses. This was still in use in 1936 when our goods and chattels were packed into it for our removal from 23 Lyndhurst Grove to 139 Grove Lane.

Round the corner, facing Camberwell Green, was the Marmite factory. Although the end product was excellent, and people who worked there said only the finest vegetables were used, the smell from the processing plant was quite awful. Also in this small stretch of road were the 'Greencoat Schools', stone-faced buildings with weather-worn figures of a boy and girl in niches in the walls. I knew very little about these schools but remember seeing in later years these two figures in the library in Peckham Road.

On the corner with Camberwell Road was a well known hostelry, the Father Red Cap. I believe it is still as popular now as it was then.[14] I can remember hearing voices raised in song and the tinkle of piano keys in the bar parlour. I never went inside. The local fishmonger, Bennett, had his premises next door. He sold fish of excellent quality and smoked kippers on the premises. He also had live eels in a metal trough and bloaters in long lines on metal rods. All his slabs were of marble and there was no front to the shop. Roller blinds were lowered at closing time.

Opposite, across the road, was Dents, a provision shop. It was very old fashioned and one had to go down four steps to the counters. He sold some excellent saveloys. Later this shop was modernised and became a post office. The last time I saw it, it was a betting shop. Next was the wide and lofty entrance to the tram yard. Many trams started or finished their journeys here and it seemed that these vehicles were constantly entering or leaving. The yard covered quite a large area and had another entrance, or exit, in Camberwell New Road, by the railway arch.

Along this stretch were many more shops and an alleyway that led to the Grand Hall, the poshest cinema in Camberwell. Along one side of the alleyway were the premises of Melhuish, the flour millers. It was almost impossible to believe that only about fifty years before I toddled around this area, Camberwell Farm grazed its sheep and cattle on the land now covered by these buildings.

In those days, Bowyer House, the seventeenth-century residence of Sir Thomas Bowyer, stood to the left of the farm. In its extensive grounds were large groves of oak, elm and yew trees. The mansion was demolished in 1861 when the London, Chatham and Dover Railway pushed its way through Camberwell from Blackfriars, and split the estate, which was sold for building. The Tramways Board erected their sheds and servicing workshops, and houses covered more of the land. An echo from the past is to be found in street names. Mansion Street marks the site of Sir Thomas's noble residence and Medlar Street is a reminder of the fruit once grown there.[15]

Some streets had names like Orchard Row and Great Orchard Row, and were further reminders of what once had been. Later their names were changed and Greens Row became Duff Place, Mazzard Row and Guildford Place. They became one of the slums in a slummy area. It had a reputation for violence and was shunned by most folk. When, in later years, I worked for the Co-op, whose store fronted this sordid area, I came to know many of the

---

14 The large public house at 319–323 Camberwell Road was still trading as the Father Red Cap towards the end of the 1990s. Built in 1853, it originally housed one of Camberwell's early music halls. The name has now changed, but the building still carries the inscription 'THE FATHER RED CAP' at rooftop level.

15 The references to 'Sir Thomas Bowyer' in this paragraph appear to be based on a misrecollection of the knight's first name. Bowyer House was actually the residence of Sir *Edmund* Bowyer (1613–1681), who had inherited the Camberwell estates of his uncle Sir Edmund Bowyer (1552–1627).

residents and became on good terms with them. Even so, I can only recall venturing in there once and felt very apprehensive all the time I was there.

At No. 266 Camberwell Road (formerly No. 2 Union Row), once lived Thomas Hood whose writings did much to publicise the terrible conditions of the working poor. He is best known for his 'Song of the Shirt', a fragment of which runs:

> *Stitch, stitch, stitch,*
> *in poverty, squalor and dirt,*
> *A woman sat in unwomanly rags,*
> *and sang the song of the shirt.*

This drew attention to the appalling plight of the women who worked at home in ill-lit, cold and draughty rooms making shirts for a pittance.[16]

Camberwell Green

Camberwell Green was at the heart of the borough and stood a green oasis among the bricks and mortar that surrounded it. In bygone days it stretched to St Giles' Church but was gradually encroached upon. Even so, it was a pleasant spot with large plane, chestnut and laburnum trees, with many bushes and well-groomed stretches of grass which displayed little enamelled notices, to 'Keep off the Grass'.

During the 1914–18 war, a Forces refreshment club and social centre was built on the side facing the Greencoat Schools. After the war ended it was taken over as a Labour Exchange but after some years the local people agitated for its removal and for the restoration of the Green. This was done about 1927 and the Labour Exchange moved to the corner of Artichoke Place and Church Street.

On the east side of the Green were fourteen houses with very long gardens, but they suffered the fate of many similar properties in the borough by being pulled down. Two quality housing blocks were built in their place, one was named Hayes Court. The rest of the site was taken over by the Peabody Trust who erected two large blocks of flats.

---

16 Thomas Hood (1799–1845) moved to Camberwell in late 1840 and took up residence at 2 Union Row soon after his arrival. He and his family remained there until the close of 1841 ('Camberwell', *Old and New London*, vol. 6 (1878), pp. 269–286). Lines 1–8 of 'The Song of the Shirt' (1843) run as follows:

> *With fingers weary and worn,*
> *With eyelids heavy and red,*
> *A woman sat, in unwomanly rags,*
> *Plying her needle and thread—*
> *Stitch! Stitch! Stitch!*
> *In poverty, hunger, and dirt,*
> *And still with a voice of dolorous pitch*
> *She sang the "Song of the Shirt".*

Church Street began at Camberwell Green and ended at St Giles' Church where it became Peckham Road. Although there were a few shops by the Westminster Bank and a few up Denmark Hill, notably Horsley's Stores and Kennedy's, whose sausages were always first class, the main shops were in Church Street. Most of the shops were small. The largest were Fuller Medley's on the corner of the Grove, and the South London Drapery Stores opposite, on the corner of Datchelor Place (a date etched in the stonework over the premises gave the date of opening as 1865).

In this famous old street were three public houses, the Artichoke, Hermit's Cave and the Stirling Castle. The local constabulary had its station near the Green. There was Pullum's Body-Building Centre, confectioners, tailors, corn and seed merchants, dining rooms, shoe shops and newsagents and, laying back, the Camberwell Baths with its clock in the apex of the building. These small shopkeepers catered for most of the families' needs and it was only for large items like household furniture that people went to Brixton or the large stores in the capital.

Around the corner from Fuller Medley's, in the Grove, was the Mary Datchelor School for Girls. This middle-class school was first established in two private houses in Grove Lane in 1877. It was taken over by the Haberdashers and it grew in importance over the years; it was considerably enlarged in 1926. Girls came from far away to be enrolled there and their standards and results were high.

Next door to the Mary Datchelor School was the Grove House Tavern. It had become but a shade of its former greatness. In its heyday it had been a centre for revelry and refreshment rivalled only by the Greyhound, in Dulwich Village, and the Rosemary Branch in Peckham. The exclusive Camberwell Club met here and it attracted many London notables who wanted a day in the country, the exhilaration of the chase, and a chance to gamble. It had extensive grounds, assembly rooms and a tea garden.

Charles Dickens is said to have been on the club's membership roll. He certainly knew it well and used it for one of his *Sketches by Boz* – 'Horatio Sparkins'. Most of its land was bought by speculative developers in the middle of the nineteenth century and the club was disbanded. Parts of the Assembly Rooms were taken over by a Mr Steinitz who founded a marquetry and joinery business. Charles Dickens purchased the marquetry for his home in Gads Hill, near Rochester in Kent, from Mr Steinitz.[17]

Opposite the Tavern was a dairy, all that remained of a farm that had been

---

17 'In 1861 C. Steinitz became the lessee of Camberwell Hall, and in addition to devoting the hall and minor rooms to public meetings as heretofore, he contrived to set a portion of the building apart for his business – the manufacture of parquetry. [...] Some of the parquetry, manufactured here, may be seen at Gad's Hill, the residence of the late Charles Dickens. In *Sketches by Boz*, Dickens gives an amusing account of a ball held at Camberwell Hall by certain "aspiring" local residents.' William Harnett Blanch, *Ye Parish of Camerwell: A Brief Account of the Parish of Camberwell, its History and Antiquities* (London: E. W. Allen, 1875), p. 306. Blanch's work may have formed one of the sources for this chapter of the memoir.

there for over 300 years. I remember buying milk and cheese for my mother from this dairy, but the greater part of the farmland disappeared under bricks and mortar about the time when the Grove House Tavern's land had been built upon. A few yards past the dairy was a footpath to St Giles' Church. This footpath once linked Loughborough House, a stately home, with the church. Part of the ancient path can still be trod from Coldharbour Lane (at the side of the Baptist Chapel) into Denmark Hill, then across the road into Love Walk and thence by a narrow passage from Grove Lane into the churchyard.

The land around Loughborough House in the seventeenth century was very marshy and nearby Monypepper had his osier plantation. About this time the Vanessa butterfly appeared here in large numbers and it became known as the 'Camberwell Beauty'. This butterfly, the trademark of Samuel Jones the maker of gummed paper, has been very erratic in returning and despite several attempts to reintroduce it, it has declined to remain. Why it came when it did still has the lepidoptera experts baffled.

Nearly halfway up Camberwell Grove, opposite Lettsom Street, stood Camberwell's most lovely and famous residence—the Thatched Cottage. It was said to be London's last thatched cottage, and was thought to have been built by Dr John Coakley Lettsom in the grounds of his Grove Hill estate. Although most of the old estate had been built upon, the thatched cottage remained as a link with the elegance and grace of the Regency period. Often on my way to school during the First World War I would stop and gaze at it and wonder if I would ever have enough money to buy it when I grew up.

This lovely residence must, over the years, have known many distinguished occupants, but according to tradition, the most famous was Mrs Maria Fitzherbert, a twice-widowed lady who became the morganatic wife of the Prince Regent, later George IV.

The Thatched Cottage was bomb-damaged during the Second World War. Instead of having it rebuilt when hostilities ceased it was demolished and a block of flats erected on the site. What short-sightedness and what a tragedy.

A few yards further up the Grove, just past the footway from Grove Lane, a plaque on one of the houses recorded that Mr Joseph Chamberlain once lived there.[18] A couple of houses further on was a very mysterious residence. The front garden was surrounded by a high corrugated iron fence with several strands of barbed wire laced around the top. The house looked dirty and neglected and ivy and creeper covered the walls. The grime of years covered

---

18 Joseph Chamberlain (1836–1914), industrialist, social reformer, radical politician, and imperialist, was born at 3 Grove Hill Terrace on 8 July 1836. He made his fortune in Birmingham as a manufacturer of wood screws and then went into politics, becoming a member of Gladstone's cabinet in 1880. He was part of the Liberal Unionist group that split with the Liberal Party over the Irish Home Rule issue in 1886 and eventually sided with the Conservatives. He served as colonial secretary in Lord Salisbury's government from 1895 until 1903.

the windows and the place had an air of death and decay. A stout iron-sheathed door locked with a huge padlock secured the entrance to the garden.

People talked about the house in whispers. Some said it was the scene of murder most foul. Others said satanic orgies and rites took place there when the moon was full. Others swore they had heard the clanking of chains and ghostly sobs from shadowy figures gliding among the bushes and trees. When I asked my mother about this mysterious house she told me she had heard that, like Miss Havisham in Dickens's story *Great Expectations*, the man who lived there had been jilted by his bride-to-be on their wedding morning. As a result he had shut himself away from the world behind his barricades. The wedding breakfast remained mouldering on the table and the curtains drawn allowing no sunlight to enter. I heard this story from other sources but no-one really knew if it was true.

As a boy I was quite scared of the place. When passing it, my chums and I would cross to the opposite path, just in case some sinister being should pounce upon us. One day in 1921 I was delivering some newspapers for Mr C. J. Bunn, whose shop was in Grove Lane, next door to the George Canning public house, when passing this strange house I fancied I heard the noise of someone trying to open the rusty door. Then I noticed the big padlock was missing. I confess my heart missed several beats and I scuttled to the security of a nearby plane tree and peered around it, ready for instant flight. I heard someone (or something) pulling the ancient door, which seemed reluctant to move. Much to my disappointment, or relief, no dragon or devil appeared, but a small man, about five feet four inches high. He was dressed in a top hat and morning suit. After securing the gate with the usual padlock, he pocketed the key and began a brisk walk down the Grove. I followed at a safe distance. He turned into Canning Passage and headed along Champion Park to Denmark Hill railway station.

A short time afterwards the place must have been sold. The new owner pulled down the iron fencing, cleared the garden, cleaned the place up and repainted the woodwork. In a very short time it was hard to picture what the old place had looked like.

This area was, in the eighteenth century, the Grove Hill estate of Dr John Coakley Lettsom. He was a Quaker who specialised in medicine. He started free dispensaries for the poor and needy, founded the Medical Society of London and was a founder of the Royal Humane Society. His estate was large and in one of its fields, experiments were conducted with a view to introducing, from the continent, wurzel and sea kale for winter cattle food.

The site of his villa is covered today by Nos. 9 to 12 Grove Park. A number of aged trees still survive, among them acacia, a cedar and a catalpa. The well, reputed to be the original Camber well, from which Dr Lettsom conducted water to his ornamental lake (now covered by Lettsom Street), is in the garden of a Grove Park house. Few people today have heard of the famous doctor and only Lettsom Street recalls his name.

Most of the houses in Camberwell Grove had lengthy gardens and between these and similar properties in Grove Lane was a wide service road. In Georgian days, horses and carriages were stabled and parked here. Most of the outbuildings are now garages. The entrance to these is still in Canning Place. Some lovely terraces of Georgian houses lay back from the Grove with access from semicircular drives. I believe a preservation order has been put on many of these properties.

Grove Lane, sister highway to the famous Grove, also boasts many Georgian houses and soon after we were married, Elsie and I lived in one of them. Until a few years ago there were many cottages too, a link with Camberwell's rural past. Mrs Blake, a friend of Mother's, lived in one of them. In 1905 a large mansion, Langley House, which was sited between De Crespigny Park and Windsor Road, was pulled down and the Denmark Hill School erected on the site. It was a co-educational school and all our family began their education there.

Although the school had no playing fields, only a hard-surfaced playground, it backed on to the Camberwell Nursery where the Council's Parks Department had its glasshouses. From this lovely little oasis went the plants and shrubs that brought a riot of colour in summer time to the parks and gardens of the borough. The public were allowed in and seats were provided for elderly folk to sit and admire the flowers and trees.

Further Afield

The tramway from Camberwell Green to East Dulwich, Stuart Road and Forest Hill, came up Denmark Hill, turned left opposite Ruskin Park and ran alongside the railway in Champion Park. It then turned left into Grove Lane and carried on uphill to the top of Dog Kennel Hill, passing the premises of the London Choir School on the left. Opposite was the entrance to Champion Hill, a private road with some lovely houses.

Dog Kennel Hill was a thoroughfare of noble proportions. It ran steeply downhill to Grove Vale and East Dulwich railway station. It carried four sets of tramlines and, because of the steepness of the gradient, only one car was allowed on a set of rails at a time. Even so, trams still got into difficulties, mainly due to faulty brakes. I have an old postcard in my collection which shows the original dog kennels once housed here. A tollhouse once stood nearby and a turnpike was sited where the railway station now stands.

At the top of the hill was an unmade road called the Glebe. From it, semicircular drives led to four imposing mansions. Their long gardens stretched the whole length of the hill. The first house of the four, the one whose grounds ran alongside the road, appeared to have been empty for some years and was derelict. The other three were occupied. Some of the bolder spirits among my school chums had been inside the ruined mansion and they came out with lurid tales of blood stains on the bathroom walls and suchlike.

Consequently, my friend Noel and I were much too scared to go through the doorway ourselves. In later years I was sorry not to have had the courage to explore the old Georgian mansion.

In the extensive grounds of the old place was an orchard, long since overgrown and covered with brambles. Here in the autumn we would go scrumping for apples. Unfortunately, some boys would not confine their scrumping to the derelict area but raided the fruit trees belonging to the other houses. This usually resulted in the maids or gardeners chasing after us with savage-looking dogs, and we had to beat a hasty retreat to the road or through the rickety wooden fence into the relative safety of the roadway. The last time I entered these grounds was in September 1922. My father had insisted that I go to see Harry Turner, my old headmaster, to ask for a free pass to evening school. It was a Thursday afternoon and I was most reluctant to ask a favour of the old Head, and I spent a couple of hours roaming the grounds trying to sum up courage. In the early 1930s the London County Council purchased the whole site and erected the tenement blocks of the East Dulwich Estate on these historic grounds.

On the opposite side of the hill, near the apex, were the gardens of the Champion Hill houses and a Scout hut. This troop was known as 'Hardy's Own'. Its sponsor, Mr Hardy, lived in one of the nearby houses. The troop, I believe, was attached to Wren Road Congregational Church. Below the scout hut grounds was the sports field of the medical school of King's College Hospital. In those far-off days there was no National Health Service and hospitals were maintained by voluntary contributions. One of the events held to raise funds was a procession through the Borough with gaily decorated floats and people parading in fancy dress. It ended up on the sports field with all the fun of the fair, stalls, swings and roundabouts.

From here the fields stretched away to Green Lane, a rustic way much used by courting couples. In between was the field and stands of Dulwich Hamlet football club. Entrances to the ground were on Dog Kennel Hill, Champion Hill and Green Lane. In my early days the 'Hamlet' was one of the premier amateur clubs of the Isthmian League and had a tremendous following. After the 1914–18 war players like Edgar Kail and Tim Coleman helped the team win many of the most coveted trophies. The prices charged for admission to first team games were 8d. for men, 5d. for ladies and boys. The fence on the further side of Green Lane marked the boundary of the Bessemer Grange estate.

Sir Henry Bessemer came to live here after having amassed an immense fortune of three million pounds. He was born near Hitchin in 1813 and became one of Britain's greatest inventors. He made lead pencils from waste, dyes that were proof against forgery, and bronze powder by an entirely new method. His most famous work, the one that gained him a knighthood, was the development of a new, inexpensive and superior steel, which became known as 'Bessemer Steel'. In 1863 he purchased the Grange Estate on Denmark Hill and lavished vast sums of money on it, making it the showplace of South London. It boasted a lake, orchards, a golf course, a massive conservatory housing rare and exotic plants, and a herd of Alderney cattle. With Ruskin Manor, which adjoined it, the two estates covered the whole area from Champion Hill to Sunray Avenue.

When Sir Henry died in March 1898 his Grange, like so many other great houses in the neighbourhood, became a private residential hotel, boasting two golf courses and country house amenities. By all accounts it never lacked a wealthy clientèle. The Grange opened its gates to the public on special occasions and it is one of my deep regrets that because I had to work on Saturday afternoons, I was never able to go. My sister, who was fortunate enough to attend a garden party there, came home with a glowing account of the beautiful grounds, the opulent buildings, the lovely lake and wonderful conservatory. These estates remained intact until after the Second World War when the local Council took the land for development.

Denmark Hill

At the Denmark Hill end of Champion Hill stood a triangular area of rough grass surrounded by a rickety wooden fence. It was called 'The Triangle'. This was reputed to be an old plague pit where victims of the Great Plague of 1665–66 were interred. The terrifying horror of those awful days is part of our history. Although Camberwell was then only a rural hamlet it was not sufficiently remote from London to escape the disease, which spread swiftly and fatally. Lytcott Grove commemorates a Colonel Lytcott who, with his wife and four children, was among thirty-five Dulwich victims. The number who died in Camberwell is unknown and no record remains of the number buried in this mass grave. At the time of the outbreak it created horror, fear and panic among a superstitious population who saw in its effect either the wrath of God, or the visitation of the Devil.

When I was a child all people feared this triangle of land, believing that if the earth was disturbed the plague germs would be loosed to create a new wave of terror in this area. Before anyone scorns their ignorance it is as well to remember that some of them, as children, may have seen the terrible effects of cholera that swept London in Victorian times. Besides bubonic plague and cholera, there were other vicious killers around like smallpox, diphtheria and typhoid fever which annually took toll of loved ones, many in infancy.

All people, rich and poor, shared the same dread of the killer plague. It was not until 1894 that the bacillus of the disease was discovered, and not until the early years of this century was it definitely established that bubonic plague is carried by fleas on black rats. Horror of this land was so real and widespread that until a tennis court was built upon it in the 1930s, the number of people I had seen on the 'Triangle' could be numbered on one hand.

From here, the long wooden fences of the Ruskin and Bessemer estates stretched for half a mile to Sunray Avenue, where one of the lodges was sited. Until around 1926 when the Camberwell Council built its 'Model Estate', the area around here was wild country where, as small boys, my chums and I went bird nesting and tadpole collecting, or built shelters of tree branches and grasses. Although there were a few allotments on one side of the avenue, habitation was sparse and the roads were unmade, full of potholes and puddles, a place where a boy's imagination could be given full rein. In the past, Sunray Avenue and Red Post Hill were the route to Dulwich Village from Camberwell.

Denmark Hill, which began at Camberwell Green, terminated at Red Post Hill and the road became Herne Hill. It was the boundary between Camberwell and Lambeth. On the Lambeth side there were still many open spaces and from the high ridge excellent views of London could be seen. The smoky sunsets were particularly fine and one road, named 'Sunset Road', had a special point to view the panorama.

Like so many of the open spaces around here, the fields were covered with good quality housing after the 1914–18 war. A wide stretch of these fields was added to nearby Ruskin Park and called the 'Extension'. During the aforementioned war, Ruskin Park was taken over by the Ministry of Pensions as a convalescent and recuperative centre for wounded service men, but the extension remained open to the public.

Ruskin Park itself was situated opposite an old hostelry called the Fox under the Hill, where the Surrey hunt used to meet, and was formed from some of the land of a Mr F. C. Benecke. It was dedicated to John Ruskin, the poet and art critic, who had resided in nearby Ruskin Manor. It was a delightful park with tree-lined walks, a rose arbour, vast stretches of lawns, colourful flower beds, and what we boys liked—a couple of ponds. A sundial near to the Ferndene Road entrance recorded that the composer Mendelssohn had written his 'Spring Song' in a house near the spot. This piece of music was originally called 'Camberwell Green'. Mr Benecke's mansion Dane House must have been a showplace before the London County Council acquired it for public use. People flocked here on summer days to listen to the band or just to stroll and chat. Part of the original house was used as a refreshment pavilion but I believe it has now been demolished.

Most of the local lads' recreation took place in Ruskin Park. No games were allowed in the park itself but the extension was large enough for all who cared to use it. Around its perimeter was a running track half a mile and forty yards long. On this we boys from the Boys' Life Brigade trained for battalion races. Here we also played cricket of a sort, and kicked a ball about. In the early days a rough unmade road separated the extension from the park proper, but in time it was rehabilitated, grassed over and absorbed into the park.

Next door to the park entrance in Denmark Hill, over the railway tunnel, was a nursery selling plants and shrubs. On a recent visit I observed that it was still there and appeared to be doing the usual business. Then came the buildings of King's College Hospital, one of the Capital's twenty-six great teaching hospitals. In my early days it always appeared to be in debt and I wondered how it could continue on borrowed money. Efforts were always afoot to raise money to keep it going. Outside the entrance, in Bessemer Road, was a large wooden thermometer showing the financial state of the hospital with boxes nearby in which the public could place donations in cash. There was also a receptacle for collecting empty toothpaste tubes.

Nearby stood St Matthew's Church, some shops and a narrow passage leading into Coldharbour Lane and the Empire Cinema, once known as the Metropole. It was a large building with its main walls in Coldharbour Lane. At this junction there were always tramway men on duty to change the source of the power supply for trams coming from, or going to, Brixton. In Camberwell the power cables were below ground, in Lambeth, overhead. I often used to stand and watch the skill and dexterity of these tram men as, with a big two-pronged fork, they collected the 'plough' from under an incoming car and directed it into a parking channel, whilst the conductor released the spring loaded arm on the roof and juggled it until it was connected to the overhead wire. The system went into reverse when a tram arrived from West Norwood or Brixton.

Opposite the cinema was the site of Dr Carr's famous Baptist Chapel and, on either side, several roads of middle-class houses. Denmark House once stood here. It had been the residence of George, Prince of Denmark, husband and consort of Queen Anne. Denmark Hill took its name from this house.

In later years Denmark House became the home of the Denmark Hill Grammar School, but in 1875 it was demolished and the school moved to Peckham Road, next door to St Giles' Church. It was given a new name, Wilson's Grammar School, and achieved a reputation as a school of high academic achievements.

Popular Entertainments

On the corner of Orpheus Street was the house of entertainment known far and wide as the Camberwell Palace, home of music hall, melodrama and pantomime. When it began life in 1896 it was known as the 'Oriental Palace of Varieties'. Its shows were immensely popular with the local folk but I never entered its portals until I was about eighteen years old. At that time a series of melodramas were staged by Tod Slaughter and his company of Barnstormers.

The plays they performed were tumultuously received and included such favourites as *Maria Marten* (or *Murder in the Red Barn*), *Under Two Flags*, *Spring-Heeled Jack (the Terror of London)*, and most famously of all, *Sweeney Todd, the Demon Barber of Fleet Street*. Tod Slaughter, who always had the leading role, had an enthusiastic following and always received a great ovation from his admirers. These old-time stars were the heroes and heroines of the working classes and I recall seeing Fred Barnes, an entertainer of some repute with a fruity voice, being mobbed by hundreds of fans as he tried to enter Henehey's pub in the New Road.

On the opposite side of Orpheus Street was an amusement arcade, regarded by many as a Den of Iniquity. It was full of penny-in-the-slot machines and mechanical bagatelles. It was most definitely out of bounds for us boys but one day, during the war, we found a French penny and Noel [Vining] and I, rather fearfully, went in the den, and when the attendant's back was turned, put it in a machine and flipped the handle. We were successful in getting an English penny in return but lost it a few seconds later and all we got in return was a few seconds of suspense. On the wall of the Bijou, as it was called, was the slogan, 'If you spit on the floor at home, please spit here. We wish this place to be as much like home as possible'.

Further down Orpheus Street was a carriage repair works and I can recall a long line of carriages, cabs and carts lined up on the road awaiting attention. I am sure that some of those old vehicles would be worth a lot of money today. Opposite the Palace was an old ironmongers and oil shop. After I left school I worked there for a week from 8 a.m. to 8 p.m., Monday to Friday, and until 9 p.m. on Saturday. All I received for this long slog was seven shillings.

Nearby was the Golden Domes cinema. It had a large gold-painted dome at each end of the roof. I seldom went there but recall seeing Conan Doyle's *Lost World* and the first of the talking pictures called *Blackmail*.[19] A large store 'Horseleys' occupied the corner site and just past the entrance to Ratcliffe's timber yard was Edwards, the pork butchers. Our family were good customers and I was often sent there for tripe, sheep's heads and brawn in a pink jelly that was made in large enamelled bowls. It was delicious. On my last visit to Camberwell I saw that Edwards still has a flourishing business.

Wren Road

Along Church Street, opposite the Green, was a small turning named Wren Road, at the end of which stood the Camberwell Green Congregational Church. This church was built on the site of the Manor House where Sir Christopher Wren resided during the rebuilding of St Paul's Cathedral after the Great Fire of London. The name of the road commemorates his stay.

Over the years the Manor House became known as 'The Old House on the Green', and it was said that around 1600, the occupant, a wealthy city merchant, murdered his wife and disposed of her body by bricking it up in one of the house walls. It is not recorded if the body was ever found, but the old house remained standing until 1850, when it was pulled down.[20]

---

19 *Blackmail* (1929), directed by Alfred Hitchcock.
20 The legend of the 'Old House on the Green' is recounted on pp.[301]–302 of William Harnett Blanch's *Ye Parish of Camerwell: A Brief Account of the Parish of Camberwell, its History and Antiquities* (London: E. W. Allen, 1875).

The Congregational Church was a rambling building with twin spires visible to travellers coming up the New Road from Kennington. Several of its many halls were named after local dignitaries. These halls were used for many weekday activities such as women's meetings, scouting activities, and male-voice choir rehearsals. The services attracted large congregations but it began to decline in the 1930s when new housing estates began to appear around the periphery of London in places like Eltham, Kidbrook, Morden, Epsom and Banstead to mention only a few. There was a Mission, Clemance Hall, in Elmington Road attached to the church.

For a brief period in the early 1930s Kimpton Mission came under its wing, but it was not a happy relationship for the Mission folk were too independent, and in time the association ended. The church was abandoned in the 1960s and the buildings and site sold. With the money from the sale a smaller, modern church was built in Grove Lane on the corner with Love Walk.

To the left of the church was the entrance to the yard where the police kept their vehicles and equipment, and on the right, the offices of the Thomas Tilling's bus company. On Sundays, the occupiers of a house in Daneville Road would allow worshippers to come through their house and garden to save a long, roundabout walk. The entrance to Wren Road from Church Street was narrow and often public meetings took place on the corner. On the right hand side was (and still is) a terrace of seven houses. My parents, with sister Con and brother Reg lived for a while in No. 3 on the first floor. I was born there on 14th October, 1907.

People didn't move very far away in those days and, as a case in point, nearly twenty-eight years later, on 7th September, 1935, Elsie and I were married by the Reverend David Vaughan in Wren Road Congregational Church, only a few yards away from my birthplace.

Contrasts and Changes

The nearby Camberwell Baths, already mentioned, possessed an imposing frontage that has remained unaltered with the passing years. It had a First Class swimming bath, with a Second Class bath round the back in Harvey Road. Mixed bathing facilities were not introduced until 1932. Women had their set evenings, men had theirs. During the winter the First Class bath was floored over and meetings and social functions held.

At the side of the swimming bath were the public baths. They were wooden baths and cost 6*d*. to use. Once inside, the attendant would fill the bath at a temperature to suit the individual. To get the water warmed up during the course of a bath, one called out 'more hot' and the attendant would turn on the hot water until told to stop. I didn't go very often, preferring to use the tin one at home.

I have referred, in general terms, to the contrasts that existed in the

Borough of Camberwell, with affluence in the south and poverty in the north. However, there were grey areas in the south around McNeil and Rignold Roads and better class properties in streets bordering the north. Along the Peckham Road there were large houses and gardens, and also elegant properties by Brunswick Park where St Giles' Hospital was sited. In Peckham Road too, were the offices of the Metropolitan Borough of Camberwell.

In this area were two big mental hospitals, called Asylums in those days. One was Camberwell House with extensive grounds bordering Vestry Road and with large buildings on either side of Peckham Road. Nearer Peckham was Peckham House run on similar lines to the other. After the 1939–45 war, both these properties were taken over by the Council, the Camberwell buildings being used as supplementary Council offices and the grounds as a public park. A school replaced Peckham House.

Around the turn of the century many street names were altered. More were changed in the 1930s. Craigallon Gardens became Grove Park, Wilby Road became Jephson Street, Orchard Row was renamed Medlar Street, to mention just three. Outer London was divided into postal areas and our neck of the woods became SE3. Church Street had 'Camberwell' put in front of it, as did the Grove. It was no doubt welcomed by the postal authorities, but I think a link with the past was lost when old names were eliminated in this way.

This then was something of the area that I knew as a child and in which members of my family were raised. I have described a few of the familiar surroundings that, good or bad, were part of my everyday life. In this neighbourhood lived people who shared the same problems as ourselves, people who were kind and generous with the little they had. A few were hard and grasping, but most were good neighbours.

Because of the 1914–18 war some inevitable changes were delayed until normality returned in the 1920s. Those of my generation were privileged to see an old order pass and a more caring one take its place. Judged by present-day standards we were poor in most material things and we knew hardship and frustration, shortages and anxiety, but we were rich in essentials like kindness, courtesy and love, and the comfort and shelter of a happy home. Although we may have been deprived and under-privileged, I look back on these times with a feeling of pride, and realise just how fortunate we had been.

THE WAR YEARS 1914–1918

1914

I recall little of the actual declaration of war or of the public reaction to the news that, so soon after the ending of the conflict in South Africa, the country and Empire were again involved in a trial of strength, and this time on our doorstep. Now though it was not against a few Boer farmers but a strong and ruthless Germany whose navy equalled ours and whose army was massive, and only the North Sea kept us apart. Even so, most people, despite the raw deal they had received from their rulers and leaders, were intensely patriotic and by all accounts the popular nationalist feeling expressed itself by parading through the streets behind the bands, singing songs and hymns, and waving Union Jacks. Politicians made inflammatory speeches urging the young men to enlist in the colours, and the hoardings bore the picture of the Army Commander-in-Chief, Lord Kitchener. There he stood with peaked cap, piercing eyes, bristling moustache and pointing finger above the caption 'Your King and Country need You'.

The people were so confident in the invincible power of the British Army and Navy that they dismissed with scorn the bogey figures of Kaiser Bill, Little Willie and the Prussian generals, believing that one Tommy was more than equal to three Jerries. All felt confident that because right was on our side victory was assured; after all, the long-standing treaty signed by the great European powers had guaranteed the neutrality of Belgium, and Germany had torn up the 'Scrap of Paper'. We were therefore fighting a holy crusade. In any case the war would be over by Christmas.

Only one scene comes to my mind with any clarity. It is of myself trotting past the railings of the Mary Datchelor school and the little parade of shops opposite the Georgian houses in Grove Lane, on my way to school. I was most dispirited because the outbreak of war had cut short the school summer holidays. I heard adults talking of husbands and brothers volunteering for the army and saw an increasing number of men in uniform appear on the streets. But the war and all that it meant was beyond my comprehension.

Although the war was beyond my understanding the serious situation that developed at home was all too real. Up to the time hostilities began we, as a family, while not living luxuriously, enjoyed a reasonable standard of living and were well clothed and shod. During the winter of 1914–1915 however, it became apparent to us children that all was not well and that our parents were in some financial difficulty. Unfortunately, Dad never confided in us. This was due, I'm sure, to the Victorian view of children that then prevailed, that they should be seen and not heard, kept in their place, do as they were told and obey their parents without question. It was a great pity that we were never told what was going on or what caused the hardship that we were to experience for many years to come. As we were involved we were entitled to know, but not a word was forthcoming. Mum, no doubt in deference to Dad's wishes, bore in silence the heavy load that was suddenly thrust upon her shoulders. What she did for us and the efforts she made on our behalf left us feeling very humble but very proud of her.

As always happens, the consequences of war seriously reduced the home market in consumer goods and services, whilst overseas business vanished overnight. Dad, a commercial traveller, no doubt relied on the commission on sales for the main part of his income. Whom he worked for I do not know, but at some point he travelled in paints and varnishes. I often overheard him mention Lever Brothers when talking to Mum, so it is possible that his firm had a connection with them. He used to take an occasional trip to Paris on business so his firm must have had European connections. When war stopped the export of consumer products, Dad's income must have plunged. While this may have accounted for much loss of income it is difficult to understand why the situation at home became so desperate. There were clues to other financial losses which I did not understand at the time but looking back, I feel they probably contributed in no small measure.

One of the articles we had at home was a large wicker-work laundry basket. On its side in large black capital were the initials 'OHL'. In it we put our soiled linen and woollens ready for wash day, usually Mondays. These initials used to puzzle me so one day I asked Mum what they meant. After some hesitation she replied 'Oak House Laundry'.[21] It didn't mean much to me but she went on to say that Dad had had a lot of money invested in this laundry but the business had failed and he had lost it all. I wondered if this failure was the cause of all our trouble. There had been another business venture that ended in financial loss that Mum often spoke about. It appeared that in the early days of their marriage Dad bought a small confectionery shop somewhere in the Clapham area, presumably for Mum to keep herself occupied while he was away from home. He purchased the goodwill and stock at valuation, but when they opened for business it was to find that the amount of trade the shop did had been grossly inflated (a common practice),

---

21 A business with this name was operating in Hendon in 1909, as is evidenced by a notice printed in the issue of the *London Gazette* for 24 December that year (issue 28321, page 9810): 'Notice is hereby given, that the Partnership heretofore subsisting between us the undersigned, Arthur Hipwell and William Samuel John Hipwell, carrying on business as Laundrymen, at No. 1, the Village, Child's Hill, Hendon, in the county of Middlesex, under the style or firm of "OAK HOUSE LAUNDRY," was dissolved as and from the 11th day of December, 1909, by mutual consent. All debts due to or owing by the late firm will be received and paid by the said Arthur Hipwell, who will continue to carry on the said business. --Dated the 21st day of December, 1909. ARTHUR HIPWELL. WILLIAM SAMUEL JOHN HIPWELL.'

and that the stock for which they had paid good money was practically worthless, being boxes and cartons of display dummies or filled with packing material. It was a common enough swindle and although they struggled to make the shop pay its way, the end was inevitable and they lost every penny they had put into it. Most dark clouds have a silver lining, however, and it was at this shop that Mum met two ladies who were to become her lifelong friends, Ada Skinner and Ethel Dornan, known to the family as Aunt Ada and Aunt Ethel. It is possible they were sisters but I cannot be sure. All the time I knew them they lived at No. 59, Treherne Road, Brixton.

Although he appears to have been a very unwise speculator, Dad was a clever man with an excellent brain, a fluent talker and great musician, playing the piano and organ equally well. He was educated at Berkhamsted School. Whilst he had academic qualifications he was not very practical, in fact the only tools I can recall seeing in our flat were a pair of pincers, a hammer, a wood chopper and an ice pick.

What Dad's shareholding in the Oak House Laundry was I never knew but it is possible that its collapse left him with debts. He was in his sixties during the war years so time was not on his side. Mum used to get bitter about misplaced confidences and swindlers who robbed, lied and cheated. Simple, trusting folk were fair game for these human parasites and predators.

In 1914 the war seemed far away and its distant echoes came to us in the form of popular songs like, 'Sons of the Sea' and 'Belgium Put the Kybosh on the Kaiser'. People spoke about the invincibility of the British Navy under Winston Churchill and it came as a shock when German naval units bombarded some of our coastal towns in Yorkshire.[22] I heard folk talk of the battle of Mons but it didn't mean much to me. More men appeared on the streets dressed in soldiers' uniforms of khaki with peaked caps and puttees. Now and again I saw a naval rating but there weren't many in Camberwell. When I saw them I remembered that I had had a sailor suit when quite young, the only difference was that my collar had been white, with a blue striped edge.

There was great excitement one day when the news was spread that the Camberwell Gun Brigade, on its way to France, would march through the Borough. Everyone who could lined the route to cheer the local lads and send them on their way rejoicing, as it were. I stood on the wall in front of St Giles' Church and had an excellent view as the contingent led by a band came from the direction of Peckham with flags flying and drums beating. Union Jacks hung from windows of the shops in Church Street, fluttering in the breeze. The noise was deafening as the tramp, tramp, tramp of heavy boots mingled with the frenzied cheers and shouts of the assembled citizens. Women rushed to the marching men and flung their arms around individual soldiers, kissing them goodbye. Tobacconists came out of their shops and

---

22 On 16 December 1914 German warships shelled Hartlepool, Scarborough and Whitby, killing more than a hundred civilians (*Annual Register for 1914*, pp. 248–9).

threw packets of cigarettes into the ranks, but some fell short and were picked up by the crowds milling on the pavements. Fruiterers pitched apples and oranges to the boys in khaki. It was a very moving sight. Gradually the sound of the band faded and the column of marching men slowly merged into a seeming dark mass as they passed from my sight round the bend in Church Street, opposite the Green. I presumed they finished their parade in Flodden Road where the First Surrey Rifles had their headquarters. Gradually the crowds, now strangely quiet, dispersed to their homes.

I heard it said sometime later, although I cannot vouch for the truth of it, that the Brigade was caught in an exposed position in Flanders and in the crossfire they were wiped out almost to a man.[23]

The boys at school used to boast that their dads were fighting in the trenches 'at the front', wherever that was. When I was asked what my father was doing I could only say, very apologetically, that he was too old to be in the Army or Navy. We heard that London motor buses were being used to take British infantry into the fighting zone at Armentières and we all thought that the Germans would soon be running back home.

---

23 On 11 April 1915, around 800 members of the newly-formed 156th and 162nd Brigades of the Royal Artillery, headed by their band, marched from their training depot in East Dulwich to the Parish Church of St Giles, proceeding by way of Denmark Hill and Camberwell Green (see 'Camberwell Artillery', *The Times*, 12 April 1915, 10c). This was probably the parade that Len witnessed.

The formation of the 156th Brigade RFA under Major Fred Hall, MP for Dulwich, had been authorised in a letter from the War Office to the Mayor of Camberwell dated 14 January 1915. In the event there were found to be so many would-be recruits in Camberwell that further authority was granted for the recruitment of the 162nd Brigade in March, and it was eventually decided that the whole of the 33rd Divisional Artillery would be raised from there. The 166th and 167th Brigades RFA and the 126th Battery of Heavy Artillery were fully formed by 1 June of the same year. (The 167th and 166th Brigades were disbanded in September 1916 and January 1917, respectively.)

The 'exposed position' referred to above was presumably the Ypres Salient, where the 33rd Divisional Artillery suffered heavy casualties between September 1917 and August 1918 (the term *salient* here refers to a projection of the forward line into enemy-held territory, exposed on three sides to enemy fire). In his *History of the 33rd Divisional Artillery in the War 1914–1918* (London: Vacher, [1921]), Major J. Macartney-Filgate writes that the Ypres Salient was 'the deadliest portion of the whole line for gunners', and that losses suffered by the 33rd Division during this period were 'appalling': '[F]ew of the men who, early in September [1917], marched up past Dickebusch and Shrapnel Corner to the battery positions beyond Zillebeke Lake were ever destined to return, while the majority of those who did came down on stretchers, the wreckage of modern war' (p. 111, 133). According to Macartney-Filgate, in a period of fifty-one days during the battles for the Passchendaele Ridge (in autumn 1917) the casualties of the 162nd Brigade numbered 315, while those of the 156th Brigade 'were almost as great'. 'A|156, a six-gun battery, had twenty-six guns disabled during the time it was in the line, while D|162, which had suffered the loss of one hundred and six casualties including six officers had had nineteen guns put out of action by the enemy. The batteries had, in fact, been practically wiped out, and it was a mere remnant of their former selves which reached the wagon-lines' (p. 133; see also pp. 112–134). See also G. S. Hutchison, *The Thirty-third Division in France and Flanders, 1915–1919* (London: Waterlow, 1921), pp. 3–4, 14, 29, 68–71, 112, and 164–6.

1915

As 1914 drew to an end and the new year of 1915 was ushered in, the early optimism faded and the adults talked of a longer, drawn-out conflict. Life became considerably drabber. Food became scarce and prices increased on all goods. As our own clothes and footwear wore out we were glad to accept any second-hand articles that came our way. We cut cardboard inner soles for our boots but they only gave temporary relief and could not keep the rain out. Mum spent long hours darning our jerseys and socks and sometimes we wore old black stockings that had had the feet cut off and the ends stitched across. Although we tied them below the knee with string, or old bootlaces, they never stayed up for long but concertinaed down around our ankles. Mum would work late into the night under the indifferent light from a hissing gas jet, mending and sewing, patching and darning. She was a fine-looking woman with soft clear skin and gentle grey eyes, and in those gloomy days she must have wished herself back to her countryside home of Aston Abbotts. One of her few breaks came every Monday afternoon when she relaxed for an hour or so at the Mothers Meeting at Kimpton Mission. The fellowship and sympathy she found there, plus practical help for the family in the way of gifts and second-hand clothing from more fortunate members, helped us all considerably.

In January 1915 we began to hear a name that gradually became more and more familiar to us, the 'Dardanelles'. This, it appeared, was a campaign to knock Turkey out of the War. Another name in that region that also became familiar was 'Kut el Amara', referred to in the newspapers as 'Kut'. It all seemed a long way away but we received a sudden jolt one day which shook our complacency and made us realise that we in England were not so safe and secure as we had thought.

Balloons had become quite common and we often saw them sailing quite low overhead. We would shout and wave to the aviators in the basket suspended below the gasbag and they would sometimes lean over and return our salute and drop a handful of sand on us, although it never seemed to fall anywhere near us. In 1915 the Germans used Zeppelins for the first time in an air raid over England, especially targeting the London area. At first they were very successful and the panic caused by these air raids was unbelievable. They always came at night and folk used to dread the approach of darkness. The authorities ringed the capital with searchlights and anti-aircraft guns but while the pencil of light could pick up an airship, its height was beyond the range of the guns, which only created a lot of noise and fear amongst the population and created an extra hazard of falling shrapnel.

The first raid by the 'Zepps' seemed to be unexpected. When it came, Mum woke us from our sleep and told us to get dressed and go downstairs. All the residents from the upper floors congregated on the first two flights of the common stairs. Fear and excited chatter intermingled, and cups of tea were made and passed around. Brother Reg, leading the bolder spirits among us, went out into the road to look for Zepps, much to Mum's dismay. I, who never liked my sleep disturbed, crept back upstairs and returned to bed. Next day we went to see the damage the bombs had caused. It was very minor. A slightly damaged house in Albany Road and another somewhere in Brixton. When I saw how little damage there was I began to wonder what all the fuss was about. As raid followed raid I became more stubborn and refused to get out of bed when the alarm was raised. In the end, Mum let me stay where I was but she took the girls down to sit with the neighbours in No. 17. Brother Reg used to revel in the opportunities that an air raid brought. As soon as the boy scouts' bugles sounded the alarm he was up and away, searching the streets for shrapnel, calming the horses in the stables in Artichoke Mews or, if things got too hot, seeking shelter in the cells at the Police Station in Church Street. He was everywhere and in everything and was exceedingly popular with everybody. He had a wonderful imagination and over our breakfast porridge, he would relate hair-raising experiences that had come his way during the emergency.

On the 8th of September the full horror of air raids was really brought home to us when a bomb fell on a crowded bus, causing many casualties. There was bitter resentment against the Germans for this atrocity and when they began dropping incendiary bombs to start fires, resentment turned to anger and mobs went on the rampage through the streets looting and smashing the windows of any shop with a German-sounding name. I recall how the hooligans, shouting and swearing, converged on the baker's shop at the bottom of Kimpton Road where they smashed all the windows, tore down the fixtures and fittings and looted anything of value in the little shop. The two young women fled for safety to a neighbour who took them in and the baker fled for his life over the rear wall. The people of the neighbourhood were disgusted with the shameful treatment these poor folk had received. Although of German origin, they had been naturalised for many years and were honest, law-abiding citizens. In time they opened for business again but the name 'Kranz' was not restored over the shop. This was not an isolated incident and many others suffered from the fury of the mob.

The Zeppelins continued their raids but on the 3rd of September 1916 civilian morale was boosted when Lieutenant Leefe Robinson of the Royal Flying Corps shot one down over the village of Cuffley, near Enfield in Middlesex. People who witnessed the sight said that as it fell it blazed like a new incandescent gas mantle when first lit. No one spared a thought for the crew who were probably burned to death. Lt. Robinson was awarded the Victoria Cross for his success and people went mad with excitement. A popular song at the time, 'Back Home in Tennessee', was parodied for this event and I recall that on a Pearson's Fresh Air outing to Hampton Court we yelled the song out of the tramcar windows:

*Back home in Germany,
That Zepp will never be,
Count Zepp he's on his knees,
He thought the world of these,
All they could think of that night,
Were searchlights shining bright,
Shells were whizzing, bombs were dropping,
Zepp was all alight.
And people out of doors,
They all sang in chorus,
Our airman brought it down,
In a place near Enfield town
We were unprepared to meet it,
But we gave quick word to greet it,
When it came down, when it came down,
To its doom near London Town.*

On September 24th further successes attended our intercepting aircraft, for over Essex that night one Zeppelin, the L33, was shot down in flames and another, the L31, was disabled and came down almost intact. On October 1st, the night of the fortieth raid, another Zeppelin was destroyed, coming down at Potters Bar in Middlesex. These losses must have seriously depleted the Zeppelin fleet and the raids gradually eased off, leading the tired folk of London to believe that the air raid menace had been overcome.

At the outbreak of war the aircraft industry had been in its infancy, but with Government money now available for research and development, there was a speedy improvement in the range, power, height and armament of aircraft. Enemy aeroplane raids during daylight hours were already frequent along the south coast in 1916 but it was not until November 28th that a German plane appeared at midday over London, dropped its bombs, and got clear away. By Spring 1917 the big 'Gothas' began heavy attacks on the south coast towns, and although we did not know it at the time, these were the prelude to assaults on the capital itself. On Wednesday and Thursday, 13th and 14th June, planes appeared over London in the blue of a perfect summer morning. At first, people thought they were British. By the time they had unloaded their deadly cargo, 104 civilians had been killed and 432 injured.

There was much ill-feeling against the authorities at the ease with which the attack was made, and as a result more defences were set up and anti-aircraft guns ringed the city. Official warning of raids was also instituted. Nevertheless the enemy came again at 11 a.m. on Saturday, July 7th, and about twenty-four machines in a triangular formation flew in and dropped their bombs, causing more casualties. There was excitement at school on the Monday following the raid, for many of the boys had witnessed the arrival of the raiding force and some had seen (or so they said) the bombs falling. I suppose I must have been busy at home for I was not an eye witness, much to my regret. We ran around the school playground with arms outstretched imitating aeroplanes in flight and in imagination, defeating the Jerry pilots in a dozen different ways. It was said at the time, and confirmed by German pilots after the war, that one of the landmarks the enemy navigated by was the Crystal Palace on Sydenham Hill.

The raiders came again on Monday, 24th September, and bombed Islington, Finsbury, Soho, Holborn and Piccadilly, but the reception they received from intercepting planes and anti-aircraft fire was so hot that they switched their attacks from daytime to night. People came to dread the bright moonlit nights. Aeroplane raids were much worse and created more confusion and panic than the Zeppelin raids for the aircraft came in lower and made more noise, and because of their speed were more elusive. No one felt secure and the nights were noisy with guns thudding and shells whining, and searchlights vainly seeking the enemy, who made full use of any cloud cover. They came too at a time when food was short and the years of war were sapping the nation's vitality. Folk were stunned by the enormous casualties, and by the numbers of war wounded who could be seen around wearing their light blue clothing, often limbless and swathed in bandages.

Back in 1915 however, this was very much in the future and people were ignorant of what was in store. People still hoped for a miracle to end the conflict and bring their loved ones home. From hoardings, the accusing finger of Lord Kitchener pointed scornfully at men still in civilian clothing and it was said that some women went around distributing white feathers hoping to shame these men into enlisting. Everywhere they went young men were encouraged by one means or another to enlist. There were parades through the street by soldiers in peaked caps and puttees and by sailors in smart blue uniforms, with flags fluttering and bands playing. Even the commercial advertisements joined in the chorus. An Oxo advert showed an insert of a soldier writing home from the trenches; the Union Jack was prominently displayed with the caption, 'Take up the sword of justice—it's our flag'.

As the year progressed life became considerably drabber. The Boat Race, cricket test matches and professional football games were abandoned until after the war. The big museums and art galleries were closed. Buses and horses disappeared from the streets when they were taken by the Army to France. Women became conductors on the trams and worked in the munitions factories. Commodities became scarce and prices for goods and services increased beyond the reach of poorer people. Much hardship was experienced and there was increasing discontent.

*

For the men who volunteered for the Army (conscription had not yet arrived), there was a brief period of training before being shipped off to France to face the horror, danger and discomfort of trench warfare, and the almost total military deadlock. The casualties were enormous and the hospital service of the day was unable to meet the enormous demands placed upon it. As a result many schools were taken over and turned into emergency hospitals. One of these was the school that we attended—Denmark Hill School—which was situated in Grove Lane just past De Crespigny Park. The reason for its acquisition was probably its location, being close to the big teaching hospital of King's College on Denmark Hill and to the railway station in Windsor Road. The school was an imposing edifice of ample proportions and one of the last to be built prior to the outbreak of hostilities. It was a modern building with light airy rooms and good-sized playgrounds. It had a wide frontage to Grove Lane with a stout iron fence and a screen of evergreen bushes to ensure privacy. At the rear it backed on to the Camberwell Nursery, a green oasis with colourful borders and greenhouses, some of which were heated. The Nursery was a cool and pleasant retreat much enjoyed by the elderly and infirm who lived nearby. The main school building, on two floors, contained all the classrooms plus two square assembly halls, while a small outbuilding in the girls' playground was for the exclusive use of the infants. It was co-educational, catering for around 900 pupils ranging in age from five to fourteen years—the school leaving age.

Classes were divided into 'Infants', 'Junior Mixed', and 'Senior Mixed', and the number of boys and girls was about the same. It was a school of contrasts, for Camberwell had its affluent areas as well as districts of great poverty, and in Denmark Hill School the extremes met. The ragged children often sat alongside the sartorially elegant. There were twenty desks in a classroom, not always filled. The girls occupied the two rows of desks on the right while the boys sat on the left.

When the requisition order came the problem that must have caused most headaches was what did one do with the pupils and teaching staff? The decision went against dispersal and on the 22nd February 1915 the school moved, lock, stock and barrel, to Lyndhurst Grove School, a mile away in Peckham. Compared with our school, Lyndhurst Grove appeared old, dirty and untidy and it was, of course, much further from home.

When the military authorities took over our school as an emergency hospital they also commandeered the pleasant Nursery Garden and the nearby Ruskin Park, leaving only the 'Extension' for public recreation. They surrounded the park with a massive wooden fence and over the school entrance a board was erected with the words 'Ministry of Pensions Hospital'. Rumours abounded amongst the schoolchildren that the hospital was just a blind and that the fence with its barbed-wire top hid prisoners of war, brought there to be shot at dawn, or tortured in newly built torture chambers. One lad with more than his share of imagination claimed to have heard the screams of German spies being made to confess.

I recall little or nothing of the evacuation. None of us liked the new location, which backed on to the railway line and was noisy in consequence. I never imagined that Elsie and I would live opposite the school, at No. 23 Lyndhurst Grove, when we married some twenty years later. The influx of a whole school into another must have created immense problems, for Lyndhurst Grove was already filled to capacity. The outcome was that, as a temporary measure during the period of the emergency, each school would attend for only half a day, one month of morning lessons followed by a month of afternoon lessons. This 'double session' was to continue until further notice.

This half-time schooling lasted well past the end of hostilities. We children thought it a marvellous idea but from an educational standpoint it was a disaster. The teaching staff under Harry Turner, our headmaster, struggled on, but they must have felt cramped and unsettled. Many of the regular teachers were serving in the Forces and had been replaced by temporary teachers and part-timers, who seemed to show far less interest in their charges. From a strictly formal school we became an unruly informal crowd doing much as we pleased. There was no curriculum, and lessons were continually interrupted. Absenteeism was a real problem, much of it caused by illness brought on by malnutrition, and queuing for food often made a child late.

I found the walk to Lyndhurst Grove dreary and tiring and tried going by different routes to relieve the monotony. I usually ended up going to school on my own. Brother Reg was an early riser, always up with the lark. When it was his turn to do so he would light the kitchen fire and make the tea. His singing would wake up most of the family. Two years and two months my senior he always left me standing, even allowing for the difference in age. He was very confident and self-assured; alas I was the opposite. We had a family tradition that whoever made the morning tea had the privilege of drinking the first cup out of the pot; the second was taken to Mum. I'm sure she appreciated this small gesture even if the brew may have left a lot to be desired.

It was a proper scramble with all of us trying to get to the sink for a wash. By the time I appeared on the scene, still only half awake, Reg would have consumed his porridge and gone on his way. I earned the very dubious title of 'lie abed sluggard', for, despite frequent callings and threats of punishment, I found it almost impossible to leave a warm bed on a winter's morning and face the cold new day. Often to get to school on time I had to miss breakfast and run all the way. I dreaded seeing the streets empty of children because this meant I was really late, and late arrivals were frequently caned before the assembled pupils. It was always a great relief when we were on the afternoon shift.

*

How I spent the extra leisure that half-time schooling brought me I have no clear recollection, but I do vaguely recall running errands and scrounging around the shops for wooden boxes to use for firewood. I also kept my eyes open for road repairs, and would take along a little sack to collect wood block chippings, which were red and tarry and used to floor the road. These would rise up in great bubbles after rain and needed constant attention to prevent accidents. Pocket money from our parents had dried up, and Reg and I used to run errands for neighbours for a halfpenny, or piece of cake. They were hard times and we were often hungry. Mum did her best with the slender resources at her disposal, but first call on the purse was always the rent. For our midday meal we would often buy 2*d*. or 3*d*. worth of bones from the butcher and Mum would put them in our big iron saucepan, cover them with water and bring them to the boil, and simmer for some hours. When the liquid was strained off it would turn into a thick jelly overnight. Potherbs (onions, carrots and turnips) would be added and sometimes a packet of Edwards' Desiccated Soup was tipped in to give added flavour. When served up hot it was a delicious meal.

Scrag end of mutton, breasts of lamb, tripe and cow heel were among the cheaper foods and we took advantage of them for variation in the diet. Rabbit sold at 6*d*. a pound and fresh herrings at 2*d*. a pound.

Our main breakfast dish was porridge made with rolled oats, often cooked overnight in a double saucepan, with Lyle's Golden Syrup or jam stirred into it; occasionally just salt was added. A variation was gruel made from fine, coarse or medium oatmeal. I hated this as much as I did semolina. These foods filled me up at the time but by mid-morning I was starving again. A new cereal called Flaked Maize came in during the war but I couldn't bear it.

Although bread was reasonably priced, 3*d*. for a 2 lb loaf, it was an expensive item for a family and sometimes Reg and I would go out and queue up for stale bread. This often meant lining up outside the bakers on Denmark Hill from about 6 a.m. until the shop opened at 8 a.m. Perhaps fifty or sixty people would be in the queue, stamping their feet and swinging their arms to keep their circulation going if the morning was cold. Often the shopkeeper would announce 'no stale bread' whereupon there would be a stampede as the waiting crowd shot off to Wilson's in Daneville Road or Price's in Coldharbour Lane to try their luck there. It was not unusual to return home with an empty bag after a long, cold wait.

*

The one day of the week that I disliked more than any other was Monday, for this day was rigidly adhered to for the family laundry. There were no washing machines, spin dryers, rotary clothes airers or electric irons to lighten the burden, and no launderettes or biological washing powders, and little drying space. All home laundry had to be boiled and rinsed, or rubbed by hand on a rubbing board. Despite all this the finished articles were as white and clean as their present-day counterparts.

The washing was first sorted on the floor and the white articles were given priority over everything else. They were put into the copper, covered with water and a packet of Hudson's soap powder sprinkled over the clothes and stirred in. This powder, which consisted of little granules of soap, was the forerunner of modern powders and detergents and cost 3½d. for a quarter pound packet. I cannot be sure but it could have been made by Lever Brothers who marketed the universally known, all-purpose Sunlight Soap and the high-quality Lux Flakes, which ladies reserved for their most delicate, dainty and flimsy articles.

When I was not on the early shift at school I used to help light the copper fire, which was not always easy because it was so close to the floor. We used a lot of wood as fuel as it was easy to come by. Most goods were packed in wooden crates or boxes which the shopkeeper, after emptying, put outside his shop for people to take away if they were so inclined. I became quite good at scrounging firewood, which was chopped up and stored in the copper ready for the following Monday boil-up.

A wooden lid covered the copper's contents but as the water began to bubble and the clothes ballooned up, this lid had to be removed and the clothes pressed down with a 'copper stick', usually a piece of broom handle. This stick had a dual purpose, for it was used to chastise Reg and myself if we misbehaved. One day Reg, anticipating some punishment, sawed two-thirds the way through it, and the next time it was used it broke into two unusable pieces.

The kitchen would fill with steam and the room became most unpleasant. There was no time to prepare a midday meal so we had to be content with bread and cheese or bread and dripping, with salt sprinkled over the dripping. This dripping, which came mainly from a joint of beef, had a delicious amber brown jelly which settled at the bottom of the basin and was much sought after. When the whites had been boiled to Mum's satisfaction they were lifted out with the copper stick and dropped into a zinc bath, and the coloured clothes took their place in the steaming water of the boiler. As there was no drain tap to the copper the waste water had to be baled out by hand using a small galvanised basin, which had a handle attached. The water was often used to wash the kitchen floor at the end of the laundry session.

Rinsing was the next stage, and as the small stone sink was only three or four inches deep it was done in a small enamelled bath, which was also used for bathing the baby. This was placed in the sink and the clothes were squeezed and swished about and then wrung out by hand. For the white items the water was tinted blue by using a dolly or Reckitt's Blue Bag. This was a small cylinder of ultramarine encased in cotton gauze and cost a penny at Thompson's, the oil shop, on the corner of Kimpton Road. After use it was dropped into a jam jar and put on the shelf ready for the next rinse. Next came the mangling, which was a great test of one's strength and endurance.

The mangle was painted green and stood about six feet high. The large wooden rollers were turned by the hefty iron wheel at the side, which operated a series of toothed, or cog wheels. Pressure was applied to the rollers by means of a large spring which could be adjusted by a large screw at the top of the mangle. It was efficient enough, but hard work, and sapped one's energy. When my time came to turn the driving wheel I had to use both hands to keep it moving. In order to get a few pence to help the family budget we used to mangle for neighbours. I would often glance out of the window as I turned the handle and wish I could join my more fortunate chums playing in the road.

The later, more modern wringers, with light rubber rollers, bear no resemblance to the old heavyweight mangles, which are now museum pieces. These monsters needed little maintenance and it was only when the wooden rollers began shredding and depositing splinters into the clothes that they outdid their usefulness. I sometimes wondered just how many broken buttons they were responsible for.

Drying clothes was also a problem. Sometimes the washed articles were taken down the forty-eight steps into the yard for a blow. This was always hazardous as the line might break or the nail come out of the wall. It could also be soiled by children chasing each other through the lines of washing. Some items might even get stolen. Thus, most of the week's laundry was draped on lines across the room or put on a clothes horse in front of the fire.

A few white articles were dipped in starch prior to ironing. Starch came in little packets with a white label showing a robin with a very red breast. This was the famous Robin Starch. A spoonful of this was put in an enamelled bowl, mixed with water and stirred until it had the consistency of thin cream, and then hot water was added. Pillowcases, tablecloths, pinafores and the like received the starch treatment; they were dipped in and wrung out by hand. I remember getting up late one morning and seeing what I took to be a bowl of soapy water in the sink, plunged my hands into it and splashed it over my face, realising too late that it was, in fact, the bowl of starch.

Ironing was yet another problem, a job for Mum and Con. They used the old flat irons which were made from one piece of iron, although the inside of the handle was hollow. The iron bore numbers like '4' and '7', which, I believe, indicated how many pounds the iron weighed. They were heated on the gas ring or on the trivet in front of fire. It was most difficult to judge the correct temperature and scorching was common. Testing was done by licking the top of the finger and lightly tapping the base of the iron. If the moisture sizzled the heat was judged about right and the ironing began. At least two irons, sometimes three, were kept on the go to ensure continuity, for the heat went out of them very quickly. Prior to use they had to be rubbed down so that no dirt from the fire or grease from the gas stove was transferred to the newly laundered linen. The iron had to be held in a glove with a thickly padded palm to avoid the hand being burnt on the hot metal.

I hated washdays almost as much as my mother and sisters did, and was glad when the last bucket was emptied and the mangle wiped down and pushed away to its home in front of the toilet.

*

One day at school some of my classmates divided themselves into two groups and began skylarking about in the playground by pitching small stones at each other. It was fairly harmless as we were all rotten shots, and it was easy for us to dodge any oncoming missiles. One of the stones I threw happened to bounce off the school wall and caught Alf Healey, one of the Kimpton Mission boys, on the leg. He let out a horrible yell. Elated by this success I pitched another the same way and it ricocheted into the opposing faction catching them unawares. I was only saved from a beating up by the ringing of the school bell ending the mid-morning break. During the following lesson it was obvious to me from the dark looks and mutterings that some reprisal was being planned, so as soon as the morning lessons ended I fled the class as fast as my legs would carry me. I was hotly pursued from the playground, but in those days I was skinny and could run pretty fast, and by the time I reached Rignold Road most of my pursuers had given up. By the end of Lettsom Street there were only two on my tail, Alf Healey, about fifty yards away, and Noel Vining, the athlete of the class, only ten yards behind me. I was about to turn the corner into the Grove when I heard Noel call out to me to stop. He came running up. 'Let's make up' he said. 'We'll join up and beat up Alf'. This made excellent sense to me and, vastly relieved, I replied 'Good idea!'

He pretended to hold me until Alf came running up. He was most surprised when we both set about him and chased him most of the way down the Grove. It plainly was not Alf's day. This pact with Noel turned into a lasting friendship and we became staunch friends for many years.

My friendship with Noel opened up new horizons for me. Until we met my little world had been bounded by home and the Mission, where I spent Sunday mornings and afternoons and a couple of weekday evenings at the Boys' Club. Noel was really his second name, for he had been christened Charles Noel, but as he had been born on Christmas Eve, 1907, the shorter name had been preferred. He was the eldest of five children, sisters Winifred and Eileen and brothers Ralph and Albert, but at the time we met Albert and Eileen had not been born.

His father, Charles, was a big, strong, dynamic man, the manager of Harris, the baby pram specialists of Rye Lane, Peckham. His mother was a small, dainty woman, very quiet and homely, who treated me like another son. Their home at No. 42 Grove Lane was a large Georgian house with a long front garden and an equally long (maybe longer) rear garden which backed on to a wide rough drive at the end of Kerfield Mews. In the past this drive had been used as a parking place for the carriages that conveyed the residents of these great houses. Once the coachman had delivered his passengers to the front entrance on Grove Lane he would have driven round Kerfield Crescent and into the mews, where little stone stables for the horses led off at right angles from the drive. On a visit many years later I noticed that the old stables were still being used, this time by a light engineering firm, and the houses and drive had altered little.

When I was first introduced to No. 42 I was immediately struck by the huge scullery, which, with the kitchen-cum-living room, occupied the whole of the basement. This scullery was so large that Noel and I played cricket in it. Of course we were only small boys then and places do tend to shrink as one gets older and bigger. Apart from a large stone sink under the window the room was pretty bare. The kitchen-cum-living room was also large and contained numerous cupboards, a large wooden dresser and a big kitchen range. It was sited under the front part of the house and a door at the side of the window led out to a small flagged area, an open space below ground level and guarded by high iron railings along the front of the house. On the ground floor was the parlour, a very large room with mahogany panelling and a marble fireplace. Behind this, looking out on the back garden, was the bedroom of Mr and Mrs Vining. At the side of the rear door was the toilet and more cupboards.

The first floor was occupied by a widow, Mrs Bradshaw, and her daughter Maisie, plus another lady who I believe was Mrs Bradshaw's sister. Maisie and my sister Con were at one time very good friends. The Bradshaw ladies were excellent tailoresses and Mum got them to make me a couple of suits with dummy waistcoats. They were made to measure and I was awfully embarrassed at the time of fitting. Mrs Bradshaw had cold hands and a dreadful-sounding sniff.

The children's bedrooms were on the second floor and an uncle and aunt occupied the top floor.

The gardens were lovely places in which to play. Behind the iron railings that bordered the Lane was a large area of lawn and many lilac bushes, plus a few bluebells that came up every spring. In front of the railings was a large paved space and three or four stone steps led up to the front door, which had a bell-pull rather than a knocker. Midway along the boundary with No. 40 grew the largest American Bean Tree I have ever seen. It was old even then and was probably part of the original Manor House gardens, long before the present houses were built. In summer it carried clusters of flowers something like those of the white horse chestnut, and in autumn the long bean pods hung down from its branches just like runner beans.

The back garden, separated from its neighbours by sturdy high brick walls, had a centre lawn with flower borders where candytuft grew in profusion, and a small tree outside the back door. A concrete path ran alongside the border to two timber sheds which stood by the door leading to the unmade drive from the Mews. Opposite the garden walls of these houses was another high brick wall running the length of the terrace, which enclosed a small orchard in the grounds of a convalescent home, whose entrance was in Love Walk. We often tried to climb this wall to get at the apples which peeped at us from the topmost branches, but we never had much success as there was always a gardener around ready to repel any boy who dared try his luck.

I loved to play in this and the neighbouring gardens, where some of our schoolmates lived. It was so different to the grim yard that comprised the play and airing space for the residents of the Mansions. Unfortunately, I had many little domestic duties to perform so my playing time was strictly limited. All the time I was at school I seldom had a Saturday morning free and I envied my more fortunate friends who could go to the park and play cricket or football.

One afternoon Noel came round and asked Mum if I could go to a party at his cousin's home. After Mum had inspected behind my ears and above my wrists, and combed my hair, she sent me off with Noel to enjoy this new experience. His uncle had an upholsterers business in the Camberwell Road and it was at the back of this shop that about twelve or fourteen children were gathered, all aged about seven or eight years old and dressed in their Sunday best. On a table in the middle of the room was such a spread of goodies that my eyes nearly popped out. Never had I seen such piles of sandwiches, dishes of blancmange and jelly, pyramids of rock cakes, plates of coloured fondants, jugs of cream and a big dish of peaches, as well as bottles of lemonade and cups set out for tea. When we sat down and tucked in I really believed that the feasting in Heaven they spoke about at the Mission must be something like this. We were all in excellent spirits and I recall how Noel slapped a large green jelly with a spoon and shouted, 'It must be Chivers', because it shivers'. When we had eaten our fill, our hostess asked if we could manage any more. All the rest of the children said they had had enough so I had to say likewise, although I'm sure I could have managed another rock cake.

Afterwards we joined in fun and party games and as was the custom, some young guests were invited to perform their party piece, which could be a poem, song or simple tune on the piano, which practically every home, however poor, possessed. Being quite unused to festive occasions I was dreadfully shy when it came to my turn. However, I was coaxed into singing Ivor Novello's 'Keep the Home-Fires Burning', which I sang all the way through. All my family had excellent singing voices and it seemed I was no exception, for my rendition was so well received that I found myself blushing with pleasure and thought how nice it would be to sing to people when I grew up.

*

The weekly magazine that we had at home, when we could afford it, was *The Family Journal*. Mum found great pleasure in its articles and stories, while we looked forward to the children's section. Another magazine that became popular during the war was called *John Bull*. As I recall it was printed on yellow buff paper and featured a short, sturdy figure with a squashed top hat and a Union Jack waistcoat. This magazine was edited by Horatio Bottomley, who put himself across as the soldier's friend, drawing attention to their hardships and grievances, and to the wickedness of the profiteers, politicians and incompetent generals directing the war effort. However, it seemed his motives were not always so honourable, for in 1922 he was brought to trial, convicted and imprisoned for his Victory Bond swindle, which caused many poor and working-class people to lose their money.[24]

In those far-off days there was no radio or television to occupy the long winter evenings. Electricity was around but it was for the favoured few. Central heating and double glazing were way ahead in the future. My sisters, brother and I would sit around our plain deal table playing Ludo, Happy Families or Snakes and Ladders, getting as near to the fire as we could and shouting for a 'penny for the gas' when the light went out. Our parents encouraged us to read and while they frowned upon the lurid literature known as 'penny dreadfuls', they allowed us a copy of a high-class comic called *Rainbow*. Week by week we followed the adventures of Tiger Tim and the Bruin Boys, Marmaduke the Magician, and the Chinese twins, Sing Hi and Sing Lo.

The newsagents had a wide range of children's fiction on sale and *Rainbow* was expensive at one penny. Most others, like *Funny Wonder*, *Lots of Fun*, *Merry and Bright* and *Chips* cost a halfpenny. Unknown to our parents, or so we thought, we swapped our *Rainbow* for more exotic literature and so were able to widen our comic horizons. I vaguely remember *Ally Sloper's Half Holiday*, *Puck* and *The Boy's Own Paper*, although the latter two would be insulted if anyone called them comics. My favourite characters appeared in *Chips*. They were two ragged tramps called Weary Willie and Tired Tim. I am sure many adults secretly read comics. Our school teacher often referred, very sarcastically, to the not so bright pupils as Dreamy Daniels, Weary Willies and Tired Tims.

One memorable day brother Reg came home from school with a copy of a boys' magazine called the *Nelson Lee Library*. This magazine, small enough to slip into a jacket pocket, was to become my favourite weekly. Recorded in it were the adventures of Nelson Lee, the world-famous detective whose consulting rooms were in the Gray's Inn Road. He was also housemaster at a mythical public school 'St Franks', a school built on the site of an old monastery where secret passages, hidden rooms, sliding doors and ghostly visitations abounded. The narrative was related throughout by Richard Hamilton, alias Nipper, Lee's capable assistant. An air of mystery hung over St Franks and many shady characters were pursued through the cloisters and the quad by our heroes, aided by room mates, the elegant Sir Lancelot Montgomery Tregellis West and the very practical Tommy Watson.

Boys of my age, whose horizons were Ruskin Park, Kimpton Mission and Peckham Rye, knew absolutely nothing about public schools. We had never

---

24 Horatio William Bottomley (1860–1933), newspaper proprietor, journalist, MP and convicted fraudster, founded the 1*d.* weekly *John Bull* in 1906.

even heard of them. It was a revelation to learn that there existed in this country schools where pupils lived and learnt, slept and ate, and that parents paid good money to send their children there, seeing them only at Christmas and holiday times. The Nelson Lee cult spread in our class and we identified ourselves with the Remove boys of St Franks, becoming totally absorbed by the weekly stories. Being war time, Nelson Lee's services were constantly sought by the Government and Secret Service; on one occasion I could not resist reading during a lesson, and had just reached the part where Lloyd George was receiving advice from Nelson Lee when teacher's ruler brought me sharply and painfully back to reality.

Another most popular boys' periodical was the *Union Jack Library*. This magazine was already twenty-seven years old when I was born, having commenced publication in 1880. As its name suggests its stories had a patriotic leaning and many famous writers contributed stories and articles to its pages. I suppose I was about twelve years old when I read my first *Union Jack*. At the beginning I found the stories hard to follow but the more I read the more absorbing they became, until I began to share my affections for Nelson Lee with a new hero, Sexton Blake. Occasionally the two detectives liaised. Blake had an assistant called Richard Carter, or Tinker, and they made a perfect team. Their adventures spanned the world, from the highlands of Tibet to the swamps of the Amazon and the back streets of Naples and Paris. In addition to their adventures in the *Union Jack Library*, Sexton Blake and Tinker appeared in their own publication, the *Sexton Blake Library*, first published in 1919. This was a pocket-sized paper-covered book of eighty-four pages and cost 4*d*. Four copies appeared every month. Few of us could afford 4*d*., so we obtained them from second-hand shops or stalls in the market for 1*d*. each. By swapping them with our classmates we were able to follow the monthly adventures at very little cost.

Books for reading at school were few and mainly extracts from popular works like *David Copperfield* and *The Pickwick Papers*. We had shortened versions of Jules Verne's *Clipper of the Clouds* and *Round the World in Eighty Days*. There was R. M. Ballantyne's *Coral Island* and Henty's *Tiger of Mysore*. We acted one or two scenes from the *Merchant of Venice* and because I was supposed to have a cultured voice, I had the embarrassing part of Portia. Once we went by tram to the Old Vic to see how professional actors compared to our own unworthy efforts.

From an early age I had a liking for poetry and found the poems we were taught easy to memorise. We recited in unison simple poems from our *Child's Book of Verse*, like Tennyson's 'Brook', and took it in turn to read verses from the *Pied Piper of Hamelin* and the *Ballad of Chevy Chase*. I gradually developed a flair for writing simple verse and hesitantly began to show around my humble efforts. Had I received the necessary encouragement and a little help at that time I might have progressed to better things, but, alas, only ridicule and scorn greeted my primary efforts. However, Harry Turner, our headmaster, was very keen on setting competitions to test his pupils' abilities; every class at some time had to participate and it was compulsory for every boy and girl to enter. He set our class the task of writing a story or poem on any subject, but it had to be the pupil's own original work.

As can be imagined most of the entries were very half-hearted, but a few had merit. My story was about a boy trapped by the tide in a cave and of the efforts he made to escape. I received much praise and was highly commended by Harry Turner. My friend Ted Thompson was quite a brainy boy; his story was judged to be exceptional and he was awarded first place in the competition. There was no prize given, for, during the war, the giving of prizes was suspended.

In the poetry competition I had little opposition and, much to the delight of Mrs Wilson, our teacher, came an easy first, my only serious challenger being Ted Thompson, who was awarded second place. I cannot recall what my poem was about but I do remember how self-conscious I was when Ted and I had to stand on the platform and read our respective pieces to the assembled school. After this small triumph my interest in poetry declined but I can recall the odd occasion when Ted and I collaborated in writing limericks, which were very popular at the time.

Our school was co-educational and each class had roughly equal numbers of boys and girls, totalling about forty. At one time girls and boys sat at the same desk but it wasn't popular and in time the girls sat in two rows on the right and the boys in two rows on the left. Each sex had its own school entrance marked 'GIRLS' and 'BOYS', with separate playgrounds and doors into the school. The boys and girls appeared to have little time for each other and the only time I can remember when the boys showed any interest in a girl was when Maud Elliot, an Australian, joined the class. She had lived somewhere in the outback and her stories of life among the kangaroos and cattle fired our imaginations. Needless to say, she was most unpopular with the rest of the girls. However, the day came when one of the lads fell for one of the girls and asked Ted and I to write a poem for him. This rather Victorian way of making his affections known was quite normal at the time, and Ted and I, despite our inexperience in these matters, decided to oblige. I can recall only the second verse, which went:

> *O when does your birthday come pray,*
> *Let me know before the day,*
> *And if you will be my very own,*
> *I'll buy you a bottle of Eau de Cologne.*

Whether this helped the romance I cannot recall.

Ted (Edward Cecil) Thompson, my other school chum, lived at No. 45A, Kimpton Road, opposite the Mission. He was the youngest member of the Thompson family, having a sister, May, and two brothers, Percy and Frank.

Percy was to become a casualty of the war. His father had a wooden leg but what caused his disability I never knew. His mother, a buxom lady, was a devoted worker at Kimpton Mission, a leader of the Mothers' Meeting and a person who could always be called upon to help out when help was needed. She was always very kind to me, as was her husband. During the war Mr Thompson ran a canteen for the Senior Boys' Club in the small hall of the Mission but there wasn't much demand for it and after a while this amenity ceased. He did not appear to have any regular work, although for a time he managed a coffee stall which was installed nightly at the tram shelter on Camberwell Green. Percy Thompson was unknown to me but both Frank and May became good friends of mine. They were very talented and put their abilities to excellent use as leaders of Kimpton's youth. Frank was like an older brother to me and I always looked up to him and held him in high regard. He left school in 1915 at the age of thirteen and stayed with his firm, Samuel Putnam & Co, Timber Merchants, during the whole of his working life, rising from office boy to Managing Director.

The desks we used at school accommodated two children sitting side by side. Each desk had a wooden top and tip-up seat bolted to an iron frame. The desk top was hinged and when raised revealed two small compartments for housing text and exercise books. In the fixed part of the desk top were two shallow trays which held the pens and pencils, and a hole at each end held a removable china inkwell. The wooden tops of the desks were made unsightly from the ink that had spilt or overflowed from carelessly refilled wells. One's fingers were never clean, for the ink seemed to get everywhere.

Because we only attended school for half a day, books, pens and pencils had to be collected up at the end of each session and stored in the cupboard until the next day, when the class monitors handed them out again. The teachers must have found this lack of continuity exasperating and no doubt longed for the day when the authorities would de-requisition the school in Grove Lane.

When it was decided that the boys and girls in our class should sit separately the teacher made an attempt to seat us according to the alphabetical list of surnames, As in the front through to Ws at the back. However we swapped about without much interference, and while I occasionally sat with Ted, I usually sat with Noel, and we spent much of our time planning what to do after class.

*

The year 1915 went monotonously on but it was noticeable how many men in blue uniforms were now to be seen around the borough. These were soldiers who had been wounded in the trenches of France and Belgium, and who had been sent back to England for hospital treatment and convalescence prior to returning to the war front. Lots of these men were to be seen in Grove Lane and around the Denmark Hill area because of nearby King's College Hospital and its ancillary premises in Grove Lane and Ruskin Park. Many had their heads swathed in bandages, arms in slings or walked with crutches. They often kept company with local girls and were seen cuddling in doorways, much to the chagrin of the local lads, who often pelted them with clods of grass. It was sad to see how many women went shopping dressed in funereal black, a testimony to the real cost of the conflict raging overseas.

*

In Grove Lane just past the railway tunnel, stood a large building rejoicing in the name of the Lava Skating Rink. Roller-skating had become very popular in Victorian and Edwardian days and these rinks had sprung up in most cities and towns throughout the country. There was another rink only about half a mile away in Coldharbour Lane next to Price's, the bakers, and opposite Hayes Laundry called, I believe, the 'Embassy'. Skating gradually declined in popularity and during the war the Lava Rink became the headquarters of 'Grandad's Army'. This was probably not their correct title but that is how we knew them. Noel and I used to stand outside and watch these men marching four abreast, arms swinging and heads held high, grey-haired and bald-headed men, veterans of past conflicts. We often had a good laugh at their expense but no doubt they would have fought hard against any invader.

Sometime later, towards the end of 1916 or beginning of 1917, the Lava Skating Rink caught fire and was razed to the ground. Grandad's Army moved elsewhere and the site remained derelict for many years until, in the early 1920s, a Scout hut was erected on its frontage. This remained until after the Second World War, when the area was grassed over and incorporated into the grounds of the Council's housing development in the Grove.

*

The summer of 1915 was hot and dry, and Noel and I played outside whenever the opportunity came. The Vining family owned a wooden horse on three wheels, two at the back and the other at the front, with pedals attached. We used to take it up Grove Lane to the wide expanse of pavement outside the school, which was on a fairly steep incline. We had a lot of fun racing down the hill, one of us sitting on the horse the other standing on the back axle. Once we threw out a challenge to Maisie Bradshaw on her scooter but in the event we were beaten from the start, and to add to our discomfiture we overturned outside the gates of the Nursery.

When we returned to school after the summer holidays, sister Con, who had won a scholarship, took her place at Charles Edward Brooke, the grammar school in Haslemere Road, near Myatts Park. It meant little to me at the time but looking back I realise what an achievement winning the scholarship was. It must have involved hard studying under adverse conditions, for there was little privacy at home. Scholarship passes were few and far between and the most any school could have was three; sometimes only one was awarded, occasionally none.

In a prominent place on the wall of the school assembly hall was the 'Honours Board', which recorded in gold lettering the year the scholarship had been won and the name of the successful scholar. There were few names recorded and for some years there were no names at all.

At the end of October another sister, Audrey Florence, was born into our family and we children were six in number. Our local doctor was a Dr Johnson, in whom Mum and Dad had great faith, and he attended Mum. When the doctor stopped his visits a Nurse Veasey, who lived in Mosedale Street, came in once a day to bath the baby and give general help.

While this addition to our family must have increased the strain on our slender resources I was not really conscious of it, and things went on much as before except that we had to make our clothes and boots last a bit longer. In those days it was accepted without question that some were born rich and others poor for, after all, one of the hymns we sang at Sunday School reminded us that 'God made men high or lowly, and ordered their estate'! Even so, there were ominous rumblings of discontent with this order that allowed the privileged classes to be almost above the law and which bore so heavily upon the shoulders of the poor. Young as I was, I often wondered why some women always had plenty of money while my mother had so little and had to look at every penny she spent.

As I trotted off to school on a Monday morning I always passed a queue of women outside Prescott's, the pawnbrokers in Church Street, waiting for nine o'clock when that worthy man opened for business. Many had pathetic bundles of clothing in prams or under their arms, which probably contained Father's best suit or Mum's best dress, or sometimes the children's Sunday garments. Others clutched mysterious brown paper parcels which concealed from prying eyes the heirloom or treasured possession that was going into 'pop'. Mr Prescott was known as 'Uncle'. He was obviously a fair man for I never recall a bad word said against him. The articles his clients brought into the office were pledged for whatever sum the pawnbroker was prepared to give. With luck they would be redeemed the following Friday evening or Saturday morning. Mr Prescott or his clerk were able to write two cards at once by using a double pen. One card was attached to the article pledged, the other was handed over to the client with the money. I was told that the three balls suspended over the pawnshop meant the odds were two to one against the person getting their goods back. In support of this the pawnbroker's window was full of unredeemed pledges and anyone with money to spare could buy valuable goods at bargain prices.

*

With the approach of the Christmas season the toy shops tried to put on the best displays they could in the circumstances. Prior to the war most toys were made in Germany but these were no longer available; in any case, nobody would be so unpatriotic as to buy German toys. There was a toy shop in Church Street and Reg, Noel and I often stopped to gaze at skates, tops, dolls, clockwork trains, steam engines and humming tops that were displayed in the window. We would fantasize about what we would buy if we were lucky enough to find a sovereign or two. We often searched hopefully in the gutters but all we ever found were used tram tickets and cigarette packets.

The festivities of Christmas 1915 were overshadowed by the war. Many men were away from home in the Army or Navy, and without them there would be little cause for rejoicing. There was talk of rationing of essential foodstuffs but nothing came of it at the time. Adults complained about the rising cost of food and of profiteering by shopkeepers. For those who were not short of money there was plenty of food to be had, although some items like raisins, currants and sultanas, necessary ingredients of the Christmas pudding, were reserved for special customers who would pay the price.

As a special treat on Christmas Day we children were allowed to drink a small glass of Stone's Raisin Wine. I am sure this would have earned the displeasure of Mr Scurr and Miss Mulley, leaders of Kimpton Mission's Band of Hope, but we enjoyed it. We would go to the service in the morning while Mum prepared the dinner. She was an excellent cook and did wonders with the food she was able to buy. I cannot remember us ever having the traditional turkey, instead we had either leg of pork or aitchbone of beef, usually the latter. This was a good family joint from which large slices of meat could be carved and the leftovers made into Shepherd's pie. Even the bones would become the basis of a good old Irish Stew.

At lunch time we ate our fill of beef, roast and boiled potatoes, parsnips and brussel sprouts, followed by apple pie and custard with a mince pie. No fruit meant no Christmas pudding, although I did scrounge a piece from Noel. Dad told us how when he was a boy all his mother and he had for their Christmas dinner was a kipper because that was all his mother could afford to buy. There were relatives living in the same town (Rickmansworth) but they never gave any assistance to their poorer relatives. As a result Dad turned his back on them and in later years completely ignored them all.

During the afternoon we amused ourselves by playing board games like Snakes and Ladders and Ludo, and card games of Snap, Beat Your Neighbours and Happy Families, and Noughts and Crosses. We roasted chestnuts on the bars of the fire grate. We sang Christmas carols and I can remember Reg singing 'God Rest Ye Merry Gentlemen'.

We ate our Christmas tea by candlelight and it was the meal I really loved. The little coloured candles with twisted stems made by Price's were still available in the early days of the war but they disappeared after this Christmas. We softened the end of the candles and stuck them on saucers or put them in little coloured jars that were hung from any convenient bracket. The danger of fire caused by candles being knocked over was an accepted risk but we managed to avoid accidents. The mottoes on the walls glowed their messages down on the family as we ate our meal. Their golden words on holly and silver backgrounds read, 'God Bless Our Home', 'Merry Xmas', 'What Is Home Without a Mother' and 'Happy New Year', and had been bought from Woolworth's at a penny each. The paper chains we had made from strips of coloured paper with a patch of gum at one end. They were always breaking and were a great fire risk. Tea was always a jolly meal and we teased each other as we ate our jam and cake and spooned away tinned fruit and blancmange. When the washing up was done and we sat down feeling full, we could be excused for feeling that God was in his heaven and all was right with the world.

1916

While the summers of the war years were hot and sunny the winters were severe, with bitter winds, hard frosts and snow. As a family, with the possible exception of Dad and Reg, we were warm-weather types and felt the cold keenly. My sisters bore the cold stoically but I always considered the winter had a personal vendetta against me and did its best to make my life a misery. My jacket, jersey and shorts gave little protection from the icy blasts that nature hurled in my direction. Whether it was due to poor circulation, inadequate diet or lack of some vital ingredient in the mysterious mixture that makes up an individual I do not know (although I suspect this to be the case), but I suffered terribly from chilblains, as did my sisters, and even mother was not immune. When we were out playing in the snow we would stamp our feet and circle our arms around our heads and across our chests to get our sluggish circulation going. Sometimes we made for ourselves 'winter warmers' out of empty Cadbury cocoa tins. We would punch holes in the tin and push a piece of string through a hole in the centre of the base. A loop was tied to one end for the hand to slip into and a knot the other end held it in place. A piece of woollen rag was then set alight and when it was smouldering well it was stuffed into the tin and the lid pushed on securely. Putting a hand through the loop in the cord we whirled the tin round and round, and the draught made the rag flame and smoke. The smell was revolting but the tin glowed almost red hot. We allowed the tin to cool a little, warmed our hands around it, and then discarded it in the nearest dustbin.

Because of chilblains I dreaded the approach of the bitter weather that winter brought in its train. It wasn't considered manly for men and boys to protect their hands with gloves and this resulted in them going around with hands in their pockets. I never had a pair of gloves until I left school. Scarves were popular and were worn around the neck and tied in front with a big knot. Most men wore boots, which were covered with dubbin to keep out the water, and the normal headgear was a cap, except for city types who wore a bowler or a top hat.

Sometimes in the winter I could not see the knuckles on my hands for chilblains, which covered my hands from wrist to fingertips. When I came into a warm room the itching was so bad that to obtain relief I would go and put my hands under a tap and let the cold water run on them. This was really very unwise. Before going to bed Mum would rub yellow Vaseline on my hands to keep the skin from cracking and to ease the irritation. I received little or no sympathy, for folk were ignorant of the cause and most told me to run around and not be a slacker. The chilblains got so bad that Mum took me to see Dr Sansom, whose consulting room was opposite the Green, a few doors from the Westminster Bank, on the corner of Camberwell New Road. His surgery was really the parlour of an old house and the waiting room, once the hall, was lined with chairs. His small dispensary was tucked into a corner by the entrance, and its window overlooked the Green. Dr Sansom was very sympathetic but could offer no quick solution. He said the only cure was to take opium but this, of course, was not allowed. He was sure that, in time, I would grow out of them.

Ladies' handbags were not so much in evidence then as they are today and most women in the area in which we lived only carried purses. To keep their hands warm in winter the female population tucked their hands into a muff, which was sometimes suspended waist-high from a fancy cord around the neck. Muffs came in various sizes, but the most popular length was about twelve inches. It was a cylindrical tube of fur, lined with wool, and the thickness and quality of the fur depended on the price that had been paid. Some muffs were very fine and toned in well with the fur coats of the ladies of quality and wealth. The muffs appeared to be very efficient in keeping hands warm. I used to try Mum's out and very cosy it was. Some muffs had a pocket in the lining, but usually a woman held her purse in her hand, inside the furry covering.

Winter slowly dragged on its inevitable course, but eventually the day came when we felt the sun warm on the back of our hands and we knew spring was on its way. The crocuses would soon be out in the park, and we could look forward to larks singing above One Tree Hill, and cricket on Peckham Rye.

*

At school one morning, two of our classmates, who never seemed short of pocket money, decided to hire a boat that afternoon on the lake in Dulwich Park. They invited Noel and myself to be their guests on condition that I was steersman. I had never been on a boat before or, for that matter, in Dulwich Park, and I was awfully excited at the prospect. Mum, somewhat reluctantly I thought, said I could go and after lunch. Noel and I set off for the park about two and a half miles away.

The easiest way there was by tramcar from Camberwell Green to Dulwich Library, in Lordship Lane, and thence a short walk down Eynella Road to the park gates in Court Lane. The lake was on the further side of the park. A child's fare on the tram was a penny each way but Noel and I were penniless, so we set off on foot. The prospective five-mile return journey we took in our stride, for walking was an accepted fact of life and nobody rode if they could walk. Of course, the distance one could cover in a short time was limited and was the main reason we seldom went more than a mile or two from home.

The weather in the previous few days had been very cold, with heavy frosts at night, but this day had seen the return of the spring sunshine. We felt light-hearted as we walked, kicking stones along the way and looking for birds' nests in the hedges bordering Green Lane. When we eventually got to the park it was to find ice on the lake and boating suspended. For a few minutes we kicked a ball around and then decided to make our way home to tea. We idled away a few minutes by the smithy watching the sparks fly, and at the Mill Pond we tossed a stone or two into its placid waters. About fifty years ago a windmill had stood here, but that, and the surrounding cornfields, had long since gone. We rejoined Green Lane from East Dulwich Grove and, a little footsore and somewhat deflated, eventually reached home.

*

In Peckham Road, opposite the Oliver Goldsmith School on the corner of Southampton Street, stood the headquarters of our local fire brigade. Its training yard was round the corner in Talfourd Road and the superstructure of its drill tower rose from its centre. Two appliances were kept here and at one side was the operations room. Fire alarms placed at strategic points around the Borough were connected to a panel on the wall. When an alarm was sounded a shutter fell down on the panel giving the position of the pulled alarm, and the bells were automatically sounded.

The present-day calling of the fire service by telephone was unknown then, for public telephones were very few and mainly to be found in shops, where the shopkeeper was responsible for collecting the money for calls. Only in the homes of the wealthy were private telephones to be found. The fire alarms (there was one in Grove Lane near Love Walk) were red in colour and in appearance something like the present day parking meter—a tubular stand with a round operating head. Behind a circle of thin glass was a red lever; around the head was embossed 'In case of Fire', and on a plate below, 'BREAK GLASS. PULL KNOB. WAIT FOR ENGINE'.

Along the routes of the water-mains were the fire hydrants, and an enamelled plate on a nearby wall or fence indicated the position of the hydrants in case snow should obliterate the whereabouts of the cast iron covers. These plates were about six inches square and bore a blue 'H' on a white background. Sometimes, at high risk points, it showed 'HD' denoting a double hydrant. Occasionally, there would be a figure '4', indicating to the fireman that below was a four-inch main.

There was tremendous excitement, especially among children, when the clamour of fire bells heralded the approach of the fire engine, with the men in black oilskins and polished brass helmets ready for action. When a call came, the 'Escape' with its ladders was always first away, for the saving of life was the first consideration. The second appliance, the pump, was never far behind, and a third always came from the next nearest station—Gresham Road, Brixton, Lordship Lane, Queens Road or Old Kent Road, depending on where the outbreak had occurred. As soon as it could be spared, the Escape always returned to its base in case of another call.

I was in Coldharbour Lane one day when a fire broke out in a factory in Harbour Road. The Brigade was quickly on the scene but so rapidly did the fire spread that the factory was gutted and remained for a long time just a blackened shell.

I was to become familiar with the workings of the London Fire Brigade when in 1938 I joined the Auxiliary Fire Service and received my training at the Peckham Fire Station. Because I was fully trained on the outbreak of war in 1939, I was put in charge of a station in Holloway, where I remained until I resigned in February 1940.

*

However peaceful the scene at home seemed at times, one could not escape the fact that we were at war and the fighting in the trenches was taking its toll of the male population. Small factories that were to be found in the back streets were called upon to make their contribution to the war effort, and in July there was a loud explosion when one of these small factories blew up, killing three people. There were other more serious accidents. We were playing out one day in April when there was a glare in the sky and the sound of a distant explosion. People said that a fire in a munitions factory somewhere in Kent had caused a terrible disaster and there were about 200 casualties. To say we were scared was an understatement of the first magnitude. We fled into No. 42 and for some time I was too frightened to go home.[25] This disaster was, however, dwarfed by another which took place on 19 January 1917. It was a mild evening for January and we were out flying paper aeroplanes on the corner of Kerfield Crescent. I remember how mine, caught in an upward current of air, went sailing around the wall of a house in

---

25 On 2 April 1916 an explosion at a powder factory in Kent killed more than one hundred men and injured more than sixty others. A single paragraph about the explosion appeared in *The Times* a few days later (see 'Fourth Air Raid/Verdun Attacks Crushed/Big Explosion in Kent/The New War Budget', *Times*, 5 April 1916, 8A). See also 'The Kent Powder Explosions: 172 men killed and injured', *Times*, 27 April 1916, 3B, and *Annual Register for 1916*, 10.

Grove Lane. It was almost dark but suddenly the sky began to lighten in the east and it became as bright as day. A few moments later the most appalling sound I have ever heard filled the air and concussed our eardrums. There was a sound of shattering glass and everyone ran for cover. Next day we heard it was caused by an explosion in a munitions factory at Silvertown. Later reports said sixty-nine people had been killed, 450 injured and damage estimated at two and a half million pounds had been caused.[26]

*

Brother Reg, Noel and I, like most boys of our age, had a passion for fishing. Our rods and lines were very crude, consisting of a length of button thread tied to a stick, with a bent pin on the other end. Our nets were pieces of old net curtaining wound round a circle of wire and fixed to a piece of cane. We pulled up tufts of grass in search of worms to use as bait, and these were impaled on the bent pin. Hopefully the fish would swallow the worm and get the pin caught in their throats. When our household duties had been completed we would sally forth with our gear and a couple of jam jars in search of sticklebacks, minnows or a humble tadpole.

The nearest ponds were in Ruskin Park. The large one with its grassy banks and willow tree is still there but the smaller one to the north, by the railway line, has long since been filled in and now lies beneath the tennis courts. One of us always had to be look-out as fishing was forbidden. We were never left in peace for long as the park keepers were very alert and unsportingly chased us off. In the end we gave up our piscatorial pursuits in Ruskin Park and looked elsewhere for our angling.

One day it was suggested that we try our luck in the canal. This stretch of water was near Camberwell Gate, alongside Albany Road. For some reason I never roamed in this direction, my instincts always led me south or west. Reg, however, was quite familiar with north Camberwell as he liked the street markets of East Street and Westmoreland Road, and knew all the back doubles of the area. Our way took us the length of Camberwell Green and we emerged opposite the tavern called the Father Red Cap, which was next to the Greencoat Schools. The road at this junction was criss-crossed with tram lines, for on the opposite side of the road was the Camberwell Tram Depot. From where we stood we could see the trams leaving for the Embankment, Waterloo and Blackfriars, but there was another exit in New Road for services to Kennington, Vauxhall and Victoria.

Next door to the Father Red Cap was Bennett's the fishmonger. He used to smoke his own kippers, bloaters and haddock. Dad was very fond of the latter

---

26 'One of the most tragic events of the month [January 197] was an explosion which occurred at a munitions factory in the East End of London [...] The total number of casualties was over 450, including sixty-nine killed and seventy-two seriously injured.' (*Annual Register for 1917*, 55).

for his tea and one or other of us used to come here for a piece of haddock, or a small whole haddock. He always preferred a piece because of the large flakes that were missing on the smaller fish. We paid 3 or 4d. for haddock, while fresh herrings were 2d. a pound and kippers 2, 3 or 4d. a pair, depending on the size. Spratts were even cheaper. The shop, which was open-fronted, was kept spotlessly clean and water was continually being sloshed over the marble slabs.

Camberwell Road commenced at the Green and went north to join Walworth Road at Camberwell Gate, where a turnpike had once stood. A few yards from the fishmongers was a squalid area of slum property known by its principal street, Buff Place. There were other equally disreputable streets like Bullace Row, Mazzard Row and Guildford Place, which backed on to the tenements of George Street where the Salvation Army has its citadel. Buff Place had a reputation for brutality, crime, squalor and dirt, and the area was shunned by all self-respecting folk. Street fights were common, especially after the pubs closed on a Saturday night, and when the police were called they only ever went in in strength. Many years later, about 1926, the Royal Arsenal Co-operative Society took over three shops between Mazzard and Bullace Rows and opened a grocery and provisions store, with a butchers attached. I joined the staff of this store on 21 March 1927, when I was nineteen years old, and worked there until the outbreak of the Second World War in 1939 when I was called up for service with the Auxiliary Fire Service.

A few shops past here was the upholsterers kept by Noel's uncle and where I had gone to that never-to-be-forgotten party. But it was a depressing walk past the little shops, all of which needed a coat of paint.

About half way to our destination we came opposite Wyndham Road, once the site of the Camberwell Mill. Now, alas, the area was covered by more slums, some of London's worst. The area rejoiced in the name of Sultan Street, although this was only one of the many squalid streets between Wyndham Road and Bethwin Road. Running parallel to Camberwell Road was Crown Street, also very notorious. It was the only street in the slum that I ventured into and this was only because the yard of the Farmer and Cleveland Dairies was there. The owner was known to our family because he was a keen supporter of Kimpton Mission and one of his roundsmen was our milkman. When I was about twelve years old I became a milkman's boy and helped with one of the rounds.

Opposite the dairy, in the main road, was a shoe and boot factory that also made clogs. It is strange to think that once clogs were worn in the streets of Camberwell. A little further along was Cambridge House, a social centre run by voluntary and residential helpers. It provided a much needed service for the people of the neighbourhood, but I never went there.

The canal was not much further and only a few yards from the main road. At its head was a timber yard. It was called the Surrey Canal, was four miles long, and part of the Grand Union Canal system. It had been cut in 1802 and was used mainly to move timber and coal. At the end of its length it joined the Thames at the Surrey Commercial Docks. It was a dark, evil-smelling stretch of water, so horribly polluted that no fish could have lived in it. We walked along the towpath for a bit and then mooched off home. After that I never wanted to go there again, but it held a strange fascination for many boys and fatalities from drowning were not unknown. One lad from the Kimpton Road area fell in and died soon after. Mum always maintained that if the evil water had been pumped from his body in time he would have recovered. After this we were forbidden to go to the canal, but the warning was unnecessary, for I had no desire to go there ever again.

Another pastime we enjoyed was making paper boats and floating them in the gutter after it had rained or when the water cart was sluicing down the roads. Later we turned our efforts to making wooden sailing boats and submarines with some success. One afternoon the three of us walked to Brockwell Park to try out our latest models.

Brockwell Park was in Lambeth near Herne Hill and sometimes Mum would take us there for a picnic. We would take our food with us, then at about four o'clock Reg or I would go home by tram (fare ½d. each way), make some tea and bring it back in a jug. We used to sit in the park near the railings in Norwood Road, where there was a screen of large trees, and watch the tramcars going to and fro. There was no pavement along this stretch of the highway. On the opposite side of the road was the firm of 'Bath's' which made rustic furniture and occupied the whole frontage between Herne Hill railway arch and Croxted Road. Many years later a parade of shops was built in front of the Bath's workshop.

On this occasion ill luck dogged our pleasures. Reg, trying to pull his yacht in, overbalanced and fell in the pond. He got out safely and wrung out his clothes as best he could in the toilets. When we reached home he received a beating for getting his clothes wet. We all thought this very unfair. We did not go back to Brockwell Park again for a long time.

At long last we found the ideal spot. It was a secluded little lake in the grounds of a large house near the bottom of Red Post Hill. There was a hole in the fence large enough for us to squeeze through. The lake had grassy banks and was screened from the perimeter fence by trees and bushes. We pretended to be Red Indians and trod lightly and cautiously as we approached the water's edge with our homemade rods and line. Sentry duty was taken in turn and once a few fish had been netted we stole quietly away with our catch safe in the jam jars. Now and again we had to run like mad for the escape hole when a servant came after us. However, we did no damage and attempts to catch us were never pressed home, nor was the fence repaired.

When Camberwell Council built its garden estate on Red Post Hill and Sunray Avenue, the grounds and lake of this big house were turned into a public park, called Sunray Gardens. In later years when I strolled through the park, it was hard to believe that once access could only be gained by trespassing, and I pictured the three of us creeping through the bushes with our homemade fishing nets, getting such pleasure from catching a couple of minnows.

*

It was in 1916 that 'summer time' was foisted on the British people and clocks were advanced one hour for the first time in our history. The Daylight Savings Bill had been introduced into Parliament around 1906 but its reception was hostile and it failed to get the necessary support to reach the Committee stage. It took a war to get this novel piece of legislation onto the Statute Book and it was perhaps ironic that the Coalition Government was concerned with it not as a progressive social measure, but as a means of stimulating the war effort.

Most people, at first, resented having to get out of bed an hour earlier than usual, but it was the agricultural community who were the chief objectors, complaining that the dew would not dry up any quicker and the cows wouldn't give their milk an hour earlier just to please the Government. However, after the initial shock the advantages of an extended evening were apparent and gradually opposition subsided. We boys were all for it. It was generally accepted in those days that 'summer time' would end with the cessation of hostilities and only those with a little more foresight could see that it was probably here to stay.

Things were becoming pretty tight on the home front, money was short, the price of food was rising and commodities were becoming scarce. The U-boats were taking their toll of shipping and the fishes fed well. As if she hadn't enough to do at home looking after her own family, Mum undertook some part-time cleaning work at a residence in Coldharbour Lane, not far from Gresham Road. The money must have been desperately needed. The people, who lived at Ardath House, were named Tanner and were members of Kimpton Mission. No doubt that is how Mum came to be involved with them. I used to go there with her and run errands for Mr Tanner, an elderly gent who bred prize-winning rabbits. Mum and I would board a tramcar at the Green bound for Brixton which, I believe, was a No. 34. The fare for Mum was a penny and she paid a halfpenny for me. When we travelled together we always sat downstairs on the slatted seats of yellow varnished wood. These seats ran the full length of the tram with the passengers facing each other, and there was always a flow of conversation between them. If I ever travelled on my own, and provided it wasn't snowing, I would go upstairs and sit on one of the slatted seats that had moveable backs. There was no roof to the tram but waterproof covers were provided as some sort of shield against inclement weather. I always felt sorry for the driver, who faced all weathers practically unprotected.

It was an uneventful ride to Ardath House, past a few shops on either side of the Lane and Denmark Place Baptist Church about a hundred yards further on. The road bore left by Hayes Laundry, which was opposite Price's Bakery and the skating rink, and about a quarter of a mile further on were crossroads, a few more shops, a church and the railway station, all known as Loughborough Junction. The railway divided here, one line going to Denmark Hill the other to Herne Hill. It was also a junction for trams, straight ahead for Brixton and left for Norwood

Ardath House, a fair-sized detached residence with a wide pillared portico, had stone steps leading up to the front door. The Tanners kept Mum busy and I resented her being there, although I knew I could do nothing about it. Once Mr Tanner gave me 2*d*. to get my hair cut at the barbers opposite Osborne and Young, the hay and chaff merchants, but in the main I thought them mean and was glad when Mum stopped going there.

*

The hot, dry summers of the war years made keeping food fresh a real problem as there were no refrigerators. Most folk bought their provisions on a day to day basis, a quarter pound of margarine, two ounces of cheese, a quarter pound of corned beef *etc*. Flies were a nuisance. They settled on any food that was left uncovered for more than a few moments. Milk was protected by a muslin cloth or little crocheted cover, weighted around the edge with large beads. Even so the pests were everywhere and people bought flypapers from the oil shop to deal with them. These flypapers were cylinders of sticky paper which we unrolled and hung from our gas bracket. In a short time they were black with flies. Despite this their numbers never seemed to diminish. On Saturday evenings shoppers would gather round the butchers and fishmongers waiting for the shopkeepers to sell their food at knock down prices, as they too had no means of storing their perishable goods.

There were two moneylenders in the Mansions, Mrs Moon in No. 3 and Mrs Roe in No. 1. They used to charge a penny in the shilling, per week, for each pound that was borrowed, which worked out at 1*s*. 8*d*. for each £1. Sometimes Mum, in desperation, would borrow a pound from one of them and thereafter was the problem of how to repay a debt that forever increased. Mum was always scared that Dad would find out about borrowing from moneylenders, and this went for most of the women in the flats. Although in later years Mum and Mrs Moon were on friendly terms and even went to Aston Abbotts together, I could never bring myself to forgive her for the heartless way she once treated my mother. Her defence was that she wasn't the moneylender, but only the agent for some nebulous person in Peckham, but she didn't convince anyone for a moment. Mrs Moon had two children. The daughter Beatrice was about Con's age and her son, a lad about Reg's age, was called 'Sonny' Moon, which needless to say brought much chaff from the local lads.

In June came a grim reminder that the country's troubles were a long way from being over when the war-weary public heard the news that Lord Kitchener, the Secretary of State for War, had been drowned on the cruiser *Hampshire* while on a mission to Russia. The *Hampshire* had struck a mine near the Orkneys and there were few survivors. People just could not bring themselves to believe that the man with the peaked cap, bristling moustache and pointing finger, whose familiar face had stared at them from the recruiting posters of 1914, was really dead. Many people were in tears and a gloomy depressed mood was abroad. Most folk seemed resigned to yet more hardships and shortages, and their pessimism was well founded. There was stalemate in France and the Somme offensive had been stopped in its tracks with casualties mounting day by day. At sea, the U-boats were inflicting grievous damage to our shipping, and on the home front the queues got longer for food which got scarcer and dearer. Excessively long hours of work did not help the sapping morale.

The hours during which public houses could remain open for business had recently been curtailed and now they could only serve drinks for a couple of hours midday and for four hours at night. This, of course, did not stop people drinking alcohol, they just had less time to drink it in. The pubs continued to do a roaring trade and their sawdust floors could scarcely be seen for feet as customers jostled each other to get to the bar. Sometimes I would hear singing as I passed the doors of the Artichoke or the Hermit's Cave, our local pubs, and to me it seemed blasphemous when the unseen revellers parodied the famous hymns tunes of Ira Sankey. One I remember used the tune of 'Over the river', and went something like this:

> *Looking for ale, yes, looking for ale,*
> *Sometimes we get it, sometimes we fail,*
> *Look at our noses, they're red as roses,*
> *When the pub closes, looking for ale*

Another I recall adopted the hymn tune 'I am so glad that our father in heaven' (Jesus loves me):

> *O what a kind hearted fellow was he,*
> *The naps and doubles that he gave to me,*
> *Trebles and long shots, they all came my way,*
> *In less than a week he had trebled my pay*

Another song that borrowed the tune of Bishop Heber's 'From Greenland's icy mountains', commemorated a popular actor and promoter whose theatre stood on an island in the Thames. Many aspiring young actors worked with Fred Karno at one time or another, including Charlie Chaplin, a local lad from a poor home in Lambeth, whose fame in early American films is well known. This chorus, I understand, was popular with the men in the trenches:

We are Fred Karno's army,
A merry lot are we,
Fred Karno is our captain,
Charles Chaplin our O.C.,
And when we get to Berlin
The Kaiser he will say,
Hock, hock, mein Got what an ugly rotten lot,
Are the ragtime infantry

Although Charlie Chaplin became a household name, his brother, Syd, was no mean actor and was instrumental in getting Charlie his job with Fred Karno in his 'Mumming Birds'. Syd was best known for his performance as Charley's Aunt in the comedy of that name.

During the school summer holidays I went with a party of boys from Kimpton Mission for a two-week stay at Hove, in Sussex. It was my first experience of a holiday organised for boys and girls by the Country Holiday Fund, a charity concerned with the welfare of deprived children in the big cities. We boys took it all for granted but a lot of time and effort by many unknown men and women must have been put into it.

I am not very clear in my mind how we got to Hove, although we travelled by train. Outside the station a group of women were waiting and about five other boys and myself were rounded up by a young woman, whom we later knew as 'Fanny', and marched off to a house in Livingstone Road. I have always believed the number was 111, but on a later nostalgic visit No. 11 was where I imagined No. 111 to be.

It was a poor establishment and we slept two to a bed in a room at the top of the house. Our first meal was a slice of bread and margarine and a slice of bread and jam (without the margarine). It was poor fare but as none of us lived very riotously we accepted it without complaint. Frances (Fanny) was the maid of all work, little more than a drudge. She scrubbed and cleaned all day long and did the shopping as well, while the large lady, who was the mistress of the establishment, strutted around issuing orders to us all. Once we thought we were all in for a treat when Fanny asked us if we liked herring in tomato sauce. We all said we did but the succulent herrings never appeared on our plates.

Hove was a dull place. The beach was very stony and a long way off. We gathered shells, but these began to smell horrible after a few days so we had to throw them away. Sometimes we went as far as Brighton Pier, but we could only look at it from the shore. We threw stones in the sea and then at each other but we became very bored. On one of the days we made our way to the Downs where we chased rabbits and butterflies and gathered harebells and wild scabious. Even so, two weeks passed quickly enough, and the time came to return home and we gathered at Hove Station for the return journey. By strange coincidence, when I was fourteen years old, the Mission received two tickets for a holiday in Hove and Ted Thompson and I were invited to go. We were over the normal age for these holidays but we were pressed to accept the offer, which we did. On arrival at Hove we were met by Fanny and off we went to Livingstone Road again. Frank Thompson, Ted's brother, came and stayed with us for a week.

Once back home Hove was soon forgotten; we went back to school and the routine of family life resumed. Mum relied on her older children to take the young ones out while she got on with the household chores. We had a big bassinet, known to us kids as 'the pram'. Reg and I, or Con and Reg, had to carry it down the forty-eight stairs to the street, and then climb up the stairs again to fetch Eileen and Audrey, put them in the pram and push them around the streets for an airing. If only one of us were available the pram had to be bumped up or down the stairs single-handed, and hard work it was. On the odd occasion a neighbour would assist, but normally one did not seek help. Like most boys I hated pushing the pram around.

Often, taking the babies out had to be combined with running errands for Mum, who relied a great deal on her three older children to keep their eyes open for some of the scarcer foods. Sugar was the first to disappear from the shelves, and when a shop took delivery of its quota the news quickly spread and queues would form. One of the shops, Fuller Medley's, on the corner of Camberwell Grove, had sugar one morning and Mum and Con managed to get 2 lb. Brother Reg, whose imagination was even more vivid than mine, spread the word around that we had bought a vast quantity of this sugar and as a result, Mum was accused of hoarding by neighbours, which upset her no end.

It was about this time, I believe, that Treasury notes took the place of the sovereign and half sovereign, and were, as far as I can recall, red and green. These notes were different from subsequent issues in that they were issued by the Treasury and not the Bank of England. From an early age I was interested in coins, perhaps because I rarely had more than a halfpenny or farthing at any one time. There were a large variety of coins in circulation, gold, silver and bronze. The gold half-sovereign was about the size of a farthing and I heard of several cases where a child had been told to take a farthing from mother's purse to buy sweets and had inadvertently taken a half sovereign. However, most shopkeepers were honest enough to see that the coin was safely returned to the parent. This error did not seem to occur with the sovereign, which was similar in size to a halfpenny. There were also £2 and £5 coins but these were mostly found on watch chains or were made into pendants. Of silver coins there seemed no end. There were lots of Victorian crown pieces and a few double florins, the latter having been minted in the 1880s, when it was proposed to go decimal. I loved to handle these huge coins which filled the palm of my hand and looked forward to owning my own one day. There were few silver coins of Edward VII around, probably because he didn't reign for very long, but George V coins were in abundance, from the half crown to the little three-pence piece.

One afternoon I was hurrying to school, late as usual, when in Rignold Road I saw a packet lying in the road. I picked it up and saw it contained a lot of blue ribbon in a variety of widths. I stuffed it in my jacket and continued on my way. When I reached home later, we examined the package in more detail and found that besides the ribbons, there was a wallet containing sixteen shillings in silver coins. It was a godsend to Mum who was at her wits end to know where our next meal was coming from. She rewarded me with a sixpence, which was quickly spent.

With the approach of winter supplies of food in the shops became scarcer and queues for what little there was grew longer. Shopkeepers took full advantage of this to raise prices and were consequently accused of profiteering. Mum, who by nature was very placid, was roused to protest vehemently when Fenner's, the greengrocers, would not let her have potatoes if she did not also buy cauliflower leaves. Thereafter most of our vegetables were purchased in the little market in Waterloo Street.

As children I suppose we were fortunate to be too young to appreciate the desperate plight we were in, but for our parents the battle to provide food and warmth was constant. Few men were around. There were women conductors on the trams, women delivered the post, many ran the shops, worked in the factories and on the farms. Life was governed by DORA, the Defence of the Realm Act. It bore down on everyone. You couldn't fly a kite, feed bread to an animal or buy whisky at weekends. It was small wonder that Reg and I became proper little scroungers. We were continually touring the shops in a quest for food. One afternoon, in the dairy opposite the Grove Tavern I bought a large piece of cheese. That evening, Mr Arkell, the Mission Superintendent, paid us a visit and his eyes sparkled when he saw our cheese. He asked us where we had bought it and no doubt hurried to the dairy the next day to see if there was still some for sale.

1917

Of the war years, 1917 was probably the worst. It was a year of confusion. I used to hear people talking and although I did not comprehend much it was apparent that all was far from well. Adults didn't discuss matters with small boys, so we were ignorant of much that went on outside our own little world. But by all accounts great battles were raging in France, and the words Somme, Verdun and Ypres were enough to make women pale. The dangers of working in the munitions factories was brought home to us in the January when the disastrous Silvertown explosion occurred. The shock of this added to the defeatism that was becoming apparent in a population that was overworked and underfed, and weary from air raids that disturbed their sleep.

The enormous casualties that filled the hospitals added to the falling morale. All recreation was now subordinate to the war effort, there was no University Boat Race or County Cricket, and the Football League Final was cancelled.

With the German submarines continuing to take their toll of Allied shipping there was a shortage of bread and flour, and potato flour was allowed to be added to wheat flour, in the proportion of one part potato to seven of wheat. Sugar was already rationed. Instead of rice one had to use flaked maize, ground rice or semolina. All were equally unpalatable.

In the midst of all these shortages, someone in authority had a brainwave and the allotment campaign was launched. The idea took off. Gardens were turned over to grow vegetables, land was provided in parks and open spaces, and with new strength and purpose the nation began to dig for victory. How much this home-grown food contributed to the nation's larder is uncertain, but it was a step in the right direction. Our Uncle Joe in Rushden, who had a plot of land, sent us a sack of spuds when things were looking grim, and they made some very welcome meals.

One day Reg and I, for want of something better to do, got hold of a couple of old newspaper bills and went along to Knatchbull Road, which we thought sufficiently far from home, and called out 'Kaiser dead—Official'. It was not unusual for boys to go around the streets selling newspapers in those days and almost at once a servant girl came running across to us to buy a copy of the paper containing the good news. When she saw us splitting our sides with laughter and without any evening papers, she cried, 'You wicked boys!' At that moment other doors opened and we ran for our lives.

In April, the United States of America declared war on Germany and a new song was added to our list. It was called 'Over there—for the Yanks are coming'. Although we didn't always know the correct words to the songs, we sang out heartily just the same. In concerts at the Mission we heard songs like 'There's a long, long trail a-winding', 'When the great red dawn is shining', 'Sister Susie's sewing shirts for soldiers' and 'Goodbye-ee' plus many others. The Mothers' Meeting and the Girls' Club kept themselves busy knitting comforts for the troops.

In the spring of 1917, Mum, unable to make ends meet, decided to take in washing. Before she was married she had worked as a children's nurse to a family in West Norwood, called Lacey. Their home was at No. 21, Kingsmead Road, a very select neighbourhood situated between Leigham Vale and Palace Road. It was a detached house which backed on to the railway. I never met Mr or Mrs Lacey, in fact I think the latter was dead. Nor did I meet the two sons, Charles and Ernest, but the two daughters occasionally came to No. 23 to see Mum and bring her small gifts. Anyway, Mum evidently agreed to do their laundry and yours truly was given the job of collecting the soiled linen and delivering the clean. I cannot say I ever enjoyed this task, but I had to do as I was told.

I used to go to collect the laundry on the half day when I was not at school.

I would get on a tram at the Green and a halfpenny child's fare would take me as far as the Tulse Hill Hotel. The route was along Coldharbour Lane to Loughborough Junction, then left around the block, passing the Salvation Army Citadel, to the junction of Poplar Walk Road and Milkwood Road. At this point Milkwood Road was too narrow to allow two trams to pass so the tram going towards Herne Hill had to deviate up Poplar Walk Road and down Lowden Road before rejoining Milkwood Road, where the highway became much wider.

Milkwood Road ran alongside the railway for most of its length and at the Herne Hill end the railway arches were in use as shops. The tram would clank across the Herne Hill crossing and run alongside Brockwell Park until it reached Trinity Rise. There was quite an area of open space here but it was built on after the war and became known as Brockwell Park Gardens. The tram continued on its way to Knights Hill and the tram garage in West Norwood, but I alighted at the Tulse Hill Hotel which was the limit of my ½d. fare. In those days this was a posh hotel at the end of the run for buses which came from Camberwell Green via Herne Hill, and there always seemed to be two buses standing on the forecourt. Norwood in those days was quiet, prosperous and very select.

My way took me past the shops to the junction of Palace Road and Leigham Vale. Here, on the corner, was Peed's Nursery with its colourful display of flowers, trees and shrubs, and with glasshouses at the back. Sometimes I would vary my route and turn into Kinsfaun Road to get to Kingsmead Road but usually I trotted up Leigham Vale to the junction of the three roads. No. 21 was about fifty yards up on the left-hand side.

Usually the house was empty but I knew where the key was hidden and I let myself in. The washing was sometimes in a parcel, sometimes in a laundry basket. How I hated the latter for it was far too big for me to carry. Most times there was a note asking me to do some shopping for scarce items of grocery. This was another of my hates, for the shops were a long way off and I knew what a hopeless task this chasing after 'under-the-counter' food was. One day I bought some 'Lemco' (a sort of Bovril) instead of Lemon Curd. Next time I went, there was a note telling me to take the Lemco back and get Lemon Curd. Although I received a copper or two for going shopping, I really resented this chore and to this day felt I was used.

The weight of the laundry was far too heavy for me. I was only nine years old, very thin and without much physical strength. I would stagger along with the basket or bundle, and rest it every few yards on a garden wall. Sometimes a good Samaritan would help me with the burden and I was always thankful when I reached Tulse Hill and could deposit it on the tram platform, under the stairs.

Once on a trip to Kingsmead Road I was stopped by a school inspector and accused of playing truant. He asked endless questions which he recorded in a notebook, and he scared me nigh to death. After that encounter I was very reluctant to go to West Norwood again and used to go with very bad grace. How pleased I was when some months later the Laceys decided to sell their house and move elsewhere.

As spring merged into summer, the Germans increased their daylight bombing attacks on London and in July there were heavy casualties. People who could moved away from the capital to the comparative safety of the country. Others found temporary escape from their distress and privations in the Bioscope or the Cinema. It was about this time that Noel and I sneaked in to the Empire Cinema and saw a Chaplin comedy. We were real cinema fans after that but since money was not forthcoming, we had to be content with the lurid posters outside. One advertised a serial, full of hair-raising adventures, called *The Red Ace;* another, entitled *The American Girl*, had a picture of a girl's face and I fancied her eyes watched me as I approached and then walked away. The most famous film of the day was *The Exploits of Elaine* starring Pearl White, but I never saw any of the episodes.[27]

Sister Con, four years older than me and the brainy member of the family, was a keen follower of the stage and screen. She seemed to know the names of most of the English and American actors and actresses of the day, and would sometimes substitute their glamorous names with her own. Although she may not have realised it, Con had quite an influence on her younger brothers and sisters and while she could be a bit scathing (especially to me), we nevertheless learnt a lot from her. She provided a link with the events and happenings that were unknown to us. Because of studying and homework she was excused the irksome queuing for food, though no doubt she contributed her share of duties in other ways.

Often of an evening when the weather was bad we younger ones would sit around the kitchen table and listen as she related stories of school, and of films and plays that she had seen. She possessed the gift of eloquence, as did brother Reg, and could build up glowing word pictures which transported us away from No. 23, Stobart Mansions to a world of make-believe. She was able to fill in for us the details of film serials we had missed, although most plots were beyond me.

That summer Noel and I went with the Country Holiday Fund to Norton Heath, near Ongar in Essex, and stayed with a Mrs Witham. This was a dream holiday. The war and air raids were far away and we had a wonderful time. Noel's parents cycled to see us and were relieved to see how happy we

---

27 *The Red Ace* (Trans-Atlantic Film Company, 1917) was a serial in sixteen episodes directed by Jacques Jaccard. The girl on the poster advertising *The American Girl* (1911) was presumably its star, Florence Lawrence (1886–1938), who was famous first as 'The Biograph Girl' and then (following her move from Biograph to the Independent Motion Picture Company in 1909) as 'The IMP Girl'. She is sometimes called 'The First Movie Star'. In *The Exploits of Elaine* (Hearst-Pathé, 1914), a serial in fourteen episodes directed by Louis J. Gasnier and George B. Seitz, Elaine Dodge (played by Pearl White) sets out to discover the real identity of the villain known only as 'The Clutching Hand', who has murdered her father.

were. The little hamlet remained unaltered for quite a while, but on a visit in 1972 I found that the cottage in which we stayed had been modernised and enlarged and the little chapel closed. The common, with its trees now fully grown, remained otherwise unaltered.

One afternoon, I think it was early September, Mum and the rest of the family except Reg were out. When we returned home Reg was missing. This in itself was nothing unusual for he and I would often sneak out to play if the opportunity arose. We both resented staying at home to look after our young sisters or going shopping or chopping firewood when our chums seemed always to escape such irksome tasks. By teatime Reg had not returned and Mum began to get anxious. After a while she went over to the eagle bracket and took down the little flowered tin that held the rent money. It was empty. So too were our money boxes, little oval mustard tins which we kept on the built-in dresser, although they seldom contained more than a few pence. It became obvious that Reg had run away.

Running away from home to seek fame and fortune was a popular theme of many stories in the boys' magazines of the day and Reg, who would have made an excellent explorer, or even a pirate, had decided to have a go. He had pocketed all the loose cash from the flat, fortified himself with some bread and cheese and departed to goodness knows where. Mum, however, was not so easily deceived and immediately guessed her eldest son's destination. 'He's gone to Granny's', she said.

Mum's hunch about Reg proved to be correct, he had indeed gone to his granny's. The story as I remember it was that on his arrival he told our unsuspecting grandmother that Mum had sent him, and a letter was in the post. He stayed about a week and then decided it was time to go. He made his way to Aylesbury and hung around the railway station trying to get the fare home by doing a bit of portering. Just outside Aylesbury, on the hill near Bierton, is a women's prison. According to Con, one of the ladies to whom Reg offered his services was the Matron. She must have been suspicious about this young lad, who was so anxious to earn a copper or two, for when Reg carried her bag to her quarters in the prison, she gave him a slap-up tea, and phoned the police. Dad and Mum had to go and fetch him home. Reg soon got over the inevitable beating and related his adventures, with a great deal of flair, to his admiring circle of friends.

With the coming of winter the situation on the home front was really grim. I spent many of my out-of-school hours pushing the pram around the various coal yards in the hope of getting a sack. Coal was supposed to be rationed but it was almost impossible to obtain. Once when I was successful in getting a half hundredweight from a street cart, I came home quite elated. We tried all sorts of things to make a fire. We twisted newspaper into briquettes, scrounged tarry blocks and wooden boxes, sawdust, shavings, in fact anything that would burn and keep the home warm. Food remained very short and it began to have an adverse effect on me. What with queuing from early morning for stale bread, roaming the streets for fuel and tramping from shop to shop for beef bones, tripe or pig's fry, or anything that was cheap, I began to feel very tired and depressed. I suppose most folk felt the same. I found myself unable to concentrate at school and my position in class dropped from the top stream to well down the second half. Dad did not take kindly to fools and failures, and poor results often merited a beating. All this left me with an inferiority complex which took many years to overcome.

Christmas 1917 was the gloomiest yet. Only in the Mission, which somehow managed to radiate an air of serenity, was there hope and confidence in the future. Our neighbours in the Mansions were really despondent and their depression apparent, and contagious, for even the children's normally buoyant spirits began to reflect the anxiety of the grown-ups. All this gloom was justified, for hardly a family had been spared grief and hardship. No one talked about victory any more and none dared predict what the coming year had in store.

Unexpectedly however, there came some good news, a ray of hope. Although there was deadlock on the Western Front, news came of the rout of the Turkish army and of the liberation of Palestine. We heard that Lord Allenby, the commander of the army in that area, had accepted the surrender of Jerusalem and had entered the city on foot. People said this fulfilled an old prophecy. Although I had heard a lot about Jerusalem at the Mission, I had never believed it to be a real city and it came as a surprise to learn that the Jerusalem that our Lord knew so well was a real place.

When I had finished my duties at home and there was nothing for me at the Mission, I always headed for Noel's home at No. 42, Grove Lane, and together we would join in a very rough game called 'Release', which was very popular with the local lads. The game took place under the leadership of Tommy Cockerton, who divided the contestants into two sides. A base was laid out by chalking a square on the pavement with a smaller square in one corner. The game was something like cops and robbers and when any prisoners were taken they were put in the square box and a guard stood with one foot in the smaller box. If the robbers could pull the guard's foot out of his box the prisoner was released. Many a time I went home with torn clothes resulting from the free-for-all that took place around the box.

It only took me about five minutes to get to No. 42. Once across Church Street I turned into Grove Lane by Frost's, the grocery and provisions store. Opposite Frost's stood the Hermit's Cave, and between the pub and a small road called Wilby Road there was a dowdy second-hand clothiers in whose window hung a large card bearing the words 'Weekly Payments Taken'. I suppose I wasn't very bright for the meaning of this notice was beyond me. Who had taken what? I should have asked someone to elucidate but I hated being laughed at because of something I did not understand.

Some years later, Wilby Road was renamed Jephson Street after one of the founders of the Camberwell Free Grammar School (Wilson's). At its entrance stood a cats' meat stall. The meat was horseflesh and always looked lean, succulent and well-cooked. Often I would gaze with envious eyes at the little squares of meat which the owner threaded on to wooden skewers. These were bought by the local cat owners at 1 or $2d$. a stick. After the war we had a cat with a tortoiseshell-coloured coat whom we named 'Minnie'. One day I sneaked a piece of her meat and ate it. It was really good.

Jarrod, the fishmonger, occupied the other corner of Wilby Road. He lived in Kerfield Crescent. He was also the local bookmaker. Once Noel and I saw him leave a half-crown on top of a stone pillar by the Kerfield Arms. A little later a bewhiskered constable stealthily collected it.

Further down Grove Lane, past Alf Jacob's fruit and vegetable business, a butcher's and a wine and spirits store, was a bakery, whose proprietor, Miss Matthews, was for many years the leader of Kimpton Mission's Women's Meeting, which Mum attended. Reg used to deliver orders for Miss Matthews until she caught him eating the cakes.

On the opposite side of Grove Lane was a row of houses with stone steps leading up to the front doors. In the one roughly opposite the wine shop was the local watch and clock repairer. A large clock filled the space in the front window. Dad's watch was always being taken there for cleaning and adjusting. This particular watch belonged to his father and, as far as I know, was the only thing he had of his. In the course of time this watch came to me.

At the end of the houses was an archway that led to a billposter's yard. I believe that a mineral water factory had stood here at the end of the last century. On the pavement outside was a huge plane tree. Then came the rear buildings of the Mary Datchelor School. A line of railings with evergreen bushes behind them occupied the space between the buildings and the pavement. All this was altered when the school was extended in 1926.

Next came a small parade of tiny shops that commenced with a newsagents and ended with a confectioners. In between was a fish and chip shop, a laundry receiving depot, builders' premises and the entrance to a yard which led to a small printer's. The newsagent's window displayed a variety of postcards. There were local views, comic cards and a series of 'Old Bill' cartoons. The latter were the creation of Captain Bruce Bairnsfather and depicted the soldier known as Old Bill and his stooge in a series of comic war scenes. One I recall showed the pair sitting by a large shell hole in a wall. 'What did that, Bill?' asks the stooge. 'Mice,' replies Bill.

The tobacconist's and confectioner's was kept by two maiden ladies who wore long dresses and ruffles round their necks. Their shop was spotless. It had an 'L'-shaped counter which extended from the window across the front of the shop parlour. On the small rear counter was kept a large china bowl covered with a muslin cloth, which had beads around its edge. From this they sold fresh milk using a half pint measure. The main wall was lined with shelves which contained glass jars of sweets and trays of chocolate bars, all in precise order. The wall to the right of the entrance door was covered with old posters, one of which showed a row of ladies in Victorian dress escorted by two bearded constables, and above this was the caption 'Wild Woodbines —Ten for Two Coppers'. Noel and I used to gaze longingly at the little bowls of sweets on display in the window. Dolly Mixtures, Favours, Liquorice and Chlorodyne lozenges, Toffee, Cachous and Lucky Dips. The latter was a sort of sugar apple. If you were lucky enough to buy one that had a pink band around the stick you were rewarded with a stick of rock. These two ladies had an air of refinement about them but how they made a living from their tiny shop I do not know.

Monday evening at the Mission saw the people of the neighbourhood come with their pennies to deposit them in the Penny Bank. We often put in a penny one week and took it out the next. It was a happy sort of banking and something which is unknown today. The queue of people outside the Vestry waiting their turn to go in and deposit their money laughed and chatted and related their difficulties and triumphs to each other. B. B. Fisher and Frank Thompson, who took their money and entered it on their cards, had a cheerful word for everyone. At a time when people were desperately short of money they struggled hard to save for a little cheer at Christmas. One could get this money out at any time but most folk tried to leave it in the bank until the second Monday in December, when all the money was paid back, with a little interest added. Many slate club secretaries defaulted with loss to the people who had trusted them, but the Mission Bank was trustworthy and in most years its deposits from its members amounted to over £1,000. This may seem a small sum today but when the average wage was only about 25$s.$ a week, it represented hard savings from the three hundred or so people.

The children's choir practice was also on a Monday from 6.30 to 7.30 p.m., when we sang and rehearsed for the Sunday School Anniversary and Parents' Meeting. The baton was in the capable hands of Mr H. MacKenzie, the Mission's Secretary. One song we rehearsed at great length was 'The Yeoman of England'. I suppose I remember this song more than any other because we were rewarded with a penny each for putting on a good show.

In winter the halls of the Mission were never very warm. The main hall was lofty and had slates over a timber roof, with huge polished beams spanning the width of the hall at the level of the eaves. From the centre beam hung the trapeze, and a thick climbing rope was attached to the beam near the entrance hall. A row of high windows lined the southern wall. There was no insulation and heating was provided by an enclosed fire whose chimney was against the wall near the steps to the Vestry. In later years gas fires were installed and while they raised the temperature, the bills they generated were always a drain on the Mission's slender resources. Although we often shivered during the services, it struck even colder when we left the building, so we usually hurried home.

During the winter I never ventured far from home if I could help it. To school, Noel's or the Mission was as far as I wanted to go. From somewhere I obtained a copy of the *Swiss Family Robinson* and although the beginning and end pages were missing, I read and re-read it until I knew the story almost by heart. It had tiny illustrations in the corner of some pages. Although my knowledge was very limited I remember having doubts about the story, which featured so many different species on an uninhabited island. A little later I read *Masterman Ready* by Captain Marryatt and in the forward he referred to the *Swiss Family Robinson* and its fantastic menagerie. I felt a thrill to think that Captain Marryatt and myself had the same reservations about Johann Wyss's book.

1918

Slowly the cold dark days of winter slipped away and the yellow and blue crocuses once again began to bloom in the parks and gardens. Outside the shops the queues of housewives waiting, more or less patiently, for the shops to open did not vary. By now most food was rationed. The exceptions were, I believe, tea, cheese and bread. Most folk grumbled and voiced their opinion of the profiteering shopkeepers in no uncertain terms. Items like eggs were unobtainable, even if one was prepared to pay over the odds. The shopkeepers had their favourite customers—usually the very well-to-do.

One day I ran some errands for Mrs Axten, who lived in No. 19. She was a kind person and I liked her a lot. She would reward me with a halfpenny or penny for small services rendered. On this particular occasion I went into her kitchen and saw, on a shelf of her dresser, five eggs in eggcups all standing in a row. Back upstairs I told Mum about these eggs but she didn't comment. That day I promised myself that when I went out to work Mum and I would have an egg for our tea. Some years later I redeemed that promise.

During the spring news came that Kut el Amara, commonly known as Kut, had been retaken and that 'Johnny Turk' had received a beating. This news did not raise any hopes, for Turkey was a long way away and the Germans too near for comfort. This pessimism was justified for the Germans launched a huge offensive and drove the British back forty miles. It was said that people on the South Coast could hear the roar of guns. An invasion of Britain seemed imminent. It was a grim and despondent time.

*

On the 23rd of April another sister was born into our family. She was named Vera Carrington. I understood that Carrington was the name of family friends, but never found out who they were. The struggle to keep her family clothed and fed had worn Mum out, and the lack of a balanced diet took its toll. Vera suffered from rickets. This was a disease of children which caused the bones to soften due to the lack of essential minerals. Although it is a rare occurrence these days, it was very prevalent at the time Vera was born. She was crippled for a time but gradually overcame the handicap. Mum, of course, was very worried, but I don't think the rest of us were aware of its seriousness. For one thing our education had been sadly curtailed by the war and we were very ignorant in many fields of learning.

The standard of hygiene was much lower in those days and poverty, squalor and dirt went together. The school nurse came round periodically and examined every child's head for nits. She used a steel comb to go through everyone's hair, dipping it in a bowl of carbolic between each examination. She was a big, rough woman doing an unpleasant job and in consequence was equally rough to boys and girls alike. The girls with long hair were often brought to tears by the tugging of their tresses.

Our family did not have the luxury of expensive toilet soaps although there were some excellent brands in the shops. Pears was the aristocrat of fine soaps with Vinolia and Wright's Coal Tar not far behind. For poorer folk it was Lifebuoy, a red soap containing antiseptic carbolic, or Sunlight, which was in reality a laundry soap. Using too much of the latter caused chapping, and it took liberal amounts of Vaseline to get the skin back to normal.

At home we ate a fair amount of bread. Fortunately it wasn't on the ration. Sometimes we went out early in the morning to join the queues outside the bakers for stale bread, although this was not always available. Our supplier for normal purchases was Kranz, whose bakery was on the corner of Kimpton Road and D'Eynsford Road. His bread was oven baked and had a nice snappy crust which Dad liked very much. Because the bread was hand made it varied in size and had to be reweighed on purchase. If it was under the statutory weight, a small piece of bread or a roll was added to make the weight up. We, incorrectly, called the odd piece the 'overweight', instead of 'makeweight'. There was always keen competition at home if the makeweight proved to be a tasty bread roll. Sometimes the baker sold Nelson cake, which today would be known as bread pudding. One could purchase quite a large slab of it for a penny. Stale cake could be had quite cheaply and we often spent any spare pocket money on it in preference to sweets. Kranz would also roast a Sunday joint in his oven for a copper or two.

Throughout the war years the public were under intense pressure from the newspapers to invest their savings in the Government-sponsored War Bonds. 'Saving for a rainy day' and 'looking after the pence' had been drummed into us since we were babies. The blunt truth however was that after paying the rent and keeping the family fed and clothed we had no money to save, and certainly nothing left for luxuries like buying War Bonds. Any odd coppers left over from household expenses were more likely to be put into the Penny Bank at Kimpton Mission rather than lent to a Government that did nothing for the poor who worked long and hard for a meagre wage.

Not all the areas of Camberwell were as poor as ours. A speaker at one of the Mission's meetings called Church Street the great dividing line of the Borough. From its north side, stretching to Walworth, were the areas of slums, mean streets and tenements where poverty, squalor and crime were the norm. In contrast, the south side contained the residences of the clerks and artisans, many of whom employed domestic help. Further out on the periphery were the homes of the professional and business men, large Georgian terraces in spacious grounds, and private hotels, while in the hamlet of Dulwich were the estates of the very affluent.

For a long time now the opposing armies in France had been bogged down in trench warfare, but around 1917–1918 armoured machines called 'Tanks' had been developed to overcome the stalemate. These tanks were huge lumbering metal monsters mounting a gun and propelled by an internal engine which drove an endless belt of tracks on either side of the machine. We had no idea at the time how much these tanks would revolutionise future warfare. During one of the War Bonds promotion weeks in Camberwell one of these Land Ironclads was put on display in a sealed-off section of Vestry Road, opposite the Town Hall. A booth was set up nearby and every purchaser of a War Bond was allowed to enter the roped off enclosure and make a personal inspection of the grey monster's exterior. Crowds milled around outside the ropes and I recall moving among them watching with envious eyes the lucky adults and children who were able to get near enough to rap their knuckles on the machine's metal sides.

At the Sunday School Anniversary Meeting, which parents were pressured to attend to hear the Superintendent's report and to see Bible stories and parables acted out by the children, the prizes and badges earned during the previous year were awarded. It was always a time of great excitement and we waited with baited breath hoping our own names would be among the prize-winners. There was always a lot of cheering as names were called and the lucky ones went up the centre of the hall, mounted the three steps to the platform and received a book or Bible from a dignitary of the Shaftesbury Society, who shook the child's hand. The girls would curtsey and the boys bow before hurrying across the platform to the steps on the other side. Friends would gather round to see what had been given for punctual attendance and good conduct for the last twelve months.

I received as my prize a book called *Froggy's Little Brother*. It was a very sad story about two orphan boys. Froggy, the elder, earned a few pence as a crossing sweeper. These were people who for a small sum would sweep away dirt and litter from the streets to allow people of quality to walk without soiling their exquisite attire. The story told of the brothers precarious living and how hardship and malnutrition caused the death of the younger boy. Froggy, now on his own, managed to obtain a situation as a servant boy in a large London house. The tale ended on a happier note when Froggy took under his protection a waif from the streets.[28]

The showing of cowboy films at the cinemas made toy pistols very

---

28 *Froggy's Little Brother* by Brenda (pseudonym of Mrs G. Castle Smith), first published c. 1875.

popular. Despite shortages of metal, many were on sale in newsagents and toy shops. There were two types of pistol to be had. One detonated a single cap while the other, a repeater, could keep firing until its coil of percussion caps was exhausted. These pistols were much too dear for us so we contented ourselves with the percussion bomb. This was made of two pieces of iron about the size of a cobnut and had a groove for string round the edge. The cap was put between the two bits of iron, a string tied around the edge, and then it was flung in the air. There would be a noisy report when the bomb hit the ground, causing many a cat to flee in terror.

As spring turned into summer the newspapers became full of scare stories of industrial troubles in the Midlands and, I believe, there was trouble in the police force. However, as a small boy, things seemed so much happier when the sun was shining, trees were in leaf and flowers were blooming in the parks. The queues outside the food shops seemed much more tolerant and the air of pessimism so prevalent in the earlier part of the year appeared to have receded, if only temporarily, into the background. When I think back to those days I can appreciate the struggle it must have been for Mum and Dad to rear and clothe their growing family in a time of shortages and rationing. We never went hungry although meals were often repetitive and monotonous. Breakfast was usually porridge, and the Sunday joint often stretched into four meals. Stews were our main stand-by and we often used beef bones which we bought from the butcher for a couple of pence. Except on Sundays, our tea was usually bread and margarine. To vary it, Mum would sometimes give me a basin and two pence and send me off to Thompson's, the oil shop, where jam was sold 'loose'. The shopkeeper would weigh the basin, add four ounces, then carefully weigh out the jam, usually a variety called mixed fruit. Most folk said it was flavoured turnips, and certainly it had a flavour all its own. One assistant I liked to be served by never bothered to weigh the basin, he just plonked a dollop of jam out of his 7 lb stone jar into it. We always got more jam from him. We only ever had bread with jam or bread with margarine, never all three together.

We usually bought our margarine from the Home and Colonial Stores, whose small shop was a few yards from the police station in Church Street. Behind the single window was the grocery counter and facing it, with its back to the rear wall, the provisions counter. Provisions was a misnomer for they sold only butter, margarine, cheese and lard. One day I went into the shop for some margarine but had to wait because a couple of ladies were being served. In front of the counter were a couple of two hundredweight sacks of sugar and lying on them I spotted a ten shilling note. My hand closed over the note and thereafter I was torn between handing it to the assistant or taking it home. It may not have been honest but I took it home where it was received like manna from heaven.

Butter came to the shops in 56 lb boxes in a solid lump. It would be tipped out on to the marble slab and the assistant would use a wooden slicer and beater to chop the butter into the amount requested by the customer, and then wrap it in greaseproof paper. Margarine seemed to come to the shops prepacked. Cheese came in big wooden plywood drums, rather like a large hatbox, and weighed about 60 lbs. The cheese had a muslin-type cloth around the rind and this had to be scraped off before it could be cut into saleable pieces. It cost 6*d*. a pound. Special cheeses like English Cheddar, Gorgonzola, Caerphilly and the like were much more expensive.

In August, during the school summer holidays, Noel and I were lucky enough to be selected to go away again with the Country Holiday Fund. This time our little party was sent off to Newbury, in Berkshire. The only part of the journey that I recall was seeing the white posts and rails of Newbury Racecourse. When we reached our destination, Noel and I and two other Mission boys were taken to a village outside the town, called Donnington, I believe. We had a great time roaming round the countryside and once we saw a stoat chasing a rabbit. We heard the rabbit scream as it was caught, but as we came racing up the stoat fled. The rabbit, however, was dead. One of the boys took it back to where he was staying and it finished up in the pot. Our lady took us to Donnington Castle where we climbed up the battlements and gazed out over the countryside. We saw the gatehouse and lots of cannon balls that had been used in the Civil War. People had etched their names and date of their visit all over the place, although I could not understand why. We paid an occasional visit to Newbury and I remember buying a salt and pepper pot at a penny each, a present for Mum when I came home. In 1919 we came again to Newbury but this time we stayed in the centre of town at No. 2, George Street. The river Kennet was nearby and we spent most of our time fishing in its small tributaries. I never revisited Newbury, although I should like to have seen it again.

After our return from Newbury the summer holidays seemed to fly by. Those August days were warm and lovely and the war seemed far away. We played in the Mansions' yard, in the street, in Ruskin Park and in the evenings, after tea, Noel and I and friends played our favourite game of Release. Noel and I were approaching our eleventh birthdays and now had sufficient confidence in ourselves to venture out from our home ground and explore the outer areas of Camberwell that bordered on to Dulwich and Forest Hill. This exciting prospect, although only two and a half miles away, was planned like an expedition to darkest Africa. It is strange to think that at that time some people never left the village in which they were born, although there was public transport which by today's standard was excellent. Shortage of money was the main cause of it being used so sparingly. The war was beginning to change all this, but travel still held a sense of adventure and romance, and the thrill of meeting the unexpected round every bend in the road.

Our first expedition was to One Tree Hill. We went to the top of Dog Kennel Hill by way of Grove Lane and at the top, to the left, was an unmade road called The Glebe. It contained four stately houses with grounds that stretched all the way down to Grove Vale. The first house, however, was empty and rapidly becoming derelict. This house was a magnet to the local boys and was reputed to be haunted. One lad, braver than the rest of us, said he had been inside and seen the words, 'God Help The Man Who Kills Me' scrawled in blood on one of the walls. I was not brave enough to venture through the doorway so cannot describe the interior of the mansion, but we entered the drive and stole up to the portico and leaned against the stone pillars surveying the broken windows and rotting frames.

We left the house and wandered through the huge garden, long since overgrown until the flower beds were no longer visible. The orchard was waist-high in nettles, spear grass and brambles. After biting into some half-ripe apples we crept out into Dog Kennel Hill through a gap in the fence. The hill was wide and steep with four sets of tramlines and at the bottom was East Dulwich Railway Station and Grove Vale with its small shops. At the end the road divided, one fork going uphill through Lordship Lane to Forest Hill, and the other one, which was our route, going to Goose Green, East Dulwich Road, where the swimming Baths were sited, and Peckham Rye Common, known as the 'Rye'. Adjoining it on its southern edge was Peckham Rye Park with its bowling greens, rose gardens, shady walks and a lake. Beyond the park were open stretches of meadowland (long since built on) which led up to the railway at Honour Oak. Once under the arch we were at the foot of One Tree Hill.

Before the school holidays ended, Noel and I made another excursion into Dulwich Village, in those days a charming rural hamlet. We felt a little uneasy in our tattered clothes as we walked beneath the huge chestnut trees. An old milestone informed us that we were five miles from the Standard in Cornhill and the same distance away from the Treasury in Whitehall. We made our way up to the Toll Gate, reading aloud from the notice board the cost of taking a flock of sheep, a horse or herd of pigs through the gate. We were pleased to see that cycles were free, even though we did not own one. Our aim was to get to Dulwich Woods but we were not successful. The gate was locked and we were further deterred by the people who passed, giving us suspicious looks.

The toll road was a rough track bordered by trees and hedges which led up to the Crystal Palace. Here and there, lying well back from the track, were the mansions and estates of the wealthy city merchants and businessmen, vast Georgian residences needing an army of retainers to run them. There were also small farms with cows and sheep and a few chickens, and most fields had a horse or two grazing in them. Off to the right, hidden from view, was the iron track of the South Eastern and Chatham Railway, formerly the London, Dover and Chatham Railway which was opened in 1860. There was one tiny station, Sydenham Hill.

We were tired by the time we reached the top of the hill and we stopped for a while to look at the Crystal Palace in front of us. It was a huge building stretching about a quarter of a mile along the parade and at either side were two large towers with the huge Nave at its centre.

Soon the holidays were over and we went back to school to the term in which we would sit the scholarship examinations. It was at about this time too that the news from France began to sound good. The German armies were in retreat to their homeland pursued relentlessly by the American and Allied armies. All through September and October there were rumours of Germany's imminent collapse. On 11 November, a grey misty morning if I remember aright, and a Monday (as Mum was doing the washing), I went shopping for milk in Grove Lane. It was nearly eleven o'clock by the clock in the watch repairer's window. As I reached the newsagents the sound of gunfire filled the air and women came running out of their homes crying out that the Armistice had been signed. In my ignorance I didn't know what an Armistice was and only later learned that each side in the conflict had agreed to cease firing. And so, four years, three months and seven days after the outbreak of hostilities, the war had ended.

I went to school that afternoon but we left early. Everywhere there were wild scenes of jubilation. People sang and danced in the streets, barrel organs played, boys marched around the houses banging dustbin lids. Flags hung from windows and with the coming of night huge bonfires were lit. Our bonfire was in Artichoke Place, outside the Camberwell Baths. We danced around it singing songs from the war and parodies of Sankey hymns. People from the Mansions and the houses over the stables in Artichoke Mews brought out old furniture and fittings and verminous mattresses to add to the blaze. The stables were raided for straw and the flames soared upwards. Some of the wilder elements got out of hand. Fenner, the greengrocer next to the Hermit's Cave, had a pony and trap which he kept in the Mews. The wild types got the trap out, put one of the Andrew's girls in it and with shouts of 'Joan of Arc' pushed it on to the fire. It could have been a nasty situation with a tragic ending but fortunately someone ran for Mr Fenner who, with help, dragged the blazing trap from the inferno. Happily the girl was unhurt.

And so the war was over. Our prayers had been answered. Nobody knew what lay ahead nor at that time did they care. Soon we would be back at our own school and fathers and husbands would be coming home from the trenches. The war to end all wars had been won. That is what we all believed.

THE POST-WAR YEARS
1919–1921

1919

The Armistice Day celebrations lasted the best part of a week, and when Sunday came the churches and other places of worship were filled to overflowing with people who came to give thanks that the horror of war had ended. I often heard the words 'never again' spoken by men and women who had suffered bereavement, injury and hardship during those four long terrible years. I heard men say they would sooner shoot themselves than return to the horror of the trenches or ever again serve under callous and incompetent officers and NCOs. Any glamour associated with war had long since been dispelled.

The ordinary people soon found that the cessation of hostilities brought no immediate solution to their everyday problems. Although the guns were silent and the womenfolk could look forward to the return home of husbands and sons, there still remained the shortage of food, fuel and clothing. Winter arrived early and in some ways it seemed harder, colder and more bitter than the winters of the war. The Christmas of 1918 was as grim as that of the previous year but now, at least, there was hope and a prospect of return to normality. Small wonder that the Watchnight services on New Year's Eve had bumper attendances and that the message of the bells as they rang out across the dark streets was of 'Peace on Earth' at last.

Somehow the people struggled on, and the first demobilised men came home amid scenes of rejoicing. The first ones home and out of uniform were the fortunate few, for they were able to take what vacant jobs were going. Those who were discharged later faced the grim prospect of unemployment. Their small gratuities were soon spent and they became bitter and angry with their leaders. Lloyd George had promised them a land fit for heroes to live in, but as one remarked, they had returned to a land that only heroes could live in. A cynical song went something like this:

> *We won the war, we won the war*
> *You can ask Lloyd George or Bonar Law*
> *We beat the Germans, Austrians and Turks*
> *That's why we're all walking round and out of work*
> *What was it for, we won the war*
> *So the next time the enemy's at your door*
> *Bring him in and shake his hand*
> *Give him some dinner and treat him grand*
> *What's the use of fighting any more*

We had expected that as soon as the war was over we would leave Lyndhurst Grove School and return to Denmark Hill School in Grove Lane. The weeks went by. There was no news of a move in November and at Christmas the military were still firmly entrenched at Denmark Hill. The New Year arrived and during the winter months we still trudged up to Lyndhurst Grove. By now the parents of children from both schools were becoming extremely angry and a petition signed by 309 parents was sent to County Hall, demanding that the return of the Denmark Hill pupils to their school be expedited, and protesting at the continuance of the 'double session' arrangement whereby each school had the building for only half of each day. Even so it was late summer before the military authorities de-requisitioned the school, and not until 6 October 1919 did Harry Turner lead his staff and scholars back to Denmark Hill School—four years, seven months and two weeks after he had led them into exile.

*

I believe it was in the early part of 1919 that I joined the Band of Hope at the Mission. I suppose 're-joined' would be more accurate, as I had belonged to it before, but because Miss Mulley wouldn't let me go to their party (I had not attended regularly), I had left in a huff. However the good lady prevailed upon me to return to the fold, as it were. We were all asked to sign the pledge, which roughly went 'I promise to refrain from intoxicating drinks as beverages'. Miss Mulley was housekeeper to her brother who had a house and builder's business in Sedgmoor Place, a turning out of Dalwood Street. She had a nephew, Fred Mulley, who became a leading drummer in the Brigade and later married sister Grace's friend Kate Norman.

Miss Mulley was not only leader of the Band of Hope but also the superintendent of the infants branch of the Sunday School. She was also the Mission's caretaker. A devoted and keen worker ever ready to help, as far as her meagre resources permitted. I well remember the Band of Hope party which took place in January. By present-day standards it would be pretty tame, but we enjoyed it immensely. After a little tea, we played games like musical chairs and blind man's buff, and then with a scarf tied over the eyes one tried to pin the tail on the donkey. Later in the evening a lady told us a poem called 'Little Orphan Annie'. We were all scared when she got to the bit about the goblins, and when we left to go home Grace and I ran the few yards home as fast as our legs would take us.

*

At eleven years of age I was old enough, and allowed by law, to find a little job. Most boys of that age wanting to earn a few coppers did a paper round, helped a baker's roundsman or assisted a milkman. It was slave labour but every penny was useful, indeed welcome, to the family income.

About a year before, I had found myself a little job with Wilson's, the baker, whose shop and bakery was on the corner of Daneville Road and Denmark Hill. I had been in the shop one day when the lady in charge asked if I would like to run a few errands, and I said I would. I used to sweep the shop, deliver cakes and bread to nearby customers and tidy up a bit. In return I received a bag of cakes or a flan. No money was ever passed over but the family always appreciated the cakes. I don't quite know what Mum thought of this 'job' but I suppose she thought it was pretty harmless even if there was no money at the end of it, and so most Saturday mornings I went along for an hour or so and returned with the bag of stale cake. There was never enough time on these days, what with helping with the shopping, cleaning the knives, turning the mangle and taking the ashes down to the dustbins in the yard. We never had much of a meal on Saturdays, everyone was too busy. Mum would make a jug of cocoa and we would have bread and dripping to eat.

Another job which I did not like was to take my two younger sisters out in the pram while Mum and Con got on with the household cleaning. In those days looking after children was considered woman's work and most men felt it demeaning to be seen out with a pram. I used to feel very embarrassed pushing the babies around and hoped that my chums wouldn't see me. I received a nasty jolt one day when coming down from Church Street with my two baby sisters. I didn't look where I was going and ran the pram into the wall of the Mansions. The pram tipped up on end and, had it not been for the fact that my sisters were strapped in, both would have been thrown out on to the pavement; I shudder to think what would have happened to them—and me.

One afternoon Dad and Mum went shopping in Walworth and in the evening Dad came home alone. He said that they had been waiting for a tram to bring them home at the stop by Westmorland Road. When it came along there was such a shocking scramble to get on board that he and Mum had become separated. He had managed to get on but found to his consternation that Mum had been left behind. I immediately volunteered to go and find her and set off through the Green and down Camberwell Road. I was very greatly relieved when I met Mum near Addington Square. She had decided to walk but was happy to know Dad was safe and sound at home.

Getting aboard public transport was always a problem, especially on a Saturday. People would push and shove and use their elbows to make sure they weren't left behind. Orderly queuing did not impress itself on the public until the outbreak of the Second World War.

One day I was delivering some bread for Wilson's and had the baker's wickerwork basket on my arm when I was stopped by a man who identified himself as a School Inspector. He asked why I was not at school. Rather frightened, I told him we attended school for only half a day. He made it plain that he did not believe me and began firing questions like 'what school did I attend?', 'who was I working for?', 'how much was I paid?', 'what was my name' and 'where did I live?'. These School Inspectors were looked upon as bogeymen and hated by parents and their offspring. I had been stopped by one of them once before when I was bringing home some washing from Kingsmead Road for Mum to launder. I was given the third degree before I was able to convince him that I wasn't playing truant. However the inspector who had caught me delivering bread called round home a day or so later to interview Mum about my breaking the law. Mum was the mildest of women but she bristled with indignation when the bogeyman explained the reason for his visit. She told him in no uncertain terms that he ought to have better things to do than go snooping around the streets persecuting small boys who were only trying to earn a little pocket money. The Inspector was evidently used to this sort of reception and he calmly stated that as I was under eleven years of age I was not allowed to be employed. That was the law. The law had been passed to prevent the exploitation of children and it was part of his duties to see that shops like Wilson's did not break the law by getting labour on the cheap. Eventually Mum calmed down and the Inspector went on to say that he intended to deal severely with Wilson's, who were trying to get round the Truck Act which made payment in kind an offence. There was nothing for it but to stop going to the baker's and, much to our regret, there was no more stale cake to be had—unless we bought it! Looking back I think that these education officials were much maligned men. They had an unpleasant task interviewing parents whose children had absented themselves from school without reasonable explanation. Catching truants was only a side issue. Many parents who had had little schooling themselves could not grasp the point that educating a child was to make him or her a self-supporting member of society.

Sometime later I teamed up with a Mr Chapman who was a milk-roundsman employed by the Farmers and Cleveland Dairies, whose shop and yard was in Camberwell Road just past Wyndham Road. The owner, or manager, I don't know which, was a Kimpton Mission supporter and he probably got me the job. This was the day of the small business, the one-man bakery, the local dairyman and the corner shop. The giant milk combines like Express and Unigate had not come into being, while the Co-operative dairy service was still in its infancy. The general public probably never realised it but they were never to have it so good again. The small man waited upon them daily and the customer was always right.

Chapman's round covered the Kimpton Road/Vicarage Road area and across Church Street into the square bounded by Camberwell Grove, Vestry Road and Lyndhurst Grove. He commenced his deliveries about 6 a.m. and I joined him about half an hour later. The milk was trundled around the streets in a small handcart nicknamed a 'pram'. It was built on the tricycle principle with three wheels, a small one in front and two large ones at the sides. The sides of the cart were metal bars and were hinged to allow for the removal of the churn for cleaning. The churn, which contained the milk, was the centrepiece and had a facing of brass on which the dairy's name was etched. Every milkman was proud of his churn and he spent much time, bluebell polish and elbow grease to keep it gleaming. At its base was a tap for drawing off the milk into the handcans and I used to love to watch the creamy, foaming milk flowing into the big cans. The key to this tap was always kept in the milkman's pocket, for bad lads had been known to turn on the tap when the roundsman was elsewhere and run away.

From the stout handlebar hung two big hooks for holding the handcans, which had a two gallon capacity. Inside each can hung three measures, a half pint, pint and quart. Each was cylindrical in shape and had a brass handle. The milkcans, which were oval with brass hinges and wire handles, came in three sizes like the measures. At the back of the can was a U-shaped brass wire fitment for slotting over the bars of the pram. Each can had the name of the dairy engraved on its lid and there were frequent rows among the rival dairymen who would accuse each other of can stealing. These cans were expensive and had to be accounted for.

Some dairies supplied their deliveryman with a 'chariot'. This was a two-wheeled cart drawn by a horse. It was much envied by the foot sloggers, for pushing a fully laden pram was hard work. These chariots had long shafts for the horse and when in motion rode at a steep angle. They carried two churns and the cans were arranged round the sides on racks. The driver stood on the sloping platform and guided his steed with reins that ran through the space between the churns. It was quite a thrill to ride on a chariot for they were speedy. They were, of course, much more expensive to operate and maintain than the common pram.

My milkman had a fine yodelling voice and his cry of 'milko' echoing in the streets brought women and children and the occasional man to their street doors with jugs or bowls in their hands. Chapman or I would take a large can and measure the requested amount into the proffered receptacle. The customers in the posher houses in The Grove or Brunswick Square who ran accounts, and who thought it beneath them to be seen with a jug in their hands, had their milk left on their doorsteps in one of the precious cans. Specially favoured clientèle (those who gave tips and were generous at Christmas) had a little oblong slip of greaseproof paper placed between the top of the can and the hinged lid. There was keen competition among the rival milkman for chance trade. This was the sale of milk to housewives who had no regular roundsman and who had no allegiance to any dairy. These people paid for their milk with ready cash, which was a novelty in those hard-up days.

After the early morning round was completed I would return home for breakfast then go to school. Chapman would return to the depot to refill his churn and have his breakfast too. He would then start his second delivery going over identical ground and serving the same people (lack of refrigeration made both rounds necessary). During the week he finished work about noon or an hour later. Saturday was a busy day. The accounts had to be settled and often it involved calling upon a customer two or three times before they came to the door and paid up. There were many 'moonlight flits' with the tradesmen running up bad debts as a result. When the money was in, it was back to the yard, whose entrance was in the notorious Crown Street, to pay in the money, scald out the churn and cans, scrub the pram and polish the brasswork. My remuneration for all this toil was four shillings a week, out of which I was allowed to retain sixpence. I used to collect a few coppers in tips, so I didn't do badly.

Most folk had a very poor opinion of milkmen, for it was universally believed that not only did they give short measure but watered the milk as well. Some people purchased measuring jugs to check the roundsman's measures. These jugs proved to be very inaccurate when it came to the test. This check, which always put the milkman in the clear, did not allay suspicion but rather served to increase it. I can say that while I never saw milk adulterated, what I did notice time and time again was that many cans had bottoms knocked upwards and sides pushed in. However, I do believe that milkmen were a hard-working body of men who often rose before dawn and pushed their little carts around the streets in all weathers so that a family could have its milk on the breakfast table.

Mr Chapman was quite a lad with the ladies. At Christmas he kissed almost every one of his female customers and drank so much wine and whisky that he hadn't a clue what he was doing. Some of the ladies gave me a sixpence or shilling for a Christmas box and insisted on kissing me as well. I was awfully embarrassed and my face went scarlet, but the cash was most welcome. Chapman had been a regular soldier and had signed on the reserve, for which he received a small payment. When the trouble broke out in Ireland he was recalled for service and left without giving me my week's pay. His deputy was a kind man whom I liked a lot and we got on well, but eventually the Irish trouble ended and Chapman returned and I got my belated earnings.

Helping to push the milkman's cart around the streets, especially up the hill that was Camberwell Grove, and in all weathers, was very hard work. In those days I was thin with little physical strength. Mum did her best but by today's standards our diet would be considered unbalanced and probably inadequate. Delivering milk was tiring and often by breakfast time I felt worn out.

One day on the early morning round I was putting a can on the doorstep of the house where a Mr Chamberlain used to live when my head started swimming and I felt very faint. Chapman made me put my head between my knees but it didn't help. I cannot recall how I got home and I became very ill. I had contracted influenza. I did not know it at the time but a virulent form of this disease was sweeping Europe and it took a terrible toll of people who had endured four years of war and privation. Like Reg and Grace I had a lovely voice and often sung solo at school and at the Mission but when, at last, I was able to get around again, I could only croak. Many months passed before I could speak clearly again and to my great sorrow my throat was permanently affected. My singing voice had gone forever. For years I had trouble with my throat and every winter had some form of tonsillitis.

After my illness I continued to help Mr Chapman but Dad and Mum must have given the matter some thought and concluded that I must give up being a milkman's boy. I wasn't sorry when the break came although I missed the money. Now and again I helped another dairyman, a Mr Jackson, who delivered his milk by chariot. I used to go more for the ride than the money.

Around 1925–1926 the glass milk bottle came into general use and sounded the death knell of the unhygienic can. The first bottles were thicker and heavier than their present-day counterparts and had a wider neck with an inside rim. A waxed cardboard disc bearing the dairy's name was inserted on to the rim as a seal against contamination. It was difficult to remove this disc without sending a squirt of milk over oneself and in time a modification was introduced whereby the disc had a circular cut in its centre so that a finger could be pushed through and the rest of the disc easily raised. This bottle was a big step in the right direction and remained in use until superseded by mechanical bottling and the use of silver and gold foil tops.

Sometimes when I think back to those distant days I cannot help wondering what became of the thousands of milkcarts, measures, churns and cans that were in everyday use and such a feature of life in the streets of our towns and cities. Where are those brass-faced containers on which men spent such time and elbow grease to make them gleam? How I wish I had had the money and foresight to keep a few of those oval cans - but alas, I had neither. It is strange, but true, that items and utensils in everyday use can disappear literally overnight.

*

A clock was a popular wedding gift; most households possessed a timepiece of one type or another and it was usually housed on the mantleshelf in the parlour. Checking the time was another matter as there was no radio signal, and the church clock was not always accurate. We were fortunate that there was a clock high up on the entrance to the Camberwell Baths in Artichoke Place. One or other of us would be continually running through the yard and down the passage of the other part of the Mansions to see the time. Schoolchildren were summoned to attend by a bell, but unless one lived nearby it could not be heard. It only needed the Bath's clock to be out of order to create panic in those households who relied upon it. Fortunately it was pretty reliable.

Quite often as I was hurrying to school I would see a Mrs Waterman escorting her two daughters, Lily and Rose, across Church Street before sending them on their way to school. Mr Waterman worked for the GPO and in addition was a keen photographer and handy with woodworking tools. They were very proud of their daughters who were always neatly dressed. In my ignorance I thought them rather 'stuck up'. I don't know what they thought of me at the time—nothing very flattering I am sure. Lily, the eldest, was in my class at school and was always in the top stream. Both girls attended the Mission and in later years I became very friendly with Lily who, in time, became Captain of the Mission's Girls' Life Brigade Company. Rose married my friend Frank Thompson and they made their home in Banstead in Surrey.

In 1919 the pupils of my class sat the scholarship examination. It was held one Saturday morning at the Oliver Goldsmith School in Peckham Road. It proved to be rather a farce. We were asked to answer questions on subjects we had hardly heard of and the outcome was a foregone conclusion. In any case there were very few scholarships to be won. When in due course the results were made known the teachers were resentful when they found that only one grammar pass had been awarded. The successful entrant was Ron Wall, son of the Church Street tobacconist. The rest of us were consoled with a half-day holiday due to Ron's success. Our class had more than its share of bright lads and lasses and I am of the opinion that Ted Thompson merited a pass, but he and the rest were condemned to an elementary education because of the Scrooge-like mentality of the SBL.

Our Brigade company that year were determined to make their mark in the Battalion sports and to that end started holding training and running practice from the springtime onwards in the recreation field off Ruskin Park, which was always referred to as the 'Extension'. There was a cinder track round the perimeter measuring half a mile and forty yards. Sometimes on a Sunday morning, before breakfast, we would meet and test ourselves over various distances. I always fancied myself as a five-miler, but the best I could manage was nine circuits of the track. Other times we would mark out a hundred yards of Kimpton Road and the sprinters would be timed with a stop-watch. In the event I was unable to take part because I was on the milk round and did not possess any suitable footwear. However the Kimpton contingent did well enough without my help, for Jim and Pete Clements, who were excellent athletes, carried off most of the track events.

*

Strange as it may seem, the shops soon began to fill their shelves once more and the windows displayed goods and articles that had not been seen for years. There was rebellious talk among housewives who could not forget the profiteering and under-the-counter sales that had gone on during the war. The United Kingdom Tea Company of No. 36, Church Street came up with an amazing offer of Butter Beans at one penny a pound, or 7 lb for 6*d*. These beans became a part of our diet for a long time. My first full-time job after leaving school was as an errand boy for the UK Tea Co. and one day whilst searching for some price tickets I came across the literature and display cards of the butter bean offer of three years earlier.

Although there were now no shortages in the shops, money was still very tight and it became rationing by price. There was a lot of unemployment and the out-of-work men were in militant mood. They paraded through the streets behind bands with their women and children pushing their pitiful belongings on old perambulators. I recall walking alongside one of these protest rallies, the band was playing the 'Flight of the Earls'. They went along Peckham Road shouting and hurling abuse at their police escort. They continued up Lyndhurst Road to Chadwick Road where there was an empty factory, backing on to the railway line. It must have all been planned beforehand for someone opened the gates and they swarmed in. They camped out in this factory for some months, a depressing and humiliating sight. This militancy smouldered and finally burst into flames in the General Strike of 1926.

That summer Noel, I and other lads from the Mission went again to Newbury under the auspices of the Country Holiday Fund. Although we would have loved to return to Donnington, this time we found ourselves staying at No. 2, George Street, just off the main thoroughfare close to the River Kennet. As I remember it, the river divided near the bridge into the main river and a smaller stream, although the latter may have been part of the Kennet and Avon Canal. On the banks of this lower water we passed the days fishing for sticklebacks and minnows with the aid of string, bent pin and worms. We had a wonderful time. The sun shone every day and we became as brown as Red Indians. Our hostess and the neighbours were very kind to us and when the time came for our departure they gave us gifts of flowers and vegetables to take back to London with us.

*

Brother Reg was destined never to return to Denmark Hill School, for we were still at Lyndhurst Grove when he attained the age of fourteen years on 13 August 1919. When school broke up for the summer holidays at the end of July he and most of the other boys and girls in his class left to seek fame and fortune in the outside world. Reg was full of self-confidence, had plenty of initiative, and possessed drive and a wonderful imagination. He could be relied on to do a good job and give value for money. But it was a grim, hard world and he had great difficulty in finding employment. There was little local work and Mum could not spare the money for fares.

For a time Reg had a job delivering for Miss Matthews who ran the bakery shop on the corner of Grove Lane and Daneville Road. This job finished when the good lady accused him of eating the cakes. He then drove a horse and cart delivering customers' orders for Fuller Medley's grocery store which was on the corner of Camberwell Grove. Finally he teamed up with Joe Fenner, the Church Street fruiterer and greengrocer, next to The Hermit's Cave public house. Fenner was a hard taskmaster, working Reg from early morning until late at night. Often Reg was up at the crack of dawn to go off with Fenner to collect vegetables from the Borough Market or fruit from Covent Garden. On the odd occasion I would go for the ride but I did not like early rising. Reg seemed happy enough but, like most young lads, was exploited by harsh employers.

It was about this time that Reg began bringing home a wider variety of boy's magazines and they were passed on to me when Reg had devoured the contents. I became a real bookworm and used to tuck myself into odd corners and, as I read, let my imagination wander. I am sure all this reading stimulated my imagination and led me on to more classic literature which, later in life, held me in good stead when conversing with those more learned than myself. Brother Reg was not one to worry about the future or to put money by for a rainy day, so he spent his money as soon as it came to him. After the weekend he was usually spent out and if he couldn't borrow off Mum he would ask his employer, Fenner, for a 'sub', or advance of pay. 'Look after the pence and the pounds will take care of themselves' was something Reg did not subscribe to.

The family was growing up fast in 1919. Reg was fourteen, I was approaching twelve years and Grace was nine years old. Our eldest sister Con became sixteen on 19 September and at the end of the autumn term she left the Charles Edward Brooke grammar school in Hazlemere Road. Like Reg, she was very self-confident, possessed a mastery of the language and had a keen and critical mind. Even so jobs were not easy to find. To give Dad his due he did exert himself on his eldest daughter's behalf and found her a position as a junior clerk with a firm called 'Nofar', so called I believe, because the business did not deal with farthings—the smallest coin. I have an idea that it was a wholesale drapery establishment. On reaching home after her first day Con dashed into the kitchen and took a swig from the milk jug gasping 'I've had a terrible day'.

Her employment with Nofar was short-lived. It was not Con's idea of a career for a grammar-school girl. I believe she had a couple more jobs then applied for a position as a girl probationer with the Post Office telephone service. She did well as a 'Hello Girl', and would sometimes relate conversations she had overheard, although how much was factual and how much imagination I know not. Con chummed up with another telephonist named Ivy Fussell and their friendship lasted for many years. They were inseparable until men came into their lives. Ivy was a fluffy blonde and good company. Her father was quite an entertainer in his way but very heavy-handed on the piano. On one occasion his thumping broke a couple of keys. One evening, Mr Fussell brought round his concertina and having lubricated his throat with some suitable refreshment, proceeded to regale us with some of the old ballads which were still popular. One of his favourite renderings was 'The Dear Homeland', a nostalgic song about an Australian emigrant. We used to love hearing the adults sing the songs they loved so well.

I have mentioned before about Con's ability—her winning of the scholarship was proof enough. She was good at storytelling and recitations and could always win applause with her monologues. Among her repertoire was 'Rover in Church', the 'Little Fan' and 'The Green Eye of the Little Yellow God'. She also had another gift—a flair for fortune-telling by cards. Con's readings made her immensely popular and ensured for her invitations to numerous parties and the like. Although she was excellent at this pastime she was vulnerable too and frequently consulted other fortune-tellers herself.

There is something fascinating about fortune-telling, whether it be by cards, palmistry or astrology. Few people can resist it, even if they are disbelievers, and the merest whisper of an interest in the subject will find members of both sexes volunteering as guinea-pigs. The gift of looking into the future, although having no logical explanation, appears to be inbred in some families. Even in 1919 to tell fortunes was illegal and there were stiff penalties if one was caught telling fortunes for profit. Dad often told us tales of his mother Francis, who was known in Berkhamsted where they lived as 'The Witch'. She was evidently a water diviner and possessed the gift of second sight. He said her divinations and predictions were truly remarkable. She had a great following, especially among the local girls who were always consulting her about romantic matters. She told one young woman that that afternoon she would meet her future husband at the local railway station, a prediction that came true. By all accounts her popularity soared and the number of visitors to their home in Paradise Road increased greatly.

Although I never saw him demonstrate, Dad always maintained he was a water-diviner. He was also a keen astrologer and one of the elite band who brought astrology to the people prior to the First World War. He was a close friend of Alan Leo (Sepharial), and E. H. Bailey, the editor of the *British Journal of Astrology,* whom I once met. I was interested in the subject from an early age and in my late teens studied Astrology with indifferent results. Sometimes I assisted Dad with some castings and on one occasion he asked me to help him in drawing up a map to find out the most favourable time for opening a new Masonic Lodge. I suppose I should have persevered but when one is at work from early morning to 7.30 or 8.30 at night, followed by night school, one had to try to get one's priorities right and I was often far too tired to think clearly, which is the first requirement of Astrology. In my early twenties I became very uneasy about it all so I shut my books on the subject and made a complete break.

*

Saturday was always a busy day at home, when the kitchen table had to be scrubbed, the knives cleaned, the floor washed and the windows cleaned, and the younger girls would often be sent down to play in the yard while the older ones got on with the chores. Doing the outside of the windows was a bit hazardous. One sat on the window sill, gripped the woodwork with one hand and tried not to look down to the ground far below. The sashes were of the up-and-down type and often the sashcords would rot and break and the top frame would come down with a crash. We would have to prop it up with a stick of wood until such time as new cords could be inserted. Saturday was also the chief shopping day and one or other of us would accompany Mum to the market in Waterloo Street to get the vegetables and sometimes a rabbit or fresh herrings. When she returned Mum would unload her purchases on the table and sort them. Some items would be put into the cupboard of the kitchen dresser, others into a little cabinet on legs with a gauze front which usually housed provisions like margarine, dripping and lard. Eggs were a rarity as was bacon. The tea tin had pride of place on the overmantle, a sort of shelf over the fireplace with a frilly dado hanging from it. On this was displayed our few treasures—a box with seashells embedded in it, a decorated biscuit tin (full of hairpins and junk), a nine-inch statue of Psyche (chipped) and our money boxes (usually empty).[29] Below was the kitchen range which in winter time was kept alight continuously, usually with our iron kettle singing away on it. Mum liked her cup of tea and she often said that she hoped there would be tea in heaven.

Such furniture as we had was practical not decorative. Our chairs had been made with rush seats but standing on them as well as normal wear and tear had made them sag and shred. We could not afford to have our chairs mended by the door-to-door repairer. These craftsmen would sit on the pavement outside the houses and thread new rushes through the holes in the framework. It was fascinating to watch them plying their trade before one's eyes. Instead, Mum would send one of us to Thompson's, the oil shop on the corner, for a shaped seat to be made out of plywood decorated with lots of holes. This would be nailed to the chair frame after first having removed the remains of the rush. Some Jackson's varnish stain suitably applied gave the seat a mahogany-like finish. Unfortunately, we did not know the art of applying the varnish correctly so it became sticky and soon wore off.

On the landing outside our flat, No. 23, was a space about six feet by four feet with a low wall and some iron railings to keep anyone from falling down to the floor below, where Mrs Fisher and her family lived in No. 20. In this space we kept our perambulator. What we would have done without this maid of all work I do not know. It had a boat-shaped chassis and four large wheels.

---

29 In Greek myth, Psyche is the beloved of Cupid (Eros). In art she is sometimes shown with butterfly wings or holding a butterfly (the ancient Greek form of her name means 'breath, life, soul or spirit' and 'butterfly'); sometimes she is depicted carrying a lamp (in reference to an incident in the *Cupid and Psyche* section of *The Golden Ass* of Apuleius.

There were seats at either end and the centre panel could be removed to allow children's feet to go down into the well. Beside transporting my younger sisters for an airing in the Green or Brunswick park, it was used for carrying shopping, coal, tarry blocks or anything too heavy to carry by hand. Neighbours borrowed it to take their bundles to the pawnbroker on Monday mornings and it was used for light removals. I do not know where it came from, or what happened to it, but it served us well. Despite being bumped up and down forty-eight stone stairs it seldom let us down and the only replacements it ever required were new leather straps where the chassis joined the springs. I look back with great affection to our true and noble friend the Pram.

Although the War was fading into memory, times were still very hard. Sometimes when we opened the landing door in the morning we would find a vagrant huddled up in the corner by the pram. I remember Grace screaming when she opened the door to get the milk. Her cries brought Dad to the door at the double and he sent the man on his way. I think that on reflection he regretted his hasty action and in later cases Mum would give the poor soul a cup of tea and a slice of bread and margarine before he went out into the unkind world again. Mum had a kind heart and I can recall her collecting half-smoked cigarettes, breaking them down, and giving the tobacco to men who came begging at the door. I regret to say that I was not so kindly disposed toward them.

*

One day our parents received a letter from Rushden in Northamptonshire, to say that Uncle Joe and Aunt Bec would like to come and stay with us for a few days. We were all very excited because visitors to our home were almost non-existent. Aunt Rebecca was Mum's elder sister and her senior by fourteen years, having been born in Aston Abbotts on St Valentine's day 1863. Her husband, Joseph Hornsby, had been a footman at the Abbey where Aunt was also employed. When they married they moved to Rushden and went into the dairy business. We believed them to be rich, which wasn't true at all, but at this time they were comfortably off. Mum could hardly contain herself with excitement as it was many years since she had seen her sister and brother-in-law. When they came they took over our parent's bedroom and Dad told them to treat our home as if it was theirs. How we packed into the rest of the flat I cannot recall.

Aunt Bec was tall and thin and she had worry lines etched in her forehead. She always looked old although at that time she was only in her fifties. Uncle Joe was a quiet man with a soft voice but he spoke with deliberation and had the habit of putting his thumbs into the armholes of his waistcoat. The four adults spent a lot of time chatting but we were not allowed to join in or listen to the conversation. They took Mum and Dad out quite a bit and sometimes

Con and Reg were included in the party. I felt grumpy at being left at home to mind house and when Reg gleefully related some special treat they had had I moaned and said it wasn't fair. To placate me and to keep harmony in the family, Uncle Joe bought us a large bag of sweets and I hope they did not take my churlish attitude to heart. Our relatives met most of our neighbours and Mission friends and the time soon passed. There were a few tears when Mum and Aunt Bec parted. After they had gone our lives resumed their uneventful courses.

*

It was during the summer that people were excited by the appearance overhead of an airship—the R34. It was a wonderful sight to see the great shining dirigible nose her way through the atmosphere. I believe this airship was one of the most successful ever built for it made the double crossing of the Atlantic Ocean. During the war we had learned to fear the Zeppelins but we were proud of this airship. In the years that followed, other airships were built at Cardington in Bedfordshire and they culminated in the R100 and R101. I remember well the announcement one Sunday afternoon when the radio gave the tragic news that the R101 had crashed in Beauvais in France whilst on its way to India. This disaster sounded the death knell of airship construction in Britain although Germany was to continue with the Zeppelin programme until the Hindenburg burst into flames near New York.

Earning pocket-money became a major preoccupation with me. Sometimes I would do a Saturday job at Fenner's and tuck into apples when I could. One day I heard that Price's bread roundsmen would pay a lad half a crown for a day's work and so early one morning I presented myself at the bakery, which was next to the Embassy Hall in Coldharbour Lane, and asked around. One man took me on so I climbed up beside him and off we went in the direction of Kennington. The round took most of the day and it was dreary monotonous work, lugging baskets of bread and knocking on doors. About 5 p.m. we returned to base and I received 6*d.* for my day's work. I never went there again.

On 6 October 1919 we returned to our school in Grove Lane and settled down to full-time work for the first time in nearly five years. To give them their due the teaching staff tried hard to cram us but we were not very receptive. As our school had no facilities for woodwork we were told to attend mensuration classes at Crawford Street school twice a week. Mensuration was hardly the word for what we were taught, for it was simple carpentry and not the science of mathematics concerned with the determination of length, breath and volume. We were here only a few weeks and then switched to Grove Vale school near Goose Green. It was a long and tedious walk, the length of Grove Lane and down to the bottom of Dog Kennel Hill into Grove Vale. How long we stayed there I cannot remember but all I managed to achieve was a pipe rack and a pair of book-ends.

The raising of funds by youth organisations was as difficult in those days as it is today. The Boys' Life Brigade at the Mission was always short of funds and various schemes were dreamed up to try and bring the money in. One popular idea (at least it was popular with the officers) was the sale of scent cards. These were little oblongs of card impregnated with a kind of talcum powder and the idea was to put them among clothes and linen to make them smell of violets, lavender, ashes of roses and other equally exotic-sounding perfumes. I hated the things but had to take my quota and try to sell them at a penny each. Sometimes I would stand outside Denmark Hill railway station and try to get the folk coming home from work to buy one. This was strictly forbidden as they were not to be offered for sale to the general public but only to friends and relatives. Few people, however, were prepared to give a valuable penny for a grubby card with an indifferent odour.

*

Christmas was an exciting time, for the toy shops were once again full of gay and colourful gifts. I used to spend a lot of time with my nose pressed against the toy shop windows in Church Street and Coldharbour Lane. The austerity of the war years had gone and the brightly lit windows bulged with steam engines and Meccano, dolls and humming tops, kites and mechanical toys, rocking horses and scooters. Everything was there to delight the eyes of young and old alike. We decorated our flat with homemade paper chains and pinned up the mottoes saved from previous years, with their seasonal messages like 'Merry Christmas', 'God Bless our Home', 'Happy New Year' and 'What is home without a Mother'.

Every year Mum did her best to make our Christmas a happy one. She always cooked an excellent meal, but I always looked forward to our Christmas tea more than dinner. We always had this meal by candlelight and I loved to watch the dancing shadows cast by the candles on the faces of the members of my family. The evening was a quiet time. Reg and Con would be invited to parties but a long time was to pass before I received a similar invitation. I didn't have much confidence and tended to shy away from mixing with others. I loved to read and would sit by the fire with a copy of Ballantyne's *Coral Island*.

With the arrival of the New Year, Mum would attend the Watchnight service at Wren Road church. I always went to bed for I hated going out in the cold night air. The New Year parties at the Mission were really something to get worked up about. By present-day standards, the fish paste and jam sandwiches would be considered poor fare, but we would tuck into them with gusto, and the cakes would disappear in no time at all. B. B. Fisher, who was my Sunday School teacher and lived in No. 14 in the Mansions (a flat that our family later occupied) would lead the community singing which preceded the conjurer and magician. Two choruses went like this:

> *Blow, blow, blow, like a pair of bellows blow,*
> *If you don't succeed at first,*
> *Blow until you nearly burst,*
> *You've only got to blow and then the thing will go,*
> *So puff out your face like a big balloon,*
> *And blow, blow, blow.*

and:

> *Oh that buzzing bumble bee stung Bertie's boko,*
> *Bertie's boko, poor thing*
> *Right on his nose,*
> *He fixed his toes,*
> *And gave him such a sting.*
> *Then Bertie Brown ran round the town,*
> *His nose stung by that bee,*
> *But oh! what a sting that bee bestowed on Bertie's boko,*
> *When Bertie went to Battersea.*

1920–1921

The cinema was now tightening its grip on the public's imagination and most people liked to include a visit to the local flea-pit once a week. The actors and actresses of the silver screen now ousted the explorers and travellers in public esteem. Soon these new heroes and heroines received the adulation normally reserved for Royalty. Charlie Chaplin, the lad from Kennington, was immensely popular and Mary Pickford, William S. Hart, Douglas Fairbanks and Lillian Gish had a huge following. Sister Con used to send for photographs of film stars and she collected quite a number. I distinctly remember one of Elsie Ferguson.

Although nobody realised it at the time, the wireless was soon to make its presence felt. Noel's father bought one of the new crystal sets and when the opportunity arose, Noel and I would put on the earphones, juggle the 'cat's whisker' on the crystal and try to pick up the broadcasts from the 2LO station on Savoy Hill, which broadcast Debroy Somers and his band playing from the Savoy Hotel in the Strand. Although it was a case of hit and miss it was immensely exciting when sound came into the earphones. Sometimes a whole evening would pass without picking up intelligible sound. We tried putting a torch battery on the aerial terminals but all that happened was the battery went flat.

The months gradually slipped away and I do not recall any outstanding events until 19 May when my sixth sister was born. She was called Iris Denise. I wasn't at all sure that I liked being surrounded by so many sisters, but most families were large and it seemed the accepted way to live. Denny, as she came to be called, was a most lovable child, plump and jolly. Most unkindly she was nicknamed 'Podge'. At that age she had no objections but as she grew older the unflattering 'Podge' was dropped by mutual consent. I liked all my younger sisters but Denny always had a special place in my affections.

As 1920 ended and 1921 began, what to do when I left school began to occupy my thoughts. One of the milkman's customers who lived in Dagmar Road, enquired of him as to whether I would like to be apprenticed to the printing trade. Dad was all for it and had it come off would probably have set me up for life. Nothing came of it however.

Until the year 1921 boys and girls reaching the age of fourteen years were allowed to leave school on their birthday, but that year the London County Council decided that pupils must stay on until the end of the month in which they attained school leaving age. This was not all. They set up Day Continuation Classes and made it compulsory for each school leaver to attend them twice a week. This evoked a storm of protest from employers and parents, but the LCC persisted with the scheme. In the end it died through absenteeism.

My last months at school were fruitful and rewarding and I gradually rose in class until I attained first place. Often I would take my work and sit at a desk in the hall as a senior monitor responsible for sounding the break bells and seeing doors were bolted back. Mrs Wilson, our teacher, had tried hard to see her pupils left school with a reasonable standard of education, but the lost years had proved to be an insurmountable obstacle to overcome, and each scholar was judged to be at least two years behind the standard considered acceptable for a school leaver. Over a period of four months every child in our class would leave to become a competitor in an already overcrowded labour market.

At the end of October, 1921, I said goodbye to the Headmaster, Harry Turner, to Mrs Wilson, and to Mr and Mrs Howard, Mr Wraith and Mr and Mrs Hills. It was only then that I realised how much I liked them all, despite the odd caning I had received for misdemeanours. Mr Turner gave me a 'Character', and I said goodbye to my classmates who for many years had been my constant companions. It really was the parting of the ways. Many of them I would never see again, and it was with a lump in my throat that I left Denmark Hill School and made my way home.

Any immediate hope of finding employment was soon dashed. I walked miles in the hope of getting an advertised vacancy, only to find the job had already been filled. I would go to the library and take my turn in the queue of men and boys who were waiting their turn to go through the 'situations vacant' section of the *Daily Chronicle* in the vain hope of finding something suitable. I never went to the Labour Exchange to ask for work. The mistaken belief was that no decent employer ever asked the Labour for workers, and that only good-for-nothings and layabouts ever went there and hung around its doors.

If anything undermined my self-confidence it was this continual rejection with the resultant feeling that I wasn't wanted. I looked to Dad for help in vain; he seemed indifferent. Mum was sympathetic but my older siblings considered me a shirker, something which even today I find hard to forget. It culminated one day when Grace told me to stop sitting about and go and get some work. I felt very sick about it. I heard of a job going at an oil shop on Denmark Hill so I went and got it. I worked from 8 a.m. to 8 p.m. and to 9 p.m. on Saturday, all for 7s. a week. At the end of the week I left.

I then got a paper round with Bunn, the newsagent in Grove Lane, for 4s. 6d. a week. It involved early morning and evening work. Then Knight, the grocer next door to Bunn's, asked me to deliver their orders. For this work I received 6s. 6d. a week plus my tea on Saturdays and an occasional flank of bacon. A resident in Camberwell Grove, whose garden was alongside the railway embankment, asked me to do a spot of gardening for 4s. a week. I managed to combine all three jobs so I wasn't doing too badly.

These jobs were alright but I wanted something regular and one day Noel spotted a card in the window of the United Kingdom Tea Company on Church Street stating 'Boy Wanted'. I did not hesitate, went in and got the job at 15s. a week. And so, for better or worse, I was on my way to becoming a self-supporting citizen.

The Years of Change
1921–1930

The branch of the United Kingdom Tea Company at No. 36, Church Street, where I started full-time employment was, even in those days, old-fashioned. The company was owned by the Tetley family whose head office was in Mincing Lane and, as its title suggests, specialised in tea. The trade mark showed three ladies in long Georgian dresses which were coloured to suggest the nationalities of England, Scotland and Ireland.

The shop had two windows which faced the main road from Peckham to Camberwell Green and was in the centre of the shopping precinct. The large window was always dressed with groceries and displayed small bowls of cocoa, coffee beans, dried fruits, muscatels and almonds, with tins of fruit and large packets of cereals. The small window was reserved for alcoholic drinks and here were displayed the well known brands of whisky like Johnny Walker, Gilbey's Spey Royal, Buchanen's Black and White, all selling at 12s. 6d. a bottle, and 30% proof. Sample bottles of Sherry, Port and Tarragona had little price tags around their necks, and on special pyramid stands, supplied by the brewers, were ales and stouts, the most popular of which were Guinness, Bass, Watney's Pale, Reid's and Hammerton's Oatmeal Stout.

A brass quadrant on which the firm's name had been etched was fixed to the tiles at the base of the windows and it was one of my tasks every morning to clean it with metal polish. Each week small posters were pasted on the windows drawing the public's attention to the special offers on groceries. The price of alcohol was never cut. Above the windows, across the whole breadth of the shop, was the fascia board displaying the firm's title in gold leaf on a green background, and protected from the weather by glass. Although the firm boasted the grandiose name of 'United Kingdom' it had only six branches, at Streatham, Clapham, Ilford and Seven Kings, plus two others whose location I cannot remember. I believe, however, that they had a big wholesale business in tea and their speciality tea named 'Silverdale' had many devotees. I think the Tetley retail business folded prior to the Second World War but Tetley tea can still be bought in high-street shops today.

The interior of the shop glowed with mahogany. All the counters and fixtures and fittings were made of it. There was a long counter on one side with numerous shelves and drawers, and on the opposite wall, on long rows of shelves, were the alcoholic liquors with their labels arranged in precise order, like rows of colourful soldiers. At the end of the shop was the manager's desk and a door that led to the warehouse and cellars. At intervals, along the centre of the floor, were displays of tinned fruit and bottled beer, and at the sides were stacks of biscuit tins without lids but protected by glass covers.

The selling of wines and spirits was the shop's main business. Much more trade could have been done on the grocery side had the shop sold provisions like butter, bacon, eggs and cheese, for the public preferred to buy these items at the same time and place as their other groceries. I wondered if there was some clause in the lease which prohibited the sale of these items because the shops at Streatham and Clapham had provision counters.

When I entered the grocery trade packaging was still in its infancy and most dry goods were delivered in bulk. Sugar came in two-hundredweight sacks, soda in a similar quantity. Cocoa, rice, dried fruit, and rolled oats came in one-hundredweight sacks or boxes. Cooking salt arrived in huge blocks and had to be cut into 1d. lumps with a saw, which had become rusty with use. Goods were delivered to the shop by contractors with horse-drawn carts, although the bigger suppliers like Peek Freans or Watney's had their own wagons. Most of the drivers would carry the heavier goods into the shop for a tip of two or three pence, which was recorded on the till roll and paid out of petty cash. Practically everything on the grocery side had to be weighed by hand (tea was the exception as it came already packaged) and while there were special bags for some items, most commodities were wrapped in blue paper called 'royal hand'. There was a lot of skill in wrapping, especially in the making of 'paper cups', and while in time I became very efficient at it there were many who were unable to master it.

Weighing cocoa was a messy business as the brown powder managed to get everywhere, in the hair, up the nostrils and all over one's clothes. Its basic price was 8d. a pound but some of it was put into different bags and sold to the unsuspecting shopper at 1s. a pound, which struck me as dishonest. I was to find that this double pricing was a feature of the trade and excused on the grounds that the inevitable losses due to breakages, shrinkage and evaporation and 'turn of the scale' had to be made up. The manager had to be sure that his books balanced at the half-yearly stock take.

The shop had a small staff. Mr Galloway was the manager, Fred Berge his deputy, and there was one other assistant and a lad who was the chief delivery boy. As I was the latest addition to the staff I was given the menial tasks to carry out, like polishing the brass, cleaning the windows, grinding coffee beans and delivering customers' orders. If the orders were too heavy to carry we used a two-wheeled cart which made delivery a little easier. Once a week I had to load the handcart with empty beer bottles and, armed with an order form, go to Fremlin's beer bottling depot in Kenbury Street, off Coldharbour Lane. Here I would hand in the order, unload the empties and bring back the full bottles to the shop. It was a job I hated. Not only was it heavy work but I found the smell of stale beer quite nauseating. All beer sold over the counter had a deposit charged on the bottles, 3d. on a pint and 4d. on a quart. All the bottles were over-stamped with the shop's name and only those bottles bearing this stamp were accepted for refund.

Whilst I was glad to have a steady job I missed the freedom of the past months when I had been going 'freelance'. Working until nine o'clock on a

Saturday night barred me from many social activities which I could have enjoyed had I finished at midday. I often fretted over this and envied my chums watching the football at Dulwich Hamlet or playing cricket in Ruskin Park. Although I tried to accept the inevitable I came to hate the restrictions of shop life. Despite this it was many years before I turned my back on the grocery trade.

Around the year 1922 there was a much publicised scheme to encourage young lads to emigrate to Australia and work on the farms where there was a shortage of labour. The brochures and boys magazines told in glowing terms of the opportunities that awaited young men of vision and determination in the land of the Southern Cross. One of my friends named Jack Southgate applied to go, and was accepted. Noel and I went along to his house in Warner Road to wish him well. There was a lot of excited chatter about Australia and as a result some of us went to the Labour Exchange on the corner of Artichoke Place to collect the necessary forms.

In my enthusiasm I had overlooked my family's reaction to this venture. They were quick to point out that once committed and out in the bush I might never see them again and that I had no experience of handling heavy horses, one of the requirements, nor had I the physique for farm work. Mum was most upset to think I had even considered leaving home. I do not recall Dad's views on the subject but I'm sure they were not favourable. The last thing I wanted to do was upset the family so I tore up the forms and tried to forget the whole idea.

I believe I worked hard for my weekly wage of 15s. I was allowed to keep 1s. 6d. for pocket money. This wasn't so bad as I used to supplement it with a few coppers which kind folk gave me when delivering their orders. As the shop faced Kimpton Road I had no expenses to meet or fares to pay, and could get home for meals. The shop hours were long, 8.30 a.m. to 7 p.m. Monday to Wednesday, 1 p.m. Thursday, 8 p.m. Friday and 9 p.m. Saturday. There were occasions when I had little to do and then time dragged wearily. At the back of my mind I cherished the notion that I would like to work in an office. Some of my old classmates had found jobs as office boys and seemed to like it well enough. Dolph Mordey was in shipping and Ted Thompson was 'somewhere in the city'. I used to imagine working in a nice warm office with Saturday afternoons free and being someone of importance, unlike errand boys who had no status whatsoever. As a result I went along to Crawford Street School and enrolled in evening classes to study book-keeping. Ted Thompson joined the same class.

I suppose I got on well enough at the start. I had to buy myself a textbook called *The Primer of Bookkeeping*, which cost two weeks' pocket money. The class commenced at 7.30 p.m. and lasted until 9.30 p.m. The instructor was not a nice person, very sarcastic, and he did his best to make us feel like a lot of half-wits. I sometimes had difficulty in getting to the class on time and would receive an embarrassing comment on my late arrival. After the class had ended Ted and I would walk home via Camberwell Green where his father managed the snack bar by the tram shelter. Ted would often go up and get a cup of tea from his father but I always held back, not wishing to embarrass him into giving me one too. After the first term I was so disillusioned about evening classes that I did not enrol for a second term.

Mr Galloway, the shop manager, was a short man in stature but he had a large corporation, which he assured us was not fat but muscle. He was bearable when in good spirits but would often arrive at the shop in a very sour temper, and it was best to keep out of his way as much as possible. Wednesdays were always very trying. In contrast, Fred Berge was always in good spirits and never lost his temper or raised his voice. We had a mutual respect for each other and I liked him a lot. I found out that he had once been employed by the Co-op, but his reason for leaving remained a close-kept secret. When in 1927 I joined the staff of the Royal Arsenal Co-operative Society I made a few discreet enquiries about him but all I could glean was that he had been a victim of a miscarriage of justice. Business at the shop was slow and trade only averaged about £150 a week and looking back I wonder if these poor trade figures were the cause of Galloway's depression.

In the outside world things seemed to go from bad to worse. Everywhere appeared to be in chaos despite efforts to get trade moving. Much of it was above my head but I could sense the feeling of despondency everywhere. The unemployed hung about the Labour Exchanges and some men went around the streets playing instruments or singing, in the hope that some kind-hearted person would spare them a penny or two. An indication of the hardship everywhere could be seen in the pawnshop windows, which were full of unredeemed pledges.

I am sorry to say that I was not much help at home around this time. My off-duty hours were taken up with my own pursuits and I didn't care much what happened at home. Mum had her hands full with her growing family but I never heard her once complain. She somehow managed to do the shopping, cooking, sewing and mending and still keep the flat looking clean and tidy. Sister Grace was a great help to her and some of the younger girls helped by running small errands. We were terribly overcrowded, for ten of us were packed into four rooms. As Dad was home only about two nights a week some of the girls slept in Mum's bed and this relieved the pressure a bit. Reg and I slept in the kitchen. I rather liked this for it was always warm and being one of Nature's cold mortals I thought sleeping in front of the fire was absolutely wonderful.

*

We didn't possess much in the way of furniture, just the bare necessities like a table and chairs, and beds to sleep in. There were always breakages to cups and saucers so our collection of china was unique in that all pieces were different. It was about this time that the Laceys, to whom Mum had been a children's nurse in her single days, sold their house at No. 21, Kingsmead Road, West Norwood and much of their unwanted furniture was passed to us. We became the proud possessors of a very handsome walnut sideboard plus many other things like tables and chairs. Whilst this furniture was most welcome it did reduce our amount of living space.

When the sale of the house and contents took place I went to Kingsmead Road with Mum and witnessed the transactions. I knew little about the sale of property but I thought it most unusual when I saw bundles of treasury notes being passed to Mum from the man who received the house deeds. There was an organ in one of the rooms and I tried to play a few notes on it. In another there were scores of books all tied up in bundles. Mum told me to take any I wanted but none attracted me. What I did find was a pair of opera glasses in mother-of-pearl and these I pocketed, and still have them to this day. While the house business was being transacted I mooched around and in a cupboard came across something very heavy wrapped in brown paper. Being curious I took one of the parcels down and untied the string. Inside was lead type, which appeared to be covered with music symbols. At that moment Mum appeared. She was furious with me and snatched the type away and put it back in the cupboard. I was amazed, for it was unlike Mum to be angry with me. I could only think that whatever I had unwittingly unwrapped I was not supposed to know about. To the best of my knowledge at that time I had never met Mr Lacey but I had heard much of him and understood he was a celebrated organist and had composed one song entitled 'A King without a Crown'. Some years later I heard it sung on the radio. The matter of the music score was never referred to again.

*

About this time I learned to ride a pedal cycle. It took me a long time to do so. Noel helped me and in the end I mastered the art of turning corners. A little earlier Noel had purchased a second-hand bike from a lad in Fowler Street for fifteen shillings. Its brand name was 'New Hudson' but that was the only new thing about it. However it was a bike and a treasured possession. Brother Reg had also bought a second-hand bicycle and was very proud of it. Physically Reg was much stronger than me and he loved speed. He tore around the streets as fast as he possibly could. His cycle had a fixed wheel of the type used by racing enthusiasts, which enables the rider to maintain fast and steady speeds. I was not so keen on this kind of cycle and considered the fixed wheel a menace.

On August Bank Holiday Sunday, Noel suggested that I try and borrow my brother's bike and go for a ride to Hayes Common in Kent. Much to my surprise Reg agreed to lend it to me, so nice and early the following morning Noel and I set off on our travels. I was a bit shaky with the fixed wheel but after a short time managed to get the hang of it. We made our way up Denmark Hill to Sunray Avenue where we carefully threaded our way through a series of water-filled potholes, then past allotments and fields towards Dulwich Village. Passing the mill-pond and Dulwich College we went through the toll-gate (no charge for cycles) and up the rough tree-lined road to Crystal Palace. The road from Crystal Palace to Penge is wide and runs steeply downhill and this was our route. It was unfortunate that the fixed wheel on Reg's bike prevented me from free-wheeling for as we sped faster and faster down the hill my feet came off the pedals. I couldn't get them back so I rested them on top of the fork bracket and let the pedals race around uncontrolled. The wind whistled through our hair as we raced on and on towards Penge. Suddenly there was a scream of tortured metal and I felt myself propelled through the air like a shell from a gun barrel. My guardian angel must have been watching over me that morning for I landed in a heap in the middle of the road about twenty feet further on. A policeman standing nearby came running over and ran his hands over me before helping me to my feet. Fortunately I had suffered nothing worse than a bruised knee. By now Noel had stopped and ridden back and all three of us surveyed the wrecked cycle.

Reg's pride and joy was a sorry mess. It did not take long to discover the cause of the accident. The cycle chain must have come loose, for the pedal crank had caught in it. The sudden stop had bent the cycle in half. We tried to force it back into shape but it was hopeless. When we got back home and Reg saw his cycle he burst into tears, and I couldn't blame him. I had sixteen shillings saved up in the Mission's Penny Bank and it cost me all of this for repairs. I vowed that I would never, from choice, ride another fixed-wheel bike.

Sometime later, Noel's father gave him a Raleigh cycle and I agreed to buy the old New Hudson from him at the price he had originally paid for it. I purchased it at 1*s*. 6*d*. a week, which was the whole of my pocket money. It was, in reality, a poor old machine but it was all I could afford. Although classified as a 'heavy roadster' it had, over the years, had different parts substituted for the originals and the makers would have had some difficulty recognising their product. Its handlebars were narrow, it had only a front brake and its wheels were twenty-eight inches, which meant that in the event of a spill I would fall further than if I had one of the newer models which had twenty-six inch wheels. I learned how to take it to pieces and reassemble it and it served me well. Reg would come out with Noel and myself and we would ride off into Kent, and were not adverse to scrumping a few apples from the orchards. In time we widened our horizons and one day ventured to Aston Abbotts and back. We hadn't told anyone of our plans and Mum was worried sick. We returned home triumphant at about ten o'clock full of our achievement.

I suppose that I had been working at the United Kingdom Tea Company for about eighteen months when my friendship with Noel Vining began to wane. It was no sudden rift, rather our lives were set towards different goals. My working on a Saturday didn't help. Noel graduated from pedal to motor cycle and met a local girl named Violet. After years of a very close friendship with Noel, during which we saw each other almost every day, I was completely lost. Noel's father left Harris's, the baby carriage people, and bought a couple of ex-army lorries and went into the haulage business. In time Noel and his brothers Wally and Albert all became drivers in the family business. The haulage business prospered and they were able to keep their lorries at the back of their home at No. 42, Grove Lane, in the old carriage driveway.

*

At this time I became very depressed with my lot. Why, I asked myself, didn't Dad do something for Reg and myself. Looking around I saw that most sons followed their fathers into the family firm, or worked in the same business. Dad was a clever man, of that there was no doubt, but he did nothing to help us and seemed content to let us sink or swim, and flounder we certainly did. One day I asked Mum if Dad could find us something better than shop work but she said Dad believed that young men should make their own way in the world as he had done. She added that he could have found an office job for me had I been attending evening school. I felt this slight very keenly because I had made an effort to further my poor education but evidently this did not count.

After I had been working for a year I was given a week's holiday. In those days a week was all one could expect, however many years' service one had given. Only managers received a two-week break. I was awfully thrilled at the prospect of a holiday and after packing a spare shirt cycled off to spend the time with Grandma Higgs at Aston Abbotts. She was old and frail and around eighty years of age at this time and not long after went to live with Frank and Ethel Halsey. Frank was one of the finest men I have ever met but Ethel's conduct towards Gran left much to be desired. After my short break I came home refreshed but with none of my problems solved.

Perhaps my parents noticed how irritable and depressed I was getting because one day Dad asked me if I'd like to go to the opera. When I said that I would he sent me off to the Old Vic in Waterloo to get tickets for *Il Trovatore*. We sat high up in the 'gods', as the cheaper seats were called. That opera was popular was evident for every seat in the theatre was occupied but I wasn't at all thrilled and found it an awful bore. Afterwards we went into a restaurant and had a meal, which was a real treat and much more acceptable. The way Dad spoke to the waiter showed he was no stranger to dining out in this fashion.

While this was a welcome interlude, it did not solve any problems and it looked as though I was destined to go no further in the employment market.

At home, Reg and Dad seemed unable to agree on anything and this worried Mum no end. Reg talked about leaving home. His hours at Fenner's the greengrocer were long and arduous and being a restless type he chaffed under the restrictions which encompassed him. It was obvious that things could not go on this way indefinitely.

However things were about to change for me. One day the firm's area supervisor came into the shop and had a long chat with the manager. Mr Galloway called me over and the supervisor asked if I would like to be apprenticed 'to the trade'. He said that if I agreed and proved satisfactory I would become a permanent member of the firm's staff and have a job for life. Without giving the matter very deep thought I said I would. Pushing the barrow and cleaning the brass had long since lost any glamour it may once have had. If my parents agreed, and subject to the granting of a 'Guarantee', I would continue with my present wage until I was sixteen years old when I would receive a 2s. rise. On my seventeenth birthday I would be given £1 a week, and wages would be reviewed when I reached eighteen years as my apprenticeship would then be over.

The prospect of spending my life in the grocery trade did not thrill me but there were millions out of work and any job was better than none. The despairing faces of the unemployed were to be seen on every street even though London and the South East were supposed to be prosperous. I went home that evening and informed my parents who seemed to think it was a good proposition and they agreed to sign the form. I went to see the Mission Superintendent, Mr Arkell, who gave me a reference and put his name to the application form as guarantee for £1,000 against my absconding with the firm's money. I then spent half a crown on a white apron and the next Monday morning took my place behind the counter. Looking back now, I feel sure it was a legal way to get cheap labour.

Really there wasn't much to learn. I soon acquired the necessary skills in weighing and wrapping the various commodities, filling in order forms and serving customers. For a short while all the change I gave was checked but in a very short time I was given freedom as far as the till was concerned. We did not have a cash register but all sales and refunds were recorded on a paper roll which moved forward one space every time the till was opened. The manager totted up the till roll early the following morning and compared the result with the cash from the till. I was never asked to explain any transactions so I assume that the cash and the till record always agreed.

A new lad was taken on in my place and one of the assistants was sent elsewhere. The new boy was in trouble from the start. He was sent to the Bank for £5 of copper coin and on his way back to the shop had the money taken from him. There was an awful to-do about it and in the end he was sacked. His place was taken by Harold Holdaway, who lived in Mosedale Street. For a short time we chummed up and he introduced me to some of his pals. One evening we were kicking a ball around at the bottom of Datchelor

Place when we were pounced on by some plain-clothed policemen who said it was illegal to play football in the street. How a tennis ball could be called a football was beyond me, but in the event we had to appear in court and were fined five shillings each. I was incensed at this harmless pastime being made the subject of an offence. Somewhere I had read that Australian Aborigines would 'point the bone' at their enemies and as I left Court I pointed an imaginary bone at the Magistrate. It gave me much pleasure when a short time later I read in the local paper that he had gone to the heavenly fields where, presumably, they do not play football. Immediately after the football incident I broke with Harold Holdaway and was on my own again. Harold left and joined Campbell Connolly, the music publishers.

My half holiday on Thursdays was a waste of time. After lunch I would clean the windows just for something to do. In the evening I would go to the central library in Peckham Road and browse around. One half day I borrowed sixpence from Mum and went to the Golden Domes cinema on Denmark Hill. I have long since forgotten the title of the film that was showing but during the interval the forthcoming attractions were flashed on the screen and to my surprise and delight one of these was to be Conan Doyle's *The Lost World*.[30]

For a long time this had been my favourite book and I had read its pages so many times that I knew whole passages by heart. My friend, Ted Thompson, had received a magnificent copy of it for his last school prize and we thought it was a true story. In the days that followed I looked forward with great anticipation to the screening of this film. It was released in a blaze of publicity and I went to see it. My disappointment at the liberties taken with the story made me wonder how Conan Doyle could have allowed the film to be made.

During the autumn and winter of 1922 a series of illustrated lectures were given at the Art Gallery in Peckham Road on a Thursday evening. The subjects were varied but always interesting. For me they became a must and, wet or fine, I would attend, becoming absorbed in the travels and adventures of men who visited remote areas of the globe and faced dangerous situations. Once every session there would be a talk on 'Camberwell, Past and Present'. From these talks I learned much of my knowledge of the Borough's history. On one occasion I persuaded Dad to come with me and we listened to a speaker whose subject was 'Popular Fallacies'.

*

I suppose I had been absent from Kimpton Mission for about a year when I met the Clement brothers, Jim and Pete, and, shortly after, Frank Thompson, who asked me to return to the Brigade. It so happened that the following Saturday the Girls' Company was holding its Annual Display. At this time sister Con was one

---

30 *The Lost World* (1925), released by First National Pictures (USA). Starring Bessie Love as Paula White, Lloyd Hughes as Ed Malone, Lewis Stone as Sir John Roxton, and Wallace Beery as Professor Challenger. The Apeman was played by Bill Montana.

of the Lieutenants and Grace and Eileen were in the ranks. Mum and the rest of the girls went along and came home bubbling with enthusiasm, for it had been a great show. In the chat that followed I mentioned that I was considering rejoining the Boys' Company. Reg was very cynical about my intentions and made me so mad that I determined to rejoin at the next meeting. This I did and at once my whole outlook on life changed. I felt it was the break I had been waiting for.

Once back in the ranks I became quite enthusiastic and for the first time in many months felt really happy. Miss Mulley persuaded me to become secretary to the Band of Hope and I went back into the Sunday School. I won the prize for semaphore signalling and was soon an active member again. The Brigade used to camp on land adjoining and belonging to the railway at Banstead Station. A camp was being held at Whitsun weekend. I could not afford to go but it was agreed in the end that I could go at the subsidised price of 2s. 6d. I was delighted and joyously accepted the offer.

The officers and lads went on the Saturday afternoon to set up camp, but I had to wait until after the shop closed at 9 p.m. The afternoon seemed endless, but when the shop eventually closed I went home, collected my cycle, loaded up some firewood and a few items of clothing and set off. I reached the camp at Banstead at about 11 p.m. where they were waiting for me with a cup of cocoa.

We were housed in a big army bell-tent and we slept in a circle with our feet toward the centre pole. During the night the weather changed and the rain came lashing down. It poured down so fast that we had to dig a ditch around the tent to divert the water, as the last thing we wanted was to get our blankets wet. When morning came everything was sodden and as it was impossible to get a fire going, we had to get by on dry rations. Jim and Pete Clements, who were resourceful lads, climbed down the side of the railway cutting and made some tea on the stove in the signal box. It was very welcome and as we drank it the rain eased off, and by the afternoon the sun was out and we were able to play football in the grounds of the golf course just across the road. We had a great time setting traps for rabbits and roaming over the Downs. I caused a certain amount of laughter at teatime by asking what we were having for breakfast. Ever since, Frank Thompson has never ceased to remind me of it. On the Monday, many of the Mission girls came to see us and we provided hot drinks for them. They had brought their own food. We all had a great time together although I was slightly embarrassed when Eileen, Jim and Pete's sister, kept me company.

*

Back at the shop, I was still learning the trade but could not help feeling I was wasting valuable time. I soon came to realise that very little skill was needed to sell groceries and wines and spirits. It was on the provisions side of the business that skill was required, and I used to watch the assistants next door in Frost's, cutting up bacon or slicing cooked meats, and using pats to mould the butter into size and shape. This was where expertise was rewarded. To break away however was impossible at this stage. Jobs were at a premium and the few shillings I earned were needed at home. Britain may have won the war but the country was seething with discontent. The unemployment caused by falling trade brought untold misery.

Some of the prices charged for commodities in those days now seem unreal until one considers the wages and salaries that were paid. Granulated and yellow crystal sugar was 2d. a pound, condensed sweetened milk 3d. a tin. A pound of dried fruits, like currants, raisins and sultanas, was 6d. and rice 4d. Jellies (pint size) were 3d. each, rolled oats (the staple diet of the working classes) 2½d. a pound. Marmalade cost 6½d. for a two-pound jar and 1s. for a three-pound jar. A twelve-pint packet of Pearce Duff's custard powder was 4½d., Oxo cubes a 1d. each and pepper 1½d. an ounce. Tea varied from 1s. 4d. to 3s. a pound, biscuits from 6d. a pound, and Lyle's Golden Syrup, whose tin has changed very little since those days, was 7½d. for 2 lb.

Sunlight soap sold for 6d. a 1 lb bar, Lifebuoy 4½d. a 12 oz bar, loose soap flakes 6d. a pound and Lux flakes, which came in two different sizes of packet, were 4½d. and 7½d. A 4oz packet of Hudson's powder cost 1½d., Vim and Glitto 4½d. a large drum, and hearthstone, 1d. a lump.

On the alcohol side, whisky at 30 under proof was 12s. 6d. a bottle but Jameson's Irish, 20 under proof, cost 15s. (Dad was partial to the latter). Wines varied in price considerably. A pint of beer cost 7½d. or 1s. a quart, but this also varied a lot, and the bottles carried a deposit of 3d. or 4d. depending on size.

After the incident of the lost change I was given the job of going to the bank with the previous day's takings and bringing back any change that was needed. We banked at the local branch of the Westminster Bank, on the corner of New Road and Camberwell Green. Galloway was not a trusting type and he personally checked the silver and copper that I brought back. Occasionally a 5s. bag of coppers was found to be a penny short and I would have to return with the bag to the bank and ask for the missing penny. This was most embarrassing for after examining the blue paper bag for identity marks and passing over the missing coin, the bank clerk's look told me that he considered I was on the slippery path to Dartmoor.

It was necessary to keep a few farthings in the till and while we often got sixpence worth from the local sweet shop, I would sometimes get a 5s. bag of farthings from the bank. I used to count the little coins into piles for the manager to check and found a certain amount of pleasure in the task. Often I would come across farthings from the reign of Queen Victoria, William IV, and even of the Georges. Many would be green with verdigris but easily recognisable on account of their larger size. Copper coins were withdrawn from circulation in 1859 and replaced by bronze (a mixture of copper, tin and zinc). Even in the 1920s good specimens of the old copper coins were sought-after by collectors, but farthings had few devotees.

One day I found among the farthings a strange coin. It was made of brass and bore the date 1837, the year of Queen Victoria's accession to the Throne. It bore the Queen's head and on the reverse a crowned horseman slaying a mythical dragon. Above the horseman's head were the words 'To Hanover'. I was sure I had found a rare and valuable coin so I swapped it for a farthing of my own. About a month later another brass coin turned up resembling a spade guinea with the effigy of George III and the inscription 'In memory of the Good Old Days'. I exchanged this also and began to ask around to see if anyone could identify my two coins, but drew a blank.

On another occasion a strange halfpenny came my way. On one side was a man sitting at a loom and on the reverse, a sheep's fleece. The date was 1791 with the word 'Rochdale'. Close examination showed that round its edge were the words 'Payable at the warehouse of John Kershaw'. These three coins started my interest in numismatics, which has never faltered over the years, although they did not ensure for me the hoped-for life of luxury and idleness. The Rochdale coin was a 'token', minted in the days when there was a dearth of copper coins. The brass spade guinea was a gaming counter, and the one 'To Hanover' is better known as the Cumberland Jack. Both the latter are worthless. Good quality tokens have their devotees but generally interest in them lies in the cities, towns, trading firms and local and ecclesiastical authorities who produced them.

*

With Con, Reg and myself each making a small contribution to the family purse, it became a little easier for Mum to keep house. She was a good manager and devoted all her time and energies to her family, but life for her must have been a terrible bore. My sisters did their share of the household chores and Grace, who was now approaching school-leaving age, was a tower of strength. Grace did not relish the thought of going out to work and did her best to prevail upon Dad to let her stay at home and help Mum around the house. In the event, Miss Stewart, the Girls' Club leader at the Mission, got her a job as a waitress at John Pearce's eating-house in the Minories where she worked.

It was a long way for a girl of fourteen to travel. She would leave home at 7 a.m., get a tram to London Bridge and walk the rest of the way. The hours were long and she did not reach home until 7 p.m. All she earned was ten shillings a week which, after fares had been paid and a little given to Mum for her keep, left her very little. Even so she seemed happy enough. Another Mission girl who worked alongside Grace and sometimes travelled with her was Eva Crocker, a slim, dark-haired girl who seldom smiled. I suppose that what with the long hours, hard work and rush hour travelling there wasn't a lot to smile about. Eva's sister Emily also worked at John Pearce's, and she had a younger sister Ruby. Their only brother, who I think was called Dick, was a member of the Mission's Boys' Life Brigade Company. The Crocker family lived in Sedgmoor Place, a few doors away from the Clements. Eileen Clements and Eva were both in the Girls' Life Brigade, and were friends.

*

At the Mission a Miss Willett became captain of the Girls' Life Brigade with Francis Stocker and May Thompson as Lieutenants. Sister Con severed her links with the Company when she teamed up with Ivy Fussell, another telephonist. The Girls' Life Brigade launched ambitious musicals like *Aladdin* and *Sleeping Beauty*, and went from strength to strength. A Mr Jones came to live in Kimpton Road, almost opposite the Mission Halls. He was an ex-army musician and became the Boys' Life Brigade Bandmaster and knocked the drum and bugle band into such good shape that they became the envy of every other band in the area. We used to parade around the streets before the morning service on the first Sunday of each month with drums beating and bugles blowing. I did my best with my tub drum but never did achieve a satisfactory 'roll'. Following behind us marched the Boys' Life Brigade and the Girls' Life Brigade and their cadets, plus hordes of children who joined in the marching as we passed along our route.

*

One day Dad came home with a grey African parrot in a cage. Dad said a friend of his had become tired of it because of the bird's untidy habits. I think the bird belonged to Mr Lacey's eldest son who was a buyer for Lever Brothers, somewhere in the Congo. We called the parrot 'Polly' and he became a very untidy member of the family, scattering his seed far and wide. He didn't like Dad at all. He was a fluent talker and could whistle, laugh and sing. He was also very vicious and cheerfully bit the hand that fed him. We had to wear a glove when dealing with him as his beak was like a razor. All members of the family were bitten at one time or another. He learned the name of our tortoiseshell cat and would call 'Minnie, Minnie!', and when the cat jumped up onto the table and rubbed his back against the cage, Polly would sink his beak into the cat's tail. The things Polly did deserve a chapter to themselves. He interrupted Mission services, yodelled like the milkman and called down workmen who were repairing the roof. We would let him out of the cage and he would walk all over the floor nipping any ankle that came his way. He lived until 1940, when he died of influenza.

*

Apart from Aunts Ada and Ethel, who lived at No. 59, Treherne Road, Brixton, Mum had no close friends. Some of the Mission ladies, Mrs Thompson, Miss Mulley and Mrs McPhun, would pop in to see how she was and she looked forward to their visits. It therefore came as a surprise when she received a letter from a Mrs Evemy. Mum was excited and in the ensuing chat told us that they had been school friends in Aston Abbotts. Mrs Evemy had left the village to get married. Letters were exchanged and we were invited to visit the Evemys at their home in Hammersmith. One Sunday we took advantage of the offer. I don't think Reg came and Dad certainly didn't. We went by tram to the Oval and thence by tube to Hammersmith.

The Evemy home was in the Guinness Buildings in a flat like our own. It was sparsely furnished and overcrowded but we were made very welcome. The man of the house appeared to do as he was told. Mum and her friend reminisced about their childhood days and caught up with more recent news. I don't recall much except that we had a nice tea and that they had a daughter, Ivy, a little younger than myself. During the week I received a letter from Ivy but cannot remember what it was about. Mum was most upset. What it was about Ivy that Mum did not like I have no idea. She need not have worried for Ivy did not interest me and when the return visit was made I was elsewhere. After a while the correspondence ceased and there were no more exchange visits.

*

One weekend Mum went to Aston Abbotts to visit her mother and I went with her. I think it must have been a Bank Holiday weekend. The old lady was now very frail and seemed to have put on a lot of weight. I wandered around the fields with Frank, who was a shepherd, and we chased a few rabbits. The weather, as I recall, was very pleasant. When we alighted from the tram at Church Street on our return, we were surprised to see Con waiting for us. She came up to me and said, 'Don't say anything to Mum, but Dad has had an accident'. This was a ridiculous thing to say as Mum heard every word and really panicked and couldn't get home fast enough.

Among his many accomplishments, Dad was an organist. He once told me he had played all the major London organs including St Paul's and the Albert Hall. Some time later he played the organ at the Brixton Astoria while the cinema organist had a break. It was while Dad was playing the organ at a church in Ascot, which he had been doing for some months, that the accident occurred. It appears that after the service, and while crossing the road, he had been knocked down by a motor cycle and had to be brought home in an ambulance.

He sustained much bruising and an injury to his ankle. An ulcer developed on the ankle that never healed. The motorcyclist was not insured and no compensation was ever paid. The accident could have been worse but Dad hobbled a bit for the rest of his life. He tried several remedies to cure the ulcer but he could only get temporary relief. Germolene proved to be the most soothing, and another household remedy, Zam-buk, quite useless.

*

In November 1924 Mum had another daughter. I was not at all thrilled about it. A brother would have been different but I already had my quota of sisters. To my shame, I refused for three days to go and see my baby sister until Mum sent for me. She was most upset and there were tears in her eyes when she asked why I had not been to see her. I mumbled something about having enough sisters already and then went to see the tiny fair-haired baby in the cradle. I suppose my scrutiny lasted a long time for Mum said 'And does she meet with our Lordship's approval?' I looked back at Mum and grinned. 'Sorry, Mum, she really is lovely'.

With the ice broken the family debated a suitable name for the new arrival and we decided on 'Doreen Pamela', Pam for short. The age difference between Con, the eldest, and Pam was twenty-one years. It was to be expected that Pam would be made a fuss of, and she was. I like to think that in her early days life was easier for her than it had been for her sisters. Mum let her hair grow and she soon had tresses that cascaded around her shoulders. I always felt I had a special responsibility for Denise and Pam, and for a while this was true.

The harmony of the house had been broken a year earlier when Reg had joined the army. When later I asked him why he had taken this step he said it was because he had had a row with the 'old man'. They certainly were antipathetic to each other and it had upset Mum no end. There was obviously more to it but I was not very bright and couldn't see things as they really were. Looking back it is clear that Reg had a mind of his own and wanted his own way, rebelling against authority and restrictions. Dad and he were frequently at loggerheads. I think they had temperaments that were very similar, with quick tempers and aggressive attitudes. I believe that much trouble could have been avoided if Dad had been home more and taken more interest in his family instead of leaving so much to Mum, who had more than enough on her plate. Had Dad so wished he could have made our start in life much easier, for he must have had many influential contacts in the business world. He was a Freemason too but no help was forthcoming when we needed it. His view that each person should stand on their own feet was, in my view, a way of opting out of his responsibilities. Most people succeed in this world 'because of' and not 'in spite of'!

When I think back to those formative years I cannot suppress the thought that as a family we were let down badly. Mum made an unselfish and magnificent effort on our behalf, but there was something wrong somewhere. It has often occurred to me that Reg and I would have done well in partnership together. He had flair, was an excellent mixer, a real go-getter and universally liked. He had a fertile imagination and could bluff people into believing his stories and imaginary qualifications. He could talk his way in and out of most situations. I had none of these qualities, but possessed an excellent memory, had the power of concentration and knew the value of money. But it was not to be.

Reg seemed destined to become a fruiterer and greengrocer for he had worked for both Fenner and Jacob's, the local greengrocers, although for a time he drove a delivery cart for Fuller Medley's. He was quicker off the mark than me where young ladies were concerned and he began to show an interest in one of the girls who lived in the flat next door, No. 22. This was the home of Mrs Bull, a widow. She had two daughters, Nora and May. She soon made it clear that she and her daughters had ambitions far above the riff-raff who dwelt in Camberwell, so Reg looked elsewhere. He next chummed up with Lily Mason who lived in a flat in one of the three-storey houses that faced the Mansions.

Lily was a good-looking blonde and as a result was disliked by all the local females. Mum wasn't very keen either, but I suppose most mothers believe that no girl is good enough for a son of hers. Lily had a brother whom we knew as 'Titch' because he was small in stature, although he was about my age. He and Reg got on well. He contracted tuberculosis and when he died Reg was very upset and often went to the cemetery to smooth out the soil on Titch's grave. The romance blossomed for some time. Lily did not impress me and we rarely exchanged a word. When Reg returned from the Army he met Lily again but after a short while they went their separate ways.

When Reg was about eighteen years old he became very frustrated, reminding me of a caged tiger. He was not earning enough money for his needs. Maybe Lily was proving more expensive than he had anticipated. The outcome was that he went along to the local recruiting centre and joined the Army. I think he immediately regretted his action but having accepted the 'King's Shilling', there was no turning back. Mum was very, very upset. On the morning of his departure from Tidworth, there were many tears and Mum was prostrate with grief, as were my sisters. They somehow hinted that I was partly to blame for his joining up, which I resented. We had had our differences but what family doesn't. Reg joined the Cavalry and after his initial training was sent to the Canal Zone in Egypt, and then to India.

*

As I approached my eighteenth birthday, Frank Thompson, the Brigade Captain, announced one evening that the Kimpton Boys' Brigade was to be disbanded. It came as great shock to all of us. I never heard the real reason but presumably there were leadership difficulties. It so happened that it took place on my eighteenth birthday and there was a big farewell party at the Mission. A lovely tea was set before us and we were entertained with songs by the sister Company. One of the items they sang was Rubinstein's 'Melody in F'. When it was over and we began to leave, Pete Clements came to see me and said that his sister Eileen would like to see me.

I had not seen Eileen for some time so I accompanied Jim and Pete to their home at No. 49, Sedgmoor Place. She told me she was going into service as a parlour maid with a Mrs Barling of No. 1a, Stirling Mansions, Canfield

Gardens, off the Finchley Road, and that she would not be coming home very often. We promised to write to each other, exchanged a kiss, and parted.

The next day I told Mr Galloway that I was now eighteen years of age and my apprenticeship was over. I had fulfilled my part of the agreement and expected a review of wages. When the supervisor came the matter was discussed and I was awarded a rise of 15*s*. a week, making my weekly wage 35*s*., which in those days was a fair amount. When I returned home and informed Mum, she suggested I pay her 21*s*. for my board and keep, retaining 14*s*. for myself. For the first time in my working life I felt I had a few shillings to play with, and opened an account at the Post Office.

I had an awful fear of poverty, for I had first-hand knowledge of the misery it could bring. All around me there was evidence of it, broken homes, malnutrition, ill-clothed children and pawnshop windows bursting with once treasured items, and all caused by lack of money. People died because they had not sought medical attention soon enough and those on poor relief seemed to lose all their self-respect. I was determined to get some money behind me and I saved every penny I could, and slowly accumulated a few pounds. I had no fares to pay and my expenses were minimal.

Reg was doing well in the Army and was promoted to Corporal and later to Quartermaster. He made an allowance out of his pay to Mum of 7*s*. a week, which I thought was most generous. Evidently Army life suited him for his letters home were interesting and well written. One day Mum had a telegram from Reg and, very agitated, she showed it to me when I came home for lunch. It read 'Wire ten pounds by return'. Mum was in a right old state. She didn't have five pounds let alone ten. Then she asked me if I could let him have it?

I must admit that I was most reluctant to do this but nevertheless went to the Post Office to arrange for the money to be withdrawn from my account and sent to India. The cost of telegraphing the money was high. However Reg must be in need of it and I believed he would pay me back in time. About a fortnight later Mum had another telegram from my brother asking for a similar sum. Again I forked out. When a third request came I had to tell Mum that £5 was all I had. She raked around and raised the other £5 and we sent it off. I did not like to ask but I was puzzled why Mum did not ask Dad to help out. Later, when Reg left the Army, the loan was still outstanding. I had heard that soldiers who served their time received a small gratuity. I asked Reg for my £25 but I never did get it back. I must say that it did not make relations between us very cordial.

It was evident that 1926 was going to be a difficult year on the labour front. All around there were signs that trouble was brewing, and the miners were in militant mood. I suppose working in a food shop cushioned one from some of the effects of the discontent around, for although pay was low people had to be fed, and, next to the rent, food was top priority. The out-of-work men paraded through the streets behind bands, with their women and children alongside them pushing old perambulators containing their few belongings. It looked, and must have felt, quite soul-destroying for both sexes.

At the shop I found Mr Galloway was becoming very morose and unsociable. Fred Berge, much to my regret, left to become manager of the Seven Kings Branch and I became the second hand which, unfortunately, carried no extra pay. One of our best customers was the London Choir School, whose premises were on the corner of Grove Lane and Grove Hill Road. One day there was a dispute over a counterfeit half-crown given in their change. Galloway, in one of his moods, refused to change it and the Matron in retaliation placed her grocery orders elsewhere. Trade was hard to obtain at the best of times and the loss of the London Choir School's business was a real blow.

Shortly after this, the supervisor, on one of his periodic visits, called me over and said they wanted me to canvass for new custom. Canvassing was a hateful job and very unrewarding, and I was most reluctant to agree. In the event I had no choice. My wages were reduced by 5s. a week and I would receive 6d. in the pound commission on orders. Although I tried to make a success of it the most commission I ever received in one week was 7s. 6d. Often it would only be 4s. 6d. I used to ride around on the shop's heavy carrier cycle and it was prone to skidding. I had a horrible skid in Coldharbour Lane and looked up to see the wheels of a bus only a few inches away.

*

Now that the Boys' Life Brigade had disbanded the close comradeship of the lads gradually disintegrated. I continued to attend the Mission but most of the others left. In late May I saw Pete Clements at the Thompsons' house and stopped and joined in the chat. The talk was chiefly about the General Strike and we were of the opinion that it wouldn't catch on. The miners had already come out and a General Strike had been declared at midnight on the third of May. I suppose it was the nearest thing to a revolution that this country has experienced. Gradually its effects became apparent. Gangs of men picketed the tram depot at Camberwell Green to prevent any cars leaving. People had to walk to work as public transport came to a standstill. One morning I accompanied Grace as far as London Bridge. Every kind of alternative transport was pressed into use, cycles, motorbikes, roller skates, pony and traps, traction engines pulling trailers and a few motor cars. In the main, though, people went to work on foot.

I had only a limited view of the effects of the Strike. In our area few people had any sympathy for the strikers, and they chaffed under the inconvenience it brought. There were no newspapers but news sheets were issued. These told us that the Government had opened depots in Hyde Park and volunteers were asked to assist in maintaining essential services. Buses were driven by students and an emergency train service run by volunteers. This had the effect of angering the strikers who saw their plans being undermined. Gangs of hooligans roamed the streets and they were kept on the move by mounted police waving truncheons and making repeated charges at them.

Galloway wouldn't venture to the bank with the takings and sent me instead. I went there cautiously but had no trouble. The gates at each end of the Green were locked to prevent the mob gathering there. I went to the bank one afternoon at the time that an attempt was being made to bring some of the trams out. The strikers let them get as far as Wyndham Road then one of their number lay down in the road across the tracks. When the trams came to a halt a barrage of missiles smashed every window in the cars and the crews were roughly manhandled. It was rumoured that one man died as a result of his injuries. A running battle with the police followed as the cars were hauled back to the yard.

It was a very frightening experience and the start of much violence. Shopkeepers boarded up their windows against looters and vandals, and for a while the streets were empty of shoppers and pedestrians. The mob roamed the streets and I remember Mum and I looking down on Kimpton Road from one of our windows and seeing the police and hooligans in a running battle. She was awfully anxious about Dad and the girls and I had difficulty restraining her from going out to meet them. Fortunately all was well. After eight or nine days the strike collapsed although the miners held out for a lot longer.

*

I was due for a holiday the first week of August so I wrote to my Aunt and Uncle in Rushden asking if I could spend a few days with them. They replied that they would be happy to have me. I would add that on Mum's behalf I had kept up a correspondence of sorts with them. I tuned up my old cycle and made a little box to put on the carrier to hold a spare shirt, and included a pineapple as a present for them. On the Monday morning I said my goodbyes and set off on the seventy-mile journey to Northamptonshire. It was the longest single run I had undertaken and was a real test for my old boneshaker. I went via the Edgeware road to St Albans and on to Luton and through Bedford for the final stretch. At Milton Ernest I stopped for a sandwich and a rest before going on to Rushden. Uncle had set off on his bike to meet me but somehow we missed each other. I felt tired after my journey but soon recovered my energies after a meal.

Aunt Rebecca Sarah was Mum's elder sister, born 1863, and was fourteen years her senior. We knew her as Aunt Bec. She had met Joseph Hornsby when they were both in service at the Abbey in Aston Abbotts. When they married they left the village and settled in Rushden, which was not far from Uncle Joe's birthplace in Raunds. They went into the dairy business and whilst Aunt Bec looked after their little shop, Uncle Joe went out selling the milk on the streets. Their hard work paid off and they became reasonably well off, owning a few houses as well as their own shop. Strangely they lived in a rented house, No. 62, Roberts Street, where they had been since 1898.

They had three children. The eldest, a boy, named Joseph after his father, and two girls Mary and Lizzie (Elizabeth). At the time of my visit Joseph was in Canada having emigrated sometime earlier. He married a girl he had met on the boat. He found employment with the Canadian Pacific Railway and at this time was the Stationmaster at a place called 'Franz'. Mary married a Herbert Hodgkins and lived in Irthlingborough, a mile or so away, and Lizzie had married Thomas Marks and lived in Harboro' Road nearby. Mary had a son named Stanley and Lizzie a son called Denys. Aunt Rebecca made a great fuss of me and showed me to my room upstairs which overlooked the garden, where Uncle grew prize gooseberries and chrysanthemums. No. 62 was the end house in a block of four and I was soon meeting the neighbours. Next door lived the Cross family who had a daughter about my age called Ena. I cannot recall the name of the next household but at the end lived the Baileys, whose son, although a cripple, managed to run a little grocery business from the front parlour.

In the days that followed Uncle Joe and I cycled around the countryside. We went to Irthlingborough and to his birthplace at Raunds. One evening we went to Kimbolton Castle and climbed an enormous ancient earthwork not far away. The area was quite interesting. Cousin Tom took over where Uncle left off and we got on very well together. Stanley introduced me to his club, and I soon felt I had known these friendly folk all my life.

Uncle Joe Hornsby was a leading light in the local Labour Party and a speaker of some renown, although I never heard him at a public meeting. He was a member of the Urban District Council and in time became Chairman (the equivalent of Mayor). He was also on the board of the local Co-operative Society. Rushden was no beauty spot. It was a small industrial town given over to the making of footwear, and the factories, built mainly of Victorian red brick, were to be found in some rather depressing streets. Even so the fields and woods were not far away and the Council had acquired an old Manor with extensive grounds and very centrally placed. It was being laid out as a public park and would supplement the recreational ground at the end of the town where the annual fair was held. From the new park one could see the spire of the church framed in the sylvan setting. One of the trees I recall was a beautiful copper beech. In the bandstand, one of the local bands would play. The town boasted about three bands and there was great rivalry amongst them. Mr Cross, from next door, played in the Temperance band.

Uncle seemed to take great pleasure in introducing me to his fellow councillors and friends, and to the staff of the local Co-op shops. I found this a complete contrast to Dad's attitude to his family. One of Uncle's close pals was John Spencer, who as well as being the present Mayor was also a member of the Co-op board and the manager of a boot and shoe factory. He personally showed me over his factory although it was closed at the time for Wakes Week. He explained the function and purpose of each machine and said that much of the cutting out of leather for the uppers was done by women in their homes. He took me to his home and introduced me to his wife and daughter, Irene. During the war, tragedy had struck this family. A son had been killed in action, and in a single week three daughters had died of diphtheria.

My Aunt and Uncle seemed very interested in me and in a quiet way had me talking about myself. They asked if I was interested in any young woman, and I said no. They enquired about my job with the UK Tea Company and said that the Co-op was a much better employer; if I so desired they were sure an opening could be found in their Society. Aunt told me I was a handsome young man, a remark that made me blush, and now was the time to take advantage of youth and looks, and to get out of the rut I was in. I had never thought of myself as handsome and I felt awfully flattered. It seemed to me that I was being invited to make my home with them. That an effort was being made to show me I was welcome socially became clear when Cousin Tom asked me to make up a foursome with himself and two girls I had already met, Ena Cross and Irene Spencer. Together we went to the fair, the cinema, and finished up at his club.

One way and another I spent a very happy week and for the first time began to lose the feeling of inferiority that lay upon me like a headache. On the last night I lay in bed thinking over my relatives' proposition. Attractive as the prospect seemed, I knew I could not leave my parents, my sisters and my friends at the Mission. However attractive the idea I knew it could not be done. I think there were tears in my eyes when I said goodbye and began the long ride back to Camberwell. However, a seed of discontent had been sown. Somehow I must leave the UK Tea Company, though how or when was not clear.

*

My nineteenth birthday came and went and I saw no chance of quitting the shop; however there must have been something in what my Aunt had said about being handsome because I began to receive invitations to parties. Most of these were held at the home of Doris and Kate Norman who lived in Vicarage Grove, near Brunswick Park, although they later moved to Champion Grove. Sister Grace and Kate were great friends. I used to like these parties, where we sang and played silly games. At the time we thought Frank Thompson and Doris Norman would marry, but it was not to be. Doris was an excellent pianist and played for our operettas and plays. Frank wrote a play called *Ghosts*, and I played the part of the villain. He used as his theme Molloy's 'Love's Old Sweet Song', before it had a revival in popularity. Grace was leading soloist and made a great impression on the audience. She had a fine voice and was always being called upon for this or that concert.

At this time Grace chummed up with the nephew of the Mission's Sunday School Superintendent, Mr Pankhurst. Most of the others had paired up and I used to feel a bit out of it when we went on rambles or to parties. The

Normans had cousins Mabel and Cecil (Fred) Knocker who lived at No. 17, Vicarage Grove and we often found ourselves in each other's company. Mabel was a dark-haired girl, very placid, and worked in a printing shop just off Rye Lane. I liked her parents much more than I liked Mabel and they often invited me to their home. We used to sing songs around the piano, their particular favourite being Sullivan's 'The Lost Chord', which I rendered very indifferently.

About the middle of November the postman brought me a small parcel. I was very surprised for nobody had ever sent me anything before. The postmark was blurred and I puzzled over who had sent it, and what it was. When I eventually opened it up, the package contained two pairs of black silk socks and there was a birthday card and covering letter from Eileen Clements. I felt awfully bucked to think she had remembered me for I had never written the promised letters to her. I wrote and thanked her and let her know the correct date of my birthday. She wouldn't be coming home until Christmas, so we arranged to meet then.

Trade at the shop was slack and Galloway wasn't very pleased when I asked him to let me speak to the superintendent about a rise. I suppose I was beginning to feel a little more confident and whilst I was always polite we began to clash over trivial things. The weather up to Christmas was cold and there was snow on the ground. Eileen came round in the afternoon and Grace and I went back with her to her home. However, I got the impression that the evening was not a success and when Grace and I left, the departure was cool. A few days later she sent me a letter to say she didn't want to see me again. I felt sad because I liked Eileen, but I would not go where I was not wanted so I replied expressing my regrets and left it at that.

In late January 1927 I upset Mr Galloway over something and he retaliated by saying that if I did not like the job I could get out. Such small incidents are often the forerunners to much larger ones. In February I went sick with a bout of influenza. Dad went to see Mr Galloway to tell him I was in bed unwell and from what Dad said afterwards, he was most rude to him. I was mad about that. I could put up with Galloway rowing with me but insulting Dad was something I was not going to have. As I recovered, I turned over in my mind the pros and cons of remaining with the UK Tea Company. I had never forgotten my uncle's remarks about the Co-operative Society.

It so happened that despite our neighbour Mrs Bull's grand talk about her daughters not keeping company with Camberwell's riff-raff, Nora was going out with a Co-op milkman. I went in one evening when they were at home and had a chat with him. He gave me some useful information and told me of the advantages of the Co-op as an employer. Next day I wrote a letter to the Staff Manager of the Royal Arsenal Co-operative Society at Powis Street, Woolwich, asking if there were any vacancies.

To my astonishment, and pleasure, I received a letter from Mr Hall, the Staff Manager, inviting me to go for an interview. I had to tread cautiously in case nothing came of it, so I got Dad to help me with a reply and I arranged to go for the interview on a Thursday afternoon, when the shop was closed for the half day. I had a 2*d.* tram ride to Woolwich, which took me all the way there, and found my way to Mr Hall's office. He received me very courteously and we had an informal chat. I told him that Uncle Joe was Chairman of the Rushden Co-op and he had suggested I offer my services to the Royal Arsenal Co-operative Society. Whether this helped or not I do not know, but he then sent me off for a medical examination by the Society's doctor. When I returned, Mr Hall said he could offer me a position at the Camberwell Green branch at a weekly wage of 34*s.* 6*d.* and there would be annual increments on each birthday until twenty-five years of age, when I would get £3 6*s.* 0*d.* a week. There would be deductions for insurance and superannuation.

This seemed wonderful, and I accepted. I would have to give my present employers a week's notice, so we agreed a starting date of Monday, 21st March, 1927. As I came home on the tram my head was in a whirl and I felt that, at last, I was getting somewhere.

When I broke the news to Galloway he nearly broke a blood vessel, and I felt a bit sorry, for he had been kind to me. When I reminded him that he had told me to 'get out' he said he hadn't meant it and asked me to think it over, but my mind was made up and there was no turning back. Mum and Dad were delighted and that evening I went and told the Knockers, and on the strength of it took Mabel to the pictures. When Saturday night came and Galloway handed me my insurance cards he said that if it didn't work out I could always come back. So one chapter of my life closed and another was about to open.

*

I was a bit apprehensive as I made my way to the Camberwell Green branch of the Royal Arsenal Co-operative Society at No. 291–295, Camberwell Road on the Monday morning. The shop was the frontage of the block bordered by Buff Place and Mazzard Row and behind it lay two of the toughest roads in the area. It was divided into three shops. Nearest the Green was the grocery shop, in the middle the provisions section including the check office and Manager's office, and the furthest away was the butchers, run separately from the other two.

The manager was a Michael Collins, very slight in stature but a real slave-driver, and strong men quaked in his presence. The foreman was Mr Sharman, a good-looking man who, soon after my arrival, married the General Manager's daughter and was rapidly promoted to Manager of the tea warehouse. Lewis Brand was first grocery hand and we liked each other immediately. For a time I was out of my depth. There was a large male staff and three young women in the check office. It was a busy shop and on a Friday evening customers would be lined up six deep at the counter. There was none of the gentility of the UK Tea Company. It was go, go, go!

It happened that my arrival coincided with the launching of a big new membership campaign. It cost 1s. 6d. to join the Society. The 1s. was entered in the new member's passbook and the 6d. was for the book of rules. Each new member was given a free box of groceries valued at 3s. 6d., which contained items like tea, biscuits and marmalade. People enrolled in their hundreds, many just to get the free parcel. The second week, I joined and persuaded Mum to do the same, and we each received the free parcel. Each member of staff was expected to be a member and it paid to do so because a bonus was paid on wages, equivalent to the dividend paid on purchases, and for staff on the top rate this could amount to about £6 10s. a half year. I had to serve a month's probation and be on the staff for three months before I could qualify for the bonus.

The staff were a rough and ready lot and I felt a bit out of place. As a family, we had been brought up with the certain, though unspoken, belief that we were a cut above common folk. It was not an acquired sense for we had had it from earliest childhood and were not allowed to indulge in the bad language and low talk of the worst offenders. I was ragged quite a bit but in the end we accepted each other and got on well together. I thoroughly enjoyed going to work in those early Co-op days and despite the really hard work liked the customers and the new incentive that the job gave.

As at the UK Tea Company all goods had to be weighed in the shop; even tea came in chests. Whereas previously a week's supply of sugar came in a two-hundredweight sack, here it came in by the ton. For the first three days of the week several men, called the 'stock gang', spent their whole time down in the cellars weighing tea, sugar, soda, soap flakes, rolled oats etc., whilst upstairs the counter staff, in any available spare time, weighed dried fruit—sultanas, currants, raisins, apricots, prunes and candied peel. At the end of the shop was the corn counter and here was sold poultry and rabbit food, pigeon mixture, plain and self-raising flour. There was a terrific trade in these items for most houses in the neighbourhood kept rabbits, poultry and pigeons.

I had to do my stint in the stock gang and despite the hard slog it was very enjoyable, for the lads sang as they worked. Mid-morning tea was not allowed and Collins was very strict about this. Even so, we managed a cup, and often a few cakes were smuggled downstairs from the shop. We would post a look-out whilst we indulged ourselves. The worst aspect of the work was that one was wholly responsible for the cash, and shortages had to be paid for. This was the source of much friction, for many shortages could be caused by writing a wrong amount on the paper check. Many staff were dismissed because of continual shortages; although each assistant had a key to their own till, the swapping of change often led to errors and some staff were not adverse to helping themselves from another's till. As there was a half day on Thursday, and all cash taken on that day was left to be included with Friday's takings, it was not unknown for staff to borrow from their till and repay it out of their Friday wage packet.

The most trouble among the staff, however, was caused by cigarette smoking. Although Collins was a chain smoker and his office could be blue with fumes, he would not allow his staff the same privilege and the men and boys would hide themselves in the toilet or an odd corner for a drag, well aware of the penalty if they were caught. Cigarettes and tobacco were sold across the counter, not in a kiosk, and this was a source of temptation; one or two staff were dismissed for helping themselves to a packet of 'gaspers'.

Orders for deliveries came in during the week, were passed to the provisions counter, and then packed and checked on the grocery side. There were hundreds of them and deliveries were made by van on Fridays and Saturdays. Sometimes I had to work an hour's overtime on a Friday and for this I received an extra 11d., which was always welcome. I began to see my account at the Post Office growing once again.

I wrote to my uncle and told him how I had taken his advice, and reported my progress. He was very pleased and wished me well. My joining the Co-op was to have an effect on the family. Mum began to buy her food there and to have Co-op milk delivered, although she still let our previous milkman, Jackson, leave a pint a day. Sisters Eileen, Vera and Denise all worked for the Society at one time, and Eileen married Sid House, who was a colleague of mine at the 'Green'.

Two months after my arrival a fresh assistant joined us, named Harold Denner. He was bronzed and fit and I took an immediate liking to him. He joined me on the grocery side; we soon found we had a lot in common, and we chummed up. Because his surname was similar to that of Reginald Denny, a film actor of the time, he was called 'Reg', and this nickname stayed with him for the rest of his life. It was not long before he came home with me, and when his family left Earlsfield for Worcester Park, I became a frequent visitor there.

*

My association with Mabel Knocker drifted on. I wasn't very happy about it, for I felt I had been manoeuvred into a friendship that I was reluctant to continue. I needed to do something about it but lacked the will to take any positive action. Mabel was a nice enough girl and I got on well with her young brother and her parents, who were fine people but who seemed to think it only a matter of time before Mabel and I came to a definite understanding. The silly thing was that it was the colour of her hair that I did not like. Blond hair fascinated me. All the members of my family had blond hair. Eileen was a golden blond. Mabel was dark. In my mind there was a continual conflict and resolving it was a problem I shirked. Although I did not know it, fate was about to take a hand.

On the first Monday in July the shop began to fill with customers bringing in the brass checks they had collected over the past six months to exchange for their 'dividend'. A desk was set up in the grocery shop, near to the side window, and one of the assistants received the checks and issued receipts for them. On this particular day I was wearing a blue shirt that Grace had given me. It was the first time I had worn a one-colour shirt and I was not at all sure that it suited me. I was at the end of the counter weighing sultanas out of the bin into half pounds and thinking of nothing in particular when I happened to look up and saw in the queue, waiting to pay her brass checks in, Eileen.

I couldn't believe my eyes. In the six months or so since we had parted she had really blossomed. She was dressed in the latest fashion and her fair hair hung around her shoulders. She smiled as our eyes met, and with a thumping heart, I went across and exchanged a few words. We couldn't say much—there were too many listening ears. She said she was home for a few days. At that moment I was called away and the opportunity to continue the conversation had gone. I wanted to go round to Sedgmoor Place to see her but having once been given the brush off, I was unwilling for another snub.

All that week she was on my mind but she did not come into the shop again. The time passed wearily and when we finished work on the Friday I decided to go for a walk and try to sort things out in my mind. Since joining the Co-op I had been in the habit of taking a long walk on a Friday evening, provided the weather was favourable. My route was, more or less, the same. Up Grove Lane into Windsor Walk, across the road by Ruskin Park and over Denmark Hill to Sunray Avenue, then along East Dulwich Road to Peckham Rye, down Rye Lane and home, via Peckham Road. It took me roughly two hours. Once home I would have some bread and cheese and a cup of cocoa. Friday night was Girls' Life Brigade night and my sisters would be sitting around chatting, although Mum usually retired to bed at about ten o'clock. I would call out 'goodnight' to her before turning in myself. Saturday at the shop was always a busy and tiring day.

On this particular Friday evening I had, for some unaccountable reason, decided to reverse my route and go to Peckham first. As I was crossing Havil Street to the Town Hall, a familiar voice called 'Len', and looking down Havil Street I saw Eileen hurrying towards me. Where she was bound for I never did ask, but soon we were laughing and chatting together. For the next three hours we strolled around. She took my arm, and anyone would have thought that we had never parted from each other. We returned to Sedgemoor Place around midnight and when I asked her if we could forget about the past six months and go out together again, she said she wanted to more than anything else, provided I broke with Mabel Knocker.

In our conversation over the past three hours it amazed me how much she knew of my actions since last Christmas. Someone must have kept her well and truly briefed about me. I was never sure who it was, but I suspected Fred Mulley, who lived opposite her home. I wanted Eileen, and agreed to break with Mabel. When I said I would write to her, Eileen was insistent that I tell her to her face. I did not like this one little bit for it seemed that Eileen disliked Mabel intensely, although, to the best of my knowledge, they had never met. Eileen was very persuasive and in the end I reluctantly agreed. When I left her and strolled home in the darkness my spirits were high.

Telling Mabel took some doing, but she was an unemotional young woman and seemed very indifferent. There had been nothing definite about our relationship - a visit to the cinema, an outing to a cricket match with her parents, but nothing further. I found out afterwards that she was furious. When I told the family that I had parted from Mabel and made up with Eileen, my sisters told me I was out of my tiny mind. Even Mum expressed her displeasure. At the Mission my standing reached an all-time low, but I was completely indifferent to black looks and snubs.

Eileen came home about once a week and we would meet and go to the cinema or spend the evening at her home. One Friday I went back with her to Cranfield Gardens. It was a long ride. Stirling Mansions was a great deal classier than Stobart Mansions, in fact it was very 'upper crust'.

That Christmas she came back home for a while, then we returned to No. 49 Sedgmoor Place. Although I had known the Clements family for a long time I began to feel a little out of my depth. They had a telephone (a luxury in those days), a horn gramophone and lots of records. They would dance in the front parlour and sing songs at the piano. Eileen was a good dancer, as were her brothers, but I had two left feet and sensed I was slightly despised because of it. When it came to quizzes, however, it was a different story.

At this time Eileen's father was working at Camberwell House, a large mental home whose extensive grounds backed onto Dalwood Street, behind the Town Hall. He had been well known in the theatrical world as a Shakespearean actor, as well as in the variety side of the business. His stage name was Ferris Carlton and a picture on the parlour wall showed him in Pierrot costume with members of Will C. Pepper's 'White Coons'. He was a charming man and he and I had long chats. Mrs Clements was a lovely lady who was always very kind to me. They had six children, three girls and three boys. Eileen was the fifth child. The eldest son was a taxi driver, but Jim and Pete were still looking for work. Jim eventually went into the R.A.F. and Pete into the Police. Eileen's elder sister, Cecilia, was dark-haired, and the youngest, Winifred, was about to leave school. I believe that the Barlings, for whom Eileen worked, were also theatrical folk.

*

It was about this time that I had the urge to try my hand at writing short stories and poems. It was only when I re-read my efforts that I realised how my education had been neglected and that my command of the language was very poor. I knew that if I was to get anywhere in the world, I would have to set myself targets, and stick to them. I started to read more and to give myself memory tests, but found concentrating very hard. For my eighteenth birthday, Dad had given me an organ and I tried hard to play it, although I would much rather have had a piano. I was at that stage in life when I fretted about lack of opportunities, for instinct told me that Eileen would never marry a shop assistant.

At No. 14 Stobart Mansions lived a family named Coles and sister Grace was friendly with them. One of the sons played a violin and came up once to give us a recital. Dad wasn't very impressed. Grace went to a party there once and said that a plate of nuts was passed around the guests with a whispered proviso of 'don't take the brazils, Mother wants them!' One day in late spring 1928, Grace came in with the news that the Coles family were moving. Their flat, No. 14, was the biggest flat in the Mansions, having five large rooms, and was at ground level, bordered by the Kimpton Road entrance and backed by the yard.

I have said how terribly cramped we were in No. 23. My sisters were growing into lovely young women but they hadn't room to move. I still slept in the kitchen. There was very little privacy. Climbing forty-eight stairs was alright for the younger members of the family but for Mum and Dad it was an ordeal. There was a buzz of excited talk, for if we could get this flat we could all spread out a bit. Dad was home that weekend and said he would go to the rent office on the following Monday morning to see if an exchange could be made. Afterwards he told us that only by bribing the clerk was he able to get the tenancy, and the rent had been increased from 15*s.* a week to £1. We were only paying 13*s.* 6*d.* for our present flat so it was a huge jump in rent.

Moving flats was arranged for the following Thursday. The Coles had left No. 14 in a shocking state and Mum was nearly in tears about it. I recall looking at the hearth of the living room fire. It undulated like desert sand dunes. Rather puzzled I gently tapped it with a hammer and it flaked. A heavier blow or two and all the accumulated hearthstone came away revealing the hearth underneath. Mum was scared about vermin in the walls and all the paper was ripped off and burnt.

On the Thursday afternoon I persuaded Reg Denner and Adams, the shop porter, to come and give me a hand and together we moved all our heavier items of furniture downstairs. By the evening all our goods and chattels were in the new flat. We had lived in No. 23 for about fourteen years and had been happy there, but we had outgrown it. We hoped the new flat would prove to be as happy.

The three bedrooms faced Kimpton Road. Mum and Dad had the one that led off from the living-room-cum-parlour. I asked for the middle room but my sisters wanted that one so I had the end room, which had the disadvantage of a street lamp outside. This was a nuisance and with the bedroom windows being right next to the pavement, there was also the continual noise of people passing by. However, for the first time in my life I had a room of my own and some privacy, and could put my few possessions, like books, into the built-in cupboard. Mum too was much happier now that she no longer had to climb those dreadful stairs. It was easier for her to get to the Monday Women's meeting, and to have her friends in for little get-togethers.

*

Eileen was still at Mrs Barling's and her visits home became less frequent, which I wasn't too pleased about. However she was home one weekend and asked me to go with her to a party given by some friends who lived opposite. They were nice folk and made me welcome. Everyone performed their party piece and it was a merry evening. Inevitably they asked me to render an item. I had anticipated this and previously my sister Eileen and I had tried out Molloy's 'Love's Old Sweet Song' and found the key of E Flat most suitable for my voice. Fortunately the pianist was able to play in this key and I received quite an ovation at the end. I'm sure this enhanced my standing with my blonde girlfriend.

We met fairly regularly after this and Eileen told me she was leaving her job and coming home to become a dressmaker. She began asking me about my financial position, how much I earned and what were my prospects. I think the influential people she met at Stirling Mansions had made her aware of her boyfriend's financial shortcomings, and I sensed that her sights were set much higher. Her parents, to their credit, tried to get me to do something positive, like getting engaged, but I knew this wouldn't help. One evening as we sat in her parlour she kept niggling me about some chap she had met. I think it was all phoney but I became angry and left in a huff, making no arrangements for a further meeting.

I think we each waited for the other to make the next move. It was August and the weather was very hot. Then we received a letter from Ethel in Aston Abbotts to say that Grandma Higgs had died and that the funeral would be on the following Monday. We were all very upset, Mum especially so. She wanted to go to the village straight away so I sent a telegram to Ethel saying Mum would come down on Sunday. Then I had a letter from Eileen saying that she wanted to see me on the same day. I was full of mixed feelings. In the event Mum decided against the Sunday visit so I went to Aston Abbotts alone to check the arrangements.

I was not very happy about it for I did not see what I could achieve. It was a lovely summer's day but the journey was difficult and irksome. I left home early and got a train from Baker Street to Aylesbury. There were no buses to the village so I had to walk the five and a half miles, arriving there at lunchtime. I talked over the funeral arrangements with Frank and Ethel. The service would be at St James, the village church, and she would be buried in the churchyard opposite the home she had lived in for most of her eighty-four years. She was laid out in the parlour but I declined going to look at her, preferring to remember her as I had known her, a very kind lady.

It does me no credit to admit that throughout my visit I was on edge, my mind constantly drifting away from the subject in hand. I did my best to be sociable and discuss family matters with the Halseys, but Eileen's letter was on my mind. I had a sensed that something unpleasant was going to happen and could not shake it off. I believed Eileen would say something I would sooner not hear. I stayed with Ethel and Frank until about four o'clock then prepared for my return walk to Aylesbury. Frank told me about a footpath from the village that might save me a furlong or two and walked a little of the way with me. It was a nice gesture but I think the distance and time saved was minimal.

I alighted from the tram at Camberwell Green at about 8 p.m. and although I was only a few yards from home, I did not stop but went straight to Sedgmoor Place and explained the reason for my late arrival. All seemed normal and my forebodings evaporated. I was invited to supper and spent a pleasant enough evening. It was only when saying goodnight to Eileen on the doorstep that she told me she was breaking off our relationship and didn't want to see me again. Although I half expected this I felt suddenly empty. I suppose I was tired after a long day of travelling and walking, and her words hit me hard. I don't recall what I replied but I returned home feeling that I had come to the end of a most imperfect day.

Mum was still up, awaiting anxiously for my return, and wanting to know where I had been until nearly midnight. I told her that Gran's funeral had been changed to Wednesday, but apart from this all would be as planned. She sensed that all was not well with me and eventually I told her that Eileen and I had parted, much to my regret. Mum was sympathetic, but not unduly so, and said I would have no difficulty finding another girlfriend should I so wish. My sisters were not so sympathetic and said it served me right for giving Mabel the brush off, and that Eileen, with her looks, would go to the highest bidder. None of this helped me at all.

When I had had a good night's sleep and could think things through more clearly, I was not so pessimistic. We had had these break-ups before and surely it would only be a matter of time before we were reconciled. My horoscope, which Dad had drawn up and given to me, showed I would be nearly twenty-eight years old before I married, so there was plenty of time as I was not yet twenty-one. I had hopes that by then I should have attained some position in life and in the meantime I would go my own way and not let any other girl play with my affections.

*

In the September I had my first week's holiday due. I had now completed a full year with the Co-op and qualified for one week's holiday. After two years I would receive nine days and after three years this would increase to two weeks, which for those days was very generous. As I could now spend my money on myself I went to Prosser Roberts, the chemists in Church Street, and bought a camera. It was a box Brownie and cost 12*s*. 6*d*. The snapshots it took were not exactly works of art and often the shutter would jam, but it was a start and I began by taking a few pictures of my family with it.

I invited myself to Rushden again and was warmly welcomed. This time I went by train. From St Pancras I could get a 5*s*. excursion ticket to Wellingborough and travel the rest of the way by bus. I borrowed a cycle and went visiting Uncle's relatives, and used my camera to the best of my ability. Compared to present-day standards the results were poor, but my Aunt and Uncle were most pleased with the copies I sent them. Time passed very quickly and I renewed friendships made on my previous visit. Uncle Joe and I spent a deal of time playing 'rings' with the disabled Mr Bailey at the end of the row. On the Friday I went to the jewellers in the High Street and bought a silver teapot for Aunt and Uncle as a memento of their kindness and hospitality.

It has been said that in life, as one door closes another one opens. Although I did not realise it, for I was still smarting over Eileen, life was beginning to open up, becoming more interesting, and I was learning to trust in my own judgement. My colleague at the shop, Reg Denner, had been friendly with a local girl named Annie. When his romance, like mine, suddenly shattered, we found we had many interests in common and together decided to ignore young women and go our own way. Reg's family had now moved to Green Lane, Worcester Park, and I became a frequent visitor there. Dad used to call us 'David and Jonathan', although I'm not sure which of us was which. A strong bond of friendship developed between us which we never lost.

On my twentieth birthday I received a rise in pay of 9*s*. a week making my weekly wage £2 3*s*. 6*d*., which was very good money. Each half year I received a bonus of 1*s*. 6*d*. for every £1 in wages earned. This was a great help and although I would give Mum a small sum from it, the rest I kept for myself, finding it useful for clothes and holidays. I used to send to my cousin Tom for shoes and he would get me a handmade pair for 15*s*. Suits were expensive but mass-produced suits were beginning to appear on the market at £2 10*s*. each. This was the beginning of the 'Fifty-Shilling Tailors'.

My sister Eileen, who had a mass of auburn hair, had left school and got a job with the Royal Arsenal Co-operative Society Lordship Lane check office, where she met her future husband Sidney Major House. I got on well with Eileen and my younger sisters and tried to help them where I could, and I think it was appreciated. It was different with Con, who could be very withering, especially when she took up with Arthur Tilley. Grace kept fairly neutral. She was nearest my age and we shared common interests at the Mission, but I used to find her bossy and resented her telling me what I should and should not do. Eileen learned to play the piano and she and I would often have a sing-song together. When Reg Denner and Sid House joined in the result was something worth listening to. Vera could play the violin and Grace, with her lovely voice, added class to our endeavours. The 'Williams' Sing-Songs' were much appreciated by our neighbours!

In the autumn of 1928 the Co-op commenced a series of evening classes for its junior employees and in a burst of enthusiasm, most of the staff of the Camberwell Green branch went along to the London County Council school in Choumert Road, Peckham, and enrolled. I took two subjects, Bookkeeping at ordinary level, and Salesmanship. If a student completed the course with 80% attendance, the fees were refunded. As the weeks went by the fervour waned and the numbers attending dwindled until only a dozen or so remained. I determined to stay the course.

With the approach of my twenty-first birthday, the family decided I must have a party to celebrate it, provided I bore the cost. I agreed to do so and arrangements went ahead with Mum and the senior sisters doing the catering. It was, in a way, a house-warming too, being the first real party held at No. 14. Most of the folk that came were Mission friends, but the girls invited some of their friends and Mum had a companion in Mrs Blake, who lived in the cottages in Grove Lane. Mrs Blake was the sister of Mrs Purdew, who lived at No. 16, above us. I had absolutely no experience of being a host, or acting as Master of Ceremonies, but somehow I blundered through the evening. Grace sang 'The Children's Home' and 'Nirvana' and we all joined in singing old music hall songs and played silly games. There was plenty to eat and drink. Mum and Dad bought me an oak writing desk which I kept for many years. In the end it was converted into bookshelves. Mrs Blake gave me an inkstand to put on the desk. I received many cards including ones from Mabel Knocker and Eileen Clements, although I did not invite either. A few days later Eileen came to see me and was prepared to renew our friendship. I was still smarting from our last tiff however and was non-committal. We parted on friendly terms and left it at that.

The Co-op had a wage scale for its junior staff and the biggest increase was at age twenty-one. I received an extra 10s. 6d., making my weekly wage £2 15s. 0d. I began to feel quite well-off and eased up on savings, deciding that I needed to widen my horizons. On our half days, Reg and I began visiting places like the British Museum, St Paul's Cathedral or a West End cinema, or played 'Putting' in Ruskin Park. Some Sundays we would go to Box Hill or Epsom Downs. It was a happy, carefree time. He would come home with me or I would go with him. If the weather was unkind we played cribbage; if fine, we would go to an area of common land opposite his home, stick a cricket stump in the ground and spend long periods bowling at it. We became very proficient.

At the end of March, 1929, I sat the bookkeeping examination and the following week had a written and practical test in Salesmanship. I was not happy about my showing in either subject but had the satisfaction of knowing that I had completed the courses and had had my fees refunded.

Adams, the Co-op shop porter, used to run a football pontoon among the staff and their friends. It cost 6d. a week to participate. Teams were drawn out of a hat and to win, your team had to get eleven goals in X number of weeks.

In the early part of 1929 I couldn't go wrong and won several times. In addition to the money prizes there were consolation gifts of tins of fifty cigarettes. I won so many of these that I gave them either to Dad or sent them to brother Reg in India. Reg always replied and thanked me for them. He was always asking if I had a young lady although I wasn't sure if he really wanted to know, or was just filling up space in the letter!

*

Having more or less completed two years' service, both Reg Denner and I were entitled to nine days' holiday. As we were low on the seniority list, holidays in the summer months were not available for us and the best we could obtain were the last three days in April and the first week of May. We scouted round for a suitable resort in which to spend our well-earned leisure. Reg's brother, Jim, knew of an address in Sandgate, near Folkestone, and he sketched in the attractions of the area, like the Hythe canal, the miniature railway, the Leas, Warren and the like as well as the activities around Folkestone Harbour itself. It sounded fine so we wrote to Mrs Flynn of No. 4, Garden Cottages, Wilberforce Road, Sandgate, and asked if she could accommodate us. She replied that she could and we accepted her terms of 35s. a week full board. The East Kent Bus Company had just commenced a daily service to the coast so we booked our seats and waited for the great day to arrive. It was very early in the year for a holiday by the sea and it had been a long hard winter, but we were young and enthusiastic and took things in our stride, and when the great day came we set off in high spirits.

Mrs Flynn made us welcome and we soon began to familiarise ourselves with our surroundings. The weather was far from ideal, being windy and cool, and the area was quiet as the summer season was some weeks away. We spent a lot of time paddling a canoe on the Hythe canal, and travelled to Dymchurch on the Romney, Hythe and Dymchurch Railway across Romney Marsh. This was a miniature railway and the engines were little replicas of the *Flying Scotsman*. The one pulling our coaches was named *The Green Goddess*. Dymchurch in those days was a tiny place and the beach was deserted. The wind swept across from Dungeness whipping up the surface of the sea into countless white caps, and the fine sand stung our faces. We did not stay there for long.

I had trouble with my camera for the shutter kept jamming and one day as we came away from the canal I became so irritated with it that I tossed it over my shoulder in disgust. Reg went to retrieve it and to our surprise we found the hard knock it received from its contact with the ground had, somehow, jolted the offending part back into working order.

We strolled along Folkestone's zig-zag path, explored the wild area of the 'Warren', chatted to the Lifeboatmen and climbed the Martello tower. We went by bus to Dover and explored the castle. One evening the Flynns invited us to the local Star and Garter Home to a whist drive, and Reg was lucky enough to win a shirt. The holiday passed all too quickly and in no time at all we were boarding the coach for the homeward journey.

*

About a month later when I was busy in the shop, one of the check office girls came to me and said I was wanted on the telephone. Telephone calls to, or from, staff were not allowed, and as I made my way to the office to take the call I was very apprehensive, fearing bad news about my family or something equally unpleasant. My hand was shaking as I picked up the 'phone. When a voice at the other end said, 'this is the Staff Manager's Office', it did nothing to allay my fears. The voice went on to say that I had been successful in the recent examination on Salesmanship and I had been awarded a Co-operative Union Scholarship. Congratulations were extended to me and a letter giving details would be put in the post that day. I would be invited to spend a week in Manchester as a guest of the Society with all expenses paid. I was in a bit of a daze when I put the receiver down, but decided to keep the news to myself until it was confirmed. The letter arrived the next morning and I showed it to Collins, the Manager, who went into ecstasies of joy to think that a member of his staff had won one of the coveted awards. He pinned my letter to the notice board for all to see and from then onwards I was his blue-eyed boy. Congratulations came to me from all quarters.

A few days later the Staff Manager sent for me and I made the long ride to Powis Street to see him. He said lots of complimentary things and hoped I would rise high in the Society's service. Unfortunately he never returned my letter. He gave me details of the Manchester visit and when we parted I felt that, at last, things were going my way. As I sat in the tram on my way back to Camberwell I let my imagination wander. I pictured myself rising in the ranks and even becoming a member of the Committee. What an illusion that proved to be.

I set off for Manchester about a week later and at St Pancras Station joined another two successful candidates and we travelled the rest of the way together. At the end of our journey, we were met at the station and taken by car to the Co-operative Wholesale Society's college hostel at Kersall. This was a large square house set in large gardens, with lawns, trees and flower beds. It was sumptuously furnished and had dining, recreation and lecture rooms on the ground floor with sleeping accommodation on the floor above. It was formerly the home of Judge Hughes, the author of the classic story *Tom Brown's School Days*. Much of his furniture was still there and when I wrote home I told Mum that the letter to her was written at the desk used by Judge Hughes to write his story. The house was on high ground and from across the road one could look down on the racecourse, canal and the city's buildings.

From the back garden one could have access to the moor. I was intrigued to see signposts pointing the way to Bury, Bolton, Blackburn, Rochdale and Burnley, places that until then I had only ever associated with football teams.

It was an interesting week. The Co-operative movement was strong in the North and many factories in the area were owned by them. We visited quite a few of them. The margarine factory at Irlam was one, and we watched as they shovelled the product with gleaming spades. Nearby was the biscuit factory at Crumpsall, and in the entrance was a giant clock shaped like a cream cracker. Most intriguing was the tobacco and cigarette works. In one section women were rolling cigarettes by hand with amazing accuracy, at so many to the ounce. One of the ladies saw I was interested and kept weighing handfuls to show me the weight of the cigarette content never varied. The speciality was 'Silk Cut' and these were machine made, cut and boxed, and produced in thousands. In those days 95% of adult males smoked and when I used to refuse a 'fag' I was regarded with amazement.

We were escorted around the factories by the Managers and often lunch or tea would be laid on. Everyone was friendly and any questions put were answered with warmth and kindness. In those few days I came to like the Lancashire people a lot. Back at the college we had lectures and demonstrations and were encouraged to take part in discussions. The meals were excellent and being served by a uniformed waitress was a novel experience.

One day we were taken to Rochdale. In those days it was famous not only for being the birthplace of Gracie Fields but also as the place where the Co-operative movement had its roots. From its small but successful start here, the Co-op eventually spread throughout the British Isles, and beyond. When I went there the 'Pioneers' old store was owned by a chap called Hopwood who sold seeds and pet and animal foods. I believe that since then the Co-op bought the shop back and opened it as a museum. From here we went to Hollingworth Lake and had a boat out, but the water was choppy and the wind cold.

We were allowed one free day and several of the students went on a tour of Manchester. Contrary to popular myth it stayed dry. We saw the home of the original Eccles cake and a maze of cobbled streets. Salford was a poor, slummy area and most depressing. It was not possible to buy a through ticket on the tram so we had to get a separate one to go through Salford. We were all glad to get back to the breezy uplands of Kersall for our evening meal.

On the last night we had a party of sorts, although no girls came to it. We had quiz games, community singing and plenty to eat. The following morning we sang 'Auld Lang Syne' and then went our separate ways. It had been a most interesting experience.

When I returned to the shop I was plied with questions about my stay at the College which I answered to the best of my ability. It created a great deal of interest and not a little jealousy. Shortly after this came the results of the

Bookkeeping exam, in which I obtained a first-class pass. In the ordinary way I would have been entitled to a week away at Brighton, but one was not allowed two scholarship breaks in one year.

*

The Co-operative movement at this time was riding high on the crest of a popularity wave and the membership, attracted by the high rate of dividend, increased all over the country. It increased so much in the London Area that the four Societies, London, Royal Arsenal, South Suburban and Enfield Highway, all reported people joining at the rate of hundreds a week. Our shop found it difficult to cope with the customers who came flooding in and often people were massed six deep in front of the counters causing lots of complaints about the time it took to get served.

The Co-op countered this by opening new branches, and in our own area a new shop was opened in Camberwell New Road, with a chap named Senior in charge. Many of our customers went there and some of our staff, including Sid House, were transferred there. In Walworth, a big store known as 'Grose Bros.' had already been bought and converted into a furniture and drapery emporium and plans went ahead to open a large grocery and provisions shop nearly opposite. When it eventually opened, our manager, Collins, was put in charge. I also went there for about six weeks. A Mr Clarke ('Nobby') took over at the Green. But this was still a few months off.

*

At home, my youngest sister, Pam, was nearly five years old and Denise was nine. I was very fond of my two little sisters and while life for them was a little easier than it had been for us older ones, I felt I would like to give them a little outing. One Thursday afternoon I took them, and Mum, on a visit to the country. We went to Peckham Rye Station and got on a train to Dorking. We alighted at Ashtead Woods and had a little ramble on the common and through the fringe of the woodland. There were some old cottages at the side of the common and in one of them we indulged ourselves by having tea in the garden. It was a small treat but I believe they enjoyed the change of scenery.

In the early autumn I went sick with a severe attack of tonsillitis and influenza and I felt very ill. I suppose the attack of Spanish 'Flu which I contracted just after the war had left me vulnerable to infection of this type. Our G.P., Dr Sansom, ordered me to bed and said I ought to have my tonsils out. He wrote out a certificate for claiming sick pay and I paid for a private certificate to send to the shop.

When one started to pay the 'Lloyd George Insurance Stamp', one had to register with a Friendly Society or an Insurance Company that specialised in the scheme, and claims for sickness benefit were submitted to them. I had joined the St Matthew's Sick and Sharing Out Society, whose offices were at St Matthew's School in Camberwell New Road, near the tram depot. The first three days did not qualify for payment but after that they paid out 15*s*. a week, for about thirteen weeks. Supervision was strict and 'Sick Visitors' would call to see that claims were genuine, and one had to be indoors by 8 p.m. at the latest. Failure to comply with the rules resulted in benefit being withheld.

The Co-op paid sickness benefit to its staff after a qualifying period of six months and subject to receiving a medical certificate within forty-eight hours. This amounted to two weeks on full pay and two weeks on half pay. After that you were on your own. Many staff used to take advantage of the concession and wheedle a certificate out of their doctor for a week or two 'on the panel', as it was called. It was noticeable that few cases of sickness exceeded two or three weeks.

In my own case I had a week in bed then, feeling the need for some fresh air, went for a walk, much against Mum's wishes. I got as far as Ruskin Park and sat down feeling all in. When I tried to stand my head started to swim and my feet couldn't seem to make contact with the ground. It felt just like walking on air. I lost track of time but eventually managed to stagger home. The exertion may have done some good for the next day I felt considerably better and sat by the fire and read a little.

That evening I had a surprise visit from Eileen Clements. She came armed with a bag of oranges and pears, and a look of concern. I don't know how she knew I was on the sick list and didn't ask. I presumed one of the shop lads had told her mother when she came in for her groceries. Mrs Clements had a soft spot for me and I liked her a lot. Eileen and I chatted as if we had parted only yesterday. She told me that her brother, Jim, had joined the R.A.F., and Pete was in the Metropolitan Police. She hinted that her latest romance had ended and she would welcome my company again.

I was at a loss to know what to say or do. Eileen had a special place in my affections and no other girl I knew could approach her in looks and figure. Why, I wondered, had she not pursued a film or stage career, like her father. Up until then she was the most attractive young woman I had met. It had been a year since we had parted on her doorstep following my grandma's death. I had been very bitter about it and had thought some harsh things about the young lady sitting opposite me now. I felt I was immature and instinct told me that she would want to be the boss and would not be content to live on a modest income. I had seen those blue eyes harden, and her voice could be sharp. Even so she could be generous and kind. I had to make up my mind once and for all. That she had great affection for me I did not doubt. We spoke about the Mission and in a haughty tone she referred to it as 'that place!' That was the decider. The Mission was part of my life and I was not going to give it up for her or anyone else. In the end we parted for the last time.

I was away from the shop for two weeks when I asked Dr Sansom to sign me off. He was most reluctant to do so and tried to persuade me to go to the coast to convalesce for a couple of weeks. I should have taken his advice but did not want to lose any money by going on half pay, and in the end he gave me a final certificate. I went back to the rush and bustle of the shop but felt unwell for a long time after.

*

Reg and I gave up our roaming around the countryside during the autumn and winter and we became fairly regular members of Kimpton Choir, which was really a social club, although we did practice once a week for an anthem, or sacred song to be sung at the Sunday evening service. Frank Thompson conducted us and eventually handed over to Ron Gardiner, who was an excellent organist. Now and again I would spend the weekend at Worcester Park and we would visit the local Methodist Church where Reg's brother Jim and his girlfriend attended. We received numerous invitations to parties and socials, and life seemed very good.

Heartened by my success in the exams earlier in the year, I enrolled for the advanced course of Co-op Bookkeeping. For this I had to attend the Society's Rye Lane Office. There were about twelve in the class and the instructor was the clerk in charge of the office. It was very complicated but I plodded on. Unfortunately interest gradually waned and the numbers attending began to fall. One day the instructor, Jock Staughan, announced that because the attendances had fallen below the required number the class was to close. Any of us remaining who wished to continue would have to go to Head Office at Woolwich and join the class there.

I felt that to stop now would mean that all my time and effort would be wasted. Woolwich was an hour's tram ride from Camberwell Green and as the class began at 7.30 p.m. and I didn't leave the shop until 7.15 p.m. I could only make it by leaving the shop before normal closing time. I approached the shop foreman who made it plain that granting time off, even for educational purposes, was not on. I went to Clarke, the manager, and he was equally unhelpful and said I would have to get Head Office consent. Rather angrily, I wrote to the Staff Manager explaining the position and requesting permission to leave the shop at 6.30 p.m. on Tuesdays. To my surprise, and much to the annoyance of the senior staff, my request was granted.

My initiative didn't do me much good for every Tuesday I was given work that forced me to be late leaving. The tram ride to Powis Street was long and bumpy and by the time I arrived I was usually in no mood to concentrate and assimilate the intricacies of advanced bookkeeping. Coming home on a winter's night was cold and boring and it was usually 11 p.m. before I reached home. I would make myself a cup of cocoa, have some bread and cheese, then fall into bed exhausted.

I kept going until the period of Christmas trade, when I was told that I could no longer be given privileges that were denied to the rest of the staff. I was not strong enough to have a stand-up fight with the manager and foreman and in the end decided against continuing the classes. In my heart I knew I should have carried on but the odds against me seemed too much. The Co-op was a good movement, but I decided that all the dictators were not on the Continent - many were employed by the Co-op.

*

About this time I became interested in the 'wireless'. It had come a long way since the time Noel and I had tinkered with the crystal set at his home. Now, one could obtain a valve set that enabled a whole family to listen through a trumpet-shaped speaker. Some of these speakers were encased in square or oblong boxes with patterns resembling the setting sun, clouds or palm trees cut out of the front by fretsaw. For £5, a princely sum, I bought a set off Lambert, one of the provision hands.

Excitedly, I displayed the new toy to the family who were thrilled to think we had joined the privileged classes, and I put the set on top of the kitchen copper, connected the terminals to the battery and accumulator, as per instructions, wound the earth wire around the sink waste pipe, and fixed the aerial around the window frame. In hushed expectancy I switched on. The set's three valves glowed and from the speaker came the traditional melody 'Blow away the mountain dew'. Mum and the girls beamed as we listened to the broadcasts and even Dad was impressed when he came home.

Of course, the copper was no place for the wireless. Its rightful place was in the living-room-cum-parlour. There was a little built-in cupboard at the side of the fireplace that seemed meant for it to stand on. The only power point we had in the flat was in the kitchen but as it was a battery-operated set that was not a problem. However, we had to have the set earthed, so on a Thursday afternoon, Reg Denner and I, armed with a steel poker and our only hammer, tried to make a hole in the brickwork that separated the kitchen from the parlour. Sister Eileen played loud martial music on the piano to give rhythm to our blows. It was a nine-inch thick wall and it took us all afternoon to get through. The hole came out in the lower part of the cupboard, which was ideal. With a red-hot poker we burnt a hole through the top wood and the job was done.

We placed the set in its new home, threaded the earth wire through the hole and connected it up. The accumulator and 120-volt battery were put on one of the cupboard shelves and the aerial was taken out of the window to the waste ground where the old cottages had stood before demolition. Here, against the wall of the Camberwell Baths, a solitary tree had been left standing, and we climbed up and attached the end of the aerial to one of its branches, making sure a china insulator prevented contact with the tree itself. This gave us a good length of reception and when we connected it to the set the results were quite impressive.

The wireless was costly to run. The accumulator lasted about a week before it had to be taken to a battery shop to be recharged, which took a day. I bought another accumulator so that we had one in reserve. Cost of recharging was 3*d*. The battery that supplied the power was a 120-volt Ever-Ready costing 7*s*. 6*d*., which was quite expensive. One had to put plugs into the negative and positive sockets, and two other plugs, known as 'wander plugs' were inserted into other sockets according to the power output required. A battery was only at its peak for about two weeks then its life was quickly spent.

We were now in touch with events as we had never been before and for a while we listened to everything we could. The British troops who had been occupying the Rhineland began to leave for home. A Zeppelin flew to New York and back again across the Atlantic. Britain won the Schneider Trophy from Italy and following a big Boy Scout Jamboree, Baden-Powell was made a Lord. However, the novelty began to wear off after a while and normality was resumed.

Meanwhile at the Mission we were involved in the forthcoming Sale of Work which was scheduled to last three days. A great deal of time and effort went into this sale and it was widely advertised, especially among the local churches, chapels and mission halls, and their support was requested. Mr Pankhurst was the driving force but every Mission helper played their part. Working the hours we did limited the help Reg and I could give but we assisted with the stalls, ran some games and took part in the concert. I sang solo – 'There's a long, long trail a winding' - and Reg and I together sang a duet - 'Where, oh where, do I live'. Grace raised the standard with 'Pale Hands I Love', one of the Indian love lyrics, 'The Children's Home' and 'Nirvana'.

At the conclusion of the sale late on Saturday night, Mr Pankhurst called his workers together for a short service of Thanksgiving. He announced the hymn 'Christian seek ye not repose', which seemed most appropriate when we looked around the hall and saw how much clearing up had to be done to get the halls ready for the Sunday services. I do not remember the exact amount raised but it was well in excess of £100. This money was used to make some essential improvements to the Vestry and the Kitchen. New toilets were installed and it seemed the effort had been worthwhile.

At home we had a letter from brother Reg telling us that his six years in the Army were nearly up and that he would be coming home next year. Everyone was delighted at the news. He told us that he had been promoted to Quartermaster and put in charge of stores and equipment. This was an achievement and we were all proud of him. Before being discharged he said that he had to attend a course, and he had chosen plastering. This didn't sound at all like Reg.

*

Despite the unemployment there was plenty of money around at Christmas and the shop did a roaring trade that persisted right up to Christmas Eve. Like most shop workers, I was glad when the door closed at nine o'clock and I joined the queue outside the Manager's office to pay in the takings. Once outside the shop all trace of weariness vanished and Reg and I sauntered off to No. 14, Stobart Mansions. He gave Mum a gift of a tea caddy and wished her and those of my sisters who were there a 'Happy Christmas' before leaving for his home at Worcester Park.

One by one the rest of the family came in with little presents received from their friends. Nothing spectacular, for times were hard. We were all happy to think we could relax and enjoy the two-day break. There were plenty of greetings cards on the mantelshelf and the postman brought more about 11 p.m. Christmas cards could be bought for as little as one penny and the cost of postage, if the envelope was left unsealed, was a halfpenny. This was known as 'printed paper rate'. The postman used to call for his 'Christmas Box' on Boxing Day and most folk managed to give him sixpence.

Not many people would have been able to afford those little luxuries associated with the festive season were it not for the thrift and loan clubs that operated in pubs and clubs and who paid out their members' savings a couple of weeks before Christmas. We used to put our savings in the Mission's Penny Bank. As usual Mum had been hard at work making mince pies, sausage rolls and cakes, and Grace had been busy decorating the flat with paper chains, tinsel and balloons. We bought 6*d.* worth of holly and mistletoe from a stall in Waterloo Street and put the prickly leaves in vases or around the picture frames. Always optimistic, the girls hung the mistletoe in a bunch from the ceiling, just inside the front door. A good fire blazed in the kitchen range and another in the sitting room. It was the time for roasting chestnuts and peeling oranges, which were cheap at eighteen for a shilling.

Christmas Eve was always a gay time. Eileen would sit at the piano and we would all gather round and sing carols. Mum would sit in the armchair and watch her children enjoying themselves. She usually indulged in a glass of wine and appeared very contented. Neighbours would come by to wish us the compliments of the season and share a glass of whatever was going. Wine did not interest me but to be sociable I would have a glass of Stone's Ginger or Raisin Wine. I used to like cordial, which was thick raspberry- or blackberry-flavoured syrup diluted with hot water. Arthur Tilley came in with Con but Dad did not arrive until Christmas Day.

After the excitement had died down and we had wished each other a Happy Christmas, I retired to bed. I lay for some time unable to sleep. The early hours of Christmas Day were noisy with passers by chatting and singing. The light from the street lamp outside my window cast enough light for me to look around my room. It was a good size and I was fortunate to have it to myself. I had a double bed which Reg Denner and I had to share when he stayed overnight with us. There was an oak dressing table and wardrobe, and a built-in cupboard which contained my few possessions, mainly my books. On the wall over the fireplace was an etching, a brown, sombre scene of a farmworker plodding up a hill. In front of the window was the desk that Mum and Dad had given me for my twenty-first birthday, with Mrs Blake's inkwell on top. From the centre of the ceiling hung an electric light bulb, electricity having been installed in the Mansions earlier in the year.

Although I was usually a sound sleeper, and could put my head on the pillow and fall asleep in seconds, this night's sleep would not come - perhaps the cordial had been over strong. I lay there turning over in my mind what the future had in store for me, and the more I thought the more despondent I became. I felt my lack of education keenly and was desperate to broaden my horizons and to contribute more to my poor fund of general knowledge. My success in the Co-op exams had turned sour and I felt I should break away and do something else, but could not imagine what. Mum relied on the money I bought in. By dint of much self-denial I had managed to save £40 this year, a tidy sum but not enough to launch myself off into unknown waters. There were two million unemployed and much poverty and discontent all around us.

Eventually I dropped off to sleep and the next thing I knew was one of my sisters handing me a cup of tea. It was a good start to Christmas Day and I was soon up and in the kitchen, where one by one the rest of the family began drifting in. Normally breakfast was a hurried meal but today it was nice to sit down together, taking time over our meal and joining in the chat.

No services were held at the Mission on Christmas Day unless it fell on a Sunday. This year it was on a Wednesday, so the Advent Service would be on the 29th. I was like a lost sheep with nowhere to go. I was not wanted in the kitchen where the preparations for lunch were in full swing, so I sat around reading until mince-pie time came at eleven o'clock. This was a family tradition when we drank coffee and regaled ourselves with hot mince pies. The postman came with some belated Christmas cards which we opened and placed with the rest on the mantelpiece and sideboard. I felt a bit low, for outside the family, I had received no greeting cards. I felt somehow that I was missing out on the things that really mattered. I nearly put my coat on to go and visit No. 49 Sedgmoor Place, but hadn't the courage to take the plunge.

Boxing Day came and went and the year drew to its close. On New Year's Eve I was invited to a party at the Knockers', and it made up a little for the dreary Christmas. Mabel was very cool toward me and I couldn't blame her, but I had no wish to renew our old friendship. For me it was Eileen, or no one. And so the bells of St Giles' Church rang in the New Year and we wished each other the traditional greetings and went our several ways through the frosty air of the first January morning of 1930.

Ellen Williams, Len's mother
b. 16 May 1877, d. 23 December 1949

Frederick William Lacey, Len's father
b. 26 March 1854, d. 15 December 1932

Leonard Ernest Williams, aged seven
b. 14 October 1907, d. 5 February 1986

Constance Mary ('Con')
Len's eldest sister
b. 19 September 1903

Eileen Margery
b. 10 December 1912

Audrey Florence
b. 30 December 1915

Iris Denise ('Denny')
b. 19 May 1920

Doreen Pamela ('Pam')
b. 19 November 1924

The view from No. 14 Stobart Mansions, overlooking Kimpton Road

Audrey, Denny and Pam on Kimpton Road

Denny and Minnie the cat, in the yard at Stobart Mansions

Ethel and Frank Halsey's home in Aston Abbotts
(Grandmother Higgs died here in 1930)

Ethel (*left*), Len's mother (*seated*) and Mrs Moon, outside Ethel's home in Aston Abbotts

Three views of Stobart Mansions, Camberwell, the Williams' home from 1910 to 1936. The family occupied three flats in the block overlooking Kimpton Road during this time, nos 21 and 23 on the top floor and no. 4 on the ground floor. The second block overlooked Artichoke Place.

Left, top and bottom: from Kimpton Road; *Right, bottom*: facing Artichoke Place, with Camberwell Public Baths at the far end

© City of London, London Metropolitan Archives; reproduced by permission

The scouts on church parade, outside Kimpton Mission; Stobart Mansions is to the left of the photograph

43rd Camberwell (Kimpton) Scout Troop, outside Kimpton Mission

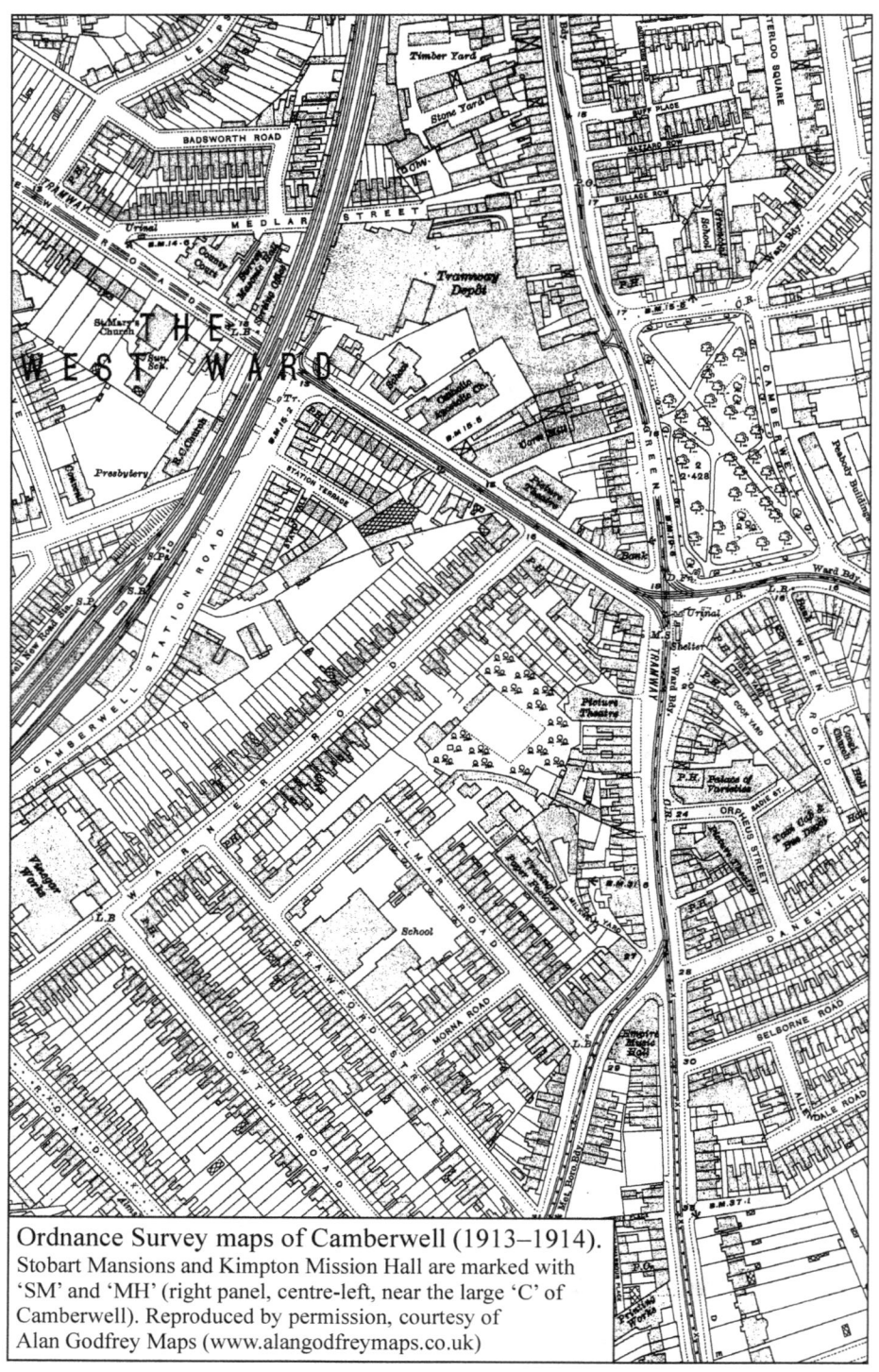

Ordnance Survey maps of Camberwell (1913–1914). Stobart Mansions and Kimpton Mission Hall are marked with 'SM' and 'MH' (right panel, centre-left, near the large 'C' of Camberwell). Reproduced by permission, courtesy of Alan Godfrey Maps (www.alangodfreymaps.co.uk)

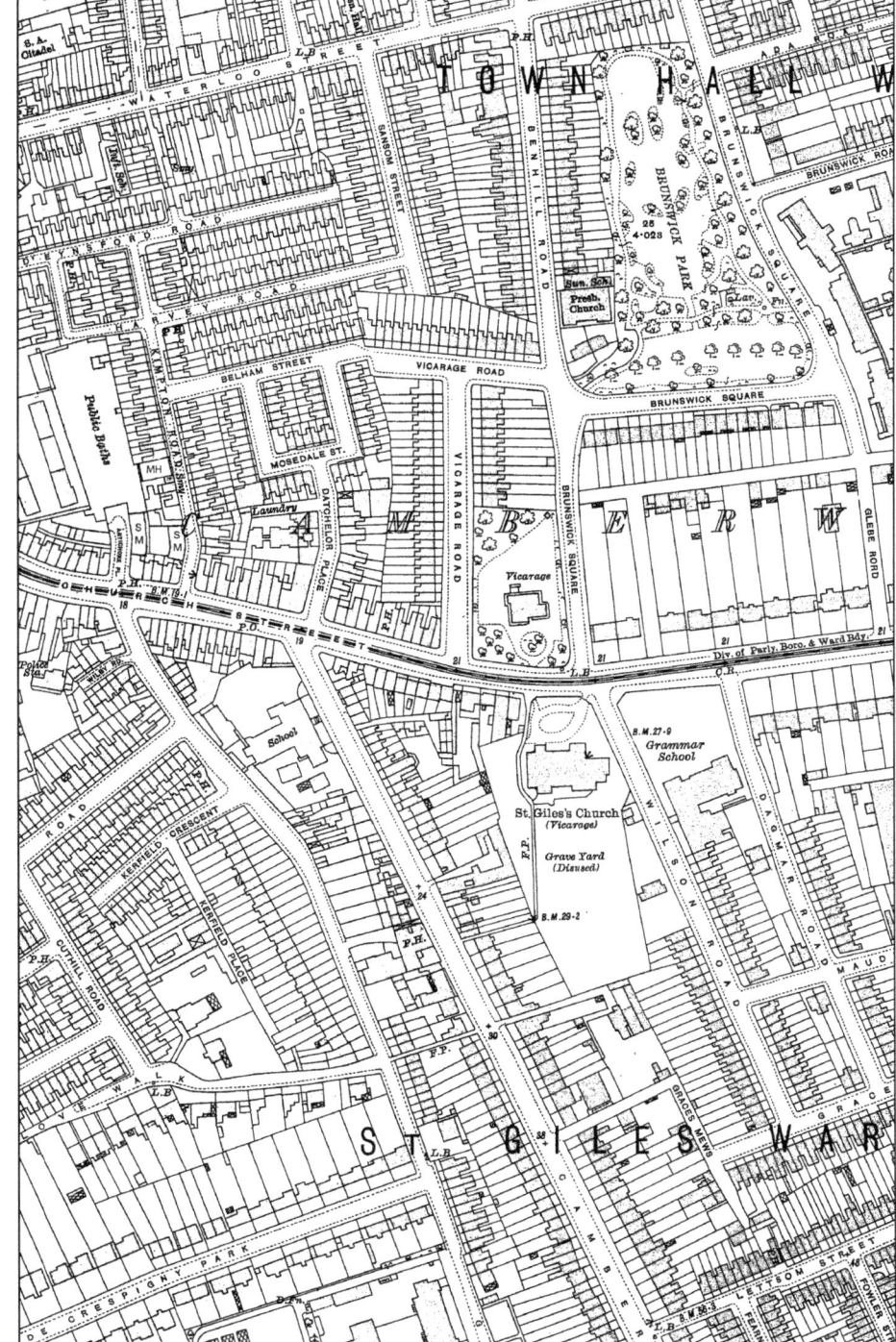

The programme for one the many dramatic productions held at Kimpton Mission

PROGRAMME
OF AN
OPERATIC CANTATA

to be held at

KIMPTON MISSION HALL,
CAMBERWELL,
on
Saturday, December 12th, 1925
in aid of Mission Funds.

Doors open 7.15 p.m.   Commence, 7.45 p.m.

Programme : One Shilling.

THE "KIMPTON" CHOIR
PRESENT

"PHYLLIS"

(THE FARMER'S DAUGHTER)

An Operetta in Two Acts.

Act I.—Scene I.
  Outside Farmer Meadow's House.
Scene II. An Evening Three Days later

INTERVAL.

Act II.—Scene I. Seven Days later.

DRAMATIS PERSONAE.

Phyllis (The Farmer's Daughter) Miss GRACE WILLIAMS
Margaret (Her Adopted Sister) Miss MAY THOMPSON
Farm Girls { Miss LILY WATERMAN
           { Miss DORIS FISHER
           { Miss KATHLEEN NORMAN
Farmer Meadows - Mr. HENRY GLADSTONE
Douglas (A Young Farmer) Mr. FREDERICK MULLEY
Chapleigh (A Dandy from the City)
                          Mr. FRANK THOMPSON
Farm Labourer - Mr. LEONARD WILLIAMS

Accompanist : Miss DORIS NORMAN.
Stage Manager : Mr. EDWARD THOMPSON.

REFRESHMENTS MAY BE OBTAINED AT POPULAR PRICES.

Denmark Hill School, where all the Williams children were educated
(it transferred to Lyndhurst Grove during the First World War)

42 Grove Lane, Camberwell, where the family of Noel Vining, Len's childhood friend, lived until 1939

Grove Lane, Camberwell
Len and Elsie lived at No. 39, Grove Lane 1936–1940

Camberwell Green
Kimpton Road is just around the corner from here

Len, aged twenty

Len, aged twenty-two,
Camberwell Green

Cousin Mary, Uncle Joe, Aunt Bec (Ellen Williams' sister), Denny, Elsie and Pam, at Rushton, Northamptonshire

The Royal Oak, Aston Abbotts
Len's brother Reg was the landlord here during the Second World War, and Audrey and Bill Brooks were the proprietors in the 1950s and 1960s

Elsie Ruth Williams
b. 25 July 1912

Leith Hill Camp, 1930

Elsie, Reg and Hilda
Camp site, near Leith Hill
Whit Monday 1930

Easter 1933

'The Caravan'
Cooke Brothers Field, Nr Abinger Bottom, Leith Hill, Surrey
Whitsun 1935

Wedding Day
7 September 1935
Wren Road Congregational Church, Camberwell

Scout Troop's
Guard of Honour

Len's visit to the premises of the first Co-op shop in Rochdale in 1936, following his Co-op scholarship award

With Elsie's brother Tim
Littlehampton, 1936

Auxilliary Sub-officer, AFS
Peckham 1939

At North London Homes for the Blind
Hanley Road, 1939

WEEK OF ENTERTAINMENT AT BLIND HOMES.

The residents of the Blind Homes, Hanley-road, Stroud Green, have had a week of entertainment. On Friday the members of the A.F.S. Alarm Post stationed at the Homes provided an hour's fun. Auxiliary Sub-officer Len. Williams, of Peckham, was compère, and he contributed songs and choruses with Sub-officer Syd Woods, of Dalston (pianist) and Auxiliary Firemen Alfred Loaden, Will Avey, Frank Bremner and William Wilson.

On Saturday Miss Madge Lebire who reads occasionally to the invalids in the Homes, brought a party of friends and gave a concert. Mr. John Borthwick played the piano and the organ. On Wednesday Mrs. A. Clarke, of Hanley-road, brought a party of friends, who gave an entertainment. Mrs. Stuart presented comedy items, Mrs. Lawler and Mrs. Phipps gave recitations and dialogues and Mr. and Mrs. G. C. Saunders sang duets.

The RAF Intake
Cardington, Beds, November 1940
(Len: centre, back row)

'Mardale', Tollerton, February 1947. Len was billeted here during his RAF service with 60 Maintenance Unit. 'Rockdale', his first billet, is on the left.

With Doreen (b. 11 April 1939) and Brenda (Sylvia, b. 26 March 1942) at 'Evergreen', Three Bridges Road, Crawley

The Williams Girls
Brenda, Janet (b. 15 January 1950) and Doreen

The Williams Family
c. 1952

Len and Elsie
Golden Wedding Day
7 September 1985

Sunshine and Shadow
1930–1935

1930

The New Year was always a busy time for shopkeepers. Most of the larger stores went in for sales to tempt the public to part with any money that might still be in their pockets, and their special offers always attracted large crowds of bargain hunters on the opening day. Some of the catalogues from Selfridges, Gamages and the Army and Navy Stores were quite bulky affairs and must have taken a lot of compiling. The Co-op held its own sales in March and September so at this time its shops went in for a general overhaul and preparation for the half-yearly stocktaking and checktaking from members.

In those days the Co-operative stores owed their immense popularity to the fact that every half year it returned its profits to its members by way of a dividend on purchases. The more a person spent the greater the return. All Co-op societies paid their members a dividend, but the amount varied. The societies in the Midlands and North paid more than those in the South and West. In Newcastle, for example, the dividend was 3s. 6d. per pound. My uncle's society, the Rushden Industrial, paid two shillings whilst the Royal Arsenal Co-operative Society returned 1s. 6d. per pound to its members. It was generally accepted that people in the depressed northern areas were more dedicated to the Co-op than those of the more prosperous southern counties.

The accounting systems, and the way customers kept a check on their purchases, differed too. The most popular system was the 'Climax'. In simple terms this meant that the counter staff recorded, in triplicate, each customer's total spent. One slip was given to the member, the second was forwarded to the Society's record office and the third was retained by the assistant as a check on the till receipts. Each member was given a share number and allocated a page in the ledger, where a record was kept of the amount of every purchase. Each half-year these pages were totted up and the Society's financial wizards calculated, once profits were known, what the entitlement would be. If a member had taken the trouble to retain each till slip they could check the accuracy of the statement they received, but in practice this was seldom done. The Climax was a costly and laborious way of returning the half-yearly surplus to the members.

The Royal Arsenal Co-operative Society had a unique system for giving its members the 'divi', which was based on brass and tin checks. The counter assistant wrote out the amount spent in his check book, making a carbon copy. The customer took the top copy to the check office where it was exchanged for brass or tin checks, depending on the amount spent. The tin checks were in denominations from ½d. to 10s. and were of different shapes and sizes. The 10s. check was oval; the 2s. 6d. check, hexagonal, the 1s. check, round, and so on. Brass checks were round and the £2 check was twice the size of the £1. The tin checks were soon accumulated and could be exchanged at the office for brass ones on the first three days of the week.

Each assistant was given a paying-in book to enter the amount of each day's sales and this, with the takings, went to the branch manager, who checked and signed the book. Next morning the office girls would tot up the check book and report to the manager if the figures did not tally. Any shortages had to be met by the assistant and this was a continual source of worry and irritation, for often the shortage was due to a duplicate check having been written out. The management seldom accepted this explanation and unless one was very fortunate the cause of the discrepancy was rarely found. One used to dread the coming of a check-office girl carrying one's own check book. It was almost impossible to guard against stealing by one's own workmates and although the penalty for this was instant dismissal, it did take place. Keys to the tills were provided but the pace of work made locking them almost impossible.

The first Monday, Tuesday and Wednesday in the months of January and July were the days when members were invited to bring their share passbook and brass checks to the shop. The shop manager would select two assistants from his staff whom he judged as suitable for this clerical work and whose handwriting was reasonably legible. I was one of the assistants selected to do this work and regarded it as a break in the monotonous routine of weighing goods and serving the customers. All the same it was a job that required concentration, and was rather exacting. From the time the shop door opened at 8.45 a.m. on the Monday morning it was non-stop until the door closed at 7 p.m.

A desk of sorts was set up in the grocery shop where my colleague and I dealt with the long queue of people who waited, more or less patiently, their turn. Our job was to examine the member's passbook and write down on a large pink form the name, address and membership number, then count the number of brass checks being paid in and enter the details. The top copy was kept by the member as a receipt and the carbon copy retained by the Society. The brass checks were put into a large biscuit tin. At the end of the day my colleague and I counted the brass checks and the office girls totalled the figures in our receipt books. The following morning checks and books were sent to Head Office.

It was usually 10 p.m. before the counting of these tokens was completed for their numbers ran into thousands. The manager was always on edge until the comparison between the written figures and counted checks had been made. It would have been no use trying to fiddle the accounts to make them balance, for a second check was carried out in Powis Street. Only once did my accounting go awry when I was shown to be about 200 checks short. This was a worry for I prided myself on my accuracy. About two weeks later, Collins, the manager, informed me that Head Office had found the discrepancy and all was well.

I was always glad of the extra money I earned by way of overtime and in the three days this usually amounted to ten hours. All the same, by the Wednesday night I was worn out and used to count checks in my sleep. The weariness was soon forgotten when, on the Friday, I received an extra fifteen shillings or so for the overtime worked.

Whilst my colleague and I had been absorbed in our clerical work, the rest of the staff, in between serving customers, were busily preparing for the stock-take. Every packet, tin and bottle had to be counted and these, and the bulkier items like sides of bacon and sacks of sugar, were entered on stock sheets. At one time the shops closed at 5 p.m. on a Tuesday but in the early 1930s this early closing was discontinued and the shop remained open for normal hours. An independent person, usually a member of the Women's Co-operative Guild, came to the shop to ensure that the number of items entered on the stock sheets tallied with the actual goods. Her job completed, she would sign the sheets as a true and faithful return, collect her fee and depart into the night. These referees were much detested by the staff who looked upon them as ignorant busybodies who could be easily hoodwinked if one should so wish.

After the excitement and frustrations of the check and stock-taking the shop settled back to its routine once again. The manager was always on edge at this time for he had to make periodic visits to the branch office in Rye Lane to agree his trading figures, check all invoices and balance his books. His fear, and one that haunted him for weeks, was that his stock might be short, with all the enquiries that would bring. It was the worst thing that could happen, for a short stock meant rapid demotion. Only once at the Camberwell Green branch was there a short stock, and it was so minor that no action was taken.

Life for Reg Denner and myself appeared settled and orderly, but events were about to change our lives radically. Reg was twenty-one years old whilst I was twenty-two. Neither of us had regular girlfriends. My sisters had often introduced me to their friends but I was wary of getting involved again after my experiences with Mabel and Eileen. My sister Grace was quite sweet on Reg but nothing came of it. Reg and I spent much of our free time together visiting some interesting places like the Tower of London, the British Museum, and Madame Tussauds, to mention a few. Our holiday at Sandgate had been most enjoyable and so we began to plan our 1930 holiday. Two ideas worthy of consideration took root in our minds. One was a trip by barge to Birmingham, a sort of working holiday, the other a hiking trek, so popular in the United States. We decided on the latter.

We purchased a book called *Hiking for Boys*. The fact that our boyhood days were receding made no difference for we were still young at heart and believed that adventures were still to be found if one bothered to look for them. We studied our little volume at great length. It contained a plan for making a tent and one Thursday we took ourselves off to the Scout Shop in Buckingham Palace Road and bought a length of canvas and a couple of thumbsticks.

When we announced our plans to our families they thought we were off our rockers! A hiking holiday in England was almost unknown; it just wasn't done. This only made us more determined to go ahead. Mrs Denner, possibly with some misgivings, allowed us to use her sewing-machine to make our tent. Our efforts were pretty fair and after we had proofed it with a mixture of alum and isinglass, it began to look like a real tent. We proudly displayed our creation to our friends but this just added to their conviction that we must be quite mad. Mum was horrified to think that two clumsy amateurs had probably ruined Mrs Denner's sewing-machine.

However, in the early part of January our holiday plans were subject to all kinds of uncertainties, not just family misgivings. The holiday list at work was not circulated until around Easter time, and as Reg and I were only junior members of staff we were limited as to choice of weeks. Also, there was no guarantee that we would be allowed to take the same time off; in fact it was most unusual for two members of either the grocery or provision staff to be absent at the same time. Ever optimistic, we kept our hopes high and continued to plan our adventure.

One Saturday afternoon in January, during a lull, Reg and I were chatting behind the grocery counter when two girls from Kimpton Mission, Lily Waterman and Hilda Stringer, came into the shop. We chatted for a while and then they invited us to the New Year party being given by the Girls' Life Brigade that evening at the Mission. Like most young men we were always ready to enjoy the fun and free food this promised and we agreed to come along as soon as the shop closed. The girls had not bought anything during their visit to the shop, and I had the feeling that this was no chance meeting and that Reg and I had been singled out for special attention. I pondered on my misgivings for a while then confided in Reg. He, too, had had his suspicions and we awaited the evening's events with interest.

All through the afternoon I thought about the coming evening and try as I might I could not put it out of my mind. It has been said that coming events cast their shadows before them and my psychic senses were alerted. Reg, I knew, had been chatting Hilda up so perhaps some understanding between them could be expected, but I had never considered Lily as a possible date. She and I were, of course, old acquaintances, having gone through school in the same class. We were of the same age and had joined Kimpton Mission at the same time. The family lived in Kimpton Road at, I believe, No. 23. She had an older brother and a younger sister Rose. Her father, like Mr Knocker, was a postman.

Lily Waterman was a very attractive young woman. She had dark eyes and black hair and was very slim. Some time previously she had kept company with Frank Thompson and it had been almost universally accepted that one day they would marry. What happened I do not know but they parted company. In the event Frank married her sister Rose and I often wondered how the family reacted to this change on Frank's part. I suppose I should have felt honoured that she gave me a second thought, but my affections were elsewhere and I still cherished the hope that Eileen and I would come together again.

The shop did not close until 8 p.m. and by the time we had cashed up, made out our paying-in slips and queued up to hand in our takings to the manager, it was 8.30 p.m. The Mission halls were only a few minutes walk away, past the Green and through D'Eynsford Road. When Reg and I arrived the revelry was in full swing and we hung up our hats and coats and joined in. Being two of the senior girls, Hilda and Lily were busy in the Vestry organising the food and making lots of fish-paste sandwiches. We exchanged greetings then went into the main hall to join in the fun and games. The Institute boys who had been invited were a mad-brained lot and Reg and I did what we could to see that there were no casualties to life, limb or furniture. At the meal we sat with our hostesses indulging in idle chatter.

It was as we lined up for the final dance of the evening, 'A-hunting we will go', that Fate stepped in and changed my life for ever. I came face to face with my dance partner, who said her name was Elsie. I was at a loss to understand why we had not met before. She was, most likely, a newcomer and outside the 'inner circle' of senior girls of the Girls' Life Brigade. I thought she was most interesting and left the party in a thoughtful frame of mind. Reg escorted Hilda home but I'm sorry to confess that Lily went completely out of my mind.

Whilst the family were at dinner the following day I dropped a bombshell into the conversation by asking the female members if they knew a girl called Elsie Squires. They stopped eating and looked at me as if I had announced I was joining the Foreign Legion, or something like it. One of them said 'Why?' I replied I had met her at the Girls' Life Brigade party and she interested me. Grace said, 'She's much too young for you, she's only seventeen'. I chose to ignore this comment and repeated my question.

There is one great advantage in having sisters: they know everything going on around them, especially among the female population. I suppose if I'd asked the same question about any local young woman they would have known all the answers. They told me Elsie lived in Harris Street, near to Linda and Bertie Brown; was a newcomer to the Brigade; worked at the Co-op; and had recently lost her young sister.

That evening I went to the Mission service and took my place next to Spud Murphy in the choir. We were the bass part. Reg Denner, when he came, sang tenor, and had a good voice. We sang the 'Homeland' as our contribution to the service. Ron Gardiner was organist and choirmaster. Mr Pankhurst, a real orator, gave the address. He was one of the finest speakers I have heard and could hold his audience spellbound. He was also a very practical man and never spoke above the heads of his listeners. By trade he was a draper and perhaps not too worldly-wise, for some time later his business went bust and it broke him in more ways than one.

I had noticed Elsie come in and sit on her own, and at the end of the Service I went and had a word with her, conscious that my actions were being closely watched by the ladies of the choir, including Mabel Knocker. It did not bother me any but I was not going to rush things, and after a few words left it at that.

The next weekend I went home with Reg to Worcester Park. It was bitterly cold and the water pipes froze. When on the Sunday evening I made my way home, the rail lines were icing up and the live rail sent out brilliant flashes of light as the trains crept slowly towards Vauxhall. Fortunately the tramcars were still running so I was soon back home in the warm.

The shop in winter was cold and draughty. The check-office girls had a little electric bowl fire to keep themselves warm but the shops were unheated. With customers entering and leaving the doors were never closed. There was a rear door at the end of the grocery counter and when this opened an icy blast swept along the counter. My hands would go white as the circulation seized up and I could only get relief by going down to the mess room and plunging my hands into hot water. The shop floor was covered with a composition, pink in colour, looking like linoleum, and each morning was covered with fresh sawdust. It looked nice enough, but the constant treading and the inevitable bits of commodity dropped, made hard lumps form behind the counters. This was agonising on one's feet and periodically we had to chip the lumps away with a garden spade.

One morning when I was fast asleep, Dad came in and woke me up. It was 5 a.m. He told me that the water pipe must have burst for a pool of water was forming on the kitchen floor and was getting worse. Very reluctantly I left my cosy bed, got dressed and went into the kitchen to see what all the fuss was about. There was a small lake on the floor although our pipe appeared to be unbroken. Then I noticed the wall was glistening with moisture, so guessed the cause of the trouble was in one of the upstairs flats.

By present-day standards the Mansions' plumbing was primitive, but no different from most other establishments of the time. There were no storage tanks or radiators, no hot-water systems or baths. A single lead pipe, direct from the main, brought in the supply, and branches from it supplied each flat. By now other neighbours were about and we traced the leak back to No. 21, where the Wrights lived. Some folk said they had heard Mr Wright hammering the water pipe the evening before. Whether that was true I cannot say, but the pipe in the Wright's toilet had a six-inch split in it, from which the water was gushing. Despite all our efforts the split could not be closed and the answer appeared to be to shut off the supply from the main until we could seek out a plumber.

That caused another problem. We could not locate the stopcock. Then someone had the brilliant idea of calling on Mr Collard. On the face of it Mr Collard was the man for the job. He lived at No. 9 in the other block across the yard. He was foreman at Trollope and Colls, the building contractors, whose depot was in Camberwell Road, nearly opposite the Co-op store where I worked. A sleepy-eyed Collard came to see what he could do. The cold was intense and most people returned to the comfort of their flats. Dad, who hadn't a clue about plumbing, went back to bed. I was no better for my education on the subject was non-existent. Soon it was only Mr Collard and myself left to find the hidden stopcock. I relied completely on his expertise. Eventually we located a metal cover and thought our troubles were nearly at an end. When we prised the cover off and exposed the stopcock, we found to our dismay that instead of the usual half-inch head, the one looking up at us was two inches.

Collard looked puzzled and kept looking from the little half-inch water key he was holding to the big square head below. 'Never seen one that size before', he muttered. I was no help. Then I had a bright idea. Why not ask the police for assistance? At the mention of the police, Collard's pinched blue face paled and I remembered that he had had several skirmishes with the law, mainly because of his drinking habits. He could be a very violent man when he had downed a few pints and these outbursts usually took place on a Sunday. One day whilst under the influence, he had smashed up his wife's piano and tossed the splintered pieces out of the window of the flat into the yard below. When he was in one of these tantrums people avoided him like the plague.

Much to his relief I volunteered to go to the police station and explain our predicament. The officer on duty wasn't really interested; he 'phoned around trying to locate a two-inch key, but at 6 a.m. all likely sources of such tools were closed. Almost frozen, I returned and told Collard the police were doing their best. At 8 a.m. I went indoors to get ready for work. The water inside the flat was icing up and everyone was unhappy. Just before I left, a man arrived with a two-inch key. A few disconsolate onlookers watched him slowly turn the rusty tap. Then heads began to appear at the windows. 'Hi', somebody shouted, 'you've turned off the gas!'. Were our faces red.

I went to work with the problem still unresolved. When I came home at lunchtime, I heard that the police had contacted the letting office in Albany Road and had got hold of a plan of the buildings. From this they located the stop-cock for the water supply. This had been cemented over. With the water shut off, a plumber was able to repair the pipe, but it was a long time before the flats were able to dry out.

For some unknown reason the holiday list at work was circulated early. The shop foreman had first choice of dates followed by the first grocery and provisions hands. After them it went to the staff in order of seniority. Reg and I had joined the firm at about the same time so there was no one in between us. With hopeful expectations we put down for the same period, 2 to 14 June. To our delight, Mr Collins, the manager, approved it. We could now go ahead with our plans. One Thursday afternoon we went to the public library in Peckham Road and asked the librarian if we might peruse some Ordnance Survey maps.

Hiking holidays at this time were virtually unknown so Reg and I felt we were blazing a trail, as it were. The librarian waxed enthusiastic when he heard of our plans and soon the three of us were pouring over maps of Southern England. Our new friend advised us to avoid the suburbs and start from a rural railway station. We thought West Humble, the station for Box Hill, Surrey, would suit us, as it was only a few stations from where Reg lived. We planned to make for Ranmore Common and then head for Leith Hill, the highest point of the North Downs. Of course, holidays were still a long way off so we had to contain our enthusiasm and carry on with the routine daily tasks.

About the middle of February I thought I would try my luck and date Elsie Squires, so on Monday the 17th I went to the Peckham Branch of the Royal Arsenal Co-operative Society where she worked in the Tobacco Kiosk. Although the shop closed at 7 p.m. the kiosk was kept open until 8 p.m. It was a fairly busy spot. Buses stopped almost outside and the tram halt was in the middle of the road. Almost opposite was the Kentish Drovers public house and Jones and Higgins, South London's 'greatest department store', and the busy shopping thoroughfare of Rye Lane was within a stone's throw.

I chatted with Elsie for a short while. The odd customer came by for tobacco or cigarettes. Elsie was surrounded by tins and packets of this and that. Player's Weights and Wild Woodbines sold at 4*d*. for a packet of ten. Player's Navy Cut, the most popular brand of cigarettes, were twenty for 11½*d*., and Empire tobacco was 8*d*. an ounce. As the hands of Jones and Higgins' clock moved towards the hour of eight, I plucked up courage and asked her if she would accompany me to the cinema. To my delight she said 'yes'. I waited for her in the doorway of the shop whilst she closed up the kiosk by pulling down the window and bolting it.

There were several cinemas in the area but we decided on the Tower, about half-way up Rye Lane. It was a most imposing cinema with a large entrance hall, marble floor and pillared walls. Usually there were long queues waiting for admission but as the second programme had started we were able to walk straight in. The film showing was *Married in Hollywood*, but I have long since forgotten the plot. When it ended we walked through the quiet streets to her home in Harris Street. We said goodnight and agreed to meet each other at the Mission on Sunday evening.

We met fairly regularly after that and one evening she invited me in to meet her family. I hoped that I made a good impression on them. I took an instant liking to her young brother Thomas (Tim). She had an older brother, George, and an elder sister Doris (Dolly), but she was not at home. I think she worked for a family in Court Lane, Dulwich, and lived in. Her father was a big man who could knock out melodies on the piano although he could not read music. Her mother was a small woman. They made me very welcome.

Thursday 6 March was bonus day. On this day the staff of the Royal Arsenal Co-operative Society received their half-yearly bonus. This was calculated on the wages earned during the half year ended on 6th January, and the amount of dividend declared on purchases. This was 1*s*. 6*d*. in the pound. I believe I collected about £4, quite a good sum in those days. Reg, Sidney House (a fellow worker) and I decided we would celebrate by taking our girlfriends to the theatre. On the advice of a member of staff who was a fairly regular theatre-goer, we plumped for the show at the Hippodrome, *Mr Cinders*, with Sonny Hale in the lead. That evening, with Elsie, Hilda and Sister Eileen, we sat in the circle and enjoyed a thoroughly good night out.[31]

A few weeks later I thought it was high time I took Elsie home and introduced her to my parents. It was no secret that I had been going out with her. It may seem strange to present-day young people that it took so long for them to meet, but in the 1930s the social niceties were entirely different to those of today. Young men were not supposed to date girls until they were earning enough money to be able to save and give the young lady reasonable expectations. There was a strict code of conduct to follow and most fathers held rigid ideas as to with whom their daughters should be allowed to keep company.

At this time I was twenty-two years of age and some of my chums were already married or courting. I believe Ted Thompson and Dolly Hurst were wed. It may have been no secret that I was seeing Elsie but I admit that on that day, 22 March, I found my heart racing as I introduced her to my parents and sisters. I need not have worried for Mum and Dad took to her instantly and later congratulated me on my excellent choice. Having their approval was edifying, although it wouldn't have made any difference had they disapproved.

Elsie and I met each other two or three times a week and on one evening at least we went to the cinema. 'Going to the pictures' was the popular recreation for young and old alike. The great majority of films were in black and white although every now and then one was shown in colour. Talking pictures were around and these made a vast difference for until then we had had to make do with subtitles and a pianist. I think the first talkie of note was Al Jolson in *Sonny Boy* and the two hit songs from this film were 'Climb upon my knee, Sonny Boy', and 'Rainbow round my shoulder'. Walt Disney's Mickey Mouse had ousted Felix the Cat, and into the cinemas came

---

31 The leading roles in Vivian Ellis's 1929 musical comedy *Mr Cinders*, a role-reversal reworking of *Cinderella*, were actually played by Bobby Howes (1895–1972) and *Binnie* Hale (1899–1984). Hale, who played the role of American heiress Jill Kemp, is remembered for her recording of one of the songs from Ellis's show, 'Spread a Little Happiness'.

the mighty Wurlitzer Organ, whose consul was made to rise slowly to the level of the stage in a blaze of coloured lights.

I recall going with Dad to the Brixton Astoria one Thursday afternoon. What the film was I have long since forgotten. The organist was named Pattman and at the end of his recital Dad went to speak to him. They were in conversation for a minute or two and when Pattman and his organ descended from view Dad returned with the news that he had been asked to deputise for Pattman the following week. I did not think this at all unusual as Dad had played all the big London organs, including those at St Paul's Cathedral and the Albert Hall. I am sure he belonged to the Royal College of Organists, and he was also a Freemason, so a good many doors were open to him. He earned quite a bit of money on the side as a relief organist and on Sundays he played the organ at a church in Ascot. It was on one such occasion whilst leaving the church that he had been knocked down by a motor cycle, badly injuring his ankle. Playing at the Astoria was therefore no surprise. What did puzzle me was what he did with the money he earned from these engagements, for we saw little of it at home.

With the coming of better weather, Elsie and I would go for walks as far as the Crystal Palace, and on Bank Holidays we went with Reg and Hilda to Box Hill in Surrey for a ramble. This area had been a favourite place for Reg and I, and now we found it even more picturesque with the addition of female company. We came across a tombstone on the zig-zag path which recorded that a late inhabitant of Dorking was buried there upside down, in the belief that the world would right itself one day.

The days sped away and holiday time drew near. Reg and I went ahead with our preparations and soon we had assembled our gear. There was a violent thunderstorm on the Sunday before our departure and Frank Thompson warned us to abandon the hike if our blankets got wet. Our hiking holiday had aroused a great deal of interest and I think quite a few would have liked to join us. We said our farewells to family and girlfriends and on the Monday took the train to Box Hill. Our packs were quite heavy for we carried food, tent and Primus stove in addition to groundsheets and blankets, and we each grasped a stout thumbstick.

We alighted at West Humble and outside the station turned left for Ranmore Common. It was a damp, sultry afternoon and we panted a bit as we went uphill to the field path that would take us to the woods. The area appeared empty of people but there was abundant wildlife in the fields and daisies and buttercups were dotted about in the grass. It was quiet in the woods. The trees arched overhead, giving a gloomy aspect and making us wonder of we were in for another downpour. We plodded on and glancing down noticed that our shoes were quite wet. Now and then we frightened a pigeon and the loud flapping of its wings disturbed the stillness. Although it was June and the days were at their longest, it began to get dismal and the views started to fade. We sat on a tree stump and ate a sandwich or two and after a short consultation decided to seek out a suitable camp site.

Although the woodland area was vast, finding the right place to pitch our tent proved most difficult. There were plenty of green 'rides' separating the belts of trees, but often these were soggy or uneven or full of nettles. We began to despair of finding a site when we came across a dry area, fairly level, beneath a spreading oak tree. It wasn't ideal but it would have to do, so we cleared a small space of twigs and bits of wood and set up our tent. It was surprising how cosy it looked. We used our thumbsticks as tent poles and pegged the side down with meat skewers. The Primus stove did not pump at all well but after a long time we were regaling ourselves with tea and cakes for our supper.

The only person we had seen since entering the woods was a man on horseback. We nodded to him but he went on his way without speaking. As the light crept from the sky and the surrounding trees took on strange, dark, eerie shapes we decided to turn in, creeping into our sleeping bags and using our folded clothes for pillows. We were soon asleep.

During the night I was woken by the plop, plop of something falling on the tent roof. I couldn't figure out what it was. I looked across at Reg but he appeared to be asleep. It was a strange sound. It couldn't be rain for it wasn't steady enough. I wondered if it was old acorns being dislodged by the breeze, but it didn't seem heavy enough. This strange sound continued through the night but otherwise all was quiet. Next morning when we arose and looked outside we saw all around the tent bits of blackened tree bark, dead twigs and husks of acorns. Reg confessed that the falling bric-a-brac had disturbed his sleep too and like me he had pondered on the cause. Whether this is normal under oak trees I do not know but we decided, in future, to give oak trees a miss as camping places.

The morning was misty and chill and we shivered a bit as we went about preparing breakfast. I suspect we were both thinking that anticipation and preparation were better than realisation when it comes to sleeping out of doors. By the time we had a cup of tea our water supply was exhausted and it was apparent that water would be our main problem. We would have to wash when we found a stream. After a rather unsatisfactory breakfast we took the tent down and packed up our belongings, shouldered our rucksacks, grasped our thumbsticks and set off on our adventures.

Sometime later we emerged from the woods and, more by luck than judgement, came to Ranmore Post Office. We had heard about this place and knew that it catered for ramblers and was a favourite meeting place for clubs exploring the area. It had a small shop and did afternoon teas. We also knew that at the bottom of the sloping field opposite was a footpath that crossed the railway line from Dorking to Guildford. The post office had not yet opened for business so we continued on our way, found the footpath, climbed over the stile and panted our way up the undulating terrain. Somewhere we crossed the ancient Pilgrims' Way that linked Canterbury with Winchester and soon after made our crossing of the railway.

After a while we came across a bubbling stream. This was a welcome sight and after unshouldering our packs, we took out soap and towels and scrambled down the bank to the water's edge. The water was icy cold and I shivered as I splashed it over my face, but it was most refreshing and left us feeling prepared for whatever lay ahead. We set off again, passing a farm before coming to Wotton Church and the main Dorking to Guildford road. Here, on the opposite side of the road, was a lovely olde-worlde inn called the Wotton Hatch Hotel, with wooden tables and chairs set out in front of it. By now the sun was shining and it was very warm. We sat there for a while and looked at the view and studied our map. Sometime later we saw a film in which the hotel was used. I wrote a card to Elsie with our address as 'somewhere in Surrey'.

At one side of the hotel was a metalled road that led through pine woods, past an estate, which, according to a notice, belonged to the Duke of Norfolk, and on into the Tillingbourne Valley. It was a beautiful place, full of the sound of rushing water. Two fountains shot water into the air, which then splashed back into the pools. Bird song was deafening. Half way through the valley we came across a waterfall that cascaded from high rocks and fell with a roar into the water below. At the side of the pool we could see a cave or tunnel which we decided to explore. We took off our packs and as we entered the tunnel we could see that it was man-made, with an arch of brick. The walls were green and dripped with moisture, so after a few yards we deemed it wise to return to the sunshine and fresh air. We continued down the valley and reached a hamlet called Broadmoor, and a couple of farm workers directed us to the Leith Hill Tower.

Some weeks after our morning in the quiet, unspoilt Tillingbourne Valley, the area was the subject of the 'Star Ramble' in the daily newspaper *The Star*. This put the area on the map and hoards of people invaded the area, with all the noise and litter that crowds bring. Soon the local people, for their own privacy and protection, started putting up fences and barbed wire in an effort to contain the mobs, who seemed to delight in annoying them and causing damage to their properties. We were glad to have visited the valley before it was 'discovered'.

Our route to the Leith Hill Tower took us steadily upwards and the air was filled with the scent of pine, for this area appeared to be a vast pine forest. Here and there we came across stretches of open rough land covered with bracken and heather, and the blackened stumps of trees indicated that the ground had been swept by fire in the not too distant past. Then we were back beneath the conifers again. Eventually we emerged from the gloom into the open and saw in front of us the tower that crowned the highest point of the North Downs.

This was our first visit to this famous vantage point and as we stood there and looked out across the Weald to the South Downs, we could appreciate why people went into raptures over the view, and why the tower was built.

The midday sun lit up the fields and glittered on the distant water. Here and there were dark areas of woodland and light patches of meadow where sheep and cattle grazed. Tiny ribbons of road snaked their way among the fields to disappear from view behind thick hedges. In the far distance the hazy blueness merged with the misty curves of the South Downs on the skyline.

A yard from where we stood the ground fell away sharply, rugged and rock-strewn, to a road, and almost three hundred feet below was the red roof of the Leith Hill Hotel. I took out a camera and tried to get a picture of the view, with the hotel as the centre point. The tower, and five acres of surrounding land, belonged to the National Trust, and a woman inside the tower doorway told us that for $2d.$ we could climb to the top. The steps led to a square roof surrounded by a low parapet. In the centre of each side was an indicator board showing the distances and pointers to various landmarks.

If the view had been good from ground level from here it was stupendous. To our left were the pine-clad hills of the North Downs and to our right was Box Hill and the village of Coldharbour, two miles away. We could see the sun glinting on the towers of the Crystal Palace, reminding us of home. We followed as best we could our route that morning from Ranmore Common. Most impressive of all was the vast expanse of woodland. Leith Hill is 965 feet above sea-level and the height of the tower increased this to over 1,000 feet.

The lady custodian sold us each a glass of lemonade for $2d.$ apiece and told us about a little general store about half a mile away where we could replenish our supplies. She showed us the path to take and we threaded our way through the gorse bushes and bracken. The little path sloped steadily downwards skirting Leith Hill Place - a pleasant country residence, home to the composer Vaughan Williams - until it ended at a crossroads. Nearby we saw the little shop and went in.

It was a typical village shop, untidy, dark, but well stocked with all the necessary goods ranging from potatoes and tinned fruit to pins and buttons. A couple of ladies were being served so we waited and looked around. On a notice pinned to a shelf were the words 'Camping Site'. When the other customers had left, the proprietor, a large country-looking gentleman, came to attend to us, and very soon we were chatting as if we had know each other for years. He told us his name was Albert Cooke and that he was in partnership with his brother. They had taken over these premises, formerly a blacksmith's shop, and had opened it to sell groceries and provisions when they were discharged from the Army.

We enquired about the camping site and he told us that he and his brother had purchased a large field in the middle of the pine woods for £1,000. They hoped that one day they would build some superior houses on it but in the meantime they had decided to let it for camping, although, so far, no one had used it. Reg and I decided we would be the first.

The cost of pitching our tent was $1s.\ 6d.$ a night and as we liked the look of the area we decided to book for two nights. We gave 3s. to Mr Cooke and purchased some supplies from him. Although the prices were higher than back home we felt that transport costs were more expensive. In any case, we were on holiday and not too bothered about a few extra pennies. Friend Cooke came to the door of his shop and gave us some very confusing directions to the field and told us of a nearby house where we could obtain water.

It was a scorching hot afternoon and as we plodded up the road the heat shimmered over its surface. Our packs seemed to get heavier and heavier and after about a mile we began to wonder if the camping field really existed. Eventually we found Broadmoor Road and the gate to the field, which we opened and entered. It was a lovely area with pine woods on three sides and a gentle slope downwards. Over the years the hedge had grown inwards and the mass of bushes and saplings, with their feet in a haze of bluebells, isolated the field from the road and ensured complete privacy. The air was heady with the scent of pine and the droning of the bees was everywhere. We fell in love with the place straight away. We found an ideal place to pitch our tent and soon we were unpacking and making ourselves at home. Once settled we went to the nearby house where Mr Cooke had suggested we get our water. We knocked and asked for our canvas buckets to be filled, but as we did not get a very welcome response we decided in future to find an alternative supply.

We built ourselves a fireplace by digging a small trench and lining it with stones. There was dry timber in abundance and an endless supply of pine cones. Soon our billycans were boiling and we were regaling ourselves with tea, eggs and bacon, and tinned fruit. Life was good. After we had washed up we decided to explore our new surroundings and made our way out of the field by the gate on the further side that was almost lost in the overgrown greenery of the hedge. We crossed a couple of fields and came to the hamlet of Abinger Bottom. A spring of water issued from a wall to join a spring that meandered across the lane. The water was clear and fresh. Here was our water supply.

That night we slept the sleep of the just. It had been an exciting and exhausting day. Fate had been kind in directing us to this lovely spot. When we awoke next morning the sun was blazing down and it was warm and still. Wood and coppice were alive with bird-song and as we prepared breakfast we decided, by mutual consent, to hike no further but spend the rest of our holiday right here.

The following Monday was Whitsun bank holiday and we thought it would be an excellent idea if our girlfriends could come and spend the day at our camp. Leaving everything where it was, we set out to go to Dorking. We found a path that led to Broadmoor village and were soon back in the Tillingbourne Valley. At the Wotton Hatch Hotel we boarded a bus into Dorking. At the main Post Office they told us that letters could be addressed to us there and we could collect them. Postal services in those days were quick and efficient and we knew there was time to write a letter and receive a reply by Saturday.

When we returned to camp we had our meal and continued our exploration of the surrounding area. There were numerous paths, most of which led to the tower on Leith Hill. The area was alive with rabbits which darted across our path, but we were never successful in catching one. The sun continued to blaze down with a tropical intensity and my arms, unused to so much exposure, began to swell to almost twice their size. At first I hoped that I could be developing bigger muscles but at night they began to itch and I tossed and turned trying to get some relief. We hadn't bought any first-aid equipment with us, which was not very far-sighted, and the only thing I could find was my tube of Shavex, a brushless shaving cream. I smeared some of this on my red-hot arms and to my joy it acted as a palliative and gave me quite a bit of relief. I decided that in future I would keep my arms covered in hot sunshine.

Next morning we strolled down to the shop to see friend Cooke. We told him how pleased we were with the site and that we had decided to spend another week there. We stocked up with supplies, enough to see us over the weekend, and made our way back to camp. Over the next few years I became very friendly with the Cooke brothers and recommended their camping site to many friends. When Reg and I formed the 43rd Camberwell Scout Troop we held our first camp here. In time a couple of caravans were installed and piped water laid on. The young folk at the Mission had two Easters here, the girls occupying the caravans and the lads sleeping under canvas. Elsie and I were guests of the Cookes on one occasion and we corresponded with each other until the outbreak of war.

The lovely weather continued and we lazed about, consumed lots of eggs and bacon and fried bread, and drank innumerable cups of tea. In the cool of the evening we would stroll to the tower and chat to anyone around. There was always someone there, for the tower acted as a magnet and was a regular meeting place for rambling clubs. We visited Coldharbour Village but it wasn't at all exciting. A bus linked the village to Dorking but it was a very infrequent service.

On Saturday morning we made our way to the Dorking Post Office to see if any mail had arrived for us. To our delight we were handed a letter apiece. Our girlfriends said they would come to see us on Monday. We went around the shops and bought some extra goodies including some fancy cream cakes, which became pretty soft by the time we got them back. Keeping food fresh in the terrific heat was a problem but we did our best by wrapping it up and hanging it in a tree.

We visited most of the hamlets and villages within walking distance. The area was very wild and one could stroll for miles through forest and rough country. Friday Street was an interesting place but it swarmed with hikers on the Sunday. Leaving the heights we walked into Ockley but didn't like it much and after that kept to the Downs.

Monday morning we rose early, had breakfast, tidied up the camp and set off to Dorking North station to await the arrival of the girls. They must have left home early for we didn't have long to wait. We boarded a bus outside the White Horse Inn in the High Street and soon arrived at the Wotton Hatch Hotel. The girls appeared to like the area as much as we did and were quite delighted with the fountains and tumbling waters of the Tillingbourne Valley. It was about an hour's walk to our camp but by now we were familiar with the little-used paths and found the field without any problem.

It didn't take long to get the fire going and we were soon chatting over a cup of tea. The glorious weather continued and we had to eat our meal in the shade of the trees. After lunch we took the girls to the Tower and climbed the stone stairs to the observation platform. We lazed on the green by the Tower and looked out over the fields, hills and woods. The time sped away and reluctantly we had to leave to return to the camp. We had a lovely tea with salad, tinned fruit with evaporated milk, and the iced cakes, which had somehow survived in the heat.

Then it was time to see our girls back to the railway station and we set off on a path we had discovered that avoided the stony track used by the ramblers. It ran along the hill and dropped down behind the cottages of Broadmoor Village. From there a well defined path took us through the valley to the hotel, where we boarded the bus. We said our farewells on Dorking North Station and watched as the train clattered on its way, eventually reaching Vauxhall where the girls would alight and get a tram or bus to Camberwell Green.

By the time Reg and I reached the Wotton Hatch Hotel it was dusk and we left the tarmac road and entered the darkness of the trees. Our feet crunched the gravel of the rough path but we could hardly see a yard in front of us. The air and the undergrowth rustled with unseen creatures and the noise of rushing water was everywhere. It was still warm and the smell of the pine woods was almost overpowering. In the darkness we must have walked quickly for in no time at all we were climbing the path at the back of the village.

We slept late the next morning and when we emerged into the open the sun was already high and the heat hit us like the blast from an oven. I went off to get the water while Reg began the cooking the bacon. Tomorrow, Wednesday, was the end of the week we had booked here. The question was, should we pay for a couple more nights? Somehow the visit by the girls had disturbed our routine and now the place did not seem quite the same. By mutual consent we decided that tomorrow we would break camp and return home and spend a day or two on excursions to the coast.

That evening we made our last visit to Leith Hill Tower. It was very quiet now for the crowds of the weekend had left. The South Downs were lost in the heat haze although the sun still flashed on the distant towers of the Crystal Palace. As it became dusk the bats began to fly around us. We felt very privileged to have enjoyed such a lovely holiday in such wonderful surroundings.

Next morning we went to the village shop and said our farewells to the Cooke family. They seemed genuinely sorry to see us go and said we were welcome at any time. We shook hands all round, expressed our thanks and said we hoped to see them again. Then it was back to camp for our final meal there. Our supplies were now exhausted, so we took our tent down, packed our blankets and billy-cans into our rucksacks and tidied the site. Apart from the flattened area of grass there was nothing to show of our nine-day occupation. We shouldered our packs, grasped our thumbsticks, took a last look around and said our thanks to the field and trees. It had been a holiday that far exceeded our expectations and one we would never forget.

When we reached home our families were surprised to see us. We spent the last few days of our holiday on day trips out. We took a coach to Margate and won a couple of teddy bears at the pin tables in Dreamland, and spent a day at the Tower of London. But these attractions could not compare with the peace and quiet of the field among the pine trees, where the only sounds to be heard were made by the birds, insects and woodland creatures.

As a boy I was absorbed in travel and adventure stories, whether fact or fiction. In my imagination I had accompanied explorers to both the Blue and White Niles, paddled along the Colorado River and braved the Congo. I had a good imagination and one of my most often read books was Conan Doyle's *The Lost World*, which told of group of British explorers and their discovery of a land of prehistoric animals in a remote region of South America. Ted Thompson and I had often discussed the story when he received a super illustrated copy of the book as a school prize in 1921.

Sir Arthur Conan Doyle was a gifted man in many fields but I think his Sherlock Holmes stories were the most widely known of his literary works. I felt very sad when the news of his death was announced in the papers on Monday, 7 July. In his later years, Conan Doyle had become intensely interested in Spiritualism and when it was stated that a memorial service would be held in the Albert Hall on Sunday, 13 July, I felt I would like to go along. Elsie agreed to come with me and although we had no tickets we had no difficulty in gaining admission to the packed hall.

The service was conducted by the Marylebone Spiritualist Association. An air of suppressed excitement filled the hall. There were hymns and short addresses, one given by the journalist Hannen Swaffer, who wrote for the *Daily Herald*. The highlight of the evening came when Mrs Estelle Roberts, Doyle's favourite medium, gave spirit readings to members of the congregation. The one that caused the most stir came from the dead suffragette who had thrown herself under the hooves of the horse in the Derby. We did not quite know what to make of these spirit messages, but felt that a solemn occasion had been used to bolster the cause of spiritualism.

Many other things were happening in the world outside our little circle. Henry Seagrave was killed in his boat *Miss England II* in June, whilst attempting to create a new water speed record. Sir Thomas Lipton made another unsuccessful bid with *Shamrock V* to wrest the Queen's Cup from the Americans. Airships were still regarded as highly important factors in aviation. Germany's Zeppelin had already flown to New York and back, and Britain had launched two airships, the R100 and R101. The first was very successful but the latter was wrecked at Beauvais, France, on 5 October, whilst en route to India. However, most events took second place in the public's imagination to the news of the solo flight to Australia by Amy Johnson. It took her nineteen and a half days and earned her a place in the record books. A more modest event, but one that nevertheless won fairly wide approval, was the decision by the First Commissioner of Works, George Lansbury, to allow mixed bathing in the Serpentine in Hyde Park.

An insignificant event, but one which became an important factor in our lives, took place when Miss Boothby, a Sunday School teacher, asked the Mission Council for permission to start a Wolf Pack. Since the Boys' Life Brigade had disbanded in October 1925, there had been little social activity for the Mission boys, who on reaching school leaving age mostly drifted away. There was an 'Institute' but it wasn't very popular. The Council readily gave their assent and Miss Boothby set about forming her Pack.

In July the Girls' Life Brigade went on a couple of weeks' holiday to Edgeware in Middlesex. In those days this was still an area of countryside. They stayed at a place called 'BoLoBo', whose owner was evidently a member of the Boys' Life Brigade. On the Thursday, Reg and I went along, as it was visitors' day. We were made very welcome, but the main purpose of our visit was to see Elsie and Hilda. There wasn't much time but we made the most of it. The day after our visit it was Elsie's eighteenth birthday, but I cannot recall what present I gave her.

When the camp was over we resumed our normal routine of visits to the cinema and each other's homes, and evening walks around Dulwich and Peckham Park. With Reg and Hilda we would sometimes make a foursome and go to places like Box Hill. In the middle of August, Elsie and her sister, Dolly, went on a week's holiday to Brighton. And so the weeks and months slipped away. Our lives were centred around the Mission, which we attended most Sundays, although every now and then we would visit other places of worship. At this time I was interested in the British Israel movement and gave a talk about it on 17 November, in the Vestry at the Mission. I'm afraid I made no converts and with the coming of Christmas was too busy with work to pursue it further.

I think Christmas that year was one of the happiest I have ever spent. I was twenty-three, Grace was twenty, Eileen was eighteen, Audrey was fifteen, Vera was twelve, Denise was ten and Pam was six. Con was engaged to Arthur Tilley and they were due to get married the coming year. Brother Reg was expected home from India during 1931. It was a family any parent could be proud of but I sometimes wondered if Dad really appreciated his children. He still continued to work but his business and where he worked were never discussed with us. Now that several of us could contribute to the family purse Mum must have found life a little easier financially. I once saw Dad, one Friday evening, pass Mum her weekly allowance, and it was £2 10s. I thought how little it was to manage on for the rent of our flat was one pound a week and three children were still at school, but I said nothing. I gave approximately half my wages to the household budget.

On Christmas day we exchanged presents and tucked into the good food. As usual, we had an aitchbone of beef, never a turkey, plus all the trimmings, roast and boiled potatoes, Brussels sprouts, parsnips and sausages with Christmas pudding and mince pies afterwards. Grace liked to superintend the cooking and serving and I think Mum appreciated taking a back seat for once. Friends would call in during the evening and there was always a full house. We used to sing songs around the piano and perform our party pieces to help the festivities. I believe I went to see Elsie and bring her home for the evening. I remember returning after seeing her home and not meeting a single person, although much merriment came from the houses I passed. Usually there was somebody about, however late, but on this occasion the streets were empty.

And so the year of 1930 drew to its close. It had been an eventful year. In it I had met my future wife and had a memorable holiday with Reg. I was beginning to look ahead and plan the future, and the outlook appeared to be favourable.

1931

The year 1931 started off quietly enough. There were the usual end-of-year parties and Watchnight services. Mum liked going to the latter and would attend the one held at Wren Road Congregational Church. The New Year parties kept the Christmas spirit alive for a little longer and I used to think how dull the winter would be without them. However, once past, the old routine began again.

At the shop it was business as usual and I was once more busily engaged in the check-taking from Monday, 5th, and took no part in the stock-taking. By the time Wednesday night came I was glad to get to bed. With the check- and stock-taking over, the goods came piling into the store ready for the weekend shoppers. The manager worried about his stock sheets and made numerous visits to the Rye Lane office to ascertain whether his shop had made the necessary profits. Around this time I was made shop steward and was responsible for collecting union subscriptions as well as attempting to keep harmony between staff and management. I received one shilling in the Pound commission on the money I collected. Once a year I was invited to a shop stewards' dinner and dance. Reg used to come with me but I had to pay for his ticket.

One of the conditions of employment' when entering the Society's service was to join, and remain, a member of a Trade Union. Anyone whose membership lapsed through non-payment of contributions lost their job. As both management and staff were bound by the same rules, one would have expected little friction between them, but most managers and shop foremen appeared to resent paying union subs and the shop steward was not popular. Looking back I can see that taking over the job of union representative probably worked against me, and may have contributed towards my lack of promotion, despite the fact that I was certified, hardworking and dedicated.

However, life continued fairly evenly and Elsie and I continued to meet two or three times a week. We decided to have a week's holiday together and booked into Mrs Flynn's Guesthouse at No. 4, Garden Cottages, Sandgate, from 7 June. Reg and Hilda had booked up there a week or two before us. About the middle of April, Mrs Squires came into the shop and informed me that Elsie had been taken to St Giles' Hospital with appendicitis. This had me worried. In those days it was a major operation and the resultant death toll was high. I went in to see her as soon as I could but visiting was very restricted and each visitor could only have a few minutes by the bedside. As well as her family, and myself, most of the Girls' Life Brigade members wanted to visit her too. Fortunately, all went well and she was discharged on 7 May with the recommendation that she have a period of convalescence.

It was about 20 May that she went away to Hastings for two weeks to a place I believe was called 'The Hermitage'. I was able to visit her there, and we spent the day strolling over the Downs to Fairlight Glen. I was most happy when her convalescence was over although it so happened that within a few days of her return home we were off on our holiday to Sandgate. It was a quiet place with little entertainment but the town of Folkestone was only a mile or two away and there was plenty to see and do there. A popular place was the Leas Cliff Hall, perched high in the cliffs and facing seawards. The Leas was a grassy stretch of land between the hotels that lined this part of the sea front and cliff edge. Here was the bandstand and numerous seats for lazing and listening.

The beach was mainly shingle and stones. The sand was to be found on the further side of the harbour, under the railway bridge and through the fish market. Here little kiosks displayed for sale saucers of cockles, mussels, whelks and winkles. At the end of the fish market was the half moon of soft sand, a favourite area with the children who delighted in building sand castles and digging channels to the water's edge. To the right stood the pier, where cross-Channel steamers sailed back and forth to the French port of Boulogne. A series of arches beneath the road that ran along the sea front was a favourite place to shelter whenever it rained.

At the end of the spit of sand were broken cliffs and on top of these a golf course had been laid out. There were three Martello towers here, just a few of the remaining towers built along the south coast when Napoleon and his armies threatened to invade. These round buildings had a central pillar which supported the cannon mounted on the flat roof. Of the three here, one was on land belonging to the golf club, another was used by the local scouts and the third was left for the public to explore, which we did.

Behind this area was a wild stretch of country known as The Warren. The railway line between Folkestone and Dover crossed part of this area before disappearing into a tunnel. One day, in a spirit of adventure, Elsie and I decided to walk through the Warren to Dover. It didn't look very far and the pier at Dover was visible from Folkestone. At first there were numerous paths leading to the waste land, but gradually, one by one they began to fizzle out, until we found ourselves scrambling over huge boulders or skirting around towering rocks. At one point we found ourselves on the edge of a sheer chasm. We had no option but to scramble up the cliff above us. I was really worried. Elsie was only now recovering from her operation and I feared the worst. Thankfully we reached the top without incident.

Fortunately the worst was over and we carried on, but Dover seemed as far away as ever. As we walked we came across a level area covered by an encampment of rude huts and tents where families and their animals were living. I particularly remember one woman making something on a treadle-operated Singer sewing machine. When we reached Dover it was 8 p.m. and we vowed 'never again!' We managed to board a bus bound for Hythe and were soon back in the parlour of No. 4 Garden Cottages, where we played records on a wind-up gramophone.

Another day we visited the Romney, Hythe and Dymchurch Railway, a passenger railway but in miniature. The train rattled and bounced over Romney Marsh and across little bridges that spanned the dykes. Periodically the driver would loose a blast on his whistle to scatter the sheep from his path. Only Dymchurch had anything of interest and its connections with the mythical Dr Syn somehow gave it an air of mystery and romance.[32] Otherwise the area was rather dull.

As with most holidays, this one passed all too quickly and we were soon saying our goodbyes to Mrs Flynn and heading for the coach to take us home. The following day we were back to the old routine. At work the busy period of check- and stock-taking would soon be upon us and at home the marriage of my eldest sister, Con, and Arthur Tilley was to take place on 22 August. The rift between my sister and I was as wide as ever, in fact her scathing tongue did nothing to improve matters. As the day approached, Dad came to me and asked if I would bury the hatchet, but I refused and said I would not be attending the ceremony. Looking back I can see how easy it would have been to bring this quarrel to an end, but there it was. I knew Mum and Dad were upset but I had made up my mind. When the day came I went to work as usual. At the ceremony Dad played the organ but I understand he left soon after.

That year the Royal Arsenal Co-operative Society employees broke with

---

32 Dr Syn was the hero of a series of novels by Russell Thorndike (1885–1972) beginning with *Doctor Syn: A Tale of the Romney Marsh* (1915).

tradition and instead of having their annual outing to Bostall Woods, near Woolwich, the organisers hired a special train and chose a new venue, Margate. Elsie took her mum and dad and I managed to get a ticket for my mother. This change of venue proved to be a popular move and thereafter, until the outbreak of war, the annual outing was always to a seaside town.

I believe it was around this time that trolleybuses were introduced to London. They were reckoned to be the quietest and most comfortable of all passenger-carrying vehicles. They were, however, confined to North London and we never saw them south of the Thames. By all accounts they were not popular with the London Fire Brigade because of the network of overhead power lines.

The effect of the Wall Street Crash in America was beginning to have an effect throughout the world, and businesses began to close, putting millions of men and women out of work. A world depression followed. The Labour government fell and was replaced by a National Government under Ramsay MacDonald of 'kiss me Duchess' fame.[33] There were cuts in the wages of the armed forces and the civil service, police force, fire service and the like. Unemployment soared to nearly three million. There were savage income tax increases and nearly all workers became liable to pay it.

Up until then I had been exempt from income tax as I was earning just under £3 a week. Now I found myself liable for about £6 a year, to be paid in two instalments, three quarters in April and one quarter in October. When I received the tax demand I took it to Dad, who often boasted of how his friends managed to diddle the taxman, and asked him if there was anything I could do about it. He took one look at it, handed it back and said, 'No, you'll have to pay!' I felt shattered for I had really thought he could help me find a way out of parting with two weeks' hard-earned pay.

Elsie and I continued to have our weekly visit to the cinema despite the blood-sucking taxman. There were plenty of picture houses locally - the Grand Hall in Camberwell New Road; the Golden Domes and the Empire on Denmark Hill; the Purple, Montpellier and Gattis in Walworth; and in Peckham, the Tower and Annexe in Rye Lane; Queens Hall in the High Street, and a couple more whose names I have now forgotten. In addition to films, many put on stage shows or had a Wurlitzer organ that rose into view in a blaze of coloured lights. The largest cinema in South London was built at the Elephant and Castle and called the Trocadero.

One Sunday afternoon, Elsie, Reg and Hilda came to tea with us at No. 14. During the course of the meal Reg informed me that Miss Boothby had asked him to form a Scout troop at the Mission. I was most surprised, for Reg had no experience in this direction. He added that he would accept if I came in as his assistant, and after some discussion I agreed to support him.

---

33 Ramsay MacDonald is reported as having uttered these words ('Tomorrow every Duchess in London will be wanting to kiss me!') on 25 August 1931, after forming the National Government. The source is Viscount Snowden, *An Autobiography* (London: Nicholson and Watson, 1934).

Elsie and I had been going out together for over eighteen months and now seemed the right time to place our relationship on a permanent basis. My first impression of her had been proved right and she had exceeded my highest expectations. She was kind, generous and unselfish, and I was certain she was the girl I would like as my life's partner. I do not remember now how the subject came up although it was probably uppermost in both our minds, but the outcome was that we decided to become engaged. At this stage I did not ask for her father's permission nor did I mention it to my parents. I was approaching my twenty-fourth birthday and Elsie was nineteen, so we were old enough to make our own decisions and ask permission later. Many of my old chums from schooldays were already married with children.

Since my childhood I had had a horror of poverty and all the miseries that resulted from it. Looking back I could well remember the hopelessness in the faces of the men and women, the hungry, ragged children, the queues for stale bread and the Monday morning line of women waiting outside the pawnbrokers to pledge the few family possessions. I had seen many marriages wrecked because they got off to a bad start with money borrowed to pay the wedding expenses, homes set up on hire-purchase and the consolation sought from a bottle. This way was not for me. Ever since I had first started work I had always tried to live within my income and put a few pence away in the Post Office bank. Elsie was of like mind and was thrifty too without being mean. We agreed to avoid paying on the never-never if it could possibly be avoided. As we discussed the future we estimated an engagement of two years. In the event, because of circumstances beyond our control, our marriage was to be four years away.

We decided to get engaged on my birthday, 14 October. In those days I was still keen on astrology and decided to calculate whether this was an auspicious date for such an occasion. In the event it appeared that the 14th was unsuitable but that the following day, 15 October , contained excellent aspects in the field of matrimony. Elsie was agreeable and so the 15th was the day on which we would purchase the ring and make our pledge to each other.

It so happened that 15th October was a Thursday when the shop closed for the weekly half day. Elsie managed to get the afternoon off and we met after lunch and took a No. 34 tram to Brixton, where the shops closed on a Wednesday. The Government had recently announced that Britain had abandoned the Gold Standard and the precious metal market was in turmoil. Until now the Pound Sterling had been linked to gold but now it would fluctuate like most other currencies. No one really knew how this would affect living standards but the cost of diamond rings was certain to increase.

We left the tram in Gresham Road outside the Police Station, and crossed to the further side of Brixton Road where a new parade of shops had recently opened. One of these was James Walker, a branch of the jewellery chain. Inside, the assistant showed us a tray of engagement rings. Elsie made up her mind quite quickly and selected a three-stone diamond ring in a cup setting. It was a modest little ring and whilst I would dearly have loved to buy her a more expensive one she seemed quite content with her choice.

When we returned to Camberwell we went to my home first to break the news. Mother did not seem surprised and welcomed Elsie to the family. Dad was equally pleased. I do not recall my sisters' reactions but I do remember Eileen being the most enthusiastic. We went on to Elsie's home where she proudly displayed her ring.

There was no engagement party or presents. People around us did not have the money to indulge in such luxuries. Times were very hard and getting enough to eat took priority. Only the upper classes could afford to spend lavishly and they were good days for the wealthy. For the vast majority there was little to spare on frivolities.

And so the year of 1931 drew to its close. Christmas was probably the gloomiest since the war. The depression was not confined to Britain; the whole world was suffering, especially in America, and there seemed to be no end in sight.

1932

As far as I recall, January was reasonably mild. The *Daily Herald*, which was the newspaper that I read, featured an article on the hiking craze and one contributor, Tom Stephenson, organised Sunday hikes. There was one early in the month that Elsie and I decided to go on. We met early and joined the party at one of the London railway stations. They were a mixed group - men with large rucksacks and hairy legs, women with thick glasses clutching Ordnance Survey maps and looking rather vacant. One thing they all had in common was that they were excellent walkers.

Elsie and I were almost running at times to keep up with the group. The Hertfordshire countryside was undulating, to say the least, and often our route lay over ploughed fields, which was hard going. It started to rain and soon the pleasant walk became an endurance test. The fifteen miles seemed endless but somehow we made it and were glad of the rest on the train home. By mutual consent we decided organised hikes were not for us.

There was always a lot happening at Kimpton Mission in the month of January. Each organisation held a social for its members and there were many invitations, especially for young men, who were in short supply. Elsie and I attended all of them. This year there was an extra one, for Mabel Knocker celebrated her twenty-first birthday on 16 January. I was pleasantly surprised to receive an invitation and thoroughly enjoyed the evening. On the 23rd the Choir had its social and on the following evening, after the Sunday service, there was a half hour of hymn singing with refreshments. This monthly feature of singing favourite hymns was most popular.

A couple of days later I went down with a bout of influenza. It was not serious but still most unpleasant while it lasted. Like most of my colds and ailments it started off with a sore throat. It was surprising that one kept as well as one did. The shop was cold and draughty and customers were never very careful with their coughs and sneezes when being served. All the same a week away from work was not all bad news.

At the end of March the Brixton Theatre put on a musical, *Lilac Time*, which I had seen some years before at the Wimbledon Theatre and enjoyed very much. I took Elsie along to see it at Brixton and I believe she liked the songs and music too.

With the approach of spring, and as the days began to grow longer, our thoughts began to turn to the great outdoors once again, and on Good Friday we went for a ramble from Ranmore Common to Westcott and back to Dorking. On Easter Monday, we walked with Reg and Hilda over Epsom Downs and Headley Heath.

On the following Whit Monday the young folk from the Mission went to Windsor for a ramble through the Great Park. We went up the 'long walk', which was about three miles long, to the statue of a past monarch, where we had our picnic. In the afternoon we headed for Virginia Water, a large expanse of water with many ducks, swans and other, rarer wildfowl. In one spot we were surprised to see some Grecian pillars scattered over the grass, apparently an artificial 'ruin' placed there in the past to enhance the beauty of the park. We had our tea at a nearby hostelry amongst beds of red tulips and blue forget-me-nots.

Derby Day was always a special event in the racing calendar and one in which the public took much interest. People who knew little or nothing about horse-racing would put a shilling or two on a fancied entry. At the shop a sweepstake was organised and for the sum of sixpence one hoped to draw the winning name and increase one's assets by a few shillings. Needless to say I was never one of the lucky ones. The race was run on Epsom Downs, which in the normal way was a public open space. Thousands of people flocked to the Downs for the race and many returned home certainly poorer if not wiser.

This year there was additional interest because the actor Tom Walls had entered a horse called April the Fifth. Tom Walls was an ex-policeman who had left the force to go on the stage. He was very successful and starred in the Aldwych Farces, along with Ralph Lynn and Robertson Hare. Already a well known name, his horse's success in this classic race made him a household word.

One year, Reg and I visited Epsom Downs after the race meeting. The litter left behind was indescribable, with paper and empty bottles everywhere. I even saw a Bible torn to shreds. The local scouts were doing their best to clear up the mess and the smoke from their bonfires drifted across the deserted stands. Looking at the appalling mess left by the racegoers, one could sympathise with the locals who wanted racing banned from Epsom Downs.

The unemployment situation was very grim and the whole country was suffering from the Depression. Many unemployed men went on hunger-marches to draw attention to their plight, but it did not seem to me that much was done, or could be done, to ease the situation. In lighter vein, mixed bathing was allowed in all municipal baths, and Elsie and I would go swimming about once a week if the weather was fine. Our evenings were spent in each other's homes listening to the radio, chatting, and playing board games like draughts; and once a week a visit to the cinema. A popular writer of American Westerns around this time was Zane Grey, and his books sold in their thousands. In the 1920s and 1930s his romances, with titles like *The Thundering Herd*, *Wanderer of the Wasteland* and *Maverick Queen*, could be found in many homes. Most of them were made into films and Elsie and I saw many of them. *Riders of the Purple Sage* was one I recall, which we saw at the Tower Cinema in Rye Lane.[34]

On 10 July, Elsie and I went on holiday to Ilfracombe in North Devon. We had been planning it ever since Elsie was able to get her holidays to coincide with mine. We went by coach from Victoria and the journey lasted all day. I have a record of what we did and the places we visited in a diary I wrote at the time.

Earlier in the year, Reg and I had had the go-ahead from Kimpton Mission Council to form the Scout Troop. We were really greenhorns in those days but what we lacked in expertise we made up for in enthusiasm. At the Scout Shop, Reg purchased a copy of *Boy Scout Tests* while I went in for *Scouting for Boys*. We completed all the necessary paperwork and were ready to proceed.

The first Tuesday night, Miss Boothby and 'Spud' (Cornelius) Murphy came along with four young lads who had shown an interest in becoming Tenderfoot Scouts. They had to pass certain tests before they could become initiated and Reg and I took advantage of this breathing space to further our knowledge of scouting matters. To this end, we were 'adopted' by the 49th group, whose headquarters were at the London County Council School in Caldecott Road, off Coldharbour Lane. They were of immense help and in a short time, Reg and I were initiated as Rover Scouts. We had to attend a training course at Frylands (or Freelands) Wood in Kent, one weekend in September. One of the Scout leaders of the 49th took us in his car and on the way tested our sense of direction by trying to lose us on Shirley Hills. It seemed to us that we made an awful mess of things and were most surprised when we later received a Certificate to say we had passed. When the Course was over Reg and I decided to make our own way home. We received our Warrants on 26th October, at Camberwell Town Hall.

On August Bank Holiday Monday a large party from Kimpton Mission went on a ramble from Epsom Downs, over Headley Heath to Walton on the

---

34 *The Thundering Herd* was first published in 1925, *Wanderer of the Wasteland* in c. 1923. *The Maverick Queen* was not published until 1950, ten years after Zane Grey's death in 1939. The 1931 Fox Film Corporation Hamilton MacFadden Production *Riders of the Purple Sage* starred George O'Brien as Lassiter and Margueritte Churchill as Jane Witherseen. The novel on which it was based was first published in 1912.

Hill. Because Reg and I knew the area quite well we were asked to lead the group. These rambles were extremely popular and enjoyed by everyone who joined in. They provided fresh air, good companionship and a taste of adventure. In those days there were many country cottages where ramblers could buy afternoon tea consisting of bread, butter and jam, plus a cake and tea, for about 1*s*. a head. Sitting in the parlour if the weather was inclement or outside on the grass in the shade of a tree made the little meal seem like a banquet. On the way home we would sing and chat and tell funny stories, and the time passed quickly.

Encouraged by the popularity of these rambles, we began to get more adventurous. Rambling by moonlight had been tried by some clubs with great success. Elsie was enthusiastic about the idea and agreed to find out how the rest of the girls felt while I did the same with the lads. The idea took on and, fortunately, there were no objections from the girls' parents. I wrote to the Railway Company for a special overnight party ticket which they issued without comment. On 17 September our party set of to Vauxhall Station to begin our adventure.

Reg and Hilda did not come with us so I took charge alone. At Dorking we were in time for a bus to take us to the Rookery, the stop before the Wotton Hatch Hotel. I had calculated that we needed a fairly long walk. At times it was quite eerie and the lads delighted in trying to scare the girls by lying in the grass and letting the beam from a torch light up their faces.

My sense of direction was put to the test that night, especially in the wild areas of Leith Hill woods and Broadmoor Common. There was little or no moon and a thin mist rose from the forest floor, but this in no way dampened our spirits. Only once was my sense of direction at fault but I soon realised my mistake and by retracing our steps for a few yards soon got back on the planned path. We reached Leith Hill Tower in the early hours and were surprised to find a number of ramblers on the hilltop. We rested here for a while and chatted to some of the other walkers; although there was no moon the darkness was far from black.

We ate some sandwiches and gazed over the Weald. Someone noticed that the door to the Tower was open, so we made our way up the spiral stairs to the flat roof. From this high point we could only make out pin-points of light and nothing more. We continued on our way and as dawn was breaking we passed the old campsite in Cooke Bros. field. By the time we reached Abinger Springs it was light. I had planned that we would breakfast at this spot as there was an abundant supply of fresh spring water, and so we unpacked our groundsheets, lit our Primus stoves and were soon absorbed in boiling water and making tea. Breakfast in the crisp, open air had an appeal all its own. Afterwards we washed up, splashed some icy cold water on our faces, and moved off to Dorking and the train home. Despite the lack of a night's sleep, we made the evening service at the Mission and it was said that we had never sung better.

Brother Reg had returned home from the Army earlier in the year. Prior to discharge and going on the Reserve, he went on a plasterers' course, to give him a trade in civilian life. He reckoned it was all a farce and never did make use of his newly acquired skill. I was glad to have my brother home but it took some adjusting to for he had been away in Egypt and India for nearly five years, during which time I had been on my own, as it were. However, he shared my room and we got on reasonably well. I cannot say the same for his Army pals who visited occasionally. One in particular, an Irishman called Mick Ryan, I disliked intensely. Sister Grace, on the other hand, quite liked him, and they went out for a while; but Mick was a drifter and in the end Grace gave him up.

Reg brought home with him from India some brass candlesticks and inlaid figures as well as a quantity of Persian silk, which was really lovely. He gave some to our sisters and to me he gave a couple of twisted snake ornaments but I cannot recall what became of them. Most of my brother's silk went, eventually, to his latest girlfriend. There wasn't much work available for ex-army personnel and in the end he got a job with either Fenner's, where he had been employed prior to joining up, or Mitchell's, the greengrocer on Denmark Hill. Both were slave-drivers!

Mum was happy to have her eldest son home and Dad and Reg seemed to tolerate each other, although there was some kind of barrier between them. Reg was a great entertainer and his listeners hung on to his every word. One was never quite sure whether he spoke the truth or used his fertile imagination. He had travelled widely and been to places with very odd-sounding names and his rise to Quartermaster proved he had ability. He had been given an inscribed silver cigarette case by his Commanding Officer, Sir Douglas Scott, whose sister had married one of the Royal Dukes. He found civilian life irksome and toyed with the idea of joining the Palestine Police, although nothing came of this. Still, he fretted quite a bit.

Soon after returning home he courted his old girlfriend, Lily Mason, but they had been apart too long and the romance was never really rekindled. I never had much time for the blonde Lily, but looking back I think my brother would have avoided much heartbreak if they had stayed together. One or two other girls flitted through his life, and then sister Grace introduced him to Ivy Curran.

Since leaving school, Grace had worked as a waitress for Pearce and Plenty at their eating-house in the Minories. She had got her job there through Miss Stewart, leader of the Mission's Girls' Club. Other Mission girls, Eva Crocker was one, also worked there. The hours were long, the work was hard and the wages pitifully low, although tips from customers helped. In time, Pearce and Plenty were taken over by A.B.C. These initials, I believe, stood for Aerated Bread Company. The son of 'Pearce' became the Managing Director of the A.B.C. but lost his position in a dispute. A court case followed and he was awarded substantial damages. Whether the waitresses' lot improved under A.B.C. management I do not know. Some time later, Miss Stewart, with Emily Crocker and her husband, opened their own shop.

Many young women worked in cafes, coffee shops and restaurants and the catering firm of J. Lyons & Co. was famous for its 'Nippies', girls dressed in smart black uniforms with white frilly aprons. Sister Audrey became a Nippy after leaving Coppins, the grocers, where she had met her future husband, Bill Brooks. Audrey did well and in a very short time became assistant manageress at the Hyde Park Corner House and stayed there until the outbreak of war, when she became the catering manageress at the Bank of England.

Grace chummed up with a young woman, Rose, and they became lifelong friends, going everywhere together. Another young woman working there was Ivy Curran. Grace had a photo on the mantelshelf of Rose, Ivy and herself. I knew that Reg was walking out with someone but it was not until I was looking at the photo one day that Grace volunteered the information that the third member of the trio was the young woman Reg was courting.

Ivy was dark, with shoulder-length black hair, and quite good-looking. We were introduced soon after. I was not sure why I did not take to Ivy. We soon met her family. Her mother was a large dynamic woman, in charge of every situation, and her brother Roy worked for a dyers and cleaners. She also had a younger sister whose name I do not remember. Ivy and Reg were soon engaged to be married.

On 14 October, I was twenty-five years old. The only thing of note about it was that I got a three-shillings-a-week rise at the shop, which put me on the maximum for a grocery and provision assistant. My weekly wage was now £3 6s. 0d. with deductions totalling 3s. 3d. for insurance and superannuation. The only possibility of earning more was to get promoted, but despite my certificates the chance of a higher position was very remote. Eileen had won an old wind-up gramophone in a raffle and we would buy cheap records to play on it. Dad gave me a record of the Egyptian Ballet music,[35] but it wasn't really my taste. I much preferred Bobbie Comber singing 'Misery Farm' and 'He played his ukulele as the ship went down'. I think my birthday was the last time I saw my father.

As I have already mentioned, Dad was seldom home for more than a day at a time. It had been so since my earliest days and so over the years we had accepted what we were told, that his business involved him in a considerable amount of travelling which took him from home quite a lot. I don't recall how we heard of Dad's illness but I remember one morning seeing a letter in my mother's hand. She was looking distraught and when questioned for the cause, she said that Dad had been 'taken ill' at Littlehampton. We gathered that he was at a friend's house and was being well looked after. I had a strange sense of foreboding and was all for going to see him, but Mum said it

---

35 *Ballet Égyptien* by Alexandre Luigini (1850–1906).

wasn't possible at present. Dad was one who liked his cigarettes so I bought him a tin of fifty Silk Cut and asked Mum if she would send them to him. As the days passed news was scant and I became very worried. I again asked if I could go and see him; after all, Littlehampton wasn't that far away. Mum said she would write and see what could be arranged.

In the days that followed we were told that there was an improvement in his condition and that all being well he would soon be home. This allayed our fears and I relaxed a little. November passed and on 3 December there was a reunion social at the Mission which I tried to enjoy despite the nagging fears about Dad, for we still lacked definite news about his homecoming. A reunion service followed the next day which Elsie and I attended. Whilst these two functions were well supported very few 'old Kimptonians' arrived and I was disappointed not to renew old friendships from the Boys' Life Brigade days.

On the morning of Thursday, 15 December, I was serving customers on the butter counter when Clarke, the Manager, called me away from my duties and said my brother wanted a word with me. Rather puzzled, I finished serving the customer and went and saw Reg, who was standing by the egg display. He came straight to the point and said, 'Dad died this morning. This afternoon Mum wants you to come with me to Norwood cemetery where they are having a service for Mr Lacey.'

I felt myself go as cold as ice. Words would not come. My head was in a whirl. Having imparted the distressing news, Reg left saying he would see me at lunch time. For the rest of the morning I was in a daze and kept hoping I would awake from a bad dream. I was not interested in Mr Lacey, who was Mum's old employer. To the best of my recollection I had never met him. However, if Mum wanted me to represent her at the funeral I would go. When I reached home I was told that Mum was in a state of shock and had to be kept quiet. A host of unanswered questions crowded my mind. Why had we been kept from visiting Dad? When was his funeral to take place, and where? Why all the secrecy about his illness? There was no one to ask and so no answers to the nagging doubts that flooded my mind.

I have no clear recollection of the family's reaction to the news of Dad's passing. The younger girls were at school. The news had come so suddenly that it would be evening before the whole family assembled to talk over the situation caused by Dad's death. Meanwhile, after a cup of cocoa and some bread and cheese, Reg and I boarded a tram for Norwood. It stopped quite near the cemetery gates and we alighted and made our way to the church.

Mr Lacey must have been well respected for there were many cars dotted around and the church was full of wealthy-looking individuals. There were no women present and Reg said it was because it was a Masonic Service. We sat at the back through a lengthy service but I did not remember one word of what was said. My mind was too full of my own sorrow and had no room for the late Mr Lacey. When the service was over we tacked onto the end of the mourners and followed them to the Lacey family grave, which had been opened up to receive the head of the family.

It was a warm and sunny afternoon for mid-December and I stood on the outside of those gathered around the graveside. Somewhere in the group was Mr Lacey's eldest son, Charles, but I did not know him. He was the only male survivor of the family - that much I had heard from Mum - and there were two daughters, Dora and Mary, but they were not present. Now and again they would visit my mother, who had been their nurse when they were children at No. 21, Kingsmead Road. They had been expensively educated. Dora had been trained as a singer. Mary, if my memory serves me right, was a demonstrator in one of the big London stores. Charles had a daughter, Muriel, whom I had met when I was about seven years old on a visit with Mum to the Lacey residence.

After the clergyman had performed his graveside duties the crowd broke up into small groups and then singly or in pairs dispersed to their various chauffeur-driven cars. Soon my brother and I were the only ones left. In all the time that we were there nobody had spoken a word to us. It mattered little. I was too full of my own feelings to care about these high-powered businessmen who had come to pay their respects to their friend and colleague. So Reg and I left the cemetery together and boarded a Camberwell tram. A long time was to pass before the fantastic truth dawned upon me that on that afternoon I had indeed been present at my own father's funeral.

That evening Con and Arthur came round but Mum kept to her room and would not see us. It was obvious Con and Reg knew something they would not divulge. Eileen, with her business instinct, talked of getting black-edged notepaper. Then Ted Thompson came to see me about something, and he was soon told the bad news. There wasn't much I could do so at about 7 p.m. I went out to meet Elsie.

As the days passed and nothing was said about a funeral for Dad, I began to get very worried and sick at heart. I could not understand why there was so much mystery. Was Dad really dead, or had he disappeared for reasons yet to be revealed? In desperation, I asked my eldest sister only to receive a blistering, 'He's dead alright!'. When Mum at last came among us she looked so ill that I did not have the heart to question her. I decided that if she did not want to speak on the subject I would not press her. In the years that followed she never spoke on the subject to me. With hindsight, I can see that Con and my brother must have known much of the truth, but they kept their own council. Had I been on better terms with Con no doubt she would have told me all for I am sure her knowledge of the truth explained much about her loathing of our father.

I only once tried to get Mum to talk, and that was indirectly. The Co-op ran an Insurance and Death Benefit Scheme for members and their families. I asked Mum if she wished me to put in a claim, but she refused even to consider it. This only increased my fears that something was wrong. One

Thursday afternoon I was sitting in my bedroom when my mother came in carrying Dad's cashbox. 'Dad wanted you to have it', she said. I took the box from her and tried to reassure her that I would do my best to look after her and my young sisters. She then put her hand on my shoulder and gave me a sealed letter. For a while I toyed with the envelope. What would it reveal? Would my questions at last be answered and my fears allayed? When I did pluck up the courage to break the seal and read the missive, I found my father had revealed nothing to set my mind at rest.

Inside it was a letter and another sealed envelope addressed to my mother. I put this aside and began reading the letter. It was dated 1930, a little over two years ago. I was disappointed. It referred to Dad's plans for my two youngest sisters, Denny and Pam, who were still at school. Pam was to have a medical training and Denny a musical one. He expressed a wish that Denny should have the piano, a Boyd pianette. He said that ample funds would be available to carry out his wishes. There was not much more, except to say that when the time came for Mum to join him, I should dispose of the home as I saw fit. He signed himself 'Dad'.

To say I was perplexed was putting it mildly. By rights, Reg should have assumed responsibility for Mum and the girls. I took the letter addressed to Mum to her and she took it without comment. Looking back I believe this was the time I should have asked her to elucidate, but I did not. I returned to my room to ponder over the letter. The deed box was empty. I had hoped it would contain some documents. I consoled myself with the thought that when the 'ample funds' came along I would be able to trace the source and take it from there. I waited and waited but not a penny ever came to carry out Dad's wishes. I am sure that Dad had made provision but for whatever reason, my family did not receive any financial help whatsoever.

Life had to go on and I tried to put my fears and worries behind me. Christmas was very nearly upon us. I had won a hamper of groceries in a raffle, but this did little to lift our spirits. I cannot say it was the happiest Christmas the family had ever spent, and the vacant chair reminded us that things would never be quite the same.

I had Christmas lunch with the family and after listening to the King's speech on the wireless, went to see Elsie and spend the rest of the day with her people.

With Christmas behind us I was left wondering what lay ahead for our family. Mum had no pension, for Dad had never paid into the 'National Health'. Henceforth she would have to rely on her children. She had been a wonderful mother in our young days, working and slaving to see that we had enough to eat. Now it was our turn. If we played our part all would be well. Only Con was married. It looked as if Elsie and I would have to wait a bit until things sorted themselves out. In the meantime, I waited for the ample funds to turn up to ease the burden and carry out Dad's wishes. It was a worrying and uncertain time.

1933

In the New Year, the parents of Sidney House came to tea. My sister Eileen and Sidney had been going out together for some time and I think they may have become engaged some time before Elsie and I. Grace and I had already been to the House residence at No. 32, Thompson Road, East Dulwich, and met the family. Like myself, Sid had one brother and several sisters. He and Eileen had met at the Lordship Lane branch of the Royal Arsenal Co-operative Society where my sister worked in the check office and Sid on the provisions counter. Soon after, he was transferred to the Camberwell Green shop, where Reg and I worked, so we came to know each other a little better.

I did not altogether approve of Sidney House and felt he was not really worthy of my favourite sister. For his part he considered I was adopting the big brother act. In course of time we learned to accept each other and got along fairly well. I need not have bothered myself over their relationship, as Eileen proved herself mistress of all eventualities. Sid never seemed short of money and I suppose he was able to keep most of his wages to himself. He bought a motorcycle and Eileen used to ride pillion. They had one or two nasty spills and it worried Mum no end.

Mr House Snr. was by trade a baker with a local firm and I believe Sid worked there too before joining the Co-op. He was a small man and Sid took after him physically. Mrs House on the other hand was a big buxom woman and had a jolly nature. They were an easy pair to get on with and Mr House related how he first made hot cross buns and put dough into the oven about the size of an average bun. When they were taken from the oven they were the size of footballs. Soon afterwards, Mr House had a serious accident, catching his hand in some machinery. He never worked in the bakehouse again and only did light work. Mrs House died during the war but her husband lived until he was over ninety. He found himself two more wives and outlived them all.

At the Mission the season of socials and parties gathered momentum, with the Girls' Life Brigade, Mothers' Meeting, the Children's parties held in January and the Scout's first birthday party in February. I managed to persuade Elsie's brother Tim to come along to this, and the Girls' Life Brigade girls supervised the refreshments. Tim brought a friend along with him and these two young men, in full scout uniform, really added a touch of class to the festivities. In due course I managed to persuade Tim to join the 43rd and his coming, more than anything else, set the troop on the right path.

Miss Boothby's Wolf Cub pack held a supper and social on 25 February, in aid of funds. As usual Reg and I, along with most of the Mission's younger element, gave it our support. The choir social followed on 4 March. In the main the same boys and girls attended all these events and a great time was had by all.

During these and other get-togethers the idea of an Easter weekend at the Cooke Bros. field at Leith Hill was suggested, and quite a number expressed interest. The large caravan that had been added to the field would be ideal for the girls, whilst the boys would bring their tents. After some discussion it was agreed that I would book the field and make all the necessary arrangements. On the following Sunday, Elsie, Reg, Hilda and I went to see the Cooke brothers at their home and booked the field and caravan for the Easter weekend. Afterwards we rambled over the area and returned to have tea with the Denners at Worcester Park.

In the middle of March my friend Frank Thompson became engaged to Rose Waterman, who lived with her parents and sister Lily at No. 23, Kimpton Road. Their marriage was a happy and successful one but during the war tragedy overtook the Waterman family when a German bomb fell on their part of Kimpton Road, killing not only Mr and Mrs Waterman and Lily, but two other friends of ours.

Elsie's father had poor eyesight, which had been aggravated by mustard gas during his time in the trenches at Flanders. Since I had known Elsie his sight had deteriorated, and his doctor now arranged for him to be admitted to Guy's Hospital for an operation. He was admitted on the 26th. Elsie and I went to see him six days later but it would be sometime before the results of the operation were known. He came home, with his eyes still bandaged, on 12 April.

Cambridge won the boat race on 1 April. It was a great event in those days and much fuss was made of it. Little bows of light or dark blue ribbon were sported as 'favours' by opposing groups and there was much discussion on the merits and demerits of each crew. Everyone who could lined the riverbanks to cheer on their boat, or wait in breathless anticipation for news of the result.

With the coming of Easter our final plans for the weekend at Leith Hill were finalised and on Good Friday we set off by train to Dorking, and bus to the Wotton Hatch Hotel. The rest of the way was by foot, but this only added to the fun. Water had been laid on and there was abundant firewood in the woods, and soon the dixies were boiling. Tents were quickly erected and the girls soon had the caravan set out to their satisfaction. Elsie and I had to leave that evening for we had to work Easter Saturday, but the others settled in. Saturday working had always riled me but it was part of shop life and had to be accepted.

That Saturday seemed endless but eventually 8 p.m. came and the shop closed. I met Elsie at about half past and we set off for Vauxhall station. By the time we disembarked from the bus it was dark but the sky was clear and for the time of year it was reasonably warm. Occasionally an animal would scuttle from our path and the route behind Broadmoor cottages was indistinct, but we enjoyed our walk and a hot cup of cocoa greeted us when we arrived. We had a lovely weekend rambling through the woods and cooking over an open fire. We built a huge bonfire of pinewood and sang songs and hymns in its flickering light. The weather stayed fine and when we finally broke camp and left for home we all agreed to come again next spring.

For the first time our Scout troop, together with the Wolf Cub pack, took part in the St George's Day service at St Giles' Church, and afterwards in the Parade. It was a very impressive show. The Mayor of Camberwell, together with the Scout Commissioner and their retinues, stationed themselves on the corner of Grove Park and Camberwell Grove, and the local Scout groups marched up the Grove with bands playing, flags flying and onlookers cheering. The Scouts, in three lines, wheeled round in front of the dignitaries on the podium. Each troop scoutmaster saluted and the scouts with 'eyes right' received the acknowledgement of the Mayor. It was most impressive. It is difficult to calculate the number of boys on the parade that day but there must have been many hundreds.

On the following Thursday, 27 April, the combined Wolf Cub pack and Scout troop held its first display. From my point of view it was not one of our most successful ventures. The Cubs did well but our lads were bashful and tongue-tied and our camp-fire routine was a disaster. We had made a fire in an old container by soaking sawdust with paraffin. It smelt dreadful and must have nearly driven our supporters from the hall. However, it was a start and later displays were much better organised and presented.

Towards the end of May, Elsie's father went back to the hospital to have his eye bandage removed and to get the results of the operation. When I reached the Squires' home that evening it was to find Mrs Squires almost hysterical, for examination revealed that the operation had been a failure and the sight of his eye had completely gone. It was a nasty shock for the family, but for Mr Squires it must have seemed like the end of everything. It meant that he had to give up work and go on the blind register, for his other eye was almost useless. There was no social security in those days and the outlook for the family was grim. It seemed that Elsie's and my marriage would have a further setback.

Sometime prior to this unhappy event my brother announced that he and Ivy would be getting married on Whit Sunday, 4 June, at Kennington Church near the Oval cricket ground. To say that I was stunned by this news was putting it mildly for I had hoped that Reg would remain at home to help the family get back on its feet after the shock caused by Dad's death. Our two young sisters were still at school and Mum needed every penny to keep the home going. I'm afraid I let my disapproval show, but I received no support from Con or Grace, who made it clear they were on Reg's side. In fairness to my brother I believe he was probably under pressure from Ivy.

However, I did not let my feelings stop me from attending the wedding, although Elsie and I did not stay late at the reception, which was held at the Curran's home. I think Mum took Reg's leaving pretty hard; after all she had seen very little of him over the past eight or nine years and his going so soon after Dad's passing must have left her feeling despondent.

Reg and Ivy lived with the Curran family and we visited them now and again. The had a little dog which loved chasing the cats. Reg took a keen interest in the garden and he made it blossom. The Currans loved the social life and were always having parties to which we were invited. We attended many of them and always had a good time. All guests were expected to entertain with their party pieces and sister Grace was always in demand as leading soprano. Mrs Curran and Roy had their own favourite item, 'The Song of the Thrush', which included the line 'Thousands of miles away', which they always sang as 'Fousands'. This tickled us no end.

A short time later they moved to a large house in Clapham Road. It had an enormous garden and in it they kept poultry and rabbits. Mrs Curran, and Ivy, with lots of spare rooms at their disposal, took in paying guests, commonly known as lodgers. One man who took a room there was an Irishman from Cork called John Ryan. Reg and John became firm friends and it was not long before he became a frequent visitor to our home. John had a mother and sister back in Eire but I think his father must have passed away when John was young. He worked as a painter and decorator but I do not remember who with, except that later he worked on some Government premises. He was of course a Catholic, but I don't believe a very devout one. Altogether he was a fine man. Later he became friends with Grace and they were married on 24 September 1939, soon after the outbreak of war.

Now that Tim Squires had joined our Scout troop we began to make good progress with recruitment. Like most other Scouts our boys wanted to experience life under canvas and were anxious to spend a week or two at a summer camp. This presented a real headache for us. I talked it over with Reg Denner, but he could not see his way clear to give up one of his precious two weeks leave allowance to take the boys away.

I pondered the matter deeply. If I didn't do something the boys could become dissatisfied and leave to join other, more adventurous troops. I talked the matter over with Spud and Tim and they agreed to support me if I organised a camp. We fixed a date for the first week in August and agreed to try for the Cooke Bros. field. That night I wrote to Mr Cooke and in due course received a favourable reply. Preparations could now go ahead.

On 25 June I took Elsie to Rushden to meet my Aunt and Uncle. I hadn't seen much of them recently and thought it time I let them know that I still rated them highly. We were made very welcome and some of the folk from Irthlingborough came to see us, as well as my cousins from around the corner. They asked about Mum, but that was all. Uncle Joe and Aunt Bec looked no different to the last time we had met.

Our local teaching hospital was on Denmark Hill, adjoining Ruskin Park, and the wards stretched backwards from the main building to the railway line. The main entrance was in Bessemer Road. On the corner of Denmark Hill a huge 'thermometer' stood with notices appealing for funds. According to the appeal, the hospital was hopelessly in debt and the income from donations was marked in red on it. I didn't know much about finances in those days and it puzzled me how a hospital owing thousands of pounds could continue to operate. They appealed for throwaway items, like toothpaste tubes with the words 'Though these may seem useless things, they help to heal the sick at Kings'.

Once a year a pageant and fancy-dress parade was held in the borough to help raise funds for the hospital. I was never able to see much of the spectacle as I worked late on a Saturday but I did manage to see one of the 'floats' as it passed by on its way to the procession. It consisted of four young men in evening dress seemingly much the worse for alcohol, sitting in a trap pulled by a donkey. A carrot was dangling in front of the donkey's nose, presumably to encourage it to go. The procession always ended at the medical school's playing fields on Dog Kennel Hill where a fair was set up with stalls and galloping horses. I once won a box of chocolates at one of the booths.

In July I took myself off to Leith Hill to discuss camp plans with Albert Cooke. He suggested that we send all our equipment to Ockley Station and he would collect it and take it up to the camping field to await our arrival. I paid him for the rent of the field and for the water we would use during our stay. I asked if he could loan us a grass hook, which he called a 'fagging hook', to cut the grass around the camp site. After leaving him I went to the field and selected what I thought to be the most suitable area for our tents. I made a rough sketch for Spud Murphy's guidance, as he would be first to arrive with the lads in the afternoon. Again, work would prevent me from arriving until past ten o'clock.

Tim made a postbox to fix on the gate for any mail, and I wrote to the Dorking Postmaster about the delivery of letters. I also informed the local Scout Commissioner to let him know we would be camping in his area, and also nearby Lemons Farm, asking the farmer to supply us with vegetables. Having done everything possible at this stage we could only hope for fine weather.

Elsie and I took advantage of the lull to go on a day's outing to Bournemouth, but whether it was the relaxing air or simply tiredness I found it hard to keep awake. We had our picnic in the delightful pleasure gardens and watched the children playing with their boats on the tumbling stream. Time passed quickly but I was quite glad when we returned to the railway station and were able to relax on the train home.

5 August arrived and the 43rd Camberwell Scout troop left for their very first camp. I had done all I could but had to leave the move to camp in the hands of Spud Murphy and Tim. By coincidence, the Girls' Life Brigade also left on the same day to their camp at Swalescliff. It was a long day at the shop and it seemed as though eight o'clock would never come. As soon as the shop closed and I had paid in my till receipts I hastened off home, grabbed my rucksack, said goodbye to Mum and the girls and boarded a tram to Vauxhall station. I managed to get on a bus at Dorking station and alighted at

the Wotton Hatch Hotel, then made my way through the Tillingbourne Valley, reaching the camp at about 11 p.m.

I found the tents set up in a semicircle around the flagstaff. A fire of pine branches glowed in the darkness and I was soon drinking cocoa in the flickering light. The boys were still awake so I went round and wished them goodnight. Spud and Tim related how they had made stretchers and thumbsticks, and had negotiated the paths without much difficulty. When they reached the field it was to find that Mr Cooke had already arranged for the grass to be cut for us. It was a wonderful starry night, quite still, and the firelight lit up the trunks of nearby trees.

We had a wonderful week. The weather was sunny and warm. There was wood in abundance and the fire became the focus of our camp, cooking our food during the day and singing songs around it at night. We were visited by some local scouts and the Commissioner paid a courtesy call. Mr and Mrs Cooke came to tea one day bringing with them three large jam sponges. We explored the surrounding countryside and practised our signalling from the cliff edge below the Tower. We were given the freedom of the Tower and from its battlements followed the lines on the indicator plates. The sun gleamed on the glass domes and towers of the Crystal Palace, so close to our homes. The week quickly passed and it was soon time to pack up, tidy up and leave for home.

At the end of the month Elsie and her sister went on holiday to Ventnor, on the Isle of Wight. I found plenty to do, the scouts were absorbing most of my spare time and numbers were increasing. We were joined by members of the 49th and began to make our mark in local contests. For their assistance in running the troop, Ted Warne and Ted Nichols were made junior A.S.Ms. At the end of their holiday, I went to Waterloo Station and met Elsie and Dolly and escorted them home to Harris Street.

7 September was bonus day at the shop. As I was now on the top rate, my bonus amounted to about £6 10s. 0d., a sizeable sum in those days. I usually gave little gifts out of it to Mum and my young sisters, and on the strength of it Elsie and I went to Eastbourne the following Sunday.

At the end of September Elsie's parents had recovered sufficiently from the shock of Mr Squires' operation to go for a well deserved holiday to Brighton. I am sure the few days away must have done them a power of good.

At the Mission preparations were put in hand for the reunion social and service at the beginning of December. All past members who could be traced received an invitation. It involved a lot of work, mainly by Frank Thompson and Rose Waterman. Many had moved from their addresses and others did not reply. All the same a goodly number turned up to the social. I kept an autograph book of the event and although not everyone entered their name, I see that my mother and sister Vera came along as well as most of the youth organisations and the Women's Meeting. There was a contingent from Wren

Road Congregational Church with whom the Mission had a working arrangement, and many past workers who had retired came along. There was the usual programme of games, dances and competitions, with refreshments and much chatting.

With the approach of Christmas things at the shop became hectic and tempers a little frayed. In late summer, the manager would be invited to a function at which Christmas goods and gifts were displayed, and he would place an order for those items he estimated his shop could sell. There was a great deal of competition among managers to see who could place the biggest order for fancy goods and many of them, in their enthusiasm, over-ordered. As Christmas Eve approached, the manager would take stock of the fancy goods remaining on the shelves. Because they would become valueless after the festivities, he would threaten, cajole and chase the staff to get rid of them by the 24th. Life became a misery with the manager and foreman standing over the salesman, urging them to greater efforts to sell the unwanted items. Many finished up in the staff raffle.

Elsie and I usually stayed in our respective homes for Christmas lunch, but for tea we would go to one another's homes. This year Mum came with me to the Squires' home and it made a pleasant break for her to chat with Elsie's parents.

On New Year's Eve we were invited to Mabel's home at No. 17, Vicarage Grove. By now her parents had accepted that I was engaged to another girl, but Mabel remained cool. However, it was a good evening and with a glass of Tarragona wine we bade farewell to the end of 1933 and toasted the arrival of 1934.

1934

The New Year was damp and very cold. The nights and mornings were foggy with frost overnight. At work we were soon immersed in the seasonal stocktaking and checktaking. The goodwill of Christmas soon evaporated and it was back to the grindstone once again. The senior staff wore worried looks and the manager was irritable and unapproachable as he pondered on the last six months' trading figures, the wage rate and percentages. During the previous year, the Society's Management Committee had approved the opening of many more shops, two of which were in Camberwell. Until then our branch had had a monopoly, and as anticipated these new branches had taken some of our trade. This did not improve Mr Clarke's fragile temper. Some staff were transferred, and Sid House went to Camberwell New Road branch.

On the social side it was a happy time. The Mission's season of socials and parties was soon in full swing and did much to brighten winter's gloom. Elsie and I did our best to attend each one although we were usually late in arriving because of the shop hours. On 22 January, the Mothers' Meeting held their high tea and social, which Frank Thompson, Reg Denner and myself organised. With one of the Girls' Life Brigade girls helping out on the piano, we entertained with songs and sketches. I was glad my mother attended and at long last she appeared to have regained some of her cheerfulness. Elsie and Hilda looked in to see how things were going.

We opened with our signature tune, 'Jolly Good Company'. Frank, who was the life and soul of the party, and the idol of all women, always sang the same songs each year, but this didn't seem to matter. His repertoire included 'The Ideal Home', 'The Rich Man Rides by in his Carriage and Pair' and 'The Night I Appeared as MacBeth'. He had an endless supply of patter which I tried hard to memorise. I did a monologue or two and Reg helped out with the sketches. Our closing tune was always the same and sung to the tune of 'In Eleven More Months and Ten More Days', went like this:

> *Now we've come to the end of our little show,*
> *And we think that you'll agree,*
> *That a couple of hours of fooling around,*
> *Is enough for you and we.*
> *We hope that you've enjoyed yourselves,*
> *And that we've caused no pain,*
> *And we promise you this, in twelve more months,*
> *We'll do it all over again.*
> *In twelve more months,*
> *In twelve more months,*
> *We'll do it all over again.*
> *In twelve more months,*
> *In twelve more months,*
> *We'll do it all over again.*

There was always much applause at the end, and some welcome food laid on for us after the show.

One day Elsie and I decided to start making something for our future home and sent away for some rug-making materials. When the parcel arrived it consisted of a printed semi-circular canvas, some hanks of wool, a pair of rug needles, and a wooden guide for cutting the wool into equal lengths. We started with a lot of enthusiasm but progress was slow and we only ever seemed to be able to complete three rows at one sitting. It became a lengthy and tedious job. It was not completed until after we were married, taking roughly three years to make.

Plans for the Easter weekend break at the Cooke brothers' field began to take shape. I wrote to Mr Cooke and on Sunday the 11th, Elsie and I visited him to sort things out. We had a very pleasant time there, booked the field for a very minor sum, including the caravan, and after a very nice tea left for home.

The following Saturday evening, if I remember correctly, we went to an unexpected party. Elsie had a cousin, Leila, and she was celebrating her twenty-first birthday at the school where her father worked as the caretaker. Leila was a pleasant young woman, in build much like my Elsie, but with darker hair. We had a lovely time. I began to feel that socially, things were looking up.

Kimpton Mission was directed and managed by a Council elected by its workers, and around this time I was elected to serve on it. This was probably because I was a scout leader and attended many of the social functions. I must admit that I never felt at ease in the presence of men and women experienced in committee work and *au fait* with law and procedures. Dolf Mordey was Secretary and a Mr Owen Byers, OBE, the Chairman. Working in a shop was not calculated to give one much familiarity with agendas, balance sheets, standing orders and the like, and it was a long time before I made any real contribution to the work of the Kimpton Mission Council.

The 1930s was a time of amalgamations in the business world, and many firms banded together to cut out costly competition and standardise operational procedures. An example was the amalgamation of London's trams, omnibuses and underground railways under the title 'London Transport'. In theory this made for more efficiency and was declared to be in the public's interest, but in practice it proved to be the opposite. Elsie's father declared that the trams would be the first to go, and although this took some years, come true it did. London Transport may have streamlined the transport, but services declined as the fares increased.

For some time there had been moves to amalgamate the four London Co-operative Societies, and a working party had been set up to examine this proposal. The four societies differed in size and direction. The London Co-operative Society was the biggest and operated north of the Thames, although some of its branches were as far away as Southend-on-Sea. It only paid one shilling in the pound as dividend. Our society, the Royal Arsenal Co-operative Society, was more compact and had its main trading area in south-east London. It paid 1*s*. 6*d*. in the pound. The South Suburban Co-operative Society operated in south-west London and also paid 1*s*. 6*d*., whilst the fourth, The Enfield Highway, covered the fringe areas of Hertfordshire and Essex. I cannot recall their 'divi'.

The working party recommended acceptance, in principle, of the amalgamation, but there was an immense amount of opposition, and it was very vocal. As far as we were concerned there was one big drawback. The Royal Arsenal Co-operative Society paid its employees a bonus each half year, which the others did not. Although we were assured that this would continue to be paid we were very suspicious and the staff, who were very well organised, decided to oppose the plan. In the first week of March, meetings were held all over the Royal Arsenal Co-operative Society area by the Management Committee and votes taken on the proposal. The employees packed the meetings and overwhelmingly rejected it. As all four Societies had to agree, the amalgamation idea became a dead duck.

On 'bonus day', 8 March, I received my share amounting to £6 10s. 0d., the equivalent of two weeks' wages, and very welcome. We all felt that we had done the right thing in safeguarding this privilege.

Easter came early in 1934. Good Friday was on 30 March, and whilst we would have preferred it to be a week or two later, we were all keen to get going. There was no weather forecasting service so we had to be prepared for all types of weather. In the end it proved to be a dry and reasonably warm weekend.

There were eleven of us as I recall, six girls and five fellows. There was Elsie and her brother Tim, Mabel Knocker and her brother Cecil, Lily Waterman, Biddy Matthews, Kitty Smith, Elsie Crocker, Spud Murphy, Dolf Mordey and myself. We took the now familiar route to the Cookes' field and were soon settled there, the girls in the caravan and the boys in their tents. Elsie and I and Biddy had to leave in the evening for work the next day. At the end of the Easter Saturday trading, I met Elsie and Biddy at Camberwell Green and we set off once again to join the others. We arrived to find our friends sitting around a blazing campfire and we joined them for cocoa and biscuits.

Despite the late hour, Elsie and I decided to walk to the Tower. We were joined by Dolph and the three of us had no difficulty finding our way. There was always someone at the Tower and this night was no different. We could hear singing and laughter but were not always sure just where the hikers were located. We stayed for a while and then retraced our steps to the camp.

The next day, after breakfast, we set off on a walk to Holmbury St Mary. It was quite rough going - the ground was soggy and the hills were steep - but we found a much easier route back. After lunch, as we relaxed in the sunshine, Mr and Mrs Cooke arrived. They were very agreeable and we invited them to stay for tea. They informed us that they were buying a much larger caravan which would be sited at the top of the field, and if we liked we could have first choice in booking it for the next year.

The time passed all too quickly and it was soon time to leave for home. We chose a route through Abinger Bottom and Friday Street but as it was crowded with hikers we decided not to hang about but to continue making our way home. We all agreed it had been a wonderful weekend and we should think about another holiday next year, possibly in the new caravan.

April was a busy month at the Mission, with a Scouts' concert and the annual Public Meeting organised by the Mission's Council and Organisations. This was always a great day, when the public were invited to come along to hear all about what went on at Kimpton Mission, and to see displays by the Girls' Life Brigade and Scouts, listen to the choir sing and partake of light refreshment. Harry Whiteman, a local Headmaster, took the chair, and two local Justices of the Peace, David Ramsey and George Hearne, spoke words of praise and encouragement to those gathered there. There was always a full hall.

On Whit Monday our ramble was from Epsom Downs to Headley Heath and Mickleham. These rambles had become very popular and many of the Mission's younger folk came along. We always bought a party ticket from the railway to keep the cost of the journey to a minimum and normally took our food with us, although we often bought a cup of tea while we were out.

In July we went to see the Aldershot Tattoo, and later paid a visit to Hastings and to Fairlight Glen, one of our favourite picnic spots. There was a fair at the King's College Sports ground on Dog Kennel Hill and Elsie and I took Denny and Pam there for an outing. On 25 July it was Elsie's twenty-second birthday.

For our annual holiday, Elsie and I had planned to go to Ventnor on the Isle of Wight. My sister Eileen and her fiancé Sid had also been planning a holiday on the island, but failed to find accommodation. So that they would not be disappointed, Elsie and I wrote to our holiday address and asked if they could share our rooms. The landlady agreed so all was set for the four of us to go. We had a great time and I kept a diary of the events and places we visited.

In early September a great Co-operative Exhibition was held at the Crystal Palace. It received a great deal of publicity and thousands of people flocked to see the displays. Elsie and I went there one evening and strolled through the vast building where demonstrations, film shows and the like were in progress. A big membership campaign was launched and everyone that joined, at a cost of 1s. 6d., received a parcel of groceries as a gift. Small wonder that many people joined just to get the introductory offer. It was the last time I visited the Crystal Palace before it was destroyed by fire in November 1936.

Before the weather broke and the long dark nights of winter came, I thought it would be nice to visit my Rushden relatives again. Eileen and Sid said they would like to come along so the four of us made the journey on the second Sunday in September. As always, my Uncle and Aunt seemed pleased to see us and made us very welcome.

The first Sunday in October was the day that Kimpton Mission held its Harvest Festival. There was always a colourful display of flowers, fruit and vegetables, plus extras like water and coal. Everyone tried to be there for the evening service and there was always a full house. Although few people in the neighbourhood had much idea about the farming year of ploughing, sowing and reaping, they nevertheless joined in the harvest hymns with great gusto. On the following day the harvest gifts were shared out among the members of the Women's Meeting and poorer folk in the immediate neighbourhood.

On my birthday that year, I was invited to a Union meeting of shop stewards at the Co-operative Hall in Rye Lane. The guest speaker was Herbert Morrison, the Leader of the Labour Group on the London County Council. He gave us the inside story of the workings of Local Government and invited questions afterwards. I'm sorry to say that most of what he said went in one ear and out the other.

And so the year of 1934 began to draw to a close. Elsie and I paid a flying visit to the Cooke family and spent a happy time as their guests. We confirmed the booking of the new caravan for next Whitsun. When our friends heard the news, all decided to put sixpence a week away towards the cost. I was given the job of collecting the 'tanners' and keeping the records.

The reunion social was again held at the Mission at the beginning of December. Although there was a reasonable attendance and all those present enjoyed themselves, there appeared to be a lessening of interest. We had had three very successful years but at the next Council meeting it was decided to have a break from it in 1935. In the event it proved to be the last get-together of its type held at the Mission.

With the approach of Christmas there was little spare time with the usual rush at the shop. The festive season came and went and I saw the New Year in with Elsie at her home.

1935 (up to 7 September)

The first three months of the year followed the usual pattern, with the check- and stock-taking at work and the round of parties and socials at the Mission. Elsie and I visited the Trocadero Cinema at the Elephant and Castle, a new cinema recently opened, and claimed to be the biggest yet. In addition to films and the mighty Wurlitzer Organ, they laid on a stage show and on the evening we visited the Western Brothers were the star attraction.

On Good Friday, 19 April, Elsie and I decided to visit Southend on Sea, a place we had not been to before. It was a very popular venue for people living in the East End of London, being easily accessible to them from Liverpool Street Station. In addition, river steamers like the *Royal Sovereign* and *Maid of Kent* plied their way between the Tower Bridge pier and the mile-long pier at Southend. Some of these pleasure boats would continue along the coast to Margate and Ramsgate.

People who had visited Southend did not speak too favourably about it, saying it smelt of fried fish and chips and jellied eels, and that the smell of the mud was atrocious. However, we were not deterred and boarded a train at Liverpool Street. When we reached our destination we were pleasantly surprised to see trees and flowers. The cafés were an education, for each one displayed in the window what a meal for sixpence, nine pence or one shilling would consist of. There were stalls selling platefuls of seafood and numerous fish-and-chip shops as we had been led to expect, but everyone seemed to be in good humour and thoroughly enjoying themselves.

We took the railway to the end of the pier and walked back, then made our way to Leigh, considered to be the posh end. In Southend there was a huge funfair and the noise from it shattered the air all around. After some tea in one of the cafes we left for home, not at all disappointed with our outing. As the train drew into London we could see, in many of the houses we passed, families sitting around their tables, on which there were lighted candles. They wore hats and shawls around their shoulders and appeared to be absorbed in prayer. It took a moment or two to realise that we were looking at the Jewish community celebrating Passover.

The following day, Easter Saturday, some of the senior scouts and Brigade girls went off to camp at Ditchling, organised by Nichols, one of the scouts who had joined us from the 49th troop. A relative of his had a farm there and had given them permission to use part of it for the camp. We joined them in the evening after work but our journey seemed endless as we had a long wait at Burgess Hill for the local steam train to complete our journey. At Ditchling we were met by Ted Warne. The brim of his scout hat was adorned with glow-worms he had collected on his way to the station. They were the first glow-worms I had ever seen. It must have been about half past eleven before we reached the camp. There was no cocoa waiting for us, so we stirred the embers of the fire into life and made our own.

The weather stayed fine and we spent our time rambling over the Downs and chatting with our friends. As always the time flew by and we were soon making our way home again.

Reg Denner no longer worked alongside me at the Camberwell Green shop. Because Hilda and he were to be married in the near future, he had asked for a transfer to a branch nearer his home, so that he could save on his railway fares. When his transfer came through it was to the big Tooting branch. To say I missed him was an understatement for we had been very close pals since 1927. We didn't see much of him at the scout meetings either, which was quite understandable.

The year of 1935 was the Silver Jubilee of King George V and there were many big celebrations to mark the event. 6 May was declared a public holiday and we took advantage of this to go on another ramble. Our numbers were smaller than usual because many of the girls went to London to see the procession. The King also made four state visits to the Metropolitan Boroughs, and on 18 May he came to Camberwell Green. It caused great excitement. There were flags and bunting all over the borough and Camberwell had never looked so gay and colourful. Even the Co-op premises were decked with garlands and bunting despite the indifference which management and staff professed. In the event, these types cheered as loudly as any when the Household Cavalry and the King's carriage clattered by.

The question of when Elsie and I should be married now occupied our thoughts. We had been engaged for nearly four years but had been going out together much longer. We had tried to do the right thing for both our families. Since Dad's death I had tried to help Mum and my younger sisters and I believe my contributions had helped cushion the financial crisis caused by Dad's passing. My sisters were growing up: Denny was approaching fifteen and Pam eleven. It was not easy for Elsie either, for her family relied on her too. However, a decision needed to be made and after some heart-searching we decided to make 7 September our wedding day.

I was quite at a loss to know how to break the news to my mother. She must have realised that I would leave home sooner or later, and would undoubtedly miss my contribution to the household budget. Unfortunately, I did not earn enough to give her an allowance. Maybe I was over sensitive, but I got the impression from my older sisters that I could have done more for the family. I felt this was most unfair; indeed Eileen said that if Elsie and I hadn't decided to marry when we proposed, she and Sid would have.

On 19 May, my sister Denise was fifteen years old and left school. She had passed her exams high enough to have entered grammar school but there was no spare money to enable her to accept a place. She was at a loss to know what kind of work to do, and any job was hard to obtain. I heard there was a vacancy coming up in the tobacco kiosk at the Royal Arsenal Co-operative Society Church Street branch. I suggested that she might like to apply, which she did. She went for an interview at Powis Street and was successful. All went well for a while and then her till takings began to be short and she was dismissed.

I knew nothing of this until sometime later when I called to see Mum and she told me what had happened. I knew that Denny was completely honest and I went to see the manager. He said that of late she was always short and because so much money was involved he had had no alternative but to send her to head office. I was very angry, knowing that someone had taken advantage of my sister's youth and inexperience and had been rifling her till. I suspected the kiosk manageress but without proof could do nothing. I came away from the interview feeling sick. However, a short time later the girl in charge was caught stealing and admitted taking the money from Denny's till. It was incomprehensible to me that she could have stooped so low as to rob a girl of fifteen. By this time Denny was working in an office, a job found for her by Miss Moffet of the Girls' Life Brigade.

On 23 May, Elsie and I went to Brixton to buy a wedding gift for our friends Reg and Hilda. After much deliberation we chose an eight-day clock. In the evening we went to the cinema and saw a film adaptation of Dickens' novel *Great Expectations*. I thought it was one of the best films I had ever seen.

Two days later on Saturday 25 May, Reg and Hilda were married at the South London Tabernacle in Peckham Road. I had secretly hoped I might be asked to be the best man, but in the event that job went to Reg's brother, Jim. I managed to get the afternoon off, which in those days was a great concession. I may have been asked to make the time up but cannot recall. Elsie was not so fortunate. She was allowed two or three hours off but was late getting back and received a severe reprimand from her manager.

The reception was held in the Burndett Hall, round the corner in Bushey

Hill Road. After the usual photographs were taken, we settled down to an excellent meal. There were a lot of people there, most of whom I knew. After the reception and speeches the happy couple left for their honeymoon on the Isle of Wight. On their return they would be living in Stoneleigh, where they were buying a new home.

From now on the time seemed to fly. Once the wedding was over we began to prepare for our weekend camp in earnest. We were unable to travel with the main party as Saturday work once again intruded, but at 8.30 on Saturday night, Elsie and I met at the Green and set off for Dorking and the Wotton Hatch Hotel. We were quite used to this route by now and reached the camp at 11.30 p.m. A small consolation for us missing out on the start of the weekend was that our friends had all settled in, the tents were erected and the kettle was boiling.

The new caravan at the top of the field was much larger than the previous one we had hired. It was roomy and had a porch, and the views from the windows were superb. During the second night of our weekend there was a terrific thunderstorm. The top of the field where we had pitched our tents was much more exposed. The lightning flashed incessantly and the thunder was deafening as it reverberated around the hills. The rain lashed down and soon our tents were awash. We grabbed our clothes and took refuge in the living room of the caravan and waited for the storm to subside. Next morning the sun shone, but everywhere was very soggy. However, it would need more than that to dampen our spirits and we made the most of our few days' holiday.

With our wedding day only a couple of months away, Elsie and I had to get down to some serious planning. I had a word with my friend Frank Thompson, and he arranged for us to see the Reverend David Vaughan of the Congregational Church, in Wren Road. Kimpton Mission had connections with Wren Road and we felt it was more appropriate than a Church of England service. The Reverend was a nice chap and helped us settle the details. Getting married in a nonconformist church meant that the local registrar had to be present, so our next step was to visit the Town Hall and make the necessary arrangements with him.

Our next visit was to the London County Council's housing office in Spring Gardens, Westminster, to put our names down for a house or flat. We hoped to buy our own home, but in the immediate future felt it best to be close to our parents. With hindsight, it was not a wise decision, for we had a lot of trouble obtaining accommodation locally and it would probably have been better to buy immediately.

Elsie decided to have as her bridesmaids her sister, Dolly, and my two youngest sisters, Denny and Pam. I pondered on who my best man should be. Reg Denner was the obvious choice but I had seen little of him since his marriage and change of job location. There were two other possibilities, my school chums, Noel Vining and Ted Thompson. I had seen Noel recently. He was now married and drove a lorry for his father, which made his movements uncertain. I had kept in touch with Ted, although he, too, had moved from Walworth to Feltham, in Middlesex. I had been to see him at his new home, and his brother Frank had kept me posted about him. In the end it was Ted that I wrote to asking him to be my best man. He agreed, and on 11 August, he and his wife Dolly invited Elsie and me to their home for tea and a chat.

Ted had left Camberwell when he transferred to the London Transport office at Chiswick. His home was on the edge of open country on a new estate, and he and Dolly took us for a stroll around the area. Ted seemed quite happy that I had asked him to be my best man.

In the meantime I ordered my suit for the great occasion from the Co-op Man's shop, in Rye Lane, Peckham.

Elsie and I now started house-hunting in earnest. The local papers seemed to be full of flats and houses to rent but in the event finding a suitable place at a rent we could afford proved extremely difficult. Finally we agreed on the upper flat of a house divided into two at No. 23, Lyndhurst Grove, opposite the school I had attended during the 1914–1918 war. The rent was 17s. 6d. a week, more than we could really afford being nearly one third of my weekly wage. We knew we would have to find somewhere cheaper eventually. If Elsie had been able to continue working after our wedding it would not have been so bad, but the rule of the Royal Arsenal Co-operative Society was that they did not employ married women, and she would have to resign.

Most of our spare time now was devoted to the preparation and planning of our wedding and the reception. We were very ignorant of protocol and the like and had no one who could advise us. We had to meet the cost of our reception and had booked the Mission for this. Grace offered to supervise the catering, an offer we gladly accepted. We ordered the cars and puzzled over the guest list. Elsie was making the bridesmaids' outfits, as well as buying linen and making curtains. Her own wedding dress was being made by our friend Miss Boothby.

We had a break from all this on Sunday, 25 August, when the firm went on its annual outing. The venue was once again Margate, and a special train was hired by the Royal Arsenal Co-operative Society. We managed to get tickets for Mum and Elsie's parents and we had a beautiful day with unbroken sunshine. Elsie and I strolled as far as Cliftonville but our parents were content to sit and relax in the sun.

I started my two-week holiday on 2 September. Elsie resigned from her job and for a few days we were free to go shopping together. We bought our dining room suite from Pearson's, on Denmark Hill. It was of golden oak and consisted of an extending table, four chairs and a sideboard, and cost £14 10s. 0d. Our bedroom suite came from the Co-operative House in Rye Lane and cost £29 10s. 0d., although the bed was extra. The kitchen equipment came from various sources. By the time I left Elsie on the Friday night we were both tired out. We hoped that we had bought most of the essentials. Tomorrow was our wedding day. Hopefully it would go smoothly and be a memorable day for us and our families.

Sleep did not come quickly that night. I lay in bed knowing that that this would be my last night in Stobart Mansions where I had lived for most of my life. The light from the street lamp filled my room and the footsteps of the passers-by echoed on the pavement outside. I could hear the trams rattling by just a few yards away. All familiar sounds I had lived with for many years.

I wondered how Mum would cope without my financial help and what the future held for my sisters. There had been no sign of my father's promised 'ample funds'. I felt despondent when I thought about the past. I was nearly twenty-eight years old and still a shop assistant earning a meagre wage. I seemed to have achieved very little and wondered what the future had in store. I had not the slightest doubt that Elsie and I would be happy together and make a success of our marriage. Money would always be a headache but we would build our home gradually and keep out of debt.

Next morning there was much activity with my sisters going to and fro between home and the Mission carrying provisions, and setting out the tables and chairs. Ted came for me about 1.30 p.m., and after a tearful farewell with Mum we strolled the few yards to Wren Road. As I passed the door of No. 3 it occurred to me that in twenty-eight years I had not strayed far from my birthplace.

The church was full of friends and relatives and the organist was playing softly. Outside the scouts and girls from the Girls' Life Brigade who were to form a guard of honour were already assembled. Ted and I took our places and waited. The bridesmaids had arrived and were ready. Two o'clock came and went and as the minutes ticked away I began to wonder if Elsie had changed her mind. Suddenly the organist struck up the Wedding March and Elsie appeared on her father's arm. She looked very beautiful and as she stood next to me whispered that they had been waiting for the car to come for them. The Reverend Vaughan made a great show although it is hard to recall much of the ceremony.

We moved into the vestry and I was relieved to see the registrar there. Ted and Elsie's sister, Dolly, witnessed the signing and after receiving the congratulations of all present, we left the vestry and walked down the aisle which was lined with friends, relatives and well-wishers. Outside our Guard of Honour was waiting and we were showered with confetti. The sun shone and the photos were taken. Then it was off to the dear old Mission, where we had met on that January evening in 1929, for the wedding breakfast and the speeches. A bucketful of confetti was tipped over us by scouts from an upstairs window as we entered the hall. This then was the start of our new life together, full of hope for the future and confident that come what may we had each other and would succeed.

THE WAR YEARS
1939–1945

This is not a history of the Second World War. That has been documented elsewhere. Rather it is a personal account of how Elsie and I, like millions of other families, met and responded to a challenge that was not of our seeking. Our lives were dramatically disrupted by events over which we had no control.

For a long time previous to the outbreak of war the Government had informed us that another war with Germany was a possibility and that the civilian population, both men and women alike, should in their spare time train as auxiliary firemen, police reservists, air-raid wardens, hospital nurses and rescue squads to provide a back-up service to the regular forces if conflict should come. There was a good response to this appeal and many civilians took up the challenge and were reasonably well trained and equipped by 3 September 1939.

There was every reason to believe that extreme peril threatened the nation for every day the press and radio carried banner headlines or thundered out warnings of imminent catastrophe if any man or woman failed to play their part in time of crisis. As the spring of 1939 merged into summer the preparations for defence were pushed ahead. Public buildings and government offices were cocooned in sandbags. Machine-gun emplacements guarded the bridges. Trenches were dug in public parks and shelters were built in gardens. White bands encircled trees. Gas masks were issued. Windows were blacked out and householders advised to criss-cross the glass with sticky tape to prevent splintering. Mothers and babies were registered for evacuation and businesses began to move from built-up areas. Barrage balloons hung over possible targets.

The conflict, when it eventually erupted, was dramatic in its intensity, fierce and terrifying, a case of overwhelming pressure unceasingly applied. After the British Army was rescued from Dunkirk, the attack on Britain itself began in earnest, and the rain of bombs on cities and towns caused terrible damage and loss of life.

It was a fearful and nerve-wracking time. Mothers and children and the elderly were especially vulnerable. Food was rationed and in short supply, with long queues forming outside shops. Supplies of water, gas and electricity were frequently interrupted. Unexploded bombs were a real hazard, and the terror from the skies began to take its toll of friends and loved ones.

I was seldom in danger but the thought of how Elsie, Doreen, and later Brenda were faring was a continual source of worry. Because of the nature of my work, which involved much travelling, it was almost impossible to have them near me, although we tried a couple of times. Elsie, with two small children, was faced with the dilemma each night the siren sounded of whom she should take to the shelter first. Fortunately she managed the transfer with such speed that the girls rarely had their sleep disturbed. I came home at every possible opportunity and my work occasionally gave me the chance to call in for an hour or two between journeys.

For me it was a complete change to serving people from behind a grocery counter. At the outset I was determined to make the most of any opportunity that came my way. During the next few years I acquired new skills and shouldered responsibilities that held me in good stead when I returned to civilian life.

When I look back on those years of enforced separation from my Elsie and my daughters I feel immensely grateful that we all survived such a dangerous time without serious injury.

Those days are far away now but I remember the comradeship and teamwork that united us all during that time and feel a glow of warmth not only to my RAF colleagues but to the many kind and generous people who welcomed us into their homes. In particular, the village of Tollerton in Yorkshire, and the residents of 'Mardale', who welcomed a stranger into their home and gave him true friendship.

1939

Saturday 26 August to Saturday 2 September

About 8.20 p.m. on the evening of 26h August, 1939, I kicked the sawdust from my shoes, waved goodbye to my colleagues who were still paying in their takings to the shop manager, bundled a few belongings together and left the Camberwell branch of the Royal Arsenal Co-operative Society to start my fortnight's holiday. I little thought as I left the shop that Saturday evening that my working days there were over. For more than twelve years I had served behind the counter and now, in blissful ignorance of what fate had in store for me, I made my way home.

The atmosphere that evening was electric. People going about their everyday affairs were tense and not a little worried about what the coming days might bring. The optimism of last September, when war had been averted following the meeting between Mr Chamberlain and Adolf Hitler, had been replaced by pessimism and despair at the news coming from Europe. During the past few days men had been busy painting white lines down the centre of main roads, and white rings encircled trees, lamp-posts and Post Office pillar boxes. Pavements too were edged in white, and black shields all but obscured the red, amber and green of the traffic lights, leaving only a pinpoint of light to guide pedestrians and vehicles. Outside police stations and on hoardings were notices instructing people on the warnings that would be given in the event of an air attack - a fluctuating whistle for an impending raid, and a long, even signal when the danger had passed. The ringing of handbells would warn that poison gas was present.

I was in thoughtful mood as I made my way home recalling what had happened since Elsie and I had married on 7 September 1935. They had been four happy years despite some financial worries. We had found the rent for our first flat at No. 23, Lyndhurst Grove rather high, so the following year we took an upstairs flat at No. 139, Grove Lane, at thirteen shillings a week. It was far from ideal but we managed. The trams rattled and clanked past the house on their journey to and from Dulwich, but we soon got used to them.

My sister Eileen and Sidney House were married at St Giles Church on 27 September 1936, and the rest of the family took this opportunity to move from Stobart Mansions to No. 24, Hawarden Grove, Herne Hill. Mum and the girls took the ground-floor flat plus a room on the first floor, and Eileen and Sid took over the upstairs rooms. My brother, Reg, had moved to High Wycombe, and Con and Arthur had a house in Shooters Hill, which we visited occasionally.

Things were not going at all well for me at the Co-op and I felt frustrated at my inability to resolve the situation. I think I had been at the branch too long and was being taken for granted. Many of the rotten jobs, like tramping the streets canvassing for orders, came my way, but the fear of losing one's job kept complaints at bay. I am sure Elsie was aware of my feelings. She had done her best to earn a pound or two at home by dressmaking and the like, having had to give up her own job at the Co-op when we married. She had kept up her connections with the Girls' Life Brigade, but I had surrendered my warrant as a Scouter. After my pal Reg Denner had resigned, I had continued with the scout troop and in 1936 took them to camp at St Lawrence on the Isle of Wight. Elsie and some of the Mission girls holidayed at Ryde at the same time so were frequent visitors to the camp. Sometime later the local Scout Commissioners forced an amalgamation on the 43rd which I did not agree with and so resigned, although I did keep up my links with the Rover crew.

Because the situation in Europe was causing such great alarm at this time the message from the wireless and posters alike urged the population to join one of the Civil Defence forces, as police reservists, air-raid wardens, auxiliary firemen and the like. The pressure was so great that most able-bodied people felt they should train for something in case war came. I considered the greatest danger after a raid would be fire and after some deliberation decided to enlist in the Auxiliary Fire Service. I received my training for this at the Peckham Road fire station and was duly issued with a uniform, helmet, gas mask and other equipment. At the end of my training I was given a £1 gratuity.

Our daughter Doreen had been born at St Giles' Hospital on 11 April. She was a beautiful baby and our pride and joy. When we knew she was on the way Elsie and I realised we would need to find more suitable accommodation, and when the ground-floor flat became available we applied for it. The rent of £1 a week was a bit of a shock so although we took the flat we decided the time had come for us to buy a place of our own.

There had also been changes in Elsie's family at this time. Their house in Harris Street was to be included in a big rebuilding scheme. They were offered a house in Morden, but because Elsie's brothers worked in Camberwell her parents decided to take a London County Council flat on an estate in Cowley Road, Brixton.

All did not seem well with my sisters at Herne Hill either. Eileen and Sid seemed often to be in dispute and Mum said she found difficulty in paying the rent. When the middle flat at No. 139, Grove Lane became vacant she decided to take it as the rent was lower. This did not please my young sisters and they did not stay there with her for long but moved back to Herne Hill. However on this evening they were still residing with Mum at No. 139.

Elsie, with Doreen in the pram, met me in Grove Lane and together we slowly walked up the hill, past the school where I had had my very elementary education and over the railway bridge to our home, three houses along from the George Canning public house. Next door to the pub there were two shops, Bunn the newsagents and Knight's the grocers. After leaving school I had briefly worked at Knight's when I could find no other work and I reflected that in all that time I had not gone very far from the scenes of my childhood. As we walked along it was clear that householders had taken notice of Government advice and had criss-crossed their windows with sticky tape and hung up black material to keep any lights from shining into the street. Most people had now registered to receive a gas mask and even little Doreen had a baby mask tried out on her. Elsie and Doreen had registered with the LCC for evacuation should war come although where they would be sent heaven alone knew. It was all most depressing. However, we were due to go on holiday on Monday and that was a ray of sunshine.

The following day, Sunday, was warm and sunny, and in between packing our cases for the holiday, we sat in the garden. A little breeze stirred the flowers and the bees were busy in and around the scarlet blossoms of the runner beans. The tomatoes were beginning to change colour from green to yellow and the first gladioli were in bloom. It was hard to realise as we sat and soaked up the warmth that in the big world outside tempers were rising and armies were mobilising. The newspapers and radio were full of what might happen in Danzig and the Polish Corridor, and experts aired their views on old boundaries, customs and disputes that were at the heart of the trouble.

At about six o'clock in the evening the doorbell rang and I opened the door to see an AFS chap standing there.

'Nobby wants you to come to the station at once', was his cheerful message. 'Some of us have been on duty all day without any relief'.

I discussed the summons with Elsie and decided that my best plan was to go and find out what it was all about. I donned my uniform and made my way to the fire station. Far from being the hive of industry I had imagined, I found the place quiet, with the lads sitting around smoking. There were no instructions on the occurrence board so I went outside. In the road I saw members of the public eyeing the AFS rather curiously and I felt it was all rather depressing. Sometime later a Heavy Unit came into the yard and we were told to load it with about twenty-four lengths of unlined hose, which we did. Half a dozen of us clambered aboard and the Heavy Unit took us to New Cross fire station where we unloaded our cargo and then returned through the crowded streets of Peckham to our base, where we were stood down. I came home feeling it had all been rather pointless.

Elsie and I were up early the next morning as there was much to do before we set off. It was a lovely morning and I took a last look around the garden. The sun shone from a cloudless sky and the dew sparkled on the flowers. As I drank a cup of tea and viewed the Anderson shelter that lay, unerected, on the left-hand side of the garden, I pondered not for the first time on why so-called Christian countries seemed unable to settle their differences without recourse to bloodshed. When trenches were dug in public parks, the population issued with gas masks and households supplied with air-raid shelters, the world seemed a sad place indeed. After breakfast I went upstairs to say cheerio to my mother and to collect my youngest sister, Pam, who was coming with us. We had to make our way to Kennington where we would get the Green Line coach to Aylesbury. It was decided that Elsie and Pam would take the luggage on the tram, whilst I would push Doreen in the pram and meet them there. It was a lovely hot day and the newly painted white lines everywhere dazzled the eyes. At Camberwell Green we passed a number of grey trailer pumps heading towards Peckham, and there seemed to be a lot more men around wearing military uniforms. Outside the police station there were sandbags stacked, and when we reached Kennington Park we saw a silver barrage balloon anchored to the ground by a steel cable. This was an object of great curiosity to the many children who gazed up at it. Doreen was asleep by the time I met up with Elsie and Pam and as there were a few minutes to spare we stood in the shade and waited for the coach. There were several other people waiting at the coach stop but fortunately most of them boarded the coach to Luton. We took Doreen out of the pram and folded it up, and though our coach was fairly full when it arrived, the conductor allowed us to take it on board. Crowds were waiting at Victoria and it seemed that an unofficial evacuation had already begun. People jostled to get on board but many were disappointed and would have to wait another two hours for the next one. We felt we had done the right thing boarding the coach where we did.

This trip had special interest for me as it had been many years since I had travelled this route. When I was about fifteen years of age my brother Reg, Noel Vining and I would rise about 3 a.m. and cycle along this road to the village of Aston Abbotts, my mother's birthplace. In those days there was still a carrier's cart to the villages, and animals would be driven along the road to market. It seemed a more carefree and happy life to the one we faced nowadays. Most of the fields we used to cycle past were now covered by factories and housing estates and it was only after we left Watford that the countryside began again. There were no white lines on the roads here. In the fields the corn had been harvested and stacked in rows over the stubble.

The old-world town of Aylesbury hadn't altered much in the intervening years. There were a few new shops around the cobbled market square and the motor car was gradually replacing the pony and trap. The peacefulness that greeted us was interrupted by the clock tower booming out a welcome. We made our way to the bus station but found that the Leighton Buzzard bus did not leave until four o'clock, another two hours. When it did come many more people had joined the queue and there was a great scramble to get aboard. After an argument with the inspector we were eventually allowed to bring the pram on board, and we settled down for the last part of our journey. We alighted at the Wingrave crossroads, reassembled the pram and made our way uphill to Aston Abbotts, and the Bull and Butcher public house where Mr and Mrs Humphreys were expecting us.

We soon settled in and after a refreshing meal took a stroll around the village, visited some relatives, and went to see the cottage where my grandmother used to live. The trees on the village green carried notices, as they had always done, only the content was different. In the evening, after Doreen had gone to sleep, we went to the bar, played darts with the local lads and listened to the local gossip, mainly concerning the price of wheat and cattle.

Next morning I strolled downstairs into the yard where the hens were busy pecking between the cobbles for seed, and nearby a large sow with a dozen piglets was snorting at a trough. Mr Humphreys was also the village baker and had been busy since 5 a.m. baking the bread he supplied to the surrounding villages. His daughter and son made the deliveries. After breakfast we strolled to the next village, Cublington, and picked our first ripe, juicy blackberries, and then bought a few postcards from the village shop to send to our relatives.

Aston Abbotts has been described elsewhere so I will not dwell on the layout of the village. Some council houses had been built at the entrance to the village and my uncle and aunt lived in one of them, having moved there from Church Row. My uncle, Mum's brother, was seventy years old and had worked on farms all his life, and had never been to London. They invited us to tea the following day and whilst we were there the news coming from the BBC seemed to be a little more optimistic. This optimism, however, proved short-lived.

The next day I borrowed a bicycle and rode into Aylesbury. War fever had gripped the town and it was like entering a different world. People were in the shops panic-buying what they could, including torches and anything that they suspected might become in short supply. Men were painting white lines, and a complete blackout had been ordered that night. I made a few purchases and cycled back to the village. In the afternoon I left Elsie, Doreen and Pam at the inn and went for a stroll in the sunshine. I could hear a wireless giving out some news and paused to listen, which was not difficult for the village was very quiet. Although the afternoon was hot I felt chilled at what I heard. The Government had ordered the evacuation of women and children from the cities. I returned to the inn and switched on the wireless. A rather monotonous voice announced that all Army, Navy and Air Force reservists were being mobilised, and all Territorials were ordered to report to their units. At night a complete blackout of the whole country was to take place, and the nation was being put on a war footing.

The next morning news came through that Germany had invaded Poland. Fighting was reported to be heavy and the cities had been subjected to massive air raids. We strolled to see Aunt Sarah who was full of the news that evacuated children were coming to the village.

Borrowing the bicycle again I rode once more into town. A group of children carrying little bundles and cardboard boxes containing their gas masks had already arrived and were being shepherded along by local officials with the help of scouts and guides from the town. The sight of these little ones, poorly clad and plainly very apprehensive was quite upsetting. The older children were comforting the younger ones while the adults, who I took to be their school teachers, tried to keep their confidence up. I consoled myself with the thought that if London were bombed these little ones would be safer in the countryside.

When I arrived back, I related what I had seen. That afternoon we joined the landlord's daughter and her cousin who were off to the nearby field where the haymaking was in progress. The girls, and Pam, had a great time throwing each other in the hay and stuffing it down each other's necks. When night came, no lights showed in the village and I knew we must be quite invisible from the air. I knew too that Elsie and Doreen would be far safer here in the village than back in London and I hoped they would be able to remain at the inn, for the time being at least. Pam's school had already drawn up plans for evacuating their pupils, but the news report had said that anyone on holiday should not return for the evacuation.

That night orders to the country's citizens came over the wireless thick and fast. Only two of the BBC's wavelengths would be used and both would give the same programme. Every reservist was ordered to report to his station, all air-raid wardens, police reservists and auxiliary firemen were mobilised. All cinemas were to be closed, football matches cancelled and many of London's underground stations were to be closed for alterations. Buses, coaches and lorries were commandeered by the Government who, by special orders signed by the King, now possessed unlimited powers over the people. All this meant the end of my holiday with Elsie, Doreen and Pam. True, no war had been declared but that final step could not be far away. I longed to remain on holiday with them, but Elsie and I knew that I had to make my contribution to the defence needs and that meant returning home at once. Mr and Mrs Humphreys agreed to let them stay for as long as the rooms were available. Most people found it difficult to sleep that night, wondering what the next few hours would bring. Little Doreen, unaware of the turmoil surrounding her, slept soundly. Her first four months of life had been peaceful and adventurous, and we hoped by the time she became more aware of the world around her, life would have returned to some sort of normality.

At breakfast the next morning a telephone call came for me. It was my sister Vera, ringing from London. She told me that the Auxiliary Fire Service had been to the house three times now and they were demanding that I return and report for duty. She agreed that Pam could stay on with Elsie if she wished, so everything was settled. With great reluctance I accepted that the time had come for me to leave Aston Abbotts and my family and return home to London. I packed my few belongings into a parcel, bade farewell to Elsie, Doreen and Pam, thanked Mr and Mrs Humphreys and waited outside the inn for the bus into Aylesbury.

In Aylesbury I discovered that the Green Line buses were no longer running, so I headed for the railway station. There were long lines of children emerging from the station, and people milling around everywhere. It was the nearest to panic that I had ever seen. I presented my coach ticket at the booking office but they would not accept it until the evening. I went back into town in the hope of finding other transport, but there was none. All the coaches and buses were being used to transport the evacuees to the outlying villages, or had been commandeered for other duties. I went back to the station and bought a ticket.

The journey to London was quiet and uneventful. The sun which had shone from a cloudless sky all week was still golden and warm, but for once I took little interest in it or the countryside gliding past. As we approached the capital the skies became dotted with silvery barrage balloons, and I observed more trenches, sandbags and shop windows criss-crossed with gummed paper.

I went straight to Elsie's parents' house in Brixton. Her family was glad to see me and asked what plans I had made for Elsie and Doreen. I explained the present situation but given the uncertainty of everything, who could make plans? I stayed for a cup of tea then boarded a tram to the fire station at Peckham. When I arrived, the place seemed to be in a state of chaos. Men and women were milling around the place, some clutching slips of paper, others looking lost, seemingly without any direction or control. After about twenty minutes I found one of the regulars that I knew. His advice was to go home, get enough rations for forty-eight hours, and then report to the sub-station in Haymerle Road.

I went home, where my mother prepared a meal for me while I related all the village news. She in turn updated me with the family news. My brother had already been called up, and Vera was being moved to Harrogate with the Post Office. After I had eaten I went downstairs to our flat, put some gear into a case, collected some provisions, including a tin of corned beef, and put on my uniform. My brother-in-law gave me a lift back to Peckham where I was issued with a steel helmet and a gas mask. I walked to Rye Lane and waited for a bus, only to find that no buses were running, so, fully laden, I had to walk all the way to Haymerle Road, where I arrived hot and despondent. When I reported in, I was sent home again for some blankets. I wondered why I had been insane enough to return from holiday.

By the time I arrived back the lads had just stopped filling sandbags, and were relaxing by playing darts or just sitting around chatting. The hours passed slowly with the inactivity. I met up with one of the acting sub-officers who had trained in the same class as me and together we went around checking the equipment, the taxi numbers, and visiting the fire alarm stations, located at various points in the area. The general plan of operation was that at each street fire alarm there would be stationed a trailer pump and crew. There were six substations to each main station where additional pumps were placed in reserve. In theory it was a good plan, but in practice it collapsed. That night we slept on bags of sawdust on the hall floor, until at around midnight a terrific thunderstorm shattered the stillness. Rain fell in torrents, drumming on the corrugated roof of the building making an uncomfortable and unpleasant situation even worse. The storm passed and then returned. We slept very little.

Sunday 3rd September

The morning of 3 September was bright, with the sun drying up the puddles from the night before. I ate a couple of rolls, which was all I had. One of the men had a radio set, and when we switched it on the news was dominated by the war in Poland. We were also advised to stand by for an important announcement. We went into the road to continue filling sandbags but when the next news bulletin was due we trooped inside to listen. The announcer explained at length the Government's position on the situation in Europe, and ended by saying that an ultimatum had been presented to Germany and that if they did not withdraw their troops from Poland by 11 a.m., a state of war would exist between our two countries.

The substation in Haymerle Road was at the furthest point from my home and I was anxious to have this anomaly remedied. At 10.45 a.m. the officer in charge asked for volunteers to man the fire alarms. I stepped forward and was sent back to the main station in Peckham Road. Before I reached there the Government's time limit had expired so I was too late to hear the Prime Minister's speech to the nation, when he announced that we were now at war with Germany. It was a terrible situation to be in. For a long time we had been filled with horror stories of what would happen if war should come. How mass bombing could flatten and destroy cities. Other stories, however, portrayed Germany as a bankrupt nation using dummy equipment, and that any war would be over by Christmas. I was old enough to remember similar statements in 1914 when the First World War started.

I reported to the office at Peckham and was told to take a couple of hours' leave. It did not seem worthwhile taking my luggage home so I took it upstairs to the canteen where I was allowed to leave it in a corner. I was about to make my way downstairs again when the air was filled with the undulating shriek of an air-raid siren. I hastened down and went out on to the pavement in front of the station. The wailing siren had brought near panic to the neighbourhood. Traffic came to a halt, police whistles vied with the siren to be heard, people raced to the air-raid shelters and barrage balloons on the ground were being hastily raised. All eyes were raised to the sky for the first glimpse of enemy planes. The crews of the fire appliances made ready and had their engines running. I seized my helmet and gas mask and went into the station yard. The faces around me, probably like my own, looked white and strained as we prepared to face what we could not know or imagine. Everyone feared the worst and believed that Hitler had sent out a fleet of bombers to coincide with the declaration of war. The streets were soon deserted and for a few minutes an unreal silence fell over the area. Then came the long continuous note of the siren giving the all-clear, and everyone breathed again.

The strain gave way to relief; people poured back onto the streets, and life returned to normality of a sort. Rumours circulated freely but the truth was that nobody knew what was happening with any degree of certainty. I went home and had a meal with my family and then returned to duty.

I met an old friend that I had not seen for many years and we stood, chatting of days gone by and what might be store for us in the future. As he said, 'The lights have gone out again. How long for this time?'

By early afternoon life seemed to have resumed its normal course. The trams rattled by and the occasional omnibus appeared in the streets. The barrage balloons had been lowered and people began to appear once more, just like any other Sunday. More auxiliaries joined Harold Holdaway and myself in the station yard and we sat on the sandbags chatting in the warm sunshine. Every now and then a London Fire Brigade officer would appear at the station and take down our names. Gradually our ranks began to thin as small groups of men were sent off to different substations until eventually only about a dozen of us remained. Then at about 5 p.m. an officer came and selected half a dozen of our number and said they were being sent to No. 66 station, Clerkenwell. The rest of us thanked our lucky stars we'd been missed but about fifteen minutes later a taxi pulled into the yard and we were told to get on board with our gear. When we asked our destination, we were told it was Clerkenwell as the high-risk areas now took priority. This did not go down at all well with the group, Clerkenwell being on the other side of the river and a long way from our homes. As we left the river and drove northward our hearts sank further as we gazed at the height of the palatial buildings and office blocks. It didn't take too much imagination to visualise these buildings on fire and collapsing on us.

Clerkenwell Fire Station soared upwards like a New York skyscraper. On arrival we were sent up to the top of the building, and from the windows we had a wonderful view of the City of London. Down below we could see the rows of fire appliances and a street of derelict houses with pane-less windows. High buildings surrounded us on all sides. After a few minutes we were called back down the many flights of stairs to the yard. Here we met up with the other AFS chaps from Peckham, whose comments about the Fire Service organisation and personnel were unprintable. We hung around for about thirty minutes and then, with another group of men from Battersea, were packed into a van and sent off again. We appeared to be heading further north through the streets of heavily sandbagged and boarded shops until we drew into the yard of the Holloway Fire station. Our spirits rose a little for the area around appeared quiet and residential, with two-storied houses, gardens and trees.

Once again we were sent to the top of the building only to be sent down a few minutes later, reminding us of The Grand Old Duke of York nursery rhyme. On *terra firma* we lined up opposite the front of the station, looking a sad little group of souls, tired and hungry. A few children who had not been evacuated came and stared at us, compounding the sense of despair we were all beginning to feel at the way the day was turning out. In contrast to Peckham, this station seethed with activity. Trailer pumps piled high with gear were moving out and heavy units and tenders chugged up and down the road. Again, our names were taken.

The Battersea contingent from our little group, now in Bolshie mood, demanded time for a cup of tea, and were given a ten-minute break. This extended to half an hour due to difficulties getting one. We went off next and managed to squeeze into a very crowded café opposite the Post Office. We didn't take long over our refreshments but even so some officers came to chase us out. However, after all the pushing around we had endured we were in no mood for this sort of treatment. Too soon though we were back in our small groups outside the station. The Battersea men, with one exception, were sent off in various directions, and then our Peckham group was split up and sent off, leaving three including myself and the orphan from Battersea. The district officer came up to me and asked if I felt capable of taking charge of a station. When I said yes, he handed me a notebook and told me to take down some particulars. We were to head for the North London Home for the Blind, Hanley Road substation at Thornhill Laundry, Regina Road, ARC 4072. We were to notify the substation immediately on arrival. At last, things seemed to be moving quickly. I had been pushed out of one station and made sub-officer in another in the space of twenty-four hours. There was no time to ponder on this, however, as the four of us were bundled into a taxi and sped off into the night. The little fellow from Battersea sat next to me and putting his arm across my shoulders whispered confidentially, 'Leave everything to me, I'll see you're alright'.

I cannot say he inspired me at all, in fact I disliked him from the start. I asked him what was his position in the crew. He answered, with some hesitation, that he worked the pump. I told him the pump was his.

After a rather uncomfortable journey we stopped in front of a long, newly built hospital on two floors. The place was in total darkness.

'I think you'll be very comfortable here', said the driver as we disembarked and he restarted the car. Soon the tiny red tail lamp of the taxi disappeared round a corner and the four of us were left stranded like survivors of a shipwreck.

On the wide white stone slope leading up to the entrance to the building, a trailer pump piled high with equipment was standing. While we were looking over it, three young men came out to meet us from inside the glass doors. I thought they were AFS but they introduced themselves as hospital staff, and seemed very glad to see us. One of them, Eric, took me inside to the telephone switchboard and showed me how to operate the day and night boards. I rang the substation and after much difficulty made them understand who I was and where we were. In what appeared to be a maze of corridors I endeavoured to find my way back until fortunately I was 'found' by Eric, who conducted me into a lofty hall. Several old people were sitting there and an organ was playing. I took it to be the hospital chapel. At the back were two small rooms that had been set aside for our use. We stowed our luggage in one of them and returned to the entrance to overhaul the gear on the trailer pump. My instincts about the Battersea chap proved right. He knew nothing about the pump and fussed around, getting in the way. We ignored him as best we could and got on with the job of preparing for possible action. As we finished, the superintendent, a Mr Kissach, came out and gave us the welcome news that a meal was waiting for us inside. It was a real feast spread out for us with a kettle on the boil, but strangely I had no appetite for it.

A local lad was stationed at the street fire alarm, about fifty yards along the road. He had reported to me when we arrived. I guessed he would be hungry sitting there alone, so we sent a mug of tea and some food along to him. Our next job was to get the trailer pump going, but this was proving difficult. Our Battersea friend, Dunkleigh, nicknamed 'Tom Thumb' by the crew, was no help, knowing less than I did, and the pump refused to start. After a while the lad from the fire alarm came by to thank us for the tea and I asked him if he knew anything about engines. He told me he was a lorry driver and he soon diagnosed that there was no petrol getting to the engine.

Once this had been resolved and we had run the pump a few times I felt we should all try to get some sleep. This was not to be, however, as just at that moment the local station officer called by. He was pleased that the engine problem had been resolved and thanked us for our efforts, but said we should run the pump every two hours as trouble was expected. We split into two watches, Tubb and myself first, then Avey and Dunkleigh. I wrapped my solitary blanket around me and lay down on the cold, hard floor and tried to sleep. I had hardly closed my eyes when the siren started wailing. As I made my way back to the appliance, the home suddenly burst into life as the staff began to shepherd the residents down the stairs to the entrance hall. The old folk, men and women, made a pitiful sight as they shuffled along, each carrying their gas mask in a cardboard box. We chatted to them and tried our best to reassure them, and our presence certainly seemed to give them some sense of security. In fact, they probably had more confidence in us than we had in ourselves.

Mr Kissach, the superintendent, appeared wearing a steel helmet and stood with us for a while gazing up into the night sky. He told us that our presence had averted a panic amongst the residents, and that the noise of the pump, far from annoying them, had made them feel safer and more secure. After half an hour the all-clear sounded and the residents returned to their beds. We stood down and I returned to the church hall where I sat in one of the pews and wrote a letter to Elsie by the light of my torch. Afterwards another chap and myself decided to check out where the fire hydrants were located in the surrounding streets. It was not easy in the dark but we returned with a fair idea of where we could connect up and felt much happier at the way things were shaping up.

Monday 4 September

Morning came at last and we began to familiarise ourselves with our surroundings at the home. We were told that it had been built less than a year ago, during the previous October. A number of the residents came out to meet us and find out more about us. They asked lots of questions, ran their hands over the pump and its controls, and thanked us for being there. It was a great morale booster for us.

The day proved to be a quiet one, but in the evening we received a call from the substation to let us know that a taxi was being delivered to us for towing the pump. We had no official driver, a 'BI' man in London Fire Brigade terms, but Avey said he could drive and the taxi arrived as promised. Unfortunately, when Avey tried manoeuvring the vehicle to link up with the pump all sorts of complications arose. Luckily, help came from an unexpected quarter. A new lad had arrived to man the fire alarm and he offered to help. He took over from Avey and much to my relief soon had things sorted out. Our antics with the taxi had attracted quite a crowd of onlookers whose amusement with our predicament was plain to see.

Alfred Loader was the name of our saviour and I felt he would be a very useful addition to our squad if we could enlist him. As it happened, Tubb was about to return to Peckham that evening and when, during the day, the sub-officer came round, I asked if I could have Loader as a replacement. It was agreed that he could stay temporarily whilst a request was put through to the superintendent. Alf Loader did not live too far away so I sent him home to collect his gear. While he was away, Sub-officer Pink phoned for more information about Tubb and Loader. During the course of our conversation he asked to speak to Loader. When I told him he was collecting his gear from the substation he got quite angry.

'Who gave him permission to leave the station?', he roared, 'His absence means your pump is disabled, and yours is the only one that is operational.'

As I understood it every fire alarm in the area was manned and I told him so.

'Well, they're not. If anything happens your pump is the only one ready to back up the red appliances. What's going to happen when you're called out? Who's going to drive?'

I replied that in an emergency, Avey could drive.

'Has he passed out as a BI man?' his voice rose.

'No.'

By now he was really angry. 'Then you are disabled, he can't take the pump out.'

I began to loose my temper. 'In case of emergency anyone could take it out and manhandle it if it came to the worst. If you don't like the way I'm handling things send me back to Peckham.'

The situation was saved when just at that moment Alf Loader reappeared. I handed him the phone and he received a dressing down. However, after tempers had cooled Sub-officer Pink phoned me again and all ended on a happier note. In fact, after that we ended up on good terms. He confirmed Alf as one of my crew members.

Alf Loader's joining us made Dunkleigh turn quite nasty, as it was the driver's job to look after the pump. I would never have trusted him with it anyway, but he began to rant about the injustice of it all and predicted that mayhem and disaster would ensue without a good man like himself in the job. With that he marched off to bed. He was really getting on my nerves.

Tuesday 5 September

By now we had, more or less, settled in. Mr Kissach supplied us with room and board on the understanding that we paid something toward it. I told him that we were not very comfortable in the church vestry so he found us a large room on the first floor which proved much more suitable. A telephone was laid on and a 'C' man (non-operational duties) joined us to man it. I continued drilling my squad to make sure each man was familiar with the other's role. Dunkleigh was hopeless, he knew nothing and wouldn't be told either. For two hours that afternoon I tried to drum into his thick skull that his place in the taxi was behind the driver. Our jumping in and out of the taxi amused one of the local constabulary who was passing by. We invited him in for a cup of tea and he said that he would tip us off if any small fires occurred.

Wednesday 6 September

I took over the watch at 3 a.m. and sat dreaming by the telephone waiting for dawn. At 6.45 a.m. the sirens started. We grabbed our helmets and axes, ready for action. Two minutes later the substation phoned a yellow warning and ten minutes later came the red. This was serious. I warned Mr Kissach and once again the old folk were shepherded down the stairs. We started the engines and waited for goodness knows what. In the distance we heard the sound of gunfire and it all began to look very threatening. Time passed without incident until at 9.07 a.m. the all-clear sounded and we were stood down.

In the afternoon the sub-officer from Holloway paid us a visit. He seemed a decent chap and appreciated our efficiency. We were told to tell the substation to put us on the rota for twenty-four hours' leave and he would drop in again to see us the following day.

Just before 9 p.m. Avey, who was manning the telephone, said our friendly copper had reported a fire at Crouch Hill. We dashed out to the pump, donned our equipment and waited for Dunkleigh, who had failed to appear. Valuable seconds were being lost. I raced back into the building to have a last look when I heard one of the crew say, 'Where the blazes have you been?'

Obviously Dunkleigh had turned up so I rushed out of the building to the taxi and trailer, which were already moving. I made a flying leap to my position at the side of the driver only to bounce of someone sitting there. I fell back into the road, fortunately clear of the pump, and staggered to my feet. Alf stopped the taxi. In my position Dunkleigh was sitting, despite all the instructions we had given him. I made him get out and take his proper place and said I would deal with him later.

In Crouch Hill we met our policeman friend who directed us to a butcher's shop. It turned out not to be a fire but ammonia fumes leaking from the cold store. We made our way down a narrow passage to the rear of the shop. I kicked open the back door. Inside was another locked door. I gave it a shoulder charge but it resisted my efforts. I ran back a few paces and charged again. In the meantime, however, Bill Avey, a hefty chap, booted it open. My rush took me through the door right into the midst of the ammonia fumes. I staggered out gasping. Dunkleigh had the pyrene extinguisher in his hands and muttered, 'Use this'.

I despaired. 'Get outside and put that back. Are you trying to kill us all?'

As I stood there trying to think what to do next I had a horrifying thought.

I hadn't notified the substation I was turning out, which was unforgivable. I went out to Loader and told him to phone the substation that we were turning out *en route* for Crouch Hill. He came back to me and said they were getting ready to back us up.

I waited for about two minutes and then went to a nearby telephone box, explained the position and said breathing apparatus was needed from the main station. Soon after a red appliance arrived and we were sent back to Hanley Road. Later we were congratulated on one of the fastest turnouts on record and received a pat on the back from Sub-officer Beck of Holloway. By all accounts we had won our spurs. I kept quiet about what had really happened.

Thursday 7 September

After my near accident with Dunkleigh, I decided he had to go, and when some top brass came on an inspection I insisted he be replaced. By now my record-breaking turnout had become the talking point of the area and I was regarded as rather efficient. This was reinforced when we were asked to report with our pump to the substation. All the area pumps were to be tested to see how quickly each crew could bring the hoses into play from a standing start. We were quicker by a good half minute. This was not because we were better than the others but because we had modern equipment.

In those days the hoses and branches used by the London Fire Brigade had what was known as 'round thread' connections, making it necessary to screw everything up and tighten with a large spanner. The pump I had been put in charge of was a Canadian Coventry Climax with instantaneous coupling. Connections were made by pulling back two springs, pushing in the hose and letting go — a matter of a couple of seconds. The speed of the action really staggered the old hands, and we returned to Hanley Road on top of the world.

Happily, Dunkleigh was transferred to the substation soon after and I was sent as his replacement a nice young chap named Frank Bremner. He had had no experience of fire-fighting equipment, but was very willing. That evening I went over to the substation, which was housed in a laundry, and talked things over with Sub-officer Pink, who couldn't do enough for me.

Sunday 10 September

Today it was my turn for a day's leave. A taxi came to take me home and it was not long before I returned to the refreshingly familiar area of Camberwell. I had decided to go straight from there to Aston Abbots to see Elsie, Doreen and Pam. Mother said she would like to have Pam home and asked me to bring her back with me.

By one o'clock I was in Aylesbury market square. There were no buses so I had no option but to walk the last six miles. At a point opposite the prison a car pulled up and offered me a lift. I accepted gratefully and in a few minutes I was alighting at the Wingrave crossroads. It was hard to realise as I made my way up the hill to the village that the nation was at war. It was all so peaceful and I didn't pass a single person.

Elsie was now staying at my uncle's house on the outskirts of Aston Abbots. I liked Uncle George, my mother's brother, although I was not so keen on Aunt Sarah. However, when I arrived they were at lunch and the atmosphere seemed cordial enough, which was a relief. Afterwards I walked around the garden and admired his handiwork, and then Elsie and I climbed up Lines Hill, the highest point in the Chilterns. We spent a lovely time together in the warm autumn sunshine, but the time soon passed, and it was time to leave. Pam was coming with me but Elsie and Doreen would stay on for a while.

I said goodbye and thanked my aunt and uncle. Elsie, with Doreen in the pram, accompanied Pam and myself to the crossroads where we waited for the bus. None came so we knew we would have to walk. We said goodbye to Elsie and Doreen and we started on our way, lugging Pam's heavy case. Looking back I saw Elsie and the pram moving slowly up the hill. After about a quarter of a mile our luck changed when a car stopped and gave us a lift into Aylesbury. We travelled without too much frustration back to London and the blackout.

The country had been at war almost a week. The news from Poland was grim. Despite heroic resistance the country was being steadily overrun. Towns and villages were ruthlessly bombed and destroyed and the capital, Warsaw, was the target for high explosives and incendiary attacks. It seemed only a matter of time before Poland capitulated. There was no action on the Western Front and the armies faced each other from behind the Maginot and Siegfried lines.

Monday 11 September to 31 December

On returning from my day's leave I found the boys had been called to Crouch Hill again to deal with another ammonia leakage at the butcher's shop. However, after this we were told only to attend fires from now on.

The days now began to pass slowly. We busied ourselves around the home for the blind, mowing the lawns and making ourselves as useful as we could. I was about to go to bed the following Thursday night when a message came over the phone that we were to pack up our belongings and report with taxi and pump to the substation at 7.30 a.m. the following morning. This was a real blow to us all. We were on good terms with the staff and residents at the home, but orders were orders. Mr Kissach was most upset when I told him we were moving out and said he would take action to have us back if possible. It was a very gloomy crew that left for the laundry the next morning and our arrival there did nothing to cheer us up one bit. The place was dirty and dingy and one room sufficed to house the AFS. Although we put a brave face on it our hearts sank at the prospect of a prolonged stay. We parked our pump alongside the others and made our way inside. We were not made very welcome, and the local lads made no secret of the resentment they felt toward the Peckham crew whose prowess was held in high regard by the top brass.

I was out in the yard supervising the cleaning of the taxi and pump in the afternoon when, at about 2 p.m., I was called into the room that served as the substation office. I went in and stood there for a moment waiting in silence for the station officer to speak. He looked up and glared at me.

'You have some powerful friends, haven't you?' he said.

This quite took me aback. 'Why, what has happened?' I replied.

'You're being sent back to Hanley Road,' came the answer. 'Somebody pretty powerful has been pulling strings and your station is being treated as a special case. Go and get your crew and take yourselves off. Phone through when you are ready for action'.

Needless to say we were all highly delighted and couldn't leave the laundry premises quickly enough. When we reached the home for the blind, Mr Kissach summoned me and said there had been near panic among the residents when we left and he had managed to persuade the fire hierarchy to reverse their decision.

Soon we had settled in again and, as things were quiet with no signs of any air raids, a routine was soon settled into. The pump had to be continually manned for the whole twenty-four hours and, as well as the extra man to answer the telephone, we were also given a relief man from the substation to cover any days off taken by the crew. Our meals were supplied by the home and in return I collected the allowances from the lads and passed the cash on to Mr Kissach.

On Wednesday 20 September, Elsie and Doreen came home. Her sister met her at Marylebone station and they had a taxi home. I think she was glad to be back home at No. 139. I had twenty-four hours' leave on the Friday and spent it with them before returning to Hanley Road the following day.

On Sunday 24 September, my sister Grace and John Ryan were married at the Church of the Sacred Heart. Elsie and Doreen went to the wedding and by all accounts it went very well. John was an excellent chap and a real asset to the family. I was sorry not to go but the duty rota did not permit my absence.

The following Sunday Sister Audrey and Bill Brooks were married at St Giles' Church and this time I was able to attend. I had the honour of giving the bride away and making the speech at the reception. They rented a flat at No. 222, Croxted Road, and stayed there for many years. Like myself, Bill had trained as a fireman, but unlike me, he stayed with the fire service throughout the war.

It was difficult to keep track of what was happening to our family and friends during this period, which later became known as the 'phoney war'. Cecil MacCarthy, who was in the Territorial Army, had been training at summer camp at the outbreak of war and was immediately drafted into the forces, and sent to France with the British Expeditionary Force. Cecil was courting my sister, Vera.

Mrs MacCarthy lived with her family, a boy and girl, in the mansions in the opposite block. There was no Mr MacCarthy around and there were rumours that he was in Australia, but I don't think anyone was really sure. Certainly Mrs Mac was left with her two little ones to rear alone. The family lived at No. 8, with her sister, Mrs Tetlow, at No. 12. Mrs Tetlow had a daughter, Patricia, but like Mr Mac, Mr Tetlow was conspicuous by his absence. I was not a fan of either lady and tried to keep my distance. Mrs MacCarthy's daughter, Rosebud, was suddenly taken ill and died. Her death was a shattering blow and I don't think the old lady ever really recovered from the shock. One day my sister, Eileen, was playing in the yard with some of the girls from the other flats when Mrs Mac came into the yard to hang out some washing. On seeing Eileen she collapsed from shock and took a great deal of reviving. Evidently, my sister could have been Rosebud's twin, having the same auburn hair and similar in height and build. For a long time Mrs Mac refused to believe that Eileen was not her Rosebud and she became a frequent visitor (sometimes unwelcome) to our flat. If ever a woman doted on another's girl it was Mrs Mac. She was quite open in her purpose that when her son, Cecil was of age, he would marry our Eileen. I thought highly of my sister and used to get quite angry about it, but in the event I need not have worried as Eileen married Sidney House on 27 September, 1936.

However, Mrs Mac did not give up that easily. She was determined that her son, Cecil (who everyone called 'boy'), would marry into the family, and her hopes were realised when he later married sister Vera.

Although things were reasonably quiet on the war front, restrictions affecting our daily lives were already taking place. Fuel was being rationed and the allowance was based on the previous year's consumption. It was rather a clumsy scheme, the allowance being 75% of the previous year's purchase, and there were no provisos. If for any reason you had not ordered a normal amount in a previous quarter, that became your allowance, and you could not claim it later.

Air-Raid precautions were stepped up. Some of the street Air-Raid Precaution wardens became little dictators who tramped the streets looking for the tiniest pinpoint of light and would gleefully shout, 'Put that light out', or hammer on door knockers at the slightest provocation. They were not averse to calling the police out to back up their demands, and they became thoroughly detested. We had trouble with one in Grove Lane when a curtain had moved a little allowing a chink of light to show through. It was only the presence of Arthur Tilley, Con's husband, a police officer, that soothed an awkward situation.

There were various leaflets explaining what one should do to make the home safe. It was all very well for the authorities to tell the public how to board up their windows or where to place sandbags for maximum effect, but the fact was that most people hadn't enough money for the necessities of life let alone black-out material and boarding for the basements. Most folk crisscrossed their window glass with sticky paper to try and reduce the blast splinters, and if they had a cellar, they cleaned it out and put a few essentials there in case it was needed as a refuge.

For those people without any obvious shelter but with garden space, the authorities distributed Anderson shelters. These were named after Sir John Anderson, the Minister for Home Security. They had to be erected about fifteen feet away from buildings and as our home in Grove Lane had a long garden we had ample space for one. They were solidly made of corrugated steel and were delivered in sections that could be put together in the shape of an arch. They had to be buried in the ground to a depth of three feet and then covered with garden soil over the arch to a depth of fifteen inches. They could accommodate four to six people and one felt reasonably secure inside, but they were gloomy places, musty and damp.

At fairly regular intervals the air-raid siren would be sounded but one never knew if it was just a practice, or the real thing. The 'take cover' warning was a horrible sound and sent shivers down one's spine. The sirens were sited at police stations and on high, strategic buildings and made a high-pitched, warbling sound and were often accompanied by sharp blasts from police or warden's whistles. Public air-raid shelters were around which people were expected to make for, but in residential areas they were in short supply.

The all-clear signal was a continuous blast for a period of two minutes, and when it came people heaved a sigh of relief and poured out of the shelters like swarming ants. The use of poisoned gas was always a frightening possibility and the Government insisted that every person must carry their gas mask with them. The warning for a gas attack would be by wardens' rattles, although, fortunately, gas was never used.

During this time, many of the children who had been evacuated prior to the declaration of war began to drift back home. Many mothers who had accompanied the youngest evacuees had been reluctant to leave their husbands and homes in the first place, and not everyone had been made welcome in their temporary lodgings.

At the outbreak of hostilities quite a few of the Government departments and some large businesses moved out to the provinces. My sister, Vera, who was a telephonist, was sent on a temporary transfer to Harrogate. She didn't stay there long before she requested a return to London, giving her mother's health as the excuse. From what I gathered, not all the young girls, often attractive and single, were made welcome, and many had found great difficulty in finding accommodation. Sometimes they were compulsorily billeted, with some unhappy results. Men, on the other hand, seemed to experience little difficulty in getting comfortable lodgings.

The tour of duty in the London Fire Brigade was forty-eight hours on and twenty-four hours off. I came home once a week, and spent the rest of my spare time exploring the neighbourhood, visiting Hampstead Heath, Ken Wood and Golders Green. At home, Elsie was searching for more suitable accommodation for us, but despite many hours trudging around the street, nothing suitable turned up, and we stayed at Grove Lane.

My old school in Camberwell was not far away from an AFS station and I could not help thinking how convenient it would be if I could get a transfer there. A shop colleague, Bill Morrow, was one of the crew stationed there. I called in to see him occasionally. The crew seemed quite happy there and had a shelter in the school playground, bolstered by sand bags. It looked very secure, but in the event it did not provide the expected safety.

With the call-up of young men and women to the forces, there were plenty of marriages brought forward. Many of our friends from Kimpton Mission and the scout and rover troops were married and then scattered far and wide. Elsie's brother Tim took it upon himself to keep everyone in touch with a newsletter, called *Den Contact*. It was very successful and he kept it going throughout the war.

I had, of course, long since written to the Royal Arsenal Co-operative Society about my call-up. It was a worrying time where jobs were concerned. Although the Government had decreed that returning men and women from the forces could demand their old jobs back, there were always loopholes for reluctant employers. I had called in the shop a couple of times but felt no confidence that my job there was safe.

I received a rather saucy letter from the officer in charge at Peckham Fire Station asking for the return of my uniform as I had not reported for duty. Elsie's sister Dolly was a telephonist there, so I asked her to explain the situation to him. I understand she did this but there must have been some confusion because I received a further letter. This time I wrote back explaining the situation and hoped that would end the matter. It did not. By now I was really angry and wrote a very sarcastic letter and this had the desired effect.

By now I was getting disillusioned with the AFS and this incident did not help. Discipline was becoming stricter and although I was in charge I received no extra pay for my responsibilities. Holloway was a long way from home and I no longer had a taxi to take me back and forth. The pay was only three pounds a week plus a small subsistence allowance that I paid directly to Mr Kissach for the food he provided. An old friend of my family, Mrs Thompson, died about this time and I began to feel out of touch with things at home. I should have liked to go to the funeral, but I was on duty that day and Elsie had to go in my place. Christmas was fast approaching and the rota showed that I would be on duty on Christmas Day. I managed to get home on Christmas Eve and we had a little party with Elsie's parents and family, but I had to return to Hanley Road early next morning. The home for the blind had a nice party and I did a little entertaining, but I missed being at home for Doreen's first Christmas. I came home again on Saturday the 30th and went with my sister Denise and my mother to my brother Reg's home in Clapham. Elsie stayed at home with Doreen and went upstairs to see the New Year in with my sisters.

1940

The New Year arrived and the phoney war continued. It was very cold weather and we were often called out on drills. I began to hate the job. Then something happened, insignificant in itself, but it gave me the opportunity I had been looking for. The substation had been numbered 76 U on the Fire Service records, and one of the lads stationed there was a sign-writer. He was given the job of painting this number on the side of each taxi and trailer pump. For this work he was made a sub-officer. This promotion caused extreme resentment among the firemen both at the substation and among my own crew. The outcome was a round robin sent to the senior officers voicing their displeasure and grievance. They had asked me to sign it but I refused, not wanting to become involved. A day or two later the top brass of the brigade descended upon us and called the squad, about ten men, to attention. They asked me to stand aside. I cannot recall the actual words said, but the lads received a real dressing down from the area chief, who evidently disliked round robins. I was extremely glad not to be a recipient of his wrath. He ended his tirade by saying that those dissatisfied with the AFS should send in their resignations and they would be accepted.

My heart leapt at hearing his words. Here was the opportunity I had been waiting for, the chance to pack it all in and get back home. I tried to stay calm but the urge to laugh was strong. I was called over to Sub-officer Beck who said I was wise not to sign the round robin, as the hierarchy wouldn't forget it. I couldn't have cared less. I could see my way out of the Fire Service. On my next visit home I talked to Elsie and we agreed that I should write to the staff manager of the Royal Arsenal Co-operative Society and ask if I could return to my old job. I received an affirmative reply and on returning to Hanley Road I handed in my resignation and refused to withdraw it.

I returned my uniform but was allowed to keep my hat badge, as a memento. Mr Kissach and his staff were sorry we were parting company as we had had a very good relationship. On the morning of my departure three of the top brass from the London Fire Brigade came to Hanley Road, thanked me for my services and wished me luck. Soon I was on my way home to Camberwell, feeling as though a great weight had been lifted from my shoulders. I told myself never to volunteer for anything else again. I returned once to Hanley Road to see the lads and that was the end of another chapter of my life, as far as I was concerned.

It was good to be back at home with Elsie and Doreen. What lay ahead for me was impossible to guess. By resigning from the Fire Service I had made myself eligible for call-up to the armed services, but I was prepared to take that chance. Things were still very quiet on the war front. There had been a raid on the Shetland Islands and a bomb had fallen and killed a rabbit. A popular song at the time, 'Run Rabbit Run', was parodied to 'Run Hitler Run', and many tried to make light of the war situation.

Contrary to expectations, the Royal Arsenal Co-operative Society did not send me back to the Camberwell Green branch, but told me to report to the Peckham shop in Nunhead Green. My first day there was on a bitterly cold morning, with snow on the ground. My welcome was warm and it looked as though things were going to be fine. However, I had not been there more than a couple of hours when the area supervisor phoned through and told me to report to the branch in Crystal Palace Road, East Dulwich, right away.

The manager at Nunhead Green took a dim view of this and was most reluctant to let me go. He told me that Mr Withers, the manager there, was a bit of a tyrant and greatly disliked by his staff. The prospect of this transfer dismayed me but, like it or not, I was soon trudging through the snow to my new workplace. One good outcome of this change was that my new destination was a little nearer home.

The shop premises in Crystal Palace Road were fairly new, compact and clean. I reported to Mr Withers who greeted me quite affably. There was only a small shop staff with a shop foreman, Jock Sawyers, and a first provisions hand, Lawrence. I was soon on excellent terms with all the staff, and didn't find the manager difficult at all.

I soon noticed how the price of goods had increased in my absence, and there were shortages. Although we put our orders into the warehouse we had to accept the allocation provided. It meant a little unofficial rationing but generally things were not too bad. I was able to get a tram to Lordship Lane close by the shop, and alight quite near home.

It was turning into a bitterly cold winter and at times the snow was very thick on the ground. The blackout was the worst thing and once in the darkness I nearly knocked myself out by walking into a tree. Although most people had torches, the batteries for some were unobtainable, making them useless. Sometimes flashes from the trains on iced-up tracks would reflect on the snow and light up the surrounding area. We all had to register for ration books and the fuel situation for private motor cars remained strictly controlled.

When spring came at last, I was able to buy a second-hand bicycle from one of the shop lads and it became very useful getting to and from work, even sometimes getting me home during the lunch break. Our Doreen was a lovely little girl and a favourite with all who met her. Elsie and I cultivated our part of the garden, and we often visited friends and relatives. It all seemed so peaceful and normal until one looked up into the sky and saw the silver barrage balloons, and in the streets the number of people around wearing uniforms of one kind or another.

I rarely went up to London but when I did it looked like a city under siege. There were sandbagged machine-gun posts on the Thames' bridges and guards outside the Government buildings. Notices on the walls pointed the way to the nearest shelters and there were more steel helmets than bowler hats to be seen.

Around this time my mother, and sister Pam, moved back to Herne Hill. They had never been very happy at No. 139, although both Grace and Audrey had been married from there. I believe Eileen and Grace and husbands occupied the flats at No. 24, Hawarden Grove, Eileen on the first floor and Grace on the second floor. Mum took the flat at No. 28 and Audrey and Bill lived nearby at No. 222, Croxted Road, so most of the family lived in close proximity to each other. Con's husband, Arthur, was transferred to the Dulwich Police Station around this time and they too were able to move closer to the others.

Elsie's parents had been on the move too, leaving Harris Street, Camberwell, and relocating to an LCC block of flats near Brixton Road. I think their actual address was No. 396, Cowley Road. At this time her brothers, George and Tim, were still living at home. As their work was deemed to be of national importance, they were exempt from call-up to the armed services, although they had to volunteer their services on the civilian front. Doris was still working as a telephonist at Peckham Road fire station.

The war situation in Europe had been fairly quiet with the opposing armies dug in behind the Maginot and Siegfried defence lines of fortification. It was a different story at sea where war had been raging with the loss of many fine ships, both merchant and naval. Even so, many people believed that Germany did not have the capacity to fight a long war and that some sort of compromise would be reached.

We were soon disillusioned. The war suddenly flared up. The Maginot Line was outflanked and the German armour poured through, sending the allied armies in full retreat. It was unbelievable that a nation supposedly bankrupt, with tanks made of wood, could inflict such chaos. These events, leading to the army evacuation at Dunkirk, are well recorded, but far from the victory portrayed by the news reports, in reality it was a bitter and humiliating defeat, with the loss of many men and much precious equipment.

On the home front, the situation turned to panic. The Local Defence Volunteers, later to become the Home Guard, were formed. They were based on the Grandad's Army of the First World War and were very ill-equipped. The beaches along the south coast were closed to the public and defended with barbed wire, mines and concrete anti-tank traps. In the fields and at strategic road and rail junctions, concrete pillboxes appeared, confirming everyone's fears that the war was closing in on us all.

Shortly after Dunkirk we met 'Boy' MacCarthy, who had had a very rough time. His khaki uniform was in a sorry state. He told us that when the order to retreat was received, all the officers departed in the motor cars leaving the men to make their own way to the coast. In the ensuing chaos, he became sandwiched between two vehicles and was badly bruised. He had managed to get to the beach where he had waited hours on the sand and in the water, until the 'little ships' thankfully arrived to rescue them.

My brother Reg was a Sergeant Major in charge of a convoy ferrying supplies to the Maginot Line at this time. When the German armour suddenly appeared out of the forest, Reg was approaching the line with a delivery, and the first indication he had that something unusual was happening was when hundreds of French troops came hurrying past them. For a while they thought they must be on their way to Paris on leave, or something, but it was not long before the truth dawned on them all that the French army was in full retreat. In a clearing in the forest they came face to face with some German tanks that were being overhauled. Each was as surprised as the other and Reg ordered his men to clear out as quickly as they could. They were strafed and bombed all the way to the coast. Of his sixty vehicles, only two were left in a usable state by the time they reached the coast, the others having been abandoned one by one on the way. He managed to get back to England in a small boat after being in the water for a very long time. The experience, and exposure, affected his health and sometime later he was invalided out of the Army and took a civilian job in the War Office.

Europe was overrun. France had capitulated. Winston Churchill became Prime Minister and Lord Beaverbrook, a newspaper magnate, took over aircraft production. The call-up went on apace, and I, in common of those in my age group, had to register at the Labour Exchange. We had to state the service we preferred, and I put down the RAF, but as they only wanted technicians I wasn't hopeful of being accepted.

Holidays, as such, were not possible during the war but we managed a few days out during the summer. We took Doreen to Brighton one day and she enjoyed her first paddle in the children's pool. Another day, we went to Folkestone with Elsie's family, but the enjoyment was tempered by the knowledge that a few miles away, across the Channel, lay the German army.

On 29 August, I was ordered to report for a medical examination, prior to call-up. So, this was it. I had a day off from the shop and with some misgivings, I made my way to the examination centre at Tooting. The medical was brief and I was passed as A1. Then came the crunch, as far as I was concerned. Would I be accepted into the Air Force, or not. There were three rooms labelled Army, Navy and Air Force and I was ushered into the latter. An elderly man in uniform was seated behind the desk and he looked me over with his light blue eyes. He fired all sorts of questions at me, presumably testing my mental and educational abilities. Then he asked the question I knew would come.

'What engineering experience have you had?'

I knew it was no use trying to bluff my way out of this for he was an expert in his field. I replied that my knowledge of the subject was limited. He seemed disappointed and shook his head at my reply. I gained some hope from this and when, in reply to another question about motor-car engines, I replied that I knew how to take the plugs out of engines and heat them over a gas ring when they wouldn't fire. This seemed to cheer him up considerably. My answer evidently gave him the loophole he was seeking.

'So you do know something about engines after all. I'll put you down as a flight mechanic. Mind you, you will have to take a trade test when the time comes.'

He shook my hand, wished me luck and I left the interview feeling elated.

By now the war was really hotting up. The Battle of Britain, as it became called, was being savagely fought over land and sea and there were raids on south coast towns. The sirens sounded almost daily and nerves were getting frayed. The Luftwaffe were doing their best to neutralise the airfields in Kent and Sussex and the bitter battles resulted in heavy losses on both sides.

At home, Elsie and I tried to keep life as normal as we could. We would take Doreen out in her pushchair into Grove Lane nursery or Ruskin Park, and make the most of the summer sunshine. It was pleasant in our own garden too with a colourful display of flowers as well as the tomatoes and runner beans. I had planted some grass seed over the Anderson shelter and this must have contained some turnip seeds, for some fine specimens came up all over the place. Elsie would visit her parents at least once a week, and I would cycle over to Herne Hill to see my mother and sisters.

7 September was our fifth wedding anniversary. It was a Saturday and I went to work as usual. The morning was sunny and quiet, and Elsie took Doreen to visit her parents in Brixton. About mid-afternoon the sirens sounded. We closed the shop and some of the staff went into the shelter in the yard. One of the lads donned his tin hat and took up his station as lookout on the roof, while the rest of us carried on with odd jobs in the shop.

It was a noisy and grim afternoon and we soon realised that this was no practice but a very heavy air raid. The air was filled with the roar of mighty engines and the rattle of gunfire, and the crump, crump of explosives. We ventured into the street and saw billowing clouds of black smoke to the north. There was no all-clear and as time passed people ventured out to buy their weekend supplies. We served those who came in. I was very anxious about Elsie and Doreen and wondered what was happening in Brixton.

The all-clear siren did not sound until after 7 p.m. We were busy until we closed at 8 p.m. At the first possible moment I grabbed my cycle and left for home. Although it was dusk the sky was as bright as day. It was an awesome sight. The horizon was aflame and great billowing clouds mushroomed into the heavens. I had witnessed the burning of the Crystal Palace, but that was a puny blaze compared to this mighty conflagration. Every few moments huge pillars of flame leapt towards the heavens accompanied by deafening explosions and the crackle of burning. Acrid smoke filled the air. People looked stunned as they witnessed the effects of the air raid. This was war and it had been loosed upon London and its people on a sunny afternoon. I pedalled as fast as I could for home. I hoped Elsie and Doreen would be there already for otherwise I would have expected to pass them on the way, but they were not. To say I was worried was an understatement. I knew it would be only a matter of time before the bombers returned, and this time the fires would guide them back to London.

I put my cycle in the back garden and set off to find them. I did not know which way Elsie would come and I hoped we would not miss each other. I chose to go via the back roads and at the corner of Caldecot Road we met, much to the relief of both of us. Elsie said they had been in the shelter all afternoon with her parents, waiting for the all-clear to sound, and as soon as it did she left for the long walk home.

I took over the pushchair and we rounded the corner into Denmark Hill. Just as we were passing the hospital the sirens sounded. The bombers were back. We hurried on our way but before we reached home the air resounded with the crump of exploding bombs and the boom of guns, with the throb of aircraft engines overhead. We reached home safely and went into the shelter in the garden, but it was so musty and damp that we came out and sat on the stairs. We sat there thinking what a wedding anniversary this had been. The noise continued spasmodically through the night and now and again the house trembled, but toward dawn the all-clear sounded and we went to bed.

The next morning we discovered that there was no gas and so we lit a fire and boiled a kettle on it. We managed a breakfast of sorts. During the morning Elsie's brother Tim cycled over to see us and check that we were alright. He wanted to see what damage had been caused in the neighbourhood and so I got out my cycle and joined him. The damage in Camberwell was severe. Some houses were now just a pile of bricks with timbers sticking out. There were large holes in the road and a motor car was sitting inside one of them. An omnibus lay on its side, and lengths of cloth and rags fluttered from the high branches of the trees. It was a depressing sight.

Elsie had somehow managed to cook a meal on the open fire and after we had eaten I went into the garden to try and make the shelter more habitable. I really didn't like it. The steel sides were cold and the earth floor musty and green. We put down anything we could find to cover the floor and found a couple of old chairs and boxes. It did little to uplift the interior and I didn't like the idea of Doreen, or ourselves for that matter, having to spend a night there at all.

Although the day was quiet, as soon as darkness fell the sirens went and once more we were faced with the problem of where to spend the night. We tried the shelter at first, placing Doreen right at the back where she went to sleep, but neither Elsie nor I could settle, so we decided to take our chances indoors. We stayed there all night although the raids seemed to get heavier.

On the Friday night, a bomb fell in the Salvation Army grounds opposite. Fortunately it did not explode, but notices were posted warning people to keep away, and a policeman kept guard. I had a word with him and he advised that we keep to the back of the house until the bomb was made safe.

By now evacuation had become the order of the day once again, and the Government announced that they wanted the civilian population out of London and other big cities, as the Civil Defence services were being stretched to their limit. Every day more houses were being reduced to rubble and there were unexploded bombs everywhere. Water mains were fractured and the gas supply continually interrupted. Supplies were not getting through to the shops and queues began forming for trams and buses. The sirens wailed constantly, both day and night. It was becoming unbearable.

Elsie and I did not know what to do for the best. Had it not been for our little girl, Elsie would have stayed home with me. It was with the greatest reluctance that she agreed to go back to Aston Abbotts to see if my aunt and uncle would take them on for a while. I hoped they would be much safer there, although as it happened, a string of bombs fell on the village the first night they were there. Fortunately, no damage was done.

I went to work as usual but things were getting difficult in the shop. The customers were becoming disgruntled with the shortages and tempers became frayed. We could not keep shutting the shop doors each time the sirens went, so we stationed one of the lads on the roof and carried on as best we could, only going to the shelters if things got really dangerous.

The day after Elsie and Doreen left for Aston Abbotts, 18th September, was particularly trying. The alert lasted most of the day. It felt as though Camberwell had become the target area and when I reached home that night I felt exhausted. I had a meal of sorts and unusually for me, I decided to spend the night in the shelter. Miss Wright, who lived in the basement flat, came and sat there with me. The raid was so heavy the ground continually vibrated. As we sat there dozing, there came the most appalling explosion, as if a bomb had fallen right outside the shelter. I thought the house had gone.

I peered outside the shelter but the air was full of brick dust and it was impossible to see anything straight away. Gradually it began to settle and I could make out the dark outline of the house, so I knew it was still there. I went inside. Every window had been blown in and there was dust everywhere. I couldn't do much, so returned to the shelter. We later learned that a landmine attached to a parachute was responsible, and it had caused immense damage in the area. It had landed squarely on top of a detached house a few doors up from Stories Road. It was a house I had always admired, detached, double-fronted, only two stories high and with a semi-circular driveway. An enormous wisteria covered the outside and I had often daydreamed that I would own it one day. Now it was just a pile of rubble.

The devastation was extensive. Houses as far away as Windsor Walk had suffered and there was glass everywhere. Our house, No. 139, had escaped lightly compared with others. It seemed impossible that one bomb could wreak such damage. Many of the houses were old, built in Georgian times, and I suppose the old mortar between the bricks had deteriorated and the blast had found other weak points in the structures. I was glad Elsie and Doreen were well out of it.

As it happened, that day I was due to go to Aston Abbotts to see them both. I went by coach, but it took a long time to get to Aylesbury, due to diversions caused by road damage and unexploded bombs. I had a meal with them all then Elsie and I went for a stroll around the village. I told her about last night's damage and she reluctantly agreed to stay on for a while until some other solution could be found.

I left early and boarded a coach in Aylesbury for Victoria. By the time we reached Watford we could see that London was under attack once again. The driver refused to go any further so I made my way to the tube station. This took me as far as Piccadilly where the train halted. The scene there was amazing. People were sitting or sleeping on the platform, on the stairs and in the corridors. Most of them had blankets or coats wrapped around them to keep out the drafts, and some had children with them. It was difficult to step over or between them but I managed to make my way upstairs only to be met by a policeman who said that the raid was a heavy one and no-one was allowed to leave. I resigned myself to spending the night below ground. Fortunately, a train arrived at the station and halted there for the night, and I was able to scramble aboard and find a seat. Even so, it was a cramped, uncomfortable night.

The next morning, feeling stiff and not very cheerful, I got the earliest train I could to the Elephant and Castle, and from there a tram home. In my absence, the council workmen had been to the house, removed most of the broken glass from the window frames, and covered the openings with some kind of mesh. I had a cup of tea and then made my way to the shop. I arrived late and the manager was not pleased, despite my difficulties.

During the following days, or rather evenings, I used my cycle to keep in touch with my mother and sisters, and Elsie's brothers, whose parents had gone to stay with friends in Leeds. One evening I was chatting to George in their flat when a bomb fell among the flats bringing down part of the ceiling. I then went on to Herne Hill and bombs followed me all the way. I was constantly diving into shop doorways or taking cover where I could. At Herne Hill the raid was particularly heavy and I was forced to stay in a shelter for a while. I was about to leave when I decided to check the directions with someone. This delayed me for about a minute. When I reached Hawarden Grove it was to discover that a bomb had hit the junction with Croxted Road just one minute before I arrived. I would certainly have been there except for that short delay at the shelter. It was a sobering thought.

Around this time a letter came in the post telling me to report to Cardington in Bedfordshire for a trade test to decide my suitability for the

RAF. This was the crunch, then. I decided to pay Elsie and Doreen another visit but this time I would cycle there. Never again would I spend the night in the underground. I had often cycled to Aston Abbotts in my teens, but I was now almost thirty-three years old, and I hadn't cycled so far for many years. Still, I knew I could do it, so I tuned up the bike, packed a few things in the carrier, and at 7 p.m. set off on my journey. I was surprised that for the first half of the ride I felt fine. It was after I left Watford that my muscles began to ache. There wasn't a lot of traffic on the roads, but one had to be most careful of what there was. All headlights had to be dimmed and in the darkness vehicles would loom like great monsters, and it became very nerve-wracking, especially along the country roads. Cyclists must have presented their own problems for the motorists too, for in the darkness very little light came from their lamps, as the top half of the glass and the bottom half of the reflector were blacked out.

On the road to Berkhamsted I met another cyclist going my way and we kept each other company until we reached Tring, where I left the main road and plunged into the narrow lanes towards the villages of Long Marston and Wingrave. It was eerie in the darkness and as all the signposts had been removed, I was a little unsure of my way. However, when I reached the tiny railway station of Marston Gate, I knew I was on track.

I remember our mother telling us of a visit she made to her mother once and how she arrived very late at Marston Gate station owing to the train being delayed. She had Con and Reg with her, and possibly me too, and we were all stranded there in the middle of the night with not a cottage in sight. Evidently she knew where the carter lived, so she set off to his house, knocked on the door, and he took her and the children to Aston Abbotts, about five and a half miles away. I wondered why she had gone to this little branch line station instead of Aylesbury.

At the bottom of the slope from the station a little stream, called locally 'the Splash', ran across the road. I approached it warily and walked across the bridge at its side, as I had no wish to risk my tyres on any hidden stones under the water. Sometime after the war on a visit to the area, I visited the station again only to find it closed and derelict, a victim of the Beeching Plan, and the little stream was no longer there.

It was a straightforward ride to Wingrave and Aston Abbotts after this and I eventually arrived at about 10.30 p.m. After a quick meal, Elsie and I went for a walk and I gave her all the news about my interview and acceptance into the RAF, and that I had to report for a trade test on 5 October. If all went well I hoped I might be given some indication when I would be called up. We made the most of the next day together but at 4 p.m. I said my farewells and was back on my cycle heading home once again.

I had hoped to be home by about 8 p.m., but although the first part of my journey was quick and easy, the approach to London proved difficult, with many diversions and a lot of traffic. Roads were closed because of craters and many unexploded bombs. It must have been close to 9 p.m. when I was cycling down the Edgware Road that the sirens began wailing, signalling the start of another air raid. Several times I dived for cover as bombs came whistling down, although I feared the falling shrapnel just as much, if not more.

In a lull, I raced down Park Lane to Victoria and had just crossed Vauxhall Bridge when things hotted-up again. A string of bombs came whistling down just behind me and I crouched down in a shop doorway. Nearby a gasometer went up with a terrific roar and a blinding sheet of flame. It was too close for comfort. I remounted my cycle and didn't stop again until I reached home. Fortunately, there was gas coming through to the stove so I made myself a cup of tea and tried to stop shivering.

Throughout the next week the coming interview at Cardington was at the back of my mind. I showed the papers to Mr Withers, the manager, and applied for special leave. This was really a formality as the firm was bound to release me. On the Saturday morning I packed a few things into a case and set off for the interview. The hangers for the airships R100 and R101 were at Cardington but when I reported, the reception was nowhere near these hangers. The contents of my case were examined and my Rolls razor for some reason seemed to cause some interest.

I was directed to a Nissen hut where a crowd of fellow recruits was already gathered. We were each given an earthenware mug (mine was cracked), and a knife, fork and spoon, and then marched off to the dining room for a meal. Once this was over, we were taken to the air-raid shelters where we formed a chain to bale out water that had flooded them. The S.P (Senior Police) officer then flogged us some raffle tickets, which we considered a real racket, meant to lighten the pockets of rookies who felt it best not to refuse. We then were taken to the NAAFI where we were able to buy tea and 'wads' (rock cakes). Inside the canteen the air was blue with cigarette smoke. A band was playing and one or two of the chaps entertained us with some of the popular songs, 'Bless 'em all' was one I recall. It was a pleasant evening.

Sunday was spent quietly. We attended a couple of pep talks, but otherwise the time passed slowly. After breakfast on Monday, we were marched to the buildings where the interviews were to take place. We were to be seen in alphabetical order, so I would be one of the last. As each man emerged from the room they were plied with questions about their interviews. By the time my turn came, I had a rough idea of what was coming. A corporal handed me a questionnaire, including some mathematical problems, to which I managed answers of a sort.

When I was eventually ushered into the room, I was faced with an officer resplendent in his uniform with gold braid. He glanced at my test paper then looked up at me for a few moments in silence. I had once again decided it would be no use trying to flannel the experts, so when he asked me what I knew about engineering, I replied that I knew nothing at all. I did however add that I was willing to learn and would do any job given me diligently and well.

This went down well. 'I believe you', he replied. 'I will send your name forward for training as a flight mechanic.'

He shook my hand and said, 'You will enjoy your time in the Royal Air Force'.

I came out slightly dazed, but delighted. My interview had lasted less than five minutes. Others had been in for over half an hour. There were many forms to be filled in and signed and much time wasted going here and there. Nothing was said about a reporting date, although one sergeant said there had been talk of drafting us in there and then. Fortunately, this was not confirmed and at about 6 p.m. I left the station by the main gate.

I stood there for a few moments debating what to do next. There was a railway station at Cardington, but it would probably take a couple of hours to get to London, by which time the nightly air raids would be in progress. I had no desire to repeat my night in the underground station. One thought was to visit my uncle in Rushden and spend the night at his home, and then go on to see Elsie the next day. This I decided to do.

Rushden was about fifteen miles away, as far as I could recall, but I had a long wait for a bus to Bedford and an even longer wait there for the bus to Rushden. The journey took much longer than I had anticipated. In my younger and more energetic days I had cycled this way, but it was too dark to recognise any of the landmarks and the journey was boring and interminable. When I did eventually arrive at my uncle's at No. 62, Roberts Street, it was ten o'clock.

I knocked on the door and presently there was a shuffling along the passageway and the door opened. Uncle Joe had aged since I last saw him and at first he did not recognise me. We had some supper together and chatted about family matters and he brought me up to date about my cousins, two of whom still lived in the neighbourhood and one in Canada. My Aunt Rebecca had died a year or so ago and he obviously missed her greatly.

It was a quiet night but I found it hard to sleep. I thought of the happy days I had spent under this roof and the kindness of my aunt and uncle when I had holidayed here in my teens. In the morning we breakfasted together and Uncle seemed glad that I had called in. I thanked him for his hospitality, wished him well and said goodbye. I could not know that this would be the last time I would see him.

The morning was sunny and warm and I did not have to wait long before the bus to Bedford arrived. A connecting bus took me to Leighton Buzzard, and from there to Aylesbury where I caught the bus to Aston Abbotts. I walked up the hill and was soon reunited with Elsie.

I related all the events of the past few days to Elsie and after lunch we took a walk with Doreen in the pram, around the village. I wanted to find out if anyone could take my mother in for a few days' break. After all, Aston Abbotts was her birthplace and many people knew her. The difficulty was that most villagers had already let rooms to Londoners who were prepared to pay handsomely to be away from the city. After a lot of fruitless searching, we found a Mrs Robinson who knew my mother and said she would be welcome.

I decided to stay another day in the village before returning to the shop, to give Elsie and I a chance to discuss what should be done when the time came for me to report to the RAF. It was obvious that we couldn't keep our flat in Grove Lane on forces pay, which worked out to be around thirty shillings a week. Elsie would receive seventeen shillings a week, plus an allowance for Doreen of six shillings. In addition to this, I would receive two shillings a day (14s. a week) of which seven shillings would be sent to Elsie, and an extra 3s. 6d. would be paid if one lived in London.

It seemed the best thing to do was to store our furniture, and for Elsie and Doreen to live with her parents for the time being. A local farmer offered to store our furniture in one of his barns, and with some misgivings, this we agreed. The following day, 9 October, I returned home.

I visited my mother and told her about the arrangements for her to stay with Mrs Robinson and she seemed relieved to be getting away for a few days. The following Sunday, I took her to Aston Abbotts and saw her safely settled in with her old friend.

Once back home I began packing up the furniture ready for transportation to the farmer's barn. Elsie came home on the 24th to collect some more clothes and to help with the packing. It was a difficult time. Neither of us knew when we would live a normal life again. She took quite a heavy case back with her and I saw her onto the 5.30 p.m. coach to Aylesbury.

She told me later that the journey turned into nightmare, with delays and stoppages all the way, and by the time she arrived in Aylesbury there were no buses in service. She did not know what to do, and she was anxious to get back to Doreen, who had been left in my aunt's care. There really was only one thing to do and she started the long walk to Aston Abbotts, carrying the heavy case. She was almost exhausted by the time she got to Bierton, about two miles on. There was no sign of life there apart from the Red Lion public house, so she summoned up her courage, and strength, and went inside for help. She was fortunate. A good Samaritan lifted her heavy case into his car and drove her straight to Aston Abbotts, to her great relief. It would have been a frightening experience to walk another four miles along the dark country roads.

We had planned the removal of our furniture for Thursday, 31 October and Elsie returned once again. In the event the removal men never arrived. On the spur of the moment we decided to pack our furniture into a large single room in the house and I later agreed with the landlord's agent to rent it at 5s. a week. I made sure that this time Elsie returned on an earlier bus.

The events of the next few days are hazy. I slept in the shelter most nights but sometimes I would go to Herne Hill and stay there. I also received my call-up papers from the RAF, together with a railway warrant and notice to report to Cardington on 20 November.

I wrote to Elsie with the news, and she returned home with Doreen, case and all. We had dinner at her mother's home and then went to spend the night at Herne Hill.

My mother had an old tin trunk and she gave this to me. In it we packed our clothes, linen and personal treasures. During that last week together we visited our friends the Gardiners and Reg and Hilda at Stoneleigh, and I finally packed up work on the Saturday. We also visited the photographer's and had a picture taken of the three of us. The ladies there were most taken with Doreen and her beautiful golden hair when Elsie combed it through ready for the photograph.

We tried to make the best of those last days together for no one could guess at what the future held for us. The Battle for Britain seemed to be over but the nightly raids on towns and cities continued. Elsie and Doreen would stay with her parents whilst I was away. We went to Herne Hill to say cheerio to my mother and sisters and to wish Pam a happy nineteenth birthday. John Ryan was now in the Army and Sid House was expecting to be called up soon, so one way or another all the male members of my family would then be in uniform.

On the Wednesday morning, 20 November 1940, I said my farewells to Elsie's family, and Elsie and I made our way King's Cross Station, where I would catch the train for the short journey to Cardington. It was a wrench for us to part when the time came, but I was determined to get through this war and come back to my family when peace returned to our country.

On the journey I met up with one of the fellows who had been at Cardington on my previous visit, so we sat together and chatted. On arrival, we were taken to a large building that served as the intake centre. There were quite a few chaps there already and gradually others drifted in. The sergeant took our names, and then we were sent off for a meal. Next we each had our photograph taken for identity purposes. We spent some time chatting and getting to know one another, but it all seemed rather confused. We were given a service number, mine was 1196094, and allocated to a 'Flight', mine being 'K' flight. I was put in hut No. 469, and among the occupants were four lads I had met up with on my last visit, and we chummed up. The hut itself was grubby and untidy and we were told to clean it up. I had the dubious honour of being placed in charge of this operation, so had to supervise their work.

I managed to find time to write to Elsie. I was a little concerned as she had to make the journey to my uncle's house once again to collect the rest of their clothes and I worried about the travelling, the buses being so erratic now. In the event she did not have too much trouble. We had been told that we would only be at Cardington for the next few days when we would be kitted out with our uniforms and receive our inoculations and vaccinations. I suggested to Elsie that she defer writing to me until I had a definite address.

On Friday 22 November we received the dreaded inoculations and vaccinations. They made me feel pretty rough, with a hot head and icy cold everywhere else. Several of the men passed out for a while. We were told to expect two more 'boosters', not a happy thought for anyone. We were then sent to be kitted out. Our sizes were estimated by a chap running his hands over us and calling out numbers to the storemen. This resulted in items being flung our way. Taking it all round my uniform fitted well and by swapping with other people I managed to get underwear my size.

The boots I had been given seemed to weigh a ton. They had steel tips and heels, thick soles and studs, and they rubbed my ankles. But they were solid and I knew they would serve me well once they had been worn in. We were told to bundle up our civilian clothes ready to be sent home. The only item I retained was a pullover that Elsie had knitted for me.

There were many forms to be completed and I gave Elsie's address as No. 396 Cowley Road, her parents' address. We were given 10*s.* advance on our pay and told that it would have to last us a fortnight. We had a group photo taken and one way or another began to feel we were part of the Air Force.

We were expecting to be sent to either Torquay or Morecambe the following day for training and drill sessions (or square-bashing, as it was commonly called), and I wrote to let Elsie know.

Sunday was a lazy day. We had a church parade in the morning, having been sorted out into denominational groups beforehand. I had put myself down as a Congregationalist under 'other denominations'. After this we were free to spend the rest of the day as we wished. In the evening I went to the church hut and saw a film, joined in a singsong and had a free cup of tea. I was beginning to like Air Force life.

On Monday 25 November I received a letter from Elsie, who had taken the chance that it would arrive before we left the station. She had received a letter from my uncle Joe inviting her and Doreen to stay with him in Rushden if she so wished. I didn't know how to advise her. I knew that she would be warmly welcomed, but Rushden was not like a village, being very much an industrial town, given over to the footwear industry. I had to leave the decision to her. As it happened Rushden was bombed soon afterwards and my uncle advised her not to come.

The powers that guided our destinies seemed undecided as to where we should be sent next. We were kept polishing and cleaning, which we did half-heartedly, and I had a haircut. We were not allowed to leave the camp. Although it was cold, there were two stoves in our hut and someone had a radio set, so we made ourselves fairly cosy. We had to rise at 6.15 a.m. and have our beds made by 6.30 a.m. Our beds were made in armchair fashion. We laid on three hard cushions, called biscuits, and making the armchair up involved putting the blanket around two biscuits which were stood upright, and the other blanket around the remaining one which was laid flat.

On Tuesday we were marched down to the railway station with our parcels of civilian clothes. We labelled them and handed them over to be sent home.

It definitely felt as though we were severing the last links with our past lives. I wrote one or two letters but did not give a return address on them. Supper was at 7 p.m. and usually consisted of saveloys and cocoa. Some lads there were not short of money and were able to dine in the NAAFI. It seemed that some firms made up their service pay to what they would normally earn, which I couldn't help thinking a little unfair on the rest of us.

On Thursday we were told that we were going to Morecambe the following day. It was a disappointment that we were going even further north. We were given another medical examination and told to get our kit ready for the move. The next day we were *en route* for Morecambe, in Lancashire.

When we arrived at the seaside town it was to find that we would be billeted in private houses. We were split up into groups and marched around the town by a sergeant. Our little group was found accommodation at No. 142, Westminster Road, in the west end of the town. Our landlady seemed alright. We handed her our ration cards and then went for a stroll along the promenade in the winter sunshine.

I had made friends with a chap from Newcastle, named Philip Siddoway, who worked in the Trustee Savings Bank there. He was a little younger than I, being only twenty-nine years old. When we were kitted out he had been given a greatcoat that almost touched his ankles, and despite much protest wasn't able to exchange it for something shorter. It embarrassed him no end. As we were walking along an officer shouted at him to stop. He demanded to know why Phil was wearing such an oversized coat. Poor Phil explained that he had been issued with it at Cardington and had been unable to exchange it.

'You report to the clothing store in the morning and get it changed', he replied, 'you're making the Air Force in Morecambe look ridiculous'. Phil duly reported and was given a greatcoat roughly his size.

We reported in the morning at 8 a.m. and were marched to one of the town's cinemas for a lecture and pep talk. At noon we were told we were free for the weekend. It struck me that ever since I had started work I had longed to have my Saturday afternoons free, and now I had.

There were about five thousand airmen in Morecambe, all being put through their paces by a team of drill sergeants who were, in most cases, physical training instructors in civilian life. Each was given a team of about thirty men and drilled them on the promenade. There were also sessions on RAF procedures and films on aircraft identification. We had lectures from all sorts of people followed by question and answer sessions, and the time passed quickly. At 5 p.m. we returned to our billets for a meal and the rest of the evening was free for us to enjoy as we wished.

Our billet, No. 142, Westminster Road, was a typical seaside boarding house run by two elderly ladies. They did their best to make us feel at home. The food was tasty and well cooked but we often felt we could have managed larger portions! There were seven of us billeted there and I considered myself fortunate to be given the one single room available, the others sharing two to a room. The ladies were allowed 3*s*. 3*d*. a day for each of us, plus an allowance for light and heating. We had a sitting room with a fire to relax by in the evenings and were made very comfortable. The sergeant came by every evening to check on us all.

We were not given any supper, so Phil and I would go along to one of the Forces canteens for a cake and cup of cocoa. One night we were given tickets for a free supper, as it was a local celebrity's birthday. We had a good time and enjoyed the free food. As Phil and I seemed to have a similar outlook on life, we joined the local male voice choir together. We really enjoyed the company and the few recitals we gave were well received. And of course, there was always a bite to eat afterwards.

Elsie wrote and told me about the bombing at Rushden and how my uncle had been shocked to see his dear old town knocked about so badly. It must have been a bitter blow for him as he had always been at the centre of things there. So, although the planned visit to Rushden was no longer on the cards, she told me that our friends, Doris and Ron Gardiner, were thinking of taking a house in Crawley, and had suggested that Elsie might like to go along with them. She also mentioned that, so far, she had not received any money from the RAF. I went along to Pay Accounts and had a word with them. It appeared that a warrant had been sent to Grove Lane instead of Cowley Road, and they assured me that it would be sorted out. By the same post I had a letter from my sister, Grace, informing me that Vera and Cecil MacCarthy were to be married on Saturday, 7 December. My mother had returned from Aston Abbotts and was busy making mince pies for the reception. I had no doubt that Cecil's mother was in seventh heaven, having managed to get her son married to one of my sisters.

Apart from church parade, which I liked attending, Sunday was a quiet day. The weather was cold but clear after recent gales, and I would stroll around the town, often on my own. Across the bay were the hills and fells of Westmoreland, white with snow and looking like a Swiss postcard. The beach was poor though and when the tide went out there was a considerable stretch of sand. There were two piers, and along the promenade the flowerbeds were empty. Being winter there was little or no colour.

The east end of the town was a poorer-looking area than the west where we were billeted, and the houses had only tiny gardens. Between the backs of these houses were cobblestone alleyways, almost like small roads. Sometimes, after drills, the sergeant would march us around them to give the lads a chance to have a cigarette, out of sight of the discipline officers.

Although we had only been there just over a week, there was talk of us having our test for foot drill. It seemed to me that everything was being rushed through and there was certainly an air of panic about the place. We were issued with another pair of boots but these had rubber soles and were much lighter than the first pair. Each week were allowed to send one shirt, two collars, a vest and underpants, two handkerchiefs and a pair of socks to the laundry.

Our landlady was a decent type and did her best to make us feel at home. We had been instructed to make our own beds and clean our rooms, but she would not hear of this. All she allowed us to do was dry the crockery after use. We clubbed together and bought her a bunch of flowers, which pleased her no end, and after dinner the next day she gave us a cup of tea.

On 12 December we were assembled to take our drill test. We were marched to the bandstand where the inspecting officers were waiting. There had been a heavy frost during the night and the paved enclosure, where in the summer the deckchairs would be set out, was like a sheet of glass. I was one of three leading the parade. As we stepped out onto the coloured slabs, my feet gave way underneath me and I slid for about ten yards. Nobody could keep their feet and we tried, in vain, to reform. We slid here and there, stumbled and skidded. It was a shambles. After ten minutes the officers abandoned the parade and passed us out. We went to a nearby café for a cuppa, and to nurse our bruises.

We were issued with some ancient rifles and marched to the shooting butts. I was quite scared of handling a rifle and even more so of firing it. After a very indifferent start, I managed to hit the bull twice. The sergeant passed round a kitty and asked each one to put in a shilling for the best marksman, which needless to say, none of our squad won.

There were more inoculations to be had and one of them made us so ill we were excused parades for forty-eight hours. We attended more lectures, sniffed some poison gas, and were briefed on the correct drill should we be taken prisoner.

Christmas was fast approaching but the lack of goods in the shops made it impossible to buy presents. In the end I managed to buy three little brooches with RAF wings and crest on them, for Elsie and our mothers.

I received letters from Reg Denner and Frank Thompson, who enclosed 3s. 6d. worth of stamps. There was also a letter from Vera, who said they had drunk my health at the wedding reception. It was good to be able to keep in touch.

Once our arms were back in use after the inoculations we spent a lot of time on the rifle range. The instructors were decent men who treated us well. They did their best to see we had a cup of tea during the morning, and when they could, a break for a cigarette. No one could understand my refusing a cigarette.

We received news of the Christmas arrangements. There would be a break of forty-eight hours, from midday Christmas Eve to midday on Boxing Day. No one was allowed leave, but I very much doubted that I would have made it home and back again in that time, due to the disruption of the railways. Our landlady had managed to get a goose for our Christmas dinner, so we fared better than most. Many other lads were not so fortunate.

On Christmas Eve I received quite a batch of mail, plus a parcel from the Royal Arsenal Co-operative Society, which although slightly battered, contained a book, cake, tin of boot polish, a tin of fruit cocktail and some sweets. It was the first acknowledgement I had received from them. Among the cards was a piece of wedding cake from our friends Ted and Kitty Warne. For the second time in as many weeks, Elsie wrote that Doreen was poorly again, and this worried me. Also enclosed was a book of stamps from her father.

We spent the morning on the rifle range as the squad underwent its firing test. We were given fifteen rounds apiece and we blazed away at the targets in true Bisley fashion.[36] There was plenty of noise and flashes from the rifles, but they did not kick back as we were told they would, so my face and teeth remained intact. We were not told the result but as it was a team effort, I expect we all passed. We had to. There was talk of moving on to technical training on 3 January, although no one knew for sure.

In the evening, there was a social at the Methodist church and I went along. There were a lot of games, singing, and an impromptu concert, during which I rendered a couple of items, including 'The Undertaker', which they all enjoyed. Refreshments were laid on afterwards and all in all it was an enjoyable evening.

The weather was warm on Christmas morning and I went for a stroll along the sea front before going to church. The wives of some of the men had made the trip to see them (strictly unofficial) and they went their own ways. I returned to the house at dinner time where the landlady had cooked the goose, with sprouts and potatoes, plus a Christmas pudding and half a pint of brown ale (which I passed on to one of my companions). A cup of coffee followed. After the meal I sat down and wrote to Elsie.

On Friday 27th, things returned to normal and in the morning we were outside drilling once again. Just before we were dismissed for lunch, we were ordered to parade at 2.30 p.m. in front of the bandstand for a review by the commanding officer. The whole RAF personnel lined up, about 5,000 in all, and we marched around feeling quite impressive. When it was over, 'K' flight was told to stand fast. About sixty names were called out, including our own, and we were told we were being transferred to RAF Hednesford, in Staffordshire, the following morning.

From that moment it was a mad, mad rush. We had to have a medical, hand in our rifles and gym kit, obtain clearance, and by the time all the formalities had been completed, it was 6 p.m., an hour past our normal mealtime. We spent the rest of the evening stowing our gear into our kitbags, and preparing to leave. We had to be up at 4.15 a.m., breakfast at 4.45 a.m. and be on parade at 5.15 a.m. We said goodbye to our landlady and thanked her for making our stay in Morecambe so bearable.

It was dark and icy cold. The roads were slippery with frost as we trudged our way the railway station, kitbags on our shoulders. We arrived there at 5.45 a.m. and had to stand around in the bitter cold until 8.00 a.m. when the train finally arrived. It was a long and tedious journey. The countryside was

---

36 A reference to Bisley Shooting Ground in Surrey, opened in the 1890s.

covered in a blanket of snow, and there were frequent delays due to snowdrifts and diversions. We were seven and a half hours on that train, during which time we had nothing to eat or drink.

The train eventually stopped in a bleak and forbidding landscape. It was evidently a halt just for the camp, and known locally as 'Kitbag Halt'. The snow was about three feet deep and we struggled up a narrow gully until we reached a high barbed-wire fence. We trudged alongside the fence for another half-mile. Inside the wire, there were rows of huts, and the whole place had an air of desolation and despair. From inside the huts we heard a cheer and words of encouragement, like, 'It's the worst place in England', and, 'Dartmoor is a palace compared to this place'. Once inside the main gate, a service police sergeant lined us up and proceeded to tell us what a miserable bunch we were, and what would happen if we stepped out of line. In words full of wrath, he told us that the place was a hotbed of thieves and we should sleep with our money under our pillows, or next to our skin. There was truth in what he said for when we went for a meal, my cutlery was stolen from right under my nose.

We trudged through the thick snow to a hut on the far side of the camp. We were all very tired and most dispirited. Once we had managed to get a fire going in the stove, we spent the evening drying out the blankets, which were damp, and wondering just what the future had in store for us. However, after a good night's sleep and some breakfast inside us, things began to look a little rosier. Word was that we were in the best wing of the camp and the officer in charge was a good man, and this proved to be true, as we found out in due course.

During the morning we were taken to see the padre, a nice chap who told us not to lower our standards just because we were away from home. He gave us a run-down on the camp activities. After lunch we lined up outside the orderly room. We had all decided to apply for weekend leave, and the senior man handed them in.

As we were standing there, one of the corporals asked if there were any pianists among us. Phil and I looked at each other then stepped forward with half a dozen others. They marched us away to the cookhouse to wash the greasy tins from lunch. Everyone thought this a huge joke. However, we were given a mug of tea and a chunk of cake, so I wasn't complaining. But I reminded myself, once again, never to volunteer for anything.

There were twenty-four beds in our long wooden hut with a circular stove for heating it in the centre of the aisle. Our beds were spaced along each wall. There were no lockers to keep our small items in and we were told that they had been used as fuel during the severe weather of last winter. Above each bed was a small shelf, but our clothes had to be stored in our kitbags. At the entrance to each hut was a small room where the NCO had his bed. He was in charge of the hut, but the day-to-day running of it was left to a senior man. I was offered the job initially, but declined it, preferring to concentrate on things I considered more important.

The snow was a nuisance. It was piled high around the huts and kept everything damp. We were constantly shovelling it off the paths, and trying to keep the camp roads clear. The weather almost halted life on the base, and falls of snow obliterated the clearances made. I had never felt so cold, and became sick of the sight of snow and the bitter weather.

As the RAF always did things in alphabetical order, the seven of us who had been billeted at No. 142, Westminster Road, Morecambe, were also assigned to Hut 24. Phil and I joined forces with two other friends, Steve and Stan, and we did most things together, to the mutual advantage of each. Everyone pulled together and this did not escape the notice of our instructors, good men who were always ready to help us with any problems.

1941

RAF Hednesford

It took me sometime to get my bearings at the camp as the snow that blanketed everything gave the whole scene a strange, eerie feel. I found out later that the camp was about two years old and had been built on part of the wild stretch of moorland known as Cannock Chase. It was a huge area and was bounded by the towns of Rugeley, Cannock, Lichfield and Stafford, and some high wooded hills. I was told by one of the civilian instructors that the winter of 1939/1940 had been particularly severe. The snow had completely isolated the camp, and supplies had to be dropped in by parachute from aircraft. Work came to a standstill because of the shortage of fuel, and sledging teams were organised to trek to Rugeley for essentials. Items, like the bedside lockers, were burnt to provide a little warmth. This winter did not seem to me to be much of an improvement.

The first week was a time for settling in. After church parade on Sunday we were free for the rest of the day. If one stayed in the camp there was a good chance of being press-ganged into fatigues, so most chaps went out just to avoid these onerous duties. I stayed in the camp, for trudging through snowdrifts was not my idea of relaxation. In the evening our little quartet—Phil, Steve, Stan and myself—went to the film show put on by the padre in the concert hall. The film was *Rome Express*, with Gordon Harker.[37] We each put 2*d*. in the plate and were given a cup of tea. When we emerged from the hall, the night was inky black, despite the snow, and had it not been for the others I would have been wandering about until next morning.

Like all new boys, we had to be initiated into the unpleasant side of forces life, like guard duties, fire piquet and crash guard shifts. I hated guard duties.

---

37 *Rome Express* (Gaumont–British Picture Corporation, 1932; re-issued 1940), a critically acclaimed and commercially successful comedy-thriller, directed by Walter Forde. Gordon Harker (1885–1967) plays Tom Bishop, one of the comic roles.

Tramping around in the bleak, cold, wet snow for two hours on and four hours off was hateful. One bright spot was the arrival of a parcel from my friends Reg and Hilda, which had been forwarded from Morecambe. It included some notepaper and envelopes, a pie and cake, which were very welcome. There was a good spirit among the lads in the hut, and any goodies received were always shared.

We were issued passes, which enabled us to stay out until 10.30 p.m. on weekdays and midnight at weekends, provided we were not on duty. The nearest town was Cannock, a sixpence ride away. Not many took advantage of these passes as 'lights out' was at 10.15 p.m., and the buses were unreliable, due to the snow.

On Friday, 3 January, as we paraded outside the orderly room to be given our duties for the rest of the day, the flight sergeant informed us that the applications for leave we had made earlier had been turned down. We were not surprised. Later that afternoon as I was cleaning the Sergeants' Mess, I was ordered to report to the aforementioned flight sergeant.

'We've been looking for you', he said. 'I don't know what tale you told the old man, but he has granted your application for weekend leave'.

I did not tell him that on my application I had mentioned Doreen's illness. Evidently this had been noted by the CO. I took the pass, collected a few essentials and made my way out of the camp. I was annoyed that the pass had not been given to me three hours earlier, when there was still some daylight left. Now, I was at a loss to know what to do for the best. In the end I decided to try and hitch-hike, so I made my way through the snow, to the main road. A lorry stopped and I clambered aboard. I chatted to the driver to pass the time, but it was a slow journey and I was impatient. Faster vehicles passed us and I fidgeted at our slow progress. Eventually the lorry driver pulled in to an all-night café and said he was stopping there for the night. This was not going well. I had no wish to spend the night here so I waited outside to see if any other vehicles were going to London.

After a short while another lorry pulled up, with an RAF chap in the cabin. He was on his way to London, and offered to drop me off at the nearest underground station. This he did, and I eventually arrived at No. 396, Cowley Road at 11 p.m. The door was opened by Elsie, who was very surprised to see me. It was good to see them all again and to hear that Doreen was on the mend.

The weekend passed all too quickly. We went shopping at Camberwell Green on Saturday, and had our photos taken at Jeromes. Sunday we had lunch with my mother but by mid-afternoon I had to leave to start my journey back. Elsie came to King's Cross to see me off. This time the journey passed uneventfully and I arrived back at Hednesford in good time.

The following morning we were marched to the workshops to begin our technical training. We were asked to split into two groups, those who wanted to work on engines, and those who preferred airframes. The latter covered everything on an aircraft except the engines. My inclination was to take the engine course, but my three friends moved across to the airframe group. I hesitated, but in the end they persuaded me to join them, and I'm glad they did.

At the end of six weeks' training, an examination would be held in all subjects, practical, theory and oral, and those not making the grade would be transferred to group five, the lowest group, and put on general duties. This really was the lowest of the low and to be avoided at all costs.

The four of us stayed together. We worked on wood and metal, attended lectures, and learned to read blueprints. It was hard going. At night we still had to take our share of guard and other duties, as well as writing up notes and swotting for the all-important tests.

It was warm in the workshops and a pleasure to be inside, away from the ice and snow. All that week there were heavy falls of snow, accompanied by high winds, which piled the white stuff high up against the buildings. At night I didn't venture out, even as far as the NAAFI, but would conceal a couple of slices of bread in my tunic, and toast them by the fire before going to bed. By Sunday, the drifts were over eight feet deep, and all day long we were shovelling the stuff in an attempt to keep the camp roads clear. It was like being under siege with relays of men bringing in supplies. All training work was halted for the time being and all we ever did was shovel, shovel, shovel! The piles of snow between the huts grew bigger day by day and inside the walls were damp and the atmosphere humid as we tried to dry our clothes around the fire.

One day, the camp authorities received an SOS from the railway officials and on the Wednesday morning about fifty of us were detailed to go and clear the track outside Stafford. We were armed with pickaxes and shovels, and were given a box of sandwiches. We floundered our way down Kitbag Hill to the railway station, called Brindley Heath. We hung around for an hour waiting. The scenery all around us was white, with pine trees standing up like white pyramids. A train eventually arrived and we clambered aboard. We alighted at a place called Richercourt, where two engines were puffing and snorting. They had been trying to push a snowplough, but the drifts were eight feet high and they had come to a halt. We dug for about two hours and managed to clear the track sufficiently for the snowplough to complete the clearance. We broke for lunch and were given two small sandwiches each.

There was a village nearby, and whilst beer was available, there was no food to be had. We managed to buy a loaf of bread from a van, and we broke this up between us, but oh how we longed for a cup of tea. At 2 p.m. we were back shovelling snow again until darkness fell and our train took us back to Brindley Heath. Once back in the camp, we were given a meal of Irish stew (the best I had ever tasted), and a shilling for the meals we had missed. About fifteen minutes later they took the shilling back saying that as we'd had a meal, we didn't qualify for subsistence.

That night the weather changed and heavy rain lashed the camp. Next morning there was water everywhere and the whole place was a slushy quagmire. Wellington boots had to be worn all the time.

On Thursday afternoons we normally went for a route march with the camp band leading the way, but because everywhere was so waterlogged, and because we had lost three days' training, we spent the time in the workshop in an effort to catch up on lost time.

The days passed quickly enough, but the weather continued causing havoc with everyday life. I still preferred to stay inside the hut every night and often my three friends and I would spend an evening going over the day's work and testing each other. I found this invaluable.

After a long delay, our letters began to arrive fairly regularly. Syd House, Eileen's husband, had been called up to the army, and I didn't envy him one little bit. There had been talk of us receiving a long weekend's leave after six weeks at the camp. This would last from midday Friday to midnight Sunday. A short weekend, from midday Saturday to midnight Sunday was of no use at all to those who lived any distance away.

At the end of each week we were given tests and had our notebooks examined by the instructors. On the whole they were a likeable bunch and although they said they would sooner be with a squadron, they showed us lots of patience. I asked one of them why he thought they had taken on someone like me, with no mechanical experience. His reply was that they wanted men who could think for themselves, who could grasp and understand what they were shown.

'The worst recruits we get are garage hands,' he said. 'They make the worst flight mechanics. It's far better to have someone we can train because he will only know our way of doing things.' I could see the wisdom of this policy.

Elsie wrote to let me know that they had all had a few peaceful nights recently, and I was relieved to hear the news. She went on to say that she had decided to share the house in Crawley with our friends Ron and Doris Gardiner, and that her parents would be going with them. The house sounded very attractive and I was extremely glad that they would, at last, be away from London.

I managed to pick up a very heavy cold and it made me feel quite dreadful. I could have reported sick, but if I had there was a good chance that I would lose my place in the entry and have to join another, and I was very reluctant to let this happen. I was able to get some Beechams Powders and a bronchial mixture, and these helped me to keep going. The weather was still awful and I began to wonder if better weather would ever come our way. I had not been outside the camp since my leave at the beginning of January, and so on the Saturday afternoon I decided to visit Rugeley. It was a three-mile trudge through the snowdrifts, but still quite enjoyable. I found the local YMCA and met some of the RAF lads inside. We enjoyed a very decent tea, listened to the radio and appreciated the change of scene. It was a scramble getting onto the bus back, and it turned into a nightmare of a journey. The bus skidded all over the place, and at one lone point on the moor where there were tall stone blocks marking the position of the road, the snow was almost level with their tops. Fortunately, we reached the camp without mishap.

I heard from Elsie that the move to Crawley was made on 1 February. The removal men turned up this time, and our furniture was delivered safely. She was in the process of changing the ration books and other formalities, and expected her parents to join them all in the next few days. She also told me the news that her sister, Dolly, was now going steady with one of the firemen from the Peckham station.

The following weekend we were due for weekend leave. One of the chaps had organised a coach to take the Londoners to King's Cross, and I booked a seat. Our passes were issued at midday on Friday, 7 February, and soon afterwards we were on our way to the capital. It was noticeable that once we left the area of the camp the snow petered out and we saw the sun for the first time for nearly a month. Once in London I paid a quick visit to Herne Hill to see my mother and sisters, and then made my way to Brixton to catch the Green Line bus to Crawley.

It was a mild evening and very dark, and I wandered up and down Three Bridges Road looking for 'Evergreen'. It took some time to find, but as I reached it Elsie appeared in the doorway, on her way to look for me. Inside, I met Elsie's parents and the Gardiners, and then was given a tour of the house. The next morning I was able to see more of the house and its grounds. Elsie and Doris had made an excellent job of allocating the rooms and outside there were large gardens back and front. I felt sure they would be very happy there. Crawley itself was a sleepy little place midway between London and Brighton. It had a Co-op, a cinema and a recreation ground.

The weekend passed all too quickly and I was soon back on the coach heading north again. On the way, we had a break at a hotel where the radio was broadcasting a speech by Mr Churchill about the war in the Mediterranean.

Back at the camp most of the snow had melted and the next morning the sun shone making the day feel quite spring-like. It cheered everyone no end. Our instruction that day was on the art of splicing rope and wire cables, which was very rough on the hands. The previous week we had taken our exams and were all very anxious to know how we had fared. During the morning, one of last week's instructors came in, his face wreathed in smiles, and asked for Phillip Siddoway. The instructor could hardly contain his excitement when he told Phil that he had attained 87 marks in the exam, a most exceptional figure. He was so pleased that he had quite forgotten the marks for the rest of the class.

Naturally the rest of us were eager to know our individual results but did not receive them until the afternoon break. I was amazed to find out that I, too, had received 87 marks, joining Phil in first place. Steve (known as the

'Duke' on account of his posh voice) came next with 86 points, and Stan Thompson (our Brighton and Hove footballer) came fourth with 80 marks. So our little quartet had taken the first four places. Our evening revisions had paid off. The instructors said it was an amazing result, 70 marks being considered a good average. Of course, there were more results to come, but that evening we were in high spirits.

It was not long before the rest of the results were out and the average marks over the whole course put me in first place with an average of 80+ and Phil and Steve in second and third place. Sadly Stan did not make the top ten. It was good to know I had done so well but there was still a long way to go. Next day I was called in to see the progress officer, who congratulated me and said the squadron leader had asked to see the 'top ten'.

A few days later the ten of us were told to report to headquarters and on arrival there, were each given a form to fill in. There were the usual questions, age, education, civilian employment etc. I couldn't work out what this was all about, and when the flight sergeant took my form he looked at it in disbelief.

'What job did you have in Civvy Street?' he asked.

I told him I was a shop assistant. 'I don't believe it,' he said. 'You've come top in our best intake for months and you tell me you were a shop assistant! It's incredible.'

'It's the only job I could get,' I said, beginning to feel rather inferior.

'Well,' he said, scratching his chin, 'the old man wants to see you, and if he sees "Shop Assistant" on your form he'll throw you out. We'll tear this form up and start again.'

'How about "Salesman"?' I enquired.

'He'll probably accept that. It covers a multitude of things.'

I wrote it down, and he then asked about education.

'Elementary,' I replied.

He put down his pen and scratched his head. 'I still can't believe this. Your exam results put you way ahead of over eighty chaps, from all walks of life, and you tell me you only had an elementary education. We've got to do better than that.'

'Well,' I said, 'I spent a lot of time at night school and hold several certificates, including advanced bookkeeping. And I won two scholarships, awarded by the firm I worked for.'

'That's better.' He brightened up considerably and started scribbling. 'Keep it up, lad. We need the best in the RAF.'

He gathered up our papers and disappeared with them through an inner door. A few minutes later we were ushered in to the presence of the commanding officer, an elderly, grey-haired man.

'Stand easy, men,' he said, smiling. 'I'm very happy to meet you. I have before me your personal records, which show how diligent and dedicated you have been in the short time you have been at Hednesford. You have set a standard, which others will envy and try to emulate, and it will not go unrewarded. I have the authority to give immediate promotion to each of you. As from tomorrow, you are each made flight mechanics and will receive the pay for the grade. From next Monday you will report for training as fitters, the Group 1 tradesman course. Good luck to each of you.'

We all felt elated. Our pay would rise immediately to $4s.\ 3d.$ a day, an increase of $1s.\ 9d.$, which was quite an achievement. I was already transferring one shilling a day to Elsie, and now I could increase that by about ten shillings a week. This would ease things considerably for her. It also meant a longer period of training, and some hard work, but the first hurdle, the biggest, had been cleared. I received a telegram from Elsie congratulating me on the promotion, which was very nice.

The weather, which had seemed so springlike a few days earlier, now changed again and the snowstorms returned, staying with us for the whole of March. Although we were now on the fitters' course, we still had to take our turn with guard and cookhouse duties. The time passed quickly and at the end of most days I felt exhausted. I was usually in bed by 10 p.m. and asleep soon after. We were up by 6 a.m. and had to do an hour's physical training before breakfast.

Meals were not well organised. Twenty chaps sat at each table and the last two had to collect the food for them all from the kitchen and dish it out. Nobody liked this job and we all tried to avoid it. If the server wasn't careful, he'd find that after serving the others there was little left for himself. At breakfast, the plate of jam at the head of the table would be set upon by men, spoons at the ready, and scooped up onto their plates. It was a free-for-all, and often there was more jam on the table than on the bread. This state of affairs lasted for about three months, until a new cookhouse sergeant was appointed and instructed the staff to serve the meals.

On 4 April I went home on a long weekend's leave. Elsie and Doreen met me in Brixton and we made our way to Herne Hill and had tea with my mother. We were updated on all the family news. Evidently things between my sister Denise and her husband were going from bad to worse. He was piling up debts and had pawned her jewellery, and she was threatening to leave him, all of which worried my mother no end. We left for the Green Line bus and were in Crawley by 9.40 p.m.

I was sorry that I would miss Doreen's second birthday on 11 April, but we made the most of our time together with a walk or two and a visit to the local cinema. On Sunday, I had to leave by 3 p.m. to start my journey back to camp. As I came through Brixton, this time in the daylight, I could see the results of the recent bombings. The Astoria Cinema, The Police Station and Quin and Axtens had all suffered damage, and there was a large area of devastation towards Kennington.

At Euston Station I met up with Steve, and after buying a couple of Lyon's individual fruit pies in the YMCA, we boarded the train. It was an uneventful, boring journey back to Brindley Heath and the slog up Kitbag

Hill was cold and cheerless. When we reached Hut 54 there was a lovely fire burning in the stove, and we decided to make ourselves a cup of cocoa. Our noise woke up some of the lads from their sleep, which upset them somewhat, but nevertheless, we did enjoy the cocoa.

Our training went ahead but the weather remained cold and damp. It was as if spring was giving Staffordshire a miss. It was probably typical moorland weather, but that wasn't much consolation.

Elsie wrote to me with some very sad news. On the night of 16 April, a string of bombs had hit Kimpton Road killing several of our friends. Among them were Lily Waterman and her parents, Joan Durrant and her grandmother, Winnie Godwin and others. It was tragic. Lily had been in my class at school, and her parents were friends of long standing. Joan and Winnie were Girls' Life Brigade girls we had known for many years. It brought the conflict very close to home. Elsie attended the funerals, which were held on Monday, 28 April.

Because of an infection that had broken out in our hut, we were moved out whilst it was thoroughly disinfected. Some of us were moved to Hut 47, where the occupants were assigned to orderly duties and excused guard duties. Since I hated guard duty and was quite happy with orderly duty, this suited me fine.

On 16 May, I left the camp for a long weekend. A coach had been organised as before, and I booked myself a seat. From London, I travelled directly to Crawley. There was a noticeable rise in temperature in Sussex, and the spring flowers were out in the garden of Evergreen. It was a lovely weekend. We enjoyed some country walks, and went to the cinema to see *The Thief of Bagdad*.[38] Doreen seemed to have shaken off the colds that had plagued her during the winter and she played happily in the garden with the Gardiner boys.

As usual, I had to leave on Sunday afternoon, but when I reached London it was to find that the coach had not turned up. There was a great deal of moaning, but the only option was to buy our tickets and return by train. We never did get our money back, and the organiser was charged with taking money under false pretences, or something similar.

As the weeks passed the weather warmed up, at last. The countryside was transformed as the trees came into leaf and bluebells appeared in the woods. The walk to Rugeley became a pleasure, in marked contrast to the bleakness of the past weeks and months.

My pal, Phil, and I began scouting round the surrounding villages in the hope of finding a room for his wife to stay for a while. He found a place in nearby Etching, and was successful in obtaining a 'sleeping out' pass. I missed his company of an evening, but saw him during the day in the workshops. I spent an evening or two with them and was always made welcome. My efforts to find a similar place for Elsie and Doreen were not so successful.

---

38 *The Thief of Bagdad: An Arabian Fantasy in Technicolor* (Alexander Korda Film Productions/United Artists, 1940).

The time was fast approaching for our 'Trade Tests'. We were being tested constantly on all aspects of our work, and on average, our marks were in the 60s. If this was maintained, we would earn a first-class rating. Our NCO instructors told us we were above average, and wished us well, but privately told us that our lack of practical experience would probably prevent us receiving a first-class pass. The time came for us to face our examiners. At the last minute they decided to dispense with the written tests, and only gave us the oral. The examiner I went before seemed completely uninterested and kept going to the door looking for the arrival of the break bar. I instinctively knew the whole thing was a formality, and so it proved. Out of all the candidates, only one merited a first-class pass, and it wasn't me. Our marks showed that I had gained 57½ and Phil had 56. We were very disappointed.

And so our period of training ended. We were asked where we would like to be posted, and I put Faygate, in Sussex. We were given all the odd jobs around the camp as we awaited the news. It came just as we were leaving the camp on our way to join Phil's wife for tea. He was off to the north of Scotland, whilst I would be going to Skipton in Yorkshire, which showed how much notice they took of our requests. It was about 11.30 p.m. before I left the Siddoways to trek the three miles back to camp, but a motorist gave me a lift, for which I was very thankful.

The flight sergeant arranged a farewell party for us all at a pub in Hednesford, which was evidently the custom at the end of training. About fifty of us went, but strange to say it was quite a sober affair, although there were the usual drinks and singing. No women were allowed to attend; perhaps past experience had shown this to be unwise.

The following day, Thursday 3 July, those of us being posted spent the day getting 'cleared'. We had to hand in our tools and the like, and sign a form to show that we were not leaving any debts. On completing the formalities, we were handed our travel warrants and posting documents, plus a pass for fourteen days' leave. I was now officially an Aircraft Fitter II and would receive the pay appropriate to the grade. At the pay office we were given an advance of pay and subsistence for fourteen days.

That evening we met in the NAAFI for a final get-together. I found three other chaps who were being posted to the same place as me, which I found reassuring. There was a lot of talk about keeping in touch, but none of us knew what was in store, or if our postings were just staging posts for overseas. We drank each other's health in canteen tea and retired to our respective huts for our last night in RAF Hednesford.

I suppose in all life's journeys there comes a time when one pauses to reflect on past experiences. We had come to this place on the moors at the beginning of the year when winter held the place in its icy grip. Now it was high summer and the land was transformed into an area of beauty. These wooden huts had been our homes for the past six months, and in the workshops we had been initiated into the use of micrometers, hydraulics and blueprints. We had arrived as raw recruits and had been moulded into tradesmen, but now the time of preparation was over. We were being sent to bases around the country to use the skills we had learned, and we stood at the parting of the ways.

Next morning we were up early and on the move. At breakfast we took a final look around. Whilst we were all eager to leave there was a feeling that in the days to come we would look back on RAF Hednesford with affection and think only of the good times. We shouldered our kitbags, slung our gas masks across our shoulders, and, gripping our cases, took a last look at the huts of Wing 4 and the administration buildings. To the cheers of those remaining we marched out of the camp and down Kitbag Hill.

On Brindley Heath Station we said our farewells. I said cheerio to Phil and Steve in particular, for they had been good friends. Although we said we would keep in touch I never met either of them again, although Phil and I did correspond for a while. The train puffed its way into the station and those going south scrambled aboard. There was much waving and cheering as the train pulled out and I was soon settled in the corner of the compartment watching the landscape sliding by. In a few hours I would be reunited with my Elsie and Doreen, ready to make the most of the next two weeks. After that, only time would tell.

Home on Leave

The journey home seemed endless but I suppose I was impatient. It was a lovely sunny day and the countryside looked green and inviting. I travelled with one of the chaps who had been posted to the same unit as me, called Jack Wilmore. We parted company in London and agreed to meet at King's Cross on the 18th for our journey north. As I had a rail warrant I went to London Bridge and boarded a train to Three Bridges Station, which was at the end of the road in which Evergreen was situated. At about 6 p.m. I was knocking on the door.

To be home for fourteen days seemed too good to be true and Elsie and I were going to make the most of it. After exchanging greetings all round and partaking of a meal, we took ourselves off to the local cinema. Although only twenty-five miles from London it was a very quiet place and the war there seemed remote. Not far away, in the direction of Horley, were Gatwick racecourse and a small flying field which, pre-war, had been used by private and commercial firms and clubs. The airfield was too small for operational aircraft and did not appear to be in use. What we did not know was that plans for the expansion of the area, and the creation of a giant airport and new town, were already on the drawing board.

Next day we put Doreen in her pushchair and went for a long walk. In a little grocer's shop near Three Bridges station were items of food that were available for 'points'. These points had recently been introduced into the rationing system for scarce goods to ensure that there was a fair distribution of them among the people. One of these items was Spam, a mixture of ham and pork, and an American import. Only a few points were allocated to each person per month and one had to be choosy when it came to using them.

We returned to Evergreen for lunch and spent the afternoon relaxing in the extensive rear garden. Doreen played happily with the two Gardiner boys, occasionally standing on the fence watching the cows in the adjoining field. Ron busied himself with a spot of digging, but for once, I felt in a lazy mood and was content to just watch.

We spent the next couple of days visiting friends and relatives. We took the Green Line to Brixton and from there to Camberwell, to look in at Kimpton Mission. The place looked very down at heel. From there we went on to Herne Hill to visit my mother and sisters and catch up with family news, and spent the night at Sister Grace's home. I also made a point of visiting the Royal Arsenal Co-operative Society shops at Camberwell Green and Crystal Palace Road, as I felt I ought to keep in touch with the old firm. It was noticeable how many women were now serving behind the shop counters. After calling in to see Elsie's brothers, we returned to Crawley in the late evening.

On the Wednesday we took Elsie's dad with us to Horsham and spent some time with Doreen at the swimming pool. Doreen loved the water and splashed about like a little mermaid. Although we were able to get a cup of tea, there was no ice cream to be had, and sweets were rationed. All the same, we had a lovely day.

On Saturday, we went to Stoneleigh to spend a few days with our friends the Denners, calling in at the Thompsons on the way. As usual, Hilda and Reg made us very welcome and Hilda fussed over Doreen. We stayed with them until the Tuesday and spent the time strolling in Nonsuch park, visiting Hilda's mother, and looking in on Reg's warden post nearby. Reg had to go to work on Monday, so leaving Elsie and Doreen with Hilda, I paid a quick visit to my family at Herne Hill.

We reluctantly left our friends, who had made us so welcome, after lunch on Tuesday. We went on to Reigate where we met Doris Gardiner and her two boys, and journeyed home to Crawley together.

As I would have to leave home early on Friday morning, we decided we had done enough travelling and would spend the rest of the week in, or around, Evergreen, and apart from another visit to the cinema, this is what we did. There were a few shops in Crawley but as everything was on ration, strolling around shops had lost its appeal. Elsie and Doris had joined the local Co-op and bought most of their shopping there. They kept a common purse. Into it went a specific amount from Elsie, Doris and Mrs Squires, and whoever made a purchase extracted the amount from the purse. This arrangement worked very well.

About two pounds of sugar for preserving was allowed on each ration book. It was a 'once only' allocation. I remember Doris bringing in some fruit and in about an hour it was jam. She was a real hustler at getting things done.

Time was running out fast and I wasn't looking forward to going back to the RAF one little bit. On Thursday afternoon Elsie's sister, Dolly, arrived with her new man friend, Ted Kent. This was the first time I had met him and he was a little older than I expected. They had met at the Peckham Fire Station where Ted was a fireman, so we had a little in common. To help pass the time and to make Ted feel comfortable, as he seemed a little bashful, I told their fortunes with playing cards. I liked to think I was good at that sort of thing, but in any case, it was a bit of fun. After tea they left to return to Peckham, and Elsie and I saw them to the bus stop in the high street.

That evening, leaving Doreen with Doris, we went for a stroll to Lowfield Heath. We came to the hostelry where the Brighton coaches used to halt, and went inside for a port and lemon. It was dusk when we came out and there were bats swooping overhead, and in the distance the drone of an aircraft reminded us of reality.

Next morning we were awake at 6.30 a.m. and the dreaded day had dawned. We breakfasted and I said goodbye to Elsie's parents, to the Gardiners and to our Doreen. Elsie had decided to come with me to King's Cross to see me off, so at half past seven we left Evergreen and walked to Three Bridges station. The train was crowded but we managed to find seats. I put my kitbag on the luggage rack and watched the fields and houses as they slid past the window.

We reached King's Cross in good time, but I failed to find my travelling companion. The train was the 10.05 a.m. to Edinburgh and it was pulled by the famous Flying Scotsman. At any other time this would have been an adventure for me, but not this time. It was a wrench for us both to part. The time of departure came and I kissed Elsie goodbye. I watched her waving from the platform until the bend in the line separated us. I sat in a corner seat feeling very dejected, wondering what fate had in store for us all and when it would all end.

On Active Service

As the Flying Scotsman sped north and the flat plains of the Midlands flashed past the windows, I speculated on what was in store for me in the next weeks and months, perhaps years. I had had my nine months of training and would now be expected to take my share of duty, pleasant or unpleasant, and I feared it would be the latter. The war seemed to be at a critical stage and although the expected invasion had not yet materialised, the country still seemed ill-prepared to meet it. Our losses of ships and their vital cargoes were a bitter blow to the war effort, and I doubted we were told the real truth anyway.

We passed the huge complex of the London Brick Works with their high, smoke-blackened heads rearing skywards. Soon afterwards the train pulled into Peterborough station and quite a few people came on board, filling the vacant seats. I pulled out my reporting instructions and re-read them. I was puzzled. My destination was Skipton, Yorkshire, but I only had a ticket as far as York. I had looked up Skipton in the reference book. By all accounts it was a pleasant enough place, situated among the Airedale moors, with an old castle and museum, but not much else. Hardly the place, I thought, for an airfield. However, time would reveal all.

It was another lovely warm day and the countryside looked green and peaceful, hardly a wartime scene. The train stopped again at Grantham and Doncaster and then, at about 2.30 p.m. steamed slowly into the huge station at York. There was a general exodus from the train, but I took my time and when the scramble was over I picked up my gear and stepped down onto the platform. Almost the first person I met was Jack Wilmore. He told me he had arrived at King's Cross early, about 9 a.m., and had sat in the forces canteen until the train left, finding a seat in the last carriage.

We climbed the stairs, crossed the permanent way and headed for the exit. At one side was the Railway Transport Office. We went inside and showed our papers, and asked how we would get to Skipton. The chap behind the counter looked a little weary and informed us that our destination was not *Skipton*, but *Shipton*. On being pressed further, he told us to get a bus to Exhibition Square and from there, one to Shipton, which was about five miles further along the Easingwold Road.

Thoroughly mystified we went outside and met another three ex-Hednesford graduates, and together we waited for the bus. It was my first sight of York, and I liked what I saw. Across the road the sun shone on the massive city wall, its feet buried in a mound of green. My musings were interrupted by the arrival of the bus. We drove through a huge breach in the wall, over Lendall Bridge, and a few moments later alighted in Exhibition Square. Had we known it was so near the station we would have walked.

As we waited for our second bus I glanced around me. The view was grand and York seemed too good to be true. Across the square was one of the massive city gates, Bootham Bar, and above it towered the huge bulk of the Minster, with its twin towers dominating the skyline. We had a few minutes before the bus was due so I left my gear with the lads and darted across the road to read the plaque on the right hand side of Bootham Bar. It read:

> *Entry from North through Forest of Galtres. In old days armed men were stationed here to watch and conduct travellers through the forest and protect them against wolves.*

My depression of the morning began to lift. If I was going to be stationed only five miles away I would explore this great city, walk its walls and, perhaps, climb to the top of the Minster.

When the bus came, we settled into our seats, paid the 5*d*. fare, and fell silent again. This was the final stage of our journey and soon we would be facing the reality of active service. Our journey took us through the district of

Clifton Without. I suddenly understood that the hymn, 'There is a green hill far away, without a city wall', actually meant 'outside' the city wall, just like Clifton Without. This had puzzled me since childhood. It was a nice ride through pleasant countryside. After three miles we stopped at the hamlet of Skelton, and soon after, the village of Shipton. We looked in vain for the airfield, but in response to our enquiry, were directed up a side road. A walk of a hundred yards brought us to a gate on which hung a sign, RAF Shipton-by-Beningbrough. We entered, and a rather tired-looking service policeman directed us to a wooden hut, made out of a large packing case, which bore the notice, 'Orderly Room'.

A pleasant-looking corporal greeted us. He examined our papers and checked a list that was hanging from a nail in a bulldog clip.

'From Hednesford, eh?' he remarked. 'Seven of you altogether, so we're two short. I expect they'll turn up before long.' He looked at his watch.

'Not time to do much today.' (It was only 4 p.m.).

He turned to me. 'You'll join No. 5 mobile section under Sergeant Leonard. We are all billeted out. Your billet is with Mrs Barker in Church Lane. Some of the lads live nearby and they'll show you where it is. Report here at 0830 hours. Hope you will be happy with us.'

I couldn't believe my ears. Mobile work. Civilian billets. Free until 8.30 a.m. tomorrow. I came out of the orderly room in a daze. There was no one to be seen. I looked around. There was a large hangar full of tyres, gantries, railway sleepers, benches and other equipment, but no personnel. There were more huts, which served as offices, and a long, low hut with a NAAFI sign outside. Close by was a long air-raid shelter with a couple of Coles Cranes and a few motor vehicles parked nearby. I suppose the whole area was not more than a hundred yards square.

I made my way round the back of the air-raid shelter and there, stretched out on the grassy slope, sleeping, chatting and smoking were the missing airmen, sergeants, corporals and the rank and file, all seeming on excellent terms with each other. I asked for Sergeant Leonard.

He proved to be a short, stocky chap. He shook hands and introduced me to the rest of the section, who were relaxing nearby. There was one corporal and three airmen. The sergeant asked me my rank, and when I told him AC2, he frowned.

'I only have first-class men on my section.'

I apologised for my lowly status, but before any inquest ensued, somebody shouted 'Time to go' (It was 4.30 p.m.). Instantly the sleepers awoke. Engines roared into life and the airmen scrambled aboard the lorries and sped noisily out of the gate. Only about half a dozen of us were left and the corporal asked if I was the one for Mrs Barker's. I nodded, and he said, 'Come with us'.

We strolled down the lane, crossed over to a turning at the side of the church, and about fifty yards on, came to a group of cottages. He pointed to the end one and said, 'Yours'.

I can't say I was very impressed with it from the outside. It was probably well over a century old. The gate creaked as I opened it and a few steps along the path brought me to the front door. The sign above it informed me that it was called 'Silver Royd'. In response to my knock an elderly woman appeared. I introduced myself and she let me in. She was evidently expecting me, for a meal had already been prepared and was set out on the table.

She was a woman of few words and although I tried to draw her into conversation, she only made non-committal replies. All the same, she was a reasonable cook and I ate what was set before me. She showed me to an upstairs room and left me. I tried to take stock of my surroundings. It was very primitive. There was no gas, no electricity, no tap water, and the privy was at the bottom of the garden. The pump for water was outside the back door. Large, flowery wallpaper, such as we had had in the Mansions flat when I was a child, decorated my room. There was no linoleum or carpet on the floor, and the bed looked as if it would collapse if I sat on it too heavily. A stub of candle in a holder was provided for illumination purposes when it was dark.

My spirits sank somewhat at my billet, but there was nothing I could do about it at present. I went downstairs and seating myself at the table wrote to Elsie telling her where I was. I told Mrs. Barker I was going to the post office and she said I should be back in the billet by midnight. What I was going to do in the meantime I hadn't the foggiest notion.

It was not hard to find the post office and I popped my letter into the box. Shipton was the usual type of rural village with a church, pub, post office and little else. As I came away from the pillar-box a voice hailed me. It was one of my Hednesford colleagues. We swapped experiences and it seemed he was housed in quite a modern place. As we chatted a car pulled up.

'Want a lift into York?' said a cheery voice.

We looked at each other and then got in and were soon speeding along the York road. Our good Samaritan dropped us at Bootham Bar and from there we walked through the arch into Petergate and entered the Minster. Although scaffolding hid much of it, there was enough of it visible to show what a wonderful building it was. Later, we strolled around the city, unsure of our bearings, and at 9 p.m. returned to Exhibition Square and thumbed a lift back to Shipton.

Next morning, those of us billeted in the village met in the lane and marched up to the camp, where we dispersed. I joined my section and the corporal took me around the various offices to be booked in. These offices were all made from huge packing cases. I reported to pay accounts, filled in lots of forms, and was issued with a third set of shirts and underclothes, plus two boiler suits and wellington boots.

Around 10.00 a.m. the NAAFI opened and we went in. There were no girls serving inside and the tea was made by a couple of old lads who didn't look as if they had the strength to balance a tray of cups. There were some nice cakes for sale, the first I had seen for a very long time. We sat and chatted in an informal atmosphere. Everyone was very friendly and my anxieties of the past few days began to evaporate.

I learned that RAF 60 MU specialised in the recovery of crashed aircraft and was responsible for the whole of Yorkshire. There were ten sections, each comprising a sergeant, corporal and four airmen, or 'erks', as they were called, *erk* being a unit of work. Once a section was sent out on a job, they were expected to work all the hours of daylight to salvage the wreck and return it to the factory. As a reward for devotion to duty things were very easy for them at the depot. There were no parades, as such, but one had to do a turn at guard duty and occasionally, the section took its turn as a working party to deal with any emergency. The few officers there were friendly, in fact it felt like one big happy family.

The unit was next door to Shipton-by-Beningbrough railway station and most of the supplies arrived by rail. That morning we unloaded a wrecked German aircraft from a lorry and stowed it in some rail wagons. At noon we were told to pack up for the day and report at 9 a.m. the next morning. It seemed to me that I was in a dream world, so different from all the hardships I had been led to expect.

That afternoon I hitch-hiked into York and found the market place. At one of the stalls I saw a man sell ten sovereigns for 39*s.* each. I had always been fascinated by old coins and I would love to have been able to buy them. Coming away from the market I met one of our lads and we strolled around together. The old streets of York are not called 'streets' but 'gates'. In St Saviourgate we came to the Centenary Methodist Church and a notice outside said there was a canteen in the church hall and all servicemen were welcome. We fancied a cup of tea so went inside.

Our entrance caused something of a stir. Khaki uniforms were there in abundance but Air Force blue seemed unknown. We were fussed over and asked innumerable questions as to where we were stationed. The tea and cake were most enjoyable and I even managed to buy some chocolate, which I put aside to take home for Doreen. Over time, I became very friendly with the folk who ran the canteen and always made a point of calling in there whenever I visited York.

I also became quite familiar with the attractions of England's second city, and allowing for the fact that it was wartime, I came to know York well. I walked the three-mile stretch of the wall, climbed to the roof of the Minster, and visited the famous Castle Museum, the Abbey ruins and all the city gates. I enjoyed it immensely.

Gradually I settled into the unit and got to know most of its personnel. As I have mentioned, all the airmen were billeted out. Some, like myself, stayed in Shipton, others on the Rowntree estate at New Earwick. Some were five miles further up the road at Tollerton, which was reckoned to be a 'punishment' billeting. A few lived out with their wives and children, and all officers were in private houses or at the local Inn. Most of the Shipton billetees were in the Transport Section and were Corporal NCOs, but classed a Grade II trade. I came to know these lads very well and they often gave me a lift into town.

For the first week things were quiet and I had about five and a half days off. I did a night of guard duty on the Friday. Then the weather, which had been fine and warm, suddenly broke with a heavy thunderstorm, which sent the temperature plummeting. I also drew some pay. I was only due one week's pay, but they gave me two, and I sent some cash to Elsie for her birthday, presents being non-existent.

Meanwhile, things on the war front were hotting up. Germany, with the help of the Italians, had invaded Greece and Yugoslavia. Some troops from Australia, helped by some Greeks, went to the area, but it proved a gesture only and before long they had to be evacuated. The German warship Bismarck was sunk, but our losses at sea were enormous. Then on May 20th the Germans invaded the island of Crete using parachute troops. Their defences seem to have been taken by surprise and after about a week, the British troops were evacuated from the island. It was all depressingly bad news.

One of the biggest surprises of the war came on 22 June when news came that Germany, with the help of Finland, Hungary, Romania and Italy, had invaded Russia. Most people hated the Communists but saw in this move a lessening of the pressure against us. Many people considered this a blunder by the Nazis, making comparisons with Napoleon's fiasco in 1812. The initial advance moved swiftly and Poland, Estonia, Latvia and Lithuania were quickly overrun. There seemed no way of halting the German war machine.

I had hoped to get some leave in August but found that each section took their leave together, and as my section, No. 5, had had their break in June, it looked as if it would be late September before I would see Elsie and Doreen again.

Our section was called out to dismantle a plane at an aerodrome near Leeds, and on our return journey, we passed through the city. There were signs of bomb damage, and the area we went through appeared depressed and very poor. The following day, back at the unit, news came in that an aircraft from Linton-on-Ouse, a big aerodrome about three miles away, had come down in the River Ouse only a few fields away from Shipton. In the darkness the pilot had mistaken the river for one of the runways and its full load of bombs compounded the problem. Our section was detailed to deal with it.

We went along to make an inspection and to plan the best way of getting it out. Some divers were working on the plane, a Whitley bomber, which had landed right in the middle of the river, completely blocking navigation. From our point of view it was going to be a difficult operation because the river had double banks, and the highest must have been twenty feet above the water level. Sergeant Leonard, the corporal and ourselves set about making plans to get the job done, and next morning, the bombs having been removed, we started work.

We had brought two Coles cranes and a wagon loaded with heavy steel cables with us.[39] We had to wear 'Mae Wests', or lifejackets, and our tools were tied around our waists. A rowing-boat was at our disposal and we rowed out to the plane and scrambled on to the top of the wings and fuselage. One of the lads was a good swimmer and he managed to screw some eyebolts into the lifting points. It took some time, but we attached the cables, the cranes took the strain, and gradually the aircraft was pulled on to the bank.

Now that we could work from terra firma, dismantling was less difficult, but even so the work took about four days. We would take a break for lunch and tea, and work on until it became dark. Several of the officers brought their wives and children to watch us and we became on friendly terms with them. An audience of villagers stood on the top bank and took a keen interest in the proceedings.

We took the engines out and loaded them onto a barge and removed any instruments that had been above the water line. Cables were put around the fuselage, the cranes took the strain and the pull began. At first the cranes started to slip so we anchored them to some stout trees nearby. We stood clear in case the cables snapped but slowly, and then quickly, the plane left the water and was pulled on to the first bank. It had suffered badly and by the time it reached the second bank it was a mangled wreck.

The onlookers gave a cheer and some small boats that had been waiting began to nose their way upstream. We loaded the wreck on to a couple of low-loaders, gathered our equipment and returned home. The powers that be seemed satisfied with our performance, but when I looked at the twisted heap on the transporters I felt slightly sick that so much taxpayer's money had been wasted because of a pilot's error.

I received a letter from my chum from our training days at Hednesford, Phil Siddoway, who was now stationed at Edzell, near Brechin in Angus. By all accounts the scenery was lovely but the place was very isolated. They all worked long hours and seemed to achieve very little. Some of the lads from Hednesford were there so they were company for each other. All the same, he seemed very envious of my posting to Shipton.

The following weekend was August Bank Holiday. It made no difference to us except that we did not have to report until 9 a.m. I tried to find accommodation in York for Elsie and Doreen to have a short break, but it was a hopeless quest. Elsie told me in a letter that my mother and eldest sister had been to Evergreen to see her and on the following day Hilda Denner, her mother and Margaret had also called in. The Gardiners had been away for a few days and Elsie's brothers, George and Tim, with Edna Neale, spent the weekend there. It was good to know that friends and relatives had not forgotten them.

The unexpected happened during the week when I was given seven days

---

39 The five-ton Coles Mk VII crane for aircraft salvage, typically mounted on the six-ton, six-wheeled Thorneycroft Amazon Lorry.

leave. Anyone living over 200 miles away was allowed the previous afternoon. The CO was quite generous in this respect. On the Friday afternoon as I was leaving I asked Mrs Barker if I could bring my wife and daughter back with me for a couple of weeks. To my surprise she said I could. Silver Royd was not really the place I would have chosen for Elsie and Doreen but it seemed there was nowhere else.

The following week passed all too quickly, most of the time spent visiting friends and relatives. On the Friday morning we set off for York together. The sky clouded over as the Flying Scotsman sped northwards and by the time we arrived at York it was raining. We stopped for some tea in the city and then boarded the bus for Shipton, arriving there at about half past six. I'm not sure quite what Elsie thought of Mrs Barker and her residence but we settled into our room.

When I reported for duty the inevitable happened. The section was to go to Topcliffe to dismantle a Whitley bomber. I went to see the warrant-officer to see if I could be put on other work as I had just brought my family back for a few days. Warrant-Officer Murton was quite a decent sort but he told me in no uncertain terms that I should have known better, and that work came first. I had to break the news to Elsie. It wasn't very nice to leave her in a strange house in a strange area but she was a capable woman and she put on a brave face.

The job at Topcliffe took us until the Friday. I was impatient to get back and would have worked all night to get the work finished, but to the others it was just another job. However, we were given a half day on the Saturday and I took Elsie and Doreen into York. She had already been there in my absence but I was able to give her a conducted tour. We had tea in the YMCA and spent a pleasant afternoon and evening. I had heard in a roundabout way that on Sunday afternoons the Lord Mayor of York would occasionally entertain servicemen who were stationed nearby. The following day we decided to visit the Mansion House to see if we could get in. A little nervously we approached the door of the famous building where we were greeted and ushered in to the hall. It was quite crowded, but we were shown to a table and Doreen instantly became the centre of attention. We had a lovely tea with iced fancies, which had long since disappeared from the shops. But our day was really made when the Lord Mayor, resplendent in his robes and wearing his impressive chain of office round his neck, came to our table and presented Doreen with a box of chocolates, amid great applause. A reporter from the city newspaper came and asked us lots of questions, where we were from, Doreen's age etc., and the following day an account of her visit to the party appeared in the *Yorkshire Evening Post*. We were thrilled.

In contrast to the previous week we had several half days together. On Monday, I finished at 11.30 a.m. and we went to one of York's cinemas and saw *Western Union*. On Tuesday we visited Leeds to see Mrs Turner, a friend of Elsie's family. I was on piquet duty on the Wednesday and in the evening

Elsie brought Doreen to the camp to see me. I had been sorting through some scrap metal and my boiler suit was rather the worse for wear. Doreen said to her mother, 'Isn't Daddy dirty!'

We spent Thursday afternoon visiting the Minster and Castle Museum. We had tea at the Centenary Methodist church then went for a fish-and-chip supper before returning on the bus to Shipton. On the Friday I was feeling rather poorly (was it the fish?) and so we spent a quiet day. Then came some rather shattering news. I was being posted on detached duty, to work on Sunderland flying boats at Calshot, near Southampton, the following Tuesday. The posting was indefinite so it meant the end of our time together in York. We enjoyed one more day in York and on the Sunday we took Elsie's case and the pram and deposited them in the left luggage at the railway station. Elsie would collect them before travelling home the following day. It had become obvious that the work I was engaged upon meant that I would never be in one place long enough for Elsie to come and stay nearby. We would have to be content with my getting leave as often as I could.

Elsie and Doreen left on the 2.34 p.m. train the following day, Monday 1 September. They stayed the night at No. 396 Cowley Road before travelling on to Evergreen on the Tuesday.

Calshot Camp

Next day the little party that was being sent to help out at Calshot left Shipton with their kits and toolboxes and headed for York station. I remember little about the journey except that it seemed endless. We arrived at Calshot at about 10 p.m. I used to think that Hednesford was isolated but although Southampton was just across the water from Calshot, a journey of eighteen miles through very rural countryside separated the two. It seemed unlikely that we would go there often.

The camp was overcrowded. All the Nissen huts were full to overflowing and we were parked in the dance hall, as there was nowhere else. Evidently there was a big job on hand as contingents from other maintenance units had also been drafted in. It was all go. We had to be up at 5.30 a.m., although occasionally we stayed in until 6.15 a.m. After parade, at 8.00 a.m., we were marched along a narrow neck of land, called Calshot Spit, where the hangars, workshops and offices were located.

We were put to work overhauling the giant Sunderland flying boats, which were being used mainly for escort duties with the merchant ships. They were huge monsters with three decks inside. Once hauled out of the sea on sloping ramps, airmen swarmed all over them, just like busy ants. We were allocated jobs individually. I chatted with chaps who had come from places like Sevenoaks, Liverpool, Pembroke and Horsham. By all accounts Horsham MU was much like Shipton and I thought how nice it would be to get a transfer there, being so close to Evergreen and my family. Across the water was the Isle of Wight, the venue of some enjoyable holidays in the past. There was plenty of shipping in the Solent and speedy patrol boats were continually racing up and down, no doubt on the lookout for enemy craft.

On Saturday, 6 September, we were given a half day but most of us lazed about until the evening, when we went to a camp concert, run by ENSA. The next day was Elsie's and my seventh wedding anniversary, but it was just another working day at Calshot. As we marched up to the spit I noticed the profusion of blackberries along the way, more than I had ever seen before. It was sad to think that because of sugar rationing it was unlikely that many would be gathered.

As we worked the following day we observed a convoy of ships sailing along Southampton Water. Each ship had its own barrage balloon flying aloft, a protection against low flying aircraft. We had an air-raid alert but it came to nothing. The weather was quite sunny and warm and during the lunch breaks we would sit on the beach and throw pebbles into the sea, much to the annoyance of the warrant-officer, who frowned on such childish behaviour. The week passed fairly quickly and on the Saturday we were given another half day off.

I took a walk to Fawley, the nearest village, and found the local YMCA canteen, where I spent a pleasant few hours chatting and drinking tea. It was dark when I got back to camp. Some of the lads had been into Southampton and they began to roll back at all hours of the night, causing much disturbance. These defaulters paid for their misdemeanours the next day by being drafted into the cookhouse, where I saw some of them stringing beans. They had a novel way of doing the job. They topped and tailed the beans and then chopped them in half. This explained a lot when I tasted them at dinner.

For no apparent reason that I could see, I was moved from sleeping on the dance hall floor and put into the catering staff hut where there was a spare bed. It was wonderful. I was given a mug of tea in bed every morning and often the odd cookie would come my way. I felt as though I was staying at the Ritz or Savoy. There was a table on which I could write my letters and I was able to catch up with my correspondence.

We had hoped that the end of our detached duty was drawing to a close, but another Sunderland arrived which meant another fortnight at Calshot. During the week we were told that a weekend pass would be given at the end of duty on Friday. I wrote to Elsie and told her the good news. At 8 p.m. on Friday I set off and after a rather roundabout journey I reached Evergreen late, but happy. It was lovely to be back with the family and for a few hours the war seemed far away. Once Sunday lunch was over it was time to return, and Elsie and Doreen saw me off at Three Bridges.

My journey back to Southampton took me via Arundel and Littlehampton, places we had visited in the past. We had once rented a bungalow at nearby Rustington, with sisters Grace and Denise, Elsie's brother, Tim, and in the second week, Hilda and Reg Denner. As the train approached Southampton I could see a vast amount of bomb damage, and the gaunt ruins of houses and factories stood rugged and black against the setting sun. I reached the city in ample time to get the bus to Calshot.

Next morning my cup of tea came at 5.30 a.m. and as I lay there I could not help but wonder why fate was being so kind to me. There were plenty of jokes about servicemen having tea in bed, and I could bear witness that it sometimes happened. After breakfast I went along to the guardroom to collect a parcel that was waiting for me. It contained a lovely fruitcake from Elsie. I took it back to Hut C4 and shared it with the lads.

Work proceeded apace on the Sunderland but I developed a painful twinge in my right shoulder. It bothered me a lot so I decided to see the medical officer about it. He was not impressed. He recommended some exercises and prescribed the usual antidote of medicine, and duty. The former was the usual spoonful of orange-flavoured liquid, a cure-all for whatever the complaint, and all those who reported sick had a spoonful from the same bottle, at 9 a.m. and 5 p.m.

It was a scrounge really, for by the time we reported at the spit it was 10 a.m., just in time for the NAAFI break, and we had to leave at 4.30 p.m. to report back to the medical room for our evening spoonful. It seemed rather absurd that they wouldn't give us our own bottle of the stuff to last the week.

The week passed slowly but no more planes arrived for overhaul. I went to the camp cinema and saw *Hotel for Women* and *Heaven with a Barbed Wire Fence*—not Calshot, but somewhere in Arizona.[40] The weather kept fine, but signs of autumn were everywhere. The nights and mornings became misty and the trees began to turn red and brown, and the blackberries were as profuse as ever.

On the Sunday morning, 29 September, we were unexpectedly told that we were to return to Shipton the following day. Our elation was tempered somewhat by the chasing around we had to do before leaving. All the jobs we had done on the flying boats had to be signed for, and we had to get camp clearance to show we were not leaving any debts behind us. I phoned a telegram to Elsie letting her know we were moving and hoping she might see me at Waterloo.

There were many delays next morning and we did not leave Calshot until past 10 a.m. We caught the 11.15 a.m. train to Waterloo, arriving at 1 p.m. Before we could leave the platform, an RTO chap arrived and bundled us, and some lads bound for Shrewsbury, into a wagon and sent us on our way. Our first stop was Paddington station, and by the time the Shrewsbury boys and their gear had been unloaded and we had set off again, it was 2.15 p.m. I was very fidgety in case Elsie was waiting at Waterloo. The Shipton lads had arranged among themselves to spend the night in London and to continue on to York the following morning. Unfortunately, as we were putting our toolboxes

---

40 *Hotel for Women*, also known as *Elsa Maxwell's Hotel for Women* (Twentieth Century-Fox, 1939); *Heaven with a Barbed Wire Fence* (Twentieth Century-Fox, 1939).

and kits into the baggage room at Waterloo, we were spotted by another RTO bloke who inspected our route form, and said we were to travel on the 3.50 p.m. train. I was in a quandary. Leaving my gear with one of the lads, I made a dash to try to get to Herne Hill, but after some irritating delays I abandoned the idea and sent a telegram to Elsie explaining what had happened.

A service policeman was waiting at King's Cross to make sure we boarded our train. Fate seemed against me and I felt dispirited. To cheer myself up I had tea on the train. For $1s.\ 2d.$ I had a pot of tea, two slices of bread and butter and a piece of cake. When we arrived at York the last train to Shipton had left so we phoned the unit for transport and arrived at camp around 9 p.m. We were told to return to our previous billets, but Mrs Barker did not seem very pleased to see me.

Next morning my disappointments continued. I found I had been taken off No. 5 section and put on No. 18. The latter were out working. Had I stayed with No. 5 I would have been due for leave the following week. Now I would have to wait longer. A lot more airmen were in the camp and the number of sections had doubled. That morning six chaps were posted to Iceland, and that made me feel a little happier. It could have included me.

Elsie and I exchanged letters and the telegram business was sorted out. She had not been able to come to London so a lot of my frustration had been unnecessary. At Mrs Barker's the number of lodgers had been increased. A chap called Levine, of Jewish decent, had taken up residence when Elsie and Doreen had come to stay in the summer, and I didn't like him one bit. Now two more chaps had arrived and the tiny cottage was overcrowded. On the unit there was not the same freedom we had previously enjoyed. It was the usual trouble, a few taking advantage of a very tolerant leadership, and we all had to suffer. Another blow came quickly. A promotion board had been due to sit in October for the purpose of regrading recommended personnel. This had been cancelled and would not now sit until January 1942. I had hoped to obtain my 'first class', but now I would have to wait another three months. The one bright spot for me was that my rheumatism had gone.

I decided, with Elsie's help, to apply for a supplementary allowance to give her a little extra to live on. It took some time but eventually we were awarded a further $10s.$ a week.

Garforth

I joined my new section. The sergeant in charge was an elderly chap and very tolerant. Nothing seemed to fluff him and we got on well. He told me that his people were in the jewellery business so I asked him if he could get me a sovereign. He said he would the next time he was on leave.

We were loading scrap metal into a railway wagon when we were called back at the double to the unit. An urgent job had turned up near a place called Garforth, in the Leeds area. We had no time to return to our billets for a change of clothing, but loaded our toolboxes on to a wagon, put the standard gear on board and were off.

It took us some time to locate the meadow where the bomber had landed. How the pilot had brought it down undamaged into such a confined space was little short of miraculous. An army unit was guarding it and around the edges of the field boys and girls from the local village had gathered to watch the events. The sergeant produced his authority, a 'DR6' (Defence of the Realm authority No. 6), and the army chaps surrendered the plane to us, although they would continue to guard it during the hours of darkness.

It was obvious that in such cramped conditions, it would take us five or six days to dismantle the plane and get it back to the factory. Leaving us to get the gantries set up, the sergeant took himself off to the village to find billets for us. From what he said, our arrival had given the villagers no end of a boost and they all wanted to put us up in their homes. In fact, the women had nearly come to blows over it. I found myself, with one of the other lads, in the house of the local policeman. They couldn't do enough for us.

We were not sure what the aircraft was that we were working on. It had the look of a Manchester, but we couldn't be sure. By the time we had our equipment in place it was nearly dark, so we packed up and left the army to keep guard overnight. Our hostess had prepared a lovely meal, and we sat and chatted with them, feeling that all was right with the world. The sergeant called round and told us that a 'do' had been laid on for us at the working men's club. When we arrived there, the whole assembly stood up and cheered us. I felt a little embarrassed: we were not Battle of Britain pilots but just six erks, doing a humble job.

Before we had even sat down about six glasses of beer were put in front of us. I managed to distribute mine among the chaps and take their empty glasses. I gathered that most of the men present were coal miners and we sat and chatted as though we had known them all our lives. They told me of working at the coalface and in return, being the only one sober, I tried to explain the theory of flight, and suchlike, to them. It was a most enjoyable evening and I salute the generous people of Garforth.

As we worked on the plane we always had an admiring audience. I think the army guard hated the sight of us. We were getting all the praise whilst they had to stay awake during the dark, damp hours, or try to sleep in a leaky tent. We had to watch the blighters though, as instruments started disappearing. After issuing some threats, they mysteriously reappeared. Souvenir hunting was a major problem for us.

We were almost ready to remove the mainplanes (wings) when I noticed that one of the wing fuel tanks was half full of one-hundred-octane fuel. It had to be emptied before we could proceed further. The lads were all for opening the drain cock and letting it soak into the ground. I protested. Men were risking their lives to bring petrol from abroad. The sergeant said we could do as we liked with it, but it had to be got rid of. Some time later that day the farmer who owned the field came across to see how things were progressing. I asked him if he had any oil drums and if he could use the fuel.

He seemed suspicious at first but I explained the situation. He had a word with the sergeant who confirmed my offer. Soon some empty drums arrived and we drained the tanks into them. One-hundred-octane fuel was too powerful for normal machines but he said he would tone it down. For the rest of our time there, his wife supplied us with afternoon tea and cake. The problem had been solved to our mutual satisfaction.

When we were ready we phoned the unit for a crane and low-loader. The whole village came to watch as we took off the wings, elevators, fin and rudder. Then with a special sling, the body of the aircraft was raised. One chap used the hand-pump to raise the wheels by hydraulic pressure whilst I slid underneath and made sure the undercarriage was securely locked in position, and we were ready. Our admiring audience gave a cheer as the fuselage was raised, then lowered on to the transport. The mainplains followed. The engines were put on a separate wagon and all the accoutrements stowed away. The army guardsmen took down their tent, threw their belongings into a truck and returned to wherever they had come from. With the help of the village children, we formed a line across the field to check that nothing of value had been left behind. We let the boys keep any nuts and bolts they came across, and the girls went home with scraps of fabric. So everyone was happy.

There wasn't time to return to Shipton that day, as a lot of paperwork had to be done. The farmer had to make a claim for the damage done to his crops and the ladies who had billeted us had to check that their forms for recompense were in order, although some did not wish to claim. We insisted that they did. That night a dance was held in the Welfare Hall and we were invited. One of my colleagues was an excellent dancer and he was kept busy on the dance floor by the local lassies. Several times I was invited to dance but I was pretty hopeless.

Next morning as we clambered aboard our wagon, the women and children turned out in force to say goodbye and shake our hands. It was a sad parting from these generous people who had made us so welcome.

Shipton

We were soon back in Shipton and I was glad to collect the letters waiting for me. It came as a surprise to realise that the next day was my thirty-fourth birthday. There were three letters from Elsie, a card from Doreen and letters from my sister Eileen and from Phil Siddoway. It was mixed news. Syd House had lost his mother, Con and Arthur's home had been burgled, my brother Reg and his wife Ivy were on the point of breaking up and I had forgotten that today was Tim's birthday. And that night I was on guard duty.

Mrs Barker's granddaughter was staying at the house. She was about twelve years old and a saucy little cat, cheeking her granny no end. She spent the daylight hours picking up potatoes in a nearby field. In a public relations exercise, I took her and Emma, a girl of about the same age who lived in the first house in the lane, to the cinema in Wiggington, where *The Good Companions* was being shown. Some of the airmen were billeted in Wiggington and the two girls and I went with them in the station wagon, which thrilled them no end.

The weather over the past few days had become very changeable and decidedly colder. One afternoon, the CO, a very decent type, lined us up outside the NAAFI hut and asked us questions about our occupations in Civvy Street, our hobbies etc. The chap standing next to me had been in the market garden business and the CO asked him about the vegetables that were being grown around the camp. Just as he was about to chat to me, a heavy snowstorm enveloped us and that chat was called off in a hurry.

The strength of our unit had doubled but at any one time there were usually several sections out on jobs. Whilst waiting, we were usually given odd jobs around the camp. We were told that providing nothing sensational happened, we would have seven days leave from 1st November. In the meantime we went out to jobs at Driffield, Topcliffe and nearby Linton. The weather was wet and horrible but each day brought us nearer that leave. We filled in our application forms.

I received a letter from an old colleague who had worked with me at the Co-op in Crystal Palace Road. He was in Leeds, and he invited me over. One Saturday afternoon I hitched a lift to Leeds in our squadron leader's car. He was a mad driver and touched eighty miles an hour on some stretches of the road. We did the journey in less than half an hour. I felt a bit weak at the knees when I alighted. A bus took me to my destination but when I got there Ted was out visiting a cousin in a nearby town. It was a disappointment, but his friends gave me a very posh tea and an invitation to call in again whenever I was in the area.

No complications arose to stop our section taking leave and we were given permission to travel home on the Friday afternoon. I travelled to London with the sergeant, who promised to try and get me the sovereign I had requested. He was as good as his word and brought one back. It cost me £2 2s. 6d. When we had left Yorkshire there had been snow on the ground but this disappeared as we travelled southwards.

I reached Three Bridges station at about 9.30 p.m. and was met by Elsie. It was good to be home again. We spent some of the time visiting friends and family but the time sped by and in no time at all it was Friday again and time to travel back to York.

It was back to the awful weather again. Rain, rain and still more rain until everywhere was soggy, and squelched underfoot. Our section was sent out to Thornaby to collect a Lockheed that had caught fire and burnt out. All we needed were shovels, hacksaws and a broom.

The sirens began to sound more frequently and during the day the wagons and transport had to be dispersed. The nearest enemy action, however, was at Ripon. One evening as we were sitting by the fire, there was a terrific 'crump' and old Mrs Barker jumped out of her chair and nearly hit the ceiling. She rushed to the paraffin lamp and turned it out. We heard later that one of our own planes had blown up.

A POR notice was pinned on the notice board asking for volunteers to work in aircraft factories. Those selected would be given indefinite leave of absence. I immediately put my application in but was told that only men with experience in aircraft factories would be considered. Another notice informed us Christmas leave would only be given to airmen who lived locally. No travelling would be permitted.

Our section was told that a job was in the offing for us at Rawcliffe, just outside York. I received a card form Ted Lenthal inviting me again to Leeds. It had turned a little milder and I went into York and the Centenary Methodist church in St Saviourgate, my usual rendezvous. Whilst there a thick fog came down. There should have been a concert party to entertain the boys, but the weather caused it to be cancelled. A 'go as you please' competition was hurriedly organised and I had a go. I was voted best turn and thereafter was often called upon to help out.

On the Sunday afternoon I went again to Leeds. This time Ted was at home. We chatted about things past, and present, and when it was time to leave he accompanied me back to York, just for the ride. The following day I went into York in search of Christmas presents, but it was a hopeless quest. I went to the cinema and saw a film called *The Saint Meets The Tiger*. It wasn't too bad.[41]

The following day we were sent to Rawcliffe aerodrome to dismantle an American plane, a Lockheed Electra. It was a luxurious private plane with a saloon seating eight passengers, with dual controls and a room for a hostess. It was called 'The City of Chicago'.

Whilst working the following afternoon the unit warrant-officer, a chap called Murton, drove up in one of the staff cars, came to me and told me to get in the car as the adjutant wanted to see me.

Thoroughly mystified I got in the car and was transported back to base. For the life of me I could not imagine why I was so urgently wanted. The adjutant, who was the CO's dogsbody, was the least liked of all the officers by the rank and file, but I had never had anything to do with him.

I went straight to his office, knocked on the door and went inside. He was busy writing at his desk. I saluted and said, 'You sent for me, sir?'.

His manner was not friendly. 'Do you know an airman named Levine?' he asked.

I replied that we shared the same billet in Church Lane.

'Were you in York last night, in Exhibition Square?'

---

41 *The Saint Meets The Tiger* (RKO Radio British Productions, 1941), starring Hugh Sinclair as Simon Templar ('The Saint').

I said I had been there waiting for the bus back to Shipton.

'Then,' he said angrily, 'what do you mean by that disgraceful exhibition, going up and down the road shouting, "I want to be sent overseas".'

I couldn't believe my ears. I was stunned. All I could reply was, 'You heard me say no such thing'.

'I heard you myself,' he retorted, 'You were with Levine, disgracing the unit and the uniform you wear'.

'I was not with Levine,' I answered. 'We share the same billet but we go nowhere together. He and I have nothing in common. It was not me you heard shouting and I certainly have no wish to go overseas.'

He was quiet for a few moments looking down at the papers on his desk.

'So, it wasn't you?'

'It certainly was not, Sir.'

From the changed expression on his face I could see that he realised his mistake. 'All right then, dismiss.'

I saluted and left his office, but I was furious. My head was in a whirl as I tried to recall the events of last night. The fact that I had been 'on the carpet' soon spread, but I kept quiet until I could think things through. I was determined not to let the matter rest.

That evening as we sat at tea, Levine tried to pump me on why I had been carpeted, but I refused to be drawn. I think he sensed that he was involved somehow and probably my manner towards him was icy. As I looked at his gross, overweight figure I felt a loathing of him. He was always in trouble but never seemed to benefit by his errors. In the end he left for his nightly trip into York and I settled down to letter-writing.

I strolled down the lane to the post office and whilst dropping my letters into the box I met one of the airmen from the orderly room. He immediately broached the subject of my interview with the adjutant.

'He knows he made a mistake and the CO won't be happy about it. My advice to you is to get out of that billet. Sam Levine contaminates everything he comes into contact with. The adj' owes you something. Make an application for another billet, you're in a pretty primitive place anyway.'

I replied to the effect that I had contemplated doing just that but really didn't relish another meeting with the adjutant.

'This is your opportunity,' he replied. 'He blundered badly. We could have told him who the culprit was if he had asked. We in the office know where the airmen spend their evenings off and I can tell you that you spend most of yours in the Methodist canteen in St Saviourgate. We have to know these things for security reasons.'

We chatted for a bit and he promised to get the appropriate form for me to fill in. I strolled back to the cottage and sat by the fire thinking what a lot could happen in a few hours.

Levine didn't arrive back until the early hours. He was in trouble again. It seemed he had met up with an ATS girl and they had gone back to her quarters and he had sneaked inside. This was strictly taboo, but Levine never thought ahead. When he went to leave, he found the gate locked and guarded and had to climb over the wall and tore his uniform in the process. Fulford Barracks, where the ATS were quartered, was a mile or so on the other side of York and he had to walk the seven miles back. On the way he was stopped, his dishevelled appearance noted, and put on report.

Next morning he was summoned before the CO who gave him ten days confined to the unit. Had the truth of where he had been come out his punishment would have been severe. He went crying to old Mrs Barker telling her he was in trouble and would she repair his uniform. It was pathetic. He used to call her 'Ma' and she always felt sorry for him.

The orderly room corporal was as good as his word and brought me the form to complete. I put my reason for seeking the interview as 'changing my billet'. He took the form and said he would put it in the adjutant's tray.

On Wednesday, 24 November, the adjutant sent for me, and this time the interview was more relaxed. I explained the reasons for my request saying, quite bluntly, that it was in both Levine and my own interest that we parted. He was sympathetic but said that billets were so scarce that nothing was available at present. As soon as one became vacant elsewhere, I should have it. Neither of us mentioned the previous misunderstanding and the interview ended almost friendly.

The dismal November days gave way to brighter December ones. In the Western Desert the Eighth Army was on the offensive, pushing the Italians back and capturing thousands of prisoners. On the Russian Front the city of Leningrad was under siege, but the German offensive had been halted.

We finished the job at Rawcliffe and then went on to one just outside Doncaster. An Airspeed Oxford had made a forced landing in a field. It wasn't much of a job and we soon had it dismantled and waited for the Queen Mary to take it away.[42] It arrived on Tuesday, 9 December, and when it was loaded the sergeant asked if I would like to accompany the driver to Portsmouth, where it was to be delivered. I jumped at the opportunity and was soon settled beside the driver and on our way.

We stopped the first night at an aerodrome overlooking Grantham and continued on our way south the next morning. It was a fairly slow journey, as we had to obtain a police escort through the towns *en route*. We arrived in London in the afternoon but as we were not allowed on the roads at night we stopped at the airfield in Northolt.

I had a quick tea then made my way to Herne Hill. It took nearly two hours and when I got to No. 28 Hawarden Grove there was no reply. I tried No. 24 and found a full house. My mother and sisters Grace, Audrey, Eileen and Denny were there, also my brother Reg, Grace's husband John, Mrs McPhun, (a friend of Mum's) and Annie Hayes (a family friend from Stobart days). It

---

42 The forty-foot-long low-loader trailers used by the RAF to transport salvaged aircraft were known as 'Queen Marys', presumably with reference to the transatlantic liner.

was a wonderful surprise to find so many of them together. Audrey cooked me some eggs and bacon and I caught up with the family news.

Reg and Ivy were now living apart. Syd was in hospital near Helperby, not far from Shipton. Mum and Denny were talking of moving to nearby Croxted Road. It was quite like old times. Next morning I had to be up at 5 a.m. to get back to Northolt. I made it, and we set off for Portsmouth where we arrived in the late afternoon.

It had been a lovely ride through Surbiton, Esher and Hindhead, but when we reached the Devil's Punchbowl, a thick mist descended which made driving difficult. We stopped in Petersfield for lunch but when we arrived at the aircraft factory they told us that our aircraft could not be unloaded until the next morning. We booked in to the local YMCA for the night and I wrote to Elsie telling her where I was and said I hoped we would call in at Evergreen on our return journey.

The driver and I made our way to the local forces' canteen, but were not greeted at all warmly by the girls serving the tea or by the sailors there. We put it down to the fact that we were in a naval town where air force blue cut no ice. Later we heard, although it had not been announced officially, that the Japanese had sunk the battleship Prince of Wales and the battle-cruiser Hood. By all accounts, they had put to sea without air cover and had been hit by Japanese torpedo bombers, with appalling loss of life.

I felt very sad about the Hood. When the 43rd Kimpton scouts camped on the Isle of Wight in 1936, we went to Portsmouth Navy week and were shown over the Hood. On deck, some officers had approached us and asked if any of the lads had thought of joining the Navy. When war was declared two of our scout troop, Ron Howland and Lew Lancaster, joined the Navy. Both lost their lives.

The following morning we collected our wagon, which had been unloaded, and set off on our return journey. I persuaded the driver to make a small detour and by afternoon we had reached Evergreen. I was able to spend half an hour with Elsie, Doreen and Mr and Mrs Squires. It made up a little for the fact that I wouldn't be at home for Christmas. After a fond farewell we continued our journey towards London and pulled in to Croydon aerodrome for the night.

Taking the driver with me, we boarded a bus to Herne Hill where we spent the evening talking with Eileen, and then had supper with Audrey. There was a lot to talk about and it was past 1 a.m. before we parked ourselves on the sitting room floor for the night. Next morning we returned to Croydon and set off north once again. We called in at Hendon but as there were no loads to carry, we returned to Shipton empty.

Back at the unit I found that I was still in the same billet, and now two more airmen had taken up residence there. The camp seemed about to burst at the seams, with the influx of many more airmen. There was a feeling that something was 'in the air'. I put in for a weekend pass but knew I had no hope of getting it. I was right, it wasn't granted.

Then, on Wednesday 17 December, the unexpected happened. A lot of new postings, many overseas, others to more distant units, were announced. We all got very jumpy, especially when one of the orderly room staff appeared with a list in his hand. Then my name was called and with a sinking feeling I reported to the station warrant-officer. He told me that I, with four others, was being sent on detachment to work with civilian engineers at Rawcliffe aerodrome, just outside York, to work on Halifax bombers. I was to collect my gear from Mrs Barker's, as a new billet would be found for me near the Handley Page works.

I could have jumped for joy! The adjutant had kept his word, and in the process I was going to an aircraft factory where I hoped to learn more about the technical side of aircraft production. It all seemed too good to be true. Why I had been selected and not one of the more senior airmen was a puzzle, although it crossed my mind that maybe it was because I had not made a song and dance over the adjutant's blunder.

At dinnertime I told Mrs Barker that I was leaving, and she seemed quite upset. I suppose we had got along reasonably well. She promised to keep any mail for me until I could call in to collect it. I gathered up my kit and after searching everywhere for my water bottle, found Levine had borrowed it as he had lost his own. It was still full of water, which must have been inside for a week or more.

Handley Page Factory

That afternoon, the five of us, complete with kits and tool-boxes, were put aboard a wagon and driven to the Handley Page factory. We reported in. Meals were to be taken with the small RAF contingent that acted as liaison with the management. We were supposed to be billeted with a Mrs Brown at No. 3 Alwyne Grove, Clifton, but for some unknown reason she refused to have us. We ended up with a Mrs Pearman at No. 46 Queen Anne's Road, only a stone's throw from Bootham Bar.

It was an old Georgian house, very scruffy and dirty, and every room seemed to have been sublet to an assortment of queer folk. There were servicemen and their wives, Irish navvies, and some very odd types who came and went at all hours. We five were allocated two rooms on the first floor.

Right from the start, Mrs Pearman, a buxom lady of uncertain age, took a fancy to us. She laid on a tea and told us we were free to use the kitchen and sit by the fire whenever we so wished. This was generous of her as the RAF only paid her a lodging allowance for us.

The weather was cold and damp and, at times, foggy. Christmas was only a day or two away and I wrote to friends and relatives wishing them the age-old greeting of a Happy Christmas. I developed a sore throat and cold and it was a job to keep going. We had to walk to and from our billet to Rawcliffe and we often missed breakfast through oversleeping. However, the hangar was bright and warm and the workforce had a fifteen-minute break at 10.15 a.m. It was possible to buy a cuppa and slice of bread and dripping in the canteen.

The work people treated us well and I chummed up with an artisan named Prosser, who took me under his wing. But it was a production line with each man doing only his job, so we didn't learn a great deal. The work-force earned high wages and did a lot of overtime, and at times, we felt like the poor relations; but of course, we didn't have to pay for board and lodgings and the like.

Living only five minutes' walk away from Bootham Bar, I spent my evenings in the Services Club in St Saviourgate where, by now, I was well known. With the approach of Christmas several groups of carol singers appeared in the streets, but there was a despondent air over the festivities. The war in the Far East had dampened any remaining optimism. The Japanese were relentlessly driving our ill-equipped forces back to Singapore and now, even Australia was threatened by the yellow peril.

I had sent Elsie and Doreen some chocolate, which was all I could get. The shops were empty and everyone was on short rations. It was a case of make do and mend. They were dark days and I think it was only cups of tea that kept the nation going.

On Christmas morning, which was a day off, I didn't get up for breakfast as my cold was at its worst. However, we all went to the camp for lunch, a decent meal of turkey, pork, baked and boiled potatoes and Christmas pudding. We all received a packet of Woodbine cigarettes, an apple, a bottle of lemonade and the CO's best wishes.

I went along to the club in the evening. I thought it very decent of the Methodist folk to give up their Christmas evening to open the canteen. There was quite a crowd there and we played games like musical chairs with the local lassies. As usual, I was called upon to do a spot of entertaining, which was well received. All the same, I felt it was one of the unhappiest Christmas Days I had spent.

We all worked on Boxing Day. In the evening my cold began to ease and I was feeling much better. I went to the Club where it was Party Night, given by the staff. They had organised a concert and during the interval we were given orangeade and Dundee cake. A general-knowledge quiz was organised between the WAAFs, ATS, Army and RAF. I was asked to represent the RAF so I mounted the platform for the ordeal. In the event I won easily, received much applause and 2*s.* 6*d.*

Next day I received my mail from Shipton, and quite a lot there was. Cards from Elsie and Doreen, Ron and Doris Gardiner, the Denners, Ted Lenthal and Mrs Barker, as well as from the family. There were presents of ties, stamps, postal orders and cigarettes, which were all greatly appreciated.

There was also sad news. It was at this time I learned that Lew Lancaster had lost his life at sea. He had been a stoker on the battleship *Barham*, which had been torpedoed by a German submarine, the U-331, in the Mediterranean, off the coast of Africa. A total of 879 officers and ratings lost their lives, although 300 survived. Lew was only twenty-one years of age.

By the same post I heard that Mrs Knocker, a friend for many years, had passed away. It seemed our little circle of friends was diminishing. The war news was not good either. The Japanese were sweeping forward, brushing aside any opposition, and on Christmas Day the great base at Hong Kong surrendered with thousands of British and Commonwealth soldiers taken prisoner. The outlook was black indeed.

The five of us settled down at Handley Page and I think we would all have been content to stay there for the duration. We had no duties to perform and had every Saturday and Sunday off. There seemed no chance of getting leave and we had to plod on, hoping we had not been forgotten. I never gave up hope of finding somewhere for Elsie and Doreen to stay and asked around the civilian work-force. Some of them said their rents were very high, 'atrocious' was their actual word.

One day seven more airmen from Shipton joined us. They told us that the unit was overflowing with new bods. Evidently something big was brewing but no one knew what.

On New Year's Eve I went to the club as usual. The canteen was full of soldiers and ATS girls from the Fulford barracks. The airmen could be numbered on one hand. One of the ladies invited me to her home to see the New Year in. We sang songs around the piano, I gave a few of my monologues, enjoyed a nice supper and generally had a good time. As I passed the Minster on my way back all was quiet. The ringing of church bells was reserved for warning of an invasion.

And so the year of 1941 ended and we all wondered what the next year had in store for us. There was little optimism despite the fact that the Americans had now joined us. The Japanese had dealt them a body blow and recovery would take time. All we could do was hold on and hope.

1942

The New Year arrived and with it came bitterly cold weather. Snow falls were frequent and there was water and slush everywhere. When I saw Mrs Pearman later on New Year's Day she asked me what time I had arrived home that morning. I had to confess that it was about 1 a.m. I expected a reprimand for arriving back so late but instead she seemed delighted and said that the first person to enter the house after midnight was a 'lucky bird', and she was more than happy it was me. Another North Country custom, by all accounts.

I received a letter from Elsie telling me that her sister Dolly and Ted Kent were getting married on Saturday, 10 January. There was no chance of getting any more leave so I made a note to send them a greetings telegram.

One piece of good news came my way. I had been expecting to go before the local 'Trade Board' for an examination to assess my fitness, technically, to be re-graded to a first-class fitter. I was therefore delighted to be told that the unit had dispensed with the exam and had given me my first class. This would mean another ninepence a day, not a fortune but every little helped. I wrote and told Elsie the good news.

Since the 'lucky bird' incident, Mrs Pearman had become very friendly. She told me she had been married three times, and she really fancied herself as Nature's gift to lonely bachelors. She was a good sort really, and although she didn't seem to believe in housework, and the place became scruffier than ever, she often dished up tea and cakes to 'her five airmen'. Elsie had sent me a Christmas pudding and I looked around the kitchen for a saucepan to heat it in. There wasn't a clean one there. Most had an inch of potato on the bottom. However, we scraped and scoured one and boiled the pudding, which we thoroughly enjoyed. We toasted Elsie's health in tea.

Work at the factory was going well and word came on the grapevine that the foreman was making discreet enquiries about me. I wondered what the reason for this might be. Could there be a chance that I would be transferred to the civilian work force? It seemed unlikely.

I began to tire a little of my visits to the club in St Saviourgate, mainly because there was little else to do on a cold winter's night. I received quite a few invitations to people's homes, although I didn't always accept. When I did, I found myself rendering monologues, or singing 'Paddy McGinty's Goat', 'On the March' 'The Gooseberry Tree' and suchlike. There was always a meal provided and the evenings were always enjoyable.

By all accounts, Dolly and Ted's wedding went smoothly, and life at No. 396, Cowley Road was quite hectic for a time. They received my telegram. It seemed that our Doreen, rapidly approaching her third birthday, entered into the spirit of the occasion, becoming more aware of what was happening around her. Elsie told me that her brother Tim and Edna Neale were also thinking of getting married, which wasn't unexpected.

I managed to get home for a weekend. It involved a lot of travelling for just a few hours, but it was worth it. The much milder weather in the south was an added bonus. Elsie came to see me off and I was soon heading back north again.

There was thick snow on the ground at York but by the next morning it had turned to slush. It was nice to be in a warm hangar doing much as I pleased. The Shipton CO had been on the phone to the Handley Page management telling them that he wanted his lads to be shown everything that was relevant to their knowledge of the aircraft. This was easier said than done. The workers were on a production line and whilst they were as courteous and helpful as they could be, time was money and they had to keep the line moving. Often we just mooched around doing much as we pleased.

A letter arrived from Jock Sawyer, the foreman of the Royal Arsenal Co-operative Society Crystal Palace branch where I had worked prior to call-up. He enclosed a book of stamps, which was very decent of him, and told me of some news about Withers, the manager. Apparently the firm had forgotten to ask the authorities to exempt him from call-up, with the result that he was now working in the cookhouse at RAF Bournemouth. What a come-down for him.

I received a cake from Elsie and also a slice of her sister's wedding cake. We five always shared any goodies that came our way and as that day there had been a heavy fall of snow, we stayed in the billet, made ourselves a pot of tea from Mrs Pearman's supply, and sat by the fire eating cake and drinking tea. Elsie's cake was voted first class.

Rumours began to circulate that our time at Rawcliffe was coming to an end, and that we would be returning to Shipton quite soon. I would be very sorry to leave Handley Page but always knew it would end sometime. We obviously had not been sent there for our health and sooner or later we would have to put our newly acquired knowledge to use. At least we had learned a little and had been sheltered from the wintry weather in the process. Towards the end of January we were told to report back to Shipton. I immediately put in for some leave.

Shipton

On our first night back we slept at the camp. It was icy cold with snow a foot thick, and I shivered all night. Next day I was given a new billet, with a Mr and Mrs Grewer at No. 32, Rowan Avenue, New Earswick, just outside York. This house was on the Rowntree Estate and had been built for the workers at the nearby chocolate factory. All the streets were named after trees and lined with the appropriate trees on either side of the road. Although it was winter it looked a lovely estate. It was a comfortable billet except that the Grewers had an unfriendly bull terrier.

My application for leave was granted and on Friday afternoon, 6 February, I left for home, arriving at Evergreen by the evening. We spent our time much as usual, visiting relatives, going on trips to the cinema and sitting at home, just chatting. We would soon have a brother or sister for little Doreen and hoped he, or she, would be an ideal companion for her.

The 13 February came all too quickly and it was time to leave my family once again. Despite the cold, Elsie and Doreen saw me off at Three Bridges station. I hoped to meet up with one of the lads, who lived at Maidstone, at King's Cross, and this time we found each other and travelled north together. We had to stand as far as Grantham but then found a seat for the rest of the journey. We had a cuppa on York station in the forces canteen, and then went to catch the bus. I arrived in New Earswick just before 9 p.m.

I was greeted by the dog, which must have forgotten me for he snapped as I entered and tore a lump out of my glove. There was no damage otherwise, but all the same I did not trust him. Fortunately, Mrs Grewer found some wool and carried out a repair job.

At the camp there had been talk of sending a detachment to Scotland, and I did not relish going there at all. Fortunately for me they had been sent whilst I was on leave. I was sent instead to do a job at Linton-on-Ouse, a peacetime station about three miles away. It only took an hour or two to do and by the afternoon I was back at Shipton.

The nation received a shock when two German warships left Brest and came through the Straits of Dover before any of our forces could stop them. We also knew that things were going badly in the Far East and on 15 February, Singapore surrendered.

Linton-on-Ouse

On Thursday, 19 February, I was told to join the section of a Flight Sergeant Warsop and work at Linton-on-Ouse. I was to leave my billet at New Earswick, as one would be found for me in the village of Tollerton, about ten miles from York. This was a big disappointment. My visits to St Saviourgate would now be few and far between. Added to this, Flight Sergeant Warsop had the reputation of being a tyrant and Tollerton a punishment posting. The icy weather had caused me to have painful chilblains and I felt quite depressed. I wrote to Elsie and told her the news.

My depression was short lived. The flight sergeant and I got on very well, and Tollerton, far from being a penal posting, was a lovely place. I got to know the villagers well and was invited to many homes. I was billeted with a Mrs Scott, an elderly lady who lived in a modern house called Rockville, next door to a bungalow named Mardale. Mrs Scott treated me very well. She kept me supplied with tea and toast, and at night it was pleasant to sit by the fire and relax.

There were about a dozen airmen billeted in the village and we were joined by another flight sergeant, a chap named Gray who was liked by everybody. He stayed at the Manor House while Flight Sergeant Warsop lived with his family in a local farmhouse. Every morning we would be taken by wagon to Linton, back to our billets for lunch, and finish work about 6 p.m. We became a very close-knit group, more like friends, and we worked, not on large bombers, but on trainer aircraft, Tiger Moths, stripping them to the bare frame and rebuilding them to perfection. We stayed on this work for about a year.

One evening I was invited to a party next door at Mardale, where two of the lads were staying. I met the owner, Miss Illingworth, her companion Miss Eva Dunnington, and a neighbour, Harry Hoyle, the local electrician, who also manned the look-out post in the village. It was a grand evening. A large Union Jack had been pinned to the wall, and a table set with good food - a big cake, pineapple and blancmange, egg sandwiches, biscuits and other mouth-watering treats.

After an excellent meal we sang songs around the piano and I performed a few party pieces. The ladies plied us with rhubarb wine and it was past midnight before I left these lovely folk to return next door. I think Mrs Scott was a little put out about it all. Next morning one of the lads was sent on detached duty to Cambridge and although we corresponded, we never met up again.

It snowed for two days and nights without ceasing and was bitterly cold. The local farmers were getting concerned and working was almost impossible. Fortunately, I was lucky enough to be in one of the Linton workshops where it was reasonably warm. Our job was to strip down the aircraft wings and re-cover them with fabric (not an easy job), then paint them with dope to tighten the covering, and colour them green and brown for camouflage. The smell of dope was overpowering and got down to the lungs. We were supposed to be given a pint of milk to offset the fumes, but this did not happen very often.

We were invited to a concert at Wiggington, just outside York. Transport was provided for us so we felt unable to refuse, although we would have preferred to stay indoors around the fire. It was very cold travelling over the frozen roads. The concert party was quite good and we enjoyed the show, but the ride back in the icy conditions was a nightmare.

Mrs Scott had a daughter who was married to a local farmer at Linton. We received the odd joint of pork from them, so we lived well. One day she visited with her daughter, a lively little girl of nine. By way of conversation I said what a nice dress she was wearing, whereupon she pointed to her mother and said, rather cattily, 'It's one of hers'. After that I decided to keep quiet, as clothing was obviously a bone of contention.

One day, the flight sergeant called me into the room that served as an office. 'How would you like to go to Bristol?' he asked.

I replied that I was quite happy where I was and asked if my work was unsatisfactory.

'Nothing like that', he replied. 'We have been asked to send four of our lads to Bristol for a course on Blenheims, at the Bristol Aircraft Works, and I thought you might like to be one of the party. Should be a nice break from routine, and it's only for two weeks. Learn as much as you can. We have to get familiar with all types of aircraft.'

I thanked him and felt awfully bucked. I seemed to be getting very special privileges. First Handley Page, now Bristol. I felt very lucky and couldn't help wondering if there was an ulterior motive behind these detached duties. That afternoon I met the other three lads and we went into Shipton for briefing, subsistence allowance and ration cards. One of the lads was John Fouracre, who was billeted next door at Mardale and who had become a good friend.

Next morning, Sunday 9 March, we were up early and left the village at 7.15 a.m. and made our way to York station. We had to change trains at Chesterfield, where we had about a two-hour wait. The place was deserted and we wandered around the long streets of terraced houses, which were as quiet as the grave. Now and again a door would open slightly and a hand would come out, grope around for a newspaper or a bottle of milk, then quickly withdraw and close the door. We were on our way back to the station when a lady from one of the houses nearby invited us in for a cup of tea. It was most welcome and we sat and chatted with the family until the train was due. When we left we expressed our thanks by slipping a few pence into a moneybox on the mantle shelf.

It was a quarter to eight when we reached Bristol. We had to find our own lodgings. Johnny Fouracre had an aunt and uncle plus cousins in Bristol and suggested that I go with him to their home. I was reluctant to land myself on them 'out of the blue' but he persuaded me to go with him. His relatives, Mr and Mrs Fry, lived at No. 10, Graham Road, Easton. They were a very happy family and very welcoming. It was yet one more example of how kind folk can be.

The next morning we reported to the aircraft works and joined a special instruction class consisting mainly of non-commissioned officers. We were told that the going would be tough, and that at the end of fourteen days we would be set an exam and the results forwarded to our unit. They were not exaggerating, and at times I found it awfully hard going.

Bristol had suffered badly from air raids. There were ruined buildings all around. The centre of the city was badly affected and the main shopping area looked like a bit of ancient Rome. The factory itself had a balloon barrage overhead to protect it against low-flying aircraft. In my spare time I went to the Clifton Suspension Bridge and walked across it, over the Avon Gorge. Although most of the shipping discharged their cargoes at Avonmouth, there were some ships right in the heart of the city.

At the works our instruction started at 9 a.m. and finished at 5 p.m. We had to rise early in the morning to get a workman's ticket, which cost 9*d.* a day. Lunch in the canteen was a shilling. We had been given £3 14*s.* to cover our expenses for the two weeks. At the end of the first week we were given the Saturday and Sunday off and I decided to try to get to Evergreen on the Friday night. Mr Fry met me at Bristol station and handed me a packet of sandwiches for the journey, which was very generous and thoughtful of them.

Although I had no official pass I managed to elude the service police, who were always hanging around the railway stations, and reached Three Bridges station without incident. It was a very short stay and in no time at all I was heading back on the night train to Bristol, which arrived at 3.10 a.m. I went to the YMCA on the station, had a cup of tea and dozed in a chair until just before seven. I arrived at the Fry's residence at 7.15 a.m. where breakfast was waiting for me.

The weather turned sunny and mild and it was nice to sit outside the workshop in the sunshine, during the lunch break. We were kept hard at it and it was difficult to assimilate all the technical information pumped into us. On Friday, we sat the promised test and I was satisfied that I had done reasonably well.

We decided not to return to Shipton until Sunday, giving us a little time to see more of Bristol. The Frys had treated me like one of their own sons, taking me with them on visits to relatives living nearby. We toured the city with John's two cousins and went to see the Clifton Gorge, and when John's mother came from Milverton to see him on Saturday, we spent an evening full of chatting and playing darts. The Frys refused to accept all the billeting money and insisted I take back 10*s*., which I was loath to do.

The following day I had to say goodbye to my most generous hosts, and I found it difficult to express my thanks. Mr Fry and one of the lads came to the station to see us off. They seemed equally sorry that we had to leave. We returned via Sheffield and were back in York by 9.45 p.m. Mrs Scott welcomed me back with a cup of tea, which was very acceptable.

The next day, as we were crossing one of the runways, a Halifax bomber came hurtling towards us. Just as we were getting ready to jump clear it lifted off, its wheels missing us by inches.

On 25 March the King and Queen came on a visit to Linton and all the station personnel, with the exception of ourselves, were lined up on one of the runways. Afterwards, they toured the base and passed close to our workshop. I wasn't able to get a close look but saw enough to note that the Queen was wearing blue and was powdering her face as they drove past. The visit caused great excitement in the neighbourhood.

The next day was uneventful but I was very anxious about Elsie, who was due to have the new baby any day now. I was having lunch the following day when a telegram arrived from the Denners informing me that Elsie had had another daughter on the 26th, and not long afterwards a letter came from Elsie informing me that all was well.

So now we had two daughters. I had no doubt that she would be as lovely as our Doreen, and was naturally very anxious to see her. I asked to have a weekend's leave as soon as Elsie and the baby left hospital. We must have anticipated another daughter for when we had talked about names I said my choice was Sylvia. Elsie's choice was Brenda. Although she was christened Sylvia Brenda, she was always known as Brenda.

I was put on guard duty on the following Saturday night, and a long cold night it was. By the morning, however, the sun appeared and the day turned into a lovely warm and sunny one. As I had the day off, I strolled into Tollerton along the now little-used Roman road, which once linked the village to York. It was very pleasant and the signs of spring were everywhere.

That evening I went with two of my closest RAF friends, Ron Bacon and Arthur Siddall, to the Methodist chapel in the village. There were only a few folk in the hall and our entrance caused quite a ripple of excitement. We were shown to seats in the choir stalls. Ron was a local Methodist preacher, whilst I had often taken the platform at Kimpton Mission, and in the days to come we were both called upon for speaking engagements.

The garden of Rockville, where I was billeted, was enormous, with a lot of fruit bushes and plum and apple trees. Now that the ground had thawed I did some rough digging for Mrs Scott and we planted potatoes and other vegetables.

I received a letter from Elsie's brother Tim, telling me that he and Edna had named Whit Saturday, 23 May as their wedding day, and inviting me to be his best man at the ceremony. I was delighted and thought it a great honour to be asked. I replied that, provided the RAF gave me leave, I would be proud to accept.

Easter came and on Good Friday I went to the service at the Chapel, and stayed for the 9*d*. supper afterwards. Later, as I helped with the washing up it seemed just like the days at the dear old Mission. I then went for a stroll as far as Alne, the next village, and had a look at the windmill, which was still in working order.

Elsie left hospital with our new daughter on Wednesday, 8 April, and I applied for, and was granted, a pass for the following weekend. I left for home on the Friday and arrived there at 10.15 p.m. Brenda was fast asleep when I saw her. She did not have much hair, but had a serene little face and, when she opened them, lovely brown eyes. Elsie looked very well. The next day, 11 April, was Doreen's third birthday. She had been staying with Reg and Hilda Denner during Elsie's hospital stay, and so we set off, with the new arrival, to their home. We were met by Hilda, her mother and, of course, Doreen. We were invited to stay the night, which we were happy to accept. I think Hilda would have loved Doreen to stay longer, but home with us she came. I stayed as long as I could, but eventually left to catch the 10.15 p.m. train from King's Cross.

I reached York at 2 a.m. and went into the Salvation Army canteen, where I had a cup of tea. I curled up in a chair until 6.30 a.m. then returned to the station and boarded the train to Tollerton to start another day. We began to get very busy. I wondered where they were finding all the old Tiger Moths - from museums I think. One that arrived had bomb-release equipment, a relic from World War I. Each one was stripped down to the bare frame, and was completely rebuilt. When we had finished, they were as good as new. I became quite adept at stringing the fabric on to the wings and painting on the dope.

As I have mentioned, dope was terrible stuff to work with and the fumes were overpowering. There were times I felt really ill. One day whilst watching the film *They Died with their Boots on*, I felt so bad I had to leave the cinema and sit by the river Ouse for a couple of hours waiting for the sickness to pass. Next day I asked the chief if I could work in the hangar for a change.

One day I was summoned to Shipton to take the trade test for my Leading Aircraftsman's badge. I was happy to know that my name had been put forward and that the flight sergeant had recommended me. All the same, I felt keyed up, for so much depended on me putting on a good show. When I entered the station engineer's office, another officer was standing there. He turned out to be one who had taken a great interest in my section when we had pulled the aircraft out of the river Ouse. He recognised me.

'Hello Williams,' he said, 'What brings you here?'

'I've come from Linton for my Leading Aircraftsman test board, Sir,' I replied.

'Do you mean to tell me you haven't got it yet.' He winked at the technical expert. 'You ought to have had it months ago.'

I thanked him. I felt elated, for I knew that his comments had made passing a certainty. I was asked two questions and the interview was over. I returned to Linton feeling very happy, although I would assume nothing yet.

But there was a matter causing me concern. It seemed that the owners of Evergreen, where Elsie, her parents and the Gardiner family were living, wanted to sell the property, and had asked them all to find alternative accommodation. The Gardiners wanted to stay in the Crawley area. Mr and Mrs Squires would no doubt return to their flat in Brixton. We had nowhere to go, and Elsie, with two small children, was in no position to go chasing around looking for a house or flat. It was a worry.

The German air force, in reprisal raids, had started bombing some of our cathedral cities. Coventry had already been badly blitzed and suffered much damage. York, with its magnificent minster, was expecting the worst, and sure enough, one night, we in Tollerton heard the crump of exploding bombs ten miles away, as the bombers loosed their deadly loads on the undefended city. The raid lasted about an hour but even our house trembled at times. For a day or so the city was out of bounds to us, but reports of the damage soon reached us.

The railway station may have been the main target, and the damage was considerable. The ancient Guildhall had been demolished and many shops and houses were in ruins. The house at No. 46, Queen Anne's Gate, where I had stayed whilst working at Handley Page, was a pile of rubble. How Mrs Pearman and the residents had fared I had no way of knowing yet. By some miracle, the minster had escaped damage, but the main post office and city museum were casualties.

I have mentioned previously that I took a lively interest in hydraulics. There were, of course, no hydraulics on a Tiger Moth, which was entirely hand operated. Whether or not Handley Page had noted my interest I couldn't tell, but one day the chief said to me, 'We're thinking of sending you to Lockheed's at Leamington Spa for a week to brush up your hydraulics. There is only one vacancy, but it's yours if you'd like to go.'

These courses were a bit of a doddle, and I jumped at the opportunity. He said he would notify Shipton. As if to dampen my joy, I had to go on guard duty on the Saturday night, another wet, cold and lonely one. I seemed doomed to get the Saturday night duty, but I mused, I couldn't expect the jammy jobs all the time. I went to the Chapel on the Sunday evening and was invited to supper at the organist's home. I never refused a free meal. We sang hymns around the piano and finished with a slap-up meal, which included tinned pineapple, a luxury indeed.

The following day I was working in the hangar when the sergeant called me into his office. He used some unprintable language about the unit office and handed me an envelope. 'You should have travelled to Lockheed's yesterday but those idiots mislaid the papers. Better get going. You'll have missed one day of your course, but it can't be helped now. I'll get George to take you to your billet. Pick up what clothes you want and he'll run you into York. Have a good time.'

It was now early afternoon. I told Mrs Scott where I was going and said I would be back by the weekend. In a very short time I was at York station perusing the timetables. I bought a cup of tea and two cakes whilst waiting. I hadn't had time to sort out subsistence money from the cashier's office but fortunately I had about £3 with me which I hoped would be enough.

Details of the journey are vague but I do remember the long delays and wondering if I would ever reach my destination. The train eventually deposited me at Leamington Spa station at 11 p.m. The stationmaster was locking up. I hadn't a clue as to where I could find accommodation at that time of night and I had never been to Leamington before. I had visions of spending the night on a park bench, or somewhere equally uncomfortable, when I had an idea. I asked a railman where the Lockheed factory was situated and was told it was about three-quarters of a mile up the hill.

I trudged up the hill in complete darkness. Being wartime, there wasn't a glimmer of light anywhere as blackout regulations forbade it. After a while I saw the outline of some buildings and soon came to the main gate. I rang a bell and it was answered by a security policeman. When I explained my position he let me in. Once my credentials had been checked he invited me into a room where there were other men sitting. They proved to be a friendly lot and soon I was drinking tea and chatting with them as if we'd known each other for years. They said there was a spare bed, which I could use, and at 1 a.m. the works canteen would open for the night shift to have their break. I could get myself a meal there and afterwards an ENSA company would be giving a concert. The star turn was Evelyn Laye, the actress. I was welcome to go along and see the fun.

I felt quite peckish after my long journey and was soon tucking in to pork pie and chips. I then found a seat and saw Evelyn Laye play to the audience, who were delighted to see her.

The next morning I reported to the course instructor and explained my late arrival. He wasn't at all bothered. The course was a scrounge, starting at 9 a.m. and finishing at 5.30 p.m., with a half-hour break morning and afternoon, and one and a half hours for lunch. A typical lesson was: 'This is a hand-pump. You know all about it. Anyway you'll get a blueprint of it. Let's go to the canteen.' A lot of time was spent strolling around the factory and watching people work.

There were twenty of us on the course and some of them were staying at the local YMCA hostel in town. In the evening I went with them and booked a room, which was very comfortable. The weather had turned lovely and warm and Leamington was a lovely place. I spent my spare time catching up with correspondence, and the week flew by. On Friday afternoon the course ended and I left the factory armed with a sheaf of blueprints.

By rights, I should have returned to Shipton the next day, but I decided to have another day in Leamington and go back on Sunday. Left to myself, I wandered around and eventually found a seat in the beautiful Jephson Gardens. The river Leam meandered through the gardens and as I sat there the scent of wallflowers was overpowering. I had some blueprints in my pocket, fully intending to study them at leisure, but finally put them down and just baked in the warmth of the sun.

I could not help but think that here I was, on a Saturday morning, idling in a park in a most beautiful part of England. Up to the outbreak of war, save for holidays, I had always worked a full day on Saturdays, winter and summer, serving people their groceries and trying to be polite, when often I felt otherwise. I boiled when I thought of some of the insults and adverse comments that I had endured, from managers and shop foremen. Because the threat of the dole queue was ever present, one kept a job at all costs, and employers took advantage of it. I mused that not all dictators were in Germany, Italy and Japan. The RAF had seen some hidden potential in me and had helped me lose the feeling of inferiority that had stayed with me for so long. Now I was being given every opportunity and felt I was being groomed for something, although I was unsure what. I felt that rebuilding Tiger Moths was only a stopgap.

Around midday, I roused myself, left the park and had a snack at the YMCA canteen. I then set off to Warwick, found the river Avon, and had a look at the castle across the water. This part of the country was delightful and I wished I had the time to visit Stratford-upon-Avon. The following morning I thanked my hosts at the YMCA and made my way to the station. As the train pulled out of Leamington Spa I felt my time there had been a happy interlude and that one day I would return. I perused the newspaper. The war news was still very gloomy, especially in the Far East. The Japanese seemed unstoppable, leapfrogging from island to island. A big naval battle was taking place in the Coral Sea, and New Guinea and Australia were threatened. Port Darwin had been bombed.

By late afternoon I was back in Shipton, and I called in to the unit. Except for the guard, the place was deserted. I took a look at the reports on the notice board and saw with pleasure that, as from 1 May, I had been promoted to Leading Aircraftsman. One ambition had been achieved. I was now entitled to wear 'propellers' on my tunic, and to receive another one shilling a day. I could also take charge of a section if necessary. I went onward to Tollerton feeling quite pleased with myself.

Quite a sheaf of correspondence awaited me. Elsie and the children had spent a weekend at West Norwood with Dolly and Ted, and had used some of the time there looking for a house, or flat. By all accounts the weather down south was very pleasant (in Yorkshire it was miserable). There was a letter from the Co-op enclosing a 2*s*. 6*d*. postal order and some cigarettes. Mrs Pearman had also written to let me know that they had escaped safely, but the house had been flattened in the air raid. I also received a letter from my old companion from Hednesford days, Phil Siddoway, telling me that he had put in for a job in Civvy Street and was working in a factory in Coventry and he hoped to be there for the duration of the war. This was the last letter I received from Phil and I often wondered if he might have become a casualty of one of the bombing raids over Coventry.

That week the Prime Minister, Winston Churchill, paid a visit to Linton. Unlike the visit of the King and Queen this was very informal. He was dressed in the uniform of an air commodore, and had the usual cigar in his mouth. He received a tremendous ovation as he toured the hangars and workshops in an open-topped car, and came quite close to our group and the Tiger Moths. He waved his cigar in our direction and everyone cheered him noisily. We all felt quite bucked by his visit.

My application for leave to attend Tim's wedding had been granted from Thursday afternoon, 21 May, so I was able to be his best man as planned. Doreen was bridesmaid, and a real picture she looked. On the great day we went to Camberwell and I looked in on Mrs Neale in Mosedale Street, who greeted me warmly. We had known each other for a long time, for Edna's brother Ernie and I had been in the same class at school. The ceremony went according to plan and I enjoyed playing my part. The reception was held in the dear old Mission in Kimpton Road and despite rationing, a good spread was provided.

In the days that followed, Elsie, the children and I visited my mother at Herne Hill and were brought up to date with the family news. Brother Reg had been invalided out of the Army and was working in the War Office. Denny and her husband had split up. Grace's husband John had been sent overseas. Audrey was in charge of catering at the Bank of England and her husband Bill was still in the AFS. Cecil MacCarthy, Vera's husband, had also been discharged from the Army and was working at a bookbinder's in the Norwood Road.

We spent time trying to find somewhere to live but our joint efforts proved fruitless. There had been so much destruction caused by the bombing that very few places were on the market. I had to return to Shipton with the problem unresolved.

The pressure of work increased. We started work early and finished late. The country was on 'double summer time' so we were able to stay on a job well into the evening. We had become very short-staffed owing to overseas postings and the Chief was desperate to keep the work schedule on target. As

I passed his office one morning he was talking on the telephone to the unit. '…any pair of hands will do. You say you've got one bod? Send him along.' He was about to put the phone down then said, 'By the way, what's his name? What?' he roared. 'Levine… Don't you send him here. I won't have him. Don't you dare mention his name again.'

I smiled to myself and went on. Nobody wanted Levine, not even Hitler.

May melted into June, and June into July. Elsie wrote and told me the good news that she had found a flat in East Dulwich. The house, which contained two flats, had suffered bomb damage, but was habitable, just about. A family called Whittle occupied the lower flat. The upper flat, which Elsie agreed to rent, had one large room across the front and three others, all in need of repair and renovation. It had a large garden.

I was not at all happy at the thought of Elsie and our daughters moving back to London, but there it was. She was lucky to find a place. My job at the Royal Arsenal Co-operative Society in Crystal Palace Road was within walking distance, so no doubt this helped Elsie's decision to rent it. The Gardiners had found a flat and moved out on 18th July, and Elsie and her parents followed three days later. It was a big undertaking for her to superintend the move, but she left the girls with her mother, and fortunately, Reg was around to help lay the linoleum. In the following days her family were very helpful and supportive.

I managed to get weekend leave in early August and saw first hand the amount of work needed to make the flat habitable. A little work had been done but there was plenty more that needed doing. There were so few workmen available and so much needing their attention. Elsie had done a magnificent job bringing order out of chaos. There were many other necessary things that needed organising, such as getting the ration books altered, registering with a local retailer for food, and finding a milkman. Blackout material had to be put over the windows, which had been sealed with some sort of mesh, the glass having been blasted away.

When I returned to the unit I was told that I had to go on a disciplinary course at Cosford, near Wolverhampton. My heart sank. Cosford had an evil reputation and had been likened to a concentration camp. The course was to last four weeks and I wondered if I would survive it. It was with a heavy heart that I made my way there and reported in.

We were drilled and chased. Everything had to be 'at the double'. There were courses on fire-fighting and digging trenches. We waded through water and went on an assault course. After a week or so the harshness eased considerably, and far from finding it a concentration camp, I came to enjoy the routine. We took turns drilling a squad and at the end we had exams testing our technical and supervising abilities. To my amazement, I received higher marks for disciplinary work than technical.

During the four weeks I was at Cosford I hardly left camp save for a walk through some nearby cornfields. It was approaching harvest time and I remember seeing one field turn white as the breeze moved over the corn, looking just like slow-moving water. It reminded me of a passage in the Scriptures, 'that the fields are white unto harvest, but the reapers are few'.

On the Wednesday morning I said farewell to the lads as we went our different ways. When I reached Birmingham, where I had to change, I found I had a wait of two hours or more. It was annoying, but normal, and I reached York in the late evening and boarded a bus to Shipton to report in. It was a wet night and I did not relish the five-mile walk to Tollerton. I stayed in the camp overnight and slept in one of the huts where there were a few beds kept for the piquet boys.

Next morning, when the camp came to life, I went to the orderly room to enquire about leave and was told to put in for it immediately, as any leave outstanding on 3 September would be lost. The best they could do for me was a week from 25 August to 3 September. In the same breath the Orderly Corporal informed me that Mrs Scott had written in during my absence, saying she could no longer billet me as she could no longer spare the room. I was astonished. I had been very comfortable there and had helped her in return, digging the garden and suchlike. They told me that a new billet would be found for me somewhere else. At that moment the van from Linton arrived, so I put my kit on board and returned Linton.

During the morning one of the chaps staying in the bungalow next door to Rockville came up to me and said that Miss Illingworth had heard about Mrs Scott's action in closing the billet and was most indignant about it. She had rung the unit at Shipton and said that I could stay at her home. This was splendid news and at lunchtime I went to Mardale and made myself immediately at home.

I received the warmest of welcomes from Miss Illingworth, Miss Dunnington and Mr Hoyle. We became good friends and it was a home from home. They had a telephone, a piano, and a nice bathroom, which, I was told, I could use whenever I wished. With Edward, the other airman staying there temporarily, we did odd jobs, like cutting the extensive privet hedge. That evening I went in to see Mrs Scott. She appeared quite annoyed that I was staying next door. I said I would call another evening to collect the rest of my gear.

In a small village like Tollerton everyone knew everyone else's business and I soon learned that Mrs Scott had arranged to let my room to a corporal and his wife who were at Linton. However, the whole squadron was moved and her plans miscarried. I did not mind. Mrs Scott had been very kind to me whilst I was there, but now that I was at Mardale, I was more than content.

The work was piling up and we worked long hours, but nobody complained. We were like one big happy family with little or no discord. I went into the Flight Sergeant's office one day and suggested we form a concert party to give the villagers an evening's entertainment. To my surprise he jumped at the chance and told me to go ahead and get things moving. He was a good scriptwriter and between us we put on a show called 'Rosser's Revels' (Rosser's being part of our title, 'Repair On Site'). It was a success.

My leave, eight days, arrived at last. Elsie's parents looked after Brenda, and Elsie and Doreen met me at King's Cross station. Together we returned to No. 11, Crebor Street, where Elsie had made a lot of alterations and it really looked like home, despite the unrepaired bomb damage. Brenda was looking very bonnie. Her hair was still very thin, but I had no doubt it would soon grow into luxuriant tresses.

As usual, we used the time visiting and being visited, and in what seemed no time at all, I was back on the train heading north.

It was now harvest time and the local farmer sent out an appeal for help getting the harvest in. A few of us went along on three or four evenings. Our job was to stack the 'stooks' of corn as the binder disgorged them. I had no idea until then just how heavy they were. I could only manage two at a time and at the end of a couple of hours I was tired out. We received a shilling an hour for our labours. Another cornfield close by was about to be cut. The villagers, armed with sticks, stood by as the farmer drove his machine round and round the field driving the rabbit population into the centre square. Then the farmer sent his dogs in. As the bunnies emerged, running in all directions, the noise was deafening, with the villagers in pursuit, shouting and waving their sticks, dogs barking, guns banging and children screaming as they chased the creatures around the sheaves. Most of the rabbits escaped into the hedges but it was great fun while it lasted. I failed to capture anything but one of the men gave me a rabbit to take back to Miss Illingworth.

Then, one morning, there came a great surprise. The flight sergeant called his team together and read out a notice from the CO at Shipton. Our three corporals had been promoted to sergeants, and five of the leading aircraftsmen, including myself, were promoted to corporal. I couldn't believe it. Was I dreaming? Two of my closest friends were among the chosen five - Arthur Siddall and John Fouracre. We were so stunned that for a moment we were silent, but soon the rest of the team was congratulating us. Our two flight sergeants came over and we murmured our thanks. "You deserve it," they said. "You'll soon be in charge of your own Sections."

The following Monday morning, 14 September, we were taken into Shipton to have our identity cards altered and to receive our corporal stripes. There was a lot of bitterness about our promotion from chaps in the unit who had been passed over time and time again, and the sarcasm was quite open. 'If you want promotion, go to Linton,' was muttered time and time again. It did not bother me one bit. The promotion brought with it an increase in pay of two shillings a day, sixpence of which was deducted and sent to Elsie.

That evening, Miss Dunnington sewed my newly acquired stripes on to my tunics and greatcoat, and I was very proud of them. In nine months I had risen from AC2 to Corporal, something I had not believed possible. I began to see the reason behind all those courses, and believed that the 'Linton Mob' had probably been carefully chosen. But only time would tell if I was right.

It was strange at first to be addressed as 'Corporal', but I soon became used to it. I wrote to Elsie with the good news. Once things were settled I would have a proportion of my pay sent to her direct, but in the meantime I would continue to send a postal order every fortnight. The pay I now received was good and for the present at least, our financial problems had receded.

As we were working in the hangar on the following Sunday morning some of us began singing harvest hymns. Soon everyone joined in and it was strange to hear the strains of 'We Plough the Fields and Scatter' to the accompaniment of banging hammers and rasping files. That evening there were six of us at the service in the village chapel.

Sunday, 11 October was Harvest Festival at the chapel and quite a few of the RAF contingent joined the villagers for the service. The chapel was well decorated with flowers and greenery and there was an abundance of fruit and vegetables on display. The service was very similar to those held at Kimpton Mission, and it made me feel very nostalgic. At the end of the service a little deputation of the chapel workers came to me and asked if I would 'chair' the weekday service on the following Tuesday. I was a little apprehensive but after some persuading agreed to do it.

Word had obviously got around, for when Tuesday came the chapel was filled to overflowing. Nearly all the RAF team was there, whether to encourage me or see what a mess I made of it I wasn't sure. The speaker was a young clergyman, the Reverend Hughes, whom I had never met before, but we took to each other immediately.

After an initial bout of nervousness, I settled down. I tried to keep things informal and called upon my Mission experiences to add a touch of humour, and told some tall tales, which went down well. The congregation responded and the place rang with laughter, which was a change, for Yorkshire Methodist chapels seemed rather dull places at times. I warmed to my subject and even Reverend Hughes seemed delighted. At the end of the service, we held an auction of the produce. Looking back I think it was my finest hour.

The ladies at Mardale were delighted and their standing in the village soared. Congratulations came to me from all sides, and when we met for work next morning the two flight sergeants praised me for my exercise in public relations. A couple of evenings later, the Superintendent Minister for the area called round and asked if he could add my name to the panel of speakers for the Easingwold area. I agreed, and until our units became mobile in early 1943, I gave the address at several of the area chapels.

One day, four of us were approached by Headquarters and asked if we would like to train as flight engineers on Halifax aircraft. It was a very tempting offer, as we would be made up to the rank of sergeant or flight sergeant, receive aircrew pay and become second pilot on the aircraft. We were given three days to decide.

We discussed it between ourselves at great length. Had I been a single man

I would not have hesitated, but I reasoned that it would not be fair to my family to go on bombing raids over Germany. The accident rate was high, and bomber planes were sitting targets for fighter planes, despite their armaments. In the end I declined the offer, as did all but one of those invited.

I paid a fleeting visit to York and whilst there I met Mrs Pearman, whose house had been bombed. She gave me her new address and said I was welcome any time to call in for a cuppa. I was pleased to see she was none the worse for having been dug out of the rubble, but I didn't take her up on her offer. These days I seldom visited York.

I received my first assignment. I was sent to RAF Catterick to collect a Tiger Moth. I took the wings off etc., and then phoned Shipton for suitable transport for it. The WO told me to 'bung it in the wagon', which I did although with some reluctance. However, the driver and I managed to get it back to Linton.

The ladies at Mardale gave me a birthday party, which was typical of their generosity. John Fouracre came from Catfoss, and Arthur Sidall and Ron Bacon came as well. We enjoyed a lovely evening, playing darts and singing around the piano. The ladies made us a nice meal and it was past midnight before the merriment ceased. I am sure the villagers must have wondered what all the noise was about. Next day, we promotees received our back pay and feeling wealthy, I sent a fiver off to Elsie.

I managed to squeeze another period of leave at the end of October and during the week we went to Wren Road Congregational Church, where we were married, and had our second daughter christened by the Reverend Vaughan. We held a little party afterwards, and Reg Denner paid us a flying visit. We managed to see a couple of films thanks to Dolly babysitting, and my mother, sister Denny and her baby visited us, as did members of Elsie's family.

Back in Yorkshire, the November weather was rough, and tempers were a little frayed at times. One good thing was that we were issued with cycles. These were a great boon for we were often faced with long walks to get equipment when no motor transport was available. They were useful in other ways too, for on Sunday evenings when Ron was giving a sermon at some remote chapel, we could accompany him. In return he would include a hymn that Arthur and I requested. If Ron was on duty, I would cover for him. Ron's wife and child were staying in the village with the Misses Charnock, and often Arthur and I would spend an evening in their company.

I liked Yorkshire, but not its wintry weather. It was lovely after a day in a draughty aircraft hangar to relax by a warm fire in comfortable surroundings. Being an NCO, I no longer had to do the irksome guard duties, although I was liable to be called upon to be 'guard commander', but never was.

To pass the time I began preparations for our next concert. Word had got back to Shipton about our previous show and offers of help came in from officers, as well as the lads. In the end Flight Sergeant Warsop and I planned our programme using the talents of our own group. To my sorrow, I was not destined to take part as I was sent on detached duty and others put on the show.

One of our sergeants became friendly with a nurse who was stationed at Myton Hall, a few miles away. He got us an invite to a party there. Myton Hall was an elegant country mansion taken over as a service hospital for the duration. It was a lovely place and the nurses made us very welcome. This infuriated the army sergeant, who gave physical training to the patients, and he complained to the Matron that the 'Brylcream Boys' were drinking the tea ration. He got a right ticking off by the Matron, who told him we were not fighting a 'private war'.

I became the subject of an argument between Mrs Scott and Miss Illingworth. Mrs Scott wanted me back. Miss Illingworth told her to take a running jump at herself, and tempers became frayed. I said I would stay at Mardale for as long as they would have me.

For a brief spell the weather turned mild and sticky, but I preferred it to the cold. We were under pressure to get more planes to the training schools, so a day off was restricted to one in nine. Christmas was fast approaching and what to get for presents occupied our thoughts. I went into York and mooched around getting very depressed at the lack of goods in the shops. I answered several advertisements hoping to get a toy or two, but was always too late. I began to scrounge bits of wood in the hope of making a doll's house or something similar. I managed to buy a book in WH Smiths on 'How to make strong wooden toys'. In the event the toys were not made until after the war was over.

As the second week of December came to a close the work slackened off and it was decided that half the workforce could have Christmas leave. All the names went into a hat and mine was drawn out as one of the lucky ones. I was granted nine days leave commencing 21 December. As if to dampen my joy we were given our annual inoculation jabs and these really upset me for a couple of days.

The Flight Sergeant was getting very public-relations-minded and he called us together and asked if we could organise a party for the village children on the Tuesday after Christmas, and also another concert in aid of the Red Cross. As I would be on leave over Christmas I had to delegate the party arrangements to those on duty. The Red Cross concert was not so pressing.

When the rebuilding of a plane was completed and it was ready to be handed over to a squadron, it was the custom for one of the flight officers at Linton to take it aloft for a test flight. It was also the custom for one of the airmen who had worked on it to accompany him in the spare seat. I had been responsible for this particular aircraft so it was my turn to go aloft. I got myself a parachute and sat down on the seat in front of the pilot. It was my first flight.

I was a bit nervous at first, but once the plane had left the ground and we were airborne, I felt a thrill of excitement. It was like being in another world. There was no noise, save the wind whistling in the bracing wires and the drone of the engine. It was cold, but I pulled my hat over my ears. The seats were exposed to the elements, but at least the sun was shining. I looked over the side of the Tiger Moth to the landscape far below and saw the patchwork of fields and woods and the tower of York Minster in the distance. The pilot started to throw the aircraft about and that was far from pleasant. I don't think there can be much difference between sea- and air-sickness and at times my stomach seemed to want to leave me. After about half an hour he turned back to base and below us I saw Linton village looking like a collection of miniature doll's houses, and the church spire like a tiny spear. Nearby the river Ouse appeared as quicksilver, twisting itself over the landscape. Then, suddenly, the pilot put the plane's nose down and dived onto the village. The houses and church reared up at us assuming huge proportions. I was sure we were going to hit the church but at the last moment the aircraft straightened and we flew into the aerodrome and landed safely. When I tried to take a few steps, my knees buckled under me for a moment or two. As I returned to the hangar I thought that having to put you life at risk was a good method of ensuring efficient work at all times.

The next three days flew by. The residents of Mardale were disappointed that I would not be with them for Christmas but found some little items for me to take home. On Monday, 21 December, I collected my rail warrant, wished my friends a Happy Christmas and headed for the bus, railway station, and home for my first Christmas since the outbreak of war.

It was good to be back with my family. They all looked well and Brenda had grown quite a bit since my last leave. Elsie had done wonders with the flat and had made it into a real home. She must have gone without quite a bit to accumulate the food she had ready for the Christmas meals. Fuel was very scarce and rationed, but it was essential to keep the place as warm as we could for our little daughters' sake, and we scrounged wood where we could.

The next day we took the girls to Herne Hill to see my mother. She looked after Brenda whilst Elsie, Doreen and I went to the Regal Cinema at West Norwood where my youngest sister, Pam, was giving a song recital in the interval. She was well received. I suggested to her afterwards that a coloured spotlight on her white dress would be more glamorous than the hard white light. In later performances she adopted my suggestion.

Elsie's parents came round the next day bringing presents for the girls. They had tea with us but left early because of the blackout. On Christmas Eve we all went shopping in Rye Lane, our nearest shopping centre. As expected, there was little to buy that was not on coupons or ration. There were no balloons or paper chains, although there was holly and mistletoe. All the same, there was an air of festivity about that even shortages and the war could not stifle.

After the girls were in bed and asleep, we collected the few gifts we had for them. Brenda was too young to get excited but Doreen was eagerly looking forward to Santa's visit. Elsie stayed up late, rolling and baking pastry, making sausage rolls and jam tarts. It was 1.15 a.m. before we turned in.

On Christmas morning Doreen awoke, delighted with what Santa had left for her. Her first words were, 'Father Christmas brought my elephant back', a reference to a toy Doris Gardiner had made for her and we had put away for today.

Elsie had managed to get a turkey for lunch plus a Christmas pudding, so it was really a traditional meal. In the afternoon we went to Herne Hill to have an evening with the family. Eileen offered to put us up for the night so we were able to enjoy a family evening together. In the morning we returned home and after lunch visited Elsie's family in Brixton. When it was time to leave, Doreen decided to stay the night with her nanny and to come back home with them the following morning when they made a return visit. They had lunch and tea with us and we spent a lot of time sitting around the fire chatting, and the hours slipped away pleasantly. We all agreed that despite the shortages and restrictions we had all had a wonderful Christmas.

A trip to the cinema with Doreen to see *Bambi*, and further visits to see relatives, and my leave was at an end. Elsie and Doreen came to King's Cross to see me off. It was a wrench for us all but it had been a wonderful break. We waved to each other until the bend in the track interrupted our view of each other.

And so the eventful year of 1942 was almost over. Our little family had grown with the arrival of another daughter. The war continued with no end in sight and we could not guess what lay in store for us in 1943.

The journey back to York was quite an ordeal. The train was packed to suffocation point and I was one of fourteen jammed between the two doors at the entrance to the compartments. It was almost impossible to move. I had to balance on one foot and try to change to the other when I could. There were patches of snow in the fields, which became more widespread as the train travelled north. I hoped Elsie and Doreen had had a safe journey back to Cowley Road. It had been a lovely leave of absence and good to see how Doreen enjoyed herself and how our Brenda was trying to walk a few steps.

The four-hour train ride seemed endless but eventually we reached York and I staggered on to the platform with very wobbly knees. I had a cup of tea in the forces canteen before continuing my travels. The city walls and embankments were white with snow. I slipped and slid my way to Exhibition Square and, in due course, boarded a bus to Tollerton.

Christmas appeared to have been spoilt by colds at Mardale and the folk there were still under the weather. However, it did not dampen their welcome and I gave them a résumé of my time with the girls. I was fussed over no end and when I retired for the night I found an electric fire warming my room, a hot water bottle in the bed, and my pyjamas warming on the hot water pipes. I wondered what I had done to merit such kindness from these lovely people.

New Year's Eve was work as usual, in fact we did not stop for lunch and worked on until 4 p.m., when we finished for the day. There were to be no more days off for the foreseeable future, but no one complained. We had been treated very decently by the senior NCOs so we accepted it and got on with the work in hand.

1943

On Sunday 10 January I was due to take the service at the Methodist Chapel in Huby, a village four miles away. During the week a blizzard had laid a foot of snow over the countryside and it had been difficult to even get to Linton. We had been booked to give a concert to the villagers on the 6th but this had been cancelled due to the appalling weather conditions. When Sunday came it rained and then froze on top of the snow, making it really treacherous under foot, and I wondered if I would ever get to Huby. I was loath to let the Chapel folk down, and as the Chief gave me a half day's leave I decided to try walking to the village, instead of cycling. I donned my wellington boots and ploughed my way through the snow. I believe the congregation was surprised to see me. We had a good service, singing many of the old 'Sankey' hymns, which we all enjoyed. Before setting off on my return journey I was invited to supper with the local farmer. The folk asked if I would return the following Sunday, so I felt I could not have done too badly.

The news from home was that Doreen had yet another cold and Brenda had cut a tooth. It was such a shame that Doreen seemed to be so plagued by colds in spite of everything Elsie did to combat them. Perhaps the monotonous wartime diet had something to do with it.

The weather suddenly turned milder and a thaw set in. It was a treat to see the grass again and for a few days it was like a rustle of spring. It appeared that the work at Linton on Tiger Moths was coming to an end, and there were many rumours circulating as to what was going to happen next. We were told by the flight sergeants that a big conference was taking place at Shipton to decide our fate, but they were just as much in the dark as we were.

Most of the Tollerton contingent were depressed. In the year we had been billeted in the village we had become part of their life, and they were no happier that we might be leaving. Miss Illingworth and Miss Dunnington told me that no matter where we went, I would always be welcome at Mardale for the night, weekend or longer.

News came through that a decision had been taken. Shipton was to be responsible for the repair and overhaul of all Halifax aircraft south of the Scottish border. Mobile repair squads were to be formed to do 'repairs on site'. There would be ten such teams equipped with a travelling workshop, with a corporal in charge and a sergeant to supervise teams where necessary. We were ordered to cancel our concert.

Things then went quiet and we continued to live in our billets and did minor jobs at Linton-on-Ouse. I was ordered to go on a 'Commando Course' at the unit. It didn't amount to much. We ran around wet, muddy fields with a rifle and bayonet, taking pot shots at imaginary Jerries. I was given a Sten gun to practise with. It was a mass-produced weapon but could be effective at close quarters. I became quite expert with it but hoped I would never have to use it in combat.

There came some very disquieting news. London had been bombed again, probably as a reprisal for an attack on Berlin. These raids continued and I was very worried. I pictured Elsie getting up in the middle of the night and taking the girls down to the shelter in the road. She had the terrible choice of which daughter to take down first. The raids continued on a tit-for-tat basis and it was an anxious time. Even when there wasn't a raid the sirens still sounded and, either way, a peaceful night's sleep for Londoners was a rarity. York was raided again, but this time the bombs fell in open fields between Strensall and Haxby, and little damage was done.

One evening, Flight Sergeant Warsop, affectionately known by the team as 'Toby' because his face resembled that on a Toby jug, invited me to go shooting for rabbits. My sympathies were all with the rabbits but I need not have concerned myself with their welfare, for although we tramped miles over the fields, Toby's shots were wild and ineffective and we returned to the village empty handed and minus some expensive cartridges.

Sutton-on-Hull

On Monday, 26 January, Flight Sergeant Grey told me he had a job for me at Sutton-on-Hull, a simple job of erecting an aircraft to be used for demonstration purposes. It sounded alright, but I was always suspicious of 'simple' jobs because they usually turned out to be anything but. He found a spare airman to assist me and when I saw who it was my heart sank - he would not have been my choice. The flight sergeant came along to introduce us to the officer in charge.

Sutton-on-Hull RAF station was a training camp for safety equipment personnel. I didn't like the CO or the atmosphere in the camp, and when I went into the hangar to see the aircraft, my heart sank. It was an obsolete Hereford, quite a big aircraft, but it was scattered all over the hangar floor. To add to my problems, there was no equipment on the station for moving the heavy sections into place. Flight Sergeant Grey said he would send some trestles and a gantry for our use. Then he left for Linton and I went along to the orderly room to book in, and find some accommodation for us. We were assigned to the station for 'special duty', and by the time all the necessary forms had been filled in and we had been put on the 'ration strength', it was too dark to go back to the hangar.

There was a depressive air about the camp. By all accounts, the CO was a martinet, a very strict disciplinarian, and he made life a misery for one and all. Airmen were put 'on charge' for minor offences and it was not unusual to see a long line of defaulters waiting outside his office every morning. One typical piece of nastiness was to halt a squad as it approached his office, take over at their head and make them double march or run around the perimeter. I saw this happen myself, more than once.

The food was reasonable and there was a YMCA canteen and club in the camp. My assistant and I spent an hour there playing cards before retiring to our beds in a crowded Nissen hut.

Next morning we went to the hangar to see what we could do and it wasn't long before the CO put in an appearance. He wanted to know how long it was going to take me to assemble the aircraft. I informed him that without lifting equipment, it could be ten days or more, but I expected some from my unit within a day or so. This did not satisfy him and he said he wanted results quickly. He obviously hadn't a clue about aeroplanes.

He then took himself off, and a corporal came and introduced himself. He said he had been appointed by the CO to liaise with me. I thought him a decent enough bloke, but a bit scared of his boss. I told him I would probably need some manpower and he said this could be arranged, but as the airmen were on a training course, would I keep my demands to a minimum. During the time we were at Sutton-on-Hull our relations were always cordial.

I checked the aircraft sections and found the essential parts were there, but how to move them into position was the problem. I went on a tour of the camp to see if any lifting gear was tucked away. In the motor transport workshop I spotted a breakdown wagon with a small crane-like lift at the back. There were possibilities with this so I found the chap in charge and asked to borrow it. With some reluctance he agreed and I spent endless time filling in forms before I could use it. When it arrived we used it to lift the front of the fuselage, which had been facing the wrong way, and tried to swing it round. Fortunately, the tail wheel was still in place and after a couple of hours we manoeuvred it into roughly the required position.

The equipment from Shipton came a couple of days later and we managed to get the other sections near to the assembly position. The biggest snag was that the centre section had to be lifted over the top of the fuselage, aligned and bolted into position. This could not be done by manpower, and a crane would be needed. When the CO came on his daily snoop, I explained the position to him. 'I'll get you a crane from Hull docks', he said. He later called me to his office and informed me that one would be coming on Saturday afternoon. He asked me how many men I would need.

'Twenty should do', I replied.

He barked at his duty corporal. 'Cancel weekend leave for twenty men and order them to stay in camp to work under this technician's orders.'

I felt awful. Getting away from this camp for a few hours meant a lot to trainees as I knew from experience, and I had just stopped that leave for a score of men. But, the job had to be done.

We hung about all Saturday waiting for the crane to arrive. It had got to about 4 p.m. before it arrived, and another accompanied it. The drivers said they had been held up and could only spare me half an hour. I explained what I wanted. A sling was attached and the huge centre section was hoisted up and then lowered over the fuselage. The two front bolts were put into place reasonably quick, but when we tried to line up the fittings for the rear bolts it could not be done, try as we might. In the end I had to let the cranes go and dismiss the airmen.

During the whole of my service career I was never again as depressed as I was on that occasion. Had the fittings on the fuselage and section been normal there would have been no problem, but they were set at an angle of forty-five degrees and it seemed that nothing we did could get the retaining bolts to fit. I don't think I slept that night.

The CO was furious when I went to see him the next morning to try and explain my problem. He raved and stormed so much that it went over my head. I told myself that the next morning I must contact Shipton and ask for help. To fail on my first job was an admission of defeat.

That evening, although in no mood for sightseeing, we took a bus into Hull. The town had been badly blitzed and the skeletal outlines of houses and shops lined the streets. We went into the cinema and saw the film version of Jack London's book *North to Klondike*. We had to leave early to get the last bus back to camp. I could not help but think that this evening I had been due to take the service at the chapel but had had to ask Ron Bacon to take my place.

I lay in bed that night feeling very sorry for myself but eventually fell asleep. In my dreams I seemed to see a possible solution to the problem, to put the aircraft into flying position by building up the fuselage and placing trestles under the tail section. It was so clear that it was like looking at an illustration.

Next morning, after a hasty breakfast, I put my dream plan into place. When the corporal came in, I explained what I wanted and the three of us, with the aid of the gantry, raised the front of the fuselage and trestled up the tail. We heaved, shoved and pulled and suddenly the fittings came together. I pushed a screwdriver through the bolt holes, nipped around the other side and drove the bolts home. I came back and withdrew the screwdriver and completed the manoeuvre. We had won, and I breathed a silent prayer of thanks.

There was fish and chips for lunch that day and for once, I enjoyed the meal and indulged in a cup of tea at the YMCA. Although the centre section and fuselage were now joined, much work remained. That afternoon we attached the tail plane, elevators and rudder, and it began to look like an aeroplane at last.

The following day I was faced with the problem of procedure. Should I get the wheels down or attach the mainplanes (wings)? I decided on the latter course as the Hereford was still in flying position. I asked for the assistance of six men, preferably volunteers, and when they came I explained what I wanted of them. None of them had been so close to an aircraft in their lives and they were enthusiastic. With slings around the plane and the gantry taking the weight, we gingerly raised the right mainplane. As it came up, I stationed myself at the front and my assistant at the rear, both of us with bolts in our hands, ready. It was a perfect line-up. I hammered home the first bolts, my assistant did the same with his, and then the second bolts were pushed into place. The left wing gave no problems. All that remained now was to get the undercarriage down, and to join the nose section.

I crawled under the aircraft and inspected the undercarriage. It was, of course, locked in position, and it was now too dark to work in safety. I also had to calculate if the aircraft was sufficiently high to allow the wheels to swing down without catching on the hangar floor. I decided to call it a day.

The weather was surprisingly mild for the time of year and it was possible to walk around in comparative comfort. There was an ENSA concert on that night and I went along to relax. It proved to be one of the best concerts I had been to. The main entertainment came from a choir of boys, but there wasn't a dud act in the whole show.

We started bright and early the next morning. The CO poked his nose in as usual, but I ignored him. I crawled underneath the plane and was successful in releasing the catches that held the undercarriage in place, without much difficulty. I rolled clear as the heavy wheels came down, and was glad to see that they locked themselves in the down position. The aircraft was now mobile and with a bit of pushing and shoving, could be moved around. The station corporal reported this news to his boss.

At lunchtime I asked for eight volunteers to help me attach the nose section (the cabin in layman's terms). It weighed about a ton and a half. I fixed the wheels so that they would not move, and with the gantry taking the main weight, brought the heavy nose section roughly into position. My plan was to slot the bottom bolts through the lugs first, and then use these bolts as hinges, and swing the nose up. The first half of the plan went well, and the fuselage and nose were joined and bolted. I sent my assistant up to the top to slide the bolts in when we raised the nose. The gang heaved and lifted for about five minutes, but there was some obstruction preventing the nose being raised.

From the floor I could not see what it was and I called up to my man and asked if he could see what the problem was. To my horror, I saw one of his hands was over the edge of the fuselage. I shouted at him to come down and I would take his place. He moved away and as he did so whatever was holding the nose back, gave way, and the heaving of the lads sent it up with a sickening crash. Had I not called my assistant away, his hand would have been severed, or severely smashed. The possibility haunted me for a long, long time.

I slipped the bolts into place, put on the nuts, and secured them with split pins. Apart from fixing cowling and strips, and making internal connections, the job was done. From now on no more assistance would be needed. I was fed up with my assistant and determined that he would never be part of my team. He was a regular and resented working under an ex-civilian. The fact that he was still an AC2 showed what value the chiefs placed on his capabilities.

After the evening meal I went back to the hangar, closed the doors, put on the lights and began work connecting up the control surfaces so that the ailerons, elevators and rudder could be controlled form the cabin. I had only put a few bolts in here and there in order to try them out, when I realised I had an audience. About twenty airmen were examining the plane. I went down and they began firing questions at me.

I took about four at a time up to into the control cabin, seated them in turn in the pilot and second pilot's seats and showed them how to use the controls with their hands and feet. They were thrilled and delighted, moving the controls backwards and forwards, and side to side, and from the windows watching the ailerons, elevators and rudder responding to their movements. After they had all had a go, I took them around the machine, trying to explain the theory of flight, and the use of things like hydraulics, which powered the control movements with the aid of jacks.

I was showing the locking devices on the undercarriage when I felt a draught of cold air, and looking up saw that we had been joined by the CO, who was standing back in the shadows. I took no notice and carried on with my chat. We went inside again and I pointed out how one could trace the various tubes by colour coding, and that pressure lines were always red, and returns, black. We all parted on excellent terms, they shook my hand and expressed their thanks. After I had locked up and switched off, I returned to the hut quite elated at my exercise in staff relations.

The next morning. I phoned the unit and said the job was done. I was told I might have to hang on for a day or so until they could send for me. We busied ourselves putting the bits and pieces into position until, save for the absence of engines and propellers, it looked a handsome aircraft.

The CO paid his usual call but this time he was not so domineering. He must have been in aircraft before, but he appeared to possess little knowledge. All he wanted this aircraft for was to demonstrate the stowing of the dinghy etc., in the starboard wing. I suggested scaffolding either side of the wing with a platform linking the two, but whether he availed himself of my suggestion I do not know.

He, rather grudgingly I thought, said he had heard my chat the previous evening and asked if I was interested in instruction techniques, as my talk appeared to have made an impression on his 'not so bright' trainees. I said 'No', and that I was going on mobile repair work for which I had been trained. He said no more and abruptly departed, for which I was thankful. In any case, I thought to myself, a Group I technician would not be sent to a Group III station. They were in too short supply.

Flight Sergeant Grey and a wagon arrived on Friday afternoon. He went off to see the CO whilst we loaded the equipment and our toolboxes and kit on the transport. I was so glad to be leaving that I did not say cheerio to anyone save the liaison corporal, who I thanked for his help. He paid me the compliment of saying that the trainees thought I was 'a decent bloke'.

I sat in front of the wagon with the flight sergeant and driver as we made our way back to the unit. I asked him if the CO there had made any adverse reports about our performance. He replied that, on the contrary, he had given us quite a good report. He then asked why I had asked the question. I told him how he had bullied us from beginning to end.

Flight Sergeant Grey was furious. 'As far as we were concerned, this was a buckshee job. He had no right to interfere, and I won't have any of my men bullied by the likes of him. I shall write and tell him so.'

From what I heard later from the orderly room staff, he sent a blistering letter to the offending CO. I was glad I never went to Sutton-on-Hull again.

It was about midnight when I got back to Tollerton. The good folk had retired for the night but they soon bustled about and made me some cocoa. I was glad to be back. By their very nature training schools are not the pleasantest of places. There is always an atmosphere about them.

There were three letters waiting for me from Elsie plus two copies of the *South London Press*, which I liked to read. I was glad to hear that there had been no raids for a few nights although in a daylight raid Elsie had looked out of the window and seen two German planes fly across her line of vision. It was quite a shock.

Hutton Cranswick

When I reported in on Monday morning I was told there was a job for me at Hutton Cranswick, situated somewhere between Beverley and Driffield. It proved to be a place of wide open spaces across which the icy wind hurled itself, making life very unpleasant. This time I had two good lads with me but the actual job I no longer recall. I do remember that we had to walk one and a half miles to the hangar, and were buffeted by the unfriendly blasts all the way. The only break in the discomfort was the arrival of the Salvation Army canteen van.

We were billeted in a Nissen hut, which resembled half a tube of corrugated iron dropped on the ground. The fire was not lit until the evening so the hut never warmed up. At night I kept waking because of the cold, despite having five blankets and my greatcoat. We were determined not to stay on the camp a day longer than necessary so we worked long hours to get the work finished.

One lunchtime we were making our way back to the main building when we passed a bloke going in the opposite direction. My mind was on other things and it was not until he barked at us that I realised he was an officer. His uniform was not the good quality of most officers, indeed it was rather rough, like an ordinary airman's, and I believe it was this that probably deceived us. We stopped and, realising who he was, saluted. He turned to me and angrily shouted, 'Don't you salute officers?'.

I assured him that it was our custom to do so.

'I am going to put you on a charge, unless you can give me the origin of saluting.'

My scouting knowledge came in useful here. I told him that it went back to the days when gentlemen of rank carried weapons, and when passing each other, raised their right hand to show they were not armed.

He looked at me and said, 'Not quite right. It goes back to the days when men wore armour and they raised their right hand to lift the visor of their helmet. However you have given me another version so I will let the matter drop.'

We saluted him and went our respective ways. It was seldom that we had to indulge in the niceties of saluting but this officer seemed a disciplinary type who liked to throw his weight around. The technicians had little time for the Group 5 'nasties' and there was no love lost between the men who kept the planes flying and the drill and guard types.

We finished the job in record time. I phoned the unit and a wagon arrived for us at about midday on Saturday the 13th. We were very glad to leave the wilds of Hutton Cranswick and return to Tollerton. The ladies at Mardale fussed around and fried me some eggs and bacon. Then I wallowed in the bath and afterwards sat and chatted by the fire.

A letter was waiting for me from Elsie with the news that her sister had had a baby daughter on 5 February, Doreen and Brenda had eye infections and the radio, which had been giving a lot of trouble, was now going again.

That evening I took the service at the Tollerton Chapel. I had been due to speak two weeks earlier when I was at Sutton-on-Hull, when Ron Bacon had deputised for me. Now I was returning the favour as he had been sent to Melbourne in Derbyshire.

Dishforth

I would love to have had leave to be home for Brenda's first birthday on the 26 March, but the next day I was sent to do a job at Dishforth. I was told it was 'right up my street', which made me curious. When we arrived and went to inspect the 'job', we found it was a B.A. Eagle, a private plane that belonged to the group captain. It was a lovely little plane and I fell in love with it. There were three seats in the cabin, which was upholstered in blue. Its wings folded back and it could be parked in a decent-sized garage. The fuselage and wings were made of plywood.

It appeared that one of the squadron leaders had 'borrowed' it for a joy-ride and when it came in to land he forgot to put the wheels down, causing a belly landing which damaged the cabin floor, amongst other things. I felt awfully bucked to think I had been entrusted with the repair work. As we were sorting things out the culprit came and apologised for the work he had caused us. He said he hadn't known how to get the undercarriage down. He must have been dreaming of his best girl, or something, for there was a big red lever at the side of the control column marked 'undercarriage'. As soon as the pilot throttled back on the engine a red light would begin flashing, and a hooter would start blaring in his ear. I bet he had a real dressing down from the group captain.

The Communication Flight chaps had a hut nearby, with a fire and radio, and we would pop in there when we had a spare minute or two. They would invite us in for a cuppa when they had a brew up. Some evenings we would go there instead of the Salvation Army canteen.

At the weekend I returned to Tollerton for my mail and stayed overnight. The following morning I set off again, catching the train to Thirsk, and then, apart from the odd lift, walked to Dishforth, arriving about 9.30 a.m. That day my assistant went sick with the flu, and the camp doctor sent him to hospital.

The repair job took longer than anticipated. All the woodwork repairs were completed but there were spares needed before it could be tested for airworthiness. As there were only three of these aeroplanes, finding spares was a problem and could take some time, so I was recalled to Shipton. My pal, John Fouracre, had also returned from detached duty so I now had company at Mardale. I went into York to find a birthday card for Brenda but, as expected, there were none to be had.

Whilst waiting for the spares for the B.A. Eagle, I was sent to supervise a job at Linton whilst the chap there went on leave. I had to cycle there and back, a journey of about four miles by road. However, by going across the fields I could save one and a half miles. It seemed very strange being back at Linton. The hangar where we rebuilt the Tiger Moths was now empty and our happy gang scattered. It seemed desolate and sad.

The weather had, at last, improved, and the tiny leaves were appearing in the hedgerows and flowers in the gardens. Elsie wrote with news of Brenda's little birthday party, where she had tucked into some of the chocolate I had sent her. The new quarter for leave was due at the beginning of April but despite my best efforts all they would grant me was a long weekend from 2nd April. I accepted it, being thankful for small mercies.

It was lovely to get home for a few hours, but so much time was taken up travelling that it meant I only had one full day, Saturday, to take my family out. It was expensive too, as free travel warrants were only granted four times a year. At other times one had to pay one's own fare, and even at the reduced Service rate, the return fare from York to London was £4 and bus fares were extra. However, the few hours spent at home were more than compensation for the expense.

I spent Saturday morning in the garden and in the afternoon we all visited Peckham Rye Park, which looked a picture with the crocuses in bloom. The sight helped one put aside the gloom and war-weariness that encompassed life in those austerity days.

On Sunday afternoon Elsie and the girls came with me to the bus stop in Barry Road to see me off. It had been a very short break but I hoped my next visit home would be soon. They waved to me as the bus moved away and, once again, we were apart.

Snaith

When I reported in the next morning I was told I was guard commander that night. However, a few minutes later I was given a job at Snaith, near Goole, where a Halifax had made a forced landing. It was all very hazy as to what needed doing. I was given one of the new mobile workshops and three fitters, plus a driver. This made me think it could be a sizeable job. I phoned the good folk at Mardale and told them where I was going. Then we set off.

When we reached RAF Snaith I checked in at the guardroom and asked where the Halifax was. I was given a vague direction and we set off round the perimeter fence to find it. One of its undercarriages had collapsed, and the port wing was broken. We gave it a quick look over and I left the lads to unload the trestles and went off to the headquarters building.

The officer in charge of aircraft on a station was the engineering officer. I found his office, tapped on the door and went inside. He was hunched over his desk and wore a worried look as he perused a mass of papers. After a few moments he looked up. I saluted and said, 'Corporal Williams from 60 MU reporting, Sir.'

He answered wearily, 'What can I do for you, Corporal.'

'You have a Halifax aircraft here that is in need of repair, Sir. I've come to do the job.'

He sat back in his chair and looked at me with disbelief. 'You've come to do what?'

I repeated my previous statement.

He went on to ask what I knew about repairing aircraft and I told him of my experience, that I had a crew with me and had already inspected the Halifax. All I needed was his permission to start and to use the station's workshop facilities, if necessary.

He brightened considerably. 'I've been puzzling over what to do with the perishing plane. I've only got flight mechanics on the station and they aren't qualified for anything except general maintenance. I never knew you mobile chaps even existed. You say you've inspected it? What needs doing and how long do you think it will take you?'

I said that the port mainplane would have to be changed but I couldn't be sure about the undercarriage until I had raised the aircraft. Possibly the jacks would need replacing. As to time, that depended on how quickly the spares and new mainplane came from Cricklewood. It would probably be two or three weeks.

'I can't get over this,' he said. 'Damaged aircraft have always been repaired by the makers. Now you come along and inform me that you are expert enough to do this job in the field. And you're only a corporal?'

'I have hopes of another stripe one day,' I replied.

He told me to come with him, sat me in his car and gave me a tour of the station, including the workshops, where he told the WO I was to be given anything I wanted. Then he drove out to the Halifax. The lads were stripping off the cowlings and the engineering officer looked impressed. We went over the plane together and examined the undercarriage, which had caused the trouble. 'I might want to borrow a crane while we jack her up,' I said. 'But I don't anticipate any problems.'

He gave me a lift back to the Station HQ where I booked the team in and requested the cigarette and sweet ration cards. I then phoned Shipton and stated my requirements for the job. I found the billets that had been allocated to us and we moved our gear in.

Our work was hampered by the bad weather, and the gale-force winds made changing the damaged wing hazardous, but the work progressed. We had regular visits from the station personnel and they gaped as we raised the aircraft and put the hydraulic jacks into position. When we took the wing off and replaced it, it was the talk of the station.

We finished the work and had it inspected by the A.I.D.[43] It had taken sixteen days, which, despite the appalling weather, was good time. The engineering officer commended us on a job well done and said he would send a good report to our CO at Shipton.

We could not leave until the gantries, jacks and equipment were loaded up and the damaged wing was sent back to Handley Page, and it was Sunday afternoon before we left Snaith and reported back at Shipton, at around 4 p.m. As there was no transport, or buses, I walked the five miles to Tollerton. It never seemed to matter what hour of the day I arrived at Mardale, there was always a warm welcome and a meal for me. After tea I went to see the chief at the farmhouse in the village and requested some leave. He told me I had done a good job at Snaith but I had to go out again, almost immediately, as there was a job waiting at Rufforth. He expressed his regret about it and said I could have my leave when the Rufforth job was done. He gave me the next day off and I spent it mowing the Mardale lawns and trimming the privet hedge.

Rufforth

On Tuesday 28 April I went to Rufforth, about four miles from York. Easter had come and gone and one day seemed to merge into another. The billeting people on the station wanted to house us in tents but I refused and after scouting around eventually found us some beds in Hut 7, on site 5, and we moved our gear in.

---

43 The Aeronautical Inspection Department.

The weather was awful, with gales and lashing rain, and working in it was impossible. I found some space in one of the hangars and had the Halifax towed in. The following Sunday I took the day off and visited Tollerton to collect any correspondence that might be waiting for me. John Fouracre lent me his cycle and I rode back to Rufforth on Monday morning.

Getting spares was a problem and we kicked our heels in frustration at the delays. One afternoon the Shipton CO came and told me that a Halifax had crashed at Marston Moor and we could take any parts from it that we needed. Using a write-off for parts was known as a 'Christmas tree'. Taking one of the lads with me we climbed into the CO's car and were driven out to the aerodrome on Marston Moor. We found the crashed plane and he left us to strip from it the parts we needed, whilst he went elsewhere.

It was a rush to get the parts we wanted before the CO returned, but with the aid of a hacksaw we managed to remove everything in time to be driven back to Rufforth. That evening I made a rare visit to York and visited the Methodist canteen and club. I hardly recognised anyone, save for the ladies serving the tea.

The following day I happened to call in at the corporals' club and saw a letter waiting for me from Elsie, which was quite a surprise. The family seemed to be dogged by colds, which I felt must be due to the cold, sunless spring weather we were suffering. One unexpected piece of news was that my mother and brother, Reg, who by this time had been invalided out of the Army, were returning to Aston Abbotts where my mother was born, and renting a cottage there. It sounded alright but in order to get the cottage, Mum would have to billet two land army girls. I looked forward to hearing more about the move.

I suddenly developed an awful cold. It was really more like a bout of influenza. I was most reluctant to report sick as I wanted to get the job done, but for several days I had to leave the lads to bear the brunt of the manual work, limiting my activities to supervisory duties. I dosed myself up with Galloway's Lung Syrup, which I bought from the village store, and felt it helped a little.

We worked very long hours, from 8 a.m. to 8.30 p.m., and some of the replacement work was very tricky, involving a lot of riveting. These rivets were hard to obtain and despite frequent calls to the unit, were only sent a few at a time. Then to compound my misery I lost my voice. Elsie told me that the air raids had restarted and they were having to use the shelters once again. One way or another I felt at a very low ebb.

That weekend I went to the unit and in a croaking voice asked for the rivets in person, and this time came away with sufficient to finish the job. At the same time I put in my application form for leave, but left the date open as I first had to finish the job. I returned to Rufforth and we got cracking again. The next morning we woke to find everything covered by four inches of snow. It was winter having a final fling, for a few hours later it turned milder and the snow melted away.

Within a couple of days the countryside was transformed and the fields and woods were alive with bird-song. I began to feel better and my voice returned. Elsie wrote that Edna had had a baby boy, that she and the girls were well but the air raids were continuing.

We finally completed work on the plane and sent for the A.I.D. inspector who passed it as OK, which was always a relief. We packed up and returned to Shipton. I was told that my leave had been agreed, from 28 May to 5 June, but I would be allowed the Friday afternoon off for travelling home. One bit of sad news as far as I was concerned was that because we were likely to be away from the station for long periods, we would have to give up our billets at Tollerton. I felt most unhappy about this, especially when they informed us that we could well have to use tents instead. Tents were alright when I was in the Boys' Brigade and Scouts, but they had long ago lost their appeal. The folk at Mardale had been especially kind to me. In fact it was a home from home, and I always appreciated the welcome I received there.

The mobile workshops were now fitted up and ready and although not elaborate, we would no longer have to rely on public transport. One team was already on its way to St Eval in Cornwall, and included my friend John Fouracre. I would love to have been included in the party and to have Elsie and the girls visit me there.

When I went to Mardale and told the two ladies what had been said about closing the billets in Tollerton, they were most indignant. In the following days Miss Illingworth phoned Shipton and pleaded so well that I was told I could stay there whenever I returned to Shipton.

Jock Sawyers, the foreman at the Royal Arsenal Co-operative Society in Crystal Palace Road, wrote to me again. This time he told me that several of the managers had been caught fiddling the stocks and they had either been sacked, or reduced to the ranks. How the mighty were falling!

The following week it was Tollerton's 'Wings for Victory', with a Spitfire on the village green. I had expected to be in charge of the event, but at the last minute was sent to Dishforth for another go at my B.A. Eagle.

Since my last visit there a squadron of the Royal Canadian Airforce had arrived at Dishforth. This was my first contact with the Canadians. They weren't a bad bunch of chaps, although I think they all came from the backwoods and had never seen flush toilets before. They were eager to have a bash at the Jerries. They loved my B.A. Eagle but I wouldn't let them near it. I didn't want any souvenir hunting.

I returned to Shipton to collect my leave pass and railway warrant, and whilst there one of the airmen working on a dismantling job came and spoke to me. I recognised him as Leslie Dawson, who had been on Sergeant Leonard's team when I joined the unit after training school. We had got on reasonably well although he had been a leading aircraftsman and I only an AC2. I observed that he was still a LAC.

We shook hands and he looked at the stripes on my arm. 'You've come up in the world,' he said. 'When you joined No. 5 you were only an AC2. Now you're an NCO and I'm still a LAC.'

'That's how it goes, Les,' I answered. 'I've been a Corporal for nine months now and getting used to it. Sorry you've been passed over. I tell you what. I'm getting my team together for going on the road and I'd like you to be on it. How about joining me if I can fix it?'

'I'd like nothing better, Len,' he replied. 'I'm tired of salvage work and would like to travel around. I promise you my full support if you can get me on your team. You won't regret the offer.'

To cut a long story short, I was able to pull a few strings and Leslie Dawson joined my team and became my No. 1. He was with me for about eighteen months when he received his corporal stripes.

On Leave

At last, Friday 28 May arrived and in the afternoon I boarded the bus to York and then walked to the station. Apart from one short weekend, five months had passed since I had a week's leave and I was really looking forward to it. The weather was warm and sunny, the trees were in full leaf and it felt good to be alive.

The train journey to King's Cross was scheduled to take four hours but trains seldom ran to time these days. Hold-ups occurred with monotonous regularity, but people accepted that these were unavoidable. The trains were always crowded. If one was lucky enough to get a seat it was possible, though not easy, to snatch forty winks. I would try to bury myself in a copy of *Picture Post*, but the scene gliding past the window always drew my attention.

It was late evening when I reached No. 11 Crebor Street and greeted Elsie and our daughters. Elsie's parents had been on a visit and we saw them on to a bus. It was so good to be home. Brenda was cutting some teeth but wasn't making too much fuss about it. Her hair was beginning to grow and she was losing the 'little boy' look. Doreen was becoming quite the young lady and developing her own personality very quickly. It was obvious that at that early age she would know what she wanted and how to get it.

As usual, we spent time visiting relatives and walking in the park. The weather, which had been kind for the first few days, broke on the Tuesday and it became unsettled thereafter. My mother was on a visit to Aston Abbotts, but we went to see Con and Arthur, and Vera and Grace, who happened to be visiting them. Their husbands were overseas. Arthur, being in the police force, was in a reserved occupation. There was much talk about family matters and the progress of the war.

Elsie's parents were very good to us and looked after the girls whilst Elsie and I went to the Camberwell Palace to see a variety show. They often came to see Elsie to give her some help with the children and the home and generally give support which, in normal circumstances, I would have been there to share.

Despite the change in the weather, we put Brenda in the pushchair and went to Herne Hill one afternoon to have tea with Grace and Vera.

On the Friday I did not feel well at all. It seemed my Rufforth cold had not left me entirely. However I felt a little better by the afternoon when Dolly, Ted and baby Barbara came to tea. When they left at 9 p.m. it was still raining. We had enjoyed their visit immensely.

And so, with the coming of Saturday my leave was at an end. We went to the shops in the morning to get the rations, bread and vegetables. The food available was most unexciting, but at least what there was, was shared. I stayed as long as I could but at 4 p.m. had to be on my way. Elsie and the girls came to the bus stop with me and we said our farewells. How long it would be before we were all together again was unknown.

Travelling back to York was, for once, fairly comfortable. I found myself a good seat and slept for most of the way. The train pulled into York station at 9.45 p.m. and I was in time to get the 10 p.m. bus to Tollerton. I gathered that the weather in Yorkshire had been little different to London's.

When I reported to the chief he told me there was a job needing my attention at Marston Moor. It seemed I couldn't get away from the place. In the event, we didn't go until Tuesday, 6 June. The plane was a write-off and we were told to strip it of all serviceable parts. I took Les Dawson and two other lads with me. I was still feeling far from well so for once I let them do the work whilst I sat in the sunshine. With the sun now shining the atmosphere began to warm up quickly and I felt my energy returning, for which I was thankful.

Marston Moor wasn't a bad sort of camp. There was an ENSA concert whilst we were there and we saw Stanley Holloway, Douglas Byng and Binnie Hale, plus supporting acts, and very good it was. Once we had taken all the useful bits from the plane, we put them on the wagon and returned to base. As a reward, we were given Saturday afternoon and Sunday off.

On Monday morning, 14 June, which happened to be Whit Monday, the Tollerton contingent boarded the wagon and went to Shipton. We mooched around until the NAAFI opened then trooped inside for tea and a wad. Four of us were sitting together in the corner of the hut chatting when we were interrupted by a chap who came over and told me I was wanted in the office.

I was quite friendly with this NCO. His people owned the big music shop in York and he borrowed items from stock for our concerts. I asked him what was up, but he didn't know. As I left the lads to report, there was a general feeling that I must have done something amiss.

I went to the office but Flight Lieutenant Newton was not in his room. I guessed he had been called away. This was the nerve-centre of the 'Repair on Site' work. On the walls were listed the number and type of aircraft being repaired. Below them, the name of the NCO in charge, and underneath, the rank and names of the team and the workshop van number. I was perusing them when Flight Lieutenant Newton returned.

'How did you like Marston Moor?' he opened, probably for something to say. 'You did a good job there.'

I murmured my thanks knowing he hadn't summoned me for that.

'I've got another job for you,' he said. 'I'd like you to take it on, but it's up to you. You can decline it if you want, but somehow I don't think you will.'

I thanked him and asked what it was that he wanted me to do.

'Oh,' he said, with a casual air, 'I want you to go to Cornwall and take charge of our detachment at St Eval.'

I couldn't believe it. I thanked him and said I would be delighted to go but added that I believed Sergeant Ensor was in charge of the detachment.

'Work has eased up down there so I am recalling the sergeant and about half the workforce. When you are there you will be under Taunton MU, but I would like you to keep in touch with me about twice a week. I know I can rely on you to maintain our high standard of work.'

This was all too good to be true. I had wanted to go to St Eval with the original party. Now I was being sent to take over.

'Might I make one request, Sir?' I asked.

'What might that be?'

'I'd like to take my No. 1, Dawson with me.'

'Please yourself,' he said. 'But if he goes with you one of the bods there will have to return with the others.'

We left it at that. I was awfully bucked at the prospect of going to Cornwall. The RAF base at St Eval was only a few miles from the holiday town of Newquay. I was sure I could find somewhere there for Elsie and the girls to spend a week or two. I went in search of Les Dawson.

My corporal pals were hovering around. They wanted to know what it was all about as normally we received our instructions from the flight sergeant.

'Jammy blighter,' said Arthur Siddall. 'You must be the blue-eyed boy here.'

I found Dawson with some others lazing in the middle of a stack of aircraft tyres. I asked him if he would like to come to Cornwall with me and he jumped at the prospect.

St Eval

There was a lot to do. I had to arrange for travel warrants and I asked them to route us via London. Then there was the subsistence allowance to collect, the tools to check and many other things to be organised. The ladies at Mardale were getting used to my coming and going and I said I would keep in touch.

Next day we were on our way. At King's Cross we put our gear and tools into the left luggage office. Les went home to see his wife and I made my way home to see the family. They were surprised to see me. I had about three hours at home then had to leave. The break was entirely unofficial, but it had been worth it.

We met up at King's Cross, got a lift to Paddington and caught the night train to Newquay. I dozed for most of the time, but whenever the train halted, I woke with a start. We had to change trains at a place called Par, and it was 8.30 a.m. when we arrived at Newquay. We had a cup of tea near the station and then phoned for transport to St Eval.

We met up with the Shipton lads and the sergeant put me in the picture. By all accounts there was little to do. I was warned that many of the beaches were mined, but a few in the town, like Tolcarne and Lusty Glaze, were open. Newquay was nine miles away. It had been pretty awful weather most of the time. We hoped it would change.

I reported to the MU officers who told me to 'carry on'. The work on hand was mainly salvage, but I didn't mind. At the first opportunity, Les and I went in search of accommodation in the town. Most of the big hotels had been requisitioned and the majority of station personnel lived out. The YMCA gave us some addresses but we drew a blank with all of them.

The road to Newquay followed the cliffs, with twists and turns and hairpin bends, very dangerous under icy conditions, I imagined. The bus fare was expensive, 1*s*. 7*d*. single or 1*s*. 9*d*. return. The camp was not impressive and the food was poor. On the Monday, the sergeant and eight of the lads left us to return to Shipton.

Work almost dried up, which was not a good sign. I made my calls to the unit as instructed. On Tuesday, Les and I spent many hours knocking on doors but everywhere was fully booked until the end of September. When we had finally decided to call it a day the last address proved lucky. The landlady, Mrs Chinn, told us she had a vacancy for two weeks, from 10 to 24 July, bed, breakfast and evening meal only. It was a nice house, called 'Ilkley' at No. 75, Henver Road. We decided to book the rooms and I wrote to Elsie with the good news.

At the camp a big clean-up was underway. Twice we had to change huts, and then we found out why. The Yanks were coming. We rather resented having to run around hewing wood and drawing water for them but it really wasn't their fault. They were young, vigorous lads bursting for action. I couldn't help thinking that they would soon be disillusioned. They seemed to have little respect for authority.

Some of the lads came to see me and said that the Yanks, using mine detectors, had made a safe path through the nearest minefield to have a swim in the sea. Could they go for a dip? I was furious. I told them the minefields were there for a definite purpose and the Yanks ought to know better. I ordered them to keep away from the mined beaches.

It was as well I did for that night a party of Yanks went down this 'safe' path for a swim. One of them trod on a mine. Three of them were killed instantly and the other three had to stay where they were all night until the plan of the minefield could be fetched from Truro.

We still had little to do. The Halifaxes at St Eval bore charmed lives and needed no attention from us. This was worrying. I was told to send three more airmen back to Shipton, reducing our number to four, plus myself. I asked about a sleeping-out pass and was told that this could be arranged. Meantime, I wrote to Elsie with as much information as I could, and she went ahead with the arrangements for the holiday.

The weather improved and Les and I went into Newquay and lazed on the beach. There were quite a number of holiday-makers there despite the war, and the children enjoyed themselves splashing about in the water. I could picture Doreen having a wonderful time and giving Brenda a paddle.

Back at the camp it was all upheaval. We were moved out of our quarters and told we were going to Porth. That fell through and we were given a house in married quarters. Then the dreaded news came through. The Yanks were taking over St Eval, lock, stock and barrel, and the Halifax squadron was to move out. We were ordered back to Shipton.

I was in a dilemma. Today was 3 July and Elsie and the girls were due in Newquay on the 10th. I wrote and told her what had happened and suggested she come as arranged and I would try to get some leave as soon as I got back to HQ. She agreed to this and I let Mrs Chinn know what had happened.

A driver arrived from Shipton on the Sunday and we loaded up ready to leave on Monday 5 July. Once again, plans for the family to spend a short holiday break near my workplace seemed doomed. It was Wednesday before we arrived back at Shipton. The wagon broke down on Bodmin Moor and this delayed us. The first thing Les and I did after booking in was to ask for leave, and this was granted without any bother. I wrote and told Elsie the good news that I would be with her for the second week of the holiday.

Elsie had a lot to do. She borrowed a cot for Brenda, as Mrs Chinn had nothing suitable. In addition to luggage, she had to take the pushchair plus the many other items required for young children. She was travelling at night but I doubted if she would get much sleep on a crowded train. I was thinking about her all the time and prayed that the few days in Newquay would be worth all the worry and effort. Having to change at Par was an added burden.

In the event she coped magnificently. Our neighbours, the Whittles, accompanied them to Paddington and saw them on to the train. On arrival at Newquay, Elsie left the luggage in the left luggage office, and then they made their way to No. 75, Henver Road. She collected the gear in the afternoon and once they were settled in she took the girls to the beach. Daily trips to Tolcarne and Lusty Glaze beaches were the pattern of the next few days.

Meanwhile, I returned to Mardale for the few days before I started my leave. I wasn't sent out on any jobs, so busied myself around the unit. Elsie phoned me at Mardale to put me in the picture, and said they were looking forward to my arrival on Saturday. Les and I collected our leave passes, rail warrants and ration cards on the Friday. We had asked for our rail warrants to be made out to Newquay, and got away with it, although by rights we should have paid our own fare from London. Les and I parted at King's Cross, he to collect his wife, Vera, while I paid a quick visit to No. 11 to see if all was well. We arranged to meet at Paddington for the night train.

We met up as arranged and travelled together through the night, arriving in Newquay at 11 a.m. next morning. Elsie and the girls were waiting on the station platform and after greetings and introductions we made our way to Mrs Chinn's, and unpacked.

It was lovely being with the family once again. The sun shone and we took the girls to Lusty Glaze beach where they played in the sand and paddled in the sea. We had picnic teas and soaked the sunshine up. Except for the odd rain shower, we spent most of the time on one or other of the beaches. In the evenings when the girls were in bed, we played cards with the Dawsons.

On the Wednesday we thought a trip to Truro would be a change. The journey there was fine and we spent our time looking around the town and visiting the cathedral, but getting home was a nightmare. We waited three hours for the bus back, and vowed never to go there again.

We went to the cinema but the beaches always called us back. Our little girls loved the sea and sand. We decided to return home on the Friday night, and the Dawsons came to the station to see us off. The porter promised to put our luggage on to the train, but when we reached Paddington it was not on board. I fretted and fumed whilst we waited for the next train to arrive. Fortunately, the luggage was there and we treated ourselves to a taxi home, arriving about half past eight. Despite these delays, we had had a lovely holiday together.

The next day, Sunday the 25, it was Elsie's birthday, but it was also the day I had to leave. Edna and Tim agreed to look after Brenda, and Elsie and Doreen came to King's Cross and saw me on off on the 5 p.m. train. As I headed North I felt a little depressed wondering how much longer this state of affairs would continue. The war had already been going for nearly four years and there seemed no end in sight.

I reached York at 9 p.m., had a cuppa in the forces canteen, then made my way to the bus stop opposite Bootham Bar for the bus to Tollerton. When I reached Mardale I had to give a full account of my holiday. The first piece of news from them was that our two flight sergeants were on embarkation leave. I was sad about this as I considered them very 'decent blokes'. I never met either if them again.

A letter was waiting for me from my sister Con. She and Arthur had been to Aston Abbotts to help Mum settle in. The cottage she had was on Lines Hill, the highest point of the village, and the front gate led on to open fields. Pam had been into Leighton Buzzard to change the ration books, and they had been trying to buy an electric cooker, without success. The local farmer had offered my brother a job, but he was not keen to become a farmer's boy. The cottage had a large garden and mum was going to keep some hens. Two land girls were already in residence.

In Shipton the following day, the engineering officer said he was doing a tour of some of the ROS sites, and invited me along. We called in at Dishforth. My B.A. Eagle was still there but the airfield was deserted as the squadron had been moved elsewhere.[44] The plane couldn't be left there and we decided to move it back to Linton in due course. The officer went off on his own somewhere and I wandered around the deserted hangars and workshops.

I found something in a corner that cheered me up no end. It was a half-gallon Thermos jar. How it had come to be left there was beyond my comprehension. These jars were almost priceless. They were carried on long-distance bombing raids and were usually filled with soup to sustain the crew on their mission. On examination it seemed to be perfect. I knew it would be very useful but I would have to keep it out of sight or risk it being confiscated, and I would have some explaining to do as to why I had it.

I was waiting at the car when the EO returned. I don't think he knew what it was that I was holding for he queried what it was. I explained that we often had to work in isolated areas and if I could fill this jar with tea from the cookhouse we wouldn't have to waste time searching for the NAAFI or 'Sally Ann' canteen. He smiled and said, 'You don't miss much. But keep it out of sight.'

A couple of days later I took my crew on a low-loader to Dishforth. We folded back the wings and manhandled the B.A. Eagle on board. We used extreme care for it was a delicate plane and wouldn't take rough treatment. We covered it with padding and secured it so it wouldn't move. I felt I had a special interest in this aeroplane, almost as if it were my own. Then we set off for Linton.

On the way back we tried to cross the toll bridge at Aldwark but the low-loader was far too wide and we had to make a long detour to get back to Linton. It delayed us a couple of hours and by the time we had unloaded it, it was getting dark. The lads went back to Shipton, but I made my way across the fields to Tollerton.

The countryside looked lovely. The corn was standing high in the fields, the birds were singing and the fruit was swelling on the trees. It was good to be alive on such a day.

The long-awaited spares for the Eagle arrived and we soon had the job done. It still had to be passed by the inspectorate, and we never knew when they would come. I was in no hurry to leave Linton as my next job could well be in some outlandish place. As the weather was so pleasant I went for a few cycle rides around the area and in one place I nearly ran over a hedgehog. I picked him up to check him over but he rolled into a ball and I had to let him go.

Elsie wrote that she and the girls had been on a Girls' Life Brigade outing to Keston Common and that she had also been to Crawley to see the Gardiners. The plums I had sent her arrived in good order and she had tried

---

[44] RAF Dishforth was closed from June to November 1943 so that runways could be laid and the airfield enlarged in preparation for four-engined bombers. See Bruce Barrymore Halpenny, *Action Stations: Military Airfields in Yorkshire* (Patrick Stephens, 1990), pp. 59–60.

her hand at bottling some. I was pleased that all was well at home.

I was asked to help out with the harvest at a farm near Alne. It consisted mainly of heaving sheaves of corn on to a cart. Whilst it made a change, it was hard work and a couple of hours at a time was enough.

Lindholme

I was sent to do a rush job at Lindholme. Evidently a plane had made an emergency landing and had collapsed at the intersection of the runways, putting the aerodrome completely out of action. I was told to clear it away so that the station could become operational again. I got the lads into one of the mobile workshops, collected all the slings and lifting gear I thought necessary, and we set off.

When we arrived, we found the aircraft, a two-engine job, right in the middle of the crossroads, as it were. It was down on its belly but didn't look too badly damaged. Leaving the lads to attach the lifting gear, I went in search of the station crane. It was in the transport yard looking neglected. I went to the MT office and asked the sergeant for a loan of the crane and a driver. He seemed an awkward type and said I would have to fill in a requisition form and have it countersigned by the officer-in-charge. I did not wish to be difficult so completed the necessary form and went to the HQ building for a signature. Here, I was told that all the officers were at a meeting, and I had to return to the MT Sergeant without the signature. He refused to release the crane without authorisation.

I told my team that I was having difficulties getting the crane and suggested they went and found some refreshments. I went back to the HQ. Time was slipping away and I had to have that crane. I waited in the building, quietly fuming at the delay. Two hours had passed since my arrival and the plane was still blocking the runways. No officers arrived. Then I lost my temper and stormed back to the MT office.

'Look,' I said. 'I've been sent here to remove that aircraft which is blocking the runways. At any moment a plane in distress may want to make a forced landing and it won't be able to. I've tried to do everything by the book and you are just being awkward.'

I took my DR6 from my pocket and threw it onto his desk. 'In case you don't know, this warrant is my authority to requisition any equipment I need to carry out my duties. I'm now using that authority. If that crane is not at my disposal within twenty minutes, I'll get on to my superiors and tell them you are sabotaging my instructions.'

He didn't say a word, but his hands were shaking and he had gone quite white. I picked up my warrant card, glared at him and said, 'Twenty minutes, Sergeant, or else.' He had tried to pull rank on me and now realised his stripes could be at stake if I carried out my threat. The DR6 had shaken him. I went back to the plane. The crane arrived within ten minutes.

The lads could see I wasn't my usual self and wisely said nothing. It took only a matter of a few minutes to raise the aircraft. We got the wheels down and locked the jacks. I put Dawson in the cockpit to handle the pneumatic brakes if necessary, had two others hold the tail section down and, with the crane taking the weight, moved off at walking pace to the hangar. This took only a few minutes and we managed to get it under cover with the nose facing the hangar doors. Without asking anyone's permission, I used what trestles were around and jacked it up, chocked the wheels to stop any movement, and left it there for the enquiry team.

We had a meal in the dining room, then returned to Shipton.

'Somebody really upset you, Len,' said Les Dawson. 'You really scared the boys, they never knew you had a temper.'

I told Les what had happened. 'In future I'll show the warrant before asking for anything.'

As far as I was concerned the incident was closed. 'The crane was being overhauled, something to do with the jib,' I lied. 'Once it was available it was a straightforward job.'

'Good,' said the chief. 'I knew you would cope. Got another job for you, a Halifax down at Upper Heyford. Need a good team for this one. It's on the doorstep of Maintenance Command at Oxford, so you may get visitors from the "scramble egg" brigade.'

'Where is Upper Heyford?' I asked, trying to appear indifferent, although I knew roughly its location and was secretly jumping for joy.

He showed me its position on the wall map. 'Bicester seems the nearest town. It's a peacetime station. Can't let you have a van at the moment so you will have to go by train. We'll let you have a workshop when we can. Alright then, Corporal. I've made arrangements for you to travel on Monday. Good luck, and keep in touch.'

Upper Heyford

The journey to Upper Heyford was frustrating and boring, to put it mildly. The train was full to overflowing and we had to squeeze ourselves into the guard's van. We had our kit, toolboxes, bicycles, plus some odds and ends like the precious Thermos jar, concealed in an ammunition box. At Oxford, we caught the local train and then had to wait two hours for transport to the camp. After a meal, we found beds in a barrack block, which were as hard as iron, and when I woke in the morning I was stiff and full of aches.

It took all of Tuesday morning to get booked in. The formalities were rigid and had to be adhered to. These peacetime camps were keen on their parades and the hoisting and lowering of the flag. They did not approve of specialist groups, like ourselves, using the camp amenities and not doing any duties, but as soon as anyone tried to lay down the law, I produced my warrant card and said we were for 'special duties' only.

That afternoon we went to find our aircraft. It was in a sorry state, down on its fuselage, its four propellers bent, the starboard wing broken and with numerous holes where shrapnel had torn through it. What else needed our attention only a thorough examination would reveal. On its side a big white whale was painted, and it was named 'J for Jonah'. Below, five little bombs were painted, showing it had been on five raids over Germany. The more I examined it the more unhappy I became. This aircraft should have been consigned to the scrapheap and not scheduled for repair. I estimated there was, at least, two months' work ahead.

It was at the farthest point away from the main buildings, and isolated from everyone and everything. One bright spot was a large Nissen hut nearby. We soon had the door open and inside it stood a stove and a crude table with a telephone on it. I cycled off, saw the administrative people and obtained permission to use the hut and have the telephone connected. We were ready for action.

I put in a preliminary report and asked for the necessary equipment. Among the items requested were, four new engines, four propellers, a new starboard wing, undercarriage gear and numerous other items, plus sheets of Duralumin for repairs. I estimated ten weeks for completion, provided the spares arrived quickly. My estimation must have caused some consternation back at Shipton for when the first batch of spares arrived, a Sergeant Weaver came with them.

I knew Sergeant Weaver from Linton days. He was made up to sergeant at the same time as I received my promotion. He was the least liked of the Linton team. He told me he had come to take charge of the repair team. This was a terrible blow. I had hoped that if I made a good job here, promotion was almost a certainty, as I knew I was well thought of back at Shipton.

He said my report on the Halifax hadn't been well received. They thought I was exaggerating. After a meeting, the CO said that if the damage was as severe as I had stated, the work should be the responsibility of a senior, not a junior NCO. He said he had been asked to take over and reassess the work needed.

I inwardly boiled but tried to remain calm. I had no option but to accept the situation, but I felt very bitter. The rest of the team showed their displeasure at the change of leadership but in the end it had to be accepted. Les Dawson was most upset. He had reckoned on getting a third stripe and to take my place as corporal. The general opinion was that Sergeant Weaver must have blotted his copybook in some way and had been sent here to get him out of the way. It took some time, but eventually we did find out the reason why he was sent to Upper Heyford.

He went off to book in at the sergeants' mess and I called the lads together and explained the new situation. I told them not to give Weaver any cause to complain and to always be on the job on time, as they tended to be a bit slack at times. They were a good bunch and I knew I could rely on them.

In fairness to Dick Weaver, he left us alone and spent his time making cigarette lighters from blocks of aluminium, and generally we tolerated each other. He made out his damage report and sent it to HQ confirming, more or less, what I had stated. Actually, the damage was worse than we thought as we kept coming across bits of flak in the control rods and other vital parts.

The work progressed slowly and now that I was not in charge I didn't hurry unduly. We took a day off once a week and I took turns in visiting my mother in Aston Abbotts and having a weekend with Elsie and the girls. Doreen had to go into hospital to have her tonsils out and all went well for her. Elsie's parents were a great help and I managed to get home that weekend for a few hours.

I enjoyed my days at Upper Heyford, despite being second in command. I supervised the work while the sergeant did all the running around. One day one of the lads came and showed me a newspaper cutting. It confirmed our suspicions that our sergeant had got himself into trouble. The report stated that Sergeant Weaver and his wife had been prosecuted for stealing articles from a house in which they were billeted. They were fined and the magistrate made some uncomplimentary remarks.

There were a lot of rabbits around and we used to set traps for them. One day we caught one. I dressed it and the NAAFI girls cooked it for us. Every afternoon our electrician would take the Thermos jar to the cookhouse and get it filled with tea, which was very welcome.

One morning at about 10.30 a.m., we were in the Nissen hut. The YMCA van had just been and we were sitting around drinking tea and eating buns when we heard a car pull up outside. The sergeant went to the door and peered out. 'Quick,' he called. 'Open up your toolboxes and look busy.'

We did as he said and the next moment the door opened and in came four 'top brass' officers. They asked what we were doing and Sergeant Weaver said we were having a tool check as the nearby communications flight were leaving and as they had been continually 'on the borrow', we wanted to be sure that everything had been returned. It was very quick thinking on his part.

Among the top brass were head of Maintenance Command, the CO from Shipton and the Chief Technician from Upper Heyford. They inspected the work we were doing and appeared satisfied. Our CO told us there had been a big conference at Oxford and he had taken the opportunity to see how we were progressing.

I used to cycle to Aston Abbotts to see my mother and sometimes met up with other members of my family. She had an enormous garden and had now bought some hens, which used to roost in the trees. My brother had found himself a job as a security officer at Tube Alloys, a big engineering firm on the Bicester Road. Sister Denise was working as a counter clerk in the Aylesbury Post Office. Pam was also with them and became a GPO telephonist, although I am not sure if she was working there at the time.

The big house in the village was the Abbey, which had been taken over by the Czechoslovakian Government in Exile, with Dr Beneš at its head. Pam was friendly with one of his personal bodyguards, named Spalenka. I met him on one occasion and thought him a decent sort of man. The meeting place for all and sundry was the Royal Oak Inn at the entrance to the village.

That year there was an enormous crop of blackberries and the hedges almost bent under their weight. Mushrooms were plentiful, and the apples in Mum's garden littered the ground. Reg had some cages full of rabbits, but getting food for them was a problem. However, he somehow managed to scrounge a sackful of grain. Mum was not looking at all well. Too many visitors and looking after the Land Army girls were wearing her down.

Back at the camp we had a disaster, or so it seemed to us at the time. Our electrician went for the tea as usual, but on the way back fell off his bike and smashed our Thermos jar. He had been distracted by some WAAFs, by all accounts. It was highly unlikely that we would get another.

The work on J for Jonah was taking much longer than anticipated and my ten weeks looked like becoming nearly four months. The days began to get cold and damp as autumn approached. I had a week's leave around the time of my birthday, in October, and one of the places we visited was Mum's cottage. Doreen saw her first mushroom here, which she called a 'fairy house'. It made a welcome break for Elsie and our little girls, and we stayed a couple of nights.

The next time I visited Mum I met my brother going the other way. He asked me to call in to see his new lady friend on my return. I found the house and met Betty Ashmore, who was the welfare officer at Tube Alloys. She was a complete contrast to his estranged wife, Ivy, being tall and blonde and well spoken. Reg was well at home, being curled up on the sofa in front of a blazing fire, listening to the radio. Betty showed me a case full of silver cups and medals, which she had won at motorcycle racing. They made me a cup of tea before I set off on my long, moonlit ride back to camp.

Christmas was approaching and we were still at Upper Heyford. The job was almost completed and we ran the engines, tested the controls and waited for the inspectors. Sergeant Weaver insisted on taking the Christmas leave, so the best I could get was a long weekend, from 18 to 20 December, which didn't please me at all. When I returned to camp it was to find the plane had been certified OK and had flown off, after circling the airfield a couple of times, which was the usual practice. Some months later, I met a lad from Upper Heyford and enquired about J for Jonah. He told me it had been on three or four missions and then never returned. I wondered if all our work and time spent on it had been justified.

Elsie and the girls spent Christmas Day with her parents at Cowley Road. By all accounts they had an enjoyable time and most members of the family called in. I had a good day at the camp with reasonable meals, considering the rationing. Being a non-drinker, I was asked to help behind the bar in the NAAFI, which was quite an experience.

On Boxing Day I was called to the telephone. The CO at Shipton was on the line. He sounded a bit irate, the Christmas spirit having passed him by it seemed. It was a terrible line but eventually I gathered that a wagon was on its way to take us to Tarrant Rushton, in Dorset, where a job was waiting for us. We had to leave by the following day, 27 December. I was disappointed that we could not stay at Upper Heyford for the New Year, but orders were orders, and we had a lot to do.

Getting clearance from the station was quite a problem and in the end I scrawled a few signatures on the certificate myself. I got the lads to pack their kit and get everything ready for the off. I wrote a short note to Elsie informing her I was on the move again. The next day we said cheerio to the many friends we had made, loaded our kit, toolboxes and equipment on to the wagon, and set off on the long, cold ride through the snow to our next port of call, the Dorset village and aerodrome of Tarrant Rushton.

1944

RAF Tarrant Rushton, Dorset

The whole team was somewhat depressed at leaving Upper Heyford. We had been there for about four months and had settled in, making many new friends. We knew it could not last, of course, and that sooner or later we would have to move on. By all accounts, Shipton was not very pleased about the time it had taken to repair J for Jonah, but the fault really lay with the plane makers and their inability to provide essential parts. I felt a certain amount of pride in the knowledge that I had informed HQ that it would be a major job, and in the end, my estimate of ten weeks had proved a conservative one. Their insistence on sending Sergeant Weaver hadn't speeded the work at all.

It was a cold journey to Dorset. We left Upper Heyford just after lunch and stayed the night at the Church Army hostel in Newbury. I would like to have looked around the town to see if I could remember any places associated with my visits there with the Country Holiday Fund during the First World War, but there was no time and after breakfast we continued on our way.

It was icy cold. The road was slippery with snow piled high by the hedges. As we travelled, the snow increased in thickness and the leaden sky did nothing to raise our spirits. I was fortunate to be able to sit in the cabin with the driver where it was reasonably warm, but the lads in the back huddled together saying little to each other.

We reached the RAF station around lunchtime and I then spent a lot of time booking in and finding accommodation for the team. It was the wildest and bleakest place I had so far come across. I shivered as I went on my rounds. The airfield was on a plateau and the wind howled as it swept across Salisbury Plain. I managed to find an empty Nissen hut but was told that as the camp had exceeded its quota of fuel, we couldn't have a fire to warm the hut, or ourselves.

For a time we stood and shivered in our greatcoats, our breath leaving us like clouds of steam. I phoned around in an attempt to get some fuel, but it proved a waste of time, and temper. A few yards away was the start of a huge forestry plantation, and we went in looking for bits of timber. One of the airmen stationed at the camp saw what we were doing and came to our aid. He told us where the fuel dump was situated and said that it was possible to raise a section of the chain-link fence and rake out some coal. We formed a scrounging party and set off.

By now a thick mist had virtually blotted out all visibility, but as we approached the dump we could hear the sound of a shovel scraping on concrete. Closer still, we could see dark figures scurrying about with buckets and shovels. We waited a moment and then went into action. We lifted the wire and set about filling our bucket. One of our chaps went inside and came out staggering under the biggest lump of coal I had ever seen. We returned to our hut without being spotted, hid the large lump under some bracken, and soon had a roaring fire in the stove. My sister Audrey had sent me a parcel containing cake, Swiss roll and other goodies and we sat around the fire with cups of cocoa and made short work of Audrey's gift. Our spirits began to rise.

The New Year came without any celebration. After some initial difficulty, I managed to get the plane, a Halifax, towed into a hangar, and we started work. Some petrol had been left in one of the tanks and as we were emptying it the plug came out and I was soaked to the skin with 100-octane. My eyes burned and my skin became irritated, but fortunately it soon passed off.

The food on the camp was reasonable but our hut was so far away from the NAAFI that we would stay in our hut at night writing letters and stoking the fire. We received some reinforcements to help us out and our strength soared to twelve. Sergeant Weaver returned from his leave but seemed engrossed with his lighter making endeavours and so didn't bother us much.

The aerodrome was home to a fleet of gliders, called 'Hamilcars'. They were huge, as big as a four-engine bomber. They were towed off the ground by Halifax bombers. These Hamilcars were capable of carrying light tanks and all sorts of equipment, and some were fitted out as troop-carriers. When the invasion of Europe started on D-Day, it was from Tarrant Rushton that the glider force operated. In the early days, these gliders crashed all around the airfield, and we were kept busy keeping their 'tugs' operational.

The weather suddenly turned milder and soon the place was a sea of mud. It was just as well that we had wellington boots or we never would have managed to get around. By studying the map I found that the camp was situated about nineteen miles from Bournemouth, five miles from Blandford Forum and nine miles from Wimbourne Minster. There were a group of villages nearby with 'Tarrant' as the first part of their name, the nearest being Tarrant Hinton. Buses were few and far between so we were fairly isolated.

Elsie told me she had taken Doreen to see *Snow White and the Seven Dwarfs* at the local cinema. It reminded me that when Elsie and I first saw it back in 1938, the programme had been interrupted to tell us that the Prime Minister, Mr Chamberlain, had returned from his meeting with Adolf Hitler waving a piece of paper saying 'Peace in our time'.

About the middle of the month, one of our mobile teams that had been at St Eval called in and stayed for a couple of days. It was great to meet up with old friends and to swap experiences. By all accounts things at St Eval had improved since my time there. The corporal was my old friend, Arthur Siddall, and we had a long chat, and pondered on the chances of a third stripe. Like me, he had had the humiliating experience of having a sergeant take over his team. He said he would try to find out more when he got back to Shipton.

Spares continued to be a problem, for there were some parts that could not be repaired, and these needed to be replaced. We were kept busy for no sooner had we finished one job than another cropped up, and as a result the St Eval boys stayed on.

We were so isolated that we received little news, but we did hear that on 21 January, London suffered a heavy air raid. These raids continued and I fretted about my family. In the end I decided to put in for some leave, and I was granted nine days leave from 12 February.

I boarded the train at Blandford Forum early on the 12th and set off for Waterloo Station. There were the inevitable delays and it was almost midnight before I reached home. The girls were fast asleep and Elsie and I chatted until the early hours.

The next day, we collected Doreen from Sunday school and went to visit Eileen and Sid, and Audrey and Bill at Herne Hill. It was a flying visit and when we reached home again the sirens sounded the alarm. Fortunately, nothing happened on this occasion, but most nights there was an air-raid alert and we would wrap our daughters up and take them to the brick shelter out in the street. Although there was always a lot of noise, our immediate area escaped damage. Getting out of bed and going to the shelter had been their pattern of life for some time, and often, Doreen and Brenda would sleep through the transfer without waking. But it was a big headache for Elsie, although the neighbours were always helpful.

Our little Brenda who was approaching her second birthday developed a nasty cough and we deemed it wise to summon the doctor. He diagnosed an attack of bronchitis, but said it wasn't serious. All the same, Elsie decided to stay at home with her whilst I took Doreen out and about. By the weekend, much to our relief, Brenda perked up and the doctor announced that she was well on the road to recovery. We had a family party on the Sunday and Elsie's parents and Tim and Edna came to have tea with us. These visits did much to boost Elsie's morale while I was away. The following day I had to return to camp. I left it as late as I could and by the time I had reached Waterloo, the sirens had started wailing once again.

There was a long queue at Waterloo but I managed to get a seat and had a reasonably comfortable journey to Brockenhurst, where I had to change trains. The local train to Wimbourne came soon after but I had a long walk to find a bus. I was back in the hut by 11 p.m., made myself a cup of cocoa, ate the sandwiches Elsie had made, and was soon in bed.

The weather was very unpredictable, going up and down like a yo-yo, but mostly it was cold. One of our team went into the village and purchased a small log saw, and we all chipped in towards the cost. Afterwards, we went into the forestry plantation and went around thinning out some of the smaller trees, which made good firewood. It was one way of keeping the hut and ourselves warm.

One day I had to return to the hut for some reason, and I saw, lying on the path, a beautiful cock pheasant. It had evidently fallen from one of the trees. It was stiff with cold, but still alive. I picked it up, took it inside and laid it near the stove. After a while it thawed out and began to walk around. I did not want to put it outside right away so left it inside. When I returned it was missing. I suspect that someone could see its culinary potential, wrung its neck and dispatched it home.

The icy weather continued unabated but it did not stop London from being the target for the German bombers. It was very worrying, although all seemed well at home. Brenda's second birthday came and Elsie threw a little party for her. It was a lovely day in London and after the birthday tea the family, with Dolly and Barbara and Edna and Clive, went for a walk around Peckham Rye Park to round off the celebrations.

We finished repairs on one plane and the second was well on the way to completion, so we hoped we would soon be leaving this cold and isolated place. Our optimism was short-lived. Several planes had mishaps and soon there was a queue of them needing our attention. It began to seem as though we would be at Tarrant Rushton for the duration of the war.

As the days passed, the weather began to improve at last and the first primroses appeared in the woods. I gathered some and sent them home. I read in the newspapers that as from next month, April, all seaside beaches, including Newquay, would be closed to the public. I was pleased we had managed our little holiday by the sea just in time.

The gang that had been staying with us and helping out were ordered back to base. As most of them lived in Yorkshire they were not sorry to leave. All the same, it was like parting with old friends, for there was a special relationship built up between the Shipton mobile teams - a real band of brothers. Arthur Siddall reiterated that he would see how the land lay with regard to our third stripe on his return.

Around this time we were issued with 'battledress', a short blouson-type jacket, rather like those worn by Spitfire pilots. It fitted me fine, but for anyone at all overweight it was not flattering.

A letter came from my mother to let me know she was in hospital waiting for an operation on her foot. Con and Arthur were both at home on the sick list; Grace's husband John, who was in the Army, was fed up with life overseas; Sid House was home on seven days leave, and Cecil MacCarthy had been awfully bucked to receive a letter from Elsie.

Easter, which this year fell on 7 to 10 April, came and went. Doreen's fifth birthday was on the 11th, but I had no chance of getting home to share it with her. She was now old enough to go to school, and she started at Friern Road School on the following Tuesday, 18 April. Time was slipping away and she was growing up fast.

One mild evening I went for a walk in the woods, which came right up to the edge of the flying field. The trees and bushes were showing a haze of green as the leaf buds began to open, and bluebells covered the forest floor. In the ditches the primroses showed yellow and green. It was lovely to walk through them on a path that was almost non-existent. I scrambled over lichen-covered walls and jumped over miniature Niagara Falls. There was lots of movement in the undergrowth but I saw no animals. Besides the normal bluebells, I saw red and white ones, and it was the only place that I have ever seen the three colours growing together. I walked into the woods for an hour and a quarter and never reached the edge, so I retraced my steps. In all that time I never met another person. When I look back on that evening walk I think it the most lovely I ever made.

I thought it high time I visited the neighbouring towns of Blandford and Wimborne, so I got on my cycle and pedalled away. I passed a poster that said the coal-miners were on strike. Not very patriotic, I thought. Blandford Forum was not very impressive. It was an Army town situated on the River Stour. I cycled around it for a while and saw some old houses but decided to continue on to Wimborne Minster without stopping. There was not much there either, so I returned on a roundabout route to camp after a twenty-three-mile ride. The one outstanding feature of my ride was the masses of primroses everywhere.

I managed to get home for a short weekend break on 15 April. I arrived there at 10.30 p.m. and had to leave again the following day. It was not long but even a few hours with Elsie and the girls was worth it. I set off from Waterloo at 7.15 p.m. and in two hours was alighting at Salisbury. I managed to get the Tarrant Hinton bus and walked from there to the camp, arriving at midnight. I didn't bother with a drink and went straight to bed and sleep.

A concert party from Bournemouth came to the camp to entertain the lads. They were very welcome, for visiting troupes were few and far between. Their show was excellent and among their repertoire was the German song, adopted by the Eighth Army, 'Lili Marlene'. Another memorable song was 'Pedro the Fisherman' from the 'Lisbon Story'. Afterwards, I bought a copy of 'Lili Marlene' to remind me of their visit.

Then came a surprise. A signal came from Shipton with the news that Les Dawson had been promoted to Corporal. We were all pleased that his talents had, at last, been recognised. At the same time came the news that I was being recalled to HQ at Shipton. I wondered what was up. It was quite a wrench to leave the team that I considered 'mine'. I spent some time getting clearance then, on Thursday, 27 April said my farewells and boarded the transport to the station. The lads came to see me off and I shook hands all round, even with Sergeant Weaver, and settled down for my journey to London. When we arrived, I went across to King's Cross and left my kit, toolbox and cycle in the left luggage, and went on a flying visit home.

Elsie was surprised to see me, but there was only time for a cup of tea and a chat. Brenda was getting to be a bonnie lass. We put her in the pram, met Doreen from school and they came with me to the bus stop. A few minutes later I was on my way back to King's Cross.

RAF Shipton

It was late when I reached Shipton but a message had been left informing me that I could stay at Mardale. When I reached there I received the usual warm welcome, even though I had been away for some months. There was a lot to catch up on and I heard all the village news. The next morning I went into Shipton and saw the CO. He said we had done a good job at Tarrant Rushton, but they weren't so pleased about Upper Heyford. We chatted at some length and then I broached the subject of promotion to sergeant. He looked genuinely sorry and said there was very little prospect of promotion for any of the corporals.

'Now that things are relatively quiet in the Middle East, quite a lot of airmen are being brought back home,' he said. 'We have had to accept our quota of senior NCOs and are now over strength. Our mobile corporals, like yourself, have served us well and we are disappointed that we are unable to reward them, but it is out of our hands.'

So that was that. I felt quite deflated at this news. We had been doing senior NCO work and had received nothing for our labours. Some of my enthusiasm left me at that moment, for I felt we had been used as cheap labour. However, I did not forget to ask him why I had been recalled.

He told me that he wanted me to go to an aerodrome at Stansted Mountfitchet in Essex.

'There is a Sergeant Colbourne there and he has to go on compassionate leave. We thought you would be the best NCO to take over while he is away. It's an American base so you'll probably get some cheap cigarettes. It is arranged that you will go on Monday. Until then you are free to do as you please'.

I cycled back to Mardale and told them my travels were starting again on Monday. They fussed over me and I busied myself in the garden. I was terribly disappointed that there was no promotion in the offing but had to accept the reasons given me and grin and bear it. I would digress here and say that when my discharge finally came through I was given my personal file to take to Uxbridge with me. I steamed it open and read the contents. It showed that in 1943 I was recommended for promotion to sergeant and against it was a note 'When a vacancy occurs'.

But such was service life that I did not go to Stansted on the Monday. Instead, I was sent here and there. A job at Linton, then one at Catfoss. Nothing spectacular, but enough to keep me busy. There was already a team working at Catfoss, but it seemed all was not well there. I was sent along to get things speeded up and to boost morale. The sergeant in charge was named Ensor, and it seemed his chief fault was to make promises, and not honour them. An example was that he would promise the lads half a day if they worked late, and then refuse to let them have it. I was inundated with complaints. There seemed little I could do except have a word with the sergeant, which I did. I told him bluntly that promises made should be kept, unless there was good reason for not doing so. Although he told me not to interfere it seemed to have some effect, and the lads thanked me for putting their case forward.

My own little gang worked well although we were on the go from 8 a.m. to 10 p.m. We had the satisfaction of seeing our repaired aeroplane take to the air and fly off to its base. There was always a nagging doubt at the back of one's mind that something might have been forgotten. These kinds of doubts were reinforced when orders to return to Shipton were cancelled and I was told to remain at Catfoss. By the sound of it, something was cooking, and we soon learned what it was. All Halifax aircraft were grounded. There had been a bad accident. One of the mainplanes (wings) of an aircraft had fallen off and it had crashed killing all six crew members. The cause was being investigated.

The Halifax aircraft were the spearhead of all bombing raids and if they were out of commission for long, the war effort could be seriously affected. We soon learned what had caused the disaster: the crash inspectors found that the shearing of a locking pin had led to a series of mishaps that culminated in the crash. The initial fault had begun in the factory, and the repair teams breathed a huge sigh of relief. We had to install a new type of bolt where the wings joined the centre section, and the chance of a similar disaster occurring was eliminated.

RAF Stansted

In due course I returned to Shipton, and on Sunday, 21st May I started my delayed journey to Stansted. I made my way to King's Cross and then on to Liverpool Street Station by service bus. I had decided to spend Sunday night with the family so left my gear in the left luggage and set off home.

Doreen was not well on the Monday morning so we kept her away from school. She had not long ago had a small pox vaccination but whether this was the cause or not I couldn't say. I left it as late as I could but had to leave at 11.30 a.m. It had been an unofficial break but I wasn't worried.

I reached Liverpool Street Station in good time and was lucky to find a seat on the crowded train. It was a lovely sunny morning and I watched the Essex countryside sliding past the window. Stansted was the next station following Bishop's Stortford, about thirty-two miles from London. As I alighted from the train I saw Sergeant Colbourne on the station waiting for the London train. We exchanged a few words.

'You're in charge now,' he said. 'One thing, though, there are two Free French officers attached to the team, presumably to learn about aircraft. During the day treat them as ordinary airmen, but off duty they resume their officer rank.'

We shook hands and he boarded his train. The sergeant was quite a decent sort. He had come from Taunton MU on promotion, with two others. We could not help thinking that some of our own corporals should have had priority where promotion was concerned, instead of bringing in outsiders.

Stansted was occupied by the Americans but there was a small liaison RAF group on the camp. I reported in, told them who I was and that I was taking over the repair of the Halifax, that had made a forced landing. They seemed totally uninterested so I found myself a billet and cycled out to where the plane was parked. I knew some of the lads there and was informed that the job was 'a piece of cake'. A minute or two later, a van drew up to take us to tea.

And what a tea it was! The Yanks lived well. Besides the normal food, we were given peaches and cream. There was a bowl of sugar on the table and fruit juice ad lib. The only drawback, as far as I was concerned, was the thick cocoa served instead of tea. I wrote a quick letter to Elsie and then set off to explore the camp.

The Yanks were a friendly lot, but very undisciplined. They seemed to spend all their spare time gambling with dice. I chummed up with a lad who told me he came from Minnesota, and he took me into their social club. By this time I was longing for a cup of tea so I got a cup from the counter. It was terrible stuff. I sipped it in disgust and happened to say to a chap sitting at the table, 'Do you always have cocoa with your meals? We usually have tea.'

He looked at me for a few moments, then said, 'Y'want some tea, Buddy?' I nodded. 'At eight o'clock go to cabin ---, and give three raps on the door.' Then he left.

I was rather intrigued and wondered if he was taking the mickey, but the desire for a cup of tea was strong so at the stated time I went to the 'cabin' and gave three knocks. I entered and the door was shut behind me, no questions asked. It was like entering Aladdin's Cave. The place was full of men drinking and smoking, and on the tables was a staggering amount of food. Kettles were boiling, tea and coffee were on the go, and I was told to 'help myself', which I did. In one corner I saw two chaps from the liaison office so I joined them. They told me that they came here every night.

It was nice to be accepted so quickly. I was given a card to enable me to buy cigarettes and goodies from the PSI (the equivalent to our NAAFI). The weekly ration was 140 cigarettes a week, at threepence for twenty, plus items like biscuits, soap and tins of pineapple juice. Although I did not smoke, I bought the cigarettes with a view to bartering them for chocolate for the girls. The Yanks were very generous and would often dish out a double ration of cigarettes to the lads.

I didn't hurry the job, for, by general consent, this was the ideal place: good food, good accommodation, no duties and within easy reach of London. Stansted was a big aerodrome with a very long runway. Our plane was about three miles from the billet, a long way to cycle or walk. Fortunately, there was always a Jeep passing by and we usually flagged a lift. Some of the Americans would come and admire our Halifax.

'Gee, that's a big baby', was their usual comment.

The food was excellent and there were times when I felt guilty about eating it, especially when I thought of the meagre rations the nation had endured over the past few years. There was pork and tinned fruit, butter and jam, fruit juice and flapjacks (similar to our pancakes). One lunchtime I was given a soup bowl full of ice-cream. When I looked at the mound in front of me I thought of my little girls, who had never tasted ice-cream. The only thing missing was tea. However, my bed was in the cook's hut and they often woke me in the morning with a mugful. Service life was not meant to be like this!

I had a phone call from Shipton to say that Sergeant Colbourne was being sent on a course and would not be returning straight away. I would have to see the job through. This suited me and I set about organising days off for everyone. I took Saturday, 27 May off and had an overnight stay at home. When I returned it was obvious that something big was cooking. The Yanks were busy painting their kites with black and white stripes. I wondered if the long-awaited invasion of Europe was in the offing.

My two Free French officers were usually conspicuous by their absence. When they were with us they usually sat around smoking numerous American cigarettes. When they went to the village in the evening, they wore their full dress uniform of dark blue and a vast amount of gold braid. No doubt the local girls were impressed by this show of splendour. My lads, however, were not. One of them remarked that, 'Solomon in all his glory was not arrayed as one of these!'

One morning at breakfast as I watched the Yanks pouring jam and syrup over their flapjack, I asked the cook if he had any marmalade. He went off and then returned with a seven-pound tin, which he placed in front of me. Every morning after that, the tin of marmalade was waiting on the table for me. Nobody else touched it. Much to my regret, I forgot to collect my tin when I left the camp.

We had one accident when one of the lads fell off a step-ladder and broke his wrist in two places. He had to go to hospital. It was a bad fall and I think he was quite lucky to get away with just that injury.

I awarded myself another short weekend break, which helped to make up for the cancellation of all leave. I hitch-hiked home without much difficulty although I used the underground to cross London. Elsie came to meet me but as I was a little later than expected, we missed each other. The next morning was sunny and warm and I played in the garden with the girls. I left at about 4 p.m. and went by bus and underground to Manor Park station, where I boarded a bus to Loughton. The girl conductress wouldn't take my fare. On the next bus to Epping the same thing happened and my fare was refused. I then hitch-hiked to Bishop's Stortford and jumped on a passing wagon going to camp. A very successful journey, I thought.

Next morning it was announced that Allied troops had entered Rome, so it looked as if things were moving well. The day, which had started bright and sunny, turned very cloudy, windy and cool. Despite the change in the weather it seemed, from hints and rumours, that something of importance was about to happen. It was no surprise therefore that the next morning, 6 June, the news was announced that Allied troops had landed on the Normandy beaches. News was very patchy, for stiff opposition had been expected. Eventually, as information began to filter through, an air of gloom settled over the Americans at the camp. It was apparent that their troops had suffered enormous casualties in the initial landings.

The weather was awful. Wind and rain and very cold. We were glad of a fire and I felt sorry for the poor blighters stuck on the beaches in such conditions. It was bad enough just working out in the open at Stansted. There was one air-raid alert and we thought there could be reprisal raids under way, but in the end nothing came of it. The repair work was now almost complete so I gave myself another Saturday off, just in case I was moved further north when the job ended.

There were a lot more air-raid alerts and an announcement over the radio stated that London was being attacked by 'pilotless' aircraft. We couldn't puzzle out what was meant. Pilotless aircraft should be sitting ducks for any fighter plane, as they couldn't take evasive action. When I went home on the Saturday I saw, near Bethnal Green, a huge area of devastation said to have been caused by one of these aircraft.

On reaching home I learned that these 'buzz bombs', as they were now being called, were a menace, and people were under continual alert. Elsie said they had spent hours in the shelter and no one seemed to know just what was going on. I saw one of these extraordinary weapons go flying past. In size, it looked like a fighter plane, had a flaming exhaust and made a horrible buzzing sound. When its engine stopped, it dived to the ground and exploded, causing terrific surface damage.

It was very worrying. These new weapons played on people's nerves, and all ears were strained as they listened for them. It was no use our aircraft shooting them down over built-up areas, and there was always a chance that left alone they might and come down in open space anyway. Evidently, they carried enough fuel to reach London and as soon as this was burnt up, they plunged earthwards.

I was loath to leave Elsie and the girls with this new threat from the skies, but I had to return. We all hoped that now our troops had landed in France, the buzz bombs would soon be a thing of the past. This did not prove to be the case, for the launching sites were almost portable and there was worse to come.

I boarded a bus in Barry Road and started my return journey to Stansted. We heard a burst of anti-aircraft fire as the bus drove down Rye Lane, although no alert had been sounded. The all-clear was sounded as we reached Camberwell Green. It looked as if a bomb had hit the Medlar Street area, for it was cordoned off and rubble and glass were scattered everywhere. The nearby bridge over the railway line looked a mess.

At the Elephant and Castle I travelled by underground, but the journey was interrupted at London Bridge where I had to get out. From there I went by bus to Moorgate, and then went back down into the tube again. The last part of my journey was by bus to Woodford, then to Epping, where I stopped for a cup of tea, and on to Bishop's Stortford, where the all-clear sounded.

The job at Stansted was almost completed and when I notified Shipton I was told that a job was waiting for us at Hunsdon in Hertfordshire. Hunsdon was a little nearer London, so in this respect it was good news. I cycled over to RAF Hunsdon, which was situated in the wilds near Stanstead Abbotts, to give the Halifax the once over. I estimated it would take four weeks to repair. I then cycled back. The date was 12 June.

We were sorry to leave the Yanks, who had been very friendly to us. The lads left loaded down with cases and boxes that bulged with American cigarettes, brands like Lucky Strike, Camels and Old Gold. I admit I had my fair share too, which I used to barter for chocolate and suchlike. We said our farewells and on Thursday 15 June set off for our new venue.

RAF Hunsdon

We settled in on the Friday. Compared with Stansted, Hunsdon was a scruffy place. As we were unpacking, an Army contingent arrived and erected their tents in a nearby muddy field. I felt very sorry for them, having to live in such primitive conditions. Once all the formalities had been completed, I gave the team the weekend off.

The Normandy invasion seemed to have halted, even if temporarily, and the flying bombs continued to pound London and the suburbs, causing panic and enormous damage. I was really worried for my family, for south-east London was suffering badly and Elsie and our little girls were getting very little sleep.

When I reached home things were as bad as I had feared, and our Friday night was spent in the shelter. Elsie was showing signs of strain, which was no surprise. Alerts sounded all day Saturday and continued into Sunday. There were several hits very close by, particularly along the line of Underhill Road. We needed to do something, for this kind of existence was unbearable.

Back at the camp there was talk of scrapping the plane we were working on, but in the end it was decided that we should carry on. I found it very hard to concentrate, although I went through the motions. Our long-absent Sergeant Colbourne came back to us after his course and seemed pleased at the way things had gone in his absence. He was a Londoner, so knew all about the flying bombs. I asked him for another weekend off and he raised no objection.

When I reached home on Friday I suggested to Elsie that I take her, and the girls, to my mother's home in Aston Abbotts the following day. She was reluctant to leave her home despite the danger, but in the end agreed to go. I was not sure what sort of reception would await us. I knew my mother would be ready to help us, but the reactions of my elder sisters would not be so positive.

The next morning we set off and caught the 11 a.m. train to Aylesbury, and then proceeded by bus to the village. We walked up the hill, past the Abbey grounds to the cottage on Lines Hill. Mum was not too surprised to see us and she welcomed her two little granddaughters. I gathered that one or two of my sisters came down at weekends so I could only hope that things would be harmonious. I knew my younger sisters would be alright but was unsure of the reaction of the others. I had to leave the following day.

The following Friday I decided to cycle to Aston Abbotts from Hunsdon. It was a cross-country route of about forty miles, but I reckoned I could manage it. I set off and although there were times when I felt I had been over-optimistic, I eventually arrived at about 9.30 p.m. Next morning we all went shopping in Aylesbury, had a meal and returned on the 1 p.m. bus. At 4 p.m. I started my return journey.

The following Saturday Elsie left the girls with Mum and returned to Dulwich to collect a few more clothes for Doreen and Brenda. I was able to meet her there and after some necessary shopping we sat and talked things over. Elsie was far from happy in the village, but agreed to stay there for a little longer.

Although work on the plane continued, my mind was always with my family and I lived from one weekend to the next. Fortunately being so near London I was able to get home, or visit Aston Abbotts most weekends. Audrey and Bill spent a week at Mum's cottage and Con and Arthur came for the weekend, so the place bulged at the seams. On the Saturday, Bill and I travelled back to London together. This weekend visiting marked my stay at RAF Hunsdon.

Back at the camp we all received nomination forms to complete. It seemed likely that an election would be held in the near future and in the event that we were posted overseas, this form was to nominate someone to vote on our behalf. I put Elsie's name forward for this dubious honour.

News of the invasion was not good. It seemed to have become bogged down and was not making the speed that everyone had expected. An oil pipeline, called PLUTO, which stood for Pipeline Under The Ocean, had been laid to get the fuel direct the forces, and a pre-fabricated harbour, called Mulberry, had been towed across the Channel to enable supplies and ammunition to land.

The flying bombs continued to come. They caused so much devastation that something drastic had to be done to prevent them continually falling on built-up areas. Along the south coast, between Dover and Brighton, batteries of anti-aircraft and quick-firing guns were set up to try and shoot them down as they came over the coast. Many were destroyed, but many others got through and their speed was too great for the fighter planes. As a second line of defence, all the barrage balloons from the towns were moved to the ridge of the North Downs, with their centre based at Wrotham Heath.

Food at Hunsdon, which had been very poor in quality and quantity, took a turn for the better. One morning we had an egg and rasher of bacon for breakfast, and at tea some tongue and tomatoes. It was well received and I wondered if it had been given as a morale booster, for we certainly needed cheering up.

On Friday 21 July I made my way to Aston Abbotts to see Elsie, whose birthday was on the 25th. I sensed that the atmosphere was a little strained, and I spoke to my mother about the apparent hostility of some of my sisters. She said that as they paid the rent of her cottage they expected to be able to stay there at weekends. She loved having the girls though. Whilst I could see my sisters' point of view, I felt they could have been a little more understanding of our position too.

There was one piece of interesting news. The Kent family, who had held the licence of the Royal Oak Inn at the entrance to the village since my childhood days, had decided to retire. My brother Reg, and his new ladyfriend, Betty Ashmore, decided to apply to the licensing authorities in Aylesbury to take over the inn. The Aylesbury Brewery Company, the ABC, who owned the premises, raised no objection. Opposition, however, came from Tom Humphreys who was the village baker and licensee of The Bull and Butcher, the other village public house where Elsie, Doreen, Pam and I were staying when war was declared. He objected on the grounds that Reg and Betty were not married. Reg replied that Betty was his financial backer and spoke of his Army service both before and during the war. He had risen to the rank of sergeant major and had been invalided out after Dunkirk. His application was granted.

He made a great success of the pub. There was a small airfield at Wing, and with the small Czech contingent from the Abbey, business was brisk and profitable. Elsie and I called in there one evening and were introduced to one of Dr Beneš' bodyguard's, who was going out with Pam. Reg converted the stables at the back of the inn into a small dance hall and although I never went there on a dance night it was, by all accounts, a great success and an asset to the village.

The job at Hunsdon came to an end and we wondered where our peregrinations would take us next. We were not kept in suspense for long. The Shipton office phoned through and told us to go to West Malling in Kent, where a Halifax was awaiting our attention.

This was good news. I had feared that we would be sent back to Yorkshire or some equally distant place, but from West Malling to home would be quite manageable. I wrote to Elsie to wish her a Happy Birthday and to tell her of my new assignment.

The flying bombs seemed to be coming further inland, and there were some crashes near the camp. One fell on the railway at Brimsdown, but the line was only out of action for about two hours. It seemed that putting a railway out of use was a very difficult job indeed.

On 25 July, we loaded our equipment and kit into our travelling workshop and set off for West Malling. We took our two Free French officers with us and were quite lucky to find them, as they often disappeared for days on end.

RAF West Malling

The day was one of hazy sunshine and cool temperatures. It had been a very poor summer altogether. As we drove through London and into Kent there were many grim reminders that Germany wasn't beaten yet. I wondered if this would be the shape of wars to come, when robot machines, and not men, would lead the attack. Today, though, we had a quiet journey with no 'doodlebugs' flying.

As we approached Wrotham we came to the 'balloon barrage', the second line of defence against the flying bombs. I had never seen so many balloons clustered together. They stretched right and left as far as the eye could see. We drove on and passed by an area of orchards and could see the trees laden with apples. Eventually we reached the airfield and booked in.

The evening paper reported that leave for the armed forces would be resumed in the near future. This was good news. It was months since I had had any leave and it was only because I had been working within a reasonable distance that I had been able to see Elsie, Doreen and Brenda at all. I put in for a day's leave on Thursday 3 August, as Elsie was due home on that date to see if all was well at home.

West Malling Aerodrome was surrounded by orchards which the airmen were strictly forbidden to enter. This did not always stop them however, and some came back with juicy plums. Our Halifax was parked out in the open not far from the barrack blocks, which was handy. There seemed to be a lull in the flying bombs and we all hoped that the menace had receded.

I managed to get my Thursday off and I made my way to Crebor Street, arriving at about midday. Elsie had arrived earlier and had already visited

Edna, who lived a few minutes' walk away in Upland Road. We had a meal together and packed up some of the furniture, and talked over the present situation and what the best course of action would be. Things at the cottage had gone from bad to worse and there had been quite an upset with my eldest sister. Elsie had very nearly packed up there and then and come home. I persuaded her, with difficulty, to remain a little longer at the cottage and in the meantime I would write to the ladies at Mardale to see if they could help.

I saw Elsie off on the 6.11 p.m. train from Marylebone Station and after an uneventful journey she arrived at Aston Abbotts at 9.10 p.m. I felt very low, wondering why my sister was being so awkward. I went straight back to camp by train and hitch-hiking. The latter was easy, as there was plenty of service transport on the Maidstone road.

That night the air raid-alert was continuous. A shout would come over the Tannoy, 'Quick, take cover'. Within a second or two a thundering crash shattered the air as a flying bomb hit the ground and exploded nearby. My chief fear was of flying glass, and I got quite expert at rolling out of bed and underneath it immediately the alarm sounded. It was just as well for one morning the room was showered with splinters of glass.

We had to change the nose section of the Halifax, in addition to other parts of the fuselage. I took advantage of the usual delay in receiving parts to hitch-hike to London for a look around. I spent some time looking around Victoria, had a meal at the YMCA, then boarded a bus to Herne Hill to see if my sister Eileen was at home. Unfortunately, she was not there. In the next turning to Eileen's house, Guernsey Grove, a bomb had fallen and it had made a terrible mess.

I then headed for home and had quite a shock when I saw that a bomb had fallen close by in Underhill Road. I wondered what damage had been done at home, but found we had got off lightly with just a couple of Mr and Mrs Whittle's windows being blown out. The garden was looking well, everything considered. I swept the flat, moved Elsie's sewing machine and Doreen's doll's pram away from the window, then slung some water over the plants and went to see Edna. She told me that the shop in Lordship Lane, where Elsie had worked before we were married, had been destroyed by a flying bomb, and some of the staff had been killed.

One evening I left the camp and cycled out to the edge of the balloon barrage and sat down on a grassy slope in the sunshine. As I sat there I heard the now familiar noise of a buzz bomb approaching. I watched its approach. It was flying very high, well above the balloons, and it tore through the sky at a fantastic rate. It went onwards towards London and I wondered where it would fall, and who would suffer. I sat there for an hour or more and saw two further bombs pass high in the sky heading unerringly towards the capital. It was frightening. There was no deviation from its set course. It seemed to me that the only ones liable to hit the balloon cable were those that had been crippled by the coastal batteries.

The nose section of the Halifax arrived and we bolted it into position. While the lads were working on the outside, the sergeant and I were inside making the controls connections. Our two Free French officers were sunning themselves outside. They appeared to have very acute powers of hearing for they could hear the approach of a V1, the new name for a flying bomb, two or three seconds before we could. One of them called out their equivalent of 'one coming'. By common consent we stopped what we were doing and watched the approaching menace, just to be on the safe side. This one came quickly into view, its course in a direct line to our plane, but its altitude meant it would be no threat to us. Suddenly, one of the new Typhoon fighters appeared and flew around waiting. As the V1 approached it began pumping shells into it.

The flying bomb's engine went quiet. Now was the moment of danger. The pilotless aircraft came down in a dive straight towards us. So this was it. Nothing could save us now, or so it seemed. It was time to take cover. The sergeant said to me, 'I say, old boy, I think it's time we got down, what!' We crouched down behind the armoured bulkhead in the flight engineer's cabin. Through the window I could see the lads' reactions. One put his head in a wooden box, leaving the rest of his body exposed; one who had been working on the wing section jumped off (a good twenty feet, which caused him to limp for days afterwards), and took refuge under the fuselage; and another appeared to be running around in circles. The rest were out of view.

Then, just as our fate seemed sealed, one of the flying bomb's wings dipped, causing it to swerve, and it ended up dropping between the barrack blocks at our side. The explosion was terrific. One of our team was doing orderly duties in the block. One moment he was at one end sweeping the floor and the next he was at the other end in a pile of plaster and broken glass. Fortunately his injuries were slight. Our guardian angel must have watched over us that August morning.

On Wednesday 16 August I left West Malling early and made my way to Aston Abbotts to see Elsie and the girls, and decided to take a chance and stay the night. I was still annoyed that my elder sisters were giving Elsie such a rough time but felt it unwise to say anything to Mum as she became easily upset with family quarrels.

It was pleasant strolling along the lanes with Elsie and our daughters. The blackberries were ripening in the hedgerows and the apples were peeping between the leaves. The earth seemed at peace, and it was only the droning of an aircraft from the nearby field that reminded us that an awful war was raging not so far away.

Mum had a huge garden but it was wild and overgrown. Her hens scraped and pecked among the bushes and undergrowth, and at night roosted in the trees like pheasants. There were a couple of apple trees which had been neglected over the years but which produced a huge crop of fruit, although on the small side. Reg called in whilst I was there and helped himself to a bucket of apples. I managed to persuade him to leave Mum a few coppers for them.

I had to leave Lines Hill at 1.20 p.m. and it was as well I walked quickly for the Aylesbury bus came along early. I was in time to catch the fast train to Marylebone, and when I arrived in London there was an alert on. I managed to get across to Victoria, where I had a cup of tea and a bun, then boarded the Maidstone train at about 5 p.m. A flying bomb had landed alongside the railway line, but the repair squads were already there dealing with the damage.

The Allied forces seemed to be making progress at last, breaking out of the Normandy beach-head and liberating Paris around the 23 August. All the same, the flying bombs kept coming.

Work on the Halifax was making steady progress and it was looking as good as new. It looked as if we would soon be on the move again, although I would like to have stayed longer at West Malling. There was some talk that our Halifax was to be flown back to its base at Breighton, in Yorkshire, and we would have to follow it there to carry out some modifications.

I was still very bothered about my family and the pressure on them to leave Mum's cottage. I paid a flying visit to Camberwell and called in at the Evacuation Office, sited in the Oliver Goldsmith School in Peckham Road. I explained the position but their answer was that Elsie would have to return home before any action could be taken. I wasn't having that so wrote to Elsie and told her the situation.

Whilst in the area, I thought I would pay a visit to the old Royal Arsenal Co-operative Society shop in Crystal Palace Road. I could hardly believe my eyes. This busy little area was practically deserted, and I only passed four people between the bus stop and the shop. Jock Sawyer, who had written to me several times, was on holiday, but I had a chat with Lane, from the provisions counter, who related all the latest news about my old colleagues. Young Blake, who was serving in the Marines, was on leave and helping out in the shop. Withers, the ex-manager, was apparently still in the RAF cookhouse on the Isle of Wight, and four members of staff had been killed when a V1 had hit the Lordship Lane shop.

I strolled home through an area of devastation. A bomb had fallen in Mundania Road, another in Heber Road. I got the key from our next door neighbour, Mrs Thompson, and went indoors. I found some dried milk and made myself a cup of tea. One of the neighbours from across the road called in and enquired about Elsie and the girls. She said Doreen was one of the prettiest girls she had ever seen and I felt very proud. In the garden the snails had had a field day, eating everything in sight. The Damson tree was loaded with fruit and I gathered some to send to Elsie, with a few tomatoes. I returned to camp feeling there was so much to do at home and I had been able to do very little.

On 30 August, we received our marching orders, and as expected, we were to go direct to Breighton to carry out the modifications to our Halifax. It was disappointing that our move wasn't a day later as Elsie was paying a visit to the flat on the 31st. However, the team decided to break their journey north and stay in London for the night, and I took the opportunity to call in home.

I was in the garden when Mrs Thompson, our next door neighbour, came over and gave me a couple of eggs for my lunch. They were the first I had tasted for some time and were very welcome. I stayed the night with Tim and Edna but had to leave early the next morning, long before Elsie was due too arrive from Aston Abbotts.

The air-raid sirens were sounding as I arrived at King's Cross, but it appeared to be a false alarm. I decided to call in at Shipton to enquire about some leave before heading off to Breighton. I was told that provided no emergency decreed otherwise, I could have nine days from 13 September. I called in to see the ladies at Mardale and received a warm welcome, and a tea of eggs and bacon. They told me there was no vacant accommodation in the village at all, and even the chapel was stacked out with beds and bedding in case it had to be used as a rest centre.

The news from France was encouraging and it was reported that most of the launching sites for the flying bombs had been captured, and the threat from them was receding. I was sure that on hearing this news, Elsie would want to return home soon.

RAF Breighton

I rejoined the team at Breighton. It was another draughty place of wide-open spaces. The nearest town was Selby but it was not a popular place to visit. The plane had been parked at the farthest side of the perimeter, and we had to cycle one and a half miles to reach it. The weather was awful, with heavy, persistent rain, and we were seldom dry. Luckily we found some fuel for the fire and managed to dry our clothes.

As expected, Elsie wrote to tell me she was returning home on 6 September, the day before our ninth wedding anniversary. It must have been quite an ordeal for her carrying heavy cases and with two children to look after, but she said Doreen was a great help and they managed the journey without any problems. They were back home by lunch-time.

The modifications to the Halifax went ahead quickly. For some reason new identity cards were issued and mine went astray. I was on tenterhooks in case its non-arrival should delay my leave. I had further bad luck when I left my tunic in the washroom for a while and someone went through the pockets and stole my fortnight's pay. I never did recover it but my new identity card arrived in time for my leave. I left Breighton on the Tuesday and stayed the night with my dear friends at Mardale. The following morning I set off for home.

Our nine days together were lovely, and very welcome, and we spent the time getting the home straight and seeing our friends and relatives. The weather was reasonable and we were able to stroll in the park and listen to a concert party, sponsored under the 'Holidays at Home' scheme. We visited the Gardiners at Crawley, and spent time gathering blackberries. We took the girls to the zoo and wandered around, pointing out the animals and birds to them. It was a pity that little luxuries like ice-cream were not to be had, but we had some sweets, which were always acceptable. It was a treat to be able to take our girls by the hand and point out little things of interest to them.

Another day we visited our friends, the Denners. Our welcome there was always warm and Doreen was a special favourite of theirs. I am sure they would have loved her to stay with them. On the way home the sirens sounded, although the all-clear went soon after. This puzzled us, for we had been told that the danger from the V1s was over. Maybe it had been a lone aircraft on a solo bombing raid.

But if we thought the Germans were finished, we were wrong. Another more terrifying menace was about to start. The V2, another of Hitler's secret weapons, was about to bring more death and destruction into our lives. It was another, more powerful rocket, with a large warhead, which was fired high into the atmosphere and targeted on London. They gave no warning. It was only a second or two after it had landed that the noise of its trajectory was heard.

On Friday 22 September I had to say goodbye and leave my family once again, and head back to Shipton. This time I felt a little more optimistic, for the war in Europe looked as if it was nearing an end. The war in the Far East looked as if it would take longer, but once Germany was beaten, more effort could be concentrated on the 'yellow peril' in the Pacific.

As usual, I spent the night at Mardale and then reported to Shipton the next morning. Warrant Officer Murton was on leave and in his place was an elderly WO whom I had met before and was on good terms with. There were no officers in the operations room so I looked on the boards and studied the locations of the repair teams. As the job at Breighton had been completed, I checked the lists to see which of the sites would suit me best, should I get a choice. I observed that most of my chums were at the crash field at Woodbridge, in Suffolk.

I went in to see the WO, who was not a technical man, and suggested to him that I go to Woodbridge and join the crash teams there. Luckily, he was quite agreeable. 'As far as I'm concerned,' he said, 'you can go where you like. All the jobs are covered so you might just as well go there and join your pals. I've been told that they reserve you for special jobs, so if they want you for something sticky, well, you are only a phone call away.'

Within half an hour I had my rail pass and authority to join the team at Woodbridge. I persuaded the orderly room staff to route me via London and set off. On arrival at King's Cross, I made my way to Liverpool Street Station where I left my toolbox, kit and cycle in the left luggage. I was concerned about leaving my Sten gun and ammunition in my toolbox, but decided to take a chance that it would be safe, and then went home for the night.

Elsie was surprised to see me only twenty-four hours after I had left.

Although it would only be for a few hours, these moments were really appreciated. I thought, not for the first time, how fortunate I had been to be put on mobile work, enabling me to get home as often as I did.

RAF Woodbridge

Next morning I collected my gear and took the train to Suffolk, changing trains at Ipswich, and then on to Woodbridge. I got in touch with the RAF camp at Sutton Heath, and they sent transport for me. I was soon reunited with many of my Linton-on-Ouse comrades, including my friends Ron Bacon and Arthur Siddall, and we were soon swapping experiences together.

I learned a lot about the airfield on which we were working. It was near the coast and had been cut out of a vast forestry plantation. It had been specially constructed as a landing field for planes that had suffered damage by enemy fighters or anti-aircraft fire. Too often in the past, damaged aircraft had made it back to their home base only to crash on landing, putting the runways out of commission for hours on end. Now, any plane that had suffered damage was diverted to Woodbridge. The one runway was three miles long with an overshoot, and either side of it was installed FIDO (Fog Incendiary Dispersal Of). On misty or foggy nights it would be lit, and two lines of flaming jets would light the runway; the resulting heat would help disperse the fog and give the pilots a reasonable chance of landing safely.

Our billets were about five miles from the camp and runway. Fortunately we had a wagon to drive us about, which helped as we had to arrive by 7.30 a.m. if we wanted breakfast. The camp's isolation rivalled that of Tarrant Rushton. There was a YMCA hut about half a mile from our sleeping quarters, but it was only open at weekends.

There was a lot of work and I was soon in the thick of things. Small areas, shaped like banjos, were either side of the runway and damaged planes were towed on to these and we worked on them there, as there were no hangars. We were now approaching the end of September and it was often misty and cold. It was quite a sight when FIDO was turned on and waves of heat would sweep over us, warming the atmosphere. Crashes were frequent and the fire tenders were on twenty-four-hour standby.

The first night I was there, several flying bombs came over, a grim reminder that the Germans were still capable of hitting back. It was said that some were now being launched from ships and submarines. Most nights three came over, but where they landed we could not tell.

On Saturday, 30 September, Elsie's elder brother George married his lady friend, Jessie, at Camberwell Town Hall. Mr and Mrs Squires were still staying in Leeds with their friends, so Elsie and Edna prepared the wedding reception, which was held at No. 396, Cowley Road. I wasn't able to get away but by all accounts everything went to plan. Until they could find a place of their own, George and Jessie would live at Cowley Road.

There were about fourteen of us from Shipton and the two sergeants in charge were both from the Linton 'gang'. We held frequent 'on the spot' meetings to plan the work and it all went well. But our happy team spirit was spoiled somewhat by the arrival of two more sergeants, repatriated from the Middle East, and things were never quite the same again. Not that they interfered much, in fact they lazed around most of the time. Neither of them knew anything about planes larger than a Blenheim, a two-engine job, and they would sit around smoking and swapping yarns about their recent escapades in Cairo.

One day, one of the newly arrived sergeants, myself and four lads were sent to an American aerodrome near Norwich to deal with a plane that had made a forced landing and damaged a wheel. The job did not take long. We had hoped for some American hospitality while we were there, but all we got was a horrible cup of coffee.

Back at Woodbridge the work kept piling up and we were on the go from dawn till dusk. The V2s continued to fly overhead, but none landed anywhere near us. The weather was wet, cold and miserable and having to work out in the open took its toll. Most of us had colds. Elsie sent me a cake for my birthday. I don't know where she got the ingredients from, but I guess she had gone without a lot in order to buy them. In addition to cards from the family I also received one from the folk at Mardale, which bucked me up no end.

The days tended to be dreary, and with November came the thick frosts. There was a lot of discontent about the lack of weekend leave. It was not something the NCOs could deal with and in the end two officers arrived from Shipton to see us and listen to the moans. Arthur Siddall and I had a private interview with them, and we asked what the chances were of receiving our third stripe. They were sympathetic, but it seemed the Government was trying to keep expenses down and all promotion in the RAF had been stopped. We felt very bitter about it.

I received a letter from my sister, Denise, to tell me that my youngest sister Pam had married her Czech boyfriend. She was now Madame Karel Spalenka, and would live in Czechoslovakia when hostilities were over. That was looking forward a bit, I thought.

London was now under attack from the V2 rockets, and one Saturday a Woolworth store in New Cross Road was hit, causing many casualties. There had been no warning, for they arrived before anyone knew they were on the way. One Saturday morning I was in Crystal Palace Road when one fell nearby, in Court Lane. The area shuddered and a few seconds later the noise of its approach came rumbling on the air. If these weapons had been available in the early days of the conflict, the war might have taken a different course.

The anniversary of my entry into the RAF came. Four years had passed, and so far I had been screened from overseas posting. While Germany was still in the war it was unlikely that I would leave the country, but when our armed might was directed solely against Japan it might be another matter.

RAF Westcott

Christmas began to be discussed, and we were told to make application for leave. Practically every airman put in for it. Then the news came that some of us were to return to Shipton taking one of the mobile workshops with us. I was included in the party. Just before we were leaving we were told to report to RAF Westcott, just outside Aylesbury, to do some urgent repairs on a Halifax that had made a forced landing on its way to India. One of the Cairo sergeants came with us. When we reached Westcott and examined the plane, I was puzzled (and still am), as to what caused the trouble.

The aircraft's wheels were down, but the jacks, which control the raising and lowering of the wheel units, were twisted out of shape. These jacks, moved by hydraulic pressure, were made of high-tensile steel, making them – I would have thought - almost impossible to buckle. I could see that the locks, which held the jacks in the down position, were in place. I was curiouser and curiouser.

The sergeant seemed to know little, or nothing, about hydraulics. I had made a study of them and was reckoned to be well informed on the subject. None of the lads could offer any explanation, so I told the sergeant I would sleep on it.

That night I lay awake for a long time trying to puzzle out the cause. If it was not sorted out there was a chance it could happen again and possibly cause the loss of an aircraft. After breakfast I had another look, but still without any inspiration. The two jacks had to be changed. The sergeant and I went to see the CO. He asked if we knew what had caused the trouble, but we had to confess that we didn't. Then he told us what we already knew, that this plane was on its way to India. Apparently it was carrying very important classified information and had to be on its way with the minimum of delay. He asked how soon the job could be done. I told him that the hydraulic jacks had to be replaced, a fairly simple job that could be done in a few hours. The delay would be in getting the replacements from Cricklewood.

'I cannot afford a delay,' he said. 'Are there no other sources of supply?'

I said we had just come from Woodbridge where there were planes with identical jacks. We could remove a couple of them, and they could be replaced in the normal way. It would save days of delay.

The group captain looked thoughtful. He addressed the sergeant. 'Will you go to Woodbridge and get this equipment?'

'Not me, Sir,' said the Sergeant. 'I've just come from the Middle East, Cairo you know. I don't know anything about four-engine jobs. The corporal's the expert. He knows all about hydraulics. He'll have to strip them, so he's your man.'

The CO looked at me and smiled. 'Go and draw a parachute, Corporal, and I'll arrange for a plane to fly you there in half an hour.'

And so it came about that within the hour I was seated in an Airspeed Oxford winging my way across the countryside. There was a crew of three, the pilot, navigator and wireless operator. As I sat there watching the fields and woods slip by below, I thought that this surely was the summit of my Air Force career. In my wildest dreams I could never have visualised having a plane and crew to fly me about in the course of my duties.

It was quite a sight, seeing Woodbridge crash dome from the air. All around were miles and miles of trees, and the men milling around the aircraft were tiny, like ants. As soon as we landed I went and saw the lads and got help to remove the wanted jacks. I had time for a quick meal and not long afterwards I was on my way back to Westcott. Once back it was all hands to the pump, and the old jacks were removed and the new ones installed.

Inside the plane we came across a toolbox. Thinking it was one of ours, it was opened. Inside there were twelve Thermos flasks. These desirable objects were as scarce as gold dust, so six were removed and the box resealed. I considered mine a reward for my efforts.

We stayed another day to test the services and hand the plane back, and then took the wagon into Aylesbury for a night on the town. I put my cycle in the wagon and we parked on an area of waste land, just off the high street. I left the team and agreed to meet them at 10 p.m., then set off on my bike to Aston Abbotts to see my mother. She was a little surprised to see me, but I had a cup of tea with her and we exchanged news. She told me that Mr Brown's farm had been put on the market, and if it was sold, she might have to give up the cottage. Reg and Betty were doing well at the Royal Oak. Cecil MacCarthy had been invalided out of the Army and was working in a bookbinder's in the Norwood Road. Denny was still working at the Aylesbury Post Office and as I knew, Pam was now married and looking forward to her new life in Czechoslovakia.

I thanked Mum for having Elsie and the girls during the flying-bomb crisis and hoped that now things were quieter, family tensions would ease up. Mum was not very happy about the approach of winter because Lines Hill often got snow-bound, as she knew from her childhood days in the village.

When I got back to Aylesbury it was to find that a pilferer had been in the wagon. My boiler suit had gone and one or two other items were missing. Fortunately, our toolboxes, which were locked, had not been tampered with. I was very relieved, as mine contained my Sten gun and ammunition.

We stayed in Westcott one more day, and then returned to Shipton. I was told I had been selected to go on a junior leaders' course, at Newcastle, in the New Year. I had heard about these courses and the thought of going on one, especially in the middle of winter, appalled me. I did my utmost to wriggle out of going, but there was no changing their minds. It was not my day. I tried, once again, to get Christmas leave, without success. We were told that there was a salvage job at Clifton, and we could take it easy dealing with it. Whilst there, I would be able to stay in Tollerton.

The ladies at Mardale welcomed me warmly, which made up for my disappointing day. They told me that Ron Bacon had had another son and Les Dawson was working at Linton. When they heard that I would be with them for Christmas, they seemed very happy. If I could not be at home for Christmas then I was most fortunate to be with such lovely people.

RAF Clifton

I wasn't very interested in the salvage job at Clifton, especially as the sergeant had announced that he was going home for Christmas. One evening I visited the forces canteen at the Centenary Methodist Church. I hadn't been there for some time but several of the helpers recognised me and before I left I had received three invitations to spend Christmas with local families. I had to decline these kind offers but I could not help thinking how generous these Yorkshire folk were. One young lady asked if I was married. She seemed disappointed when I told her I was, and that I had two daughters. I was invited to the Christmas social on Saturday, 23 December. During the social the sirens sounded the alert and we heard a couple of distant thumps. We heard later that a couple of flying bombs had crossed the coast and landed nearby.

On Christmas Eve I left the camp to go to Mardale. Officially we were given no time off. A dense fog blotted out the countryside and the buses stopped running. A thick white frost came down and it was bitterly cold. I decided to stay put. There was plenty to eat and I sang a few songs at the piano. Miss Dunnington and Miss Illingworth loved hearing comic songs and we passed a pleasant hour or so. Elsie phoned and said Dolly and Ted had come over for lunch and shared the Christmas chicken, which had gone down well, and our daughters had enjoyed themselves. Les Dawson came over from Linton to see me and we had a long chat.

I did not return to camp until Wednesday morning, the 27th, to finish off the job. I was just getting the various sections loaded when I was called back to base. I was informed that on 21 January, I was to report to RAF Woolsington, just outside Newcastle, for the junior leader's course. I was given a list of what to take with me and then they wished me luck. I felt I would need it.

On making the usual request for some leave, they surprised me by saying I could have nine days' leave from 1 January. This, at least, was good news, and it revived my flagging spirit no end. I went to the operations room to see Flight Lieutenant Newton, who asked how the Clifton job was progressing. I told him that loading was in progress and it should be on its way by late afternoon. I informed him that I was having some leave from 1 January and on my return I had this junior leaders' course waiting. Could he get me off it? He said he couldn't, the decision was made elsewhere. They could ill afford any of their best men being taken off duties, but they had no choice. Quite often promotion resulted from a good showing.

I had heard this old flannel before and it didn't deceive me one bit, however he said I had done some good work and could have the rest of the week off, but told me to stay within call, just in case.

I returned to Clifton and superintended the loading of the remaining bits and pieces. It had to go to Southampton, and I let one of the lads, who lived in London, accompany the driver as 'second man'. Then the rest of the team tidied up and returned to camp. I managed to get them the following day off. One never knew if we would all meet up together as a team again, so I thanked each one for supporting me so well.

With time to spare I went into York to see if the shops had anything for me to take home for the girls, but there was nothing. As I strolled around I came to the Castle Museum and went inside. I found it fascinating to see the old street of shops, and told myself that one day I would bring Elsie and the girls to see these wonderful exhibits.

I went back to Mardale and spent the remainder of the time there. It was frosty and cold and I was glad to sit by the warm fire and chat with my hostesses. At the back of my mind though was the dreaded 'course', which loomed like a black cloud in my thoughts.

The last day of 1944 came. It had been another eventful year. I hoped that by this time next year the war in Europe would be over. We went to the Chapel in the evening and everyone there wished each other a Happy New Year. We returned to Mardale and sang a few songs around the piano. At midnight I went out of the back door and came in through the front. It was the old Yorkshire custom of the 'Lucky Bird'. The two ladies, Mr Harry Hoyle and myself, drank each other's health in a cup of tea and sang 'Old Lang Syne'.

And so the year of 1944 ended. The Allied armies in Europe were pushing forward, giving us all hope that this was the beginning of the end of the war.

1945

Starting the New Year with nine days' leave was, I thought, a good omen. We could not guess what the months ahead would bring but hopes were high that 1945 would see the end of hostilities in Europe. The Japanese were another matter though, and it could take years to clear them from the islands they had overrun. However, as I sat in the train speeding southwards and watched the snow-covered fields go gliding past, I sensed an air of optimism among my fellow passengers.

It was dark when I reached home and greeted Elsie and the girls. The icy weather had caused many water pipes to burst, including one of ours. The plumbing at No. 11 Crebor Street was primitive, just one tap and no hot water. Elsie had to heat every drop of hot water on the gas stove, or in the gas boiler she had brought with her. There was no point in complaining as these kinds of shortages were likely to be with us until the war was over and domestic items began to be manufactured again.

Despite the shortages, Doreen and Brenda seemed to have enjoyed Christmas. They had received a few toys, mostly home-made ones like woolly dolls and wooden pull-along carts. Elsie had managed to buy a second-hand tricycle, which, although rather cumbersome, was at least something 'on wheels'. It made me determined to make up for the things they had missed once the war was over.

Elsie was in the habit of lighting the fire in the downstairs flat ready for the Whittle family when they returned home each evening. Mr Whittle had lost his sight as a child but it was quite amazing how he managed to get around. He worked at the National Institute for the Blind, in Peckham Road. Mrs Whittle, whose name was Rose, worked at a theatrical agency in town, although she later worked at the Royal Eye Hospital in St George's Circus. George was a nice chap, but I was not keen on his wife. They had two children, Angela and Gwen.

On the Tuesday, we took the girls to the Regal Cinema in Forest Hill, to see Sabu in *The Thief of Bagdad*, the story of the genie in the bottle. Doreen enjoyed it but Brenda, who was not yet three years old, slept through it. The following day the family, with Dolly and Barbara, Edna and Clive, and Mrs Squires senior, saw the pantomime Cinderella, at the Empress, Brixton. I stayed behind and spent the time chatting to Elsie's father at No. 392, Cowley Road.

We went to get our rations on Thursday morning and whilst in the shop the manager asked me if I would help out with the stock-taking. A few extra shillings were always welcome so I agreed to go in on Friday afternoon and all day Saturday. Tim, Edna and Clive came to tea and spent the evening with us. During the day we heard the distant crump of falling rockets, a reminder that Germany was not beaten yet.

I made my way to the shop, as promised, and whilst checking the stock in the window the whole place shook as a rocket fell in Court Lane. A few seconds later there came the rumble of its approach. This lack of any warning meant that it was impossible to take any avoiding action. Elsie took the girls to the Sunday school party at Kimpton Mission in the evening and returned home about 8 p.m., and I finished about half an hour later.

Doreen had a little party with some of her friends on Monday afternoon, and by the time they left, at about 7.30 p.m., the snow had started falling and continued until a thick covering blanketed the ground.

Tuesday 9 January was my last full day at home, so despite the wintry weather we all went to the Odeon Cinema in Coldharbour Lane to see a film called *Rainbow Island*. The building was not very warm and we were all glad to get home and have a meal by the fire.

And so my leave ended. An eagerly-awaited break of nine days seemed to have passed in a flash, and I was saying goodbye once again. I headed for King's Cross and set off on the journey north. The thick snow lay everywhere and it was bitterly cold. Mardale was like a friendly oasis in a hostile environment and I dreaded the thought of going to Shipton the next morning. This had to be done, however, to show that I had not overstayed my leave. Because of the snow I did not attempt to cycle in and went instead by bus. This proved a wise decision as the bus skidded and slid its way along the route.

The service policeman on the gate was used to our coming and going at all hours and never once do I recall having to show my pass. I put my head round the orderly room to show I was back and then called in to the operations room. I had hoped that some urgent work might have cropped up that needed my attention, causing the dreaded course to be cancelled, but no such luck. To fill the intervening ten days, they suggested I join Les Dawson out at Linton. This suited me fine. I could cycle there from Mardale, weather permitting, but it was small compensation for the ordeal to come.

I went to the NAAFI and enjoyed a cup of tea and a wad as I waited for the transport to take me to Linton. There was a fairly regular service between the two places and I was in no hurry. There was very little to do at Linton but it was good to see the old place again. Les and I talked about our days at Upper Heyford and Tarrant Rushton and the different places we had been to since.

Junior Leaders' Course, Woolsington, Newcastle

The dreaded day came and I set off for Newcastle and the junior leaders' course. There were thirty-three others beside myself, from various maintenance units around the country. They included officers, sergeants, corporals and a couple of erks. There was no distinction between ranks whilst on the course. The weather had not improved and it was still icy cold, making it hard to breathe at times.

We were told the course would last for eighteen days and at the end, should we survive, we would be given a seventy-two-hour pass. Whilst the sergeant was examining the documents I had brought with me he looked up and said, 'You somebody special?'

'Not that I know of,' I replied. 'Why?'

'Oh,' he said. 'I see you are screened from overseas posting until 19th of October, and you are to be kept in England.'

I will draw a veil over the days at Woolsington. It was a commando course, pure and simple. We crawled through snow-drifts, waded through icy rivers and practised climbing over barbed wire. We threw hand-grenades, hung from trees and climbed nets and generally did unpleasant things thought up by depraved minds. I made a chart and ticked off the quarter hours. We were always wet and my hands became so numb that I couldn't hold a rifle. On one occasion it looked as if exposure would finish us off, and we were made to drink rum, much to my disgust.

The hours were not long, 8 a.m. to 5.30 p.m., but we did have to go on night exercises. The food was very good. Most of our evenings were spent drying out our clothes. Towards the end of the course the weather turned mild and everywhere became a sea of mud. We had to make notes, draw maps and find our way across country by map and reference points. Had it been summertime I might have enjoyed it, but I think it was the most miserable time of my life.

We finished the course by tackling an assault course with some of the top brass looking on. All around us thunder flashes and grenades were being thrown, and machine-guns were chattering. I lost my footing half-way across a foaming river, but someone pulled me to my feet. We had to fire our rifles at moving targets and luckily I hit the bull twice. We then crossed another river using planks, like a bridge. This time, though, there was a rope to grab if we slipped.

And so the junior leaders' course ended. A report on our performance would be sent to our CO. I collected my seventy-two-hour pass and left RAF Woolsington without looking back. Strange to say that despite the cold, ice and snow and the frequent soakings, I did not get a cold, or any other ill effects. Even so I looked back on those days with horror and hoped they would never be repeated.

It was a long journey from Newcastle to King's Cross but I was home by 8.30 p.m., thankful that I could relax for a few hours.

Doreen was now attending school, and the next morning I escorted her there. It was a pleasant afternoon, so Elsie, Brenda and I met her at the school and made our way to the park, and the swings. Saturday morning was spent shopping, and in the afternoon we visited Elsie's parents at Cowley Road. Next day it was back to Yorkshire once again.

I stayed the night at Tollerton and on reporting in at HQ the following morning, was quite bucked to learn that Sergeant Colbourne had asked for me to join him at Earls Colne, near Colchester, in Essex. This was good news. I had worked with the sergeant several times and we got on well together, so I was happy to accept. I made my way to Pay Accounts, drew some cash, collected a rail pass and travel documents, phoned the ladies at Mardale and waited for the transport to York station.

Earls Colne

I reached King's Cross and got transport to Liverpool Street Station, left my tool box and equipment in the left luggage, and set off home. This was getting to be a regular habit, calling in between jobs, even though it was only for a few hours. I left home the next morning, collected my gear and continued my journey to Earls Colne. The camp was some distance from the station so I phoned for transport. It didn't take long to locate the plane and the team, most of whom I had worked with before. They already had a billet lined up for me. Sergeant Colbourne was pleased to see me. He told me they were waiting for spares to arrive and the job would probably last another couple of weeks. However, despite the warm welcome, I sensed that something was worrying them.

I was not wrong. When the sergeant and I were on our own he unburdened himself. He told me that one of the lads had had his rifle stolen, and the loss of a firearm was a court-martial offence, as we knew. To make matters worse, it seemed that the loss had not been immediately reported and the sergeant was 'on the carpet' for not having carried out a daily firearm inspection. He would have to attend the court martial and could lose a stripe over it.

This was disconcerting news, and I could see the sarge was really worried; in fact he admitted he had never been so worried since joining the RAF. It was while he was being told that he would have to return to HQ to give evidence that he heard I was on the commando course. He asked if I could take over the Earls Colne job during his absence. Apparently the CO had told him I was earmarked to return to Cornwall (which was news to me), but that it would be put to me on my return. The decision was mine.

We had always got on well and I said I was glad he had asked for me. I could get home from Earls Colne reasonably well and he said I could have a free hand with the leave rotas. After this job was finished, we would be going to Woodbridge.

Although it was still February the weather warmed up a little and there were already signs of spring in the hedgerows. The long-awaited spares arrived on the 21st and we set about fitting the parts. I managed to get home for a few hours every weekend. I cycled to the railway station and was able to leave my bike in a cottage shed nearby. The old folk charged sixpence to park there. The tumbledown shed contained dozens of bikes and despite having no checks on them, my cycle was not interfered with.

The work was completed and all we needed now was the AID clearance. On Tuesday, 6 March, the sergeant was summoned to Shipton together with the lad who had lost the rifle, to the court martial. I wished them both well and, once again, found myself in charge. About midday, I was called to the telephone. It was the CO from Shipton. He told me to pack up and return to base. This was a blow for I thought that Woodbridge was our next destination, but orders were orders.

I didn't hurry. It was always possible to hang things out, and I did this so we could have the weekend off. I was in no hurry to go back north. I arranged for us to leave Earls Colne on the Tuesday and then received a letter from Sergeant Colbourne asking me to get the lads and equipment to King's Cross, where he would meet us. We would spend the night in London before leaving for York the next morning.

Everything was packed up and I requisitioned transport to take us to the station. Some of the lads lived in the north and were looking forward to returning to their home territory. Everything was loaded on to a trolley ready to go into the guard's van and we waited for the train. It was just steaming in when the station-master came hurrying out of his office.

'Are you Corporal Williams of the mobile repair unit?'

I said I was.

'You're wanted on the telephone urgently!'

It was HQ. They told me to return to Earls Colne as another damaged aircraft had landed and we were to attend to it immediately. I was delighted, but not so my northern lads. So, back we went and settled in again. I thought of the sergeant waiting in vain at King's Cross, but I had his home address and was able to phone him there. I suggested he have a couple of days off, as I could manage.

Elsie wrote that Doreen was not very well again, but, hoping that a change of air would help, she had taken the girls to Crawley to see the Gardiners. They had a nice break but on the Thursday, Doreen came out in a rash, so Elsie brought the girls home. She called the doctor who diagnosed measles.

Sergeant Colbourne returned in due course and told me he had had a rough time at the court mrtial because of his lack of supervision over the firearms. He had received a reprimand but had retained his stripes. The offending airman was 'awarded' fourteen days CB.[45] He decided that the solution to the problem was to put our arms in the station armoury to avoid a repetition of the trouble. I agreed. Half my Sten gun and ammunition was in pieces in my tool box and I was glad to have it put in a safe place.

Despite the severe winter, the war in Europe did not slacken. The Germans made a big counter-attack in the Ardennes, which became known as the 'Battle of the Bulge', but it was contained. Churchill, Roosevelt and Stalin met at Yalta, in the Crimea, to discuss tactics. President Roosevelt looked terribly ill. In Russia, the appalling weather had taken its toll of the German armies and the onslaught of the avenging Russians sent them reeling back. In the Far East the Japanese were fighting a rearguard action.

Even so, air-raid alerts continued to wail, and one night a flying bomb passed overhead. Occasionally the crump of a distant bomb falling to earth could be heard with the odd burst of gunfire, but these raids were on a minor scale.

I had hoped to be home for Brenda's third birthday and although at one point it didn't seem possible, I made it in the end. Doreen had been very poorly but she was recovering well and more like her cheery self. Brenda was getting quite sturdy and when they were together many people asked if they were twins.

Easter arrived and we were all given three days off. I delayed taking mine for a bit and arrived back at camp on Wednesday, 4 April. On 9 April we were ordered to leave Earls Colne and sent north to Lindholme, near Doncaster.

RAF Lindholme

As we headed north the weather became a lot colder, with gales and heavy rain. RAF Lindholme seemed crowded with RAF personnel. As I was working on the damaged plane, I managed to squash my middle finger pushing some parts

---

45 'Confined to barracks'.

into position. It was fortunate that I was wearing leather gloves for the damage could have been far worse. The job did not take us long and I had the satisfaction of seeing the aircraft take off when we'd finished.

Spring arrived in Yorkshire at last. In the fine weather, it was a lovely county. The seemingly constant winds that swept across the landscape from the North Sea made life very unpleasant, but in the calm, sunny weather it was like a different world. We did not have to wait long for our marching orders. The teams were broken up and sent to different destinations. I was told to report to Lissett, near Driffield, in East Yorkshire. I said my farewells to Colbourne and the lads, and we went our various ways.

RAF Lissett

There was another crash dome nearby on the lines of the one at Woodbridge, but RAF Lissett was much more compact. I arrived there on 15 April and had hardly settled in when my leave pass came through and I set off home on the 20th. The newspapers were full of optimistic reports that the end of the war in Europe was in sight and there were no more air-raid alerts, which was a great relief. I arrived home in time to meet Doreen from school.

We had a hectic time visiting friends at Banstead, helping Edna and Tim to move to No. 290, Uplands Road, and boating with the girls on Dulwich Park lake. We made a quick visit to Aylesbury to see my mother and sisters, did some shopping and called in on Elsie's parents. As I prepared to return to Lissett on the 29th, it started snowing.

It was still bitterly cold in Yorkshire and the snow followed me there. I began the six-mile walk from the station to the camp but after a mile a motorist gave me a lift, for which I was very thankful. There was a terrific amount of work to do at Lissett and, as usually seemed to happen, the sergeant went on leave, leaving me in charge.

It was quite a large team, which included three young women flight mechanics. I'm afraid we did not hit it off at all well. One of the girls looked after the paperwork and was quite efficient, but the other two were a menace. I tolerated them as long as I could, but the crunch came when a mainplane was being unloaded on to the gantries. The lifting crane unloaded the two-ton section with a sling around the mainplane. This was always a tricky business and needed concentration from everyone. As it was being lowered, the two girls started chasing each other around the gantries. The fellows began watching them instead of keeping their minds on the job in hand. I saw the mainplane start to slip from the sling. I shouted at the lads and we managed to retrieve a dangerous situation. If it had come down it could have crushed someone, besides costing hundreds of pounds. I was furious and ordered the WAAFs back to the hangar and threatened the lads with a charge should it happen again. It was the only time in my RAF career that I had really used my authority.

The news from the European battlefield was good and the end of hostilities was in sight. There was talk that groups of servicemen would soon be released, but in a controlled way, no mass exodus as at the end of the First World War.

At the same time I developed a bout of influenza and felt really awful for a while. When I began to feel a little better, I thought a cycle ride into Bridlington for some fresh air might be beneficial. I was not impressed and thought it a scruffy place. At one time I had thought I would try to find somewhere for Elsie and the girls to stay, but one look at Bridlington quashed that thought.

The End of Hostilities in Europe

On 8 May, news was broadcast that Germany had surrendered and the war in Europe was over. There was great rejoicing. I listened to the radio commentators describing the wild scenes in London and elsewhere. We were all given the rest of the day and the following day off. Most of the lads lived locally and I sent them home and held the fort on my own. There was still a ban on travel over twenty miles, so getting home was not possible anyway. That evening I cycled into Bridlington to see their celebrations, but although the town was decorated with flags it was very quiet. Maybe the residents were celebrating at home, for the weather was enough to dampen anyone's jollity. When the lads returned on Thursday most looked the worse for wear.

Although the war across the Channel was now over, a much tougher situation remained in the Far East. Despite this, there was much talk of demobilisation. From what I gathered, the technical airmen, especially the NCOs, would be the last to be released. This was understandable. The atmosphere in the camp relaxed and at times it seemed as though only our small group were doing any work.

From Elsie came news of the celebrations in Dulwich. The children were delighted to see the bonfires and fireworks, and the streets ablaze with light. They had had a little party in the garden for their friends. I could only hope that the nightmare of sirens, explosions and sleeping in shelters would soon fade from their memories.

My thoughts inevitably turned to the future. I could be sent to the Pacific, but I hoped not. In a way, the thought of leaving the RAF filled me with anxiety, and returning to shop life appalled me. I had always tried to make a success of it, but with hindsight I could see that I had never really settled there. I had always considered myself worthy of something better. The RAF had treated me with respect and given me responsibilities. I had been consulted on vital matters, like whether an aeroplane should be repaired or scrapped, and had learned how to handle men and to liaise with officers. Above all, I was looked on as one who knew his job and could be relied on. Had I been single I would have stayed in the RAF, but with family responsibilities that was out of the question. Elsie had soldiered on alone for far too long, and besides, the

RAF would no doubt be very different in peacetime.

Financially too I would be at a big disadvantage. The wage being paid to shop assistants was about £4 a week. Taking Elsie's and the children's allowances into account, our weekly pay was well over £7 a week and I did not have to bother about food, clothing and accommodation. But it seemed I had no option but to return to shop life until I could see what other openings became available.

There no longer seemed any urgency over the repair jobs, due in part I suppose to the many years of concentrated and time-consuming work. Many airmen were transferred to the Army, presumably to reinforce them for the big push against the Nips. The population who had expected a quick end to food rationing had a nasty shock when it was announced that rations were to be cut. It seemed a poor reward for putting up with years of shortages.

The weather did little to help, with gale-force winds and lashing rain. Whitsun came, but with the travel ban still in place, I was unable to use the forty-eight hours' leave to get home. I thought I would have another look at Bridlington, but twice I set out and twice the howling gale drove me back. In the end I stayed in the camp.

Elsie wrote that the weather down south was better and our daughters had been to several parties. Some urgent repair jobs had been done to the flat but no decorating had been carried out. They had also had storms over the Whitsun holiday, but she had still managed quite a lot of visiting.

Now that the war in Europe was over the coalition government came to an end and the decision was made to hold a general election in July. Who would win this election was anybody's guess. There had been one or two by-elections and the new Commonwealth Party had had some successes, but in reality no one took them very seriously.

I calculated that we had about three more weeks' work at Lissett, so I was very surprised when, on 23 May, I was told to take half a dozen lads with me to Doncaster airport to carry out a job on a plane that had made a forced landing there. This was one of the delights of the job, being uncertain of where one would be on the morrow. It proved to be a simple job that took only a few hours. I had a chat with the pilot who said he had flown from the West Country and that the temperature was ten degrees warmer there.

As soon as the plane took off I phoned Shipton for instructions. I was bucked when they said there was a job awaiting me at RAF Odiham, in Hampshire, and the necessary paperwork would be with me the next day. Most of the lads with me were southerners and the thought of leaving the frozen north cheered them no end. We travelled south on the Saturday, crossed to Waterloo where we left our equipment in the forces' lock-up, and went our separate ways until the next day. There was a distinct rise in temperature.

It was wonderful to be home for a few hours. I spent most of the time in the garden, encouraging the plants. Doreen had her own little patch where she had planted some seeds. I revelled in the warmth after the cold, biting winds of East Yorkshire.

RAF Odiham

The nearest railway station to Odiham was Hook, about five miles from Basingstoke. The rail service was a good one and quite fast but with a main road nearby there was always a chance of cadging a lift. Sure enough, the following weekend I thumbed a lift and the driver dropped me at the bottom of Rye Lane in Peckham, no distance at all from home. But that was exceptional. The down side was that the return journey to camp had to be by train.

Elsie was upset to lose her engagement ring whilst out shopping but luckily she recovered it from the fish shop! Our daughters were invited to a party downstairs and we took advantage of it and paid a visit to Herne Hill to see my sister Eileen.

We finished our work on the plane, but as it was about to leave it developed engine trouble. One of the engines needed changing so the servicing crew had to return to their base at Melton Mowbray for a spare. We hung on to give them a hand.

Other odd jobs cropped up keeping us employed there a little longer. Most weekends I managed to get home for a few hours. The election campaign was hotting up and I went to a meeting in the village and listened to Tom Wintringham, the Commonwealth Party candidate, who had fought in the Spanish Civil War.

I was strolling across the airfield one day when I noticed a lot of mushrooms growing. I did not like them myself so they did not interest me, but soon the lads were out collecting them, and enjoying a fry-up. One enterprising chap took a lot to town and sold them to a grocer.

One day, Les Dawson and his team arrived at Odiham to 'give us a hand'. In truth, there was nothing for them to do, but it was good to have them with us. I hoped that if he was able to stay for a while I would be able to take some leave, and sure enough, my application was granted and I was given twelve days' leave, starting on 30 June.

Now that hostilities were over things were much more relaxed, but all around were the results of the awful bombing. Camberwell had suffered greatly, and some of the rubble was being cleared and prefabricated bungalows erected on the sites. Elsie and I looked over some of them and in our opinion they were quite good, and we would have liked one ourselves. However, there was very little chance of this happening as there were many in more need than we were.

As well as the usual visits to family and friends, we spent a lot of the time decorating the flat. There was no paint to be had so we had to use distemper on the bedroom, kitchen and dining room walls instead. The fine weather enabled us to spend time in the garden and one day we took the girls to Brighton for a breath of sea air. They played in the paddling pool and had a lovely time. We visited Eileen at Herne Hill and whilst there Mum and Pam arrived, and they all made a return visit to us a few days later. Mr and Mrs Whittle and their girls had booked a holiday at Scorrier, in Cornwall, and I went with them to Paddington and saw them on to the train. Then my few days' holiday at home were over and it was time to return to Odiham.

The work at Odiham had come to an end and we hung around hoping more would turn up, but none materialised. A few days later we were told to return to Yorkshire. We left on Friday, 20 July, and broke our journey in London for a few hours' break with our families, and met up next morning to continue our journey to York. We had to wait a while for transport to arrive to take us to Shipton. Whilst there a terrific thunderstorm hit the area and for a time we were forced to stay under cover until it abated. Once booked in, I left the camp and caught the 6 p.m. Tollerton bus and made my way to Mardale. I was welcomed back and given an egg for my tea. The rest of the evening was spent relating my adventures and catching up with the village news.

On reporting in the next morning I was told that a party of us were being sent to St Athan, in South Wales. This was not good news. St Athan had the reputation as the RAF equivalent to Alcatraz or Devil's Island. What made it worse was that we had to get cleared from Shipton as we might not be returning there. This did nothing to raise our spirits. Nobody seemed certain, we could be away for three months or for good. I wrote to Elsie with the sad news. It was her birthday in a couple of days and I hadn't been able to get her a card. I returned to Mardale that evening and the ladies put their minds to solving the birthday card problem. Next day I visited York and was lucky to find one, which I sent off there and then. I returned to Mardale to find that the ladies had also been successful in their search so I sent that card to Elsie as well.

RAF St Athan, South Wales

There were twenty of us in the party that left for Wales on 25 July. It was a long, tedious journey with a change of trains at Gloucester and Cardiff. We arrived at midnight but it was another couple of hours before we turned in for the night. It was pouring with rain, which did not revive our flagging spirits.

St Athan was a huge place with a flying school and a training school, as well as the maintenance unit. For us, it was like working in a factory. The hours were 8 a.m. to 5.30 p.m. but from 1 August the starting time was brought forward to 7.30 a.m. We had to march to and from work like a lot of rookies, which was not what we were used to at all. The aircraft in the main were American Liberators and Flying Fortresses.

The countryside around the camp looked inviting, but we spent most of our time indoors so saw little of it. We were given the weekend off and I took the opportunity to visit Barry Island and the amusement area complex. It was full of holiday-makers and lots of children. The queues for beach trays seemed endless. The sands looked very nice and across the Bristol Channel one could see the hills of Somerset. I wished I could have been on that side of the water. I did not stay long and made my way back to camp.

There was great excitement in the NAAFI as the results of the general election came in. The Labour Party was sweeping the board and it looked as if the Tories had been decimated. All four Camberwell seats, even Dulwich, were now Labour. I suppose it was to be expected. Churchill had proved himself a great war leader but his peacetime record did not inspire the working man. I believe people expected Mr Attlee to right all the wrongs overnight, but this was never likely and in fact for a while things only got worse.

I managed to get a seventy-two-hour pass and arrived home on 4 August. Elsie related all the happenings of the past few days. They had been to the fair and Brenda had managed to put lipstick all over her face. They had also booked a holiday at Deal with the South London Campers, from 26 August, and her parents would be going as well. This was good news.

Then came some staggering news. American airmen had dropped an atomic bomb on the Japanese city of Hiroshima, causing thousands of casualties, and soon afterwards another on Nagasaki. I had read a little about the power inherent in the atom, and the destruction it could cause if ever it was loosed. It seemed that the scientists had found a way to harness this power. Few people at the time had any sympathy for the Japanese. Their treatment of British and Allied prisoners had been barbaric, causing misery and death to untold numbers of men who had been forced to build roads and bridges under the whip and lash, and without adequate food, clothing or shelter.

I was asleep in bed when somebody swiped me over the head and shouted, 'The war is over. The Japs have surrendered.' In a few moments the camp was in uproar. Bonfires sprang up all over the place and everything that could be burnt was being tossed into the flames. I quickly got up and dressed. Some of the lads were going crazy, doing war dances around the flames. I was appalled at the senseless destruction going on around me. Notice-boards had been wrenched off the walls, bus shelters were being uprooted and tossed into the fires. In the distance I heard the 'dong, dong' of the camp's fire bell. Two chaps arrived carrying the bell in its wooden frame, and with a final dong it was thrown into the flames. The piano was dragged from the NAAFI and a singsong began with Welsh voices raised in harmony.

I made my way to the ablutions and found one lad in there, shaving. 'I'm off!' he said.

'Don't be daft,' I said. 'The war is over. Demob has already started and now things will be speeded up. You've everything to lose if you go now. Hang on for a day or two. Don't forfeit your gratuity by absconding.'

'I'm still going,' he said. 'And don't you try to stop me.'

I could see he wasn't open to reason so I left him there and made my way to the cookhouse to see if there was any tea on the go, but there was nothing doing. In the end it was the heavy rain that put a stop to all the craziness.

The commanding officer came on the Tannoy and appealed for calm. He said a twenty-mile limit had been put on all travel and the railways would not issue cheap tickets. As soon as it could be arranged, two days' leave would be given to everyone, and in the meantime there was to be a free cinema show.

According to the demob tables my turn would come with Group 21. Age, length of service and whether the serviceman was considered essential to the air force governed these tables. A revised one put my group as ready for discharge in October, but only time would tell.

Elsie wrote with news of their VJ-day celebrations. A few of them had got together for a little party but unfortunately Doreen had been troubled by toothache, which meant a trip to the dentists. He could not do anything straight away and arranged for Elsie to bring her back the following day. He made a couple of extractions after giving Doreen gas, and charged 8s. 6d. Another problem that upset Elsie no end was that the girls had contracted impetigo, and no matter what she did the attacks kept recurring.

On 20 August, the Group 20 chaps were recalled to Shipton to prepare for demobilisation, so our hopes were raised that we too would soon be leaving Wales. At least it seemed that we still belonged to our old unit, which was something.

Then the unexpected happened, which was to delay my release. I displaced a cartilage in my left knee. It was extremely painful and I was obliged to report sick. The medical officer said I must have a sitting-down job and I was put in the orderly room. I could only hobble about and every step made me wince. I hoped it would ease, but it never did.

Elsie and the girls and her parents went to Deal on 26 August and enjoyed their week's holiday there. Elsie's dad played the piano of an evening and by day they played games or visited other resorts like Folkestone and Ramsgate. I had a letter from my sister Eileen telling me that Sid was in hospital in Cardiff with a leg injury, and could I visit him there as she was very worried. She had not been well herself and wasn't able to make the journey. Grace's husband John was also in hospital having had a bad injury to his legs.

I saw the medical officer who tried manipulation to get the cartilage back, but without much success. All the same, I hobbled my way to Cardiff and managed to see Sid House in hospital. He seemed quite cheerful and told me he had arthritis in his legs, but reckoned he would soon be up and about. We chatted for an hour or so, and I was given a cup of tea. I told him I would write to Eileen and then left to return to St Athan.

One of the jobs given to me in the orderly room was that of compiling a list of airmen to take part in the church parade on Sunday. About one hundred and twenty men were needed and I asked the MU chaps if they would like to be included. They all declined. I had another idea. Since all Welshmen enjoyed singing and were all church-goers, or so we had been led to believe, I spent one afternoon picking out Joneses, Hugheses, Davieses' and so on, and put their names on the notice-board for Sunday's church parade.

There was a storm of protest. Most of the Welshmen lived out and were not happy to come in at the weekend. I was asked to alter the list, but refused. For a while it seemed I had provoked an international incident, much to the amusement of the English lads. The list remained unchanged and the Taffs had to come in, drill and march off to enjoy the church service. Soon after that I was removed from the orderly room and given the job of looking after the barrack block.

This was good news and the job suited me fine, in fact it was a doddle. I pottered around the garden in front of the block and cut the grass on the four small lawns surrounding the flowerbed.

The release of airmen slowed down, much to the annoyance of the groups who should have gone. There were posters in the NAAFI and cookhouse advising the men to 'Carry on with the job you know', 'Think before you move' and 'There's a lot to be said for the RAF'. Some of the notices were torn down and trampled underfoot. So far my own group had received no date, although rumour said it was likely to be November.

My knee continued to give me a lot of pain and it seemed that once a cartilage was displaced there was always a danger of a recurrence. If it was torn, it would have to come out, and that made me anxious. Any operation would be best done whilst I was still in the RAF. The alternative meant a hefty hospital bill, for these were the days prior to the National Health Service.

My orders to return to Shipton came on 4 September. I left St Athan on the 5th and travelled to Paddington on the overnight train. I found it difficult with my damaged knee to carry my kit and heavy toolbox and it took some effort to cross London to leave my belongings in the forces' left luggage. I had decided that no matter what, I would call in home and I eventually arrived there at 7.30 a.m.

The following day was our tenth wedding anniversary, and I hoped that this would be the last one we would spend apart. The day passed quickly and at 9.30 p.m. I set off for the night train to York. When I arrived at Shipton I booked in and then made my way to the MO's office. He arranged for me to see a specialist at Weeton Hospital, in Lancashire, and then gave me the weekend off. I had to pay my own fare, but soon I was home again.

Elsie had been busy decorating the front room of the flat. It was a large room, the width of the house. I managed to help her move the furniture around and it began to look really nice. Like a lot of houses built around the turn of the century, it was badly planned. A steep flight of stairs led up from the entrance hall, and a further small staircase led to our bedroom and the lounge. There was a small bedroom where our daughters slept. At the end of the hallway towards the back of the house was a small landing where an inside staircase led to the garden. This 'room' had been made into the kitchen with a copper in the corner, a gas stove and in the corner a toilet cubicle. The dining room was next to it, at the rear of the house. It was far from ideal but we managed.

Weeton Hospital

I returned to Yorkshire on the Monday and went straight to Tollerton to stay with my friends. I received my appointment to see the consultant at Weeton Hospital, and his verdict was that the cartilage should be removed. Back at Shipton I waited for the admission date to come through. It arrived quite quickly and I was given 20 September as my admission date. This time I did not have the tedious journey by train to the hospital as there was a 'stretcher case' going there and I travelled with them in the ambulance. The ride across the moors was rather spoilt by the mist but we arrived without any problems and I was shown to a bed in Ward 8. It was the first time I had ever been a patient in a hospital.

In due course the offending cartilage was removed and a period of rest and recuperation followed. The surgeon told me I had opened my eyes during the operation, which gave them all a bit of a shock. I had sessions in the gym under supervision, and was told that I was to go on a rehabilitation course at either Loughborough, in Leicestershire, or Chessington, in Surrey. I asked for Chessington, for obvious reasons.

All was not well at home. Elsie had been having trouble with her teeth, and little Brenda had been similarly troubled. Doreen was unwell with another bad cold. I wished I could have been around to help. The days passed slowly and still I waited. It was not until 30 October that I came south to Chessington and was able to break my journey with four days' leave.

Elsie was not well at all. She had influenza and was very groggy. Despite being ill herself she had taken Mr Whittle to hospital to see his wife. It was a kindness that rebounded on her and on Wednesday the 31st she had to visit our GP, Dr Mushlin. He ordered her to bed and prescribed M&B tablets. I did what I could in the way of shopping, housework and suchlike, although I felt unwell myself. Edna and Tim came round on the Saturday but I had to report to Chessington that evening and I left home feeling very concerned about Elsie.

On Monday morning I was called to the orderly room and told that during the night a message had been received saying that my wife was very ill. There were no other details but I immediately put in a request to see the officer in charge. I explained the situation as best I could but he was most unsympathetic, and despite my pleadings for a short period of leave he refused my request.

Despite being worried, I was also furious. I knew that Edna would do what she could but she had her own household to look after. The hours passed but my mind was not on my exercises and at lunchtime I went to find the sergeant. He was a decent type and I told him that if I wasn't given any leave I would take some unofficially and chance the consequences. He advised me not to do anything rash and he would see what he could do. The annoying thing was that had I been with my own unit it would have been granted without hesitation.

I made preparations to abscond but decided on one more attempt to get leave officially. I returned to the orderly room and saw the sergeant. 'I'm glad you called in,' he said. 'You've been granted forty-eight hours' leave.' It was a huge relief and I thanked him. In a few minutes I was on my way home.

Elsie looked very ill. Edna had called in and got Doreen off to school, but otherwise she had been on her own all day. She'd had nothing to eat or drink until Doreen came home from school. Although only six years old Doreen had shown her capabilities and made a meal, of sorts, for her mother and sister, opened the door to Dr Mushlin and taken the prescription to the chemists, and collected the medicine. It made me very proud of her.

By the next morning Elsie had begun to show signs of improvement. The doctor called in again and diagnosed bronchial pneumonia and said she should stay in bed and keep warm. I told him that I had only been given forty-eight hours' leave. He said it was not enough and gave me a letter to take back with me recommending I be granted a further nine days. Elsie's mother came and took Doreen home with her, and Edna said she would look after Brenda. It was with great reluctance that I returned to Chessington. Next morning I went to see the CO. He read the doctor's letter and much to my relief, gave me the leave period suggested. I was soon on my way home again, arriving at about 2.30 p.m.

Elsie was looking a little better, Brenda was with Edna, and Mrs Whittle had given her a meal. I was very relieved to see folk rallying round. A little later, Edna brought Brenda back. I lit a fire, for the days were turning chilly, and soon had Brenda tucked up for the night.

When Dr Mushlin called in the next day, he said that Elsie was making satisfactory progress. I thanked him for his letter, which had enabled me to be at home at such a difficult time. In the afternoon Mr and Mrs Squires arrived with Doreen. We had tea together and then they left for home.

The next two days proved to be critical ones, and the doctor put Elsie back on M&B tablets. I was not the only one worried for on the Wednesday Elsie's parents visited again. Leaving them with Elsie, I took the opportunity to take Doreen and Brenda to Herne Hill for a little outing and to tell my sisters about Elsie's illness.

There was better news on Thursday when the doctor said he was satisfied with Elsie's progress and she could get up for an hour or two. Now, it seemed, it was my turn to feel unwell. I suppose I hadn't had the rest necessary after my operation, and the strain of recent events took its toll. However, it was a case of soldiering on and gradually the ill effects wore off.

Elsie continued to make good progress and by the time my compassionate leave expired, she was up and about. On the following Thursday she went out of doors for the first time since her illness.

The MO sent for me on my return to Chessington and said that although I could return to my unit almost immediately, he advised me to stay another week, and I agreed to do so. I had a dental appointment whilst I was there and although nothing major needed attention, he decided to give my teeth a good clean. They were scraped and brushed and I ended up with very sore gums indeed. One day we went to the Odeon cinema in Surbiton to see *The Seventh Veil*, but I wasn't impressed. Afterwards I paid a visit to my pal Reg's home in Stoneleigh, but he and Hilda's brother, Sid, had gone to see a football match between Arsenal and Moscow Dynamos. It was a foggy day and I later learned that it had been almost impossible to see the ball.

I paid a quick visit home at the weekend and was pleased to see that Elsie looked a lot better. We had a trip to the shops but it had turned much colder and we did not stay out long. Back at the rehabilitation centre I was told that I could now go back to Yorkshire. As I was due for some leave I persuaded them to let me take it from Chessington, and return to 60 MU at its conclusion. They raised no objections and so, on 30 November, I came home on seven days' leave.

On the Sunday, we met Doreen and Brenda from Sunday school and walked to Herne Hill to see Eileen. My mother and Pam were there and we chatted and had tea together. Grace also called in and it was quite a family party.

Doreen was having more trouble with her teeth and I took her to the school clinic where they extracted two of her teeth. When she emerged she was sobbing and they appeared to have been very rough with her. I was furious and very nearly went in and walloped the dentist. I managed to curb my anger and took my little girl home. No more school dentists for her, I vowed.

Goodbye to the RAF

On Friday, 7 December, I left home for my last journey to my unit in Yorkshire. It was with mixed feelings. I looked forward to being home with my family, of course, but at the same time I had warm feelings for the RAF, and 60 MU in particular. They had shown me another side of life, treating me as someone who mattered and giving me responsibilities I otherwise would never have had. I had met some lovely people along the way, who had accepted me and made me welcome in their homes. I had done more travelling and seen more parts of the country than I would ever have before, plus a little flying, including my own special chartered flight, all in the course of my duties. These memories would never leave me and I would treasure them always.

On arrival at York I went straight to Tollerton to see my friends at Mardale. We had corresponded all the time I had been away and they had insisted I stay with them on my return. It was always a pleasure to be welcomed back. One surprising piece of news was that 60 MU had moved from Shipton to Rufforth, just outside York. I knew the camp because one of my first jobs as an NCO was there.

When I reported in the following day they were surprised to see me. Evidently I had been 'lost'. Most of my close RAF colleagues had already left the service but because of my spell in hospital and rehabilitation, I was now overdue. The officers there were new to me, and they knew me only from their records. Nevertheless, they did their best to persuade me to sign up as a short-term regular. I was offered a £25 bonus if I took up the offer, and my corporal rank would be honoured. I was flattered but my mind was made up and would not be changed.

Filling in the necessary forms took time and I also had to have medical and dental checks, hand in my tools and firearm, and generally get clearance. Finally, on 19 December 1945, my discharge papers were received and I said my last farewell to No. 60 Maintenance Unit. I was handed a thick brown envelope that contained my service record and discharge papers, plus a rail warrant and some pay to cover immediate necessities. Although 20 December was my release day, I was still officially in the RAF until 14 February 1946, the intervening period being counted as release leave. I would be entitled to pay until the latter date. My release book contained some details of my service, and for my skill as a tradesman I was pleased to see that I was classed as 'Superior'.

I had to report to No. 100 Dispersal Centre at Uxbridge the following day but I made time to visit my good friends at Mardale. It was a tearful parting but I promised to return in the days to come. This I did on several occasions and their welcome remained as friendly as ever.

I reached home that evening. Tomorrow would be my last official day in the Royal Air Force. I left early in the morning, having first steamed open the large brown envelope I had been given. There was a detailed report of my career in which I was 'Highly Commended'. I read the note that said I had been screened from overseas posting until 19 October 1945. More interesting was the note recommending my promotion to the rank of sergeant when a vacancy occurred. It was good to see it there but it really didn't matter much now.

At Uxbridge I had to hand in my greatcoat and second uniform, although I was allowed to keep my battledress. I was issued with a civilian suit and a pair of shoes. I had a meal, shook hands with a 'college' type who wished me luck, and then, with my bundle under my arm and my release book in my pocket, I left the camp, and the RAF.

Christmas at Home

Christmas was almost upon us and my little family would all be together to celebrate it in our home. Despite the rationing we had a lovely time. Elsie's parents joined us for Christmas lunch, and on Boxing Day, Edna, Tim and Clive came over for a double celebration, Christmas and my release from the RAF.

Civvy Street

When the New Year came I decided to return to work, and on 5 January 1946 I returned to the Royal Arsenal Co-operative Society, Crystal Palace Road. I hated every minute of it. I tried to settle back but food was still rationed and at times it was hard going.

On 14 February I received my final discharge from the RAF. With it came a notice informing me that my war gratuity amounted to £74 5s. 0d. and that I would be issued with a Post Office Savings book for this sum. I also received £26 14s. 1d. as the final settlement of my pay and allowance.

So this was it. My weekly pay had plummeted and I was now more than £3 a week worse off in Civvy Street than I was in the forces, a fact that did my ego no good at all. As the weeks went by my frustration deepened. Elsie encouraged me to take the plunge and find something else, but I had no idea what. It all came to a head when the branch manager, a snake in the grass by the name of Tanner, told me I was being transferred to the Kennington Road branch. This would mean that I would no longer qualify for travelling expenses of 4s. a week. A postman came into the shop and seeing my glum face, asked the cause. I told him I was sick of shop life and was looking for something else.

He replied that the Post Office was recruiting staff and although the pay was about the same as I was receiving now, he encouraged me to have a go. Elsie said I should try my luck. And so it was that I made my way to the Forces Resettlement office at Deptford and obtained an application form, which I filled in and despatched. After a while, I was called for an interview, given an intelligence test and a medical examination, and was told they would let me know.

Elsie and the girls, with Mr and Mrs Squires, went again to the holiday camp at Deal. While they were away, I received a notice from the GPO asking me to report to the Mount Pleasant office. I dithered. When Elsie returned she said I should accept and join the Post Office.

As often seems to happen, the foreman's job became vacant at the same time as I was considering leaving the shop. I asked for the job but the supervisor refused. His words were, 'We are going to look after the men who stayed to work in the shops, not those who hid in the forces'.

This really was the last straw. I wrote to the GPO apologising for my delay in replying, saying that I had been on holiday, but after giving my firm a week's notice, I would join them at Mount Pleasant. I put my notice in, only to be told that I could have the foreman's job after all. I refused, and on the day stated joined the GPO as a postman.

It was a completely different way of life. The hours were a little awkward but I liked the work and earned lots of money in overtime. I spent most of my time in the sorting office with an occasional spell of collecting. In my third year there I was selected to take the Higher Grade examination. This I did, and passed. As it happened, I had also sat the Civil Service Clerical Officer exam during the year and after an initial disappointment, was accepted, and joined the Ministry of Health in November. I was to stay there until my retirement at the age of sixty-five as an executive officer.

I had only been in the Civil Service about three weeks when my mother died at her home in Croxted Road, Herne Hill. It was a bitter blow, but she was in great pain and one could not wish to see her suffer so.

Then, on 15 January 1950, our little family was joined by another daughter, Janet Ruth. She completed our trio of clever, lovely girls, of whom Elsie and I were very, very proud.

And so our lives continued and we looked forward to the days of peace and normality so long denied us. The war had been long and bitter and we had experienced privations and hardships, witnessed immense destruction of lives and property, and had lost dear friends. But we had also met new people and found kindness and generosity. Now it was time to get on with our lives again.

Appendix I
The Family Research of Janet Eaton

The following was written by Janet Eaton, Elsie and Len's youngest daughter, and details her efforts to track the Lacey/Williams family tree via historical records.

Frederick William Lacey

Ever since Dad had told me, as long ago as 1978, that our family name was not Williams, as I had always presumed, but Lacey, and that he had attended his own father's funeral believing that it was the funeral of his mother's employer for whom she took in washing, I had been completely intrigued to know more about this story.

Dad himself, with his sister Pamela, had done some research, but had come up with very little. Racking their brains for pieces of long forgotten information, they had remembered (incorrectly as it happened) that Mr Lacey had been a lawyer, and they spent many fruitless hours searching law registers for his name. They had also searched birth certificates and found, correctly, that Frederick William Lacey was the illegitimate son of Frances Lacey and had been born in Berkhamsted in 1854. Their father had told them that in his childhood he and his mother were so poor that their Christmas dinner one year consisted of only a kipper. How he could then have managed to get an education at Cambridge University and become a lawyer they had no idea, but presumed that the boy's father had acknowledged him in some way and provided for his education. Making even more presumptions, they had cast around for a local landowner with plenty of money and had landed on the Lord Carrington of the time. At the time of Dad's revelations, the current Lord Carrington did bear an uncanny resemblance to Dad, and indeed their sister Vera's middle name was Carrington. However, there is no real evidence that any of this is based on truth.

In those distant days, research was time consuming. My own researches centred on the music which Frederick William Lacey was supposed to have written, and his life as an astrologer, about which we knew some things; but I came up with very little. After Dad's death in 1986, I asked Mum several times whether she had any knowledge of Dad's father, but all she would say was that she believed that Dad's Mum and Dad had not married—she knew little else, and her relationship with Dad's family had never been a comfortable one. As far as we were all aware, no pictures of Grandad Lacey existed.

It was only after Mum had died and with the advent of the internet that I was able to take the researches any further. In about 2002, I did the classic search and entered Frederick William Lacey's name into the internet. This then led me to an astrology website, and I posted a request for any further information about his life. About this time also, I was able to find out through census records and various BMD websites, that Frederick William Lacey had existed and that his family lived in Herne Hill; also that his wife had died in 1915; but I could find no trace of a marriage between him and Ellen Bierton. Things really then came to a standstill for several years. We visited the Lacey family war graves in France, and had already visited their family plot in Norwood cemetery, but could find no other way of tracing any family descendants. We had been bemused by the fact that the same Christian names were used by both families, which did rather seem to mean a lack of imagination if nothing else!

This all changed, however, in July 2008 when I had a phone call from someone who said 'You don't know me, but my name is Florence Murphy and my mother was Mary Lacey'. To say this was a surprise was an understatement. She had absolutely no knowledge of our family, and had never suspected that we existed. To cut a very long story short, Brenda and I met up with Florence, and she was able to provide us with a huge amount of family information. More importantly, she gave us photographs and even a memoir written by her mother about their 'faithful family nurse Ellen Bierton'. She seemed to believe completely in our family story, as all the facts fitted with what she knew of her grandfather. The sad part of the story was that although Frederick William Lacey had ten legitimate children, Florence's mother and the eldest brother, Charles, were the only ones who had married and had children.

As a final footnote, the recent release of the 1911 Census has led me to discover that Frederick William Lacey completed a census return at his Herne Hill address with full details of his family and his correct age. He also completed one at Stobart Mansions, Camberwell, with details of himself and his second family, but giving his name as Frederick Williams, and deleting 13 years from his age! The population of Great Britain had been over estimated by one person, but even he couldn't disguise his handwriting. He fooled some people for his whole life, and I do wonder whether we will ever find out his true story—there's a book in there somewhere!

APPENDIX II
THE RECOLLECTIONS OF MARY LACEY

The following passages are taken from the written recollections of Mary Lacey, youngest daughter of the Lacey family (Len's father's other family). They concern her memories of Ellen (Len's mother) and Grandma Lacey (mother of Frederick William Lacey and, thus, Len's paternal grandmother). They provide a further insight into the relationships, background and motivations of Frederick William Lacey.

Ellen

My mother had a saying which she was very fond of using: 'She is one of nature's gentlewomen' meaning the person in question, though of humble birth, acted and spoke like a lady and such a person was Ellen.

She was Mother's help-cum-maid-cum-nurse, in that order, and was loved wholeheartedly by the entire family.

Ellen was the daughter of poor parents and one Saturday, when about fourteen years of age, having done the morning's shopping for her mother in pelting rain and with her boots squelching uncomfortably, due to the uppers having almost parted company with the soles, she had the temerity to ask if she could have a new pair of boots. Dinner was just finished and at her words, her father laid down his paper where he had been consulting the probable winners of the three thirty and said repressively 'If you want a new pair of boots you had better go and earn some money. Your mother hasn't any to spend on you'.

Tears sprang to Ellen's eyes at his words, uttered in such a harsh tone of voice, and she wiped them away unobtrusively, being too full of emotion to reply.

Having helped her mother to wash up the dishes, she put on her hat and coat and made her way to Brixton Public Library where she scanned the vacancies column in the local paper. There she saw my mother's advertisement for a home help and straight away went to apply for the post.

My eldest brother, then about ten years of age, answered the door and on being told her mission, shouted at the top of his voice 'Ma, there's a girl here in answer to the advertisement'.

More than once Ellen has described to me this scene that always remained in her memory. Harold, my second brother, was leaning over the banisters, watching and listening, while Charlie regarded her intently and after a short interval, Mother came and asked her indoors. She was very conscious of her squelching boots on the clean hall floor, but Mother took no notice. I don't know what was said at that interview but there must have been something about Ellen that went to Mother's heart for she was engaged on the spot and her loyalties from that moment remained with us until, years later, she left to be married, an action she deeply regretted all her life.

Trained by my mother in all domestic tasks, she became the perfect servant and in course of time, parlour maid and nurse. So much loved was she that my father had her photograph taken by a professional photographer that eventually found its way into our family album. It shows a young woman with dark hair and a face it is difficult to describe. My sister always said she had the face of a Madonna but that depends on one's individual idea of what the Madonna looked like. One's first impression on seeing her was of the perfect mother, but overall was a look of complete serenity such as I have never seen on anyone else and this expression persisted in spite of later setbacks, anxieties and poverty. She is dressed in the usual uniform of a domestic servant at that time; black dress with white embroidered cap and apron and Ellen was very proud to wear it.

She loved children and nothing pleased her more than when she learned that Mother was about to add still another baby to the family. My youngest brother, Wilfred, was her favourite, perhaps because of his intensely red hair, but mostly I think, because he was not very popular owing to a tendency to crying and getting into a flaming temper. The epithet 'cry baby' was constantly used of him as also myself but once his screaming was over he was the sunniest little soul one could wish to see. As he grew older he remained Ellen's champion - not that she ever needed one! And never missed an opportunity of visiting her when on leave during the First World War. She nearly broke her heart when the news came that he had been killed in action, the day before his twentieth birthday.

My father was an astrologer and with the late Alan Leo was co-editor of *The Astrologers' Magazine*. He had erected the horoscope of all his children, indeed, his most impressive injunction to the doctor and nurse when we were about to be born was not the care of Mother and child which he undoubtedly took for granted, but to note the exact time of birth—that is the moment 'when God breathed into him the breath of life'.

When I was about to make my entrance into the world he foretold I should be born at nine pm on March 10th and that I should be a girl. Mother, doctor, monthly nurse and Ellen all laughed at him saying it could not happen at that time but he only shrugged his shoulders at them and muttered 'Well, we shall see'. On the morning of March 10th Mother remained in bed and Ellen saw him off at the front door, after brushing his coat collar and seeing that he was fit to appear in public.

'Take your mistress up a cup of tea, Ellen, will you?' he said on leaving. She gave him a penetrating look and laughing, said 'Oh, of course, it's March the tenth!'

When he returned at dinnertime he was told he was the father of another daughter. I had been born at eighteen minutes to eleven—just nine hours earlier than he had foretold.

'How he did crow' Ellen would tell us fondly in later years and mixing her metaphors, add 'he was as pleased as a dog with two tails'.

The monthly nurse was so interested in the subject of astrology that she spent far too much time in the drawing room discussing the movements of the stars that she was given notice as soon as my mother found out (no doubt with Ellen's connivance) and Ellen was installed as my nurse from that time. This was a great advancement for her and she was well equipped for the job since by that time she was well experienced in the management of young children. My father has often described to me how she would hurry up with the work in the morning so that she could take me out in the afternoon. Perambulators were not then invented and my bassinet not yet bought but Ellen would set forth with me on her arm as proud as a queen.

Occasionally my father found it necessary to visit Paris on business and when I was about four my mother went with him leaving Ellen in charge and we had the time of our lives. She let us do all the things we liked, cooked all the dishes we most loved and I have a very vivid recollection on one occasion of us sitting round the kitchen table with the oil lamp in the centre, eating kippers for tea, followed by a fruit cake she had made specially for us. How she enjoyed herself and so did we!

It must have been shortly afterwards that she left to be married to a Mr Williams, a traveller in confectionery. She had a large family and was always very poor, so much so that after awhile she had to take in washing, much to my mother's consternation. In those days bakers would sell off all their surplus bread at a reduced price just before closing time and her children would hang round the shop waiting for the right moment to rush in and buy as much as they could afford, for bread must have been their staple diet. Our cast-off clothes were always given to her for her own children and whenever she visited us to show off her latest baby we would give her all the crusts that were left over to make a bread pudding for her hungry family.

After saddling her with eight children Mr Williams left her for good, but it seemed to me she regarded this with some relief for it meant no more babies and the older children were by then earning their own living and thus able to help her.

Nowadays people think that the poverty of those times brought great unhappiness and discontent. My experience is that riches cause just as much distress and frustration while poverty can be the means of drawing a family together. Today there is far too much insistence on material things which do not bring happiness. In Ellen's day the stress was on moral and spiritual values—everyone tried to better themselves in every way; all her children did well, three of them gaining scholarships to grammar schools and once their education had been completed she was never allowed to want for anything.

Where there is love, no matter what the home background, loyalty and devotion will flourish. After leaving our home, Ellen's children took over where we left off, giving her the care and affection we had given her. She would have been the first to admit that in spite of many privations she has been richly endowed throughout her life with blessings beyond compare.

Grandma Lacey

She was born in 1827, the youngest of five children. Her mother came of an old Berkhamsted family who were acquainted with William Cowper, the poet, himself the son of the vicar of Berkhamsted, then a very small town where everyone knew everyone. Her mother appears to have been the only member of the family to have settled in London, although she kept in touch with all her relatives and no doubt paid periodic visits to them when circumstances permitted. When one lived in Clerkenwell or Islington at that period, in spite of its being quite a nice neighbourhood with its Georgian houses and squares, an occasional visit to the country must have been a delightful change.

It is not known at what age Grandma married, but my father, her only child, was born when she was twenty-seven and she stayed in Berkhamsted with her aunt, Mrs Grover, for her lying-in. My father used to say that Berkhamsted was famous as being the birthplace of two famous men, William Cowper and himself. Alas there is no mention of him in the parish registers.

He did not remember his father and seems to have known little about him except that he died, when Father was very young, of a broken heart—a euphemism for a severe shock in those days—due to a reverse on the Stock Exchange. Grandma had a very difficult time thereafter. As so often happened in past times she was gradually forced to sell all her treasures in order to keep herself and her little son, and the few remaining pieces—various bits of china and silver and a little mahogany—are now in my possession. In course of time she took to dressmaking and as she was a beautiful needlewoman this no doubt helped to keep the wolf from the door, but such work was badly paid and my father's recollections were of the strictest economy.

For some reason her husband's family were unable or unwilling to help her and her chief succour came from her brothers for whom she had a great affection, particularly Uncle Tom, my father's favourite uncle.

In the early years they must have lived in two or three rooms where they had no kitchen for Father could remember, as a boy, taking the Sunday joint surrounded with potatoes, in a baking tin, to the local baker to be cooked—a common practice when facilities for cooking were almost non-existent for some people. He once told me she had her own way of cooking smoked haddock by placing it in a pie dish covered with a clean cloth, pouring boiling water over it and placing it on the hob, until it was done. I have tried this method myself but without success; possibly I did not give it long enough, and anyway I do not possess a hob which might make all the difference in the world.

When Father was eleven years old she married again—it is possible she was finding it more and more difficult to feed and clothe a growing boy who was always hungry, but her husband did not live long, and after his death her brother William, himself now a widower, took them into his home in Stoke Newington, and she kept house for him until he died. It must have been while she was living with Uncle William that Uncle Tom decided to go to Australia. This caused great consternation in the family, but the Laceys had always been great rovers and he was only being true to his blood. He returned a few years later laden with presents and his pockets bulging with money. I still have the carved, black ebony casket which he brought her when the ship docked at Bombay and it still bears the ugly crack caused through it being put too near the engine room. He also brought her a lovely carved ivory fan delicate as a cobweb. He was the soul of generosity and after blowing all his money he returned to Australia. A few letters were subsequently received from him and then—silence! One can picture the anguish suffered by Grandma as day by day she watched for the letter that never came. As her own father and Uncle William both died of heart trouble it is safe to assume that this was the fate of Uncle Tom, for they never received any news of him afterwards.

Looking back it is easy to understand that Grandma's life was wholly concentrated on her son. He was a gifted musician and composer of whom she was very proud, so when he announced his intention to marry my mother, one can easily sympathise with her in the circumstances. She must have felt that her whole world was about to collapse. Before, she had been all in all to him, now someone else was about to take her place in his life. The fact that my mother was a charming and attractive girl did nothing to mitigate her animosity. She was against the marriage from the start and never became reconciled to it, resolutely refusing to attend the wedding in spite of all inducements. My mother was therefore not responsible for the intense enmity that existed between them. However, in spite of her frequently repeated refusals to attend the ceremony, she did at the last moment have second thoughts and came to the church and afterwards to the reception at Grandma Odell's house (she was Mother's maternal grandma). The unlooked for appearance of the bridegroom's mother has been aptly described to me by Aunt Nell, who was a bridesmaid. 'She was dressed in deepest mourning' said my aunt. 'She wore a voluminous, black cloak that completely enveloped her person, and sometime during the reception she suddenly dived into its capacious folds and brought forth a little packet wrapped in tissue paper which she gave to your mother.' On being opened, a set of George III silver teaspoons was revealed. They are beautiful spoons and because they are now very thin with age, I use them for grapefruit as they easily cut the sections that a knife has failed to sever. I value them highly not only because of their intrinsic worth but because of their association.

As I have already said Grandma never became reconciled to my father's marriage. As far as I can tell she never saw my mother again. The pitiful part is that at no time did my father's new-found happiness affect her apart from the fact that he no longer lived with her. He visited her every week and took my eldest brother to see her as soon as he was able to walk. I have been told how, at Christmas when carving the turkey, he would place the first slices of the breast on a plate to be taken to her on Boxing Day so that she could partake of the meal—she refused to attend in person.

She died at the age of sixty-three, faithfully attended by her niece, Rosina, her sister's daughter.

Grandma Lacey must have been a very striking woman, with long black hair and dark eyes. My sister was the only member of the family to resemble her in any way, but that was only in looks - Dora could not possibly have resembled her in character. She had a gift for telling fortunes by the cards, and once told Rosina she would meet a dark man at a railway station and marry him. This came to pass a few years later; I have a photograph of them, and he is very dark. It is obvious she could not only read the cards but she must have had a strong psychical streak in her which has passed down in the family for my father was a successful astrologer and foretold my birth within nine hours.

Grandma Lacey had a very sad life, but from what I can gather it was largely her own fault as she would have derived much happiness from her numerous grandchildren had she been able to overcome her antipathy to my mother. She did not get on at all well with Rosina's mother, her sister Jane, who was a precise, prim sort of girl, while Grandma was just the opposite, full of life and probably what today we call glamour. She had more in common with her brothers who thought the world of her and she of them.

I was born long after she was laid to rest, but strangely I seem to have been the only one who ever took any interest in her. I feel we might have got on well together.

Oh, how I wish I had known her!

Appendix III
The Recollections of Sandra Pearse

The following was written by Sandra Pearse, the daughter of Pamela (Len's sister) and Karel Spálenka, the Czech bodyguard she married.

Pamela's Story

During Hitler's invasion of Europe in the Second World War, some European Royalty and foreign governments fled their countries and set up governments-in-exile in countries like the UK and various neutral countries. President Edvard Beneš of Czechoslovakia took up residence with his staff in Aston Abbey, Aston Abbotts and other places in the vicinity, and maintained an Embassy and offices in London. He was protected by Czech army security guards, who lived in Nissen huts in the village, and a secret service bodyguard, a trained marksman who accompanied the President when he left Aston Abbotts by car for London and elsewhere. His name was Karel (Charles) Spálenka.

Pamela met and later married Karel in London in 1944, and sometime in 1946 after the end of the war, returned to Prague with him, where Karel resumed life as an Editor of a major newspaper. Their happiness was to be short lived. Czechoslovakia was taken over by the communists in late 1947/early 1948, and all the people who had been loyal to the government-in-exile, and the ex-President, were rounded up and taken away—Karel being amongst them. Pamela never saw him again. She was then in great danger, being both a war bride and English to boot. Borders were being closed and people being imprisoned and she was forced by the authorities to sign a paper divorcing Karel.

The family in the UK approached the Czech underground movement through contacts, and they raised a large sum of money between them to get her out of the country. Pamela, with her young baby daughter and a few other passengers, was secretly flown out in the hold of a German Junkers aeroplane. She took only the clothes she stood up in, a few mementoes and her baby. To this day she remembers the plane as having two missing windows and how bitterly cold it was. She was met at a Kent airport by two of her sisters.

She had in a sense entered the country illegally, so had a hard time getting repatriated and obtaining a legal divorce under British law, but did so eventually and in 1953 married Hampton Roy Butcher. I, of course, was the baby. Many of the unfortunate foreign war brides left behind, remained in Czechoslovakia until the fall of communism.

Pamela often attempted to send care packages to Karel's relatives. Most were returned, or heavily censored, but in 1968 during a brief lull in the cold war under the Alexander Dubcek government, she did visit the family in Prague for a week, and subsequently a couple of relatives came for a short trip to London. Things tightened up again after this and visits and contacts ceased.

INDEX

'A-hunting we will go' (song), 163
Abbey, The, Aston Abbotts, 7, 111, 135–136, 324–325, 337–339, 379
Abinger Bottom, 172, 200
Adams (porter at Royal Arsenal Co-op), 144, 148–149
Adams, Stephen, 1844–1913 (composer), 27–28
Aerated Bread Company (ABC), 186–187
Aeronautical Inspection Department (AID), 311, 313, 354
affluence, 57, 93–94
air raids, 53–56, 84–85, 289, 320, 312–313, 328–329, 335, 340–341, 343, 349
airships (R34, R100 and R101), 112, 175–176
Airspeed AS 10 Oxford (twin-engined trainer), 277, 348
Albany Road, Southwark, 24, 53–54, 76, 165
Albert Hall, 130, 175
Alcohol, 22–24, 71, 100, 117–118, 127, 165, 197, 272, 352
Ali Baba (pantomime), 18
'All Things Bright and Beautiful' (hymn), 70
Allenby, Edmund, 1st Viscount Allenby, 1861–1936, 89
Ally Sloper's Half Holiday (comic), 65
America, 85, 182
American Girl (film), 87
Anne, 1665–1714, queen of Britain and Ireland, 44
anti-aircraft defences, 53, 55–56, 339
Ardath House (home of the Tanners), 79–80
Arkell, Mr (Kimpton Mission Superintendent), 84, 124
Armentières, 52
Arments (eel and pie shop), 20
Armistice, 98, 99
Armstrong Whitworth Whitley (bomber), 265, 267
Around the World in Eighty Days (Verne), 66

Art, 13
Artichoke (public house), 23, 29, 37, 81
Artichoke Mews, 53–54, 98
Artichoke Place, 27, 29, 36, 98, 105, 119
Ascot, 130
Ashmore, Betty, *see* Williams, Betty (LEW's sister-in-law)
Ashtead Woods, Surrey, 152
Aston Abbotts, Buckinghamshire, vii, xii, 1–8, 53, 80, 111, 122–123, 129–130, 145, 213–214, 236–238, 240–241, 312, 319, 324–325, 337–341, 348
Astrologer's Magazine, ix–x, 374
Astrology, 109, 146, 181
asylums, 47
Atlantic Road, Brixton, 19–20
Australia, 119
Auxiliary Fire Service (AFS), vii, 75, 77, 211–213, 216–226, 229–230
Avro Manchester (bomber), 272
Axten, Mrs, 92
Aylesbury Brewing Company (ABC), 338
Aylesbury, Buckinghamshire, 4, 5, 7–8, 88, 145–146, 214, 224–225, 337, 348, 356
BA Eagle (light aircraft), 308–309, 313, 319–320
'Back Home in Germany' (song), 54–55
'Back Home in Tennessee' (song), 54–55
Bacon, Ron, 287, 297, 304, 345, 349
bag-snatchers, 20
Bailey, E. H. (editor of the *British Journal of Astrology*), 109
Bairnsfather, Bruce, 1888–1959, 90
bakers, 34, 59, 69, 93
Ball games, 12
Ballad of Chevy Chase, 66–67
Ballantyne, R. M., 1825–1894 (author), 66, 113
Balliol College, Oxford, xi
balloons, 53
Bambi (1942 film), 300
Band of Hope, 23, 25–26, 71, 100, 126
Banstead Station, 126

Barker, Mrs (LEW's landlady in Shipton), 262–263, 266–267, 271, 273–275, 277, 279, 280
Barling, Mrs (Eileen Clements's employer), 132–133, 143, 145
Barnes, Fred (entertainer), 44–45
Barnstormers (theatre company), 44
Barrel-organs, 18, 26–27, 98
bassinet (pram), 83, 101, 110–111
Bath's (furniture maker), 78
Bathing, 46, 183–184
battledress, 329
Belgium, 49
'Belgium Put the Kybosh on the Kaiser' (song), 51
Benecke, F. C. (landowner), 43
Benes, Edvard, 1884–1948, 7, 324–325, 338–339, 379
Bennett (fishmonger), 35, 76–77
Berge, Fred (deputy manager of the UK Tea Company), 118, 120, 134
Berkhamsted, Hertfordshire, vii, x, 51, 109, 238, 371, 376
Bessemer Estate, 42–43
Bessemer Grange, 41
Bessemer Road, 43–44, 194–195
Bessemer, Harry, 41–42
Bethwin Road, 77
Bierton, Buckinghamshire, xi–xii, 5–6, 241
Bierton, Ellen (LEW's mother), *see* Williams, Ellen
Bierton, George (LEW's uncle), xii, 8–9, 225
Bierton, Mary (LEW's maternal grandmother), *see* Higgs, Mary
Bierton, Rebecca (LEW's maternal aunt), *see* Hornsby, Rebecca
Bierton, Sarah, 9, 214–215, 225
Bijou (amusement arcade), 45
bioscope, 22, 87
bird nesting, 74
birthdays, 148
Blackfriars, 35
Blackmail (film), 45
Blacksmiths, 33–34, 74
Blake, Mrs (friend of Ellen Williams), 40, 148, 157–158

Blenheim, *see* Bristol Blenheim (bomber)
Blitz, the, *see* bombing
'Blow away the morning dew' (traditional melody), 155
'Blow, blow, blow, like a pair of bellows blow' (song), 113–114
Boat Race, The, 56, 84–85, 192
boating, 73
Boer War, 49
BoLoBo (camp in Middlesex), 176
Bombing, 38, 53–54, 87, 192, 234–239, 243, 245, 256, 289, 320, 335, 340–341, 343, 349
Bon Marche, 19–20
Bookkeeping, 119–120, 148, 151–152, 154
bookmakers, 90
Boothby, Miss (Sunday school teacher), 176, 180, 184, 191, 206
Borough Market, Southwark, 21, 107–108
Bottomley, Horatio, 1860–1933, 64–65
Bowyer House, 35
Box Hill, Surrey, 148, 165–166, 168, 171, 176
Boxing Day, 157
Boy Scout Tests, 184
Boy Scouts, *see* Scouts
Boy's Own Paper, 65
Boys' Brigade, 27, 43, 113, 125–126, 128–129, 132, 134, 176
Bradshaw, Maisie (neighbour of the Vinings), 63, 69
Bradshaw, Mrs (neighbour of the Vinings), 63
Brand, Lewis (first grocery hand, Royal Arsenal Co-op), 139–140
Breighton, Yorkshire, *see* RAF Breighton
Brighton, 82–83, 196
'Bringing in the sheaves' (song), 27
Bristol, 285–286
Bristol Blenheim (bomber), 285, 346
British Aircraft Eagle, *see* BA Eagle
British Israel Movement, 176
British Journal of Astrology, 109
British Museum, 148, 161
British Summer Time, 79

Brixton, xii, 19–20, 44, 53–54, 204, 234, 255, 300
Brixton Astoria (cinema), 168, 255
Brixton Theatre, 183
Brockwell Park, 78
Brook, The (poem by Tennyson), 66–67
Brooks, Bill (LEW's brother-in-law), 226, 232, 292, 337
'Brown bread, brown bread, brown bread, brown bread' (song), 3
Brunswick Park, 1, 25, 46–47, 110–111, 137
Brunswick Square, 103
bubonic plague, 42
Buckingham Palace, 32–33
Buckinghamshire, 6
Buckshee Bunce (rabbit), 18
Buff Place, 77, 139
Buffaloes, see Royal Antidiluvian Order of Buffaloes
Bull and Butcher (pub), Aston Abbotts, 5, 8, 338
Bull family (No. 22, Stobart Mansions), 132, 138
Bullace Row, 77
Bunn, C. J. (newsagent), 39, 116
buses, 29, 46, 52, 54, 56, 134–135
butchers, 77, 80
butterflies, 82–83
Byng, Douglas Coy, 1893–1987, 315
Cadbury's (confectioner), 24–25, 72
'Cairo' sergeants, 346–347
Calshot, Hampshire, 268–270
Camberwell, vii, xiii–xiv, 35, 42–44, 46–47, 51, 57, 94, 342, 359
Camberwell Arms (public house), 34
Camberwell Baths, 29, 37, 46, 98, 105, 155
Camberwell Beauty (butterfly), 38
Camberwell Brotherhood Sick and Sharing-out Society, 152–153
Camberwell Club, 37
Camberwell Council, 78–79
Camberwell Farm, 35
Camberwell Gate, 20, 76
Camberwell Green, 19–20, 29, 34, 36–37, 40, 43, 45, 51–52, 67–68, 73–74, 76–77, 79, 85–86, 110–111, 119–120, 127, 134–135, 138–139, 203

Camberwell Grove, 37–40, 62, 69, 102–104, 116
Camberwell Gun Brigade, 51–52
Camberwell House (asylum), 47, 143
Camberwell Mill, 77
Camberwell New Road, 35, 73, 127, 152–153
Camberwell Nursery, 40, 57, 69
Camberwell Palace, 44, 314–315
Camberwell Road, 18, 36, 64, 77, 102
Camberwell tram depot, 76
'Camberwell, Past and Present' (lectures), 125
Cambridge House (social centre), 77
Campbell Connolly (music publishers), 124–125
Camping, 126, 161–162, 169, 171–172, 175–176, 192–193, 195–196, 203, 205
Canadian Coventry Climax (pump), 224
Canadian Pacific Railway, 136
Canning Passage, Camberwell, 39
Canning Place, 40
canvassing, 134
card games, 71
Cardington, 112, 237–240, 242
Carlton, Ferris (stage name of Mr Clements), 143
Carr's Baptist Chapel, 44
Catfoss, see RAF Catfoss
cats, 89–90
Catterick, North Yorkshire, see RAF Catterick
cellarmen, 21
chair-repairer, 17
Chamberlain, Joseph, 1836–1914, 38–39, 104–105
Chamberlain, Neville, 1869–1940, 328
Champion Hill, 41–42
Champion Hill Estate, 26
Champion Park, 39, 40
Chaplin, Charlie, 81–82, 114
Chaplin, Sydney, 82
Chapman, Mr (milkman, LEW's employer), 102–105
charity workers, 34
Charles Edward Brooke (grammar school), 69–70, 108

Charley's Aunt (Thomas), 82
check-taking, 177, 202
cherry cider, 24
Chevy Chase, The Ballad of, 66–67
Chilblains, 72–73
Child's Book of Verse, 66–67
Children's games and pastimes, *see* Games and pastimes, children's
'Children's Home' (Victorian parlour song), 148, 156
Chinn, Mrs (of 'Ilkley'), 317–319
Chips (comic), 65
Chivers' marmalade, 25, 64
chocolate, 24–25, 264, 333–334, 336
cholera, 42
Choumert Road, Peckham, 148
Christianity, 34
'Christians seek ye not repose' (hymn), 156
Christmas, 71–72, 89, 91, 99, 100, 104, 113, 138, 143, 154–155, 157–158, 176–177, 182, 190, 197, 202, 229–230, 246–247, 279–280, 298–300, 325–326, 347–349, 367
Christmas cards, 157
Church Street, Camberwell, ix, 29–30, 32, 37, 45, 51–54, 70–71, 93–94, 102–103, 106–107, 113, 117, 130, 146–147
Churchill, Rt. Hon. Sir Winston, 51, 292, 361
cigarette cards, 12
cigarettes/tobacco, 111, 141, 148–149, 151, 166, 187–188, 245–246, 280, 333–334, 336
Cinderella, 3
Cinema, 35, 81–82, 87, 94–95, 114, 125, 139, 143, 148, 166–168, 176, 180, 183–184, 202, 204, 215–216, 270, 273–274, 288, 300, 304, 351, 365–366
Clapham, 50–51
Clarke, Mr (manager of the Camberwell Green Co-operative), 152, 154, 188, 197
class, 140
Clemance Hall (mission), 46
Clements, Cecilia, 143
Clements, Eileen, 126, 132–133, 138, 141–148, 153, 158, 161–163

Clements, Jim, 106, 125–126, 132–133, 143, 153
Clements, Pete, 106, 125–126, 132–134, 143, 153
Clements, Winifred, 143
Climax (accounting system), 159
Clipper of the Clouds (Verne), 66
clocks, 105
clothing, 63, 147
Co-operative Society, vii, 35–36, 77, 102, 120, 136–142, 147–155, 157, 159–161, 163, 166, 167, 179–180, 189–190, 197, 199–202, 204, 206–207, 210–211, 229, 231, 234, 236, 259, 274, 282–283, 292–293, 313, 342, 368
Co-operative Union Scholarship, 150
Coal, 21, 88–89, 327
coalmen, 21, 31–32
Coca Cola, 24
Cockerton, Tommy, 89
Codd, Hiram, 1838–1887 (inventor of Codd bottle), 24
'Codds' (bottles), 24
coins, 83–84, 127–128, 264, 271, 274
Colbourne, Sgt., 331–334, 337, 353–356
cold, LEW's fear and dislike of, 10, 72, 91, 164, 249
Coldharbour Lane, Camberwell, 37–38, 44, 59, 69, 75, 79, 113, 134, 184
Coleman, Tim (footballer), 41
Coles Cranes, 266, 273
Coles family, 144
Collard, Mr (resident of No. 9, Stobart Mansions), 165
Collins, Michael (manager of Camberwell Green Co-operative), 139–140, 150, 152
comics, 18
commando training, 301–302, 352–353
Commonwealth Party, 358–359
Confectioners, 37, 50–51, 90–91
Confectionery, 24–25, 50–51, 375
Congo, 129
conscription, 57
Cooke, Albert (proprietor of shop at Leith Hill Place), 171–173, 175, 185, 192, 194–196, 198, 200, 202
Coral Island (Ballantyne), 66, 113
corn and seed merchants, 37

corporal punishment, 58, 115
corporal, LEW promoted to rank of, 295
Cosford, *see* RAF Cosford
costermongers, 16–17
costume, 72–73, 73
Country Holiday Fund, 82, 87–88, 96, 107, 326
court appearance, 124–125
Covent Garden, 107–108
Craigallon Gardens, 47
Cranfield Gardens, 143
Crawford Street school, 112, 119
Crawley, 252–253, 256
Crebor Street, East Dulwich, 293, 295, 314, 339–340, 350–351, 363
Cricket, 43, 56, 63–64, 73, 84–85, 118–119, 143, 148
crime, 20, 23, 77, 160, 204, 343, 348
Crocker, Emily (Kimpton Mission girl), 128–129
Crocker, Eva (Kimpton Mission girl), 128–129, 186–187, 200
Cross, Ena, 137
Crown Street, 18, 77, 103–104
Croxted Road, 78
Crumpsall, Greater Manchester, 151
Crystal Palace, Sydenham, 55–56, 97–98, 121–122, 171, 174, 196, 201, 234–235
Cuffley, Hertfordshire, 54–55
Cumberland Jack (token), 128
Curran, Ivy, 186–187, 193–194
Cycling, 121–123, 134–136, 237–238, 297, 330, 354
D-Day Landings, 335–336, 338
D'Eynsford Road, 14, 32, 93
Dagmar Road, 115
Daily Chronicle, 115
Daily Herald, 175, 182
dairies, 34, 37–38, 77, 84, 111
Dane House, 43
Daneville Road, 59
Dardanelles, 53
Darling, Grace Horsley, 1815–1842, heroine, 27
Datchelor Place, Camberwell, 37
Datchelor, Mary, *see* Mary Datchelor School for Girls
David Copperfield, 66

Dawson, Leslie ('Les'), 313–319, 322–323, 330–331, 349, 352, 359
Daylight Savings Bill, 79
De Crespigny Park, 40, 57
De Havilland DH 82 Tiger Moth, *see* Tiger Moth
Deal, Kent, 2–3, 362, 368
'Dear Homeland' (song), 108–109
debt, 80
Defence of the Realm Act (DORA), 84, 272
delivery boy, LEW works as, 116
Demobilisation, 357, 362, 367
Den Contact (Tim Squires's magazine), 229
Denmark Hill, 37–38, 40–43, 57, 59, 68–69, 116, 142, 206–207
Denmark Hill Grammar School, 44
Denmark Hill School, vii, 57, 100, 107, 115
Denmark Hill Station, 39
Denmark House, 44
Denner, Harold ('Reg'), 141, 144, 147–150, 154–158, 161–164, 167–168, 173, 176–178, 180, 183–185, 192, 194, 197–198, 203–206, 211, 242, 246, 249–250, 259, 280, 287–288, 297, 344, 365–366
Denner, Hilda, 162–163, 167–168, 173, 176, 178, 180, 183, 185, 192, 203–204, 242, 249–250, 259, 266, 280, 287–288, 344, 365–366
Denner, Jim, 154, 204
Denny, Reginald, 1891–1967 (actor), 141
Dents (provision shop), 35
'Derby Brights' (type of coal), 21
Derby Day, 183
diaries, 184, 201
Dickens, Charles, 1812–1870, 37, 39, 66, 204
diet and food, 9, 33–34, 53, 58–60, 71–72, 80, 82, 84–85, 88–89, 92–93, 95, 101, 104, 315
dining rooms, 37
diptheria, 42, 136–137
Dishforth, North Yorkshire; *see* RAF Dishforth
Ditchling, East Sussex, 203

Dividends, 159–161, 199
Dog Kennel Hill, 40–41, 96–97, 112, 195, 201
domestic service, 26, 132–133
Donnington Castle, 96
DORA, see Defence of the Realm Act (DORA)
Dornan, Ethel ('Aunt Ethel'), 50–51, 129–130
Doyle, Arthur Conan, 1859–1930, 45, 125, 175
DR6 (warrant), 321–322
draymen, 21
Dreamland (amusement arcade), 175
drunkenness, LEW's resentment of, 22–24
Duff Place, Camberwell, 35–36
Dulwich, 16, 73–74, 93–94, 97, 176, 357
Dulwich, 42, 96
Dulwich Hamlet (football club), 41, 118–119
Dunkirk, 232
Dunkleigh (AFS), 219–224
Dunnington, Miss, see Mardale
Durlstone Manor, 26
Durrant, Joan (resident of Kimpton Road), 256
Dymchurch, Kent, 149
Earls Colne, see RAF Earls Colne
East Dulwich, 40, 293, 295
East Kent Bus Company, 149
East Street, 76
Eaton, Janet, vii, 369, 371–372
Education, 92–93, 115, 123, 143–144, 158, 254
Edwards (pork butchers), 45
Edwards' Desiccated Soup, 59
eels, 20
Egypt, 132
Electric Avenue, Brixton, 19–20
Electricity, 15, 31–33, 65, 157–158
Elephant and Castle, 20
Elliot, Maud (LEW's Australian classmate), 67
Elmington Road, 46
Elsey, Arthur J., 1860–1952 (painter), 13
Embassy Skating Rink, 69

emigration, 119
Empire Cinema ('Metropole'), 44, 180
engagement to Elsie Squires, 181–182
ENSA, 269, 290, 305, 315
Ensor, Sgt., 332
entertainment, 44
Epsom Downs, 148, 183–185, 201
Essex, 55
Evacuation, 58, 213–216, 228, 236, 342
Evemy, Ivy, 130
Evemy, Mrs (Ellen Williams's friend from Aston Abbotts), 129–130
evening classes, 123, 148, 154
'Evergreen', 245, 253, 258–259, 266, 269–270, 278, 283, 286, 289
Exploits of Elaine (film serial), 87
Express Dairies, 102
Extension, The, to Ruskin Park, 43, 57, 106
Fairbanks, Douglas, 1883–1939, 114
Family Journal, The, 64–65
'Farmer wants a Wife' (game), 12
Farmers and Cleveland Dairy, 18, 77, 102
Father Red Cap (hostelry, Camberwell), 35, 76
Fenner's (greengrocers), 84, 98, 107–108, 112, 123–124, 132, 18
Ferguson, Elsie, 1883–1961, 114
Ferndene Road, 43
FIDO (Fog Investigation and Dispersal Operation / 'Fog Intense Dispersal Of'), 345
Fields, Gracie, 1898–1979, 151
Finsbury, 56
fire alarms, lever-operated, 74
fire hydrants, 74–75
Firs, The, 6, 8
First Surrey Rifles, 51–52
First World War, 36, 38, 43, 47, 49, 50–51, 67, 68–69, 71, 75–76, 79, 81, 85, 87–89, 92, 96, 98, 111, 115, 136–137
First World War, effect on LEW's education, 115
fish, 19
Fisher, B. B. (slate club secretary), 91, 113–114
Fisher, Mrs (of 20 Stobart Mansions), 110–111

Fishing, 77–78
fishmongers, 35, 80
Fitzherbert, Maria Anne, 1756–1837, 38
Five-stones, 11
Flaked Maize, 59
Flanders, 52, 192
fleas, 42
'Flight of the Earls', 107
Flodden Road, 51–52
flu, *see* influenza
flying, 299
Flying Scotsman, 260, 267
Flynn, Mrs (landlady at No. 4 Garden Cottages, Sandgate), 149–150
Folkestone, Kent, 149–150, 178
food, *see* diet and food
football, 43, 56, 64, 118–119, 124–125, 148–149
Forest Hill, 40, 96
Forfarshire (steamer wrecked in 1838), 27
Fortune-telling, 109, 260
Fouracre, John ('Johnny'), 285–287, 295, 297, 309, 312–313
Fowler Street, 16
Fox Under the Hill (hostelry), 43
France, 56, 81
Franz, Ontario, 136
Free French officers, 333–334, 339, 341
Free Salvationists, 27
freemasonry, 109, 188–189
friendly societies, 152–153
Froggy's Little Brother, 94
'From Greenland's Icy Mountains' (hymn), 81–82
Frost's (grocery and provisions store), 89, 126–127
fruiterers, 34, 51–52
Fry, Mr and Mrs (relatives of Johnny Fouracre), 286–287
Fuller Medley's (shop), 37, 83, 107–108, 132
Funny Wonder (comic), 65
Furniture and furnishings, 12, 206–207
Fussell, Ivy (Con's friend), 108–109
Fussell, Mr (heavy-handed pianist), 108–109
Gads Hill, Kent, 37

Galloway, Mr (manager of the UK Tea Company), 118, 120, 124, 127, 133–135, 138–139
Games and pastimes, children's, 11–12, 30, 62, 65, 89, 96
gardener, LEW employed as, 116
Gardiner, Ron (conductor of Kimpton Choir), 154, 163–164, 242, 245, 252–253, 259, 266, 280, 289, 293, 320–321, 343–344, 355
Garforth, West Yorkshire, 271–273
gas and gas appliances, 14–15, 31–33, 65
General Post Office (GPO), vii, 368
General Strike, 1926, 107, 134–135
George Canning (public house), 39
George IV, 38
George Street, Camberwell, 27, 77
George V, 203
George, Prince of Denmark, 1653–1708, 44
Georgian houses, 40–41, 93–94, 97, 236–237
Germany, 49, 71
Germolene, 130
Ghosts (play by Frank Thompson), 137
Girls' Club (Kimpton Mission), 85, 186–187
Girls' Life Brigade, 105–106, 128–129, 142, 162–163, 176, 178, 191, 195–198, 200, 203–204, 207, 211, 256, 320–321
Gish, Lillian, 1893–1993, 114
Glebe, The, 40–41, 96–97
'God Rest Ye Merry Gentlemen' (carol), 71
Godstone, xi
Godwin, Winnie (resident of Kimpton Road), 256
Gold Standard, 181
Golden Domes (cinema), 45, 125, 180
Good Companions (film), 273–274
'Goodbye-ee' (song), 85
Goose Green, 112
'Gooseberry Tree' (monologue), 282
Gotha (German bomber), 55
'Grace Darling' (song), 27
gramophones, 143
Grand Hall, Camberwell (cinema), 35
Grand Union Canal system, 77–78

Grandad's Army, 69, 69
Grange Estate, 41–42
Great Expectations, 39, 204
Great Orchard Row, Camberwell, 35–36
'Green Eye of the Little Yellow God' (monologue), 109
Green Lane, 41, 74, 147
Greencoat School, 19, 34, 36, 76
Greengrocers, 21, 34, 84
Greens Row, Camberwell, 35–36
Gresham Road, Brixton, 19–20
Grewer, Mr and Mrs, 283, 283
Grey, Zane, 1872–1939, 183–184
Greyhound, Dulwich Village (tavern), 37
grocers and the grocery trade, 34, 77, 117–119, 124, 126–127
Grove Hill, 39
Grove House Tavern, 37–38, 84
Grove Lane, Camberwell, 34, 37, 39–40, 46, 49, 57, 62–63, 68–69, 74, 89–91, 96–97, 112, 116, 122–123, 142, 227
Grove Park, Camberwell, 39, 47
Grove Vale, 25–26, 112
Guildford Place, Camberwell, 35–36, 77
Guinness Buildings, Hammersmith, 129–130
Haberdashers (Worshipful Company of Haberdashers), 37
Hale, Binnie, 1899–1984 (actress), 167, 315
Hale, Sonnie, 1902–1959 (actor), 167
Halifax bomber, *see* Handley Page Halifax
Hall, Mr (Staff Manager, Royal Arsenal Co-operative Society), 138–139
Halsey, Frank, xii–xiii, 123, 130, 145, 146
Hamilcar (glider), 327
Hammersmith, 129–130
Hammerton's Stout, 23–24, 117
Hampshire (cruiser), 81
Hampton Court, 54–55
Handley Page factory, Rawcliffe, 279, 281–283, 289
Handley Page Halifax (bomber), 279, 287, 296–297, 301, 310–312, 317–318, 322–325, 327, 332–334, 336, 339–343, 347

Handley Page Hereford (aircraft), 302–306
'Hardy's Own' (scout troop), 41
Harris Street, 163, 166, 196
Harris's (baby pram specialists), 62–63, 122–123
Hart, William S. (William Surrey), 1864–1946, 114
Hartley's Marmalade, 25
Harvey Road, Camberwell, 23–24, 46
Haslemere Road, 69–70
Hastings, East Sussex, 178
Havisham, Miss (character in Great Expectations), 39
Hawker Typhoon (fighter), 341
Hayes Common, 121–122
Hayes Court, 36
Hayes Laundry, 69, 79–80
Hayes, Annie (friend from Stobart Mansions), 277–278
Healey, Alf (Kimpton Mission boy), 62
Heber, Reginald, 1783–1826, 81–82
Hednesford, Staffs., *see* RAF Hednesford
Henehey's (public house), 44–45
Henekeys in the Strand, x
hens, 30, 33
Henty, George Alfred, 1832–1902 (novelist), 66
Hereford, *see* Handley Page Hereford
Hermit's Cave (public house), 23, 37, 81, 89, 98
Hermitage, The (convalescent home in Hastings), 178
Herne Hill, xii, 43, 78, 211–212, 232, 234, 237, 241–242, 253, 255, 259, 277–278, 292, 299–300, 314–315, 340, 359–360, 365–366, 369, 371–372
hide-and-seek, 11
Higgs (LEW's maternal grandfather), xi–xii
Higgs, Mary (LEW's maternal grandmother), xi–xiii, 1–3, 6, 8, 10, 88, 123, 130, 145–146, 153
Hiking, 161–162, 166, 169–170, 182
Hiking for Boys, 161–162
Hills, Mr and Mrs (LEW's teachers), 115

Hippodrome, London (theatre), 167
Hitchcock, Alfred, 1899–1980, 45, 280–281
HMS Barham (battleship), 280–281
HMS Hood (battlecruiser), 278
HMS Prince of Wales (battleship), 278
Hodgkins, Herbert, 136
Hodgkins, Mary (LEW's cousin), 136
Hodgkins, Stanley, 136
hokey-pokey (forerunner of ice cream), 25
Holborn, 56
Holdaway, Harold, 124–125, 218–219
Holidays, 3–4, 8–10, 82, 96, 123, 135, 146–147, 149–150, 162, 165–166, 168–175, 178–179, 201, 205, 210, 213, 318–319, 361–362, 368
Holloway, 75
Holloway, Stanley, 1890–1982, 315
Home and Colonial Stores, 95
'Homeland' (song), 163–164
Honours Board, 70
Hood (battlecruiser), *see HMS Hood*
Hood, Thomas, 1799–1845, 36
hooliganism, 134–135
hoops, 11–12
hopscotch, 11
'Horatio Sparkins' (story by Dickens), 37
Hornsby, Elizabeth ('Lizzie'), *see* Marks, Elizabeth ('Lizzie', LEW's cousin)
Hornsby, Joseph (LEW's cousin), 136, 147
Hornsby, Joseph (LEW's uncle), xii, 111–112, 135–139, 141, 159, 194, 201, 240, 243
Hornsby, Mary, *see* Hodgkins, Mary (LEW's cousin)
Hornsby, Rebecca (LEW's maternal aunt), xii, 8, 111–112, 135–136, 147, 194, 201, 240
horoscopes, 146
Horses, 2, 5, 21, 29, 33–34, 40, 56, 103, 107–108, 119
Horsley's Stores, 37, 45
House, Sidney (husband of Eileen Williams), 141, 147, 152, 167, 191, 197, 201, 211–212, 232, 242, 273, 278, 329–330, 362
Housework, 13–14, 17, 27, 61–62, 101

Hove, Sussex, 82–83
Howard, Mr and Mrs (LEW's teachers), 115
Hudson's Soap Powder, 14, 60, 127
Hughes, Thomas, 1822–1896, 150
Hulcott, Buckinghamshire, 6
Hull, 304
hunger, 59, 181
Hunsdon, Hertfordshire, *see* RAF Hunsdon
Hurst, Dolly, 167, 206
Hutton Cranswick, *see* RAF Hutton Cranswick
Hydraulics, 289, 306, 347
hygiene, 93
Hythe Canal, 149
'I'm a navvy, I'm a navvy working on the line' (song), 20–21
'I'm on Tom Tiddler's Ground' (game), 12
'I'm so glad that our father in heaven' ('Jesus loves me'), 81
ice cream, 25
Il Trovatore (opera), 123
Ilfracombe, Devon, 184
Illingworth, Miss, *see* Mardale
Income, 100–101, 103–104, 115–117, 119, 124, 128–129, 133–134, 138, 141, 147–148, 176–177, 180, 187, 196, 200, 255, 257, 271, 282, 286, 291, 295, 358, 368
income tax, 180
India, 132–133, 148–149, 176–177, 347
indicator board, 26
industrial unrest, 95, 133–134
inferiority complex, 137, 291
Influenza, 104–105, 138, 152–153, 182–183, 312, 357, 364
insurance, 152–153
invasion, fear of, 92
Ireland, 104
Irlam, Greater Manchester, 151
ironmongers, 45
Irthlingborough, Northamptonshire, 136, 194
Islington, 56
Isthmian [Football] League, 41
itinerant steet traders, *see* street traders

'J for Jonah' (Halifax bomber), 323, 325–326
Jackson, Mr (milk roundsman), 105
Jackson's Dairies, 18
Jackson's Varnish Stain, 17, 110
Jacob, Alf (fruiterer), 90, 132
Jarrod (fishmonger), 90
Jephson Street (formerly Wilby Road), 47, 89
John Bull, 64–65
Johnson, Amy, 1903–1941, 175–176
Johnson, Dr, 70
'Jolly Good Company' (song), 198
Jonah, *see* 'J for Jonah'
Jones, Mr (Boys' Life Brigade bandmaster), 129
Jones, Samuel (maker of gummed paper), 38
Junior Leaders' Course, 348–349, 352–353
Kail, Edgar (footballer), 41
Kaiser, The, *see* Wilhelm II
Karno, Fred, 81–82
'Keep the Home-Fires Burning' (song), 64
Kennedy's, 37
Kennet (river), 96, 107
Kennington, 3, 112, 114
Kennington Theatre, Kennington Park Road, 3
Kent, 121–122
Kent, Ned (carrier), 4–5
Kent, Ted, 281, 292, 315, 349
Kerfield Arms (pub), 90
Kerfield Crescent, 75–76, 90
Kerfield Mews, 63–64
Kersall, Nottinghamshire, 150–151
Kimbolton Castle, 136
Kimpton Mission, vii, vii, xi, 13, 18, 23, 25–26, 34, 53, 62, 64–68, 71, 77, 79, 82–83, 85, 89, 91–93, 96, 100, 102, 104–107, 111–114, 122, 124, 128–129, 132, 134, 137, 143, 148, 153–154, 156–157, 162–164, 166, 173, 176, 180, 182, 184–188, 191, 196–202, 205–207, 229, 259, 287–288, 292, 296, 351
Kimpton Road, Camberwell, vii, 14, 16, 29–30, 32–34, 46, 60–61, 67–68, 93–94, 106, 119, 135, 162, 256

Kimpton Village, Hertfordshire, 32
King George Street, *see* Lomond Grove, Camberwell
'King Without a Crown' (song by F. W. Lacey), 121
King's College Hospital, 19, 43–44, 57, 68–69, 194–195
Kingsmead Road, 85–87, 101–102, 120–121, 189
Kissach, Mr (superintendent, North London Home for the Blind), 220–223, 225–226, 229–230
Kitbag Hill and Kitbag Halt, 248, 255–256, 258
'Kitchen Nuts' (type of coal), 21, 31
Kitchener, Herbert, Earl, 1850–1916, 49, 56, 81
Knatchbull Road, 85
knife-cleaner, 17
Knight (grocer), 116
Knocker, Cecil ('Fred'), 137–138, 200
Knocker, Mabel, 137–139, 141–143, 146, 148, 158, 161, 164, 182, 197, 200, 281
Kranz the Baker, 14, 54, 93
Kut el Amara, 53, 92
Labour Exchange, 115, 119–120
Labour Party, 136, 201–202
Lacey, Charles (F. W. Lacey's son), xi, xiii, 85, 129, 189, 372–374
Lacey, Dora (F. W. Lacey's daughter), xi–xiii, 85, 189
Lacey, Florence (F. W. Lacey's wife), xi–xii, 85
Lacey, Frances (LEW's paternal grandmother), x–xi, 109, 371, 376–378
Lacey, Frederick William (LEW's father)
  astrologer, ix–x, 109, 146, 371, 374–375
  attitude to and treatment of LEW and siblings, x, 49–50, 88–89, 123, 131, 136–137, 176–177
  composer, 121
  death and funeral, xiii–xiv, 187–188, 371
  financial affairs and difficulties, 49–51, 80, 176–177, 180
  Freemason, ix–x, xiii–xiv, 131, 188–189
  injured in road accident, 130, 168

leads double life, ix–x, 85, 189, 372
marriage, xi
organist, ix–x, 51, 121, 130, 168, 179
parentage, early life and education, xi, 371
physical appearance, habits, ix–x, xiii
relationship with LEW's mother, xii
see also, vii, 3–4, 10–11, 19, 23–24, 27–28, 41, 46, 49–52, 65, 70–72, 76–77, 80, 85, 88–90, 93, 95, 101, 105, 108, 111–112, 115–116, 119, 123–125, 128–130, 133, 135, 138–139, 144, 146, 148–149, 155, 164, 167, 180, 182, 186–190
Lacey, Harold Ernest (F. W. Lacey's son), xi–xii, 85
Lacey, Mary (F. W. Lacey's daughter), xi–xiii, 85, 189, 372–373
Lacey, Muriel, xi, xiii, 189
Lambeth, 43–44, 78, 81–82
Lambeth Council, xii
lamplighters, 32–33
Lancashire, 151
Lancaster, Lew, 280–281
Land Army girls, 312, 325
Langley House, 40
Laundry, 14, 59–62, 85–86, 98
Laurie's Marmalade, 25
Lava Skating Rink, 69
Laye, Evelyn, 1900–1996 (actress), 290
Leas Cliff Hall, 178
Leave, 250, 252–253, 255–258, 266–267, 269, 274, 282–283, 293, 295, 297–300, 309, 311, 313–314, 328, 335, 337, 339, 343–344, 348–353, 356, 359–361, 364–366
lectures, 125
Leeds, 265, 271–272, 274
Leith Hill Tower, 166, 170–171, 173–174, 185, 192, 195–196, 200
Lemco, 86
lemonade, 24
Lenthal, Ted, 274–275, 280
Leo, Alan (astrologer and co-founder with F. W. Lacey of the *Astrologer's Magazine*), ix–x, 109

Leonard, Sergeant (LEW's CO), 262, 265
Lettsom Street, Camberwell, 39, 62
Lettsom, Dr John Coakley, 1744–1815 (Quaker, philanthropist), 38–39
Lever Brothers, xi, 50, 60, 129
Levine, Sam, 271, 275–277, 279, 292–293
licensing laws, 81
Lifebuoy (soap), 93
lighting, 31–32
Lilac Time (operetta), 183
'Lili Marlene' (German song), 330
Lindholme, *see* RAF Lindholme
Lines Hill, 7–8, 319, 337, 342, 348
linoleum, 15
Linton-on-Ouse, North Yorkshire, *see* RAF Linton-on-Ouse
Lissett, Humberside, *see* RAF Lissett
'Little Fan' (monologue), 109
'Little Orphan Annie' (poem), 100
Littlehampton, West Sussex, xiii, 187–188
living standards, 34, 34, 47, 49–50, 144
Lloyd George Insurance Stamp, 152–153
Lloyd George, David, 1st earl Lloyd-George, 1863–1945, 99
Loader, Alf (AFS), 222
Lockheed Electra ('City of Chicago'), 275
Lockheed factory, Leamington Spa, 289–290
Lomond Grove, Camberwell, 34
London, 53, 55
London Choir School, 40, 134
London County Council, 41, 43, 115, 148, 201–202, 205, 212
London Fire Brigade, 74–75, 180, 224
London Transport, 199, 206
London, Chatham and Dover Railway, 35, 97
Longstone lighthouse, 27
'Looking for ale, yes, looking for ale' (song), 81
'Lost Chord' (Sullivan), 137–138
Lost World, The (Doyle), 45, 125, 175
Lost World, The (film), 45, 125
Lots of Fun (comic), 65
Loughborough House, 37–38
Loughborough Junction, 79–80

Love Walk, Camberwell, 37–38, 46, 63–64, 74
'Love's Old Sweet Song' (Molloy), 137, 145
Lowenfeldt, 'a Belgian millionaire', 8
Lowenstein, Alfred, 1877–1928, 8
Ludo, 71
Lugard Street, Peckham, 16
Lux Flakes, 60, 127
Lyle's Golden Syrup, 127
Lyndhurst Grove School, Peckham, vii, 57–58, 100, 107
Lyndhurst Grove, Camberwell, 34, 58, 102–103, 206
Lyons & Co., 187
Lytcott, Colonel, 42
MacCarthy, Cecil ('Boy'), 226–227, 232–233, 245, 292, 329–330, 348
MacDonald, James Ramsay, 1866–1937, 180
Madame Tussauds, 161
Malley, Miss (secretary and deputy of the Kimpton Mission's Band of Hope), 23
malnutrition, 58
Manchester, 150–151
Manchester bomber, *see* Avro Manchester (bomber)
Mansion Street, Camberwell, 35
marbles, 11, 24
Mardale (LEW's billet in Tollerton), vii, 210, 284–285, 294–301, 308–311, 313, 316, 318–319, 331, 339–340, 343–344, 346, 348–353, 360, 364, 366–367
margarine, 151
Margate, Kent, 175, 179–180, 206
Maria Marten; or, *Murder in the Red Barn*, 44–45
markets and market stalls, 19, 20, 34, 110, 157
Marks and Spencer's 'Bazaar', 19–20
Marks, Denys (son of Thomas and Lizzie Marks), 136
Marks, Elizabeth ('Lizzie', LEW's cousin), 136
Marks, Thomas, 136–137
marmalade, 25, 127, 334

Marmite factory, Camberwell, 19, 34
marriage of LEW and Elsie Squires, 46, 203–207
Married in Hollywood (film), 166
Marryat, Frederick, 1792–1848, 91–92
Marshall, Florence (F. W. Lacey's wife), *see* Lacey, Florence
Marston Moor, *see* RAF Marston Moor
Mary Datchelor School for Girls, 37, 49, 90
Marylebone Spiritualist Association, 175
Mason, Lily (Reg Williams's girlfriend), 132, 186
Mason, Titch (Lily Mason's brother), 132
Masterman Ready (Marryat), 91–92
Matthews, Biddy, 200
Matthews, Miss (leader of the Kimpton Mission's Women's Meeting), 90, 107–108
Mazzard Row, Camberwell, 35–36, 77, 139
McKenzie, Mr H. (Kimpton Mission Secretary), 91
McNeil Road, 46–47
McPhun, Mrs (Kimpton Mission lady), 129–130, 277–278
Meccano, 113
Medical Society of London, 39
Medlar Street, Camberwell, 35, 47, 336
Melhuish (flour miller), 35
'Melody in F' (Rubinstein), 132
Mendelssohn, Felix, 1809–1947, 43
Mentmore, Buckinghamshire, 7–8
Merchant of Venice, 66
Merry and Bright (comic), 65
Methodist services, 296, 301, 308
Metropole, The, *see* Empire Cinema
Metropolitan Line, 3–4
Metropolitan Police, 153
Milkmen, 17–18, 31, 77, 102–104
Milkwood Road, 85–86
Milton Ernest, Bedfordshire, 135
mineral water factory, Grove Lane, 90
miners' strikes, 133–135, 330
Ministry of Health, vii, 368–369
Ministry of Pensions, 43, 57

Minnie (Williams's cat), 89–90, 129
mission halls, 23, 26–27
Mitchell's (greengrocers), 18
mobile workshops, 262, 310, 313, 321–322, 329, 339, 347
Moffet, Miss (of the Girls' Life Brigade), 204
Molloy, James Lynam, 1837–1909 (composer), 137, 145
money-lenders, ix, 34, 80
Monypepper, 38
Moon, 'Sonny', 80
Moon, Beatrice, 80
Moon, Harry (resident of Stobart Mansions), 18, 30
Moon, Mrs (money-lender), 80
Moore, Doreen (LEW's first daughter), vii, 209–212, 215–216, 224–226, 231–238, 242–243, 246–247, 250, 255–256, 258–259, 267–268, 273, 280, 282–283, 288, 292, 295, 299–301, 308, 310, 314, 319, 324–325, 328, 330–331, 334, 336–337, 339, 342–344, 351, 353, 355–356, 358, 362, 364–366
morale, 84–85, 89
Mordey, Dolph (LEW's classmate), 119, 199–200
Morecambe, Lancashire, 244–245
Morrison, Herbert, 1888–1965, 201–202
Morrow, Bill (AFS), 229
Morton, Major (owner of The Abbey, Aston Abbotts), 7
Mosedale Street, 70
'Mothers and Fathers' (game), 12
Mothers' Meeting (Kimpton Mission), 85
Mr Cinders (musical), 167
Mulley, Fred, 100, 142–143
Mulley, Miss (leader of the Kimpton Mission's Band of Hope), 71, 100, 126, 129–130
Mumming Birds (Fred Karno's troupe), 82
munitions factories, 75–76, 84–85
Murphy, Cornelius ('Spud'), 163–164, 184, 194–196, 200
mushrooms, 9–10
Music, 22, 26, 35, 147
music hall, 22, 26–27, 148

Myton Hall, North Yorkshire, 298
NAAFI (Navy, Army and Air Force Institutes), 239, 243–244, 257, 262–264, 270, 315, 320, 324–325, 327, 333–334, 352, 361, 363
'Nancy Lee' ('Of all the wives as e'er you know'; song), 27–28
National Insurance Act (1911), *see* Lloyd George Insurance Stamp
National Trust, 171
navvies, 20–21, 279
Nelson cake, 93
Nelson Lee Library (magazine), 65–66
New Road, Camberwell, 44–46
Newbury, Berkshire, 96, 107
Newquay, Cornwall, 316–318, 329
newsagents, 37, 90, 94–95
newspapers, 134–135, 170, 175
Newton, Flt. Lt., 349
nippies, 187
'Nirvana' (song), 148, 156
Nofar (drapery business), 108–109
Nordock Farm, 2
Norman, Doris (sister of Kate Norman), 137
Norman, Kate (Grace Williams's friend), 100, 137
North to Klondike (1942 film), 304
North London Home for the Blind, 219–221, 225–226, 229–230
Norton Heath, Essex, 87–88
Norwood, 86
Norwood Cemetery, xiii, 188
Norwood Road, 78
Novello, Ivor, 1893–1951, 64
Numismatics, 127–128, 264, 271, 274
'O what a kind-hearted fellow was he' (song), 81
'O when does your birthday come pray' (poem), 67
Oak House Laundry, 50–51
Oakey's Emery Paper, 14
Oakey's Knife Polish, 17
Oddfellows, 22
'Of all the wives as e'er you know' ('Nancy Lee'; song), 27–28
'Oh that buzzing bumble bee stung Bertie's boko' (song), 113–114

oilcloth, 15
'Old chairs to mend' (street cry), 17
'Old House on the Green', 45
Old Vic Theatre, London, 66, 123
Oliver Goldsmith School, 74, 106, 342
'On the March' (monologue), 282
One Tree Hill, Camberwell, 25–26, 73, 96–97
opium, 73
oranges, 21
Orchard Row, Camberwell, 35–36, 47
organ, 143–144
Oriental Palace of Varieties, Camberwell, 44
Orkney, 81
Orpheus Street, 44–45
'Over the River' (hymn), 81
'Over There' (song), 85
Oxford, 322, 324
Oxo, 56, 127
packmen, 4
'Paddy McGinty's Goat' (monologue), 282
'Pale hands I love' (song), 156
Palestine Police, 186
Palestine, liberation of, 89
palmistry, 109
Pankhurst, Mr (Kimpton Mission Sunday School superintendent), 137–138, 156, 163–164
pantomimes, 3, 18
Paris, 3–4, 50
Passover (Jewish festival), 202–203
pawnbrokers, 34, 70, 110–111, 120, 133, 181
Paxton (vicar of Aston Abbotts), 7
Peabody Trust, 36
Pear's Soap, 93
Pearce Duff's Custard Powder, 127
Pearce, John (owner of eating-house in the Minories), 128–129, 186–187
Pearman, Mrs (LEW's landlady), 279, 281–282, 289, 292, 297
Pearse, Sandra (LEW's niece), 379
Pearson's (furniture retailer), 206–207
Pearson's Fresh Air Outing, 54–55
Peckham Fire Station, 75
Peckham House (asylum), 47

Peckham Road, Camberwell, 34, 37, 44, 46–47, 107, 142, 165–166
Peckham Rye, 65–66, 73, 97, 142, 309
'Pedro the Fisherman' (song), 330
Peed's Nursery, 86
Penny Bank (Kimpton Mission), 91, 93, 122, 157
penny dreadfuls, 65
Pepper, William C., 143
Pepsi Cola, 24
percussion bombs, 94–95
phonograph, 27
Photography, 146–147, 149
piano, 27–28, 64, 143–144, 155, 166–167, 177
Piccadilly, 56
Pickford, Mary, 1892–1979, 114
pickpockets, 20
Pickwick Papers, 66
picnicking, 78
Picture Post (magazine), 314
Pied Piper of Hamelin, 66–67
pigeons, 33
Plague, 42
pledge, the, 23, 100
'Podge', *see* Williams, Iris Denise ('Denny')
Poetry, 66–67, 143
police, 53–54, 95, 134–135, 153, 165
Polly (grey parrot), xi, 129
'Poor Jenny is a Weeping' (game), 12
Portia, from *The Merchant of Venice*, played by LEW, 66
Postmen, 157–158
potatoes, 21
Potters Bar, 55
poverty, ix, ix, 26, 46–47, 57, 93, 133, 158, 181, 375
pram, *see* bassinet
Prescott's (pawnbrokers), 70
'Pretty little girl from nowhere' (song), 27
Price's (bakers), 69, 79–80, 112
Price's Candles, 71–72
Priest's (greengrocer and removals man), 19, 34
printing, 115, 137–138
profiteering, 92, 106–107

394

promotion to sergeant, 331–332, 346, 367
Prosser Roberts (chemists), 146–147
Psyche, 110
public houses, 22, 26–27, 157
Puck (comic), 65
Pullum's Body Building Centre, 37
Purdew, Mrs (resident of No.16 Stobart Mansions), 148
Putnam, Samuel (timber merchants), 67–68
Queen Mary low-loader, 266, 277, 320
Quin and Axtens (store), 19–20, 255
R. White of Albany Road, 24
R34, R100 and R101 (airships), 112, 239
rabbit seller, 19
Rabbits, 33, 79, 82–83, 96, 110, 126, 130, 140, 295, 302, 324–325
Radio, 27, 65, 114, 155–156, 183–184, 190
RAF 60 MU (Maintenance Unit), 264–367 *passim*, 264–265, 366–367
RAF Breighton, 342–344
RAF Catfoss, 332
RAF Catterick, 297
RAF Clifton, 349–350
RAF Cosford, 293–294
RAF Dishforth, 308–309, 313, 319–320
RAF Earls Colne, 353–355
RAF Hednesford, 247–258, 263
RAF Hunsdon, 336–339
RAF Hutton Cranswick, 307–308
RAF Lindholme, 321, 355–356
RAF Linton-on-Ouse, 265, 274, 284–285, 287, 289, 292, 294–297, 299, 301–302, 309, 320, 323, 332, 352
RAF Lissett, 356
RAF Marston Moor, 312, 315
RAF Odiham, 358–360
RAF Rufforth, 311–312
RAF Shipton-by-Beningbrough, 257, 260–262, 264–265, 270, 273, 283, 285, 291, 294–295, 297–298, 301, 309, 311, 313, 319–320, 326, 331–332, 344, 347–348, 354, 358, 363
RAF Snaith, 310–311
RAF St Athan, 360
RAF St Eval, 313, 316–318, 328, 328

RAF Stansted Mountfitchet, 331–334, 336
RAF Sutton-on-Hull, 302–303, 307
RAF Tarrant Rushton, 325–327, 329, 330
RAF Upper Heyford, 322, 324–326, 331
RAF West Malling, 339, 341–342
RAF Westcott, 347–348
RAF Woodbridge, 344–348, 354
RAF Woolsington, 352
Rainbow (comic), 65
Rainbow Island (film), 351
Rambling, 183–185, 201, 203
Ratcliffe's timber yard, 45
rationing, 92, 358
rats, 42
Rawcliffe, North Yorkshire, 279–283
Reading, 65–67, 91–92, 108, 113, 143–144
Reckitt's Blue Bag, 60
Red Ace (film serial), 87
Red Post Hill, 42–43, 78–79
Regal Cinema, West Norwood, 299
Regent Street, 32–33
Regent's Park, 2–3
religion, 34, 243
rent, 144, 206, 211
rickets, 92–93
Rickmansworth, 71
Riders of the Purple Sage (Grey), 183–184
Rignold Road, 46–47, 62, 84
Roberts, Estelle, 1889–1970 (medium), 175
Robertson's Golden Shred (marmalade), 25
Robin Starch, 61
Robinson, [William] Leefe, 1895–1918, 54–55
Rochdale, 128, 151
Rochester, Kent, 37
Roe, Mrs (money-lender), 80
roller-skating, 69
Rome Express (film), 249
Romney, Hythe and Dymchurch Railway, 149, 179
Rosemary Branch, Peckham (tavern), 37
Ross, James Clark, Sir, 1800–1862 (arctic explorer and discoverer of magnetic pole) , 6–7

Ross, John, Sir, 1777–1856, 6–7
'Rosser's Revels' (show), 294–295
Rothschild family, 7–8
Rothschild, Hilda, 7–8
'Rover in Church' (monologue), 109
Rowntree's (confectioner), 24–25
Rowsham, Buckinghamshire, 6
Royal Air Force, vii, 143, 153, 210, 233–234, 237–239, 242–367 *passim*, 243, 245–247, 249, 291, 357–358, 363, 367
Royal Antidiluvian Order of Buffaloes, 22
Royal Arsenal Co-operative Society, *see* Co-operative Society
Royal College of Music, ix–x
Royal Flying Corps, 54–55
royal hand (wrapping paper), 118
Royal Humane Society, 39
Royal Navy, 51
Royal Oak Inn, Aston Abbotts, 4–6, 8, 324–325, 338–339, 348
Rubinstein, Anton, 1829–1894, 132
Rufforth, North Yorkshire, *see* RAF Rufforth
'Run Rabbit Run' (song), 231
Rushden, Northamptonshire, xii, 85, 111, 135–136, 147, 159, 194, 201, 240, 243, 245
Ruskin Estate, 42–43
Ruskin Manor, 43
Ruskin Park, 27, 40, 43, 57, 65–66, 68–69, 76, 96, 106, 118–119, 142, 148, 153
Ruskin, John, 1819–1900, 43
Ryan, John (LEW's brother-in-law), 194, 226, 242, 277–278, 292, 329–330, 362
Rye Lane, Peckham, 62–63, 137–138, 142, 201–202, 206, 336
Saint Meets the Tiger (film), 275
salesmanship, 148
Salford, Greater Manchester, 151
Salvation Army, 23, 27, 34, 77, 307, 309
Samuel Jones (maker of gummed paper), *see* Jones, Samuel (maker of gummed paper)
Samuel Putnam & Co (timber merchants), *see* Putnam, Samuel (timber merchant)
Sandgate, Kent, 149, 161, 178

Sankey, Ira David, 1840–1908, 27, 81, 98, 301
Sansom Street, Camberwell, 23–24
Sansom, Dr, 73, 152–154
Savoy Hill, 114
scams, swindles, and sharp practices, 18, 50–51, 64–65, 118
scent cards, 113
scholarship examination, 106
School, 10, 57–60, 65–70, 88–89, 93, 98, 100, 103–104, 106, 112, 115
school inspectors, 86–87, 101–102
Scott, Mrs (landlady at 'Rockville', Tollerton), 284–285, 287–288, 290, 294, 298
Scouting for Boys (Baden-Powell), 184
Scouts and the Scouts Association, 27, 69, 173, 184, 191, 193–196, 200, 203, 211
scrumping, 41, 63–64, 122
Scurr, Mr (leader of the Kimpton Mission's Band of Hope), 23, 25–26, 71
Second World War, 38, 77, 101
Sedgmoor Place, 128–129, 132–133, 142–143, 146, 158
self-confidence, 116, 137
Senior, Mr (Manager of Co-operative shop on Camberwell New Road), 152
Sepharial (pseudonym of Alan Leo), 109
Servants, 26
servants' indicator bell board, 26
Seventh Veil, The (film), 365–366
Sexton Blake Library (periodical), 66
Shaftesbury Society, vii, 23, 94
Shakespeare, William, 1564–1616, 66, 143
Sharman, Mr (foreman of the Royal Arsenal Co-op), 139–140
Shavex (brushless shaving cream), 173
sheep, 16, 35
Shipton-by-Beningbrough, North Yorkshire, *see* RAF Shipton-by-Beningbrough
shire horses, 21
shoe and boot factory, 77
shop steward, LEW serves as, 177, 201–202
shopkeepers, 19, 37, 92

Short Sunderland (flying boat), 268–270
sick benefits, 152–154
Siddall, Arthur, 287, 295, 297, 316, 328–329, 345–346
Siddoway, Philip (LEW's friend), 244–245, 248–254, 256–258, 266, 273, 292
Silk Cut (cigarettes), 151, 187–188
'Silkstone' (type of coal), 21
'Silver Royd' (LEW's billet in Shipton), 263, 266–267, 276, 279
Silvertown, 75–76, 84–85
'Sister Susie's sewing shirts for soldiers' (song), 85
Sketches by Boz, 37
Skinner, Ada ('Aunt Ada'), 50–51, 129–130
skipping, 11
slate clubs, 22, 91
Slaughter, Todd, 1885–1956, 44–45
Slums, 18, 35–36, 77, 93–94, 151
Smith, Kitty, 200
Smith, Mrs G. Castle (author), 94
smoking, *see* cigarettes/tobacco
Snaith, Humber, *see* RAF Snaith
snakes and ladders, 71
Snow White and the Seven Dwarfs (film), 328
Soho, 56
Somers, Debroy, 1890–1952, 114
Somme, 81, 84–85
'Song of the Shirt' (poem), 36
'Song of the Thrush' (song), 194
Songs, 3, 16–17, 20–21, 26–27, 35, 64, 98, 145, 147, 177, 299
'Sons of the Sea' (song), 51
'Sorbo' sponge rubber balls, 12
South London Drapery Stores, 37
South London Press (newspaper), 307
South Metropolitan Gas Company, 15, 31
Southampton, 268–270
Southend on Sea, 202–203
Southgate, Jack (LEW's friend), 119
Spalenka, Karel ['Charles'], 7, 324–325, 338–339, 346, 348, 379–380
Spencer, Irene (daughter of John Spencer), 136–137
Spencer, John (manager at Jaques & Son boot factory, Rushden), 136–137
spinning tops, 11

Spiritualism, 175
'Spring Song' (Mendelssohn), 43
Spring-Heeled Jack (The Terror of London), 44–45
Squires, Doris ('Dolly', Elsie's sister), 166–167, 196, 205–207, 232, 253, 260, 268, 281, 292, 297, 308, 315, 329, 349, 351
Squires, Edna, 319, 328–329, 340, 343, 345, 351, 356, 364–365, 367
Squires, Elsie Ruth (LEW's wife), *see* Williams, Elsie Ruth
Squires, George (Elsie's brother), 166–167, 232, 237, 259, 266, 345
Squires, Mr (Elsie's father), 166–167, 179–180, 192–193, 196–197, 199, 212, 232, 259, 289, 293, 299–300, 324, 345, 351, 353, 356, 362, 365
Squires, Mrs (Elsie's mother), 166–167, 179–180, 196–197, 212, 232, 266, 289, 293, 299–300, 324, 345, 351, 353, 356, 362, 365
Squires, Tim (Elsie's brother), 166–167, 191, 194–196, 200, 229, 232, 235, 282, 288, 292, 319, 328, 343, 351, 356, 364, 367
St Eval, Cornwall, *see* RAF St Eval
St Giles' Church, Camberwell, 36–38, 44, 51–52, 158, 193, 226
St Giles' Hospital, 46–47, 178, 211–212
St James the Great, Aston Abbotts, 145
St Matthew's Church, 44
St Matthew's School, 152–153
St Matthew's Sick and Sharing Out Society, 152–153
St Paul's Cathedral, 45, 130, 148
St Saviourgate, York, 264, 275, 280–282, 284, 349
'Stables' (Camberwell), 29
Stansted Mountfitchet, *see* RAF Stansted Mountfitchet
Star, The (newspaper), 170
Staughan, Jock (LEW's bookkeeping instructor), 154
Steinitz, Mr C., 37
Sten gun, 301–302, 344, 348, 355, 367
Stephenson, Tom (contributor to Daily Herald), 182

Stewart, Miss (Girls' Club leader at Kimpton Mission), 128, 186–187
Stirling Castle (public house), 37
Stirling Mansions, 132–133, 143, 145
Stobart Mansions, vii, xii, 10–11, 15, 23, 29–33, 64, 80, 87, 96, 98, 105, 143–145, 164, 207, 211, 277–278, 372
Stobart Mansions, interior décor and furnishings of, 13, 15, 30–31, 157–158
Stock-taking, 161, 202
Stone's Raisin Wine, 71, 157
street lighting, 32–33
street names, 47
street traders, 16–18, 76, 84
Stringer, Hilda, *see* Denner, Hilda
Stuart Road, 40
students, 134–135
sugar, 83, 127, 140, 259, 269
Sullivan, Arthur, 1842–1900 (composer), 137–138
Sultan Street, 18, 77
Sunday School, 94, 100
Sunderland flying boats, *see* Short Sunderland (flying boat)
Sunlight Soap, 60, 93, 127
Sunray Avenue, 41–43, 78–79, 142
Sunray Gardens, 78–79
Sunset Road, 43
Sutton-on-Hull, *see* RAF Sutton-on-Hull
Swaffer, Hannen, 1879–1962 (journalist), 175
Sweeney Todd, the Demon Barber of Fleet Street, 44–45
Swiss Family Robinson, 91–92
tailors, 37
tallymen, 34
tanks, 94
Tanner family, 79, 80
Tarrant Rushton, Dorset, *see* RAF Tarrant Rushton
tea, 78, 110, 117, 118, 127, 140
Telegrams, 133, 145, 281
Telephones, 74, 108–109, 143, 150, 323–324
television, 27, 65
Temperance League, 23, 100, 136
tennis balls, 12

Tennyson, Alfred Tennyson, Baron, 1809–1892, 66–67
tents, *see* camping
Tetley family, 117
Thatched Cottage, The, 38
theatre, 44, 87, 167
'There is a green hill far away' (hymn), 261–262
'There's a long, long trail a-winding' (song), 85, 156
Thermos flask, 320, 322, 324–325, 348
They Died with Their Boots On (film), 288
Thief of Bagdad (film), 256, 351
Thomas Tilling's bus company, 46
Thompson, Edward Cecil, *see* Thompson, Ted
Thompson, Frank (slate club secretary), 91, 125–126, 154
Thompson, Frank (Ted Thompson's brother), 67–68, 105–106, 137, 162–163, 192, 196–198, 205, 246
Thompson, May (Ted Thompson's sister), 67–68
Thompson, Mr (Ted Thompson's father), 67–68, 119–120
Thompson, Mrs (Ellen Williams's friend), 129–130
Thompson, Percy (Ted Thompson's brother), 67–68
Thompson, Rose (Frank Thompson's wife), 105–106, 162–163, 192, 196–197
Thompson, Stan (LEW's friend), 249–254
Thompson, Ted, 67–68, 82–83, 106, 119–120, 125, 167, 175, 189, 205–207
Thompson's Oil Shop, 60–61, 95, 110
thrift clubs, 157
Tiger Moth (biplane), 284, 288–289, 291–292, 297–299, 301, 309
Tiger of Mysore (Henty), 66
Tilley, Arthur (LEW's brother-in-law), 147, 157, 176–177, 179, 189, 211, 227, 232, 273, 314, 319, 329–330, 337
Tilling, Thomas, *see* Thomas Tilling's bus company
'Tin Soldier' (song), 27
tobacconists, 51–52, 90–91

tokens, 128
Tollerton, North Yorkshire, 210, 264–265, 284, 287–288, 291, 294, 301, 307–309, 313, 315, 320, 348, 353
Tom Brown's Schooldays (1857), 150
tonsillitis, 104–105
Toulon Street, 18
Tower of London, 161, 175
toys, 1, 19, 71, 94–95, 113, 298, 300, 351
trade unions, 22, 177–178
tradesmen, 31
tram men, 44
Trams, 19–20, 29, 35, 40, 44, 54–56, 74, 76, 78–80, 84–86, 97, 101, 119–120, 130, 134–135, 138–139, 151, 154, 164, 189, 199, 207, 211, 216, 218–219
Tramways Board, 35
Treasury notes, 83–84, 121
Treherne Road, Brixton, xii, 50–51, 129–130
Triange, The, Champion Hill (suspected plague pit), 42
Trocadero Cinema (Elephant and Castle), 202
trolleybuses, 180
Trollope and Colls (building contractors), 165
truancy, 86–87, 101–102
Trunk Act, 101–102
Tube Alloys (company), 324, 325
Tulse Hill, xi, xii, 85–86
Turkey, 53, 89, 92
Turner, Harry (LEW's headmaster), 41, 58, 66–67, 100, 115
'Tyne Main Cobbles' (type of coal), 21
typhoid, 42
Typhoon, *see* Hawker Typhoon (fighter)
U-boats, 79, 81, 85
Under Two Flags (play), 44–45
Unemployment, 34, 99–101, 107, 115, 120, 124, 126–127, 133–134, 158, 180, 183–184
Unigate, 102
Union Jack Library (periodical), 66
Union Row, Camberwell, 36
United Kingdom Tea Company, 106–107, 117–120, 122–123, 126–127, 137–140

upholsterers, 77
Upper Heyford, *see* RAF Upper Heyford
USAAF, 333–346
V1 Flying Bombs, 335–345
V2 Rockets, 344, 346, 349, 351, 355
vagrants, 111
Vanessa (butterfly), 38
variety theatres, *see* music hall
Vaseline, 73, 93
Vaughan Williams, Ralph, 1872–1958, 171
Vaughan, Rev. David, 46, 205, 207, 297
Veasey, Nurse, 70
Verdun, 84–85
Verne, Jules, 1828–1905, 66
Vestry Road, 47, 94, 102–103
Vicarage Grove, 102–103, 137–138, 197
Victory Bond Swindle, 64–65
village life, 4–5, 8–9
Vining, [Charles] Noel (LEW's friend), 45, 72–74, 76–77, 87–92, 96–97, 107, 114, 117, 119, 121–123, 205–206, 213–214
Vining, Albert (Noel Vining's brother), 62, 122–123
Vining, Charles (Noel Vining's father), 62–63, 87–88, 122–123
Vining, Eileen (Noel Vining's sister), 62
Vining, Ralph (Noel Vining's brother), 62, 122–123
Vining, Winifred (Noel Vining's sister), 62
Vinolia (soap), 93
Violence, 35–36, 77, 135, 165
WAAFs, 325, 356
Wakes Week, 136–137
Wall Street Crash, 180
Wall, Ron, 106
Walworth, 101, 152
Walworth Road, Camberwell, 20
War Bonds, 93, 94
Warsop, Flt. Sgt. ['Toby'], 284, 294–295, 297–298, 302
water divination, 109

Waterloo Street, Camberwell, 19, 34, 84, 110, 157
Waterman, Lily, 105–106, 162–163, 192, 200, 256
Waterman, Mr (GPO worker), 105–106, 192, 256
Waterman, Mrs, 105–106, 192, 256
Waterman, Rose, *see* Thompson, Rose
'We are Fred Karno's army' (song), 81–82
'We Plough the Fields and Scatter' (hymn), 296
'We won the war, we won the war' (song), 99
Weatherly, Frederick, E., 1848–1929 (lyricist), 27–28, 148
Weaver, Richard, Sgt ('Dick'), 323–327, 330–331
Weedon, Buckinghamshire, 7–8
Weeton Hospital, 363, 364
West Humble, 166, 168
West Malling, *see* RAF West Malling
West Norwood, 44, 85–86, 120–121, 292, 299
Western Brothers (music hall and radio act), 202
Western Union (film), 267
Westminster Bank, 37, 127
Westmoreland Road, Camberwell, 20, 76, 101
WH Smith, 298
'When the great red dawn is shining' (song), 85
'Where, oh where, do I live' (duet), 156
whipping tops, 11
whist, 149–150
White, Pearl, 1889–1938 (actress), 87
White, Sylvia Brenda (LEW's second daughter), vii, 209–210, 287–288, 295, 297, 299–301, 308–310, 314–315, 318, 325, 328–329, 331, 337, 339, 343–344, 351, 353, 355, 361, 364–365
Whitley bomber, *see* Armstrong Whitworth Whitley
Wilby Road (later renamed Jephson Street), 47, 89–90
Wilhelm II, 1859–1941 (Kaiser Wilhelm), 49, 85
Willams, Iris Denise ('Denny', LEW's sister), 114–115, 131, 141, 152, 176–177, 190, 201, 203–206, 255, 277–278, 292, 297, 324
Williams, Audrey Florence (LEW's sister), 70, 83, 176–177, 187, 226, 232, 277–278, 292, 327, 337
Williams, Betty (LEW's sister-in-law), x, 325, 338, 348
Williams, Constance ('Con', LEW's sister)
  hostility to father and estrangement from LEW, x
  see also, xi, xiii, xiv, 3–4, 10, 46, 61, 63, 69–70, 83, 87, 101, 104–105, 108–109, 111–114, 116, 125–126, 128, 130, 147, 157, 176–177, 179, 189–190, 211, 232, 238, 273, 314, 319, 329–330, 337, 339–340
Williams, Doreen (LEW's first daughter), *see* Moore, Doreen
Williams, Doreen Pamela (Pam, LEW's sister), 7, 131, 176–177, 190, 201, 203–206, 213, 215, 224–225, 232, 242, 299, 319, 324–325, 338–339, 346, 348, 359–360, 366, 379–380
Williams, Eileen (LEW's sister), 4, 10, 83, 125–126, 141, 147, 155, 157, 167, 176–177, 182, 187, 189, 191, 201, 211–212, 227, 232, 273, 277–278, 300, 340, 359–360, 362, 366
Williams, Ellen (LEW's mother)
  parentage, early life, xi–xii
  see also, vii, ix–xiv, 1–6, 8, 10–12, 14–16, 19–20, 23–25, 27, 31–32, 39–40, 46, 49–51, 53–54, 58, 60–61, 63–65, 70–71, 73, 77–80, 83, 85, 88, 90, 92–93, 95–96, 98, 101–102, 104–105, 107, 110–113, 116, 119–126, 128, 129–133, 135, 139, 142–148, 152–153, 155, 157–158, 167, 176–177, 179–182, 186, 188–190, 193, 196–198, 203–204, 207, 211–212, 224, 232, 238, 240–242, 245, 250, 259, 277–278, 297, 299, 312, 314, 324–325, 329–330, 337, 341, 348, 356, 359–360, 366, 369, 372–376

works for Lacey family, xii, 85, 188, 373–375
Williams, Elsie Ruth (LEW's wife), vii, x, 46, 58, 163–164, 166–168, 173, 175–180, 182–185, 188–189, 192, 194–198, 200–207, 209–211, 215–216, 224–226, 229–238, 240–241, 243, 245–247, 250, 252–253, 255–256, 258, 265, 267–268, 273–274, 280–283, 287–289, 292–293, 295–297, 299–301, 307–310, 312–315, 317–321, 324, 328–331, 333, 335–343, 349–350, 353, 357–362, 364–365, 367–369, 371
Williams, Ethel, xii–xiii, 2, 123, 145–146
Williams, Frederick (LEW's father), see Lacey, Frederick William
Williams, Grace (LEW's sister), 3–4, 10, 29, 100, 108, 111, 116, 120, 125–126, 128–129, 134, 137–138, 142, 144, 147–148, 156–157, 161, 176–177, 186–187, 191, 194, 206, 226, 232, 245, 259, 277–278, 314–315, 329–330, 362
Williams, Janet (LEW's third daughter), see Eaton, Janet
Williams, Pamela, see Williams, Doreen Pamela
Williams, Reginald ('Reg', LEW's brother)
  army career, 131–133, 156, 217, 233
  character, 131
  relationship with F. W. Lacey, x, 123–124, 131
  researches family history, x
  runs away from home, 88
  see also, x–xi, xiii, 1, 4–5, 9–10, 13–14, 16, 18, 25–26, 46, 53–54, 58–60, 65, 71–72, 76, 78, 82–85, 87–88, 90, 104–105, 107–108, 111–113, 116, 120–126, 128, 131–133, 148–149, 156, 176–177, 186, 188–190, 193–194, 211, 213–214, 217, 233, 238, 273, 277–278, 292–293, 312, 319, 324–325, 338–339, 341, 348

Williams, Sylvia Brenda (LEW's second daughter), see White, Sylvia Brenda
Williams, Vera Carrington (LEW's sister), xiv, 92–93, 141, 147, 176–177, 196–197, 227, 228–229, 245–246, 292, 314–315, 371
Wilson, Mrs (LEW's teacher), 67, 115
Wilson's (baker, Daneville Road), 101–102
Wilson's Grammar School, 44
Windsor Road, Camberwell, 40
Windsor Walk, 142, 236–237
Wingrave, Buckinghamshire, 6, 7–8, 238
Winter, 72–73, 91–92
'winter warmers', 72
Wintringham, Thomas Henry (Tom), 1898–1949, 359
wireless, see radio
Witham, Mrs, 87–88
women workers, 56, 84
women's prison (HM Prison Aylesbury, Bierton Road), 5–6, 88, 224–225
'Won't you buy my sweet lavender' (street song), 16–17
Woodbridge, Suffolk, see RAF Woodbridge
'wooding', 9
Woolsington, see RAF Woolsington
Woolworth's, 19–20, 71–72
Worcester Park, 147
'Work, for the night is coming' (song), 27
workhouse, 26
World War I, see First World War
Worshipful Company of Haberdashers, 37
Wotton Hatch Hotel, 170, 173–174, 185, 192, 195–196, 205
Wraith, Mr (LEW's teacher), 115
Wren Road Congregational Church, 41, 45–46, 113, 177, 196–197, 205, 207, 297
Wren Road, Camberwell, vii, vii, 29, 45–46
Wren, Christopher, Sir, 1631–1723, 45
Wright family (No. 21 Stobart Mansions), 164
Wright's Coal Tar Soap, 93
writing, 143–144
Wyndham Road, 18, 77, 102, 135

Wyss, Johann, 91–92
'Yanks are coming' (song), 85
'Yard' (Stobart Mansions), 29–30, 33
'Yeomen of England' (song), 91
YMCA, 269, 286, 291, 303, 317, 324, 340, 345

York, 261–262, 264, 267–268, 275, 289–290, 297–299, 309, 312, 315, 320
Yorkshire Evening Post (newspaper), 267
Ypres, 84–85
Zam-buk, 130
Zeppelins, 53–56, 112, 156, 175–176

www.ingramcontent.com/pod-product-compliance
Lightning Source LLC
Chambersburg PA
CBHW060103170426
43198CB00010B/748